A Just Peace Through Transformation

Published in cooperation with the
International Peace Research Association

A Just Peace
Through Transformation

Cultural, Economic, and Political Foundations for Change

Proceedings of the
International Peace Research Association
Eleventh General Conference

EDITED BY

Chadwick Alger
and Michael Stohl

Westview Press
BOULDER & LONDON

Westview Special Studies in Peace, Conflict, and Conflict Resolution

This Westview softcover edition is printed on acid-free paper and bound in softcovers that carry the highest rating of the National Association of State Textbook Administrators, in consultation with the Association of American Publishers and the Book Manufacturers' Institute.

Published in 1988 in the United States of America by Westview Press, Inc., 5500 Central Avenue, Boulder, Colorado 80301, and in the United Kingdom by Westview Press, 13 Brunswick Centre, London WC1N 1AF, England

Library of Congress Catalog Card Number: 88-20601
ISBN: 0-8133-7557-6

Printed and bound in the United States of America

The paper used in this publication meets the requirements of the American National Standard for Permanence of Paper for Printed Library Materials Z39.48-1984.

10   9   8   7   6   5   4   3   2   1

Contents

Contributors

Judit Balazs
   Magyar Tudomanyos Akademia
   Budapest, Hungary

Anders Boserup
   Center of Peace and Conflict Research
   Copenhagen, Denmark

Birgit Brock-Utne
   University of Dar es Salaam

Wytze Brouwer
   University of Alberta
   Edmonton, Canada

Michael Brzoska
   Universitat Hamburg
   Hamburg, Federal Republic of Germany

Robin Burns
   La Trobe University
   Melbourne, Australia

Philip Everts
   University of Leiden
   Leiden, Netherlands

Ann FitzSimmons
   University of Colorado
   Boulder, Colorado, USA

Ryuhei Hatsuse
   Toyonaka, Osaka
   Japan

Theodore Herman
   Colgate University
   Hamilton, New York, USA

Gunilla Herolf
   Stockholm International Peace Research Institute
   Stockholm, Sweden

Egbert Jahn
    Center of Peace and Conflict Research
    Copenhagen, Denmark

Graham Kemp
    Richardson Institute for Peace Studies
    Lancaster University, England

Ravi Kumar
    Chetput Madras
    India

Pierre Lemaitre
    Center of Peace and Conflict Research
    Copenhagen, Denmark

Brigitta Lutz
    Federal Republic of Germany

Peter Magnusson
    University of Gothenberg
    Gothenburg, Sweden

David Menham
    W. Yorkshire
    United Kingdom

Andree Michel
    Paris University
    France

Lutz Michel
    Federal Republic of Germany

K. P. Misra
    Jawaharlal Nehru University
    New Delhi, India

Bjorn Moller
    University of Copenhagen
    Denmark

Kjell-Ake Norquist
    Uppsala University
    Uppsala, Sweden

Thomas Ohlson
    Centro Estudios Africanos
    Maputo, Mozambique

Harold E. Pepinsky
    Indiana University
    Bloomington, Indiana, USA

Mindy Percival
    New York, New York, USA

Roger Rawlinson
    Nottingham, United Kingdom

Jacobo Schatan
    Center for Economic Research and Teaching
    Mexico City, Mexico

Jose A. Silva Michelena
    Santiago, Chile

Narindar Singh
    Jawaharlal Nehru University
    New Delhi, India

James Skelly
    University of California
    La Jolla, California, USA

Paul Smoker
    Lancaster University
    United Kingdom

Georg Sorensen
    Aalborg University
    Aalborg, Denmark

Jomo Sundaram
    Wolfson College
    Cambridge, England

Toh Swee-Hin
    University of New England
    Armidale, NSW, Australia

Elling Njal Tjonneland
    International Peace Research Institute
    Oslo, Norway

Ines Vargas
    Norwegian Institute of Human Rights
    Oslo, Norway

Laszlo Valki
    Eotvos University
    Budapest, Hungary

Clara Venema
    Polemological Institute
    Groningen, Netherlands

Ole Waever
    Bronshoj, Denmark

Paul Wehr
    University of Colorado
    Boulder, Colorado, USA

Preface

Preparation of a volume that includes contributions from people living in many countries, and in all continents, offers severe challenges in transnational cooperation, communication and editing. The International Peace Research Association (IPRA) is grateful to UNESCO for financial support that made this volume possible. We also wish to thank the forty-one colleagues whose work appears in this volume for their cooperative spirit. We are particularly appreciative of their good natured acceptance of our efforts to shorten many papers. This has helped us to include more chapters in the volume, thereby fulfilling our aspiration to present a wide diversity of subjects and points of view.

When chapters are written by many scholars whose native language is not English, the editing challenges are great. We have been most fortunate to have the assistance of Linda Chene who has done a masterful job of both editing and thoughtful communication with authors. Many authors have expressed appreciation of the care with which she has preserved the meaning of their writing while enhancing clarity.

The papers in this volume were selected from those presented at the Eleventh General Conference of the International Peace Research Association (IPRA), held at the University of Sussex, England. Ms. Wendy Coons of the Mershon Center, The Ohio State University, played a prominent role in organizing this conference, as administrative assistant to Chadwick F. Alger, then Secretary General of IPRA and organizer of the conference program. At the same time she was involved in the early stages of preparation of chapters for publication, and was assisted in this task by Ms. Kim Orth of the Department of Political Science, Purdue University.

Finally, we hope that scholarly colleagues who read this volume will be encouraged to learn more about the International Peace Research Association, and about our Newsletter, conferences, and Study Groups. For further information we urge you to contact the present Secretary

General, Clovis Brigagao, Rua Paulino Fernandes, 32 CEP 22270, Rio de Janeiro RJ, Brazil.

This is the tenth volume of selected papers from IPRA conferences, earlier volumes are available in many libraries. Copies of the most recent volume, <u>Conflict and Crisis of International Order: New Tasks of Peace Research</u>, 1985, are available from the Mershon Center, The Ohio State University, 199 West 10th Avenue, Columbus, Ohio 43201.

Chadwick Alger
Michael Stohl

Introduction

Chadwick Alger

From one perspective the twentieth century has been a time of dramatic setbacks in humanity's aspiration and struggle for peace. On the other hand, encouragement is to be found in the growing array of worldwide peace movements and voices whose origins range from Chile to Canada, from Finland to South Africa, and from Ireland to New Zealand. Aided by growing possibilities for global communication, these movements have produced a global dialogue on peace issues in grassroots movements, in meetings of international nongovernmental organizations, in transnational scholarly meetings, in organizations of the UN system and in special UN conferences on global issues. Particularly significant have been the increasingly audible voices from the Third World and from the grassroots in all continents.

This global dialogue has produced an expanded notion of peace (see, for example, the Proceedings of IPRA Third General Conference, 1970), incorporating not only the absence of violence ("negative peace") but also the presence of social justice ("positive peace"). This in turn has provoked a searching dialogue on the meaning of "positive peace" that has been centered on explication of the meaning of development, of human rights, and of ecological balance. As a consequence, peace is increasingly seen to be the maximization of four overlapping, and sometimes conflicting, values: absence of violence, development, human rights, and ecological balance. The meaning of each value is now the subject of intense debate, as in the conflict between ecological balance and development, and the increasing challenge from the grassroots which asserts that the very notion of development violates the human rights of traditional peoples.

As an expanded definition of peace has received wider acceptance, approaches to peace have necessarily

1

become more varied, encompassing not only an array of issues but also a diversity of arenas, ranging from global organizations to the grassroots. These approaches offer a striking contrast to earlier "peace plans"--from Pierre Dubois (1306) to Grenville Clark and Louis B. Sohn (1958)--which tended to emphasize the development of central institutions that would restrain the warmaking proclivities of states. In the present context this centralized, or world government, approach to peace is rejected by many who fear that it could impose a status quo that consists of widespread unjust relationships (peacelessness) both between and within states.

Some observers also react negatively to the more decentralized approach. As peace research has moved beyond the traditional core of "negative peace," they criticize peace research for assuming an amorphous, boundaryless quality. On the other hand, many see that the broader peace agenda has at least two advantages. First, it reveals ways in which a diversity of kinds of people--in a variety of professions, disciplines and locations--can participate in an ever expanding peace movement. Second, wider participation creates ever deeper insights on how people in a diversity of life circumstances around the world define peace. It becomes increasingly obvious that a feasible and enduring peace must be responsive to the needs expressed in an array of definitions of peace.

This volume offers a panoramic view of the diversity of research now being undertaken by those who identify themselves as peace researchers. The thirty-six chapters were written by researchers from sixteen countries who contributed papers to the Eleventh General Conference of the International Peace Research Association (IPRA) whose theme was " A Just Peace through Transformation." The papers presented at an IPRA conference offer very appropriate material for gaining a comprehensive view of the peace research enterprise. This organization, founded primarily by Europeans, has gradually acquired global scope, despite the fact that membership and participation are still strongly weighted toward Europe, North America, India, and Japan. IPRA conferences have made significant contributions to the continuing global debate on the meaning of peace, on the global scope of peacelessness and on the kinds of research that would contribute to progress toward peace.

The papers that appear in this volume were selected from the more than one hundred and fifty presented at the conference. An effort has been made to maximize quality, coverage of a broad array of topics, and inclusion of contributions from as many countries as possible. Because an effort has been made to permit a diversity of voices of self-identified peace researchers to be heard, no single criterion of good research has been imposed. On the other hand, because the length of chapters had to be limited, most of the papers were shortened, some quite severely.

It is important to recognize that the conceptual framework of a volume--as reflected in the grouping of topics and the order in which they are taken up--may have implications for both theory and action. Thus we feel obliged to share with the reader the rationale for the organization of the volume. The difficulties we confronted in efforts to group the papers under topics reveals a significant characteristic of current peace research. For the most part the papers constitute a seamless web, or a spheroidal network. The present table of contents is but the last of a dozen or more attempts. At one point we were even tempted to present the papers in alphabetical order preceeded by a keyword index, thus permitting readers to construct their own table of contents. In the end, however, we followed a more traditional approach by grouping papers under nine topics grouped into three parts. Yet the reader should be conscious of the limitations of this effort. For example, although there is no peace movements topic, three topics include chapters on peace movements. (A, B, C, D). Militarization is a concern in at least three topics (E, E, H). And peace education is covered in at least three topics (A, C, D).

Once we had decided on the nine topics under which chapters would be grouped, a decision had to be made on the order of the topics. The first effort followed the customary order to be found in many peace research books and curricula, such that the more traditional peace research topics were placed at the beginning, and newer topics followed in the order in which they were placed on the peace research agenda. This approach would place the three topics in Part III, entitled "Security and Conflict," at the beginning of the volume, followed by the two topics in the section on "Economic Aspects of Peace." With this approach the four topics under "Societal Foundations of Peace," would have come last in the volume. But this approach raised concern over placing at the end of the volume papers on creating

cultural and political contexts of peace; nonviolence;
women, militarization and education; and peace education.
The tradition of placing topics such as nonviolence,
women, and education at the end tends to suggest that
these topics are of low priority, thus perpetuating the
widespread assumption that thinking and acting about
peace necessarily begins with conflict and security
issues.

Although we acknowledge that the topics covered in
this volume are linked together in a tight network, there
are persuasive reasons for placing <u>first</u> those topics
gathered under the heading "Societal Foundations of
Peace." Increasing evidence suggests that peacelessness
in the world cannot be overcome only by efforts to
directly transform the policies of states. Also required
is transformation of the structure of the state system
and transformation of assumptions about the special
responsibilities and privileges of state authorities in
the state system. But these transformations can come
only with broader participation in peace issues, both
within and across societies. Building the foundations
for expanded participation in peace issues requires
creative approaches for constructing peace cultures as an
alternative to existing militarized cultures. Yet the
building of peace cultures will continue to be treated as
a task of secondary concern so long as "security and
conflict" issues (i.e., military security and arms races)
are presented, both implicitly and explicitly, as
priority tasks in the quest for peace. Thus, by placing
the "Societal Foundations of Peace" first, we are
asserting that building peace cultures within and across
societies merits priority status in peace research and
action strategies. On the other hand, we are definitely
not suggesting that more traditional concerns, such as
"security and conflict," are irrelevant to a
comprehensive peace research and peace action strategy.

Primarily because this is a collection of individual
research papers assembled by the editors from a
conference, the nine topics do not receive comprehensive
treatment. The fundamental contribution of the volume
lies in the panoramic view that is provided of approaches
to peace research by scholars in different social
contexts. As scholars attempt to respond to aspirations
to overcome peacelessness in their particular context,
they are contributing to an ongoing global dialogue that
is creating a comprehensive view of peace and an array of
strategies for achieving it. Although the scientific and

political validity of each voice must in the end be
tested, each voice deserves a hearing if the global peace
movement, of which peace research is a part, is to be
understood. Those who would contribute research useful
to this movement need to be aware of this larger context
of their work.

In a volume with such a diversity of topics and
approaches, a variety of themes could be emphasized in an
overview. We have chosen to mine the papers for insights
on transformation toward a just peace. In our view the
transformational nodules scattered throughout the volume
provide a challenging agenda for future peace research as
well as provocative ideas for peace activists in many
contexts. Our assessment will be made in the context of
the nine topics under which chapters have been grouped.
The first four topics are grouped in Part 1," Societal
Foundations of Peace."

Topic A, Creating Cultural and Political Contexts
of Peace. The five chapters under this topic pose
transformation strategies for the discourse and
organization of peace movements, linking personal peace
to peace in more extended contexts, making peace a topic
of news reporting, and turning decentralization and
information sharing into peace strategies.

In Chapter 1, "Power/Knowledge: The Problems of
Peace Research and the Peace Movement," James Skelly
argues that the peace movement needs a long-term strategy
that gives attention to knowledge, ideology,
consciousness, and discourse. He asks for studies in
discourse analysis, semiotics, and literary criticism
that will deconstruct the global military system and
allow "people to understand the fundamental sources of
this oppression and to therefore begin to liberate the
subjugated knowledge of peace." As an example he claims
that the acceptance of the dominant arms race discourse
by the freeze movement permitted the SDI strategy to
respond to the movement's challenge while still
preserving the Pentagon's role.

In Chapter 2, "The Impact of the Peace Movement on
Public Opinion and Policy-Making: The Case of the
Netherlands," Philip Everts emphasizes the importance of
the peace movement's placement of its concerns on the
agendas of "established institutions" such as churches,
trade unions, and moderate parties of the political
center. In the past the peace movement in the
Netherlands exhibited a cyclical pattern, with peaks
reflecting temporary coalitions based on very specific

issues. Constraining a more sustained peace movement is widespread acceptance that elites should make defense and foreign policy. But Everts senses that a breakthrough has been made in the Netherlands through the outreach of the peace movement into "established institutions."

In Chapter 3, "Indices of Japanese Militarization," Ryuhei Hatsuse asserts the importance of the "obsession with private peace" and the need to awake people from a "dream of personal satisfaction." What he finds puzzling is the "quiet militarization" in Japan in a political and economic context that is not yet overly military--a context suggesting that militarization can proceed even within the limits imposed by a demilitarized society. Hatsuse sees the need to link people's definitions of personal peace to communal peace and also to notions of world peace.

In Chapter 4, "Can Peace Become a Topic in News Reporting?" Lutz Michel and Brigitta Lutz urge that journalistic ethics must be adapted to the norms of journalism concerned with peace. Their recommendation flows out of an exploratory study of the treatment of peace issues in the West German daily Suddeutsche Zeitung, which has revealed low attention to peace coupled with much greater attention to military affairs. At the same time, they note a bias in peace reporting whereby peace is dealt with only when someone in the Western political elite is involved.

In Chapter 5, "Information Sharing as a Human Right," Harold Pepinsky argues that people are freed from fear and inclination to violence by their participation in decentralized political structures. Decentralization gives security through access to information that reveals new ways to adapt to environmental contingencies. Pepinsky has reached these insights through his cross-national study of crime--a study that has revealed striking differences in definitions of unlawful behavior and in factors that affect willingness to punish. He offers this challenging conclusion: "the world will become more peaceful only as we learn to increase the unexplained variance in human action."

Topic B, Nonviolence. The four chapters in this section on nonviolence seek transformation potential: by extending perception of the contexts in which nonviolence can be applied, by rejecting the assumption that human violence is inevitable, by insisting that the organization and leadership of nonviolence movements remain consistent with nonviolent principles, and by demonstrating the power of successful nonviolence movements to encourage nonviolent struggle in other countries.

In Chapter 6, "Six Views of Nonviolence for Peace Research," Theodore Herman proposes nonviolent "alternatives to attitudes, institutions and practices that withhold peace and justice." In urging intensified attention to nonviolence by peace researchers he calls for new histories that include nonviolent heroes, education that involves cooperative learning, national policies for fairer sharing of resources, markets and knowledge as insurance against future strife, and local and global networks for meeting people's needs. In explicating six different approaches to nonviolence he enriches our understanding of the essence of nonviolence and extends the array of opportunities for using nonviolent strategies. Whatever the approach, he sees "working with others in groups as essential."

In Chapter 7, "The Biology of Nonviolence," Graham Kemp sees transformation potential in rejection of the assumption that human violence is inevitable. While some believe that ethology supports the biological inevitability of human violence, Kemp asserts that the opposite is true—that violence is culturally induced, through programs that override nonviolent tendencies. Thus, what "ethologists see as the practical path ahead is the 'cultural re-engineering' of our society to allow a biological tendency to be nonviolent in our interhuman confrontations to re-establish itself."

In Chapter 8, "Nonviolent Grassroots Movement for Social Change in Rural India," Ravi Kumar draws on the experience of Vahini (the Student Youth Direction Action Force) in specifying the kind of nonviolent movement that would be compatible with transformation. His requirements offer a severe challenge to those who would bring about what he calls a Total Revolution. Collective leadership at all levels is superior to democratic centralism. Revolution "cannot be brought piecemeal. To be complete a revolution must be a simultaneous process working at different levels and in different fields of life." Satyagrah or other peaceful techniques must be used "to win over the forces of police and administration to the side of the revolutionaries, thereby breaking the teeth of repression." At the same time the "revolutionary political instrument must be capable of effectively controlling the politically ambitious at such time as the revolution succeeds."

In the final chapter in this section, "Three
Nonviolent Campaigns--Larzac, Marckolsheim, Whyl--A
Comparison," Roger Rawlinson emphasizes the importance of
community unity and suggests that the manner in which the
nonviolence idea is introduced in conflict situations is
important to success. Also important in these campaigns
against enlargement of a military base, construction of a
chemical firm, and building of a nuclear power station is
the way in which the campaigns have influenced and
learned from one another. They have also influenced
similar struggles in England and France and have led to
direct contact with similar efforts in Japan and Kanaki
(New Caledonia).

Topic C, Women, Militarization and Education. The
four chapters in this section focus on the concerns and
perspectives of women and discern transformation
potential in a unified effort of peace movements and
feminist movements, in the refusal of women to
participate in the military, in the direct involvement of
women as peacemakers and peacekeepers, and in the
development of an alternative feminist science that
overcomes the sexism, racism and militarism of existing
science.

In Chapter 10, "Military-Industrial Complexes and
Violence Toward Women," Andre Michel sees transformation
potential in a unified effort between peace movements
(with their concern for the dignity of citizens) and
feminist movements (with their concern for the dignity of
women). Scientific-bureaucratic-military-industrial-
banking complexes are not at all neutral with respect to
the status of women. They are new "patricharchal systems
which tend to perpetuate the oppression and exploitation
of women through exerting violence." Unlike other
patriarchal systems, they are global systems that
encompass families, schooling, occupational systems,
information systems, prostitution systems, and cultural
systems.

In Chapter 11, "Women in the US Military: A Setback
for Feminism," Mindy Percival perceives the participation
of women in the military "as contrary to the goals of
sexual, racial, democratic and economic equality, and
positive global transformation." The increased
participation of women in the U.S. military is viewed as
a setback for feminism in that the military (1) reflects
the secondary status of women in American society, (2)
imposes its own unique forms of sexual discrimination,
which are detrimental to the achievement of women's

equality and full participation, and (3) is antithetical to feminist aspirations because it embraces patriarchy, hierarchy, authoritarianism and violence. Through participation, therefore, women encourage "a system of warped values that demeans, objectifies and destroys life" and "maintains an unjust world order."

In Chapter 12, "The Development of Peace and Peace Education Concepts Through Three UN Decade for Women Conferences," Birgit Brock-Utne sees transformation potential in the participation of women in decision making regarding peace and in peace education that includes a feminist perspective and acknowledges the peace contributions of women. From this perspective women should be included in delegations to international conferences not primarily because their exclusion would be discriminatory but because they have special insights to offer. Progress has been made in the course of the 1975, 1980, and 1985 UN Women's Decade Conferences. In particular, the 1985 Nairobi Conference "indicates a paradigm shift from a liberal to a more radical feminist perspective. It puts women on the agenda both as peacemakers and peacekeepers."

In Chapter 13, "Women, Science Education, and Action for Peace," Robin Burns discerns transformation potential through teaching science in a way that conveys an understanding of its cultural base and a critical examination of its relationship to society. Scientific culture includes sexism, racism and militarism. A women's perspective would provide a firm guideline for an alternative feminist science that offers new relationships between "subject" and "object" and new approaches to ethical-moral issues in seeking and applying knowledge. The basis for building a more peaceful society can begin in the classroom, as a microcosm of the wider world.

Topic D, Peace Education. The four chapters in this section discern transformation potential in making the pedagogy of peace more consistent with the goals of peace education, in adopting more long-term strategies, in developing educators that are models rather than preachers, and in teaching about peace education in a more universal way.

In Chapter 14, "Neo-Conservatives and Controversies in Australian Peace Education: Some Critical Reflections and Counter Strategy," Toh Swee-Hin seeks transformation through responding to conservative criticisms of peace education and by means of a constructive peaceful

strategy that counters and defuses criticisms. Bias
charges should be dealt with by including conservative
literature in course readings. The conservative agenda
should be demystified by clarifying how it would affect
the condition of the poor and unemployed in contrast to
the impact of the peace agenda. Peace educators are
obligated to teach about peace in a peaceful way that
would not include indoctrination.

In Chapter 15, "A Survey of Peace Education in
Canada," Wytze Brouwer discerns the advantages of a broad
definition of peace education that would build on topics
that are already an integral part of Canadian education,
such as world hunger and development, human rights and
social justice, and ecological concerns. Goals of peace
education should be made explicit through describing the
characteristics of successful graduates of a peace
education program. These graduates should be "young
people who have the desire and skill to participate in
shaping society, in their own community, their nation and
in the world." Peace education must be part of a
long-term process that involves parents, teachers, and
schoolboard members. It must be conducted in an
environment that stimulates responsibility and
independence, offers room for experimentation with
behavior and learning, and involves educators that do not
preach values but, rather, model values through their
conduct.

In Chapter 16, "Education: A Force for Change in the
Northeast of England: What Are The Global Implications?"
David Menham advocates education for world citizenship
that combines multi-ethnic education, world studies,
development education, disarmament education, human
rights education, environmental education, peace studies,
and global peace education. Confusion arises when the
word peace is identified with the peace movement (in
particular, the unilateralist movement) and when peace
education and disarmament education are confused with one
another. Unless peace education is universal in concept,
it can be as divisive as education for war.

In Chapter 17, "Hunger for Weapons: Education on
'Armament and Development' for Twelve to Sixteen Year
Olds," Clara Venema advocates combining peace education
and development education, in the regular secondary
educational curriculum, through education on armament and
development. The topics she covers include: (1) the
increasing military expenditures in the Third World, (2)
the growth of arms trade from the North to the South, and

(3) the social, economic, and political consequences of increased military expenditures and armament in the Third World. India is the subject of a detailed case study.

The next two topics are grouped under Part 25 Economic Aspects of Peace.

Topic E, Peace and Development. For the most part the transformation strategies discussed in this section's four chapters are implied. Their value is in illuminating the economic causes of peacelessness as they reveal the inhibition of "authentic development," by the militarized state, the way in which a stagnating economy can lead toward authoritarinism and dissent, the questionable use of spurring industrial development based on a drive for an independent domestic arms industry, and the inability of labor analysis developed in industrialized countries to cope with the disruptive nature of underemployment and hidden unemployment in the Third World.

In Chapter 18, "Peace and Development in a Counter-Elitist Perspective," Narindar Singh focuses on the compatibility of "genuine peace" and "authentic development," both of which require a drastic attenuation of state power. Basic to the success of disarmament is "industrial disarmament," which would require liberation from both liberalism and Marxism. At stake is not the legitimacy of this "ism" or that one but, rather, the legitimacy of the "modern hyper-militarized state." The capacity to raise questions about the legitimacy of militarized states requires a "counter-elitist" world view.

In Chapter 19, "The Limits of Import Substitution: Emerging Authoritarianism in Kenya," Peter Magnusson illuminates the roots of growing authoritarianism and militarism in Kenya. In the process he suggests that overcoming economic stagnation is a necessity if this tendency is to be overcome. Yet dependent capitalist development based on the export of agricultural primary goods and industrialization by import substitution sustained by foreign investment have reached their limits. At the same time, the stagnating economy is accentuating ethnic dissent in a state whose borders are not coincident with those of African nations. This dissent, too, is contributing to the involvement of the military in Kenyan politics, as well as to the intrusion of military aid from abroad.

In Chapter 20, "Arms Manufacture: The 'Pulling' Industry in Industrialization Aimed at Import

Substitution: The Case of Turkey," Judit Balazs analyzes
efforts to develop a domestic arms industry both as a
basis for a more independent defense system and as a
foundation for industrial development based on more
advanced technology. The development of import-
substitution strategy partially funded by assessments on
the salaries of active officers resulted in Armed Forces
Mutual Aid Fund acquisition of majority shares in the
Turkish automobile and agricultural machinery industries.
But the military and industrial independence goals of
this strategy are not being fulfilled.

In Chapter 21, "The Right to Work and the Situation
of Workers," Ines Vargas sees little chance for the 800
million people living in absolute poverty to improve
their situation in the foreseeable future. Particularly
in the Third World, more and more people find it is
increasingly difficult to earn a living. The probable
consequence will be social violence. Unfortunately, work
force approaches for analyzing the problem, based on
experience in industrialized countries, are woefully
inadequate in the Third World because they overlook
underemployment and hidden unemployment.

Topic F, <u>World Economy</u>. The four chapters in this
section seek transformation in the world economy through
public debate on the arms trade fomented by more open
reporting, the overcoming of Third World debt bondage by
delinkage from Western lifestyles that favor waste,
injustice ficticiousness, and ostentation, and the
effective participation of the masses in decisions
concerning the economy.

In Chapter 22, "The Arms Trade: Facts and
Implications," Michael Brzoska and Thomas Ohlson see a
potential for restraining arms exports given the greater
long-term development potential in the exchange of
civilian goods. Also useful, they maintain, would be
open reporting on trade in and production of conventional
arms, which would stimulate public debate in both
supplier and recipient states. Such debate, in turn
would stimulate reconsideration and reevaluation of the
interests and determinants of the arms trade and of ways
to control it. They perceive increasing activity by
trade unionists working in the arms industry in support
of reduction of arms production for export.

In Chapter 23, "Third World Debt Bondage," Jomo
Sundaram documents the growth of Third World debt—a
tenfold increase in a decade, with 108 percent of new
debt going to debt servicing by 1984. Sundaram concludes

that "it all seems somewhat hopeless" and believes that a solution will require challenging some of the very premises on which the financial system has been built. "For example, neither bank capital nor profits are sacred."

In Chapter 24, "Debt and Dependency: The Case of Latin America," Jacobo Schatan characterizes the outflow of raw materials to service the Latin American foreign debt as a plundering of Latin American resources in the name of "development" and "interdependence." In response he urges dissociation from "a false notion of "progress" that results in deterioration of the quality of life of vast numbers of human beings. A new path would involve reduction of imports to essentials, import substitution, and no borrowing. This delinking process would favor equitable and rational behavior and the disconnection from a lifestyle that favors injustice, ficticiousness and ostentation.

In Chapter 25, "Transforming the International Order," Jose A. Silva Michelena discerns the potential for a transformation in Latin America that could create a self reliant Latin America by the year 2000. The deepening of liberal democracy would advance a new conception of development whose main purposes would be the betterment of the quality of life and the assignment of resources to satisfy a new order of priorities. Elite corporatism would be replaced by effective participation of the masses in decisions concerning the economy. At the same time, this kind of democratization would offer better conditions for South-South relationships, which in turn could facilitate "real regional integration" in the Caribbean and Central America as well as greater coordination and exchange between Latin America and other Third World countries.

The volume concludes with three more traditional peace research topics viewed from a nontraditional and transformational perspective; grouped under Part 3, Security and Conflict.

Topic G, Alternative Security. Focusing primarily on Europe, these four chapters in this section seek to diminish potential for an East-West war through transformation of military forces to a more defensive posture. Among the suggestions presented are the importance of evaluating the credibility of one's own military doctrine in the context of the opponent's system of logic, the need for nonoffensive defense as a basis for no first use of nuclear weapons, an attrition net as

an approach to nonoffensive defense, and the importance
of transparency and decentralization in alternative
defense.

In Chapter 26, "Uncertainties About WTO and NATO
Military Doctrines," Laszlo Valki observes that,
originally, the military doctrines of both WTO and NATO
were defensive in character but concepts of deep
interdiction and conventional weapons systems for
carrying it out have enhanced the dangers of preventive
strike, particularly during a prolonged and escalating
crisis. At the same time, neither NATO nor WTO have a
single official document saying which military doctrine
would apply if an attack took place. Regrettably there
is a tendency for analysts to evaluate the credibility of
their doctrines only within their own systems of logic--a
practice sometimes called "self-deterrence."

In Chapter 27, "No-First-Use of Nuclear Weapons and
Nonoffensive Defense," Bjorn Moller argues that
nonoffensive defense (NOD) makes possible no first use
(NFU) of nuclear weapons. Both NOD and NFU serve the
same strategic purpose--the avoidance of any
unintentional armed confrontation between the blocs. NOD
will make NFU possible by increasing defensive potential
while replacing deep-strike conventional strategies that
would bring escalation leading to nuclear strikes. Both
NFU and NOD aim at stability, and they function
reciprocally. NFU without NOD might worsen the problems
it was supposed to solve, and NOD without NFU is
impossible.

In Chapter 28, "Common Security and the Concept of
Non-Offensive Defense," Anders Boserup argues that a
"balance" of forces can have catastrophic consequences
because forces suited for attack invite preemptive
attack. He points to the transformational potential of
basing conventional defense in Europe on attrition
through essentially stationary forces which would be
widely scattered. This attrition net would consist of
tiny defense units dispersed evenly over the entire
theater of war so that there would be no way of bypassing
the net and no need to move forces about. This would
present a potential attacker with three unattractive
options: (1) push through to an objective of no real
military value, (2) settle for a long and costly war of
attrition or, (3) escalate to a large-scale war.

In Chapter 29, "From Deep Strike to Alternative
Defense: The Role of Technology," Gunilla Herolf seeks to
replace the destabilizing effect of new deep-strike

weapons with an alternative defense whose most important
characteristic is transparency, which makes its defensive
character clearly recognizable. Another characteristic
of an alternative defense system would be its
decentralization, which would increase flexibility as
well as reduce vulnerability. Future technologies, such
as sensor technology (for detection and homing) and
miniaturization (for including advanced technology in
small weapons), are thought to favor the defensive side
more than the offensive and are expected to become
increasingly cost-effective. But in alternative defense
the role of technology would be reduced and a more robust
type of defense would be emphasized.

Topic H, <u>Conflict Analysis</u>. Three of the chapters
in this section offer suggestions for enhancing the value
of conflict analysis, by employing local and international multidisciplinary teams and by giving separate
attention to the conflict generation process, the
conflict process, and the conflict settlement process.
The fourth chapter illuminates the ways in which conflict
in South Africa has encouraged reform, which in turn is
leading to militarization.

In Chapter 30, "Getting Theory and Practice
Together: The Conflict Resolution Working Group," Paul
Wehr and Ann FitzSimmons report on an effort to enhance
the usefulness of conflict resolution research by
eliminating discipline-bound languages and conceptual
frameworks, and by overcoming jealous guarding of
disciplinary turf. Involved were researchers from law,
sociology, business, psychology, geography, and political
science who joined in the development of a methodology
for resolving a zoning conflict in Boulder County,
Colorado. In actually applying their methodology, they
overcame the meagre opportunity for conflict resolution
researchers to test their work. They concluded that
close collaboration among researchers, conflict
resolution practitioners, and disputants is a "sine qua
non for future understanding and regulation of
contentious relations."

In Chapter 31, "Unintended Nuclear War: An Emerging
Academic Concern," Paul Smoker advocates the creation of
an international multidisciplinary committee for moving
toward a deeper understanding of factors that could
contribute to an unintended nuclear war. The topics to
be investigated include suggestions for overcoming
accidental nuclear war, such as joint crisis-control
centers and an international satellite-monitoring agency.

Of growing urgency are such indicators as the decrease in
decision time permitted by new nuclear technology, the
increasing role of computers in command and control
systems, and human factors such as drug abuse, stress,
and psychological disorders.

In Chapter 32, "The Settlement of Border Conflicts:
A Theoretical Model with Empirical Illustrations,"
Kjell-Ake Nordquist presents a model for analyzing border
conflicts and presents some results from preliminary
application of the model to twenty-four conflicts being
waged over the location of interstate borders.
Nordquist's model is in response to the severe lack of
theorizing about causes of border conflicts and about
conditions for settlement. A basic assumption of
Nordquist's analytical framework is the need to
investigate three distinct phases of conflicts: the
conflict generating process, the conflict process and the
settlement implementation process. Nordquist emphasizes
that "a border is a matter of common concern between
states". And that no state can have "sovereighty" over
a border.

In Chapter 33, "The Dynamics of Reform and
Repression in the South African Conflict and the Emerging
Role of the South African Defense Forces," Elling Njal
Tjonneland probes the strategy being used by the South
African regime to prevent a radical social
transformation. At the same time, the regime recognizes
that change is needed, and it is seeking new allies among
Asians, Coloureds and urban blacks. The result is a
combination of repression and authoritarian reforms from
above—a situation that is leading to growing
militarization and the emergence of an increasingly
military-bureaucratic state in response to the black's
rejection of reforms. But the increasing role of the
military will exacerbate racial cleavages and tensions,
thereby further impeding civil liberties.

Topic I, What is Security? This last topic
underlines the connections among all of the topics in
this volume inasmuch as it could also be an appropriate
beginning topic. Each of the three chapters in this
section argue for broadening the traditional definition
of security beyond an emphasis on military factors, thus
complementing the trend toward a broader definition of
peace. They draw attention to the fact that defining
security must be democratized because different groups
within countries have different security interests. They
also express the concern that parochial and timebound

definitions of security can stifle creativity in the quest for new forms of security.

In Chapter 34, "National Security in the Third World: Need for a New Framework," K. P. Misra argues that security is multidimensional, encompassing economic-social, political-cultural, and ethnic and identity factors as well as military factors. Problems arise in applying definitions of security, particularly when the ruling elite assumes that its security is identical with the security of the country. Other difficulties are created by potential differences between national security and international security, and between the security definitions of small and big states. Hence there is a need for research that more clearly delineates the conditions that will enhance the security of the peoples of the Third World.

In Chapter 35, "Peace and Security: Concepts and Strategies," Georg Sorensen argues for broad concepts of peace and security but chooses security as the best starting point. The state presents a contradiction with respect to security in that it is "the single most important provider of security for its citizens," but it is also a depriver of security. Thus the content of security must be defined through a democratic process, and that definition must combine security against the threat of war and the threat to welfare. At the same time security must be approached at individual, state and systemic levels.

In Chapter 36, "Understanding the European Security Configuration Through Concepts of Security," Egbert Jahn, Pierre Lemaitre, and Ole Waever use concepts of security as lenses through which elements of the structure of East-West conflict can be discerned. This conflict involves both physical security (fear of being annihilated) and security against the imposition of social structures and values, through military superiority as well as other means. Complexities arise within countries because different social groups have different security interests and fears. Especially in the case of certain nonmilitary (i.e., political, ideological and economic) threats, certain elite groups have the most to fear. Sometimes different groups act independently across state borders. European security must be seen as a nonmilitary continuation of the East-West conflict under the condition of military mutual security. Otherwise one must assume that the present sociopolitical and interstate status quo should be

18

eternally stabilized. The latter assumption would
exclude a more utopian concept of European security—a
concept that would permit the possibility of a future
political constellation in which both capitalist and
communist systems would vanish and be replaced by a
common European sociopolitical order.

The potential for transformation toward a just peace
is illuminated in the thirty-six chapters that follow.
This sampling of peace research reveals how the
employment of a diversity of approaches produces results
that contribute to an increasingly deeper understanding
of what peace can mean. At the same time, it
demonstrates how peace researchers from a diversity of
origins can explicate an increasing array of roles and
tasks through which peace strategies can be practiced.
We hope that readers will engage in a critical analysis
of these chapters. Much remains to be done before the
peace research movement reaches its full potential as a
vital part of the larger global peace movement. We
invite all to join us in research that will illuminate
paths that lead toward a just peace.

PART ONE

Societal Foundations of Peace

TOPIC A: CREATING CULTURAL AND POLITICAL CONTEXTS OF PEACE

1

Power/Knowledge: The Problems of Peace Research and the Peace Movement

James M. Skelly

INTRODUCTION

I have been consistently impressed, especially in the United States, by the lack of attention given to knowledge, ideology, consciousness, and discourse. It has seemed to me that the peace movement has, with but a few notable exceptions, always been on the defensive, because it has had no long-term strategy at the level of knowledge. Its entanglement in the dominant discourse of the arms race has reduced its tactics to the intellectual equivalent of throwing bricks and bottles at tanks -- occasionally, the tank is forced to halt, or to maneuver around some road block that activists have brought down in its path, but the tank's longterm movement is inexorable -- the challenges it has faced have been largely insignificant.

In terms of the traditions of peace research, this paper attempts to build on certain theoretical issues raised by critics of peace research, particularly Schmid, Carroll, and Reid and Yanarella. 1/ It strives to further some of their insights by developing a critique from structuralist and post-structuralist thought, and contemporary literary criticism, while remaining sensitive to the theoretical land-mines embedded in these approaches. 2/ The paper also attempts to outline a strategy for future efforts in peace research that can be utilized effectively by peace movements.

In his article, Schmid criticized many peace researchers for assuming a systems perspective that "aims at control of and integration of the international system." 3/   In adopting this perspective, he noted that both the perspective and its accompanying value orientation were "identical with those of the existing international institutions and lies very close to those of the rich and powerful nations" 4/ and, I would add, those who are rich and powerful within those nations. Thus, "peace research becomes a factor supporting the status quo of the international power structure ..." 5/ He suggests that peace research "should formulate its problems not in terms meaningful to international and supranational institutions, but in terms meaningful to suppressed and exploited groups and nations." 6/   I will argue that the nuclear threat globalizes Schmid's challenge so that all of us now belong to suppressed and exploited groups.

Implicitly building on Schmid's critique, Berenice Carroll 7/ argues that peace researchers have been preoccupied with "the cult of power" such that they have failed "to challenge the prevailing conception of power as dominance." She questions whether "peace -- even negative peace" is realizable "in the prevailing nation-state system of international relations," and whether "a commitment to peace requires a commitment to revolutionary social change." 8/   Carroll then suggests that peace research focus on the power of those deemed powerless in the paradigms of those concerned with power as dominance -- the suppressed and exploited groups of Schmid's concern. She would do this by contrasting power as dominance with "the idea of power as independent strength, ability, autonomy, self-determination, control over one's own life rather than the lives of others, competence to deal with one's environment out of one's own energies and resources, rather than on the basis of dependence." 9/

Reid and Yanarella 10/ come closer to my concerns by arguing for a "critical peace research." They suggest that American peace researchers appropriated an image of science derived from the natural sciences at the very time that a paradigm shift was being brought about by developments in post-modern philosophy that raised fundamental questions about the nature of science and the theory of knowledge. In playing out their concern with knowledge as an imperative of power, they cite Merleau-

Ponty to the effect that what is needed is a "return to
that world which precedes knowledge, of which knowledge
always speaks, and in relation to which every scientific
schematization is an abstract and derivative sign-
language, as is geography in relation to the countryside
in which we have learned beforehand what a forest, a
prairie, or a river is." 11/ Critical peace researchers
they contend must therefore "develop an awareness of the
less visible sources of elite power and mass quiescence,"
12/ and cite Carroll's 13/ note that "no solution to
the war problem will be found until we have a better
understanding of why peace is not an urgent demand of the
'powerless' despite their pacific inclinations and of how
or when it might become so."
      Implicit in these works is the criticism that peace
researchers have failed to be reflective about their
production of knowledge -- knowledge which should be in
the service of peace and often is not. Schmid's concern
with formulating problems in terms meaningful to
oppressed groups suggests the need to understand peace as
what Michel Foucault 14/ has characterized as one of the
"subjugated knowledges" -- those sets "of knowledges that
have been disqualified as inadequate to their task or
insufficiently elaborated: naive knowledges, located low
down on the hierarchy, beneath the required level of
cognition or scientificity." Carroll's challenge to
focus on the concerns of those deemed powerless and to
explore the question of why peace is not one of their
principal demands, similarly implies a need to reflect on
the "culture of silence" 15/ that is manifest on peace
issues and to engage in a pedagogy that will empower
people to speak on these issues. In like manner, Reid
and Yanarella 16/ argue that peace research must
relocate "the theorist and his theoretical-activity
within the totality," and thus force theorists to give
"up the claim of being able to speak authoritatively and
indifferently about a world they do not inhabit." In
other words, they must cease their accommodation with the
"regime of truth" 17/ as applied to peace, by detaching
the power of the regime from the forms of hegemony.
      Since the focus of many peace activists and
researchers has been on the nuclear balance of terror, I
will explore the regime of truth that has developed
around nuclear weapons and the difficulties that challenges to the regime have confronted. Conceptually
central to this regime as it has developed in our times

has been the notion that the deterrent function of
nuclear weapons has maintained peace.

HISTORICAL BACKGROUND -- CONSTRUCTION OF THE REGIME

In order to develop a fundamental critique of
nuclear weapons we must understand the core of the regime
of truth that has developed around them. The theoretical
underpinning for nuclear weapons has, since the late
1940s, been the notion of deterrence of the Soviet
threat. 18/   Deterrence, as a rhetorical system, has
provided the justification for nuclear weapons, and the
structures of power associated with them in the federal
government. At the center of this rhetoric has been the
concept that nuclear weapons were offensive systems
designed to deter the Soviet Union from launching an
attack on the United States or its allies. The post
World War II peace that has existed between the superpowers, as defined in that rhetoric, has relied on the
notion that both nations were mutually assured of each
other's destruction should either launch an attack on the
other. Thus, nuclear weapons were central to the maintenance of U.S. national security because they were said
to be the principal mechanism used to deter the Soviet
Union's aggressive impulses. The U.S. readiness to use
nuclear weapons therefore neutralized the Soviet threat.

George Orwell, it seems to me, foresaw the character
of the Cold War and its latent function. The passage
below from 1984 suggests the deeper significance of what
Mary Kaldor has called "imaginary war" 19/:   The war,
therefore, if we judge it by the standards of previous
wars, is merely an imposture. It is like the battles
between certain ruminant animals whose horns are set at
such an angle that they are incapable of hurting one
another. But through it is unreal it is not meaningless.
It eats up the surplus of consumable goods, and it helps
to preserve the special mental atmosphere that a hierarchical society needs. War, it will be seen, is now a
purely internal affair. In the past, the ruling groups
of all countries, although they might recognize their
common interest and therefore limit the destructiveness
of war, did fight against one another, and the victor
always plundered the vanquished. In our own day they are
not fighting against one another at all. The war is
waged by each ruling group against its own subjects, and

the object of war is not to make or prevent conquests of territory, but to keep the structure of society intact. The very word "war," therefore, has become misleading. It would probably be accurate to say that by becoming continuous war has ceased to exist. The peculiar pressure that it exerted on human beings between the Neolithic Age and the early twentieth century has disappeared and has been replaced by something quite different. The effect would be much the same if the three superstates, instead of fighting one another, should agree to live in perpetual peace, each inviolate within its own boundaries. For in that case each would be a self contained universe freed forever from the sobering influence of external danger. A peace that was truly permanent would be the same as a permanent war. This -- although the vast majority of Party members understand it only in a shallower sense -- is the inner meaning of the Party slogan: WAR IS PEACE. 20/

If we are fully to understand the dilemma of the nuclear arms race therefore, we must not only look to its obvious manifestation in the confrontation between the United States and the Soviet Union. We must look, as Orwell would have, at the arms race in terms of its social functions and in terms of what it cloaks. We must look at how war has become peace. I am arguing that the superpower confrontation covers a hidden discourse of power within each of the societies and that nuclear weapons have been fundamental to the concentration of political power in their respective state structures.

Nuclear weapons have served more fully in the United States than in the USSR because the Soviet government had already achieved a much higher concentration of political power than the United States had when nuclear weapons were introduced in 1945. The Soviets had set out consciously to centralize power and their ideology served to justify it. Nuclear weapons, which communicate their threat through the discourse of deterrence, have justified an enormous concentration of power in the U.S. government since World War II as manifested by elaborate national security structures and the integration of the military with the industrial sector. Since this integration of social structures had already been accomplished in the Soviet Union, nuclear weapons have had much less to do with the establishment and maintenance of domestic social control within that nation. However, the relationship between the superpowers as it has developed over the past forty years now functions to justify, each for the other, the continued, largely unchallengeable, concentration of state power. Due to the enormity of the nuclear threat to the future of the human project, we now exist in a global system that consists largely of functional collusion of the United States and the Soviet Union. If Mr. Gorbachev understands that nuclear weapons are more important to the U.S. than to the USSR, his current moves on arms control may be an outgrowth of that understanding.

The theoretical underpinning for nuclear weapons has since the late 1940s been the notion of deterrence of the Soviet threat. Deterrence, as a rhetorical system, has provided the justification for nuclear weapons, and for the structures of power associated with them in the federal government. Deterrence transformed the orientation of both the military and American society toward war and, in the process, transformed American society. No longer would we draw on our heritage and criticize concentrations of power in an American government.

If one defines the Bomb as a deterrent, then "the chief purpose of our military establishment must be to avert wars." 21/ But what this would require would be a full scale mobilization of our armed forces at all times before the outbreak of hostilities! Thus, atomic bombs, characterized as deterrents, required constant mobilization of state resources. It is thus in their requirement for mobilization, rather than their awful destructive power, that nuclear weapons have become ultimate weapons. Deterrence was to be war by other means -- war as peace!

Because the post-war American political elite wanted to integrate nuclear weapons into political and military structures, and because they could only be integrated as "deterrents" to the very kind of war they embodied, there was some difficulty in the early years mustering support for the mobilization that nuclear weapons required, especially for a war that was never going to be fought. But they succeeded. The deterrent quality of nuclear weapons had ended total war and replaced it with total mobilization or "pure war." 22/

Remember that the mobilizations required in traditional wars had had the short term effect of centralizing more power in the state. When the wars were concluded however, demobilization resulted in a loss of the governmental power acquired during the war and, in the U.S., the demand of citizen-soldiers for greater political participation. The mobilization required by nuclear forces defined as deterrents, however, never requires a demobilization and therefore allows the government to accrue ever more power with little significant internal challenge to its imperatives, especially since no soldiers have died, and the war has remained in many ways invisible. The Minuteman, now a missile, would not question the actions of the political leadership, nor demand greater political power. The citizen-soldier has been automated and the political significance of bearing arms is essentially nullified. As one social critic has noted "the Total Peace of deterrence is Total War pursued by others means." 23/

THE PARADOX OF DETERRENCE

The more recent attacks on deterrence, although not tied to the broad societal upheaval of the Vietnam War, were in many ways more challenging to its continued status. The origin of these attacks can be traced to the serious rift which developed in the Washington policy elite following the Tet offensive in early 1968. That portion of the policy elite that understood that the war was eroding support for the regime put in place a new policy that attempted to sever limited war from the theory of deterrence, and sought detente with the Soviets as a way of attempting to stabilize the strategic relationship. As Paul Warnke put it, "What happens in Southeast Asia is of only marginal importance to the Soviet Union," and therefore, to the United States. 24/

The new policy would depend at the strategic level on arms control negotiations like SALT and a more traditional balance of power perspective with regard to Soviet intentions in peripheral areas. The new relationship with the Soviets however, was not in itself enough to achieve the domestic social control functions of the regime of truth in the U.S. since detente called into question the foundational assumptions of deterrence. Detente, at the rhetoric level, implicitly asserts that the Soviet threat is not all pervasive and therefore begins to call into question the structures of power associated with deterrence of the threat. Just as

Becker 25/ demonstrates with regard to the Church and sin, the institutions associated with the vast post-World War II national security apparatus had come to depend upon deterrence of the Soviet threat as their raison d'etre. I will demonstrate that because Detente began to unmask the paradoxes of deterrence, it became necessary to repress it by revivifying the threat.

Most notable in this revival effort was the reconstituted Committee on the Present Danger. 26/ The CPD, in accord with other conservative and right-wing groups, mounted a massive public relations campaign predicated on two notions: that the Soviet threat was being underestimated -- the infamous Team-B report; and that arms control negotiations and detente amounted to "appeasement." 27/ The effect in the United States has been the massive buildup oriented to military superiority that was begun in the Carter administration and continued in the Reagan era.

The difficulty in stabilizing Detente requires that we analyze the rhetorical paradox of Deterrence and thus recognize how various actors become imprisoned by their own discourse. It is here that we can see how taking a position in favor of Deterrence, however minimal, the position inevitably undermines any stable relationship between the US and the USSR, fuels an arms race, and contributes to the continued political disempowerment of the citizenry at large. To begin, we must recognize that nuclear weapons cannot communicate their threat directly but must rely on the discourse about them embodied in the strategy of nuclear deterrence to complete their threat potential. Thus, as McCanles 28/ points out, one of the paradoxes of Deterrence "is that we have discourse that has meaning only insofar as it refers to arms, while arms in turn only have meaning insofar as they are articulated in discourse." Since "nuclear weapons exist to be talked about, not to be used," Strobe Talbott 29/ says, nuclear deterrence as a "threatening text allows itself to be read as a 'mere threat.'" 30/ This in turn leads to periodic arms buildups on either side in an attempt to gain superiority and counter the perception that the existence of all those weapons is "mere threat." Thus, deterrence inevitably leads to destabilization of the very equilibrium that it is supposed to maintain. "Stabilization, like parity," Theodore Draper 31/ notes, "is a will-o'-the-wisp because it means, in reality, repeated stabilizations at increasingly higher levels."

The U.S. shift to counterforce strategy in the mid-70s provides an excellent example of this paradox at work.

CONTEMPORARY CHALLENGES TO THE REGIME

Despite (or perhaps, on account of) the revitalization of Deterrence and the accompanying arms buildup beginning in the later years of the Carter Administration, the regime of truth around nuclear weapons met three powerful challenges in the early 1980s: the nuclear freeze, the American Catholic bishops pastoral letter on peace, and the Green movement in Germany. With the analysis developed above, however, we should be able to see why these movements have ultimately been reduced to throwing the intellectual equivalent of bricks and bottles at tanks. We should also be able to understand some of the rhetorical potency of the Strategic Defense Initiative (SDI).

The Nuclear Freeze Campaign attempted to build support in the U.S. for a mutual and verifiable freeze on production, testing, and deployment of nuclear weapons in the U.S. and in the Soviet Union. From the perspective being developed here, the strength of the freeze was that it attempted, somewhat successfully at first, to break out of the constraints of the dominant discourse. It did this by putting forth a simple, straightforward proposal that would stabilize Deterrence and thus halt the built-in imperative to an arms race. This of course began to unmask the paradox in Deterrence strategy and undermine its threatening force. 32/ At the textual level, the freeze began to deconstruct the threat and reveal Deterrence as "mere threat," since Deterrence, as it was discussed above, cannot exist unless each side attempts to make its deterrent credible by seeking superiority.

The achilles heel for the freeze was its rootedness in arms control. In designing their proposal, freeze leaders wanted "an initiative that would be ... acceptable to experts." 33/ It was this desire, that the freeze become authoritative at the textual level, that would ultimately undermine it. Arms control positions do not ultimately challenge any of the fundamental underpinings of the dominant discourse and therefore, however radical they may be, they ultimately reinforce the discourse.

The challenge of the American Catholic bishops'
pastoral letter, which was being considered publicly at
the same time as the freeze, lay in its attempt to use a
totally different discourse than the dominant one. As
articulated by the bishops, the language of moral theology faced some difficulty in confronting the relatively
new discourse of nuclear deterrence associated with the
hegemony of the state. The bishops' pastoral was not a
fundamental critique of the discourse of deterrence or of
the state of pure war. It equivocated on deterrence (and
this would limit its impact), quoting Pope John Paul II
to the effect that, "in current conditions 'deterrence'
based on balance, certainly not as an end in itself but
as a step on the way toward a progressive disarmament,
may still be judged morally acceptable."

Nonetheless, the bishops' letter was strongly
criticized from within the regime. Then National
Security Advisor William Clark 34/ attempted to place
nuclear deterrence within the discourse being articulated
by the bishops. Clark wrote a very public letter in
response to a draft of the pastoral letter that argued
that, "our decisions on nuclear armaments, and our
defense posture are guided by moral considerations as
compelling as any which have faced mankind." There was
also criticism of the bishops' "competence to speak out,"
35/ -- a classic tactic of discreditation at the level
of knowledge. In the end, the problem with the bishops'
letter was that it, like the freeze, argued for arms
control negotiations. Thus, though it raised carefully
crafted moral questions its equivocable position on
deterrence and its support of arms control allowed it to
be largely assimilated by the dominant discourse.

The challenge that the German Green movement posed
for the regime is that it attacked it where it does not
seem at first glance to be vulnerable. When the Greens
indicate that "the either/or situation created by the
emergence of the two power blocs after World War II has
resulted in a loss of self-determination for the allies
of both the Soviet Union and the United States" 36/ they
are striking at a fundamental underpinning of the regime.
Deterrence requires global extension. The Greens would
have Germany first ban nuclear weapons, then withdraw
from NATO, and ultimately move to a policy of social defense. 37/ If the Germans could escape reliance on
nuclear weapons, the justification for the entire regime
might begin to unravel even to the extent of questioning

the domestic measures necessary to preserve striking
power.

THE STRATEGIC DEFENSE INITIATIVE

If the reader keeps in mind the challenge that the
bishops, the Greens, and the freeze brought to bear upon
the regime at the level of rhetoric, the political
function of SDI should be evident. The bishops were
considering the pastoral letter in a public manner in the
fall of 1982, the same time that the nuclear freeze was
appearing in the form of referenda in scores of states
and municipalities throughout the United States. Large
numbers of congressmen and senators were attempting to
jump aboard one freeze proposal or another in response to
the freeze's extraordinarily high ratings in public
opinion polls. At the same time, the Greens were
campaigning for seats in the West German parliament and
throughout Europe there were mammoth demonstrations
against the planned deployment of Pershing IIs and
Tomahawk cruise missiles. The Greens, the first new
party to elect representatives in thirty years, took
their seats in the Bundestag on March 22, 1983. On March
23, Ronald Reagan gave his "Star Wars" speech.
Like the bishops, Reagan fundamentally criticized
Deterrence by saying that "I've become more and more
deeply convinced that the human spirit must be capable of
rising above dealing with other nations and human beings
by threatening their existence." Like the bishops, he
too was for arms negotiations: "If the Soviet Union will
join with us in our efforts we will have succeeded in
stabilizing the nuclear balance." But he "one upped
them" at this point by saying "Nevertheless, it will be
necessary to rely on the specter of retaliation, on
mutual threat. And that's a sad commentary on the human
condition. Wouldn't it be better to save lives than to
avenge them?" Implicitly, the President was indicating
that he was not mired in Old Testament sensibilities, as
the bishops were apt to be with their justification of
Deterrence as a "transitional strategy."
Then Reagan held out a vision of a post-Deterrence
world in which "free people could live secure in the
knowledge that their security did not rest upon the
threat of instant retaliation to deter a Soviet attack"

and where "we could intercept and destroy strategic ballistic missiles before they reached our own soil or that of our allies," laying the ground work for the change of the key conceptual mechanism in the entire regime of truth. That key conceptual mechanism had been offensive Deterrence. One of its selling points had been that "it undermined the claims of the indigenous pacifist movements." If it is successfully articulated in the future (and this is why I think Reagan has not wavered in his assertion that SDI is for the protection of people), the new vision could keep the entire national security structure that has developed around nuclear weapons in place and would revitalize the Pentagon's role as development bank.

DEVELOPING A STRATEGY AT THE LEVEL OF KNOWLEDGE

The real challenge for peace research then is how to hone a strategy at the level of knowledge that cannot be readily absorbed by the dominant discourse and which can therefore more fully empower those in the peace movement and expand their numbers. The ease with which SDI has blunted the challenges the regime has recently faced, as well as its potential ability to relegitimize national security structures, should help to emphasize the ease with which power can transform its imperatives into knowledge. It should also emphasize the difficulty that those with very little or no power have in sustaining a challenge at the level of knowledge. The dangers of challenging from within the dominant discourse, as did the freeze, and the bishops to a lesser extent, should be evident. Peace is a subjugated knowledge.

To begin, peace researchers must attempt to uncover the hidden discourse of power within the discourse of Deterrence and the larger regime of truth associated with nuclear weapons. This is a formidable task, though I think many of us have begun to understand that it is the only way that the "culture of silence" around nuclear weapons can be broken. Berenice Carroll's charge to develop "a better understanding of why peace is not an urgent demand of the 'powerless' despite their pacific inclinations" should perhaps be our starting point. This will require, among other things, some fundamental reconceptualizations about the nature of the human self —— of subjective identity and the manner in which that identity is tied to the nation state and its regime of truth.

Robert Lifton's 38/ discussion of the "double life" that one is forced to live in the nuclear world might provide the beginning point for such a reconceptualization. Lifton argues that psychic numbing is a consequence of being born into a nuclear world where one experiences craziness, the unmanageability of life, and death as extinction while behaving "as if all this were not the case." This furthers a "fundamental gap ... between knowledge and feeling. For in order to go about 'business as usual,' one has to deaden one's feelings about what one knows." Just as peace is a subjugated knowledge, so too is the horror of war subjugated in one's consciousness. Derrida's 39/ suggestion that we need conferences of people "who are not military professionals, and not professionals of strategy, diplomacy, or nuclear techno-science" is the kind of suggestion that may help to foster speech among those who have been mute in the face of the regime. Foucault urges upon us an "insurrection of subjugated knowledge." He also suggests that politically the most significant thing that individuals can do is resist the identities that others would impose on them. I would argue that nowhere is this more important than in the identification with the nation-state that is fostered by nuclearism and the regime of truth associated with it.

I would further urge upon my colleagues studies in the fields of discourse analysis, semiotics, and literary criticism as we attempt to deconstruct the regime. The discussion of the subject in the works of Lacan, Althusser, Brecht, Barthes, and Kristeva 40/ might prove valuable since institutional power needs subjects that have internalized a fixed subjectivity so that the institutional imperatives of power can be brought to bear. The willingness to kill and be killed is the ultimate expression of a fixed subjectivity. To kill another is to think that you know who he or she is, to give them a fixed identity and then to take it away. This is the case whether one is killing Communists, Christians, barbarians, or businessmen. To kill another is to think that you know who you are as well. He is that and therefore I am this. Their reality against ours. You can't have one without the other. It is the final discourse which is expressed not only in words, but in an action that is definitive. If I can define you, tell you who you are, then I have taken the first step in a discourse the logic of which can lead to murder or nuclear holocaust. This isn't a process, however, that is exclusively psychological. Rather it is evidence of the way in which institutional politics enters our consciousness and works on our bodies. We learn to accept our fixed subjectivity in the institutions we inhabit and we impose, we subject, others to a similar identity. Only when people accept who they've been told they are can power within institutions be exercised. Drug abuse, alcoholism, and many so-called "mental disorders," are escapes from the responsibilities imposed on our imposed identities. They are ways of escaping power because they undermine the fixity of one's identity. These are tragic responses, however, because the individual still fixes the problem in self instead of confronting the powers that work against him. The challenge for peace research and the peace movement is to engage in work that allows people to understand the fundamental sources of their oppression and to therefore begin to liberate the subjugated knowledge of peace.

NOTES

1. Herman Schmid, "Peace Research and Politics," Journal of Peace Research, Vol. V, 1968, 217-232; Berenice Carroll, "Peace Research: The Cult of Power," Journal of Conflict Resolution, Vol. XVI, 1972, 587-616.; and Herbert G. Reid and Ernest J. Yanarella, "Toward a Critical Theory of Peace Research in the United States: the Search for the 'Intelligible Core,'" Journal of Peace Research, Vol. XIII, 1976, 315-341.
2. See for example, E.P. Thompson's The Poverty of Theory, 1978, to gain a sense for the explosive character of the debates.
3. Herman Schmid, 218.
4. Ibid., 221.
5. Ibid., 229.
6. Ibid., 219.
7. Berenice Carroll, 593.
8. Ibid., 600, emphasis in original.
9. Ibid., 607.
10. Herbert G. Reid and Ernest J. Yanarella, 315.
11. Ibid., 321-322.
12. Ibid., 325

13. Berenice Carroll, 611.

14. Michel Foucault, Power/Knowledge: Selected Interviews & Other Writings, New York: Pantheon Books, 1980, 82.

15. Paulo Freire, Pedagogy of the Oppressed, New York: Seabury Press, 1970.

16. Op.cit., 332.

17. Michel Foucault, 131-133. In general, we can argue that the vast discourse that has developed around nuclear weapons, from the works of the nuclear strategists, to arms control proposals (even including the nuclear freeze), to official Soviet and American policy statements, have become part of a regime of truth about peace constructed around the concept of Deterrence. As a discourse, nuclear Deterrence has become a truth that justifies the existence of the weapons and has been accepted as such by the vast majority of our citizens. A regime of truth, according to Foucault also includes:

> the mechanisms and instances which enable one to distinguish true and false statement, the means by which each is sanctioned; the techniques and procedures accorded value in the acquisition of truth; the status of those who are charged with saying what counts as true.
> The mechanisms that enable individuals to distinguish true and false statements can be seen working at almost any conference or meeting on peace and security, as can the means by which such statements are sanctioned.

18. Charles Nathanson with James M. Skelly, "The Social Construction of the Soviet Threat," paper presented at the American Sociological Association annual meeting, San Antonio, August 27, 1984.

19. Mary Kaldor, "The Imaginary War," in D. Smith and E.P. Thompson (eds), Prospectus for a Habitable Planet. London: Penguin, 1987.

20. George Orwell, 1984. New York: New American Library, 1961.

21. Bernard Brodie, The Absolute Weapon. New York: Harcourt Brace & Co., 1946, 76.

22. Paul Virilio and Sylvere Lotringer, Pure War, translated by Mark Polizotti. New York: Semiotext(e), Inc., 1983.

23. Ibid., 25.

24. Quoted in Jerry W. Sanders, Peddlers of Crisis: The Committee on the Present Danger and the Politics of Containment, Boston: Southend Press, 1983, 142.

25. Howard S. Becker, Outsiders: Studies in the Sociology of Deviance, New York: The Free Press, 1963.

26. Jerry W. Sanders, 1983.

27. Ibid., 164.

28. Michael McCanles, "Machiavelli and the Paradoxes of Deterrence," Diacritics, Summer 1984, 14.

29. Strobe Talbott, Deadly Gambits, New York: Alfred A. Knopf, 1984, 5.

30. Michael McCanles, 15.

31. Theodore Draper, "The Western Misalliance," in Walter Laqueur and Robert Hunter (eds.), European Peace Movements and the Future of the Western Alliance, New Brunswick, N.J.: Transaction Books, 1985, 66.

32. Michael McCanles, 19.

33. Edward M. Kennedy and Mark O. Hattield, Freeze! How You Can Help Prevent Nuclear War, New York: Bantam Books, 1982, 115.

34. William Clark, "Letter to Archbishop Joseph L. Bernadin, chairman of the National Conference of Catholic Bishops Committee on War and Peace," The New York Times, November 17, 1982.

35. Jim Castelli, The Bishops and the Bomb, Garden City, N.Y.: Image Books, 1983, 115.

36. Fritjof Capra and Charlene Spretnak, Green Politics, New York: E.P. Dutton, 1984, 59.

37. Ibid., 61.

38. Robert Lifton, The Broken Connection, New York: Basic Books, 1983, 366.

39. Jacques Derrida, "No Apocalypse, Not Now (full speed ahead, seven missiles, seven missives)," Diacritics, Summer 1984, 22.

40. Jacques Lacan, Ecrits: A Selection, New York: Norton, 1977; Louis Althusser, For Marx, London: Penguin Press, 1969; Bertolt Brecht, Brecht on Theatre, John Willett, (ed.), New York: Hill and Wang, 1964; Roland Barthes, Mythologies, London : Granada Publishing Ltd., 1973; Julia Kristeva, Desire in Language, New York: Columbia University Press, 1980; and Julia Kristeva, Revolution in Poetic Language, New York: Columbus University Press, 1984.

2

The Impact of the Peace Movement on Public Opinion and Policy-Making: The Case of the Netherlands

Philip P. Everts

PUBLIC OPINION AND FOREIGN POLICY: THE NORMATIVE DEBATE

Traditionally the making of defense and foreign policy has been an elite affair, and to many observers this seems unavoidable. The preparation and conducting of foreign policy, which seeks to defend and promote the highest interests of the state, requires, it is argued, a great deal of expertise. Coherence and continuity, a refusal to yield at certain moments and a willingness to compromise at others are vital ingredients for a successful foreign policy. Secrecy is another vital element. In order to be successful foreign policy should not be subordinated to domestic squabbles. Considering the national interests, foreign policy should be bipartisan if not nonpartisan and according to Henry Kissinger, it should be conducted "by stealth, out of sight of the public, the Congress, or the bureaucracy." It is difficult to equate these requirements with the nature of the democratic process.

The proponents of this, the traditional or classical, view of the foreign policy process can draw support and inspiration from some of the great writers on democracy and on political affairs of the 18th and 19th centuries: Hobbes, Locke and Rousseau rejected the suitability of the democratic model in conducting foreign affairs. De Tocqueville thought democracy unsuitable for foreign policy because of the tendency of democracies to think and act in terms of white and black rather than shades of gray, their unwillingness to compromise, and their preoccupation with the present rather than with the problems of tomorrow. The case against democratic control and the public voice in making foreign policy has been put eloquently by Walter Lippmann:

The unhappy truth is that the prevailing public opinion has been destructively wrong at the critical junctures. The people have imposed a veto upon the judgment of informed and responsible officials. They have compelled the government (...) to be too late with too little, or too long with too much, too pacifist in peace and too bellicose in war, too neutralist or too appeasing in negotiation, or too intransigent. 1/

Others, however, have equally strong arguments in favor of the opposite view. And their arguments can also be traced back in the long history of the debate. Their arguments are two-fold: The first centers on the nature of the democratic system and the question of whether toreign policy is so ditferent from domestic politics as to allow or even force us to deviate from the general democratic norm. The second refers to the results, in terms of policy outputs, be expected from a (more) democratic foreign policy. A democratic foreign policy would be conducive to peace. These arguments can also be traced back in the long history of the debate.

If one accepts the premise that those who are affected by political decisions should have a voice in the making and control of such decisions, democracy should be applied to the most vital decisions affecting the nation. In the famous words of Lord Bryce:

The general principles which should guide and the spirit which should inspire a nation's foreign policy are too wide in scope, too grave in consequence to be determined by any authority lower than the people. 2/

There is no reason to decide that only a particular group of initiated experts is qualified to determine what the national interest is and how it should be promoted. The nature of these national interests, moreover, is by no means self-evident and noncontroversial.

Indeed, the answers to the question of what these interests entail are as varied as those concerning domestic affairs. Their variety becomes even more obvious as domestic and international affairs come to be seen as the extremes on a continuum with a large middle section where both merge as we move from the traditional realm of "high" politics (issues of power and status) to the bread-and-butter issues of "low" politics. Flexibility and coherence may be necessary and secrecy sometimes required, but their importance is often grossly overstated and used as an excuse to stifle domestic criticism. Broad domestic support is also vital to the durable success of foreign policy and it is difficult to see how this support can be gained other than through open and intense debates. Moreover, the record shows that governments have often made a disastrous use of their freedom to act in international affairs. Finally, if public opinion is overly emotional at times and lacks a basis of interest and knowledge, this may be remedied by education and information and serve to provide the basis for an informed and enlightened public opinion. If there is a lack of interest today, it may be due just as much to a traditional lack of influence on policy-making as the other way around.

The plea for a more democratic foreign policy is usually based not only on the democratic ethos alone, but also on the results which are to be expected in terms of policy output. Again, these ideas are not new. Central in the ideas of the Enlightenment is the conviction that people can be liberated from ignorance, sickness and war and "will learn by degrees to regard war as the most dreadful of all calamities, the most terrible of all crimes," de Condorcet wrote in 1794. At that time public opinion (the concept appeared for the first time in the Oxford Dictionary in 1781) began to be seen as a factor conducive to peace. The idea that a democratic foreign policy would also be a peace promoting foreign policy has caught on since then. In this century, to mention but two examples, the idea has found expression in Woodrow Wilson's plea to introduce democracy into the conduct of international affairs ("open covenants openly arrived at") and in President Roosevelt's optimism that the Second World War would make the world "safe for democracy" and that democracy would lead to the abolition of war. The peoples of the world, or the United Nations, would see to that. Democratically governed states would solve their problems peacefully. That optimism turned sour very soon, but the popular belief in the peace-promoting role of public opinion lingered on. Its tenability calls for closer investigation, to which this paper aims to contribute.

The above debate has not only academic and theoretical but practical relevance, as "the people" become more and more directly involved in international affairs; the preparation and conduct of war in particular. Conscription was introduced in the Napoleonic wars and remained afterwards. The nineteenth century also experienced the introduction of those forms of production and organization which would lead to the mass wars of the twentieth century. And it was in the nineteenth century that powerful ideologies such as socialism, liberalism and nationalism, militarism and antimilitarism began to emerge. These developed into powerful tools to inspire, shape and mobilize public opinion and became the driving force behind the wars of the present age. Since the early nineteenth century organized peace movements have been on the scene. They attracted the interest of only small groups at first, but now reflect a growing interest in international affairs among "the public."

THE ROLE OF THE PEACE MOVEMENT

The history of the peace movement is characterized by two main features. First, it has been an amalgam of groups with widely different ideological origins, such as the liberal, the socialist, the Christian/humanist and the anarchist traditions. Over time these traditions have varied in prominence within the peace movement as a whole. The liberal tradition was strong at the turn of the century, but has weakened. On the other hand, the Christian/humanist element is stronger today, due to an increased involvement of the major churches. 3/

The second major characteristic is the cyclical pattern of periods of growth and decline. In order to understand and explain this cyclical pattern we should, of course, look to the societal conditions within and between nations. 4/ It is important, however, to note that within the peace movement, in the broad sense, two kinds of organizations with rather different sociological structures and aims should be distinguished: the prophetic minorities and the coalition movements. 5/

Characteristic of the first type of organization is a "totalitarian," often sect-like nature. Their aims are all-encompassing: a radical transformation of society and oneself. The movement requires total involvement of the individual. Participation in the movement is not only a means to realize alternative policies, it is also seen as the alternative itself: the building of "islands

of peace" in a warprone society. The necessary changes
of society are expected to result less from influence on
others than from changes in one's own life and behavior.
Due to their radical demands the potential of the
prophetic minorities for recruitment of new members is
usually restricted. Sectarism and fanaticism are the
main threats to the movement. They lead to a sharpening
of the difference between "them" and "us." Joining the
movement is a matter of conversion, and breaking with it
is often considered treasonous behavior, so the number of
adherents to the prophetic minorities tends to remain
very small.

In the second type, the coalition movement, the
goals are not the total transformation of society, but
are more restricted and more concrete: to stop one
particular war, or to prevent the introduction or to
abolish one particular gruesome weapon. People move in
and out of the movement quite easily and on a large
scale. Coalition movements are usually aimed at changing
government policies. This requires the formation of
broad coalitions with limited aims. In this connection
one cannot pick and choose one's allies, and while most
groups in such a coalition will usually have other more
encompassing aims, these are pushed to the background for
the time being. While prophetic minorities are
threatened by factionalism and marginalization, the
coalition movements run the danger of becoming coopted
into existing power structures or of falling apart after
the issue which gave rise to the coalition is decided or
loses its political relevance in another way.

It is the small prophetic minorities which
constitute the historic continuity within the peace
movement as a whole. The troughs and peaks above this
undercurrent are largely formed by the periodic rise and
decline of the coalition movements. The formation of
these coalitions takes place primarily at what we have
called the level of structured public opinion, when the
peace movement in a more restricted sense succeeds in
drawing support from large societal institutions, such as
the churches, the trade unions, women's and youth
organizations and political parties. Developments in the
Netherlands in recent years present a striking
illustration of the relative success of such a "long
march through the institutions."

·   The success and impact of the peace movement can be
measured in different ways. One of these is the growth

of the movement itself, the number of organizations and adherents. Effectiveness in raising support is, however, not the same as political influence, that is, influence on the outcome of the political process in terms of government policies.

To have political influence a movement need not always be a success in terms of the goals of the movement. Thus the effects of the recent activities of the peace movement have partly been counterproductive. Its perceived success in stopping the introduction of the neutron warheads around 1978 has probably increased the stubbornness with which the NATO governments held to the double-track decision of 1979 to introduce cruise missiles and Pershing missiles. Moreover, its emergence as a political factor to be reckoned with (in the form of the Freeze movement) has strengthened President Reagan's (false) appeal to make nuclear weapons obsolete through SDI and has facilitated the emergence in Europe of an "unholy alliance" between antinuclear forces and those who plead for increasing conventional weapons for quite different reasons.

Since the peace movement will usually not have direct access to governmental decision-makers it is mainly dependent on the indirect road, working through 'public opinion'. Below I shall discuss its effectiveness in doing so in the case of the Netherlands in recent years.

TWO FORMS OF PUBLIC OPINION

I have found it useful to distinguish between two major forms of public opinion, which I refer to as structured/organized and nonstructured/nonorganized opinion. Below I shall argue that the two influence the political process in very different, even contradictory, ways. Structured public opinion is represented by the views held by organized and institutionalized groups, such as parties, churches, trade unions, women's organizations, peace groups and others. These views come into the political play through the statements and other activities undertaken by the respective groups to promote their views. Public opinion in this sense concerns the views held or supposed to be held by groups as such and which are publicized on their behalf. If public opinion refers to opinions voiced in public, this applies here.

It applies much less in the case of nonstructured opinion. Here we refer to public opinion as the collectivity of views held by a public, be it the general mass public, or any subsegment of it (such as "the attentive public" or "the elites").

PUBLIC OPINION AT THE MASS LEVEL

Even if one restricts oneself to public opinion at the mass level, as it appears from opinion surveys, it is difficult to present an overview without exceeding the available space on the one hand or indulging in sweeping generalizations on the other hand. Recently some efforts have been made to summarize the major findings so far. 6/ Looking at the data it is difficult not to agree with Flynn and Rattinger that at the mass level the findings will comfort none of the protagonists in recent debates. It is difficult to find evidence that the public at large has become a driving force in shaping alternatives for current security policies, but it is equally difficult to argue that no public perceptions have changed with respect to security. 7/

Unfortunately the mass of survey data is of the single-shot variety and does not allow us to make comparisons with earlier or later data. The number of polls in which the same questions are put to the respondents with some regularity and, hence, make it possible to see whether or not changes have occurred over time are, at least in the Netherlands, much rarer. If there is any trend which can be discovered, it is one of continuity and stability "more of the same." To the extent that changes do occur, they are either statistically insignificant or temporary fluctuations.

The peace movement enjoys significant support for its goals among public opinion at the mass level, but—and that is what is important here—it has not been successful in bringing about changes in the distribution of public attitudes on the problems with which it is concerned. It has not shifted the parameters of the political process in this respect. Other data support this conclusion. In 1977 the major Dutch peace organization Interchurch Peace Council (IKV) started a campaign for the removal of all nuclear weapons from Dutch territory and from the Dutch armed forces. 8/ Poll data suggest that this goal found widespread support, even from a majority at the level of mass opinions. But that support preceded the campaign or was already available before it began. Thus in 1975 two-thirds of those interviewed had already agreed that the nuclear tasks of the Dutch armed forces should be abandoned, and this figure did not change in 1979 or 1983. At the beginning of the IKV campaign one poll found that 54 percent of those interviewed already supported the campaign slogan "Rid the world of nuclear weapons, let it begin with the Netherlands," and later polls found comparable outcomes. 9/

The same continuity and lack of effectiveness in changing people's opinions can be seen with respect to the issue of the cruise missiles -- one of the main issues in Dutch politics for over six years. While opposition has remained strong, it has not, in general, increased over time. The number of proponents has even increased somewhat between 1983 and 1985. The data, on the other hand, present little evidence that people tend to support their government once it decides a controversial question, whatever that decision is. We should be able to distinguish such an effect after the preliminary governmental decision in the cruise missiles issue in June 1984 (conditional deployment) and the final decision in November 1985 to deploy in 1988, but the evidence is unclear.

As to the content of public opinion, the data suggest that despite massive efforts to inform the public that in the nuclear age traditional military policies have lost their meaning and relevance, large majorities continue to subscribe to them.

With respect to the opponent against whom our military preparations are directed, the Soviet Union, it is remarkable to note that antinuclear attitudes are not accompanied by more benevolent attitudes toward the Soviet Union. If anything, images of the Soviets have become more negative since the early seventies. The Soviet Union is seen by large majorities, left or right, as an adversary, and not a benign one. 10/ Evidence does not support the contention, however, that if people understood the nature of the Soviet threat better and knew the facts about the relationship of forces, they would be willing to support a stronger defense. People are generally not willing to spend more on defense, in spite of their negative images of the Soviet Union. The threat that is perceived seems to come as much from the

system of mutual deterrence between the two superpowers
as from the Soviet Union alone. Although, as the data
show, there is strong potential public support for the
idea of military defense, this support is bound to erode
if defense policies are not pursued within a general
framework which aims at living with the Soviet Union
rather than defeating it. Risky politics of
confrontation enjoy no sympathy. This seems to be true
for the Netherlands as well as for other European
countries.

Looking at the situation in the Netherlands again,
we can distinguish three main groups which gradually
merge into one another: one is convinced opponents of
the present security system, especially of the nuclear
element in it. It is composed of both nuclear and
"total" pacifists. It consists of 35-40 percent of the
population, mainly on the political left. On the other
side we can distinguish the group of loyal supporters of
NATO and the policies it stands for. This group is
smaller than the former, about 25 percent. A third and
middle group consists of those who are uninterested and
turn up as the usual 10 percent or so in the "do not
know/no answer" category and those who are torn between
nuclear rejectionism and fear of then being
"defenseless." Their main argument against the
antinuclear group is: "Okay, nuclear weapons are
dangerous and wrong, but what is your alternative?" The
political battle is over the "hearts and minds" of this
group. If the peace movement's aim is to reach a
political majority that at least can prevent certain
negative developments, then it should be able to make
political headway with this group.

Above I concluded that the peace movement in the
Netherlands has not been successful in changing the
content of non-organized public opinion. The question
is, however, whether that is all there is to say. We
have to turn to the concept of saliency. If major
changes have taken place in the opinion climate,
especially with respect to nuclear weapons, we cannot
substantiate this premise by pointing at changes in the
content of public opinion, for indeed there have not been
such changes in the last ten years or so. It is,
however, probable that the already existing concern about
nuclear weapons and the attendant attitudes have remained
latent for lack of a suitable means of political
expression.

The peace movement's success has been to heighten the saliency of these attitudes. Due to its activities and developments in the superstructure of organized opinions, people are now willing to act upon their convictions, and they can be mobilized, at least for some time. Saliency has fluctuated over time with the peaks coinciding with periods of intense political activity, the mass demonstrations of 1981 and 1983. Since then a gradual decline has set in, which is probably due, among other things, to fatigue and a growing belief that the missiles would finally be deployed (the percentages of those believing that the missiles would be deployed rose steadily from some 45 percent in 1981 to 87 percent at the end of 1985). In view of this decline, the success of the petition drive organized in the Fall of 1985 was remarkable. Some 3.75 million people, or 75 percent of the "constituency" of the peace movement signed the petition, which in terms of mobilization is impressive (although not sufficient to prove that a majority opposed the cruise missiles).

The available evidence suggests, in sum, that the peace movement was the catalyst rather than the source of the attitudes which became manifest since 1977 and which became visible and politically relevant in the events of recent years, and especially of the changes in structured opinion.

THE PEACE MOVEMENT AND STRUCTURED OPINION

Since public opinion at the mass level is seldom an actor-in-its-own-right but rather a mobilizable resource, it has to be structured and organized in order to be politically effective. If the peace movement in the Netherlands has been effective to some degree in changing the political climate, it has been so at the level of structured public opinion. This appears clearer if we compare events of recent years with those of the late fifties and early sixties. In those years the peace organizations (also known as the "Ban the Bomb" Movement) were not able to gain a foothold in the established institutions like the churches, the trade unions or the moderate parties of the political center. Nuclear weapons were introduced in the Netherlands without any large-scale public or parliamentary debate. The necessity of taking part in nuclear defense was generally taken for granted, and the peace movement remained marginal. 11/

When the two major church-related peace groups, IKV and Pax Christi, embarked in 1977 on the campaign to remove nuclear weapons from the Netherlands, they were overtaken quickly by two more immediate and concrete issues: First, the plans to introduce neutron warheads (1977-1978) and then, from 1979 on, the NATO double-track decision, which would include deployment of 48 cruise missiles in the Netherlands. 12/ For many--including those who accepted nuclear deterrence in principle but thought that the cruise missiles (and the neutron bomb) were militarily unnecessary and one further step in the arms race--this was too much. The task of the peace organizations was to give political shape to this widespread opposition. They succeeded in doing this, and in bringing about an ad hoc and informal (if sometimes shaky) coalition of groups and organizations which stretched from the far left (the traditional recruiting ground of the Peace Movement) to parts of the center, including not only the peace organizations themselves, but also groups such as the churches, the trade unions and some of the women's organizations.

Churches

Although the evidence suggests that there is much opposition to the peace movement among the church members, church leaders and leading bodies (like the National Council of Churches) have adopted increasingly critical and concrete statements against nuclear deterrence and new nuclear weapons. The churches have continued, often despite strong criticism, to support morally and financially the church-sponsored peace organizations, thus giving them a strong degree of legitimacy. 13/ Together with others (such as former military and political leaders from abroad with an impeccable record for supporting established ideas about security) they have contributed to the emergence of a "crisis of faith," concerning nuclear deterrence. It is unlikely that the former confidence in it will be restored easily, now that the elites themselves have become uncertain.

Additionally, the debate has had an impact on groups such as trade unions and the (more traditional) women's

organizations, which (in the Netherlands at least) were
not previously noted for their interest in defense
matters. Their support of the coalition against the
neutron bomb and the cruise missile has sometimes been
lukewarm, but its importance should not be
underestimated.

Political Parties

Apart from the small political parties on the left,
who traditionally support the peace movement, the peace
movement has had considerable impact on the Social
Democratic Party (as it has had in other West European
countries). Since the last sixties, and after pressure
by the peace movement, this party has come a long way,
from a staunch supporter of NATO particularly with regard
to its nuclear policy, opposing the introduction of the
neutron bomb and the modernization of NATO's INF. Since
1981, however, it has taken a firm position on the latter
issue to the extent that it has ruled itself out as a
coalition partner in government.

The Dutch multiparty system and its coalition cabinets

Within these coalitions a pivotal role is played by
the centrist Christian Democratic group. In the period
under review here, the country has been ruled by a
center-right coalition, governed of Christian Democrats
and the (conservative) Liberal Party (briefly in
1981-1982). During this period the three original
Christian Democratic parties (two Protestant and one
Roman Catholic) went through the difficult and
time-consuming process of merging into one group (CDA).
This merger was opposed by the left (mainly Protestant)
wing of the new party to be formed. Members of
parliament representing this group selected a few issues,
mainly "symbolic" in nature and with little material
consequences, to emphasize their "leftist" image,
including an oil embargo against South African and, which
is important for our subject, the nuclear issues which
arose during this period. Because the government during
recent years has enjoyed the support of only a small
majority in parliament (77 out of 150 seats), this group
of "dissidents" was able to exercise considerable

influence by blocking decision-making on the nuclear issues. The result was a six-year postponement of the decision on the cruise missiles. The statements and activities of the churches, with which most members of the "dissident" group tended to agree, were if not instrumental at least helpful in maintaining societal pressure on this group. Gradually, however, the position of the "dissident" group eroded and the government was able, with the help of the few votes of the religious parties on the (far) Right, to secure a majority in parliament for its decision of November 1985 to proceed with the deployment of the cruise missiles. This majority was essential, since the increased intensity of the societal debates on questions of international affairs and foreign policy had been accompanied by an increased desire of parliament to share in the making of foreign-policy decisions. One of the major findings of a recent study on the role of domestic factors in the making of Dutch foreign policy has not been only that domestic groups can under certain circumstances exercise considerable influence on foreign policy, but also and more specifically, that in order to have this influence, it is essential to secure parliamentary support. 14/

The ad hoc coalition in which IKV and Pax Christi had played a central role was able to block the more radical actions espoused by the prophetic minorities within the coalition. It was able to sustain the opposition against the neutron bomb and its influence had helped parliament block the introduction of the neutron bomb. (Under a petition against the neutron bomb, 1.2 million signatures were collected .) After gaining what many considered to be a resounding victory, the peace movement wanted to score again when the cruise missile appeared on the scene. The government, together with its NATO allies, wanted to prevent a recurrence of peace movement success. For both contending parties it was a second round and led to a paralysis of the decision-making process which was not be be overcome until 1985. In the 1986 general elections the ruling coalition kept its majority. Time was of central importance in the whole issue. Initial delays allowed the movement to continue its strategy of the "long march through the institutions" with some success: 400,000 participants demonstrated in Amsterdam in 1981 and there were 550,000 in 1983 in The Hague. Time, however, is a two-edged sword. As the issue dragged on, the peace groups were confronted with the problem of keeping up the momentum, as fatigue set in. Moreover, it became difficult to keep the coalition together, as some of the more radical groups wanted "direct action." "Direct action" appealed to only a few and would risk alienating others. As the cruise missile issue seemed to be settled for the time being, the frailty of a coalition based on one specific issue appeared more clearly. Some wanted to perpetuate the ad hoc organization Komitee Kruisraketten Nee (Committee Cruise Missiles No), while others like IKV and Pax Christi, fearful of being identified with the political parties of the left and of losing support among the Christian Democrats, wanted to loosen their ties somewhat and return to other "more political" issues.

SOME CONCLUSIONS

At the beginning of the paper I noted that an important current of thinking stresses that foreign policy-making by nature and necessity is elitist in character. Others would de-emphasize the difference between domestic and international affairs and apply the democratic model to foreign policy. Some expect positive effects from a larger influence of public opinion on foreign and defense policy-making. This view is based on three assumptions: (1) that the public (if fully informed) would favor peace and disarmament more than would the ruling governments, (2) that public opinion can have a decisive influence, and (3) to the extent that these conditions do not yet exist, they can be brought about by conscious political action.

How do these assumptions fare in light of the evidence presented here? In order to get a better grip on the multifaceted concept of public opinion we introduced a distinction between structured and nonstructured opinion. At the latter (mass) level, contradictions exist, not only among various groups with strong and consistent convictions, but also between a tendency to subscribe to conventional ideals concerning defense and foreign policy on the one hand and equally strongly held critical beliefs concerning nuclear weapons on the other hand. Assuming for a moment that the policies espoused by the peace movement are "right" in the sense that they would promote peace in a better and more effective way than established policies would, it is not clear that these policies enjoy more than, at best, the support of 40 percent of the population. Condition one is thus, at best, fulfilled only partially. The evidence concerning condition three, the possibilities of changing public attitudes, is, again, not wholly positive. Despite the activities of the peace movement and its efforts to inform people on a massive scale, the sum of the evidence is that public attitudes at the mass level have not been affected to any substantial degree. Support has been maintained, but it has not increased over time.

With regard to structured opinion, however, the situation is somewhat better. We have illustrated the process whereby the peace movement was able to make headway among established societal situations acting as the voice for opinions which found considerable, though often not manifest, support among segments of the public. The peace movement's strategy to gain as much of a foothold within the political center as possible and to remain within the parameters of the parliamentary system was effective to some extent. It is difficult to see how other strategies, much less those based on (nonviolent) direct action, could have been more successful (admittedly this has not been proven).

At the same time the limits of the strategy of the coalition-type peace movement have become quite visible, c.q. its concentration on one particular weapons system. Once such concrete issues lose their political relevance the coalitions which crystallized around them are bound to fall apart with the concomitant disarray in the movement.

To conclude, there is some evidence that public opinion in its structured form can have some influence once specific conditions are fulfilled (condition (2). It may be worthwhile to speculate about the future of the peace movement at this point. While its history suggests a continuation of its cyclical pattern of rise and fall, it is not a foregone conclusion that we shall see a recurrence of this phenomenon this time. On the one hand, we have seen that the large coalitions which account for the peaks in the movement's history are almost necessarily a temporary affair because they are tied to specific issues. On the other hand, unlike earlier periods, the peace movement (at least in the Netherlands) has made a major breakthrough to other institutions. Thus, it is in a much better position to mobilize people again on a large scale, if the occasion arises in the coming years. And given what we know about the dynamics of the arms race, these occasions are bound to recur.

NOTES

1. W. Lippmann, Essays in the Public Philosophy, New York: Mentor Books, 1956, 23-24.
2. J. Bryce, Modern Democracies, Vol. 2, London: MacMillan, 1921, 403-404.
3. See Ph. P. Everts and G. Walraven, Vredesbeweging, Utrecht: Spectrum, 1984.
4. See e.g. N. Young, "Why Peace Movements Fall," Social Alternatives, 4, 1984, 1, 9-16.
5. Everts and Walraven, Vredesbeweging, 9-16.
6. Data for six European countries and the United States are presented and discussed in G. Flynn and H. Rattinger (eds.), The Public and Atlantic Defense, published for the Atlantic Institute for International Affairs, Totowa, N.J.: Rowman and Allanheld, 1985; London: Croom Helm, 1985).
See also:
B. Russett and D.R. Deluca, "Theater Nuclear Forces and Public Opinion," Political Science Quarterly, 89, 1983, 2, 179-196;
R. Flickinger, "The Peace Movement and NATO Missile Deployment," Peace and Change, 9, 1983, 17-30;
D. Yankelovich and J. Doble, "The Public Mood: Nuclear Weapons and the USSR," Foreign Affairs, 1984, 1, 33-46.
A collection of all data for the Netherlands can be found in Ch.H.J. Vaneker and Ph.P. Everts (eds.), Buitenlandse politiek in de Nederlandse publieke opinie, 1975-1984, The Hague: NIIB "Clingendael," 1985.
See also:
Ph.P. Everts, Public Opinion, the Churches and Foreign Policy: Studies of domestic factors in the making of Dutch foreign policy, Leiden: Institute for International Studies, 1983, 225-302.
idem, "Public Opinion on Nuclear Weapons, Defense and Security: The case of the Netherlands," in Flynn and Rattinger (eds.), The Public and Atlantic Defense, 221-275.
idem, "Ontwikkelingen in de publieke opinie," in Jaarboek Vrede en Veiligheid, Alphen aan den Rijn:

Samsom), 1983-1984, 233-240; 1984-1985, 273-282; and 1985-1986, 223-241, and 1906-1907 (forthcoming).

For a more detailed analysis see also H.J. Rebel, Defensie in Nederland, The Hague: Ministry of Defense, 1985.

7. Flynn and Rattinger, The Public and Atlantic Defense, 365.

8. See on this campaign:

Ph.P. Everts and B.J.T.ter Veer, "Disarmament and Peace Action: Report on a campaign for unilateral initiatives toward disarmament in the Netherlands," in M. Haavelsrud (ed.), Approaching Disarmament Education, Guildford: Westbury House, 1981, 147-181.

Ph.P. Everts and L.J. Hogebrink, "The Churches in the Netherlands and Nuclear Disarmament," in J. Will (ed.), The Moral Rejection of Nuclear Deterrence, Cincinnati: Friendship Press, 1985, 23-88 (this volume also contains studies on similar developments in the Federal Republic of Germany, the German Democratic Republic, Poland and the United States).

9. Everts, Public Opinion, 263-270.

10. Flynn and Rattinger, Public Opinion and Atlantic Defense, 369-370.

11. It is interesting to know that, unlike in the seventies and eighties, when the Netherlands, rightly or wrongly, were seen as a source of the "new peace movement" (cf. the ill-defined concept of "Hollanditis"), the Netherlands played a much more passive, receptive role in the first ban-the-bomb wave, when activities in the Netherlands were imported from abroad (Great Britain and the Federal Republic of Germany in particular).

12. These issues and the campaigns around them are described in more detail in Ph.P. Everts and A.van Staden, "Domestic Factors in the Making of Defense Policy: The Case of the Netherlands," Defense Analysis 2, 1986 2,122-135, which is a summary of the relevant chapters in Ph.P. Everts (ed.), Controversies at Home: Domestic factors in the foreign policy of the Netherlands, Dordrecht: Martinus Nijhoff, 1985).

13. See for details:

Ph.P. Everts, "The Churches and Attitudes on Nuclear Weapons: The case of the Netherlands," Bulletin of Peace Proposals, 15, 1984, 3, 227-242;

Everts and Hogebrink, "The Churches in the Netherlands and Nuclear Disarmament."

14. See Everts (ed.), <u>Controversies at Home</u>, Ch. 16 for details.

3

Indices of Japanese Militarization

Ryuhei Hatsuse

INTRODUCTION

In this paper we discuss contemporary Japanese society with respect to militarization and demilitarization. We define "militarization" as (1) strengthening the military establishment and capability, (2) increasing the influence of the military establishment and its capability, and (3) the increasing insertion of military values into civilian arenas. We define "demilitarization" as (1) weakening the military establishment and its capability, (2) decreasing the influence of the military establishment over civilian affairs, and (3) the increasing rejection of military values in civilian arenas.

Modern Japan has passed through three stages of militarization and demilitarization: militarization in the political and social spheres from 1868-1945; demilitarization in the political sphere 1945-1950 and the social sphere from 1945 to the present; and remilitarization in the political sphere from 1950 to the present.

1868-1945

In 1868, the first year of Meiji Restoration, Japan adopted militarization as a national goal. The slogan to build a "strong military, rich country" prevailed as Japan achieved victory over China (1895) and Tsarist Russia (1905). Then, after a decade long intermission of the process during the Taisho period of the 1920s, Japan continued to strive once again in the 1930s, to become the major military power in the world. During this period militaristic attitudes permeated Japanese society and Imperial Japan emerged as a classic militarized state.

The militarization of politics exemplifies the militarized state: Since the establishment of the cabinet system in 1885 and until the end of the War in 1945, thirteen of Japan's twenty-nine Prime Ministers came from the military establishment. A military career was a political asset to all who sought a top political position. Additionally, the Meiji Constitution (1889-1947) contained no explicit division of power between the military and civilian offices. The two were equal in power and responsibility and, in practice, inseparably fused. Military opinion often prevailed. Militarism was widely accepted in villages and towns, among children and adults, men and women, schools and companies, and in private and public life.

1945-1950

The period of demilitarization was imposed after the collapse of the militaristic Japanese Empire in 1945. All military forces were dissolved as a condition of surrender to the Allied Powers. In complete contrast to the previous period, militarism seemed to have disappeared from both private and public life all over the nation. The so-called Peace Constitution was introduced in 1947. Article 9 renounced war, proclaiming that "land, sea or air forces, as well as war potential, will never be maintained" and it prominently repudiated the "belligerency of the state." The people were at first confused but willing to accept the constitution, and they strove to maintain it as a symbol of a demilitarized Japan.

Anti-nuclearism was a natural outcome in the minds of a people who had experienced the nuclear bombings of Hiroshima and Nagasaki. A nation- wide anti-nuclear movement sprang up in Tokyo and Hiroshima in 1954 when a fishing boat was showered with radioactive fallout caused by the U.S. hydrogen bomb test at the Bikini Atoll, Marshall Islands.

Defeat in war also brought disenchantment with the military, for the violence, of any kind, was prohibited, and bullying, which had been acceptable in earlier times, in public or private, was depreciated, and gave way to better treatment.

1950-the present

Remilitarization started at the end of the 1940s and an organized military apparatus reappeared in 1950 in the form of the National Police Reserve, which was renamed the National Safety Force in 1952 and then the Self Defense Forces (SDF) in 1954. Despite Article 9 of the Constitution, the SDF has continued to expand and to improve itself militarily although remilitarization was the most controversial issue in Japanese politics from the 1950s into the 1970s. The SDF has become one of the biggest military forces in Asia. In society, bullying at school, especially in junior high schools, has recently become one of the most serious social issues in Japan. Small-scale violence appears quite often in animated cartoons and dramas.

Nevertheless, post-war attitudes of demilitarization also continues to survive and the Peace Constitution is still alive in the minds of most people. Antinuclearism is still supported by the Japanese people but their concern for peace is directed more strongly toward individual or family peace than toward social justice or world peace. On the other hand, if the government is to build up Japan's military power if must be done within the demilitarized limits imposed by the constitution and public opinion. Thus militarization in contemporary Japan has been gradual, silent, and dependent upon U.S. nuclear strategy. It must, however, be noted that the process itself is steady and incessant.

In order to grasp this gradual, silent, dependent but incessant militarization as a whole, we need to clarify "militarization" in the military, the political, the economic and the social senses, carefully examining the indices of militarization.

DEMILITARIZATION OF SOCIETY

The effects of the demilitarization of Japan since 1945 are readily apparent. For example, most Japanese would not know how to use a pistol or a machine gun. SDF officers and soldiers go shopping or to leisure activities, wearing civilian clothes rather than uniforms. Most of them prefer civilian clothes to a uniform. The military look attracts only a small number of young people. However, it should also be noted that many young people enjoy playing war games on personal computers--a mixture of militarization and demilitarization.

In a sense, Japanese society remains peace-oriented. But it must be added at once that the meaning of peace has been changing slowly during these forty years. Three points should be mentioned and interpreted in regard to the Japanese attitude toward militarization: peace, defense, and the nation.

In the demilitarized years following the end of the World War II, peace was generally accepted as a desirable symbol--certainly a respectable symbol. In the naming of companies, for example, data show that the number of companies founded with investments of more than ten million yen, given names starting with "peace," (e.g., Peace Real Estate, Peace Food, Peace Manufacturing, or Peace Taxi Co.), were 26 in 1946-50, 17 in 1951-55, 10 companies in 1956-60 and none in either 1976-80 or 1981-85 (Source: Directory of Companies in Japan). We think the decline of peace as a symbol in business reflects Japanese involvement in the defense industry.

A peace orientation has persisted in the society as a whole, however. And people's concern with peace has begun to rise again in the 1980s. An examination of books published with "peace" in the title may be used to illustrate the public concern with peace. We find that concern has revived in recent years. However, the peace image itself has changed from world or national peace building to individual peace or peace education. Table 1 shows the concept associated with peace in book titles, for example, For Peace Independence and Democracy or Peace Education and Human Rights. While the old image of peace was associated with political symbols of independence, democracy and the peace movement, the recent image is associated with the social symbols of human rights, education and non-political disarmament. Such an orientation would not call forth direct political action against militarization of the military, politics and economics.

People's attitudes towards defense appear to be contradictory. For example, while a majority has increasingly supported the Peace Constitution, a greater number have also constantly supported the SDF. Half of those polled support the U.S.-Japan Security Treaty.

The people's support for the SDF does not necessarily include the young, however. Since 1980, fewer young people have applied for jobs in the SDF. The ratio of applicants to selectees was 7.46 in 1960, 2.51

Table 1: Concept Associated with Peace in the Title of Books

	1948-50	1951-53	1954-56	1957-59	1960-62	1963-65	1966-68	1969-71	1972-74	1973-75	1976-78	1979-81	1982-84
Independence	2	1	1			1	1	1					
Democracy	1	1				1	1			1	1		
Movement		2		1		2		3	1	1			
Revolution	2												
Rights	1			1		1		1	1	1		3	1
Education	2		1						2	2	7	2	5
Disarmament										2	2	1	2
War	2		1	1	1	1	1	1	2	1			1
Constitution					1					2			1
Co-existence	1	6	1	4	6				2	2		(1)	1
Treaty	2	2	1										1

( ) signifies "negative"

Source: For 1948-74, the date of book publication and acceptance identified in Index Books of the Diet Library.
For 1973-84, the date of book publication identified in Index Cards of the Diet Library.

in 1982 and 1.98 in 1983. Fewer people have participated in short training programs, such as the one week program offered by the SDF. The number of participants was 80,000 in 1979, 93,000 in 1982 and 61,000 in 1984. Thus people try to separate themselves from the SDF, while supporting them as a defense force.

Antinuclearism exists firmly in the attitudes of the people. An absolute majority would refuse to support Japan's nuclear armament, supporting instead the three antinuclear principles adopted as a resolution in the Diet in 1971, which prohibits the manufacturing, possession and introduction of nuclear weapons into Japan. On the other hand, all Japanese know that Japan has been actively involved in the U.S. nuclear strategy, whether they approve of it or not. Most doubt that the U.S. would fight for Japan. Most want to believe in the deterrence theory and that nuclear forces will never be used again. In essence, the Japanese people have hired defense, subcontracting to the SDF and the U.S. forces.

The Japanese want peace. A recent newspaper poll shows that the Nakasone Government gained the popular support of 53 percent among the post-War Governments ("Asahi Shimbun", March 15, 1985). People, however, have felt insecure about Nakasone's defense policy. Support has been withdrawn whenever he has said or done something "hawkish." Support dropped in 1983 soon after he said that Japan should become an "unsinkable aircraft carrier." A drop occurred again in 1985 when he officially visited the Yasukuni Shrine. The majority support the defense expenditure ceiling of one percent or less of the GNP, almost irrespective of their party identification (78 percent of the Liberal Democrats, of the Clean Government, 88 percent of the Democratic Socialist, 89 percent of the Socialist and 90 percent of the Communist Diet members. "Mainichi Shimbun", Dec. 18, 1984).

The Japanese tend to keep their (individual and social) peace concerns separate from defense issues within certain limits. But their demilitarized peace resolution still works effectively against a great deal of militarization of politics and against a great deal of strengthening of the SDF. Contradictory attitudes toward peace could persist as long as defense can be subcontracted to the professionals.

An analysis of Japanese attitudes toward the nation itself shows that people have been more concerned with their private lives than with public affairs and

politics. They have been increasingly more satisfied
with their daily lives and social milieu. They have also
been increasingly less concerned with the nation and
public affairs than formerly. They have become
increasingly more confident in the Japanese nation: 95.6
percent felt happy about being Japanese. In 1983, 70.6
percent considered the Japanese more competent than other
nationalities. Already by 1971, 40 percent of Tokyo
residents considered Japanese economic power more
advanced than that of other countries, with only 15
percent considering Japan less advanced. Their
nationalism, however, is not so strong as is generally
assumed. Little more than half of the people are
emotionally attached to the national anthem and the flag:
57 percent to the anthem and 56 percent to the flag
(Source: 1975 NHK polls). They have been increasingly
less inclined toward political action, and they have been
enjoying the Pax Economica of Japan. Thus nationalism
has emerged almost without public participation.

In summing up the militarization process in Japanese
society, we noted that Japan has been more or less
demilitarized. A peace orientation and antinuclearism
has stubbornly persisted and has worked effectively
against much militarization in politics and defense. But
these attitudes are more concerned with individual and
social peace than with political peace, and are viewed as
separate from defense issues. Hence the political
influence of popular concern for peace will recede.
Nationalism has also emerged virtually without the
people's participation.

MILITARIZATION OF POLITICS

There are three salient indications of the
militarization of politics. First, an increasing defense
expenditure indicates that the government's attitude
favors militarization. A second indicator is an increase
in "militarized" political actors. Third, the growth of
defense industries is an additional indicator of
increased militarization.

Japan's military expenditures have steadily
increased in real as well as nominal terms during the
past thirty years. In nominal terms, the budget was 135
billion yen in 1955 and 3,344 billion yen in 1986, hence
it has increased about 25 times in thirty years. In real
terms, the increase is approximately 10 times. The

annual rate of increase seems to have slowed down
gradually in the 1980s. But other budgetary items than
defense and overseas economic assistance have decreased
more rapidly in the 1980s. The former two items have
maintained a constant rate of more than six percent
annual increase during these years of slowdown.
Recently, the government's budgetary policy has been
"more for defense and overseas assistance, less for
education and welfare." The weight of defense in
national economic activities, which had dropped in the
1970s, has started rising again in the 1980s especially
under the Nakasone Government (from 1983). If we do not
include the national debt and the local subsidies in the
government's expendable income, the defense budget has
been as large as almost ten percent of the total
expenditure. In addition, the rate has been increasing.

One of the recent defense issues concerns the one
percent of GNP ceiling on defense expenditure, as
formulated by Prime Minister Miki in 1976. The ceiling
was almost reached by the Nakasone Government. If the
ceiling were raised to, say, two percent of GNP as the
"hawks" demand, the SDF in scale and quality would be the
third strongest in the world. The one percent ceiling of
today is already higher than is needed for defense
purposes, given the size of Japan's GNP.

An examination of the militarization of political
actors yields an example in Yasukuni Shrine--a national
religious symbol of Japan's past "expansion" into Asian
countries--where 2.5 million war dead are enshrined
together with convicted war criminals, e.g., General
Prime Minister Tojo who was sentenced to death at the
Tokyo International War Tribunal (1946-1948) as
ultimately responsible for the "war of aggression." In
1975, the then, Prime Minister Miki made the first visit
to Yasukuni after the War. He claimed that this was in
his private, not official, capacity. In 1978 Prime
Minister Fukuda again made a private visit. In 1979
Ohira did not visit. But in 1980 Prime Minister Suzuki
made a private visit and in 1981 he did so with all his
cabinet members except those who were abroad. In 1982 he
visited without commenting that his visit was either
private or official. In 1983 Nakasone visited as Prime
Minister, denying that his visit was official. In 1985
Prime Minister Nakasone made an official visit on
Memorial Day for the first time in the post-War period.
This time he was accompanied by all cabinet members
except two who were abroad. A step forward with regard

to peace concerns, his official visit incurred the strongest protests from China, Korea and other Asian countries. They filed protests, claiming that the Prime Minister's visit, in essence, justifys Japan's past aggression and colonial policy in neighboring Asian countries. It must be added, however, that less protest occurred from <u>within</u> than from <u>outside</u> Japan. The protests from other countries worked effectively against the Japanese government. This <u>series</u> of <u>slight changes</u> in the visiting of Yasukuni reflect well the silent, gradual but increasing militarization of politics.

A possible further militarization may have developed with the appearance of Prime Minister Nakasone, ex director-general of the Defence Agency. The present secretary general of the party, Shin Kanemaru, was also in the position under the Fukuda Cabinet in 1977-78. It might be a new phenomenon of political militarization that both of the key positions in the cabinet and in the party are occupied by two ex defense director-generals. And, it should not be overlooked that the two highest staff officers of the SDF have obtained seats in the upper house, one from the ASDF since 1962 and another from the GSDF since 1977. Within the ruling party defense pressure groups have been salient: these are composed of dozens of the upper and lower house members, with several ex-defense director generals and several ex-defense under-secretaries. The above two also participate in these groups. Thus militarization of politics has been proceeding slowly and gradually. However, one should realize that not all of the factions in the ruling party are hawkish. Some are against militarization--and Nakasone's leadership is not strong enough to persuade all factions to support his hawkish stance.

MILITARIZATION OF ECONOMICS

The military-industrial complex is not yet very strong in Japan. Defense production was only 0.46 percent of the total national manufacturing production in 1982. But this figure is often misleading. Although defense related products of the telecommunication industry are only 0.73 percent of its total production, that 0.73 percent turns out to be a large amount: 201.4 billion yen (calculate 200 yen = $1), the second largest amount among all defense industries. Except for arms and ammunition, which cannot exist without defense sales, aircraft, telecommunication and shipbuilding are the biggest defense industries. Nippon Electric Company (NEC), which leads the electronics industry, has climbed in rank from the seventh, in 1978, to the second, in 1983, in defense procurement contracts. This case can indicate that Japan posseses an electronic sophistication of weapons like missiles and jet fighters and that their more highly technical industries would be involved in defense industry from now on. Judging from the desire of Japanese companies to participate in the U.S. SDI project, a new type of military/electronic industrial complex might emerge. The export of weapons is, in principle, prohibited; the only exception is the export of sophisticated electronic technology to the U.S., against which the prohibition was withdrawn in 1983 using the argument that the U.S. is an ally.

In summing up the militarization of politics, the Nakasone government has been conspicuous in its advancement of a militaristic policy. But militarization of political actors should be examined in a longer term perspective. Militarization has quietly intruded into the political arena, step by step, without being fully noticed.

MILITARIZATION OF THE MILITARY

The militarization of the military has two salient aspects: (1) the increasing strength of the SDF per se. (2) the SDF's dependence upon or involvement in the U.S. nuclear strategy.

Japan stood tenth in military spending in the world in 1984. If we consider that Iran and Iraq were at war, Japan stood eighth. According to military expenditure per head of the armed personnel, Japan stands eighth again, which indicates the high level of sophisticated or highly technical equipment that the SDF possess.

Japan is 28th with regard to the number of army personnel, 23rd in the number of combat aircraft and seventh in naval tonnage. The biggest weight is on the Maritime SDF, which had an air capability of 84 combat aircraft and 64 helicopters in 1984. The air SDF is next. Mobility of both forces is heavily weighed. However, military capability cannot be counted independent of military considerations vis-a-vis neighboring countries. With reference to three categories of nations (the superpowers, Japan's Asian neighbors and West European countries), although Japan is behind both of the superpowers it is still one of the strongest in Asia. Japan is behind but very close to the U.K., France, and West Germany, which are all similar to Japan in economic activities and in national territory. The U.K. and West Germany are dependent upon the U.S. in nuclear strategy, even though both have strong conventional capability. In that sense, too, Japan is similar. Hence, Japan's military capability is almost the same or equal to the nations of Western Europe, including France. If the defense expenditure ceiling of Japan's GNP were to be raised to two percent, the military capability of the SDF would be the third largest in the world.

The SDF's fighting ability has improved very rapidly during this decade. There have been large increases in equipment acquisition and in training. Missiles are continually being required by all of the tri-services: the GSDF, the MSDF and the ASDF. That fighter interceptors have the relatively short life cycle of ten years, also suggests a sophistication of weapons.

The SDF have, over the years, become involved in American nuclear strategy. Japan-U.S. joint exercises and training have grown in size and scale in recent years (since "Guidelines for Japan-U.S. Defense Cooperation" was adopted in 1978). Command post exercises started with the GSDF in 1981, the MSDF in 1984 and the ASDF in 1983, which signifies closer collaboration in the case of actual warfare.

We have two misgivings about those joint exercises. First, they may lead to joint combat actions beyond areas near Japan. Such actions would constitute "collective defense" which is prohibited by the constitution. The SDF were to have been interpreted as forces to be used only for Japan's defense. They should not be deployed overseas even for the defense of the U.S. The U.S.-Japan Security Treaty recognizes as the common danger only an armed attack against either of the two forces in the territories under Japan's administration. Second, the joint exercises are part of the U.S. nuclear strategy against the Soviet Union. More involvement does not imply more security. It does imply more military action.

The U.S. has asked Japan to share the burden of defense. It is realistic to assume a nuclear strategy is intended. Japan's policy recently seems to be moving gradually from passive dependence to active involvement. U.S. outposts of C^3I in Japan also indicate that Japan is deeply involved in the U.S. nuclear strategy. Outstanding are elephant cages in Okinawa and Aomori (Misawa), giant talk stations in Okinawa(Kadena) and Tokyo(Yokota) and VLF transmitting towers near Nagoya(Yosami). Japan has been increasingly willing to share the defense burden with the U.S. by financially supporting U.S. troops stationed in Japan. By 1985 assistance had risen to 80.7 billion yen from 37.4 billion in 1980 or 6.2 billion in 1978.

In summing up militarization of the military, Japan as an independent power is closely behind the U.K., France or West Germany in military capability, but lacks the same type of large offensive weapons. The SDF have grown to the fullest in conventional defensive weapons, but being alone, still lack offensive capability. Japan alone cannot be offensive in military policy. Dependent upon the U.S. for offensive weapons, Japan is closely tied to U.S. nuclear strategy, first with passive dependence, then through active involvement. Increasing military buildup of the SDF would not mean more security for the Japanese people.

CONCLUDING REMARKS

We have analyzed the indices of militarization in contemporary Japan. Quiet militarization has been proceeding gradually, incessantly, but steadily, even in politics and economics, which have not been overly militarized thus far. In Japanese society, demilitarization has stubbornly persisted and often works effectively against the above processes. Peace in demilitarization, however, has turned to individual or social peace, and is satisfied with the Pax Economica of Japan and less concerned with peace outside Japan's small private world. This obsession with private peace would lead to less influence of people over the political processes of peace and over defense issues. The people's confidence in the nation might lead to their acquiescence in a greater buildup of the SDF.

Japan's remilitarization shows that militarization of the military, politics and economics can proceed even within the limits imposed by a demilitarized society.

The Japanese people need to know about the danger of quiet militarization that is increasing while they are preoccupied with personal satisfaction. They need to transcend their quest for personal peace and look beyond their borders to the nature of their relationships with the rest of the world.

4

Can Peace Become a Topic
in News Reporting?
A Content-Analytical Approach

Lutz P. Michel and Brigitta Lutz

"The mass media have an important part to play in the strengthening of peace and international understanding and in combating war propaganda, racialism and apartheid" - with these words begins article III of the Unesco Draft declaration on mass media, adopted by the Unesco General Conference in Paris, August 1978. 1/ The declaration appeals to professional organizations of journalists all over the world to place particular emphasis on these principles in drawing up professional codes of ethics.

What contribution does the mass media actually make in combating war propaganda and in strengthening peace? Critical public opinion has dealt with this question above all in connection with press resonance to activities of the peace movement. These voices, as have many people working in mass media as well, have determined that armament propaganda and enemy image making still dominate West German media. 2/ Unfortunately, this problem has been largely neglected by communication science up to now. Only a handful of studies have analyzed press coverage of selected military topics and of the peace movement. 3/

The question which we have asked ourselves - in the light of this kind of deficit analysis - is: What chance does peace have to become a media topic? This means the question of the journalistic contribution to the weakening of peace is not to be asked. Instead, we want to rephrase the question positively: What do they contribute to peace?

A possible approach to answering this question would be to study the communicators, that is journalists in the press, radio, and television more closely, to study their views regarding responsible reporting on war and peace, to study their working conditions, and the like. A first, small study using this approach has already been

presented. 4/   It demonstrates, among other things, that
critical reporting on questions of armament and
disarmament, military strategies, and the peace movement
has been heavily influenced by the economic and political
elite in West Germany.

The present study presents the analysis of media
content. We chose this approach in order to gather the
first results from the texts which are produced daily by
professional journalists and which constitute the result
of journalistic selection processes: that which the
audience perceives. Within this context we were not,
however, attempting a comparison of media content with
"reality" but instead an immanent analysis of "media
reality" within a selected period of time.

With our exploratory study we intend to analyze the
present treatment of the peace issue and its context in
the West German press and furthermore to develop
questions for future, more extensive research. This also
means that this study does not yet make statements about
the relative proportion of peace coverage--for instance
in comparison with the proportion of war and conflict
reporting. We assumed that due to the present state of
research on this question it was first necessary to gain
access to the very area of peace coverage for empirical
analysis. One might think of, for example, theoretical
and methodological problems such as the definition of
fundamental terms and of their operationalization.

What do we mean when we speak of "peace?" A few
explanatory remarks shall briefly outline our notion of
peace. Even today in theoretical definitions as well as
in everyday use of this term, peace is defined by its
antipode: as the absence of war, or as "non-war."
Critical peace research attempts to replace this reduced,
negative peace concept, one which traditional peace
research has largely continued to use up to this day,
with a "positive peace concept." The contents which
should characterize such a peace concept are such terms
as "integration" or "cooperation." 5/

If we ignore for the present the linguistic
construction "the cold war" (so to speak a non-peaceful
non-war) it can then be said that "war" is an empirical
term - that peace on the other hand has largely remained
a theoretical one (and moreover a highly disputed
political-ideological term). C. Wright Mills has pointed
out quite correctly that "we are not able to give the
word peace any certain meaning without giving it a

political meaning and thereby making it a disputed term."
6/ As far as we can determine, there is no one,
singular notion of peace. Even 150 years after
Clausewitz's theory of "Vom Kriege" (On War) a definition
of peace corresponding to the scientific definition of
war has not yet been developed. If we integrate both
approaches (that is the traditional one "ex negativo" as
well as the "positive" one), three dimensions of a peace
notion can be differentiated. They correspond to three
levels of international and national politics: an
ethic-political, a military, and a social dimension.

Within the first dimension peace is a norm, an
ethical postulate to which human thought and action
should correspond - an idea. Within the second and third
dimension (military and social) peace can be studied
empirically. Whether a military-political measure
contributes to the end of military conflicts (that is to
say, to the "non-war") or whether it hinders the outbreak
of war can, in principle, be just as well empirically
determined as can the question whether a socio-political
measure contributes to more cooperation and integration
(that is to "positive" peace). That peace is also given
a political meaning in these dimensions and that it
becomes a term which is - in C. Wright Mills' sense -
empirically disputed as well, is not to be denied.

To neglect these dimensions - especially the social
one - appeared to us, however, not to be advisable, since
we would have had to take a problematic reduction to the
terminological construction of "non-war" into account.
How can peace, then, become a topic in news media?
Before getting to our concrete questions, let us
introduce briefly some results of communication science
which are especially relevant for our study.

As with all other events, "peace events" too are
subject to the restriction of selection immanent within
the system of mass media. If the place of the event is
far away from the media location (which is the case with
the peace issue, as in all other not primarily local
political topics), an event must overcome at least two
selection hurdles until it reaches the audience as news:
first, the news agency, which selects from the multitude
of information reaching it daily a limited number
(something in the area of one out of a hundred); second,
the editor's office: here the incoming news agency
stories are again subject to selection (here, too, at
about one to a hundred.) 7/

However, the fact that selection takes place does not concern us here - it being as old as news itself. Instead, our interest focuses on the criteria according to which selection is carried out. A number of studies, inspired by the "classic" study by Galtung and Ruge, "The Structure of Foreign News," 8/ have been carried out within the field of empirical news research since the 1960's. Of primary interest are the news factors, which determine within a given media system, whether an event will or will not become news.

The following factors can be said to be the decisive ones; on the whole some twenty such news factors have been investigated in research since Galtung and Ruge. 9/
1. Negativism. To quote Galtung and Ruge, "the more negative the event is in its consequence the more probable that it will become a news item." 10/
2. Elitism. "The more the event concerns elite people, the more probable that it will become a news item." 11/
3. Ethnocentrism. Cultural and political proximity of a country increases the chances of an event becoming news.

On the basis of knowledge about selection criteria of the news media we developed a number of questions and hypotheses, which we proceeded to examine in an empirical content analysis of the West German press.
The essential questions of our study are the following:
1. Is peace above all else a topic of foreign or domestic political news reporting?
2. Is peace given high attention value in the press?
3. Does peace mainly become a topic when it is connected with political action, that is to say that the attention threshold is passed? (Galtung and Ruge refer in this context to their threshold-hypothesis.)
4. Is peace dealt with by the media when the political elite participates?
5. Is there a strong ethnocentrism within the area of peace reporting; is the Federal Republic of Germany dominant?
6. Which of the three dimensions of peace form the core of press reporting?

Before we present our results, a short explanation of our method is required. The content analysis limits itself - due to the exploratory nature of our study - to a single daily West German newspaper. The "Suddeutsche Zeitung" was selected; it is the largest of the four national quality newspapers and is placed by communications scientists of the most varied political viewpoints approximately at the middle of the political spectrum. 12/

The time frame chosen was four weeks: specifically, the first week of the months of September, October, November and December of 1985. This sampling should guarantee that, on the one hand, the presentation of thematic connections can be grasped. On the other hand, a dominating subject of a given month (for instance, the Geneva Summit in November) cannot destroy the study.

We did not define peace formally, that is using the word "Friede" and its derivatives, but by its content, reporting either on direct actions for peace, peace demands, peace conditions, etc., or on indirect demands, actions, and so on, which are directed against non-peace, that is to say against war, conflict, and political tension or against war material, weapons above all.

Each paragraph of an article was chosen as a unit of analysis, whereby the topic of peace must dominate the paragraph in terms of content and space. By selecting the paragraph instead of the article, the amount of analysed texts has increased significantly since the peace topic only dominates a few paragraphs in a great number of articles.

Now to the results of our study:

Firstly, the rather large number of cases is to be named: the final tabulation showed that in the 24 issues studied a total of 107 articles containing peace news had been published. The paragraphs totalled 182. The figures varied between zero and 11 articles per issue and between zero and 23 paragraphs.

Together with our well-distributed sample, this number of cases offers a solid foundation for pregnant interpretations. In the newspaper we analysed, there appeared 107 articles with 182 paragraphs in four weeks. Apparently the chance for peace is not too small, at least not in the quality newspaper we analysed. What do these articles look like, however; what about the context in which peace becomes a topic here? And what conclusions concerning the chances of peace becoming a topic in an article can be drawn from these contexts? What must happen so that peace receives attention? Some of our most important results can answer these questions.
1.   Peace receives contradictory attention.

We established the following indicators of attention: the journalistic genre of the article (for example, short news story, report, etc.), the number of paragraphs containing peace in relation to each article, and, thirdly, the headlines. As to the genres, short news story and reports dominate at a rate of some 40 or 60 percent respectively. Commentary amounts to only 2 percent; documentation concerning our topic do not appear at all. This allows us to conclude that journalists do not make peace their own topic.

The very large proportion of 80 percent of the articles with only one or two paragraphs on peace - this too in long articles - also allows us to deduce a very low attention level. On the other hand, the tendency in the headlines is contrary. In about half of the cases peace is a topic in the headline. This is true for short news as well as for long reports. The surprisingly high proportion of the headlines in longer articles with few paragraphs on peace allows us to deduce an attention-getting function of the peace topic.

2.   Peace is hardly a topic in domestic reporting.

In this case indicators are, firstly, the section of the newspaper, e.g., home news or overseas news, and secondly, the nationality of the respective agent. The result of the analyses was that about three-fourths of the cases appeared in the "foreign" section, only one-fourth in the home news section.

These findings were confirmed by the results of the tabulation of the agents. Three-fourths were foreign persons or institutions, only one-fourth were agents from the Federal Republic of Germany.

3.   The focus of peace reporting is the military dimension. As can be seen in Table 1 the reporting clearly stresses the military dimension. Of the 70 percent which the military dimension constitutes, the

Table 1:   The Focus of Peace Reporting

Thematic dimensions	
ethic-political	8
social/domestic	13
social/foreign	9
military/"hot"	20
military/"cold"	50
(n = 182)	100

main portion (half of the cases) pertains to the area of disarmament, armaments limitation etc. (which we have named military "cold"). The area military "hot" (that is topics such as truce, peace negotiations, and the like) appears in second place.

Peace as the absence or reduction of structural violence (that is the social area domestic and foreign) only amounts to less than one-fourth of the cases. Finally, peace as an ethic-political topic is only mentioned in less than one-tenth of the cases.

From these findings we conclude that peace, as a topic, is largely dependent upon military themes, that means as an event it must have something to do with preventing wars or ending them.

4. To become a topic peace does not require any concrete action.

Table 2 shows the seven types of topics which we differentiated. One can see that in as many as one third of the cases peace appears as a demand. The first three types of topics are characterized by a low rate of concreteness, of factualness. Here no realities are being altered - verbal activity that occurs here

Table 2:   Seven Types of Topics

Type of Topic	%	%
statement	21	
demand	33	74
intention, suggestion	20	
negotiation	12	
treaty, agreement	2	22
concrete action	8	
condition	4	4
(n = 182)	100	100

brings about no consequences as a rule. If we summarize these three topics then they clearly dominate the cases at a rate of three-fourths.

Less than one fourth of the cases pertain to the more concrete area: negotiations, treaties and concrete action. As far as journalism is concerned these findings allow for the positive conclusion that for peace to become a topic, although an event is necessary, a factual result, however, is not. Negative in our point of view is the low level of attention given to concrete actions, a finding by the way, that was confirmed by the correlation of type of topic to agent. It seems that the possibilities for actions of the elite are reflected in these types of topics - on the other hand, the frame of action of the non-elite, grass root movements for instance, is hardly represented.

5.   Peace is dealt with by the media when the political elite takes part in the event. The tabulation of the data on the agents (see Table 3) as well as the correlation of agents to types of topics (see Table 4) show a very heavy orientation of peace reporting to the elite.   In over two thirds of the text government or leading politicians were the focus of attention.

Table 3:   Tabulation of Data on Agents

Function of agent	%
country, government leading politicians	68
other politicians (parliamentary)	15
other politicians (non-parliamentary)	2
movement, special interest group	2
professional orga- nization, union	6
supranational organization	7
(n = 205)	100

Agents who were not part of a governmental or supra-national system or in the party system make up no more than one-tenth of the cases.

Table 4: Function of Agent/Type of Topic

	state-ment	demand	inten-tion	nego-tia-tion	treaty	con-cr. act.	con-di-tion
	%	%	%	%	%	%	%
country gov't	86	48	83	65	50	63	100
other	14	52	17	35	50	37	--
	100	100	100	100	100	100	100
(n)	(44)	(58)	(36)	(23)	(4) !	(16)	(3) !

Finally, within the types of topics it was the case that, apart from the first group of agents, all others were concentrated on the area of demands.
6.   Reporting on peace is not ethnocentric in a narrow, national sense; it is, however, in a broader, political sense. Table 5 shows the nationality of the agents. It can be seen that in less than one-fourth of the cases

Table 5: Nationality of Agents

Western world	51 (incl. 23% FRG)
Eastern world	19
Third World	22
supranational	7
(n = 203)	100

West Germans appear. From this data, then, one may not deduce a strong ethnocentrism in a national sense. On the other hand, the Western hemisphere clearly dominates - including West Germany - with more than half of the cases. Accordingly in a broader, political sense - Galtung and Ruge speak of "cultural proximity" - one may

76

certainly deduce that peace reporting is characterized by
a pronounced ethnocentrism. Let us now turn to Table 6.

Table 6: Nationality of Agents/Thematic Dimensions

	ethic-political	social/dom.	social/for.	milit./"hot"	milit./"cold"
	%	%	%	%	%
Western World	40	65	33	38	59
Eastern World	40	--	--	7	28
Third World	10	30	56	48	5
supra-national	10	5	11	7	8
	$\overline{100}$	$\overline{100}$	$\overline{100}$	$\overline{100}$	$\overline{100}$
(n)	(10)	(23)	(18)	(42)	(109)

Here, the nationality of the agents is correlated with
the thematic dimension. It becomes very clear that there
is a low political proximity to the socialist countries
and that the journalists are especially disinterested in
the domestic and social politics of these countries. As
one can see, there is no single paragraph containing this
topic. Table 7 correlates nationality to type of topic.
The main finding here is that the non-concrete topics are
distributed in an above-average manner inthe area of the
Western world, whereas in the Eastern and the Third World
the more concrete types of topic dominate. The nearer
the nationality of the agent to home, we can conclude
from our findings, the more likely the less concrete
topics can overcome the attention threshold of news
reporting.

Table 7: Nationality of agent/Type of topic

	statement, demand, suggestion %	negotiation treaty, con- crete action %	condition %
Western World	57	40	33
Eastern World	19	32	--
Third World	15	21	67
supra- national	9	7	--
	100	100	100
(n)	(149)	(47)	(3) !

In briefly summarizing the results of our study we reach three essential conclusions.

1. Peace reporting orientates itself clearly to the traditional peace concept. This becomes especially evident in the placement of most of the texts in the foreign news section as well as in the heavy dominance of the military dimension.

2. Peace reporting orientates itself to the central news factors which were verified in research for all foreign news. We are able to determine that the chance of a peace event becoming news is significantly increased by participation of elite persons as well as by the political proximity of the place of event (which means by the news factor ethnocentrism).

3. Finally, the minor importance which the topic peace is given by West German journalists points to a further news factor: the factor negativism which obviously leads to the fact that peace events have fewer chances than events in which conflict dominates. At least readers in Western countries will certainly have had the same experience in reading their daily newspaper as we had:

negative news far outweighs the positive news - or, as a
news researcher and journalist once put it: good news is
no news. 13/

This observation again points to the urgent
necessity of journalistic ethics to be adapted to the
norms of journalism concerned with peace. As long as
this does not occur, as long as the professional rules of
journalism are maintained, all well-intentioned appeals -
like the article of the Unesco declaration quoted at the
outset - will remain futile.

NOTES:

1. Quoted by Jorg Becker (ed.): free flow of
information. Informationenzur Neuen Internationalen
Informationsordnung. Frankfurt 1979, p. 224.

2. See Lutz P. Michel: The Topic "War and Peace"
in the Mass Media of the Federal Republic of Germany.
In: Tapio Varis (ed.): Peace and Communication. San
Jose/Costa Rica 1986, pp. 67-98.

3. Cf. Jorg Becker: Methodological Problems of
Dealing with Disarmament in the Press. In: Current
Research on Peace and Violence, 1, 1983, pp. 29-51.

4. Lutz P. Michel, op.cit.

5. Cf. Johan Galtung: Strukturelle Gewalt.
Beitrage zur Friedens - und Konfliktforschung. Reinbek
1975, pp. 37-60.

6. Charles Wright Mills: Die Konsequenz. Politik
ohne Veranwortung. Munchen 1959, p. 158-9; quoted after
the German edition; my translation

7. Manfred Steffens: Das Geschaft mit der
Nachricht. Hamburg 1969,p. 9-10.

8. Johan Galtung/Mari Holmboe Ruge: The Structure
of Foreign News. In: Journal of Peace Research 2, 1965,
p. 64-91.

9. Cf. Sophia Peterson: International News
Selection by the Elite Press. A Case Study. In: Public
Opinion Quarterly 2, 1981,pp. 143-163.

10. Johan Galtung/Mari Holmboe Ruge, op.cit.,p.266.

11. Ibid., p. 265

12. Klaus Schonbach: Trennung von Nachricht und
Meinung. Freiburg 1977; Klaus Merten: Die Struktur der
Berichterstattung der deutschen Tagespresse. Bd. 1.
Bielefeld 1979; Hans Mathias Kepplinger: Die aktuelle
Berichterstattung des Horfunks. Freiburg/Munchen 1985.

13. Cf. Bernd-Peter Arnold: Nachrichtenwert und Nachrichtenauswahl. In: Media Perspektiven 1, 1982, pp. 28-34.

5

Information Sharing as a Human Right

Harold E. Pepinsky

INTRODUCTION

I spent the spring of 1986 in Oslo, drawn there by an extraordinary coincidence in Norwegian literature from two disparate fields -- peace research and criminology. The work in peace research is Johan Galtung's (1969) "Violence, Peace, and Peace Research." The work in criminology is Nils Christie's (1981) <u>Limits to Pain.</u> Each author is concerned about the same problem: Galtung calls the problem "violence," while Christie calls it "pain infliction." At issue for both is how to reduce that problem. Galtung argues that governmental efforts to suppress violence with violence (which he calls "negative peace") are self-defeating. The extraordinary coincidence is that Galtung and Christie propose that social control be directed <u>away from</u> concern for what offenders have done.

Galtung and Christie are vague about what the targets of peacemaking efforts ought instead to be. Galtung proposes that peacemaking efforts be directed toward "structural violence" -- conditions like economic inequality. Christie proposes that we focus on matters like what parties to conflict want that the other side has to give. Each of the authors recognizes that the alternatives he seeks are elusive and hard to describe. Christie especially concludes by acknowledging that he is very nearly at a loss for words to describe what social control ought to aim against and instead aim for. The difficulty, I think, stems not from Galtung and Christie's shortcomings but rather attests to how far their thinking has advanced. They have entered a realm beyond normal discourse in the culture we share.

A longer version of this paper has appeared in Vol. II of <u>Humanity and Society</u> (1987).

The limits of normal discourse are perhaps more apparent in criminology than in peace research. Imagine not being able to discuss causes of war -- whether normative or empirical -- without reference to trends in the "real" levels of evil behavior governments faced. That is the position of us criminologists. I think people in peace research have come a little further in their thinking. If I were to express interest in why military expenditure is so much lower a fraction of the Norwegian national budget than of the American counterpart, I would be surprised to hear the answer, "But of course the world confronts Americans with a far higher concentration of evil acts than face the Norwegian people." Still, the most common pretext for armament and warfare these days is defense against ongoing or threatened violence, or retaliation against past violence, just as criminologists this of punishing offenders as "social defence" against crime.

Practically from the outset of my criminological career, I have had the nagging feeling that what people do to those they call offenders has nothing to do with what "offenders" have done to them or to anyone else. And my more or less formal field experience since has repeatedly supported the feeling -- from daily interaction between pairs of people at home and at work, to formal and informal complaints of having been victimized, to allegations in and around criminal justice agencies, to evidence cited in research and by policy-makers. For reasons I shall summarize early in this essay, Christie is absolutely right that "crime" is not a thing, but a concept we apply or not for reasons that have nothing to do with "offenders'" behavior.

Until recently, I persisted in trying to figure out what makes crime statistics go up and down. This was in fact the theme of an entire book (Pepinsky, 1980), where I found it as trivial as it is impossible to find out whether crime "really" is increasing or decreasing. The answer is simply that crime figures can and have been made to go up and down independent of unlawful behavior in countless ways as people have found more ways to measure crime and criminality.

Some statistics, however, have a significance beyond counting crime and criminality, indicating what people do to "offenders." The proportion of Americans sitting in jail, prison or a juvenile institution has doubled since the early 1970s, to about 400 of every 100,000 Americans.

One of every twelve black American men in their twenties
is spending the day in jail or prison, with more than
twice as many on probation or parole (a correction of
Pepinsky and Jesilow, 1985: 11, 161-62). 1/ Incarceration has been the dominant mode of punishing offenders
over much of the world for more than a century, and
incarceration trends are well worth trying to explain.
To borrow Christie's term, they are a key index of "pain
infliction." American incarceration trends are linked
to warfare. It is striking that rates have climbed
steadily at all times except during major wars -- against
the Spanish and Filippinos in the first decade of this
century, during World Wars I and II, during the Korean
War, and during the Vietnamese War (Cahalan, 1979). It
is as though the balance of a mounting scale of national
violence has shifted periodically from domestic enemies
to foreign enemies and back again. This suggests that
the pain infliction against offenders discussed by
Christie is a manifestation of the same forces that
underlie the international violence with which Galtung
ultimately is concerned.

Time spent in the political culture that spawned
Galtung and Christie has helped me to begin to see a
radically new way of describing what moves people to
violence to see what other than offensive behavior it
might be that drives people to punishment and violence
against one another. One object of the human rights
movement as described by another Norwegian (Eide, 1978)
offers particular hope for building peace in a wartorn
world -- participation or information sharing.

ON THE IRRELEVANCY OF CRIME TO PUNISHMENT

The deeply ingrained idea that the urge to punish is
occasioned by crime or other sin can be questioned at
several levels.

At the societal level, a political tautology
operates to ensure that those most likely to hurt others
while breaking the law are least likely to receive
punishment. The tautology is that both crime and punishment are exercises of power, so that being more powerful
practically by definition means having greater capacity
to get away with crime and resist punishment.

First, as to the capacity to get away with crime,
some empirical evidence is beginning to support the

intuitively obvious. Two recent compilations of such evidence are in Reiman (1984) and Pepinsky and Jesilow (1985). Pepinsky and Jesilow feature evidence from realms where American doctors work -- featured not because there is reason to believe that doctors are inisually crooked, but because doctors both have power and enjoy high social standing, such that most people presume doctors to be unusually law-abiding. Suffice it to note just to bits of such evidence, which in themselves give clear indication of a large underlying reality.

The Federal Bureau of Investigation compiles crimes recorded by American police, and these days reports that Americans lose a total of $6 billion per year to offenders of all kinds. These figures, however, cover only the kinds of offenders police look for -- those who commit what are generally known as "street crimes." In any case, the figures are speculative. If for instance a theft is recorded and a suspect arrested, and the suspect is later acquitted of the crime in court on grounds that the theft did not really occur, the "theft" usually remains on police records. A preliminary police belief that the crime could well have occurred is thus sufficient to create an American crime statistic.

The search for and recording of "economic" or "white-collar" crimes is at best minimal. One example of the kind of crime the police almost totally ignore is fraud in medical insurance claims. It is standard American practice that evidence supporting a claim come from a physician or hospital, and indeed the impression of investigators for medical insurers is that practically all fraud is the result of periodic inflation of claims by most doctors. Among estimates medical insurers have obtained are those that the largest American private medical insurer, Blue Cross-Blue Shield, loses $6 billion per year in fraudulent claims, while government insurers lose another $7 billion per year. These estimates are no less speculative than police statistics, but even allowing for gross error, the figures suggest that crime among the more powerful members of American society dwarfs the kind of crime police look for, which in turn is the kind of crime criminologists habitually look for, even in independent victim and self-report surveys (Pepinsky and Jesilow, 1985: 51, 166-67).

A typical response to such figures is, "Yes, people at the top commit more property crime, but the underclass has a monopoly on violent crime." Not so. Let us again begin with Federal Bureau of Investigation estimates, this time of the number of what they call "murders" for short and in full, "murder and non-negligent manslaughter." (This according to FBI guidelines can include even killing in self- defense; only "justifiable" killing by police officers is specifically excluded.) These days the FBI tells us that around 20,000 "murders" occur annually.

One place the FBI and police seldom look for murder is in hospitals, where doctors reign supreme. Consider American legal doctrine (acknowledging that laws vary both within the US and from country to country, but that roughly equivalent arguments can be made under various penal codes). It is generally recognized that in order for a patient's consent to be touched by a doctor or by the medicine the doctor delivers to be valid, the patient must have been fully informed about the risks and necessity for the bodily contact. Otherwise, the contact is an "assault." If someone dies as the direct result of an assault, the crime is "voluntary" or "non-negligent manslaughter," although such reckless disregard, as in locking fire exits in a building that burns down resulting in death, has even been ruled to be outright "murder."

Estimates are that 10-16,000 patients die each year of unnecessary surgery (presumably without having been told that the surgery was unnecessary when "consent" was obtained), that another 20,000 hospital patients die each year from getting the wrong or unnecessary drugs and that an additional 20,000 die from such reckless contamination as being examined with unwashed hands. Both these figures and police counterparts are estimates, but again, even allowing for gross distortions the figures suggest that what powerful people of which doctors are a tiny proportion and hospitals a minor realm do what logically could be deemed unlawful and violent harm on a scale police barely begin to tap when police look for crime "in the streets" rather than "in the suites." A doctor is just a special instance of the general fact that someone who wields a lot of physical power can do a lot more unlawful, physical damage, with much less risk of being called crooked, than the violent offenders who are the target of law enforcement (Pepinsky and Jesilow, 1985: 61, 167).

The underclass young men police typically catch and courts punish are the stuff of media publicity, criminological literature and folklore about crime. Public fear of street crime in the U.S. runs high, along with the belief that underclass young men be punished even more severely, even executed in large numbers, to make us safe. At the same time, the norm even for those white-collar offenders who are caught is to forgive them and even to elevate them beyond punishment (Korn, 1971). This consensus on whom to punish and whom to forgive norm is strong across societies (Brogden, 1982), a view even taken in The Communist Manifesto (Pepinsky, 1986). immense disparity between whom we punish and where the heart of the crime problem has barely begun to be recognized by criminologists.

The disparity cannot be ascribed to simple ignorance. Our inclination to excuse or justify or rationalize them transgressions by highly placed people is just one step removed from rationalizing what we ourselves do, as when embezzlers claim that they have only "borrowed money" Cressey (1953). The other side of the coin is that once we have decided that certain persons or groups are criminal or deviant, we may recast virtually everything they do as wrong or dangerous (Tannenbaum, 1938, for which Lemert, 1972).

American anthropologist Sally Engle Merry (1981) has graphically portrayed the disparity between crime and the urge to punish at the level of the urban neighborhood, where those who reported least victimization (some ethnic subgroups of the older residents) reported and behaved as though they were most threatened by crime, while younger persons who reported most victimization minimized the crime problem. It also happened that the local young people whom the elderly thought posed the greastest threat were wrongly suspected of crimes that occurred (which were actually committed mostly by visitors from other neighborhoods).

It was my privilege this January to be able to attend the annual conference of KROM, the Norwegian Organization for Criminal Reform. My family accompanied me to a beautiful mountain lodge for the weekend gathering. On the bus, at the lodge and actively participating in the meeting were twenty inmates from the Norwegian prison reserved for the longest term offenders. Among them were some of the country's most notorious robbers and murderers. None of the three of us knew

until we reached the lodge that most of the friendly
people we had met on the bus were among these inmates.
My daughter and I played a game at mealtime of trying to
guess who were inmates, until she observed, quite
appropriately I thought, "Dad, they shouldn't be in prison."

We may tell ourselves myths and spread stories
through the media about particularly heinous killers,
rapists and pillagers as though to reassure ourselves
that those we punish or want punished for crime look and
act very distinctively. The reality is that distinctive
criminals are few and far between. The reality is that
our inclination to punish people is unrelated to how much
crime we suffer at their hands. In part, our willingness
to punish others is a function of their social distance
or status. But is must also be recognized that some
groups of people are simply less inclined to think of
punishing anyone than others. I surmise that this is
true, for instance, of the average Norwegian as against
the average American. In both countries, there is vastly
more behavior that could be punished as crime but is not,
while particularly in the US there is also punishment of
those who give precious little cause. The proposition
that Norwegians punish less than Americans simply because
Norwegians suffer less crime is seemingly implausible and
certainly undemonstrable. The explanation has to be
sought elsewhere than in what offenders do.

PUNITIVENESS AND MILITARISM

Clues to the nature of the urge to punish appear at
the top of political orders, where policies concerning
criminals and other enemies of state are made and
implemented. To some extent, politicians choose their
vocation and are selected and groomed by elites on
grounds independent of the general nature and
circumstances of the general populace. But to a
significant degree, who chooses and is chosen to try
politics, and who rises in power thereafter, is shaped by
the social setting in which the politicians operate, much
as Darwin proposed that selection of species operates, in
what biologists today would call a "stochastic" process
(Bateson, 1980). This produces certain political reg-
ularities that transcend form of government we might
otherwise distinguish. Melossi and Pavarini (1981) have

noted one regularity among European and North American governments over the past several centuries: When unemployment is low, politicians favor rehabilitating criminals by putting them to constructive, socially valued work. When unemployment rises, criminals are deemed unfit or undeserving of meaningful employment, and policy shifts to punishing and confining offenders as a demonstration of pure intolerance for unlawfulness. Care of the underclass is referred to "private charity."

This pattern fits American history well. The two most recent major surges in imprisonment, accompanied by resurgence of resort to the death penalty, have occurred in the U.S. as we moved into the Great Depression at the end of the 1920s, and since 1974 when the oil crisis signalled an enduring boost in unemployment. Parallel political rhetoric for these two periods looks just like the punitive rhetoric described by Melossi and Pavarini (Kramer, 1982). The earlier wave of punitiveness shifted somewhat away from the domestic front as the U.S. entered World War II. The latter wave of punitiveness continues unabated, and although it characterized the years of a so-called "liberal Democratic" Presidency -- that of Jimmy Carter -- it has now come to be identified with the rhetoric of Ronald Reagan and of his Attorney General, Edwin Meese. It is not that American incarceration declines at other times, but that increases are particularly steep when unemployment threatens.

Norway presents a contrast from the 1840s to the mid-1890s, the Norwegian incarceration rate fell persistently and dramatically, at a time when Norway neither fought wars nor armed for any. Between 1814 and 1844, the average daily proportion of Norwegians serving prison sentences had more than tripled, to 179 of 100,000 Norwegians, an incarceration rate that today would rank among the world's highest. Fifty years later, the rate had dropped to under 50 per 100,000. Christie (1966) has described these trends, and has proposed that the rate declined so as time became more precious to Norwegians.

A preliminary reading of Norwegian history indicates a striking contrast between how the political climate shifted as the decline stopped at the end of the century. Compare these two passages translated from Jensen (1971). The first concerns changes that began to take hold in the latter 1830s, which in Jensen's view were times dominated by the spirit and thinking of Henrik Wergeland.

Describing Wergeland and the times together, Jensen writes (p. 69, trans. from Norwegian):

It was a time when ideas of romanticism were used in the service of reaction, but in and of themselves were not reactionary. They could therefore also be used by the new classes which gained power in England and France in the 1830s. The concepts of freedom, equality and brotherhood took on new power because they partook of the deep feelings romanticism had created. The view of the nation as an organism was bound in the final analysis to create demands for accord across international and national borders, and the demand became a revolutionary force thereby, the most powerful in Europe at the time. But national feeling was not directed against other peoples. On the contrary it represented the profoundest meeting of minds among all those who marched under its banner.

In 1895 a Liberal government had been pressing hard for autonomy from Sweden. King Oscar II of Sweden had responded with a military show of force. The move for sovereignty buckled, and a Conservative Party leader became Prime Minister. Jensen writes (pp. 187-88):

The defeat was a dear lesson and made a deep impression on all those who thought responsibly. The shortsighted theoretical idealism in policy, which had been so closely associated with our spiritual life, had proven fallible, as it had in 1864 [when the decline in incarceration was also reversed for several years]. The attitude became more cautious... Now, it became clear that a bold national policy could only be built on a strong army, and the old distrust of the army changed as suddenly as the weather. From 1895 there was mobilization as for war, and the earlier proponents of disarmament on the far Left were as eager as the old proponents of defense on the Right. Major appropriations were made for extraordinary purposes time after time. New, modern armored ships were acquired, fortifications were constructed in major tons and along the Swedish border, and artillery was modernized. Both defense ministers of the time, Conservative W. E. Ollson and Liberal Georg Stan, were able businessmen who understood how to get the most for their money.

Jensen goes on to report that the policy persisted even as the Liberals gained strong majorities in the 1897 and 1900 elections. So did the rise in incarceration. The anxiety, the mobilization and incarceration all fell off after 1902, as separation from Sweden became settled.

According to Jensen, the onset of the spirit of Henrik Wergeland in the latter 1830s coincided with legislation that gave renewed authority to local Norwegian governments. This was followed by a new penal code in 1842, which was part of the new mood of accommodation to individual differences. In sum, the political process was one of what the British would term "devolution" or of what is more generally known as "decentralization."

This contrasts sharply with the first twenty years of Norwegian "independence" after 1814, and with events at the close of the nineteenth century. Within a year of formal separation from Denmark in 1814, the Norwegian parliament or "Storting" had elected the Swedish King as the Norwegian sovereign, and Norwegian currency had collapsed on the international market. Just as Norwegians had thought themselves to have attained national autonomy, they suddenly felt themselves possessed of larger international forces. Power seemed wrested from them, by a world they had to accede to with very little chance to exert their own influence over the course of events.

Jensen reports a similar setback for the Norwegians in the 1890s. The Liberals came to power in 1891 on a promise of arranging diplomatic autonomy from Sweden. They were reelected on the same platform in 1894. The Swedish King made a show of preparing to go to war. The Norwegians were not mobilized for war, and they knew their weakness. The Liberal government accordingly collapsed, as the Storting accommodated the Swedes. This was the crisis that brought on rearmament, and with it, expanded use of prisons.

In sum, when economic and political forces Norwegians faced appeared to be becoming centralized, Norwegians responded as though threatened by war, and in the process, became more punitive toward offenders. When conditions permitted political and economic authority to move back into local hands, punishment of offenders abated.

With minor fluctuations the level of incarceration level today (Norway Central Bureau of Statistics, 1985) remains roughly where it fell in the first decade of this century -- at a daily population of roughly 50 Norwegians per 100,000. One has to go back to before 1860 to find as low a rate in the U.S. (Cahalan, 1979: 12).

Placed beside Norway's experience, the entire history of the American nation state bears a remarkable resemblance to the periods when Norwegian incarceration shot up. Fed in part by warfare and militarization themselves, the history in the US is one of continued centralization of economic and political forces, as Zinn's (1980) remarkable study of American history makes plain.

Political consolidation occurred as the American States moved from Articles of Confederation to a Federal Constitution in 1789, which gave Congress legislative control over foreign and interstate commerce. In the early decades of the nineteenth century, currency regulation, central banking and tariffs followed. The major reason for the secession of Southern States and the ensuing Civil War (1861-65) was not slavery, but whether foreign trade and domestic commerce would be regulated for the South so as to suit the interests of Northern industrialists. In the decades that followed the Northern victory, giant monopolies over such businesses as the production of oil and steel and the building and running of railroads virtually captured national, state and local governments. Once control of the continental United States had been secured, attention turned to establishing economic hegemony abroad, beginning with the wars against Spain and the Philippines at the turn of the century. When the United States emerged from World War II as the only national giant with its economic infrastructure intact and booming, American-based corporate interests were in a position to move in where European and Japanese interests had dominated. Massive national subsidy of producers of war materiel during World War II became favored industries and defense contractors thereafter, so that when the President of General Motors was appointed Secretary of Defense in 1953, he could unabashedly testify to the US Senate at his confirmation hearing: "What's good for General Motors is good for the country." (See also Mills, 1956, for a classic study of the history of the American "power elite" and its consolidation.)

Foreign wars and wars on crime have provided American politicians a way to deceive a violent and troubled public. People are constantly threatened not merely by uncertainties like adverse weather, but in a consolidating economy, by seemingly intractable human forces that throw people out of jobs and otherwise throw resources like food and shelter out of reach. Identifying a foreign or domestic enemy allows politicians to attribute these threats and misfortunes to forces which appear manageable, thereby inviting the public to join the politicians in further consolidation of the economic forces which have put the politicians in office. If the "enemy" looks different enough to the public and safe enough to fight, members of the public will quite readily join in venting their frustrations and anxieties in the enemy's direction. The convenience and catharsis of joining such a fight can easily carry away a distressed public.

Norwegians have described life in their communities as "close" or "tight" (Torgersen, 1974), although Christie (1982) argues that this special quality of Norwegian life is eroding. Eroding or not, it is commonly conceded that the closeness or tightness in Norwegian communities far exceeds the American norm. The sense of closeness or tightness is a corollary of decentralized power. Torgersen and Christie describe the sense as one behaving thoughtfully or responsibly toward others because one is aware (a) of one's impact on others, and (b) of severe repercussions to oneself of hurting others. Closeness gives members of a community a special stake in recognizing one another's individuality, for the consequences of mistakenly and prematurely categorizing a person are more varied and immediate than where large and impersonal forces appear to dominate the life of one's society. In a phrase, life in the tight community requires accepting responsibility for one's own actions.

The larger the forces that dominate social life appear to become, the less important responsibility for one's own actions becomes. One's fate is out of one's own hands. Finding someone or something upon which to pin responsibility for what is happening to oneself becomes a paramount concern, and among equally anxious powerbrokers in the society, passing the buck becomes a survival skill.

These differences explain how what constitute serious threats of crime to some people can constitute minor incidents to others. The Norwegian sheriff or schoolchild has more confidence in being able to manage an unacceptable situation with less effort and with greater confidence that the drunk or the bully, for instance, will listen to reason when called upon to do so (see Christie, 1981). At the other extreme in American society, the urban elderly are especially prone to feeling powerless and dominated by larger and even incomprehensible forces. Mere proximity to young strangers may call this threat to mind. Worse yet, having even a small amount of money taken by stealth may signify vulnerability to forces and people who for all one knows could take one's life without a moment's pause or regret. What to others might be an innocuous personal encounter can to so vulnerable and frightened a person serve mainly as a reminder of one's isolation, impotence and social irrelevance. Seen thus, it becomes rational and comprehensible that one person's traumatic victimization or threat of victimization becomes another's routine and passing if not necessarily pleasant encounter.

Understandable as the urge to punish and fight might be among those who feel generally powerless, the urge is also bound to be ineffectual. The larger social forces that dominate the lives of punitive people remain generally untouched by isolated acts of punishment, and the act of punishment can even compound a person or group's isolation. On the whole, the propensity to warfare and punishment that prevails among todays Americans is scarcely an advance over "primitive" purification rituals like burning witches. The objects of punishment are for the most part coincidental to the distress that makes people want to hurt offenders. Worse yet, mobilizing to punish offenders and enemies usually entails consolidating power such that one's social fate is even further romoved from one's own hands, increasing the threat one aims to purge.

The irony of the American situation is that a wealthy and powerful people stand out as driven by a sense of social impotence. This is as true for the punitive American power elite as for the punitive working class in the same society. Within the centralized order,

those at the top of the political and economic hierarchy
are as driven by as great a sense of insecurity as those
who suffer material deprivation. In fact, if one takes
non-Native Americans as a whole, their history seems to
indicate that one's desperation and recourse to violence
grows stronger the higher one's group rises in a process
of centralization. Thus, outwardly, materially
comfortable people--the image in which Ronald Reagan is
cast--also turn out to be frightened, superstitious
militarists who themselves have fallen victim to
centralization. As such, they genuinely achieve broad
consensus that war against foreign enemies and a domestic
underclass of offenders is imperative. This shared sense
of desperation fits the description of what Weber (1958,
originally 1904-5) called "the Protestant ethic and the
spirit of capitalism," which need be neither Protestant
nor capitalist. There is a moral to the contrasting
course of American and Norwegian history: It is not the
material wealth or power people gain, but the extent of
participation in decentralized political structures that
frees people from fear and inclination to violence.

THE KEY TO PEACE

Insofar as tension of economic and other varieties
become too large, and insofar as this does not leave room
for change through political participation and individual
freedom, peace will not long be maintained, even with the
most advanced means to power. The most modern weapons
technology will not suffice to uphold calm and order.
There is a limit to what will be tolerated, and when
respect for human rights reaches so low that the boundary
is crossed, an explosion is likely. (Eide, 1978: 166-67;
trans. from Norwegian)

Human life consists of energy that craves outlet in
interaction with others; the more constructive
participation of people in community life can be
expanded, the more social peace will reign . . . It
is not [penal] law, but engineering and tolerating
diversity of economic, social, and political
arrangements, of organizations and enterprises in
each of our communities, that makes people behave
civilly toward each other. (Pepinsky and Jesilow,
1985: 138, 142)

What is it about centralization of social order that drives rich and poor alike to violent desperation? What, by contrast, gives rise to security among people who participate in relatively decentralized social orders? Taken together, what do rich and poor people lose together in centralized structures that people gain together in participative structures?

The answer, I think, is "information." When I allow my action and objectives to be affected by what others communicate, I gain new ways to adapt to environmental contingencies. When the others allow themselves to be affected by how I am affected by them, they learn, too. The more people use each other's information about how each is affected by responses to the environment, the more knowledge everyone gains. Information increases by being used, instead of getting used up like material resources (i.e., information is synergetic rather than entropic; Fuller, 1975, 1979).

Survival of the human species to-date has rested heavily on exchange of information among members. Humans differ from other species such as cockroaches in two important respects. Humans reproduce slowly, and have a narrow tolerance for change in the physical environment, as in food supply, air supply and temperature. Meanwhile, as Charles Darwin pointed out, the physical environment changes often, drastically and unpredictably. Our species could not have learned to survive several generations, let along 100,000, unless information sharing, or cooperation were the overwhelming reality of human existence. All in all, Darwin's (1968, originally 1859) reasoning leads one to suppose that human survival has rested on preserving a variety of human lifestyles and information sets, and on each member's willingness to attend to others' information and learn from it.

At a mundane level, the reasoning is the same as that of the trade unionist who tells management that they had best listen to workers' reports of problems on the assembly line, lest problems and innovations managers could not have foreseen be lost and production be slowed or stopped. More abstractly, the imperative for nurturing and exchanging information with others is essentially what mysticism calls for in all manner of religious belief systems, from Judaic justice to Christian love to Buddhist and Sufi Moslem compassion. The miracle of human survival, from the level of each individual's survival into adulthood to the level of

human survival through millions of years, suggests a
human inclination to draw satisfaction from pooling
information with others, and to have a low threshold
alarm when exchange of information is curtailed. One
would expect those who attain wealth and high position in
a fixed production system become just as alarmed over
their failure to learn from subordinates as the
subordinates are over their subjugation. There must be
an instinctive foreboding that to persist even in winning
ways, without holding oneself open to being warned and
changed by others' experience, is a good way to prepare
to die when the world changes. People who remained open
and accountable with others would feel most social
serenity even when physical conditions were spartan or
severe. Their prospects for survival would be maximized
come what may. This openness and accommodation to
others' information presupposes flexible, small-scale,
participatory organization of social life.

It is noteworthy that this imperative is sounded
time and again in literature that emerges from relatively
peaceful Norway.

One place to look for such literature in any culture
is the women's movement, where participatory organization
is a leading theme. The women's movement has an
exceptionally long and prominent history in Norway, which
for instance is among the first countries to have given
women the right to vote. Norwegians are doing pioneering
work in the field today. In May 1986, the Prime Minister
and over forty percent of the cabinet became women -- a
world record. Domestically, for example, the field of
Women's Law has been established in the University of
Oslo's law faculty. Introducing a two volume collection
of essays on the subject, Dahl (1985: 87-88; trans. from
Norwegian) writes:

By the methods of women's law this classification
[of the subject matter of law] is not grounded from
above, as an axiomatic application of justice from
superordinate principles. Many philosophers to be
sure have asserted that the ethics and choice of
moral values should be grounded from above, from
general principles of an axiomatic character which
are correctly applied as long as the axiom itself is
correct....The women's law perspective on justice is
based on mapping women's needs and wants generally,

and particularly on their perceptions of what is just.

This Foundation for framing issues in women's law seems appropriate to feminists from any culture. However, it is customary for example in American defenses of women's rights to see them founded in the kind of axiomatic reference to general or established legal principles which Dahl and her coworkers in the field reject. It is, I would argue, a more participatory culture like Norway in which the more participatory premises are to be found even in feminist literature.

The author of the only book to ground peace studies in explicitly feminist principles happens to be Norwegian. Brock-Utne (1985) has written a seminal work in peace studies in which equal participation in every sphere of human decision-making is the cornerstone of understanding and building peace among nations.

In criminology, Christie (1981) stresses that attaining intimate knowledge of others and recognizing mutual dependence in participatory structures are key conditions for peaceful community life. And in the human rights movement in the field of peace research, Norwegian commentator Eide (1978: 173; trans. from Norwegian) stresses:

The organization of the political system such that everyone receives an equally large real possibility for joining in the government of their own community [or society], is the most important mechanism for implementing [human rights]. It is also the only satisfactory way of deciding desirable priorities at anytime.

Time and again, Norwegians return to the fundamental importance of extending participation in how information is created and applied. As Norwegians are quick to point out, theirs is not a perfectly participatory or peaceful society. But the recurring ability of Norwegians to be able to describe and defend participation implies that they have experienced a fair measure of it, and given the chauvinist tendencies that shape the thinking of the best of us from any culture, it is a fair guess that Norwegian social analysts are moved in part by an awareness of what other peoples lack relative to Norwegians.

Given the fact that Norwegians are relatively inclined to peace and disinclined to punishment and violence, we might do well to take special note of the central place participatory decisionmaking occupies in

Norwegian thinking. In the Norwegian view, protection of human rights has paramount importance, and among these rights, as Eide notes, participation stands foremost. Corollary Norwegian experience indicates that establishing this right is the key to making the people and leaders of nation states peaceful at home and abroad.

CONCLUSION

A comparison of Norwegian and American experience supports Galtung's (1969) proposition that "negative peace" -- trying to repress offenders and offenses -- only escalates violence. This has been the American approach and the American result. Norway by contrast succeeded in becoming more peaceful at home and abroad in the nineteenth century, and has been relatively successful at containing its own violence since. It appears that this success rests on having stressed local, grassroots participation in decision making. The importance of this "human right" is a prominent and pervasive theme in Norwegian social control literature today. Participation means conveying the sense that each person's experience of the world influences what others in a community aim to achieve and the ways they try to achieve it. By preserving this people remain free of violence.

Just as it is mistaken to suppose that the threat of crime can be curtailed by building bigger prisons and police forces, so it is mistaken to believe that peace among nations can be built by imposing one system of government, one set of rules, or larger systems of resource allocation and political accord. Politicians will become more peaceful only as tension dissipates among the people they purport to govern. And that tension will dissipate the more variously local groups of people are permitted to arrange their affairs. To borrow the statistical jargon so common among today's social researchers and planners, the world will become more peaceful only as we learn to increase the unexplained variance in human action (Pepinsky, 1982). Within the field of peace studies, this emphasis is well expressed by stressing nurture and protecting participation as the most fundamental of human rights.

NOTES

1.   Pepinsky and Jesilow's estimate, that one in four black men in his twenties is spending the day in jail or prison, is wrong. In figures cited there which I used to derive the estimate, I <u>mistakenly</u> inferred that the proportion of men in their <u>twenties</u> incarcerated is twelve times the proportion of <u>all</u> men incarcerated, while the <u>correct</u> interpretation must be twelve times the proportion of men <u>of other ages</u> incarcerated.

BIBLIOGRAPHY

Gregory P. Bateson, <u>Mind and Nature: A Necessary Unity</u>.
    New York: Bantam Books, 1980.
Birgit Brock-Utne, <u>Educating for Peace: A Feminist</u>
    <u>Perspective</u>. Elmsford, N.Y., U.S.A.: Pergamon
    Press, 1985.
Michael Brogden (with Ann Brogden), <u>The Police: Autonomy</u>
    <u>and Consent</u>. London: Academic Press, 1982.
Margaret Cahalan, "Trends in incarceration in the United
    States since 1880: A summary of reported rates and
    the   distribution   of   offenses."   <u>Crime   and</u>
    <u>Delinquency</u>, 25:9-41, 1979.
Nils Christie, "De fratagbare goder" ("The deprivable
    commodities"),   <u>Tidsskrift   for   Samfunnsforskning</u>
    (Journal of Social Research). 2:119-29, 1966.
Nils Christie, <u>Limits to Pain</u>. Oxford, U.K.: Martin
    Robertson, 1981.
Nils Christie, <u>Hvor Tett et Samfunn?</u> (<u>How Tight [or</u>
    <u>Closely Knit] a Society [or Community]?</u>), Oslo:
    Universitetsforlaget (University Press), 1982.
Donals R. Cressey, <u>Other People's Money: The Social</u>
    <u>Psychology of Embezzlement</u>. New York: Free Press,
    1953.
Tove Stang Dahl (ed.), <u>Kvinnerett I</u> (Women's Law Vol. 1).
    Oslo: Universitetsforlaget   (University   Press),
    1985.
Charles Darwin, <u>Origin of Species</u>. London: Penguin
    Books, 1968, originally 1859.
Asbjorn Eide. <u>Fattig, Ufri og Mishandlet: Om det</u>
    <u>Internasjonale   Menneskerettighetsvernet</u>   (Poor,
    <u>Unfree and Mistreated: Concerning International</u>
    <u>Defense   of   Human   Rights</u>).   Oslo: Universi-
    tetsforlaget (University Press), 1978.
R. Buckminster Fuller, <u>Synergetics: Explorations in the</u>

Geometry of Thinking, 2 vols. New York: Macmillan, 1975 and 1979.

Johan Galtung, "Violence, peace, and peace research," Journal of Peace Research, 6:167-91, 1969.

Magnus Jensen, Norges Historie: Unionstiden 1814-1905 (Norway's History: The Time of Union, 1814-1905), 3rd ed. Oslo: Universitetsforlaget (University Press), 1971.

Richard Korn, "Of crime, criminal justice and corrections," University of San Francisco Law Review, 6:27-75, 1971.

Ronald C. Kramer, "From "habitual offenders" to "career criminals": the historical development of criminal categories," Law and Human Behavior, 6:273-93, 1982.

Edwin M. Lemert, Human Deviance, Social Problems, and Social Control, 2nd ed,. Englewood Cliffs, N.J.: Prentice-Hall, 1972.

C. Wright Mills, The Power Elite. New York: Oxford University Press, 1956.

Sally Engle Merry, Urban Danger. Philadelphia: Temple University Press, 1981.

Harold E. Pepinsky, Crime Control Strategies. New York: Oxford University Press, 1980.

Harold E. Pepinsky, "Humanizing social control," Humanity and Society. 6:227-42, 1982.

Harold E. Pepinsky, "Post-Marxist criminology: lessons from British policing," Law and Human Behavior, 10:265-77, 1986.

Harold E. Pepinsky & Paul Jesilow, Myths That Cause Crime, rev. ed., Cabin John, Maryland: Seven Locks Press, 1985.

Jeffrey Reiman, The Rich Get Richer and the Poor Get Prison, 2d ed. New York: John Wiley, 1984.

Frank Tannenbaum, Crime and the Community. Boston: Ginn, 1938.

Ulf Torgersen, "Political institutions." in Natalie Rogoff Ramsoy, ed., Norwegian Society. Oslo: Universitetsforlaget (University Press), 1974.

Max Weber (Talcott Parsons, trans.), The Protestant Ethic and the Spirit of Capitalism. New York: Charles Scribner's Sons, 1958, originally 1904-5.

Howard Zinn, A People's History of the United States. New York: Harper Colophon Books, 1980.

6

Six Views of Nonviolence for Peace Research

Theodore Herman

One of the most encouraging trends of the 1980s in many parts of the world is the growing interest in non-violence. One does not overlook the rise of terrorism, whether perpetrated by governments or private groups, but terrorism is still a fringe effort with little popular appeal anywhere. People do seem to be searching for another way.

Nonviolence has many meanings but essentially it offers alternatives to those attitudes, institutions, and practices that withhold peace and justice. It encourages people everywhere to explore new ways of thinking and acting for a more peaceful world. Therefore, a broadened understanding of nonviolence as both an attitude and a way of action provides a rich field for peace research.

"New ways of thinking and acting" may mean re-writing history to include peace heroes and acts of reconciliation both at home and from other times and places. In education it may lead to changing school curricula toward cooperative learning instead of students vs. teacher or student vs. student. It may mean prescribing national policies for fairer sharing of resources, markets, knowledge etc., as insurance against future strife. It may lead people to form groups to meet local needs or even to form global networks to meet wider needs, regardless of age-old loyalties to clan, church, or class. Whatever the prescription, working with others in groups is essential.

As a guide to research in nonviolence we offer six different approaches or views. These are derived from human experience as the stuff from which theory can be made:

1. Personal awareness or
    psycho-spiritual change

2. Pacifism or non-
    retaliation in kind

3. Development of a
    creative relationship
    with an adversary

4. Nonviolent resistance
    as civilian-based
    defense

5. Prevention   of
    violent conflict

6. Development of a sound
    relationship with the
    earth

PERSONAL AWARENESS OR PSYCHO-SPIRITUAL CHANGE

Personal awareness or spycho-spiritual change is an ancient theme in almost every philosophy and religion. It rests on self-respect or self-love based on an awareness of the worth or good in oneself and then, through respect, touches the good in others. In Gandhi's behavior this was part of the truth-in-action that marked his whole life. It was expressed succinctly in 1656 by George Fox, founder of the Quakers, as "to walk cheerfully over the earth speaking to that of God in everyone" 1/ in contrast to living defensively in fear of others.

One of the psychological elements of this positive view is the assurance of safety and control of one's immediate concerns, such as personal values, livelihood, family and friends. The opposite occurs when helplessness creates terror. To threaten that psychological safety with change can be disturbing, and therefore many people resist change unless it comes through some strong personal experience or transformation. Such an experience is a notable feature in the accounts of many people whose lives have changed abruptly to a single pursuit, often of religious or social impact. Recall Gautama leaving the palace, Ashoka forsaking warfare, Paul on the road to Damascus, soldier-of-fortune Ignatius Loyola founding the Society of Jesus, Joan of Arc envisioning French freedom from England, Gandhi sitting all night on the railway station platform, Martin Luther King one lonely midnight at the kitchen table, Charles Coulson emerging from prison after his Watergate conviction.

There are many people in the world to whom inner transformation never comes. They are either already at peace with the world, kind and loving by nature, or the prospect of inner change is not important to them. But there are others whose lives have been completely transformed by a vision, or by a shattering experience and they have gone on to change society around them. Accounts of such changes are becoming common. Research on such psycho-spiritual events is needed in each society for a fuller record of human experience and as a guide to understanding social change.

One evidence of developing awareness is the increasing attention given to the roles of men and women in society. Countless articles, books and conferences are challenging the age-old patriarchal domination in many societies which is often expressed in violence and war. An indication of growing worldwide concern was the highly visible UN Nairobi Women's Conference and NGO Forum in 1985 attended by some 14,000 women from all over the world who were there to raise consciousness and give support. At the local level there are increasing challenges, by both men and women, to the double standard of education, treatment, and expectations in every aspect of life. To extend such views into specific societies and into their educational systems would be an additional contribution to peace research.

PACIFISM OR NON-RETALIATION IN KIND

Pacifism or non-retaliation in kind is probably the most widespread and mixed view of nonviolence. It is seen in many lights: as cowardly expedience, realistic acceptance, a clear example of masochism, true psychological riposte, or loving care. It is the refusal to respond to evil and injustice with force or anger, and the willingness to respond instead with meekness and even the willingness to suffer. The injunction comes from the Sermon on the Mount in the New Testament and from the teachings of the Buddha and of Mahavira of the Jains. Because the reasons for non-retaliation differ, it is important to understand what traditions might be evoked in various societies.

In the Biblical Old and New Testaments returning good for evil is noted as "heaping coals of fire on an enemy's head," whether as an expression of enlightenment or punishment in this life or some form of punishment in another life. It is believed that in some way God will reward the victim who forbears. 2/ The Sermon on the Mount, from which Gandhi drew directly for his development of satyagraha, goes further in exhorting the return of good for evil as an act of love that follows the example of God. In Jewish tradition, a similar practice is reinforced by Talmudic teaching. 3/

In Hindu, Buddhist and Jain teachings, a person experiences reincarnation until goodness finally brings release, and nonviolence as a part of benevolence lessens the number of re-birth cycles and suffering. 4/ Thus, as in the Christian view, there is reward in a future life for doing good in this one. Ferguson notes that Gandhi "more than any other individual ... brought ahimsa (non-violence) into the active moral consciousness of Hinduism" drawing upon "Jesus and post-Christian European and American practitioners of nonviolence." 5/ In Islam, charity is extolled as a social act, but a better after-life is not promised for nonviolent behavior.

This second approach, willingness to suffer without retaliation in kind or even without hatred, is basic not only as a psychological tactic or "moral jiu-jitsu" in Gregg's phrase 6/ to arouse the conscience of the oppressor, but also to strengthen the commitment of the oppressed. It is the ultimate form of purification of one's motives.

Again, the problem for peace researchers is to find and report examples of those who have "turned the other cheek" so that the idea becomes worth thinking about. Such people are often seen in the news being hauled into court for refusing to pay the military portion of their income taxes or for refusing to register for military service or for similar acts on the grounds of conscience. An earlier model that has influenced many people including Gandhi was Henry David Thoreau who went to jail for one night for refusing to pay the Massachusetts poll tax in protest against the American government's Mexican War and slavery policies. His famous essay, "Civil Disobedience and Non-Violent Resistance," on the right to exercise conscience has become a classic.

The whole idea of willingness to suffer without retaliation in kind raises many questions, including the question of responsibility for the welfare of others and the question of the unity of one's nation. Such challenges have been raised by President Kenneth Kaunda of Zambia and deserve attention. 7/

DEVELOPMENT OF A CREATIVE RELATIONSHIP

Development of a creative relationship seeks to extend the previous view by transforming a confrontation into a relationship of unity. This form of nonviolence has been given positive names in English in place of the customary but negative term "nonviolence": "creative conflict," "all-win action," "transforming power" or, added to our vocabulary, "satyagraha" -- Gandhi's "clinging to truth" or "soul force." For Gandhi it evolved from a sense of mutual fairness (the Golden Rule) into an ethic of universal caring and love which would not be conditional on its return. Strongly moved by the lives and writings of Thoreau, Ruskin, Tolstoy, and by the Sermon on the Mount, and his own devotion to the Bhagavad Gita, he moved beyond passive nonviolent resistance to active nonviolent resistance. Civil disobedience was a last resort, but he was ready to suffer to strengthen himself and to move his adversary. Gandhi's idea of victory was not over his opponent but over the fears and attachments that keep people from reaching the good in themselves and in others.

This third form has to do with both personal change and groups at all levels. The principles are grounded in direct individual contact and change. Two striking examples of the development of a creative relationship at the international level are the formation of the European Coal and Steel Community after World War II -- the fulfilled dream of Jean Monnet and Robert Schumann to bring France and Germany together and in 1975 the Barcelona Agreement of most of the Mediterranean countries (including bitter adversaries) to monitor marine pollution -- a starting point for cooperation. 8/ (This latter move was initiated by members of the Religious Society of Friends (Quakers) in various parts of the world.)

While Gandhi's creative nonviolence is well-known, others have used it in somewhat similar ways. William Penn established colonial Pennsylvania in 1683 as a warless community which would give equitable treatment to the Indians; the community lasted for 73 years. In 1952 Albert Luthuli tried Gandhi's methods unsuccessfully in

South Africa. 9/ Martin Luther King led the civil rights struggle in the southern United States from 1954 to 1968, drawing on his own religious and personal background, and learning from Gandhi's examples how to apply the ethics of Jesus to social change. In these examples and in countless smaller ones the means are as important as the ends because they provide guidance for efforts elsewhere.

Are there some exceptional societies that are basically nonviolent? Such a question emerged in an interview in 1984 with Fr. Jose Blanco, a Filipine Jesuit who was discussing various responses to the oppression in his country. He was speaking as a churchman who was dedicated to nonviolence (not all were) and as a concerned Filipino:

... counter-violence cannot change the heart and mind of the opponent. But active nonviolence tries to change the one doing the violence. People are changed not by threats but by signs of respect; by signs of love and real charity.

But let me stress that I don't argue from arguments. I argue from experience with the poor themselves. The poor rejoice that they have found an alternative that is in keeping with their conscience and their heart. Even before their conversion to Christianity, the Filipinos were culturally a nonviolent people. Our saying is: It is better not to destroy. 10/ (Underlining added)

The relatively peaceful overthrow of the Marcos regime in February 1986 bears out his claim that nonviolence is an accepted method of public behavior in the Philippines. A great challenge remains in the social changes they will need to reduce that country's systemic violence. 11/

The peace researcher will ask if there are ways in which the principles of creative nonviolence can be discovered and applied within and between different countries. Does nonviolence depend upon a religious influence? How can nonviolence be spread over a large group and made permanent in its institutions and behavior? The following three views deal more with the traditions, customs, and the behavior of groups than of individuals.

NONVIOLENT RESISTANCE AS CIVILIAN-BASED DEFENSE

Nonviolent Resistance as Civilian-based Defense differs from the experiences of Gandhi and King both in its ultimate intentions and in its historical background: When it is faced by superior force, a nation or group devises nonviolent methods of resistance to an invader or to an internal oppressor. Although they were not all successful, there have been several such efforts, especially in the 19th and 20th centuries. They have been based on the idea that the power to control rests on the willingness of people to obey. Thus if people can be united to oppose a specific situation, they can be organized to obstruct in countless nonviolent ways. The aim is to make the cost of domination high enough to defeat the purpose of the oppressor.

While this method does not take the spiritual well-being of the "tyrant" into consideration, in an effort to make his forces feel ashamed and demoralized, attention drawn to his brutality by ridicule and by isolation is part of the treatment. Reprisals for obstruction certainly fall on civilians, even those involved, but suffering is at least more nearly equitable than in conventional war. Overall costs would be less for the victims and the chances of longterm success less for the invaders.

Principles of civilian-based defense have been most persistently developed by Gene Sharp from his many years of study of the history of wars, resistance movements and nonviolence. He argues largely from European experience that as people are trained for such participation, war will be discarded as an instrument of national policy.

Broad visions have marked the work of Gandhi, King, Luthuli in South Africa, the Green movement in FRG which began in 1972, the present opposition in Poland, and many community action groups operating in other parts of the world. Such groups operate outside of government, often with their own rules and leaders. This is the strategy of the current movement in Poland in the effort to "work around the government ... (so that) there would occur an epidemic of freedom in a closed society." 12/ However, unlike several other examples cited, the Polish opposition is not directly based on religious teachings, although the Catholic Church is generally recognized as the centuries-old guardian against outside domination.

There are many accounts of untrained groups trying to throw off oppressive regimes, both foreign and domestic, nonviolently. We recall the long struggle of Hungary against Austria, 1849-1867, the Czech resistance to Warsaw Pact invasion (1968-1969), the fall of the Shah of Iran in 1978 and of President Duvalier in Haiti in 1986. In most societies there are traditions of resistance in songs, stories and historical records. The less-known nonviolent ones need to be published and discussed also.

PREVENTION OF VIOLENT CONFLICT

Prevention of violent conflict, a fifth view of nonviolence, is work for social justice and conditions that remove the causes of violent conflict. Gandhi once said "Poverty is the worst kind of violence." We are coming to recognize material poverty, intellectual poverty, spiritual poverty or the denial of opportunity for achievement as the denial of human rights. All of them can be considered systemic violence: domination by large, impersonal forces.

We are living in the revolution of rising expectations. This revolution begins with people believing that change is possible. It is carried on by organizing and training to advance the realization of human rights by nonviolence. Changes in Third World economic systems are pointed toward small-scale agriculture and light industry, using improved technology to escape the demands of commercial production for distant and uncertain markets and for central government revenue. Efforts at alternative nonviolent local political organization have appeared in Danilo Dolci's work since 1952 to build communities among the poor in western Sicily 13/ and in the Green movement in FRG since 1972 for peace, ecological preservation, sexual equality and economic justice. 14/ In an urban setting the Movement for a New Society in Philadelphia has been trying since 1969 to change the socio-economic system by establishing working communities in neighborhoods with low cost housing. 15/ Adapting such efforts to various countries requires sharing information among researchers and social leaders.

At many levels conflict resolution is a new and welcome activity. Skills are being developed and used by

officials and others to resolve disputes between
countries and, within countries, to resolve community
disputes. 16/   Less well known is the Peace Brigades
International, founded in Canada in 1981 to "establish
and monitor a cease-fire, offer mediation, or carry on
works of reconstruction and reconciliation." 17/ Unlike
UN peacekeeping forces, PBI volunteers do not accept
government troop units or carry arms. Their efforts to
date have been on the borders of Central American
countries.

DEVELOPMENT OF A SOUND RELATIONSHIP WITH THE
EARTH

Development of a Sound Relationship with the earth
supposes that no civilization can endure unless its
people can make an acceptable living, and therefore
environmental care is vital. The values, institutions,
and technologies of any flourishing society reveal this
mutual relationship between the people and the planet.
The fragility of this relationship is exposed when a
man-made disaster, such as that of Three Mile Island,
chemical spills, toxic waste poisoning of soil and water,
failure of a central power plant, etc. occurs. People
lose confidence in authority and seek their own safety,
and thus the social fabric is imperiled.
        One of the most striking studies made is by the
anthropologist Colin Turnbull on the disintegration of
the Ik people in northern Uganda in the 1960s during a
long drought and government restrictions on their nomadic
herding circuits. Traditional values of caring vanished
as famine took over. The very old and the very young
were abandoned, the young who survived formed predatory
gangs, and the community fell apart. A culture of
despair and endemic violence was born. 18/   Similar
changes appear in many other places as displaced people
swell urban slums where desperation and violence are met
in turn by government repression.
        Now near the end of the 20th century we are assured
that the earth can support everyone. What we do not yet
have are the attitudes, customs, laws, and the techniques
that translate an ethic of reverence for all life on a
planet of interlocking systems and infinite beauty into a
world to be preserved for ourselves and our descendants.
We have not yet learned to curtail excessive life styles,

to invest in the safe disposal or conversion of toxic
wastes, to preserve natural habitats against continued
species destruction, or even to protect farm land,
forests, air and water from misuse. The new ethic of
moderate sustained living has not yet replaced the
ancient fears of scarcity that lead to rapid
exploitation. The warnings in The Limits to Growth seem
to have been forgotten. 19/

Recent famines in much of Africa and rapid
exploitation of the resources of the Amazon Basin have
aroused numerous specific warnings that "balanced
ecosystems must be maintained if sustainable economic
development is ever to have a chance of succeeding." 20/
Perhaps the approach of such catastrophes will underline
the urgency of spreading the movement for low-cost
chemical-free farming and related techniques to farmers
everywhere. Environmental issues in industrial societies
are slowly being settled through regulation, though more
because of injury to people than to the environment.
While the Greenpeace actions against nuclear testing in
the South Pacific and against whaling have had some
international support, it is only in the FRG that
environmental issues are on the program of a national
political party, the Greens.

As our pressures on the earth increase, nonviolent
action by research, education, legislation, public demonstration, civil disobedience, product boycott, dispute
resolution and other means becomes important. The need
for action extends across, above and beneath the world's
political boundaries, as does life itself. Those who
pursue any of these six paths in nonviolence study will
soon encounter some persistent questions about human
beings in society. Finding some answers and turning them
into action can move us along to peace.

NOTES

1. John L. Nickalls, ed., The Journal of George
Fox, Cambridge University Press, London, 1952, 263.
2. For many of the ideas on various religious
views about nonviolence see John Ferguson, War and Peace
in the World's Religions, Oxford University Press, New
York, NY, 1978.

3.   Ibid., and Allan Solomonow, ed., Roots of Jewish Nonviolence, Jewish Peace Fellowship with the Fellowship of Reconciliation, Nyack, NY, 1981.

4.   Ferguson, 1978, and Walpole Rahula, What the Buddha Taught, Grove Press, New York, 1959, 40 ff.

5.   Ferguson, 1978, 36.

6.   Richard B. Gregg, The Power of Nonviolence, Schocken, New York, NY, 1966, 43-51.

7.   Kenneth Kaunda, The Riddle of Violence, Harper and Row, New York, NY, 1980.

8.   Theodore Herman, "Two Quaker Conferences for Reconciliation in the Mediterranean, 1974-1975," unpublished paper, 1979.

9.   Mulford Q. Sibley, The Quiet Battle: Writings on the Theory and Practice of Non-violent Resistance. Boston: Beacon Press, 1963, 256-287.

10. "Throw Away Your Weapons: A Conversation with Jose Blanco," IFOR Report 9.5, December 1985, 10.

11. Not all societies are culturally nonviolent. There are many examples of societies which contain groups which strive violently to maintain their identity or very existence. Such a vendetta society is described in Milovan Djilas' account of his youth in Montenegro: Milovan Djilas, Land Without Justice, Harcourt, Brace, Jovanovich, New York, NY, 1963.

12. Jonathan Schell, "Reflections: A Better Today," The New Yorker, February 3, 1986, 59.

13. Danilo Dolci, Report from Palermo, Viking, New York, NY, 1970; A New World in the Making, MacGibbon and Kee, London, 1965; Monthly Review Press, New York, 1965, and in other languages; Jerre Mangione, The World Around Danilo Dolci, Harper and Row, New York, NY, 1972.

14. Petra Kelly, Um Hoffnung Kampfen. Bornheim-Merton, FRG: Lamuv Verlag, 1983. Translated as Fighting for Hope. London: Chatto and Windus, 1984, and Boston: South End Press, 1984, 17-23.

15. Susanne Gowan et al., Moving Toward a New Society, New Society Press, Philadelphia, PA, 1976; and Marjorie Hope and James Young, The Struggle for Humanity, Maryknoll, NY: Orbis Books, 1977, 11-39.

16. In various countries there are professional organizations for resolving disputes and to train others. An unusual one that trains school students is the Community Board Center, 149 Ninth Street, San Francisco, CA 94103.

111

17. Daniel N. Clark, "Transnational Action for Peace," Transnational Perspectives 9.4, 1983, 7-11.

18. Colin M. Turnbull, The Mountain People, Simon and Schuster, New York, 1973.

19. Donella H. Meadows et al., The Limits to Growth, Signet Books, New York, 1972.

20. Mark C. Trexler and Laura H. Kosloff, "International Wildlife Conservation," Development Forum, XIV.2, March 1986, 7.

7

Nonviolence:
A Biological Perspective

Graham Kemp

This paper intends to show that, contrary to popular belief, Ethology has not produced a theory of the inevitability of human violence. It has instead, strongly argued that as far as human biology is concerned, humanity is predominantly nonviolent by nature, and violence is predominantly the product of culture. I will begin arguing this point with a brief description of Ethological science.

Initially the science developed as a discipline concentrating (as the word ethology implies) on animal behavior within observable natural habitats. 1/ That is, habitats in which they evolved or are normally located; but not for example, zoos or laboratories. From here the science has broadened its scope, not only by correlating its descriptions of observed behavior patterns from one species to another, but also, as ethologist Eibl-Eibesfeldt writes: "in trying to understand WHY an animal behaves the way it does, ethologists search for the functions of the observed behavior patterns, in order to learn what selection pressures have shaped its evolution." 2/ Thus Ethology has moved from a science of observations to one of behavioral function. Ruwet writes:

> Ethology, then has expanded, has reached out toward other branches of biology, integrating their resources and co-ordinating their efforts in the study of behavior. Ethology has become the science of synthesis. It is no longer a merely descriptive study of animal habits. It has taken on such broad dimensions that today ethology can be defined as the biology of behavior. 3/ (my underlining)

It is in this light that ethologists have joined the social sciences in the study of human behavior, supplying a methodology which evaluates behavior in terms of evolutionary function, aiming to give the science of humanity a broader perspective. Tinbergen wrote:

> No informed person can doubt any more, that Man has evolved, slowly and very gradually from ancestors which were far more similar to other mammals than Man is now. This means, that everything Man is and does now must have evolved ... <u>from what his ancestors were and did</u>. 4/ (my underlining)

Thus in biological terms, human behavior must conform to the evolutionary trends of all animal life and can be analyzed against the general evolutionary background of animal behavior development. Ethologists feel this can give an added perspective to the sciencesof human behavior which will help to reduce the subjectivity from which such sciences often suffer.

Ethology's first entry into the debate of human behavior was on the question of human aggression and violence, where it felt it had a lot to offer from its own findings on the general nature of animal aggression. The work that began this entry was by Konrad Lorenz's book <u>On Aggression</u> 5/ first published in 1963. The result of this work, for Lorenz and his fellow ethologists, can be regarded as a significant failure. For, as Eibl- Eibesfeldt argues, social scientists such as anthropologists and ethnologists completely misinterpreted it. 6/ For many from Montagu (1968) 7/ to Siam (1985) 8/ the assumption was that Lorenz sought to establish that aggression was an innate instinct in the human species. In other words, it seemed to put forward a concept of the biological inevitability of human violence, ignoring any role for learning, environment or cultural influences. As Montagu wrote on this and other subsequent ethological works, "In these books the authors argue that man is by instinct an aggressive creature, and it is this innate propensity to violence that accounts for individual and group aggression." 9/ Lorenz viewed aggression as a drive, like hunger and sex, which could occur--independent of any environmental or cultural influences. Social science greeted this with hostility for two major reasons. First, such a concept ignored the accumulated evidence of the last half century from sociology, psychology and anthropology, that learning, environment and culture do play a major and significant role in the determination of human aggression. Lorenzian ethology appeared to them reminiscent of the old instinctivists of the nature- nurture debate--and such outdated concepts as Freud's death instinct. J.P. Scott entitled his review of Lorena as just "That Old-Time Aggression." 10/ Secondly, and probably the more significant objection, was that Lorenz seemed to be re-establishing the pessimism of the human condition. Montagu entitled his review, Lorenz's scenario is, "A New Litany of innate depravity, or Original Sin revisited." 11/ While Denkler wrote that ethology seemed to give excuses to humanity and to deny "self-responsibility" for violence and aggressive depravity. 12/ And as Lumsden expressed it:

> The dangers with the instinct of aggression theory is that, far from emancipating man, it may enslave him, to a reactionary ideology by apparently demonstrating the biological necessity of an authoritarian social system organized for internal and external repression. 13/

David Pilbeam said: (this is a scientific) "...Idea we could live without." 14/
But ethologists say the criticism is a complete miscomprehension of what Lorenz and ethology have attempted to assert. They stress that ethology is not suggesting a biological inevitability of human violence, but the opposite. They state that Man, in his aggressive behavior, as far as his biological or evolutionary inheritance is concerned, should conform to an evolutionary trend in the avoidance of injury and violence. The misinterpretation can be thought to occur for several reasons. One, as Tinbergen 15/ suggests, and Lorenz' biographer Nisbitt 16/ points out, Lorenz' book, On Aggression, is for various reasons badly written and unclear and therefore easily open to mis-interpretation. Nisbitt argues that even its English title can be regarded as misleading and a mistranslation of the original title; that it should have been translated as "On Aggressivity," a term which indicates its definition by function rather than manifestation. Second, the hostility to the political and social implications of what is assumed Lorenz was attempting to

say, led reviewers to concentrate on this unclear book
with the aim of isolating the danger it posed. Thus
they tend not to go beyond that work and evaluate
Lorenz' other works and the work of other ethologists.
Such further evaluation would have shown that what
ethology has come to refer to as aggression is not what
is normally accepted as aggression. Nisbitt stresses in
his discussion of Lorenz' book, On Aggression, that:

> Quite simply aggression as most people understand
> the word is not what the book is about. In its
> common meaning, aggression equals violence, which
> is not the instinct itself but the end product of
> its suppression. 18/

The ethologist Manning 17/ stressed that aggression is
not defined on the basis of behavioral manifestation but
on behavioral function. In this light, violence is seen
as one manifestation of the aggressive function, and
nonviolent activity can be regarded as another.

Initially ethology began by labeling observed
belligerent and violent behaviors aggression. But
ethologists wanted to evaluate observations in terms of
survival function. So they asserted that belligerent
behavior could be separated into two functions. First,
there was belligerent behavior related to predator-prey
behavior, whose object is killing for food. The second
was fights between rivals for the same resources. The
latter behavior pattern was almost predominantly
intra-species, since different species tend to become
defined by their occupation of a particular niche of the
available environmental resources. Thus the only rivals
that met, tended to be members of the same species. The
function of this resource rivalry was, not as in
predation, to kill, but to space out, or establish a
hierarchial "pecking order" over the available
resources. Nisbett writes that:

> [The] survival function is to space out individual
> (or pairs or groups) over the available habitats to
> ensure the most favourable exploitation of a region
> and the food sources it contains. 19/

This meant that an individual species could not, as a
whole, over-exploit its resources. There would be
always a central core that would obtain sufficient
resources for survival.

Thus, fighting behavior could be defined as two functionally different behaviors. The first they termed, "predatory behavior", and the second, intra-species rivalry, they termed as "aggression...in the proper and narrow sense of the word." 20/ In fact, many mammal species which showed considerable intra-specific rivalry often proved to be herbivores. In conclusion, there are two important points here. One that ethology defines aggression in terms of its function not manifestations, and two, that it does not therefore regard all acts of belligerence and killing as aggression. In fact aggression is behavior related to the spreading out or establishing of a hierarchy of individuals (or groups) over available resources, such as food, breeding ground, mates and so on. How aggression, when regarded in this way, functions in man, ethologists note, is not necessarily relevant. There is still too little human ethological study to make an authoritative statement. But what is relevant is that man has inherited, through this evolution, aggression (or aggressivity as Nisbett attempts to reterm it), 21/ as part of his behavioral repertoire. It is argued that aggression has become too embedded in evolution for humans to have biologically escaped from it. Eibl-Eibesfeldt shows through his human ethological research of the findings of anthropology:

> There are certain cultural differences [manifestations] in human aggression ...[but]...convincing proof that any human group is wholly lacking in aggressive behavior has not yet been produced. 22/

Ethologists also point to the physiological evidence this contention. 23/

As ethologists further examined aggression in terms of function they found that fighting and violence which aimed at harming rivals was merely one manifestation of aggressivity--and very rare. Craig wrote in 1918: "When an animal fights [a rival] he aims, not to destroy the enemy but only to get rid of its presence." 24/ Since such behavior is intra-spective, rival confrontations that could lead to injury of any kind to loser and victor would hardly benefit the species. Thus they found a strong evolutionary trend of natural selection for aggression (intra-species rivalry) to be resolved harmlessly and nonviolently, making violence a rare and often accidental or pathological demonstration of aggressivity. How this was achieved is significant to the present debate, since man should, through evolution, biologically conform to this pattern. What they found was that, although the maintenance of nonviolence in intra-species confrontations varied with different species, there were certain common themes and one central theme.

This central theme was that for every confrontation there would be two components to the behavior: (1) the attack response which initiated aggression and (2) a flight response which ended the aggression. They point out that evolution has developed or utilized a sense of fear in order for a weaker conspecific to recognize defeat quickly and, in his flight response, cause the stronger to cease the attack. Manning notes in his general work on ethology, 1972:

> During fighting we can observe attack or escape behaviour to the virtual exclusion of the other. Prolonged fighting behaviour is extremely rare under natural conditions, the weaker of the two contestants usually breaks away and escapes before any serious damage is done. Clearly selection favours individuals who recognize defeat. 26/

It is important to note the reliance on communication between conspecifics. First the communication of superior status to a resource; second the communication of defeat, which the victor recognizes and which inhibits him from continuing the attack. (This communication could be through physical contact, i.e. fighting.) But what observers noted was that animals with dangerous weapons designed for prey-predator behavior did not utilize them in aggressivity. The confrontations became formalized or ritualized in a manner in which harm from the weapons was minimized. For example, with horned ungulates (i.e. deer, sheep, etc.) whose horns could prove lethal to the flank or underside of a predator, aggressive fighting is strictly formalized to head to head confrontations which minimizes the chance of injury from these horns. 27/ Rattlesnakes in their intra-species confrontations do not use their fangs or poison. They instead indulge in a form of Indian wrestling with their bodies. 28/ Since communication is essential in aggressivity, many species have come to rely on just signalling status, as physical contact always carries the possibility of harm. Superior status can be signalled visually, by sound (e.g. birdsong) or even by scent. A weaker individual will recognize his rival's status by the signal and withdraw. If an equal rival ignores the signal, duel by physical contact may occur. But evolution seeks to avoid this by utilizing the signals as the weapons of duel: A duel of signalled threats, rather than a fighting duel.

The signal of defeat remained, for most species, flight. But among socially organized animals, flight did not form a desirable signal. Thus flight was replaced by simulated signals of flight. These are called appeasement signals for, as with flight, they appease or inhibit the attacker. Appeasement comes in various forms. One is to simply hide all signals of counter aggression. Second is to imitate defeat. For example, dogs and wolves can be seen, in their acceptance of defeat, to bare the nape of the neck or underside. This apparently suicidal response has become equated in their evolution with a flight response.

A third way is to arouse conflicting tendencies in the aggression mood of the victor. An example of this is baboon behavior where the subordinate baboon of either sex turns away and crouches in a sexual presentation posture. Another example, observed among social mammals including man, is the use of infantile gestures to arouse parental feelings from the aggressor.

In the above ways evolution has led intra-species aggression, in the over-whelming number of species, and in all mammals, to a non-lethal and nonviolent form of behavior. But the key point is the reliance of this behavior on communication between conspecifics of respective status and on the recognition of defeat. If one prevents an individual from fleeing or signalling defeat, then the attack mood persists with the aggression becoming more and more physical and violent until victory is achieved by death. This has been shown experimentally 29/ and can be seen to be the principle behind the "sport" of fighting cocks and fish. 30/

After they had identified an overwhelming evolutionary tendency in animal life to avoid violent resolutions of aggression, the question ethologists wanted to answer was why man has proved the exception to the rule. It is highly unlikely that man, as a product of evolution, should have become so radically different in his aggressivity. Ethologists argue that human violence is caused by something beyond human biology. This was Lorenz' contention, that violence in man represents a "misdirected aggression." How has it then become misdirected?

One line of enquiry was to examine the kinds of circumstances under which (other) animals divert from the norm and indulge in violent and lethal aggression. They discovered that animals placed in unnatural environments such as zoos or in situations of stress and crowding demonstrated pathological behaviors including violent and lethal aggression. Could this formulate the pattern in humans, with their overcrowded cities and increasingly "artificial" environment? Certainly, studies such as C. and W.M.S. Russell's "Violence, Monkeys and Man" 31/ indicate that there is some truth in this. But such studies could not supply a complete understanding of human violence. Certainly overcrowded cities tended to show greater levels of violence. But a direct correlation between overcrowding and violence could not be demonstrated. 32/ Charlotte Otten 33/ in her work Aggression and Evolution observed that equally crowded cities in different cultures showed differing levels of violence. Also modernization could not be the full answer. Societies of lower technological levels and in more "natural" habitats could be observed to demonstrate even higher levels of violence than our modern cultures. 34/ Finally, a pathological violence could not really explain pre-meditated and organized violence such as war, systematic persecution of sub-groups and structural or institutional violence. It is hard to accept the premise that thousands, even millions of people of diverse background could act pathologically in unison. And, John Sabini added that there is a need to understand why "... people with no desire to harm anyone" can be organized to kill. 35/ To answer this ethologists point to another means by which aggression in man has become misdirected, and to understand it one needs briefly to comprehend how ethology sees the means by which behavior patterns develop in an individual.

Ethologists do not see behavior as fixed, either by genetics alone or through learning alone. They see genes as determining behavior potential in the initial creation of the individual and the realization of that potential, resting with its environmental interaction through the individual's maturation to adulthood. In other words, genes are the source that programs a behavior pattern into the animal's behavioral repertoire; but how that behavior subsequently manifests and develops itself is determined by environmental interaction. Lorenz writes:

> The contrasting of the "innate" and the "learned" as mutually exclusive elements is undoubtedly a fallacy, ..., it is perfectly possible that a particular motor sequence may owe to phyologenetic processes all the information underlying its adaptedness and yet be wholly dependent on individual learning for the "decoding" of this information. 36/

Learning acts by increasing the survival potential of an animal by allowing the animal to adapt its genetically determined behavior to differing environmental factors. For example, an animal may be, as a species, programmed to be predatory. However, its prey may vary with its learning processes. Thus when Lorenz argued that aggression in humans was innate, he meant that initial information for that behavior's existence in humans was fixed by their genes. But how that aggressive potential developed and into what manifestations, could be significantly influenced by learning. Learning, thus could be the source of the misdirection. But ethologists refer to a more considerable force in human development which gives humans a greater aptitude to modify their behavior—to a unique level as compared to other animal life. They point out that human's greater potential for learning and greater aptitude for social communication (verbal language) and the use of conceptual thought, has allowed them to modify culturally their behavior. Culture is seen as a considerable social force in human behavioral development—not to the point that it can eliminate genetically fixed behavior, but that it can significantly restructure human behavior to meet its own social needs. Thus humans are genetically aggressive. But, as such, they would tend to share with other animal life the strong tendency to resolve aggressive confrontations nonviolently. For humans to behave violently in such contrast to other animal life, it is argued, must be due to this unique aptitude to interfere culturally and alter behavior—to override those strong natural tendencies. 37/

Why cultures should seek to do this can be explained in that, for many cultures or social groups, violence (particularly war) has proved for many centuries beneficial to their own survival and advancement. Up to this century European societies saw war as a legitimate means of national advancement. 38/ But to be successful in such organized violence, cultures needed in some way to override the human biological tendency to be nonviolent. How this was achieved is where ethology, with its wider perspective of the overall biology of aggression and how it maintained a nonviolent tendency, can be of particular practical support to peace science.

As stated, aggression in all animals is identified as basically nonviolent and relying on personal communication and a recognition of the signals of superior status and of defeat. It is interference here ethologists say, that alters human aggression to violent manifestations. They suggest that this is achieved in a number of ways, some of which I put forward here for discussion.

First, the most successful killing weapons tend to be those that prevent personal communication. They either kill too quickly or at a distance which prevents communication from taking place. Tinbergen writes:

> Very few aircrews who are willing, indeed eager, to drop their bombs "on target," would be willing to strangle, stab, or burn children (or, for that matter, adults) with their own hands; they would stop short of killing, in response to the appeasement and distress signals of their opponents. 39/

Eibl-Eibesfeldt refers to the considerable military effort utilized to prevent opposing troops from fraternizing with each other. The perception of the aggressive confrontation is altered particularly through the use of propaganda. Another is to prevent your social members from recognizing the enemy (or victims) as fellow human beings. Johnson 40/ stressed in writing that "de-humanization legitimizes killing" by altering the perception of the conflict to prey-predator behavior. Tinbergen writes:

> ... man engaged in war, or other forms of intra-specific killing seems to be able to fuse

> these different motivations into one super
> motivation: the enemy is to the warrior not merely
> another human being, he is at the same time a
> dangerous predator, a parasite ... 41/

That the language in war (hunter-killer, wolf pack, "the
nazi animal" and the facist beast, and warriors) often
assumes predator names or disguises (e.g. Aztec
warriors),reenforces this point.

Another way cultures alter the perception of human
conflict is to give it a game status; a business. This
can be seen in the language of war, where technical
terms are used to describe the human conflict: Free
fire zone; collateral damage. Dehumanization also
allows one's cultural members to fail to recognize the
appropriate human signals of status. The systematic
manner in which the Jews were first dehumanized is
possibly what made it easier for humans to inflict such
mass horror. Eibl-Eibesfeldt stresses that what is "of
central importance remains our ability to see others as
fellow human beings." 42/

A third means is the conditioning of warriors to
prevent them from recognizing defeat signals; to make
flight socially unacceptable; an act of cowardice. 43/
And, at the same time, socially reinforcing attitudes of
attack. A quick reference will be made here to the
identified nonviolent society of the Semai in Malaya,
44/ where they respect a man who walks away from a
confrontation, comparing it to our culture placing
respect upon those who "stand their ground," and do not
show fear. Cultures such as ours use other behavioral
techniques to counter human's natural nonviolent
tendencies, like their possibly stronger tendency to
bond socially and to identify themselves in social
groups. Thus humans can be induced to kill by making
killing an act of social recognition in that refusing to
kill would be considered a denial or rejection of
family, country, regimental identity, et cetera.

These are some of the ways ethologists argue that
cultures have engineered human behavior to override his
nonviolent tendencies for the "benefit" of a culture's
"advancement." What ethologists see as the practical
path ahead is the "cultural re-engineering" of our
society to allow a biological tendency to be nonviolent
in our interhuman confrontations to re-establish itself.

The purpose of the paper has been to correct a
common misunderstanding about what ethology, the biology

of behavior, has to offer peace science and to show what this science has offered that could help to establish a practical path to nonviolence. Violence is not a product of the human biology of aggression but of human culture. Eibl-Eibesfeldt stressed: "The great significance attached to war propaganda shows how strongly men, left to themselves, incline towards peaceful contact." 45/ Thus culture is the source of the problem of human violence. And in ethology's general understanding of how evolution has developed, nonviolent aggression can be seen as the means by which a culture has achieved violence and, correspondingly, how a culture can reverse it. Essential here is the importance of human contact and communication, the promotion of nonviolence, and an awareness of the need to maintain a perception of others as fellow human beings.

NOTES

1. N. Tinbergen, "On War And Peace in Animals and Man," Aggression and Evolution, ed. C.M. Otten, Xerox College, 1973.

2. I. Eibl-Eibesfeldt, Ethology--The Biology of Behavior, 2nd ed., London: Methuen, 1975, 9.

3. J. Ruwet, An Introduction to Ethology (translated by J. Diamanti, New York: International Universities Press, Inc., 1972, 198.

4. N. Tinbergen, "The Search for Animal Roots of Human Behaviour (1964)," in The Animal in its World (Explorations of an Ethologist 1932-1972), Vol. 2, with a foreword by Sir Peter Medawar, London: George Allen and Unwin, 1973, 162.

5. K. Lorenz, Das Sogenannte Bose, zur Naturgeschicte der Aggression, Schoeler Verlag, Vienna, 1963. K. Lorenz, On Aggression, translated by M. Latzke, London: Methuen, 1966.

6. I. Eibl-Eibesfeldt, "Phylogenetic Adaption as Determinants of Aggressive Behaviour in Man," in Jan de Wit and W.W. Hartup (eds.), Origins of Aggression, Hague: Mouton, 1974, 52-74.

7. A. Montagu (ed.), Man and Aggression, 1st ed., 1968.

8. G. Siann, Accounting for Aggression, Boston: Allen & Unwin, 1985.

124

9. A. Montagu, "Introduction," in A. Montagu (ed.), Man and Aggression, 2nd ed., New York: Oxford University Press, 1973, xi.

10. This ignored Lorenz' own specific denial in the Introduction of his work On Aggression that although he felt similarities existed with his theory of aggression and Freud on the dynamics of innate behavior, there was no similarity at all between his theory and Feud's death instinct concept.

11. J.P. Scott, "That Old-Time Aggression" from The Nation, 9/1/67, 53-54; reprinted in A. Montagu (ed.), Man and Aggression (1973).

12. A. Montagu, "The New Litany of 'Innate Depravity' or Original Sin Revisited," The Human Revolution, New York: Bantam Books, 1967, material added 1968, 3-18.

13. M. Lumsden, "The Instinct of Aggression: Science of Ideology?"

15. D. Pilbeam, "An Idea We Could Live Without: the Naked Ape.," Discovery, 7, Spring 1972, 110-121. Reprinted in A. Montagu (ed.), Man and Aggression, 1973.

16. N. Tinbergen, "Ethology (1969)," The Animal in its World (Explorations of an Ethologist 1932-1972), Vol. 2.

16. A. Nisbett, Konrad Lorenz, London: Methuen, 1975.

17. Ibid., 148.

18. A. Manning, Introduction to Animal Behaviour, 2nd ed., London: Edward Arnold, 1972.

19. A. Nisbett, Konrad Lorenz, 1975, 153-154.

20. K. Lorenz, On Aggression, 1966, 22.

21. A. Nisbett, Konrad Lorenz, 1975.

22. I. Eibl-Eibesfeldt, Love and Hate, translated by G. Strachan, London: Methuen, 1971, 71.

23. I. Eibl-Eibesfeldt, Ethology--The Biology of Behaviour, 2nd edition, 1975, 365-367.

24. A. Manning, Introduction to Animal Behaviour, 2nd edition, 1972, 100-101.

25. I. Eibl-Eibesfeldt, Ethology--The Biology of Behaviour, 2nd edition, 1975, 357-360.

26. Ibid.

27. For a full discussion of this see A. Manning, Introduction to Animal Behaviour, 2nd edition, 1972. Eibl-Eibesfeldt, Ethology--The Biology of Behaviour, 2nd edition, 1975, Chapter 15; on human behavior: Eibl-Eibesfeldt, Ethology--The Biology of Behaviour, 2nd edition, 1975.

28. I. Eibl-Eibesfeldt, Ethology--The Biology of Behaviour, 2nd edition, 1975.

29. K. Lorenz, On Aggression, 1966.

30. C. Russell and W.M.S. Russell, Violence, Monkeys and Man, London: Methuen, 1968.

31. P. Erlich and J. Freedman, "Population, Crowding and Human Behaviour," in C.M. Otten (ed.), Aggression and Evolution, 1973.

32. C.M. Otten (ed.), "Introduction," Aggression and Evolution, 1973.

33. N. Chagnon, Yanomamo: The Fierce People, New York: Holt Rhinehart & Winston, 1968.

34. J. Sabini, "Aggression in the Laboratory," in I. Kutash, S. Kutash and Schlesinger et. al., Violence, Perspectives on Murder and Aggression, London: Jossey-Bass, 1978.

35. K. Lorenz, On Aggression, 1966, 65.

36. N. Tinbergen, "On War and Peace in Animals and Man," in C.M. Otten (ed.), Aggression and Evolution, 1973.

37. B. Tuchman, The Proud Tower, London: Macmillan, 1966, chapter 5.

38. For example see: N. Tinbergen, "Ethology in a Changing World," in P. Bateson and R. Hinde (eds.), Growing Points in Ethology, 1976; I. Eibl- Eibesfeldt, Ethology--The Biology of Behaviour, 2nd edition, London: Methuen, 1975, 357-360; I. Eibl- Eibesfeldt, Love and Hate, translated by G. Strachan, London: Methuen, 1971; I. Eibl-Eibesfeldt, "Phylogenetic Adaption as Determinants of Aggressive Behaviour in Man" in Jan de Wit and W.W. Hartup (eds.), Origins of Aggression, Hague: Mouton, 1974, 52-74; R. Johnson, Aggression in Man and Animals, W.B. Saunders C., 1972; R.A. Hinde, Biological Basis of Human Social Behaviour, New York: McGraw Hill, 1974; N. Tinbergen, "On War and Peace in Animals and Man," in C.M. Otten (ed.), Aggression and Evolution, 1973, 111-112.

39. N. Tinbergen, "On War and Peace in Animals and Man," in C.M. Otten (ed.), Aggression and Evolution, 1973, 111-112.

40. R.N. Johnson, Aggression in Man and Animals, 1972.

41. N. Tinbergen, "Ethology in a Changing World," in P. Bateson and R. Hinde (eds.), Growing Points in Ethology, 1976.

42. Reference to Churchill's wartime use of this term.

43. For example, the Aztecs warriors dressed in the skins and feathers of predators.

44. I. Eibl-Eibesfeldt, "Phylogenetic Adaption as Determinants of Aggressive Behaviour in Man," in J. De Wit and W.W. Hartup (eds.), Origins of Aggression, 1974, 90. See also J. Sabini on experimental work of dehumanizing prisoners: "Aggression in Laboratory," in I. Kutash, S. Kutash and Schlesinger et. al., Violence, Perspectives on Murder and Aggression, 1978, 367-369.

45. N. Tinbergen, "On War and Peace in Animals and Man," in C.M. Otten (ed.), Aggression and Evolution, 1973.

46. R. Dentan, The Semai--A Non-Violent People, New York: Holt, Rhinehart and Winston, 1968.

47. N. Tinbergen, "Ethology in a Changing World," in P. Bateson and R. Hinde (eds.), Growing Points in Ethology, 1976.

48. I. Eibl-Eibesfeldt, Love and Hate, translated by G. Strachan, London: Methuen, 1971.

8

Nonviolent Grassroot Movement for Social Change in Rural India

Ravi Kumar

In the early 20th Century, after Mahatma Gandhi initiated the nonviolent political reform movement which gained India's independence, he predicted that removing India's internal corruption would prove harder than ousting the British. Today we find Gandhi's words prophetic as we struggle to free 260 million Indians from socio-economic and political repression.

The independence of India left the working class oppressed by its own government and by wealthy industrialists. Inequality and oppression still remain for the lower classes of India and democracy as it is practiced now is fraudulent. It is a system in which all the benefits have been granted to feudal landlords, capitalists, and intellectuals. These classes dominate the political spectrum. The poor and the underprivileged have not been able to achieve genuine representation. Most of the rural masses are completely unaware of even their most basic political and economic rights and are frightened of agitating because the rural power structure is so formidable.

It has been more than a quarter of a century since the assassination of Mahatma Gandhi, the leader who launched a nonviolent revolution against British colonialism and racism in India. Although his struggle for equality for the oppressed has created an attitude of awe and admiration throughout the world and his philosophy has been adopted by such people as the Black civil rights leader Martin Luther King, Gandhi's ideals have not been fulfilled in India. Established political parties have ceased to be instruments of social change. They appear incapable of fulfilling even the minimum role expected of them. Elected representatives do not raise the basic issues which affect the daily lives and struggles of people. Nor do these parties have any place for the idealism of their young people. There was a time

when routes to electoral politics were more refined; only
those with social work to their credit could enter the
political arena. But in the seventies, this trend took
another direction. Now even hijackers and criminals are
welcomed. Politics has become a commercial venture with
loyalty of a "boot-licking" variety the only criterion
for admission.

Disillusioned with this approach many young men and
women have concentrated on transformative politics and
have been organizing the poorest of the poor in various
parts of the country. They belong to various schools,
from neo-Gandhian to neo-Marxist. Although their
ideological perceptions vary, field experience has
brought about a common approach. Their aim is to raise
consciousness among the poor, enable them to fight caste
and class domination, and create people's power in order
to change the socio-economic order that has oppressed and
exploited them.

In 1974 several youth and student organizations in
Bihar (North India) joined hands to build a massive movement to fight corruption, eradicate unemployment, and
struggle against other socio-economic evils. Some of
them were politically motivated and they simply wanted to
use the opportunity to eliminate the party in power.
Others believed that the party in power was primarily
responsible for all the evils that prevailed. They
united under the banner of the Chhatra Sangharsh Samiti
(Student Struggle Committee) and later agreed to work
under the leadership of Jayaprakash Narayan (J.P.). J.P.
also agreed to lead them because he was in search of an
opportunity to arouse youth power to bring about a
comprehensive revolution which he called "Total Revolution." He tried to give this movement a revolutionary
direction. He called upon the students to struggle, not
for petty political aims but for Total Revolution which
alone, in his opinion, could solve the problems they were
faced with.

The general mass of students and youths were very
much inspired by J.P.'s revolutionary call and they
rallied under his banner in large numbers. Total
Revolution became their motto. But J.P. knew that the
Chhatra Sengharsh Samiti was dominated by youth organizations that were linked with certain political parties of
the opposition, most of whom had nothing to do with Total
Revolution. J.P. therefore tried to disengage these
youth organizations from their parent bodies and

integrate them into a revolutionary force. But he was jailed, and they continued to be guided by the leaders of the political parties they belonged to. It was in this context that J.P. decided to build a new student and youth organization committed to the ideas and methods of Total Revolution. The Chhatra Yuva Sanghrsh Vahini (Student Youth Direct Action Force) was established in January 1975. J.P. had expected the Vahini to become a rallying point for all students and youth that were not linked with any political party or group. Accordingly he called upon all nonaffiliated students and youth to join the Vahini and work for nonviolence and Total Revolution with single minded devotion.

The Vahini continued to work under the banner of the Student Struggle Committee and implement its program of action. It was too small then to take over the leadership of the movement. But before it could grow into a massive student and youth force, a state of emergency was declared in the country. This changed the situation radically. The most important issue that concerned the students and youth and also the people at large at this point was not Total Revolution. Restoration of the democracy that had been suppressed by the emergency regime of the late Prime Minister Indira Gandhi was paramount.

In 1977 parliamentry elections were announced. The same issue of democracy versus dictatorship marked this election. J.P., as the leader of the 1974 movement, appealed to the people of the country to vote for the forces of democracy represented by the Janata Party (People's Party) and to defeat the forces of dictatorship represented by the ruling congress led by Indira Gandhi. Democracy won with the victory of the People's Party and a united front of opposition parties--parties that have supported and worked for the J.P. movement, although not to achieve Total Revolution, but to capture power and with the defeat of the ruling congress both at the center and in most of the states, the political goal of these parties has been achieved. The youth organizations that had played a dominant role in 1974 and also 1977 became occupied with consolidating the political or partisan gains of their parent organizations.

The student struggle committee ceased to function, and only two years later they disintegrated with the disintegration of the Janata Party. But J.P., as leader of the people and of the youth, had already passed the torch of total revolution to the Vahini and other non-party youth and student organizations inspired by it.

Vahini is committed to bringing about J.P. and Mahatma Gandhi's vision of a nonviolent revolution to create a just society. Its ideological basis is "grassroot democracy" consisting of nonviolence, decentralization, egalitarianism and a casteless society. The members of this group are committed to the task of awakening and organizing the people to participate in a nonviolent struggle for a better society. It seeks to liberate the most oppressed groups in India such as untouchables, tribals and women. It tries to inform and educate people so that they know when they are not being treated fairly.

The Vahini appears content to build its base slowly, making sure the individual villager's sense of powerlessness is replaced by a new consciousness of his/her political rights and capabilities. It may be correct, therefore, to characterize the Vahini more as a catalyst and less as a vanguard force. Vahini's belief is that, once awakened, the oppressed rural masses will not refrain from exercising their rights.

The group is seeking ways of improving the lifestyle of India's millions of rural poor. Its members want to educate people to help them live better, healthier, more productive lives. The Vahini works to see that the real representatives of the peasants, landless poor, and the tribals, are sent to parliament and to the state assemblies. Only then will the interest of the people be guarded effectively. Democracy cannot be imposed from the top. The capture of political power without grassroot organization is useless. What is necessary is the development of a mass movement and mass mobilization from the lowest level.

The Vahini's adherence to peaceful methods for social transformation has met with both praise and skepticism. In Bodh Gaya, participation by large numbers of rural women (60% of the movement) is mostly attributable to the Vahini's peaceful tactics. The Vahini do not encourage the villagers to gain their rights by the exercise of violence. Violence frequently provides an easy excuse for the police, often in league with the rural elite, to retaliate harshly against defenseless villagers and workers.

The Vahini has worked in some selected areas in the past several years. It has adopted the cause of the

rural proletariat and has succeeded in building, in
certain pockets, what may be described as the
organizational base of Total Revolution. The most
spectacular success of the Vahini consists of the
creation of class conciousness among the agricultural
laborers in a large part of Gaya in north India. This
has produced a prolonged struggle by the Vahini against
the illegal occupation of thousands of acres of land by
the Bodha Gaya monastary. Thanks to Vahini's leadership,
the laborers have been able to liberate several thousand
acres of monastary lands by the nonviolent methods of
Satyagraha. This success has created an impact, forcing
the administration to acquire a part of the monastary
lands and distribute them among the laborers of the
village concerned. Apart from struggling for the
economic rights of the working people, the Vahini has
brought about a social awakening, especially among the
rural women. As a result, women belonging to the working
class have come forward to resist not only the atrocities
of the police and monastary musclemen, but also the
brutal treatment meted out to them by their own husbands
who often beat their wives mercilessly. The awakened
women, under Vahini's leadership, have succeeded in
putting an end to much of this practice in urban areas.
The Vahini has also been working for the emancipation of
slum dwellers. It has championed inter-caste and
inter-religious marriages. It has often joined hands
with other student and youth organizations to fight for
the preservation of civil liberties and democratic
freedom, including freedom of the press. In Bihar,
especially, the Vahini has played a significant role in
the struggle waged jointly by all youth organizations
against a draconian measure which sought to curb the
freedom of the press. The struggle succeeded and it
forced the government to withdraw the measure.

The Vahini does not believe in ivory tower
theorizing: Believers that "You have to be part of the
community if you hope to lead," its members have been
living among the poorest of the poor; alongside the poor
untouchables, eating food made of pounded rice or corn.
They drink the sub-soil water of the villages and as a
result suffer from the dysentary that constantly afflicts
the untouchables. They walk miles a day from one village
to the next. They face the laths and iron rods of the
police and the monastary's musclemen and are forced to
fight countless cases in court as victims of harassment.

In the daytime they work in the fields, and in the evenings they talk and plant the seeds of the coming peaceful revolution. At night they sleep on the hard earth beside the tethered goats.

The very concept of nonviolent Total Revolution pre-supposes a broad unity of all radicals working for social change by peaceful methods. There are several groups and organizations that seek to bring about radical change in society. Some of them are like-minded in their social approaches and political perceptions, but they differ in their emphasis on the various aspects of the technique adopted. Their priorities also differ. Some emphasize the need to capture power as a first step towards revolution. Others favor prolonged "spade work" at the grassroots level before launching political struggle. Some of the radical groups give top priority to organizing the working class and waging class struggles for accelerating economic change, while others stress the necessity of changing socio-cultural relationship before launching struggle in the economic and political fields.

Total Revolution by its very nature cannot be brought about piecemeal. To be complete a revolution must be a simultaneous process working at different levels and in different fields of life, which means that all radical groups that broadly agree on the ideals and methods of revolution must develop an integrated approach and agree to work together. Total Revolution must also be an all-inclusive process of change. The logic of peaceful technique helps to broaden the social base as a revolutionary movement. Class struggle may be necessary to organize the exploited section of society. But class action alone cannot lead to a social revolution.

Class action may at best lead to a class revolution. All of the communist revolutions in history were class revolutions and not social revolutions. They ended with the overthrow of the ruling class and capture of power by an organized group of the revolutionary class in action. They were minority revolutions which excluded and even alienated the social majority and tried by force to impose on it the will of the minority. As a result, the so-called socialist state, which was in fact a new class state, became dictatorial and physically eliminated large sections of people who refused to abide by the minority will. Wherever such minority revolutions have taken place, the ideal of a new classless society has receded further and it is as distant today as it was before the revolution. This experience of history teaches us that a social revolution is possible only through a united social action by all social forces working together at different levels and in different fields of life.

In a country like India where the people are divided into a number of classes and castes, even class action is not possible without the integration of the people on a social basis. In other words, integration of social and economic classes is an important pre-condition of class action as well as social action. Social classes in India are often limited in their approach and vision. The task of a Total Revolutionary would be to broaden people's vision and to prepare them for a wider struggle aimed at socio-economic transformation. And once this broad unity of social forces is achieved it may be easier to integrate the processes of change emerging in different forms and under different leadership.

The most difficult task is to achieve unity among various organizations which claim to be radical and yet pull in different directions. Although they agree on the fundamental principles of Total Revolution, they find it difficult to come together and work together for a common goal. They not only maintain their separate existence but also insist on working separately. They have developed different work styles and they function separately. Ideological rigidities or organizational loyalties may prevent them from forming a single platform. In spite of these differences, circumstances can force different organizations to unite against common dangers and to achieve common aims. In order to re-strengthen these action groups which define themselves as radical, they must refer to the lessons of the J.P. movement. The first lesson was that revolution requires a previously organized force of the people and the youth.

Second, leadership of a revolutionary movement must vest in the people's committees organized at the grassroots level, with a coordination center at the regional or state and national levels. Democratic centralism does not fit in the buildup of decentralized democracy. Efforts must be made to build collective leadership at all levels, from the village upwards. Third, the technique of Satyagrah or other peaceful techniques must necessarily be so fashioned and practiced as to win over the forces of police and administration to the side of the revolutionaries, thereby breaking the teeth of repression. Fourth, the political leadership of the movement must not be allowed at any stage to pass into the hands of such groups or individuals that may not be committed to the values and goals of the movement. A truly democratic and revolutionary political instrument must be capable of effectively controlling the politically ambitious at such time as the revolution succeeds.

Last, apart from building a revolutionary organization of youth like the "Student Youth Direct Force" (Vahini), a broad based organization of committed activists representing different sections of the people must be built, to coordinate the activities of different action groups and individuals working at different levels. Certain other lessons may also be extracted from the experiments carried out under the leadership of Gandhi and J.P. and other leaders who have believed in nonviolent social transformation. A closer analysis of their successes and failures may help us to shape the ideological basis on which future leadership and future organizations need to be built to achieve revolutionary ends by peaceful means and by active participation of the people at large.

Such a revolutionary organization could become a rallying point for all nonaffiliated youth organizations and students who are committed to nonviolent total revolution. For only a united revolutionary youth force can collect the sparks of revolution and work for it. Members may be college teachers and professors, workers, journalists, social workers and others. Unity of all these organizations is a must.

9

Three Nonviolent Campaigns— Larzac, Marckolsheim, Wyhl— A Comparison

Roger Rawlinson

A study of three cases appears to indicate that nonviolence is more likely to be accepted and succeed in a rural area where there is a strong community spirit and one major source of livelihood:

LARZAC

The Larzac is a large plateau in Southern France suitable for sheep farming. The peasant-farmers make their living mainly from flocks of ewes which provide milk for making Roquefort cheese.

The Military Base

In 1901 a 3000 hectare army camp was established near La Cavalerie, a village in the center of the plateau. This camp posed no problem for the farmers, but in the 1960s they became concerned about the damage done to the land by tanks which often exercised outside the camp. Low-flying helicopters caused abortions among the ewes. In 1970 a plan to enlarge the base was revealed. Later the defense minister confirmed that it would be extended by a further 14,000 hectares.

First Reactions

Backing for the project came from the local MP, the Mayor and Council of Millau (the nearest town) and from shopkeepers in Millau and La Cavalerie who hoped to gain economic advantages from the project. A new council later opposed the plan. Environmental, peace and left wing groups demonstrated against it, but the peasants were reluctant to become involved with political parties. The peasants did, however, make useful contacts with workers in Millau. The Safeguard Association was formed which, with the help of the Chamber of Agriculture, published a study of Larzac which indicated that the extension would lead to the closing of 58 farms while 40 others would be affected. The peasants expected full support from the Farmers Union but although it gave some local backing, the national body was reluctant to oppose the government. The cheese-makers of the town of Roquefort helped to publicize the issue in the country. The Occitan regionalists, who represented the aspirations of southerners for recognition of their own language and greater control over regional matters, also became actively involved. But the farmers felt that still stronger action would be necessary.

Nonviolence

Abbé Jean Toulat (author of "The Bomb or Life") and Lanza del Vasto, founder of the Gandhian Community of the Ark, came to Millau to talk about "Active Nonviolence." That the Church, through the Bishop of Rodez, gave its blessing to nonviolence was important to the predominantly Catholic farmers. In March 1972 Lanza del Vasto came to La Cavalerie to fast for a fortnight. The farmers took turns at fasting with him. During this period people unified and a pledge (signed by 103 peasants out of a possible 107) not to sell their land to the army was agreed upon. They now met regularly to discuss their strategy and plan actions. Soon there was active support from Larzac committees all over the country. Eventually there would be over 100 of them.

After a public inquiry which took place at La Cavalerie merely served to solidify the government's decision, a group of peasants took 60 ewes to Paris to graze under the Eiffel Tower. This symbolic action helped the Larzac to become a national issue. In January 1973, 26 peasants left on their tractors for a week-long journey to Paris. The gendarmes stopped them at Orleans, but they reached the capital by train and put their case forward at a large public meeting. The 103 pledge signers were always willing to speak to officials; however, meetings with the Sub-Prefect at Millau had come to nothing, nor did the talks held later in Paris with ministry officials achieve any change. The authorities were interested only in implementation of the plan.

Civil Disobedience

As the campaign proceeded, there were acts of civil disobedience as well as legal activities of all type. Sixty farmers returned their military papers to the Defense Ministry. A stone building to shelter 500 sheep was built without permit by volunteer workers. Many young people from outside the area came to work on the plateau. Some stayed to help in the campaign or even settled there as peasants, sometimes squatting on abandoned army land. When the army began to purchase land from absentee landlords, a trust was set up to buy land for agricultural purposes. Ploughing and sowing unused land bought by speculators was also a creative way of protesting. The crops would be sold to help starving people in the Third World. Farmers and residents of the plateau entered the camp and destroyed files concerning land purchase by the military. After being evicted with tear gas they were given prison sentences of up to three weeks. A peace center was set up for research into nonviolent civilian defense. Manned by young people, it also served as an enquiry center where visitors could learn about an ongoing nonviolent battle. Conferences and cultural activities took place there. Large rallies which were held on the plateau in 1973, 1974 and 1977 helped to keep the issue in the public eye.

The Legal Situation

The 103 also took a legal approach, but by the end of 1978 the government had won the legal right to buy the land. There were fasts in 50 towns while 20 farmers walked to Paris. They were met by 40,000 supporters, and eleven delegates were received at the Ministry. When the expropriation judge visited the plateau, inhabitants stopped him from entering each village by standing silently, with the Mayor at their head. Once, when 300 gendarmes tried to clear the road, protesters were injured. Finally when Francois Mitterrand was elected President in May 1981 the project was cancelled. An international peace meeting was held on the plateau in August and among the 3,000 attending were ten foreign

138

delegations including a group of Japanese protesting the development of Narita airport.

MARCKOLSHEIM

Marckolsheim is the administrative center of a rural canton of 17,000 inhabitants where nearly one third of the working population make their living from the land. In March 1974 the village council was told for the first time that a lead factory was to be established by a German chemical firm, Chemischewerke Munchen (CWM), on a site near the Rhine which was part of forest land earmarked for a plan to industrialize Alsace and which had largely fallen into abeyance.

The administration began working on the CWM dossier according to provisions made for the installation of polluting plants. The factory, however, was presented as virtually free from toxic emissions. Emile Astaud, a teacher, heard by chance that CWM had already been turned down in Lorraine. Together with two colleagues and other villagers he formed the Information Group for the Safeguard of the Environment of Marckolsheim (GISEM). An inquiry opened in April, and when members of GISEM were able to examine the dossier they discovered mistakes and inconsistencies; safety precautions seemed inadequate. Emile and his friends wrote to the administrative services, the head of CWM, university experts, etc. As the answers came, a regular bulletin was sent out. The three teachers produced a technical report -- CWM would be manufacturing lead stearate which is highly toxic and enters the metabolism of all living organisms. It is particularly dangerous to children and young animals. León Siegel, the local veterinarian and member of GISEM, warned the peasant farmers that milk, meat, cereals, and vegetables would be contaminated. The threat to the Rhine forest with its unpolluted streams, fauna and flora (including a beaver colony) was also an important factor in motivating people against the project. Seven hundred citizens attended GISEM's first public meeting to which scientific experts as well as the promoters of the project had been invited. The promoters seemed badly prepared and their arguments unconvincing while GISEM people were well informed.

Three thousand letters demanding the rejection of the plan were sent to the inquiry commissioner, and on May 27 he advised against accepting the factory.

Impartial experts, he said, should be invited to speak on the dangers of emissions. The Regional Council voted for the project 43 to 3. The Marckolsheim council voted against it 11 to 9. In June the Mayor refused to sign the permit for the factory. Although a supporter of the project, he felt it was his democratic duty to respect the majority opinion of the council and citizens. The prefect, representing the government, nevertheless signed the decree authorizing the installation of the lead factory. The eleven councillors then resigned.

On July 28, 2000 people took part in a march from the village to the site. Eighty tractors joined in; some were from Germany. The people of Baden were already concerned about a plan to build a nuclear power station at Wyhl, across the Rhine from Marckolsheim. The proposed lead factory would also affect them. The village priest also joined the march and ordered the church bells to be rung. Later he issued a statement supporting the campaign. In August over 3000 citizens from both sides of the Rhine marched through Wyhl. A decision was made to occupy both the Marckolsheim and the Wyhl sites.

The Occupation

The occupation of Marckolsheim site began on September 20, 1974. Work had already started, but people of all ages stood in the holes intended for the huge posts. The workmen eventually agreed to leave. Tents were erected and later a large round wooden house was built on a framework of tree trunks. This "Friendship House" became a place for talks, discussions and cultural activities in which both French and Germans participated. The success of the occupation was due in no small measure to the women who spent most time on the site while the men were at work. Students and conscientious objectors, some of whom came from a Gandhian Christian group in Freiburg, also helped. A training session in nonviolence was held, but the gendarmes never intervened. In supplementary elections in October candidates opposing the project were returned with a 70% majority. The mayor was replaced by the veterinarian, León Siegel, and the new council held a press conference on the site. The Minister of the Environment became convinced that the decision had to be reversed. On February 25, 1975 the

government cancelled the project. Ecology and peace
activists turned their attention to Wyhl.

THE WYHL

In the early 1970s plans were developed to build
nuclear power stations at Fessenheim in Alsace, Breisach
in Baden and Kaiseraugst in Switzerland. Fessenheim was
finally built in spite of strong local opposition. A
campaign against Kaiseraugst continued until 1986 when
Chernobyl made it unlikely the station would be built.
Breisach was cancelled after a vigorous campaign led by
the vinegrowers of the Kaiserstuhl, a collapsed volcanic
massif rising from the plain of the Rhine. In July 1973
citizens learned that the Baden-Wurttemberg regional
government had switched the nuclear plan to Wyhl, north
of the massif, near a forest site near the Rhine.

Wyhl citizens were divided over the issue. Some saw
economic advantages in the project but in all other
villages the majority were against the plan.
Burgerinitiativen, or citizens action groups, were formed
in most villages as the campaign progressed. Nonviolent
training sessions were held. At first the peasant-
farmers and vinegrowers of the area where tobacco and
other crops are also grown, were concerned mainly with
the threat to their livelihood. Temperature inversion
acting on the plumes from the cooling towers would
produce mist, drastically reducing sunlight. Humidity in
the atmosphere would encourage vine diseases. The Rhine
forest would be damaged by a lowering of the water table.
Later they learned of the dangers of radiation and
possible accidents. Fishermen who caught most of their
fish from the unpolluted forest streams also saw their
livelihood threatened. Scientists were invited by the
Burgerinitiativen to speak at public meetings all over
the region so that all citizens would be informed.
Demonstrations were organized including a 400 strong
tractorcade touring all parts of the Kaiserstuhl.
100,000 signatures were collected in the town of Freiburg
and rural areas including the Kaiserstuhl. Municipalities and local associations sent in their objections. A
public hearing was held at Wyhl in July. Outside the
hall banners stressed that the regional prime minister
and economics minister could not be impartial since they
were respectively chairman and board member of Badenwerk,
the firm given the contract to build the station.

Government experts spoke most of the time. Representatives of the farmers and wine-growers unions seemed unable to argue a good case. The audience eventually walked out in disgust and a coffin marked "Democracy" was carried out.

A referendum in Wyhl gave its citizens a chance to vote on whether or not to sell communal land to Badenwerk. Fifty-five percent approved the sale of the land while 43.2% voted against. The BI warned that the population of the whole region would decide whether the station would be built. Six local councils and ten citizens (representing the BI) filed a case against the licensing of the plant with the Freiburg administrative tribunal. The court decided work should not begin before it had given its ruling.

Occupying the Site

In spite of the Burgerinitiativen warning, work began on the site on February 17, 1975. The next day about 300 people from Alsace and Baden persuaded the workers to leave. Local police sent out to disperse them simply asked them politely to leave; some wore anti-nuclear badges in their caps. By evening 50 tents had been set up and 150 men, women and children stayed there all night. Special police were sent in at dawn on February 20, 650 of them in riot gear and with dogs. Prearranged sirens started wailing in the nearby villages. Thousands of people arrived at the site. The squatters, sitting around a campfire, linked arms and sang the "Wacht am Rhein" (to new words about Wyhl and Marckolsheim). The police, using water canon, evicted them from the site. The workmen then returned and erected a barbed wire fence all around the site. The next day local people came back to protest. Some camped outside the site and from Friday to Sunday they spoke through loudspeakers to the police inside. Eventually a dialogue became possible; some policemen were unhappy about what they were doing. A major demonstration had been called for Sunday. Soon 28,000 demonstrators had massed along the Rhine facing 1000 police. They broke through the fence and poured onto the site. It was a moment of great tension but also of great satisfaction. The police chief was forced to evacuate his men. A few policemen were weeping -- the strain had been too much. They had expected dangerous "radicals," but instead they found ordinary peaceful citizens. Tents were again erected on the site and the occupiers blocked all pathways leading to it. The police made an attempt to return. They had tear gas but it was foggy and they had no gasmasks. The camp was now organized in similar fashion to that at Marckolsheim although the friendship house was larger. A folk high school was set up where lectures and lively debates on nuclear power, ecology, alternative energy, and nonviolence took place. Singing and theater plays also became part of camp life. This "people's university" strengthened local involvement in the struggle.

The Offenberg Agreement

The occupation lasted over a year, when negotiations took place between the BI and the government at Offenberg. The two sides agreed that no work would start before November 1976; no actions would be brought against those involved in the occupation; independent expert advice would be sought on the dangers of radiation. The BI continued their activities and the people's university sessions were transferred to the villages.

Legal and Political

In 1977 the Freiburg court unexpectedly ruled that the station could not be built because of the danger of a major accident. The case went to appeal. The Mannheim court finally reversed the Freiburg decision on March 30, 1982. The nuclear project could now go ahead. The people of the region reacted with demonstration, tractorcades and another petition. Finally, in October 1983 the regional prime minister, Lothar Späth, announced a new energy plan and declared that Wyhl nuclear plant would not be required until the year 2000 -- in political terms, as good as a cancellation.

A COMPARISON

There are some important similarities among the three struggles, the communities involved and environmental features: The Larzac is an isolated plateau surrounded by canyon-like valleys. Marckolsheim lies in the Rhine valley with its agricultural land and forest bordering the river. For historical reasons Alsace has its own separate identity. Wyhl lies on the eastern side of the valley with the low massif of the Kaiserstuhl to the south, and the Rhine forest to the west.

The People

In all three regions the people have a strong sense of community. In each case the majority are engaged in a particular economic activity: sheep-farming on the Larzac, mixed farming in the Marckolsheim canton, wine-growing in the Kaiserstuhl. Each community shares in the same cultural tradition of its own greater region: Larzac shares Occitan, the Latin-based language and the culture of southern France. Marckolsheim and Wyhl share the same Germanic dialect spoken everywhere in the upper Rhine. The people of the three regions have a traditional outlook. In general they tend to be independent-minded, hardworking, disciplined, patient and politically conservative. They are also friendly to outsiders.

The Political Parties

No support came from local MP's, although there were some exceptions in the Kaiserstuhl area owing to West Germany's two-tier electoral system. Dr. Hans-Erich Schott, for instance, was returned in an otherwise Christian-Democrat victory. As a Free-Democrat he felt it his duty to give up his work in order to back the campaign in the regional parliament. He played an important part in the Offenberg negotiations. Opposition parties played a limited role in the three campaigns. The French Socialist Party was favorable to the Larzac. The Communist Party largely ignored Larzac and Marckolsheim. The Social-Democrats (SPD) and Free-Democrats (FDP) opposed the nuclear energy program of Baden-Württenberg.

The Unions

In Larzac the farmers' union gave limited support, but the Peasant-Workers (a union of small farmers) gave considerable support and organized the 1974 demonstration on the plateau. In Wyhl the farmers' and wine-growers' unions gave limited backing.

The Governing Powers

The governments and local administrations concerned made no serious attempt even to compromise. In the end the power of nonviolence made them capitulate. This was particularly true of the CDU government of Baden-Württemberg led by Prime Minister Lothar Späth. President Giscard d'Estaing came to power partly because of his support for ecological issues and for "development with a human face." It would have been difficult for him to ignore the will of the people of Alsace. President Mitterrand had taken a personal interest in Larzac and his decision to cancel the project was no doubt also prompted by political considerations. It had become a national issue.

The Police and the Army

In the campaigns the police were reluctant to use more than the minimum amount of force against citizens who clearly were not violent. There were exceptions, but few protesters were injured. Riot police called to clear the Wyhl site came from 200 kilometers away. Two companies (100 men in each) failed to arrive; one claimed it could not find the place, the other simply refused to go. On the Larzac when the army (illegally) exercised on private land, peasants and others would gather from miles around and insist that the troops leave. If they didn't, they risked having their vehicles painted with slogans. A dialogue was sometimes possible with conscripts who would come over in their spare time to have a chat or even to help with the harvest.

SOME DIFFERENCES

The Campaigns

Larzac, unlike the other campaigns, was deliberately organized to mobilize support from all over the country. This was necessary because members were too few in number (103 farmers with, at first, only limited support). The strategy succeeded since anti-militarists, pacifists, nonviolent activists, ecologists, regionalists and many others saw in the Larzac something of their own concerns -- something they could actively work for. The two other campaigns were conducted entirely by activists within the region with maximum participation of the population. The one exception occurred when the Wyhl site had to be reoccupied and large numbers were required.

The Church

The Catholic church gave its full support to the Larzac peasants from the beginning. Young priests influenced by the Vatican Council were, perhaps, largely responsible for this support. In Marckolsheim, however, only the local priest gave his full support. The Catholic clergy in the Kaiserstuhl area distanced themselves from the struggle. When Catholics in the BI found their priests would not give them even spiritual support, they organized their own religious meetings and events. The Protestant ministers were more helpful, and some took an active part in the campaign. The Catholic and Protestant bishops would not commit themselves.

INFLUENCE AND EVOLVEMENT

The Campaigns

The three campaigns influenced one another. Lanza del Vasto spent a few days at Marckolsheim and spoke at Friendship House. Marckolsheim made success at Wyhl possible. Activists from the Upper-Rhine region worked on the Larzac Plateau and came back with new ideas. Wyhl became a symbol of the growing anti-nuclear movement in Germany. When the Swiss Kaiseraugst site was first occupied more than half the squatters came from Alsace and Baden. The Larzac influenced many similar struggles not only in France but in other countries: The idea of plowing land on the Molesworth (England) USAF cruise missile base, then sowing and using the harvest for Eritrean famine relief, was taken out of the Larzac example.

Evolution

The people of all three communities evolved in many kinds of ways though less so in the case of Marckolsheim where the campaign lasted only a year. In general they began to adopt ideas and practices usually associated with the nonviolence of women's liberation, anti-racism, concern for the Third World, alternative energy, organic cultivation, etc. The Larzac continues to be the venue for meetings and conferences and the peace center of Le Cun continues its research work in alternative civilian defense. A fine library on the subject has been assembled. The farmers have organized their agricultural activities on a more cooperative basis. Delegates of the 103 visited Japan (the Narita struggle) and more recently Kanaki (New Caledonia) now in the throes of decolonization.

CONCLUSIONS

Evidence from this study seems to indicate that nonviolence is more likely to succeed in rural areas where there is a community of interest and where the people share a common faith or outlook. The most important ingredient for success is unity. The manner in which the nonviolent idea is introduced in conflict situations is of vital importance. Only a low input appears to be necessary. Once introduced it acts like leaven spreading throughout society. Nonviolence became deeply rooted in the population of the Larzac and the Kaiserstuhl. While no conclusion can be drawn from three examples alone, other examples of a similar nature could contribute to a wider study. One can speculate that if nonviolence had been introduced to the people of the mining villages during the recent miners' strike in Britain, the result might have been very different than it was. Nonviolent activists should be alert to the opportunities of this type which exist today and will no doubt appear in the future.

147

BIBLIOGRAPHY

More detailed accounts of the Larzac campaign by Roger
Rawlinson are to be found in the following: Chapter
4, "The Battle of Larzac," in Liberation without
Violence, A. Paul Hare and Herbert H. Blumberg,
eds., London: Rex Collings, 1977. "Larzac--A
Victory for Nonviolence," Quaker Peace & Service,
Friends House, London, 1983. (Also available in
Arabic: Palestinian Centre for the Study of
Nonviolence. PO Box 20317, Jerusalem via Israel or
PO Box 35, Wapakoneta, Ohio 45895, USA).

"L'Occitanismequ'es aquo?" in Aspects of Occitan
Regionalism, St. Georges, AOPA, year needed here.

A number of books on nonviolence in its various aspects
have been written by Lanza del Vasto. Perhaps the
most important are: Le Pelerinage aux Sources,
Paris: Denoel, 1943.

English edition -- Return to the Source, London: Rider,
1971. "Technique de la Non-violence," Denoel,
Paris, 1971.

"Communities of Resistance", London: Quaker Peace &
Service, 1986,(Marckolsheim, Wyhl and other
campaigns in the Upper-Rhine region).

"Wyhl, Kein Kernkraftwerk in Whyl und auch sonst
nirgends," Bernd Nossler and Margret de Witt, eds.,
Freiburg: Dreisam-Verlay, 1976.

"Wyhl. Der Widerstand geht weiter..." Christoph Buchele,
Irmgard Schneider and Bernd Nossler, eds., Freiburg:
Dreisam-Verlay, 1982.

Jim Coulter, Susan Miller and Martin Walker, "A State of
Siege, Miners' Strike 1984," in Politics and
Policing of the Coalfields, City: Canary Press,
1984.

10

Military-Industrial Complexes and Violence Towards Women

Andree Michel

This research commenced with two hypotheses drawn from the cross national literature. First, military-industrial complexes are not neutral, new, social structures with regard to the status of women. They are patriarchal systems which tend to perpetuate the oppression and exploitation of women through exerting violence. Second, military-industrial complexes are not like other patriarchal systems. Unlike other patriarchal systems, they are global systems which integrate the totality of the subsystems which make up society, hence their virulence and their efficiency in establishing a "world military order" which is based on the traditional stratifications of social class, gender, and the domination of center countries over those in the periphery.

THE MILITARY-INDUSTRIAL COMPLEXES AND THE PATRIARCHAL SYSTEM

In feminist circles, it is customary to identify the patriarchal system as one of oppression and exploitation of women. Yet the military-industrial complex is rarely examined as other than a specific modality of the patriarchal system—in the same way as other social subsystems (the family, the educational system, the organization of labour, or the economy). I have previously demonstrated that the military industrial complex can be regarded as the most advanced, the newest, and the most powerful social structure of the patriarchal system.

Translated from the French by Agnes Bertrand.

Military-industrial complexes (MIC) are intricate social structures which consist not only of high ranking military officers and industrialists who manufacture weapons, but also of scientists who manage laboratories, of bureaucrats (men from political parties or senior civil servants) who are devoted to the cause of militarism. They consist, also, of bankers who lend money to the private or nationalized firms which produce the weapons and to the countries which buy these military products. The term military-industrial complex (MIC) is used instead of the more accurate but cumbersome term scientific- bureaucratic-military- industrial-banking complex. This complex binds together the highest ranking members of the scientific, administrative, political, military, industrial and banking hierarchies--the hierarchies of power and of prestige, but also of finance. One example is a scientific community study of UNESCO which reveals that scientists and engineers working for military research and development (R&D) receive higher salaries than their civilian counterparts. 1/

MICs are social structures whose implicit (if not explicit) purpose is to maintain the privileges of the ruling classes over the dominated classes; of rich countries over poor countries. This purpose has been demonstrated by various authors. 2/ These authors maintain that such structures have all the characteristics of a patriarchal system whose aim is to maintain the subservience of women to men--The division of work within the military-industrial complexes discloses their sexist nature. The "old boy network" which the studies of the Oxford Research Group on the decisionmaking process in nuclear policy has identified, is composed of men. When, exceptionally, a woman succeeds in "rising" within a MIC, it is in the role of "great priestess" 3/ of the patriarchal system. She is devoted to the interests of the MIC, and is mandated for the implementation of the goals and strategy as defined by the men heading the MIC. This expression is used by Camil e Lacoste Dujardin to describe the repression exerted by Maghrebin mothers towards women devoted to the interests of the MIC, and mandated for the success of the implementation of goals and strategy defined by the men heading the MIC.

The Characteristic of a Patriarcal System

The characteristic of a patriarcal system is to
define women as tools to be used in the fulfillment of
the goals of the men in the system. They would not
perceive women as equals with their own goals and
fundamental needs of justice and dignity. MICs treat
women as instruments and reward them when they are
allies, and punish and discriminate against, sometimes
tortur and even kill, them when they oppose and fight the
system.

The rationale of the patriarchal system with regard
to women is wrapped up in the pretense of scientific and
"general" interest to convince women of the worthiness of
the goals that are pursued. Even today, it is in the
name of child psychology or family well-being that women
are required to remain at home to be servants of their
husbands. In the same way, it is in the name of
"defense" or "national security" (because the assumed
enemy might possess greater means of mass destruction)
that the fundamental needs of women throughout the world
(food, health, hygiene, contraception, education,
professional training, information, and decisionmaking)
are consistently denied for the sake of the arms race.
The male goal is to satisfy a mania for warfare while
women are confined to the traditional role of wife and
mother. The propaganda for a higher birth rate is now in
full swing in tiny overpopulated Europe, the continent
with the highest concentration of nuclear weapons.

The nationalist ideology in eastern and western
Europe is in fact the necessary complement of the
militaristic ideology. Both were born at the same period
of development of human history; both survive thanks to
the inertia of the patriarchal system, in times when the
"population bomb" has become a threat. Gaston Bouthoul
has argued that wars are "retarded infanticides": "the
only constant demographic characteristic of war is that
it provokes a rise in mortality". 5/ With its
stubbornness in confining women to reproduction and
excluding them from decision-making, it is as if the
military-industrial complex ignores the idea that there
are other ways than war for limiting births while
forgetting that the use of nuclear weapons would probably
kill everyone. Both ideologies lead to a quasi
pathological specialization of the roles of women and men
in the name of general interest, or allegedly threatened

national interests; both are characteristic of the patriarchal system.

MILITARY-INDUSTRIAL COMPLEXES ARE POWERFUL PATRIARCHAL SYSTEMS

These systems have managed to integrate, to their ends, the traditional subsystems (family and state) plus the most modern subsystems (education, information, and the market system) in order to strengthen their hold and oppression over women.

The Family Subsystem

When women in affluent countries have managed to emancipate themselves and demanded access to employment and freedom from home confinement, MICs have moved their production, which is chiefly geared towards military needs, to the global factory of planetary dimensions. In those Third World countries women between 18 and 25 years of age are introduced by members of their family to the electronic factories (global factory) and hired for miserably low salaries with abominable work and hygiene conditions. These women are replacing women from developed countries who have gradually and partially emancipated themselves from the family stronghold and organized to defend their rights. Because of modernization and competitiveness, these women are now victims of unemployment or precariously held job positions. This situation inevitably sets them back to renewed dependence upon their husbands.

The Nation-State

The nation-state reinforces the development of militarization by the MICs by sacrificing the jobs and social services needed by women. The labor policy of the MICs is a sexist policy, since it aims at favoring the employment of men over women. Studies from UNESCO show that for the same amount of money invested, one job is created in the military sector versus two in civilian sector. Yet the defense industry employs a highly qualified labour force (59 percent engineers and corporate executives, versus an average of 30 percent in civilian sectors) predominantly male. (Only 6 percent of the engineers are women in the United States.) Social needs, like education (which employs two-thirds of the women) are neglected and degraded. The nation-state, invaded by the military-industrial complexes (as in the USA) , or managed by nationalized industries working for defense (as in France or in the USSR), favors, supports, and promotes this sexist labor policy.

The Market Economy System

The market economy system is a sexist economic system which, throughout all countries of the world, favors men and disadvantages women. The economic yardsticks of the system (GNP) ignore the domestic production of women, and thus deprive them of income. And the market system systematically devalues professional qualifications of women in monetarized labor. Consequently, though they yield 66 percent of the total working hours (monetarised and non monetarised), women throughout the world only receive 10 percent of the total income, and own but one percent of the land. 6/ Yet it is this economic subsystem and its mode of development which deprives women of income, that the MICs back up when they support, in the Third World countries, governments devoted to this market economy and when they suppress any attempts to install any different, fairer, economic system which might be based on the needs of the most deprived women.

The School and Occupational Subsystem

That this subsystem is clearly a sexist system can be observed in France, in the United States, and throughout the world. Sexist representations of men and women; of boys and girls prevail in spite of some attempts to change. 7/ The advice of parents and teachers tend to orientate boys and girls according to sexual stereotypes. Thus in France, 80 percent of the female jobs fall into 30 categories while the same percentage for men fall into 300. The MICs invest in this subsystem, when (as in France with the inter-administrative Hernu-Savary Agreements) they promote regulations which escape parliamentary control and when they penetrate the school directly with propaganda which favors the sexist institutions of the army—and when they contract women for military employment in typically traditional roles. 8/

The Information Sub-system

The news and information delivered by the media, the written press, radio, and television constitute a sexist information system which is reinforced by the MICs who use them to transmit a militaristic ideology—an ideology which is used to justify choices in favor of nuclear weapons, arms sales, and the neo-colonialist policies of the super powers. Pacifist women (whether feminist or not) are rarely read or heard from. Only the "macho" comments of the defenders of the world military system, are generally heard. Here we are facing the phenomenon of a traditional gender distribution of speech and silence which serves to reinforce the MICs.

The Sub-system of Prostitution

This sub-system is equally developed and reinforced in the wake of wars, military occupations, and the setting up of foreign military bases engineered by the military-industrial complexes. The submission of women as instruments of pleasure for men is a general phenomenon around military bases—whether the American ones of the Philippines or Honduras, or the French ones in Africa, Tahiti, or French Guiana. The organized prostitution which was established in Asia to satisfy the needs of several generations of soldiers (in South Korea by the Japanese; of French and American wars in Vietnam...) have been reconverted to "transnational tourism" according to the expression used by Soledad Perpinan. When these occupations and wars ended, all the places of prostitution, originally used by military men became visited by consumers from affluent countries during the Sex Tours organized in the Philippines, South Korea and Thailand by foreign travel agencies. There are numerous studies dedicated to revealing the misery of the prostitutes in these countries. 9/

The Cultural Subsystem

The cultural subsystem is also widely affected by the militarization of society. The spreading of pornography on the front page of the written press and on the walls of buildings illustrates how the "pin-up" culture has invaded the whole of popular culture. How could it be otherwise when society has so fast become militarized? Just as easy pleasures were offered in compensation to those submitting to unconditional obedience (including orders to murder), the citizens whose critical minds are neutralized by the censorship of military choices and other choices pertaining to one's future are offered some compensation. Pornography offered as a reward for their silence and for allegiance to the interest of MICs. And powerless citizens compensate for the impotence and manipulation fostered by the MICs through sado masochistic fantasies engendered by pornography, where men are depicted as dominating and torturing women. This invasion of everyday culture by pornography bears heavy consequences. The research of Pauline Bart has led her to conclude that pornography is a "propaganda for rape". 10/ This opinion is suggested by the statistics which show an increase of rape. (In France the number has doubled between 1972 and 1981; in the U.S. risk of rape increased by 38% between 1976 and 1983.) 11/

Conclusion

Through this short analysis, I have supported my two initial hypotheses on the nature of the MICs as a patriarchal system which tends to invade the subsystems of which society is composed. This partiarchal system maintains and reinforces the oppression and exploitation of women worldwide. At the same time it reinforces the power of the ruling classes over the poor working classes and of rich countries over poor countries. Further research should advance in two directions:

First. It is necessary to examine the strategies MICs use in order to maintain the oppression they exert over women. I have partially answered this question by identifying the existence of a "feminine social rempart", or women's "alibi," which the MICs have created in order to win to their causes the privileged women of rich and of Third World countries. 12/ Dividing women is an old recipe used by the patriarchal system to perpetuate its power.

Secondly. We need to analyze why social movements such as peace and the feminist movements, which have such close aims have not yet succeeded in combining their effort to build a fairer, more democratic and humane society, and to free themselves from the feudal hold of the powerful MICs. Betty Reardon attempted to answer these questions in her last book, Sexism and the War System. 13/ But the analysis deserves to be continued.

NOTES

1. Ulrich Albrecht, "Les communaute de al R&D militaire," Revue

2. Particularly by Andre Gunder Frank, Political Ironies in the World Economy, University of Amsterdam, Department of Economy, Memorandum N 8423, July 1984. Internationaledes Sciences Sociales, 1983, N95.

3. This has been demonstrated by various authors, particularly by Andre Gunder Frank, Political Ironies in the World Economy, Univ. of Amsterdam, Dept. of Economy, Memorandum N 8423, July 1984.

4. See C. Lacoste Dujardin: "Des meres contre les femmes," Paris, La Decouverte, 1985.

5. Gaston Bouthoul, Traite de polomologie, Sociologies des Guerres, Paris, Payot, 1970.

6. Statistics from the United Nations Organization, 1980.

7. This appears in several researches, in particular Andree Michel: Vaincre le sexisme dans les livres pour enfants et les manuels scolaires Paris, UNESCO, 1986.

8. See in particular Wendy Chapkin (ed.), Women and the Military, Amsterdam, Transnational Institute, 1981.

9. See in particular the works of K. Barry, C. Bunch and S. Castley: "Feminism International, reseau contre l'esclavage sexuel," in Nouvelles questions feministes, N 8, Winter 1984; Sister Mary Soledad Perpinan: "The geopolitics of prostitution," in Balai, Vol. 11, N 4 (Manila). Khin Titsa: "Providence and prostitution: Image and reality for women in Boudhist Tahiland," Change, London, September 1980.

156

10. Pauline Bart, Linda Freeman and Peter Kimball, "The different worlds of women and men: attitudes toward pornography," Interdisciplinary congress on women, Groningen, Holland, 1984.

11. For France see, "Aspects de la criminalite en France en 1982 constate par les services de police et de gendarmerie" and for the U.S., see Diana Russel and Nancy Howall: "The prevalance of rape in the U.S. revisied," Signs, Summer 1983.

12. Andre Michel, "Military-industrial complexes and violence towards women".

13. Betty Reardon, Sexism and the War System, Teasher College Press, 1985.

11

Women in the U.S. Military: A Set-Back for Feminism

Mindy Percival

A common and natural result of an undue respect for law is, that you may see a file of soldiers, colonel, captain, corporal, privates, powder-monkeys, and all, marching in admirable order over hill and dale to the wars, against their wills, ay, against their common sense and consciences, which makes it very steep marching indeed, and produces a palpitation of the heart. They have no doubt that it is a damnable business in which they are concerned; they are all peaceably inclined. Now what are they? Man at all? or small movable forts and magazines, at the service of some unscrupulous man in power? Visit the Navy Yard, and behold a marine, such a man as an American government can make, or such as it can make a man with its black arts--a mere shadow and reminiscence of humanity, a man laid out alive and standing, and already, as one may say, buried under arms with funeral accompaniment.

--Henry Thoreau

The participation of women in the U.S. military has been, and continues to be, widely debated. Feminists are both staunchly opposed to it and supportive of it. The National Organization of Women (NOW), for example, favors the integration of women into the military. The position rests on the belief that in order to realize equality, women must not only share in social duties and responsibilities but also be assured of their rights. Increasingly, however, the relationship between the achievement of feminist goals and the use of nonviolent practices and the attainment of peace has become a subject of interest, research, and discussion. Feminist scholars have argued, on a variety of levels, that the means and ends of the movements for peace and feminism are, in fact, the same. World order studies highlight the ways in which the attainment of goals in one field is dependent on, and connected to, the attainment of goals in other fields; they also make a case for the interrelational nature of feminism and nonviolence. Although some explanatory discussion is necessary, this chapter does not intend to explore all the connections between feminism and nonviolence. Rather, it attempts to underscore, within the framework of these theories, the way in which women's increased participation within the military is inconsistent with specific feminist visions and can be seen as exemplifying, supporting, and encouraging sexism and male chauvinism. The interconnectedness of patriarchy, authoritarianism, violence, and militarism and their supporting systems ensure this outcome. These characteristics are most evident in military institutions, philosophies, and practices which are in direct conflict with feminist values and goals.

Equal participation of women in the armed forces may appear to be a move toward equity and equality, but numerous and substantial arguments point to the contrary. The history of women and the U.S. military [female images viewed by the military], the treatment of women in military establishments, the general economic and political ramifications of militarism for women, and the sexist and chauvinistic values upon which our military institutions are based have been pointed up as evidence in keeping with the contention that sexist attitudes and policies are supported, and feminist attitudes and policies hindered, by increased female participation in the military. The values that predominate are those "that underlie stereotypes and rationalize discrimination and oppression." 1/

The role played by the military in today's world and the ideals, beliefs, and behaviors it encourages are contrary to the goals of sexual, racial democratic and economic equality, and positive global transformation. Although individual situations or expressions may appear to signify increased female "liberation," the military aims to support and glorify all that is injurious to women in particular and society in general. It also interferes in the achievements of betterment. According to Donna Warnock,

Both feminism and non-violence see that power, in
its healthy form, comes from the strength and
sensitivity of...wholistic understanding and leads
naturally to the cooperative and nurturing behavior
necessary for harmonious existence. 2/

Specifically, women's increased participation in the U.S.
military can be seen as a setback for feminism for the
following reasons.
1.   It represents the precarious and secondary status of
women in American society, highlights the obstacles
impeding the participation of women in traditionally all-
male bastions, and reproduces workplace discrimination,
harrassment, and the exploitative use of female labor.
2.   The military imposes its own unique forms of sexual
discrimination and male chauvinism. It also promotes
attitudes, policies, and practices detrimental to the
achievement of women's equality and full participation
through its conception and portrayal of the relations
between gender and militarism, its use of female symbols
and images for military purposes, and the reactive
attitudes it expresses in response to women's increased
participation.
3.   The philosophies and characteristics on which the
military is based--patriarchy, hierarchy, authoritarianism, and violence--are antithetical to feminist
aspirations, moreover, women are not just part of the
list of victims of militarism; their condition is part of
the explanation of militarism. 3/

If we agree with the feminist assertions that
social, cultural, or biological differences between the
sexes should not be grounds for discrimination, that
women needn't adopt masculine attitudes and behaviors in
order to attain equality, or buy into unjust and discriminatory institutions in order to enter the public sphere
and achieve economic, social, and political power, and
that values, traits, and talents traditionally considered
feminine needn't be negated or devalued for women to
transcend the social structures and practices that maintain women's inferior position to men, then the military
can, more obviously, be seen as inherently antifemale.

There is a great and urgent need to deepen and
broaden the popular understanding that while
women certainly have the right and capability

to be soldiers, for women to become like men
have, would not be a step toward anyones
liberation. 4/

As will be seen, the military establishment is based on
assumptions that are literally opposed to the assertions
stated earlier.

As suggested, the historical and contemporary
relationship of women to the U.S. military is indicative
of the second-class status assigned to them and the
workplace discrimination, harrassment, and exploitation
of labor suffered by women. The earliest discussions of
women's role in the military centered on insistence upon
and rationalizations for exclusion. Physical and mental
incapability, the unfeminine nature of military involvement, the proper role of women as mothers, wives, and
homemakers and the belief that women's inclusion in
battle eliminates the purpose of fighting wars—to
protect women and children—have been popular arguments.
"What use is it to defend a nation that sends women to
the meat grinder? What are we defending?" 5/ With few
excep- tions, these arguments have kept women formally
out of the military for centuries.

Yet despite the successes of formal exclusion, women
have participated in military activities since the
beginning of military history. Women informally involved
in military activities have been called "camp followers,"
and they have worked primarily in the support services as
cooks, servants, wives, laundresses, nurses, prostitutes
and sometimes hopeful combatants. During the American
Revolutionary War and the U.S. Civil War, women "labored
in their traditional support role—their functions a
logistical one—to cook and sew and bandage, to bury the
dead and repair weapons, to nurse and help with baggage
trains." 6/ Today, the U.S. military is an administra-
tively and technologically complex organization requiring
even greater support systems, and women still largely
provide such support. As in the Israeli army, the sexual
division of labor in the U.S. armed services

constitutes both a part and an extension of the
sexual division of labor in the civilian labor
market. Within the military women occupy
occupational jobs similar to those in which
they are engaged in civilian life—clerical,
educational and social services. 7/

Practically speaking, women who provide such support serve useful and often essential purposes; yet they are often considered annoying, threatening, peripheral, and unimportant, and their functions are "kept ideologically marginal to the essential functions of militaries-- combat." 8/ When women are actually engaged in combative functions, their tasks are redefined as supportive or noncombative. Women are constantly reminded of this marginality and the low esteem associated with their roles within the military. According to Cynthia Enloe, "In the late 20th century women mobilized to serve the military's needs are still vulnerable to the stereotype of camp follower...no matter how professional their formal position in the military." 9/ And it can be easily maintained that the reason women are excluded from combat and combative functions is not because they provide support services such as nursing and secretarial work, but because they are women.

> Women as women must be denied access to "the front",to "combat," so that men can claim a uniqueness and superiority that will justify their dominant position in the social order. And yet, because women are in practice often exposed to the frontline, the military has to constantly redefine "the front" and "combat" as wherever women are not. Women may serve in the military, but can never be permitted to be the military. They must remain "camp followers." 10/

At all times women's involvement in the military has been strongly controlled by men to suit both the personal and the professional needs of the moment. As long as women provide what the military needs but would rather not provide itself, they are encouraged to enlist. When military conditions change, however, they are excused and the military remains confident that replacement will be readily available when conditions change. Women can be seen as pawns in the military labor situation, called to service when needed and eliminated as needs wane. Pearl Harbor, for example, "speeded up plans for an elite corps of 10,600 auxiliaries and 340 officers." 11/ Following the Vietnam war, the personal problems caused by the end of the draft and the reinstatement of the all-volunteer army caused planners to reconsider the usefulness of female participation in the military. Dramatically increased female participation, however, caused planners to reevaluate the role of women once again, and in 1980 the army announced a pause in recruitment, reinstated the all-male draft, and soon afterward resegregated basic training. 12/ Moreover "the thousands of women who are joining the army may well be part of a deliberate government plot to expand the recruitment pool in a time of declining birth rates." 13/

The extent of participation by women in the U.S. military is indicative of their problems in a society structured in such a way as to limit their choices. These limitations (which are caused by militarism) have been exploited by recruiters who play on desires for independence and economic security. Enlistment presents opportunities to escape the confines of a stifling family, job, or marriage. As with male recruits, these options are most tempting to women with the fewest alternatives in the areas of education, income, and autonomy, as evidenced by the disproportionately large percentage of black women presently in the service. Black women constitue 11 percent of the population, but they make up 25.7 percent of the population of the armed forces and 42.5 percent of all enlisted women. 14/ Since the 1970s, women "must be seen as replacements for men who prefer to remain civilians" 15/ and have other and better options.

Militaries have recruited and deployed women to suit their needs, exploited the limitations placed on women in our society, institutionalized support functions, and continued practices that ensure women's inferior position in the workplace. As in the business world, women face sexual harrassment and the sexually ascriptive allocation of roles, and "are concentrated in the lower ranks." 16/ The military market also reveals how the state treats different groups of women differently "for national purposes." 17/ Under the guise of equal opportunity, the military has made American women active participants in the patriarchial war system, which maintains inequality and perpetuates sexism. Increased participation should not be seen as a step toward equity and equality but as a successful outcome for militarism and male domination, and as a symptom of women's precarious and exploited position in American society. As Nira Yuval Davis has pointed out,

The Israeli case suggests that the incorporation of women into the military may change the nature of, rather than eliminate, the subordination of women. Women's formal inclusion in the military does not guarantee their equality, either in terms of the actual tasks they fulfill or in terms of the power they exercise. On the contrary, as the Israeli case illustrates, the extremely hierarchical and bureaucratic nature of the modern army can contribute to a gender differentiation and gender inequality even more institutionalized and extreme than in the civilian labor market. 18/

The military also imposes its own unique forms of male chauvinism and promotes attitudes, policies, and practices detrimental to the attainment of equality and the values of feminism. It is an institution that has "sanctified rape and murder and violence against us for too many, many centuries." 19/ It does so by exploiting female images for military purposes based on its own notions of the relationship between gender and militarism. It often defines the ideal of male militarism through "a degraded definition of nonmilitary womenhood that justifies women's second class citizenship and sexual exploitation." 20/ It also encourages attitudes of emotional coldness, desire for power, feelings of superiority, reliance on domination, aggression and physical violence. According the Helen Michalowski, "The military is blatant hierarchy. Power and privilege correspond directly with one's rank, but feelings of superiority are encouraged throughout." 21/ In the male recruit, all that is undesirable in terms of attitude and action is associated with qualities stereotypically considered feminine or characteristic of male homosexuals. Misogyny and homophobia are perpetuated throughout the military and most enthusiastically during training. "Basic training encourages women-hating (as does the whole military experience) but the way it does so is more complex than women sometimes suppose." 22/ "One is continually addressed as a faggot or girl." It seems the system breaks down when people are seen as people or when caring or questioning of authority is present. As Cynthia Adock puts it,

It is not an accident that the greatest threat to all human life, militarism, is also the most virulent expression of woman-hating and contempt for the feminine. Both sexism and militarism grow from a common root. They feed on fear and hatred of the "other," be it female or male foreigner, the tribal enemy. 24/

Both sexism and militarism are manifestations of misogyny, which is the underlying threat of the war system. And according to Betty Reardon, "Misogyny is the core of both militarism and sexism, and unless it is completely torn from the social soil in which the male power structure cultivates war, there is no hope to uproot the war system." 25/

The images of "moral mother" and "women warriors" are used for both military and antimilitary purposes. Militarists and nonmilitarists, feminists and non-feminists, rely on these sentimental images to promote a variety of reactions. The U.S. Army proclaims that "Some of the Best Soldiers Wear Lipstick," and women combatants in liberation armies are familiar, well-publicized images. Pacifist-feminists, on the other hand, have countered these images with those of women as moral reformer, mother, close to nature, and nurturers. As women are innately more pacifistic, these feminists have argued, they will renounce war and reform violent, patriarchial institutions.

We will meet, all of us, women of every land, we will meet in the center, make a circle; we will weave a world web to entangle the powers that bury our children. We, as life-givers, will not support any life-threatening force. Nuclear madness imminently endangers our children, their future and the earth. 26/

The problem with relying on notions of traditional femininity and motherhood to counteract the militariza-tion of women's lives is that the images can be used against women as well.

Women may be particularly good at opposing global militarism then, not because we are morally superior nurturers, but because gender is at the center of recurrent contradictions in the militarization process. We should fight to "junk all received notions of traditional femininity and motherhood" because they cannot be transformed and will always be used against women. 27/

The association of pacifism with maternalism and traditional feminist characteristics to dispel the images of female warrior is best replaced with the association of pacifist implications and feminism for a more just world and increased democracy. To carry this argument further, we can say that

> the antithesis of peace and justice is violence (that is, the unnecessary and avoidable harm to life and well-being) and oppression (the humanly devised barriers to the exercise of choice and self determination) which characterize and bind together sexism and the war system...and substantive progress toward either peace or justice cannot be achieved without the elimination of sexism. 28/

The military, then, uses and fosters images of women that are counterproductive to the elimination of sexism and discrimination. Women should participate in military functions according to their own decisions and their own consciences, and they should not be manipulated by male-induced images. If they resist war and military participation, they should do so on the basis of their personhood and on the available evidence highlighting its contradictions to feminism. As Reardon has noted, "The recent effects of budget-cuts and the elimination of social programs in favor of military programs has the most negative effect on women and exemplifies the way in which sexism and militarism are linked." 29/

However, beyond the discrimination against women in employment practices and policies within the U.S. military (until 1967, for example, no woman could become a general or an admiral, women required parental consent not required of men, and there was a policy of compulsory childlessness), the manipulation of the female labor forces, the exploitation of female images, and other specifics regarding female participation, there are more fundamental reasons for insisting that military involvement is obstructive to feminist goals. The military is inherently antifemale inasmuch as violence against women and war are part of the same system: "Both are justified by sovereignty, hierarchy, and the notion that relationships between people must be based on dominance rather than mutuality, interdependence and empowerment." 30/ As long as violence is encouraged in men through socialization and training, lasting peace and security are unlikely to be realized. Persons are encouraged to commit violence and to seek authoritarianism in a patriarchial society, and it is the willingness to use violence on which the military depends. Both war and sexism depend on the acceptance and the manifestations of social violence.

> Is peace possible in a patriarchal society? If we define peace as a condition in which world order values prevail for the majority of the earth's people the answer is clearly no...Peace and patriarchy are antithetical by definition... Patriarchy has legitimized the use of force to assist those in authority to impose their will on those subject to them--based on the assumption that the will of the authority is in the best interest of all concerned because it stems from superior knowledge and wisdom. 31/

Only by studying the reciprocol causation between sexism and war, violence against women and other forms of violence, overt and structural violence (which appears to disproportionally affect women as indicated in The Feminization of Poverty), militarism and reactionary trends, 32/ (exemplified by, among other things, women in the U.S. military who "have sometimes opposed policy changes apparently beneficial to women and...seemed so opposed to equality as least as repressed in the ERA" can we hope to understand the problems sufficiently to overcome them.

Yet, as victims, women must realize they are not the only ones being exploited. According to Ghandian philosophy and as indicated by the slave-holding societies of the past, not only the victim but the exploiter, too, is debased and degraded in the process of oppression. As a movement of liberation, feminism cannot succeed if it fails to realize that men, be they corporate or military executives, have to be liberated too. It matters little whether the inhuman character of the relationship is perceived by either side in its true light, or whether the exact nature of the relationship is

worked out analytically and rationally, if the ingredient
necessary to bring about change is absent--hence the
"splendid failures" of all kinds of liberation movements
in the recent past. While concentrating on understanding
the true nature of exploitative relationships, feminists
must communicate the same to "fellow victims" 33/ and
ensure that the insight is in some way shared and
accepted by "the other side." Short of violent
confrontation with the "other," feminism has to do the
job of convincing "fellow victims." What this means when
the military powers of countries are concerned presents a
difficult, but by no means insoluble, problem.

Women must realize the extent to which they
contribute to sexism through the acceptance of male
superiority, intimidation, and force, and through their
willingness to buy into the system that exploits them by
adopting the philosophy "if you can't beat them, join
them." Women should not allow men to determine the
extent of female participation in the military--that is,
whether they should be included in the draft, what
functions they should serve, and so on. "For many women
the issue is about the reclaiming of power for
themselves, and not remaining victims of a male defined
world characterized by violence." 34/ The issue is also
about rejecting the traditions of thousands of years of
history that have allowed men in power to make decisions
in opposition to female needs and wishes. Women need to
say no to the sick mentality (perpetrated by the U.S.
military) that is based on greed, arrogance,
competitiveness and disrespect for human life and human
needs. Women need to say no to a mentality that reduces
people to the level of numbers and things, manipulates
and stereotypes our thoughts in the name of education,
and allows the destruction of life through the
manipulation of language and abstractions such as
patriotism, responsibility, and freedom. They need to
say no to a system in which following orders is seen as a
greater good than following conscience. As Thoreau so
eloquently noted, "It is not desirable to cultivate a
respect for the law, so much as for the right." 35/ And
they need to say no to a system that could alleviate
starvation and disease but prefers instead increased
military expenditures and what the established order
deems "security." Women would benefit greatly from
studying the linkage between feminist goals and a
redefinition of security that

includes all aspects of the human experience which permits people to live reasonably free of fear and to pursue the multiple goals and tasks of human beings in society...a condition based upon the expectations that human needs will be met and that people will not suffer harm at the hands of other human beings. 36/

Finally, women need to say no to a system that labels them unstable, weak, irrational, naive, oversensitive, or unrealistic if they oppose prevailing ideologies, circumstances, measures, or social or government policies.

These are the real reasons for which women's participation in the military must be seen as a setback for feminism in the United States and throughout the world. Such participation encourages a system of warped values that demeans, objectifies, and destroys life, maintains an unjust world order and prevents a just one, and supports apartheid and state terrorist activity while discouraging the peaceful overthrow of dictatorial and cruel regimes, expecting women to support this policy.

NOTES

1. Betty A. Reardon, Sexism and the War System, p. 3.

2. Donna Warnock, "Patriarchy is a Killer," in Pam McAllister, ed. Reweaving the Web of Life: Feminism and Nonviolence, p. 29.

3. Cynthia Enloe, Does Khaki Become You? The Militarization of Women's Lives, p. 208.

4. Helen Michalowski, "The Army Will Make a Man Out of You," in McAllister, ed., Reweaving the Web of Life: Feminism and Nonviolence, p. 335.

5. Helen Rogan, Mixed Company: Women in the Modern Army, p. 22.

6. Enloe, Does Khaki Become You?, pp. 1-6, 22, 122.

7. Nira Yuval Davis, "Front and Rear: The Sexual Division of Labor in the Israeli Army," in Feminist Studies, Vol.2, No. 3 (Fall 1985),p. 671.

8. Enloe, Does Khaki Become You?, p. 1.

9. Ibid., p. 2.

10. Ibid., p. 15.

11. Rogan, Mixed Company, p. 129.

12. Judith Hicks Stiehm, "The Generations of U.S. Enlisted Women," Signs: Journal of Women in Culture and Society, Vol. 2, No. 1 (Autumn 1985), p. 159.

13. Enloe, Does Khaki Become You?, p. 133.

14. Ibid., p. 135.

15. Stiehm, "The Generations," p. 160..

16. Ibid., p. 161.

17. Davis, "Front and Rear," p. 672.

18. Ibid., p. 649.

19. Karen Lindsey, "Women and the Draft," in McAllister, ed., Reweaving the Web of Life: Feminism and Nonviolence, p. 324.

20. Micaela di Leonardo, "Morals, Mothers and Militarism: Antimilitarism and Feminist Theory," Feminist Studies, Vol. 2, No. 3 (Fall 1985), pp. 610-611.

21. Michalowski, "The Army," p. 328.

22. Ibid., p. 327.

23. Ibid., p. 330.

24. Cynthia Adock, "Fear of 'Other': The Common Root of Sexism and Militarism," in McAllister, Reweaving the Web of Life: Feminist and Nonviolence, p. 210.

25. Reardon, Sexism p. 58.

26. Catherine Reid, "Reweaving the Web of Life," in McAllister, ed., Reweaving the Web of Life: Feminism and Nonviolence, pp. 289:290.

27. di Leonardo, p. 615.

28. Reardon, Sexism p. 26.

29. Ibid., p. 28.

30. Barbara Roberts and David Millder, "A Peaceful World for Women: Peace Education Taking Gender into Account," The History and Social Science Teacher, Vol. 20, No. 3/4 (Spring 1985), p. 45.

31. Reardon, Sexism pp. 37-38.

32. Stiehm, "The Generations," p. 174.

33. Betty Friedan, The Feminine Mystique, New York, Norton, 1963.

34. Alice Cook and Gwyn Kirk, Greenham Women Everywhere, p. 87.

35. Henry Thoreau, "Civil Disobedience," in Carl Boder, ed., The Portable Thoreau, p. 111.

36. Betty Reardon, Militarization, Security and Peace Education: A Guide for Concerned Citizens, p. 14.

12

The Development of Peace and Peace Education Concepts Through Three UN Women Decade Conferences

Birgit Brock-Utne

THE UN DECADE FOR WOMEN

In 1972, the General Assembly, in Resolution 3010 (XXVII), proclaimed 1975 International Women's Year. That year was to be devoted to three main goals: (1) intensified action to promote equality between men and women; (2) the full integration of women in the total development effort; and (3) an increase in the contribution of women to the strengthening of world peace.

In 1975 the World Conference of the International Women's Year was held in Mexico City. We would do well to remember that Resolution 3010 by the General Assembly, as well as the following world conference in Mexico City, would never have happened had it not been for the strength of the women's movement and the intense lobbying of nongovernmental organizations. Although the non-governmental pressure groups were very instrumental in bringing it about, they quite naturally played a less important role in the conference itself. The conference included UN member states. It adopted a World Plan of Action for the Implementation of the Objectives of the International Women's Year and it suggested that the decade 1976–1985 should be named the UN Decade for Women. The General Assembly of the UN in its Resolution 3520 (XXX) endorsed the World Plan of Action and officially proclaimed 1976–1985 the United Nations Decade for Women: Equality, Development, and Peace. The General Assembly decided to hold a new conference in Copenhagen in 1980 to review and evaluate the progress made in the first half of the decade. The nongovernmental organizations, which had worked hard to get the conferences off the ground, knowing that they would be state conferences, organized alternative conferences at the same location and partly overlapping in time with the official conferences. In

Mexico the alternative conference was called "Tribuna", in Copenhagen and in Nairobi they were called "Forums." The alternative conferences have been growing in size, in magnitude, and in the types of activities they present.

In 1980 the Copenhagen World Conference adopted the Programme of Action for the Second Half of the United Nation's Decade for Women. The programme was endorsed by the General Assembly later the same year (Resolution 35/137), when the additional decision was made that a new conference would be held in Nairobi in the summer of 1985. The General Assembly confirmed the goals and objectives of the Decade (equality, development, and peace), stressed their validity for the future, and indicated the need for concrete measures to overcome the obstacles to their achievement during the period 1986-2000.

In this chapter we shall look at the development of the peace concept as it has been used in the official documents coming out of the three conferences--the first one in Mexico in 1975, the second in Copenhagen in 1980, and the third in Nairobi in 1985. We shall also look at what the documents say about the participation and insights of women in decisionmaking regarding peace.

PEACE CONCEPTS

The definition of peace has been the object of much controversy among peace researchers. (For a discussion of the way the peace concept has been used in the Journal of Peace Research in the first seventeen years of its existence, see Wiberg, 1981. For another overview of the peace concept in various cultures, see Ishida, 1969.) Here I use a distinction developed by Johan Galtung (1969) more than fifteen years ago. Galtung defines peace as the absence of violence; he also makes an important distinction between personal or direct violence and structural violence: "We shall refer to the type of violence where there is an actor that commits the violence as personal or direct, and to violence where there is no such actor as structural or indirect." (Galtung, 1969, p. 170). In the last case the violence is built into the structure and takes the form of unequal opportunity. In this chapter I use Galtung's term structural violence in the way he has defined it. I reserve the phrase direct violence for the use of physical violence that leads to maiming, to a shorter period of life, or to death. I also make a distinction between violence on the micro-level (usually involving one victim) and collective violence on the macro-level (involving thousands or millions of victims). Using these categories I have arrived at the following four fold diagram:

	direct violence	structural violence
personal violence (micro-level)		
collective violence (macro-level)		

This four fold diagram is useful when analyzing the violence women are subjected to (see, for example, Brock-Utne, 1986). When women are raped, beaten, and/or mutilated in their homes; they are victims of both personal and direct violence against women. In India the many cases of dowry deaths have received increased attention (Kelkar, 1983) They are clear examples of direct violence against women on the personal or micro-level. Wars are examples of direct violence on the macro-level. In modern warfare (as in Korea or Vietnam) more civilians have been killed than soldiers. Examples of structural violence at the micro-level are the uneven distribution of resources within the family units. Even within the refugee families in refugee camps one finds this uneven distribution. To quote the UN High Commissioner for Refugees: "Relief workers have become familiar with the sight of well-fed men alongside under-fed and sickly women and children" (UN High Commissioner for Refugees, 1980, p. 7).

We find examples of a more collective type of structural violence against women when we look at the statistics presented at the Copenhagen conference. These statistics reveal that women do more than 65 percent of the work of the world, receive ten percent of the salaries, and own one percent of the property.

Johan Galtung applied the various concepts of violence to the situation of women in 1969. In this study he notes that "when one husband beats his wife, there is a clear case of personal violence, but when one million husbands keep one million wives in ignorance, there is structural violence" (Galtung, 1969, p. 171). Likewise, women peace researchers have argued for a peace concept that rules out violence and atrocities against women in so-called peacetime (see, for example, Reardon, 1985; Brock-Utne, 1981a; Brock-Utne, 1983a; Brock-Utne, 1985). Some radical feminists who have warned women against joining the peace movement have asked: What is in it for us? Whose peace are we fighting for? (See, for example, Breaching the Peace, 1983.) They are afraid that women are once again fighting for a "cause that is bigger than our own liberation." They remind us of all the times in history (or rather herstory) that we have suspended our own fight against oppression and then have been relegated to the lowest positions once that fight was won. At those times we have been even worse off than before we fought alongside our men for some big cause like the abolition of a war or a revolution. We are still at war with male society.

The anger voiced by these feminists is understandable. They feel that women are asked to help men clean up the mess they have created; just as mothers generally help small boys clean up. But what guarantees do we have that the war against women will cease--that we are not merely helping one group of men hold on to their share of the 99 percent of the world resources against another group of men? Do we, the women of the world, get some of that 99 percent? Or shall we continue to own the one percent that the UN figures say we own?

Feminist analysis has shown that women's oppression is fundamental to the maintenance of a system that is the backbone of our destructive society. It is not a secondary issue to be attended to "after the revolution" or after general and complete disarmament has been reached. You can't transform a destructive society without dealing with the oppression of women.

How much of this feminist understanding is reflected in the peace concepts used in the three conference documents? What is said about peace in these plans of action?

In the world plan of action from Mexico very little is said about peace at all. A feminist perspective on peace is not developed in the text. What is said about the content of the peace concept is found in paragraph 50: "An essential condition for the maintenance and strengthening of peace is the promotion and protection of human rights for all in conditions of equity among and within nations..." This paragraph does not say very much. The human rights concept may be as inclusive as the peace concept. It includes the right to life in peace, the right to food, and the right to express opinions freely. But the concept has not been made gender-specific. Paragraph 50 (like the remaining peace paragraphs in the Mexico document) is gender-neutral and does not take account of the fact that so-called private violence against women, mostly committed within the family, has not been singled out for special attention as part of the human rights concept.

In the Programme of Action for the Second Half of the UN Decade for Women (the Copenhagen document), we find that the peace concept is explicitly dealt with only in paragraph 5:

> Without peace and stability there can be no development. Peace is thus a prerequisite to development. Moreover, peace will not be lasting without development and the elimination of inequality and discrimination at all levels. Equality of participation in the development of friendly relations and co-operation among States will contribute to the strengthening of peace, to the development of women themselves and to equality of rights at all levels and in all spheres of life...

Again there no acknowledgment of the gender-specific problems of women. The document maintaines that the participation of women in the development of friendly relations among states will contribute to peace. Here peace is taken to mean the absence of direct and collective violence between states (i.e., the absence of war). It does not mean the absence of direct personal violence against women in so-called peaceful times.

In the same document we find other paragraphs dealing with violence against women. But they are not made part of the peace concept. We find this insight in paragraph 11, for instance:

> ...Women have often been regarded and treated as inferior and unequal in their activities outside the

domestic sphere and have suffered violations of their human rights. They have been given only limited access to resources and participation in all spheres of life, notably in decision-making, and in many instances institutionalized inequality in the status of women and men has also resulted...

In contrast to the plan of action from Mexico, the Copenhagen document singles out women as a special group with respect to violations of human rights. Paragraph 11 deals with the collective structural violence experienced by women. We find another paragraph (141f) in the Copenhagen plan of action dealing with direct violence against women on the micro-level (so-called personal violence), but this paragraph does not occur in the context of the peace concept. In particular, paragraph 141f makes reference to

...policies and programmes aimed at the elimination of all forms of violence against women and children and the protection of women of all ages from the physical and mental abuse resulting from domestic violence, sexual assault, sexual exploitation and any other forms of abuse...

Of the three documents analyzed, only the one from Nairobi sees the absence of personal, collective, direct, and structural violence against women as part of the peace concept. In paragraph 257 we find the following sentences:

The questions of women and peace and the meaning of peace for women cannot be separated from the broader question of relationships between women and men in all spheres of life and in the family. Discriminatory practices and negative attitudes towards women should be eliminated and traditional gender norms changed to enhance women's participation in peace.

And in paragraph 258 we find a definition of peace for which feminist have been arguing. There is no peace as long as women are being beaten, as long as so-called private violence exists in the home.

Violence against women exists in various forms in everyday life in all societies. Women are being beaten, multilated, burned, sexually abused and raped. Such violence is a major obstacle to the achievement of peace and the other objectives of the Decade and should be given special attention... National machinery should be established in order to deal with the question of violence against women within the family and society...

In short, the Nairobi document acknowledges that there is no peace where domestic violence exists.

THE PARTICIPATION OF WOMEN IN DECISIONMAKING REGARDING PEACE

All three documents contain wording that pertains to the participation of women in decisionmaking regarding peace. Peace is taken to mean the absence of collective and direct violence between states. It is interesting to note the feminist perspective underlying the statements about the participation of women in questions relating to peace. I shall not analyze all of the feminist perspectives that could have been applied, but I will roughly delineate two: the liberal feminist perspective and the radical one. The liberal perspective was (already worked out) by John Stuart Mill, but we find it practiced by many contemporary feminist writers (e.g., Lin Farley and Sheer Hite) and by large organizations (such as the National Organization of Women or NOW). According to this perspective, women should participate in decision making because they may feel unfairly discriminated against if they are left out of it. Equality with men means being represented in the same number as men in whatever job or institution men have created. During debate with Johan Galtung some years ago I remember him asking: "Will you women be content if you constitute half of the members of the KGB?" His point is well taken in that it expresses the same criticism radical feminists have had of the liberal paradigm in women studies. Of importance to this paradigm are phrases such as equality with men, equal opportunities, and no discrimination. Equality is a value in itself within this paradigm. The question "equal to what?" is rarely asked by anyone.

Researchers using a radical feminist perspective for their analysis are more concerned about liberation than about equality. They are concerned about liberation from capitalist and patriarchic structures. When they talk about equality, they generally pose the question "on whose premises?" Women do not want to become equal to leading men; rather, they want the opportunity to develop their own frameworks and insights. When they express a desire to participate in decisionmaking regarding peace, it is not because they feel that they will be left out if they do not participate but because they believe that women (especially if they are feminists) have valuable new insights to offer and special qualifications and abilities that would be useful around the negotiating table. The radical feminist perspective has been and is being developed by such women as Shulamith Firestone, Dale Spender, Adrienne Rich, Ann Ferguson, Christine Delphy, Ann Oakley, Berit As, Runa Haukaa, and Birgit Brock-Utne.

In the world plan of action from Mexico women are encouraged to participate on an equal footing with men in their endeavors to secure peace. Women should be co-equals in this struggle. The underlying perspective is a liberal one. There is no mention of women having a special role to play. The claim is made that women should be more involved in the strengthening of peace, but only as supporters and co-equals of men. To quote paragraph 50:

> In order to involve more women in the promotion of international cooperation, the development of friendly relations among nations, [and] the strengthening of international peace and disarmament...the peace efforts of women as individuals and in groups, and in national and international organizations should be recognized and encouraged.

The role of women as supporters of the peace efforts of men is stressed in paragraph 51:

> Women of all countries of the world should proclaim their solidarity in support of the elimination of gross violations of human rights condemned by the United Nations and contrary to its principles involving acts against the moral and physical integrity of individuals or groups of individuals for political or ideological reasons.

And in paragraph 52 we read that

> ...Women should be given every encouragement to
> participate actively in the endeavours of inter-
> governmental and non-governmental organizations
> having as their aim the strengthening of
> international security and peace...

Paragraph 53 deals with the proclamation of a special day
to be devoted to peace and celebrated every year. This
day should be proclaimed by the United Nations. On this
day, meetings and seminars about peace should be
organized and given wide coverage in the press and other
communication media. And the role of women? "Women
should lend their full support to these objectives and
explore, as co-equals with men, ways to overcome existing
obstacles to the strengthening of international peace..."
Again, the supporter role is delineated in the absence of
other perspectives.

The Mexican document is built on the liberal, equal-
opportunity paradigm. According to paragraph 56:

> Women should have equal opportunity with men to
> represent their countries in all international
> forums...and in particular at meetings of the
> organizations of the United Nations systems,
> including the Security Council and all conferences
> on disarmament and international peace and other
> regional bodies.

The Copenhagen document contains the same liberal
feminist perspective as that found in the Mexico document
with respect to the role of women in decisionmaking
related to peace. The importance of women working for
peace alongside men is again stressed. But the wording
is more "impatient." Women should not only have equal
opportunity to represent their countries (as stated in
the 1975 document); they should be equitably represented.
(as stated in the 1980 document). According to paragraph
73, "Women should be equitably represented at all levels,
especially the senior levels, in delegations to international bodies, conferences and committees dealing with
political, economic and legal questions, disarmament and
other similar issues..."

This impatient wording can be found elsewhere as
well. In paragraph 71 governments are asked to establish

goals, strategies, and timetables, and to undertake special activities for increasing the number of women in public functions at all levels, in order that women should be equitably represented. This objective is further detailed in paragraph 72.

The impatience of this language is understandable. In 1979, despite the references in the Mexican document to equal opportunities for women to participate in disarmament conferences, there was not a single woman present in the strategic arms limitation talks (SALT) in either of the delegations of the superpowers. Nor was a single woman present in the U.S. Senate hearings in connection with the SALT negotiations (Lall, 1979).

But both the Copenhagen document and the Mexican document state that women should be in the delegations not because they represent a special insight but because their exclusion would be discriminatory. And so it is.

It is only when we come to the Nairobi document that we find either an acknowledgment of women's special role in peace building and maintenance or the use of a radical feminist perspective. Women want to participate in decisionmaking related to peace in order to provide woman-made solutions to man-made problems. Women do not want to provide the same man-made solutions that men have developed because they do not seem to work.

First we turn to two paragraphs in the Nairobi document that call to mind passages in both the Mexican and Copenhagen documents having to do with the participation of women in decisionmaking concerning peace issues. Paragraph 235 of the Nairobi document states that "universal and durable peace cannot be attained without the full and equal participation of women in international relations, particularly in decisionmaking concerning peace..." And in paragraph 237 we find the following sentence: "All obstacles at national and international levels in the way of women's participation in promoting international peace and cooperation should be removed as soon as possible."

It is up to women to discuss what these obstacles are and how they can be removed. It was not difficult for an observer at the official conference like myself to notice that women speakers spoke on the widening of the peace concept, on violence against women, and on prostitution and rape while the men in the delegations took over when issues concerning the arms race were under debate. A ten-minute discussion on weapons in space,

(Star Wars), was conducted in Commission II between two males--the one representing the USSR, the other representing the United States. Why did the men move into the delegations when issues concerning the arms race were on the agenda? Part of the reason is the fact that these issues are normally dealt with by foreign ministries and very few women have qualified jobs in these ministries. The civil servants dealing with peace issues are almost entirely male. Governments are given the following advice in paragraph 267 of the Nairobi document:

> Governments which have not done so should undertake all appropriate measures to eliminate existing discriminatory practices towards women and provide them with equal opportunities to join, at all levels, the civil service, to enter the diplomatic service and to represent their countries as members of delegations to national, regional and international meetings, including conferences on peace, conflict resolution, disarmament, and meetings of the Security Council and other United Nations bodies.

Paragraph 268 goes even further. Here governments are not only asked to eliminate existing discriminatory practices preventing women from joining the civil service and representing their countries. In paragraph 268 they are also asked to give women financial support to acquire the traditional qualifications in the field of international security: "Women should be encouraged and given financial support to take university courses in government, international relations and diplomacy in order to obtain necessary professional qualifications for careers in fields relating to peace and international security."

These paragraphs point to one measure that can be taken if the aim is to have more women participate in disarmament negotiations. More women should be recruited as civil servants. But another way to get women into these negotiations is to recruit them from outside the regular governmental channels and the diplomatic services. We know that women possess both the skills and the knowledge necessary to participate in disarmament negotiations. Women are extremely active participants in nongovernmental peace movements. And women have

organized their own peace movements all over the world;
consider, for instance, the Australian Women for
Survival, the British Women at Greenham Common Air Base,
the Nordic Women for Peace, and the Argentinian Mothers
of Plaza de Mayo. (For further documentation, see
Brock-Utne, 1985, p. 45-61.) The knowledge base within
these women peace movements is quite wide. Women have
studied military documents. They have also learned to
talk about the technicalities of the arms race. Yet they
have not forgotten such important factors as the social
and human consequences of the use of modern weaponry.
Clearly it would be a good idea to recruit women from
non- governmental peace movements to the disarmament
negotia- tions. A provision to do so is given in
paragraph 266 of the Nairobi document.

The organizational means that could be taken to
facilitate the participation of women in the decision-
making process related to the promotion of international
peace would be the opening up of delegations to include
women peace researchers and peace activists who have
acquired their competence outside of government. If
women are to be equitably represented in the
decisionmaking on peace issues, they will also have to be
recruited from grass-roots and professional organizations
working for peace. The equitable representation of women
is stressed in paragraph 269 of the Nairobi document.

All of the paragraphs quoted so far deal with the
participation of women in decisionmaking related to peace
within a more liberal feminist perspective. Women should
be equally represented in the interests of fairness. But
the Nairobi document is more concrete when it comes to
actions that have to be implemented in order to increase
the number of women in decisionmaking on peace issues.
In this connection governments are encouraged to give
women financial support to get the necessary qualifications to participate on an equal footing with men.

Is the absence of women from decisionmaking on
global issues wrong only because it points up the
discrimination against women and the lack of equality
between men and women? Or is there also reason to
believe that this exclusion will be detrimental to
humankind because women could otherwise bring to such
decisionmaking different and highly needed perspectives?
The Nairobi document clearly acknowledges that humankind
is worse off because the women's perspective is lacking.
We know that women politicians often have priorities

different from those of male politicians of the same
party when it comes to questions concerning military
expenditures. Opinion polls all over the world tell us
that women in general object more strenuously to war toys
than men do, oppose the stationing of nuclear missiles to
a greater degree than men do, and are more sympatheti-
cally inclined toward conscientious objectors (see
Brock-Utne, 1985, pp. 33-34). According to paragraph 16
of the Nairobi document: "The need for women's
perspective on human development is critical since it is
in the interest of human enrichment and progress to
introduce and weave into the social fabric alternative
development strategies and their approach to peace..."
This paragraph clearly gives credit to the women's
approach to peace. The Nairobi document, with its
acknowledgment of women's special insights, marks a
paradigm shift from a liberal to a radical feminist
perspective. Women are invited to participate on an
equal footing with men not only because it is unfair if
they are not equally represented but also because women's
perspectives are needed. This radical feminist
perspective is seldom acknowledged in public debates.

The question arises as to how this approach can best
be cultivated. How many women have been asked to sit on
a male-dominated committee simply because a woman is
needed on the committee? But when women do serve on such
committees, they are supposed to behave exactly like men.
In many respects it is difficult for women not to use a
stereotypical male approach because much of their
training is in male-oriented thinking. Women receive
this training in the university system, in government,
and in diplomatic service. But women need to have their
own institutions and organizations, and to develop their
own thinking even if it collides with the "official" male
thinking of their time. In the Nairobi document we find
acknowledgment of this insight. According to paragraph
32,

> To promote their interest effectively, women must be
> able to enjoy their right to take part in national
> and international decision-making processes,
> including the right to dissent publicly and
> peacefully from their Government's policies, and to
> mobilize and increase their participation in the
> promotion of peace within and between nations.

Governments have agreed that women should be able to express public dissent against the policies of the male-dominated governments of the world. Women are encouraged to make their voices heard on matters that promote peace within and between countries.

The paragraphs we have studied so far legitimize, even encourage, women to cultivate their own approach to peace. Several other paragraphs encourage women to unite in working out their own perspective and to fight the oppression facing them. For instance, paragraph 33 states that

"success will depend in large measure upon whether or not women can unite to help each other to change their poor material circumstances. Networking will increase the effectiveness of the political action taken by women so that they can obtain a much greater share in political decision-making than before.

In paragraph 241 women are urged to support one another when dealing with universal issues such as disarmament. In paragraph 90 women are encouraged to help one another get elected and to participate in the political process on all levels. And paragraph 348 suggests that "training programmes for and consultations between women already engaged in political life should be organized." These training programmes can be organized on the local or national level. They can also be organized on the regional or international level. Such meetings among women already engaged in political life would be good places to discuss a feminist approach to peace. Indeed, women politicians working for peace, women peace researchers, and women peace activists would benefit greatly from meeting one another regularly to work out women's approach to peace. To quote paragraph 360:

Networking of women at high decision-making levels related to peace and disarmament, including women leaders, peace researchers and peace educators, should also be encouraged in connection with United Nations system activities such as the International Year of Peace (1986). "Women and peace" should be a separate item in the programme for that Year.

But, alas, we know that the International Year of
Peace was given very limited funds by governments, and
there is little money available for the networking of
women at high decisionmaking levels. Nevertheless, as
noted in paragraph 276: "Women Parliamentarians should
always be included in delegations to inter-parliamentary
meetings organized by the inter-Parliamentary Union and
regional interparliamentary organizations." And in
paragraph 276 women peace researchers are singled out for
attention:

> The participation of women in peace research,
> including research on women and peace, should be
> encouraged. Existing barriers to women researchers
> should be removed and appropriate resources provided
> for peace researchers. Cooperation amongst peace
> researchers, government officials, non-governmental
> organizations and activitists should be encouraged
> and fostered.

These ideas certainly need to be implemented. Women
peace researchers have priorities different from those of
male peace researchers (see, for example, Boulding,
1981; Brock-Utne, 1985). A dialogue between women peace
researchers and World Women Parliamentarians for Peace is
bound to be of particular interest and to come up with
new ideas. In her study of women peace researchers, the
American sociologist Elise Boulding (1981) quoted these
researchers as saying that there had been too much
mindless data-gathering in peace research, too much
preoccupation with the technicalities of the arms race,
and too little research on alternative conflict solutions
and on the human and social aspects of the arms race.

In paragraphs 335 and 355 of the Nairobi document,
the United Nations system is encouraged to give
assistance to women working for peace. However, it ought
to be rather obvious that if governments want women to
work out "women's approach to peace," women have to be
given the necessary infrastructure to do so. In other
words, technical assistance is needed along with economic
resources so that women can take time off from other work
to travel and meet each other.

PEACE EDUCATION

We shall now take a look at the way the three documents treat the concept of peace education and women's role in peace education. What is said about the content of peace education? Is there any acknowledgment of the fact that women have worked very hard and in their own ways to promote peace between nations? (For documentation, see Brock-Utne, 1985.) A more radical feminist perspective would certainly not overlook this fact. From such a perspective peace education would not be seen as gender-neutral. The fact that some boys are taught the role of oppressor and girls the role of the oppressed, and that violence and outward aggression are discouraged in girls but encouraged in boys, is a topic of concern for any analysis of peace education from a feminist perspective.

In the Mexican document, the term peace education is not mentioned. But paragraph 55 deals with education for global understanding. This paragraph is gender-neutral and seems to suggest that it is the responsibility of parents to instill the values of international cooperation, peace, and security in the world in their children. The role of the schooling system in this respect is not mentioned.

In the Copenhagen document, too, there is no mention of the term peace education. But concepts normally included in the category of peace education are contained in some of the paragraphs (for an analysis of the peace education concept, see Brock-Utne, 1981b; and Borelli and Haavelsrud, 1983). In paragraph 167 we find the concept of "education for nonviolence," in paragraph 185 human rights education is encouraged; and in paragraph 168 the term education against violence is used. What these paragraphs are saying is that men and women should be trained not to use violence against each other. The gender-neutral form used in paragraphs 167 and 168 conceals the fact that where violence in relationships between women and men is concerned, men are usually the aggressors, and women are usually the victims. Hence such education is more sorely needed for men than for women.

One of the priority areas for action within the educational sector mentioned in paragraph 185 of the Copenhagen document is to

> develop programmes at the secondary, tertiary and
> adult education levels to encourage a basic
> understanding of human rights, including the
> Declaration of Human Rights and other relevant
> instruments. Such courses should stress the
> fundamental importance of the elimination of
> discrimination on the basis of race and sex.

This paragraph may be said to contain a feminist
perspective, albeit a liberal one, inasmuch as it sees
the elimination of sex discrimination as forming part of
a human rights concept.

Whereas the Mexican document deals with education
for peace, the Copenhagen document (with its emphasis on
educational programmes) deals with an education about
peace, nonviolence, disarmament and human rights--even
though it never uses the term education about peace.

Paragraph 76 legitimizes the provision of a more
formal peace education in this case, for women
especially. But it says nothing about the inclusion of a
feminist perspective in the lectures on international
affairs. Rather, women may simply become trained in
mainstream (or rather malestream) thinking and learn
little about the peace activities of women through the
ages.

In the Nairobi document the term peace education is
used several times. When we look at all three documents
resulting from the three UN conferences, there is no
doubt that peace education as a distinct area of concern
for educators and policy planners was first introduced in
the Nairobi document. It is there that we also find a
distinction between nonformal education for peace and for
disarmament and more formal education about or on peace.
Paragraph 255 states that "peace education should be
established for all members of society, particularly
children and young people. Values, such as tolerance,
racial and sexual equality, respect for and understanding
of others, and good-neighbourliness should be developed,
promoted and strengthened." The following paragraph
stresses that peace education "should be part of all
formal and informal educational processes as well as of
communications, information and mass-media systems."
Paragraphs 272 as 274 and 263 deal with the role of women
in peace education. Paragraphs 273 and 274 deal with
the content of peace education. The first concerns what
should be discouraged in a child's environment in

the interests of peace education; the second concerns what should be encouraged and included in peace education.

But nothing is said in these paragraphs about the fact that boys and girls are educated very differently in all societies, and that games favoring aggression and violence are aimed at and played by the boys in particular. This fact ought to be given more attention in research studies.

In paragraph 274 governments, educational institutions, professional associations and nongovernmental organizations are asked to cooperate in the development of high-quality programs, books, and materials on peace education. But we have to turn to paragraph 344 to find that the role of women in promoting peace should constitute an important element in peace education. Here international machineries that promote and support education for peace are asked to "coordinate their efforts and include the role of women in promoting peace in their curricula."

This document from Nairobi signifies a big leap forward in feminist understanding; indicates a paradigm shift from a liberal to a more radical feminist perspective, and puts women on the agenda both as peacemakers and peacekeepers. It is now up to women to follow up.

BIBLIOGRAPHY

Borrelli, Mario and Magnus Haavelsrud, August 1983. The Development of the Concept of Peace Education Within the Archipelago of Peace Research. Monograph synthesizing papers presented to the 10th General Conference of IPRA, Gyor, Hungary.

Boulding, Elise. 1981. "Perspectives of Women Researchers on Disarmament: National Security and World Order." Women's Studies International Quarterly, Vol. 4, No.1, pp. 27-41.

Breaching the Peace. 1983. A Collection of Radical Feminist Papers. London: Only Women Press, Ltd.

Brock-Utne, Birgit. 1981a. "The Role of Women as Mothers and Members of Society in the Education of Young People for Peace, Mutual Understanding and Respect for Human Rights." Paper commissioned for a UNESCO expert meeting on the role of women in peace education. New Delhi, India, December 7-11. (ED-81/CON.609/2 and PRIO publication S-12/81).

Brock-Utne, Birgit. 1981b. "Disarmament Education as a Distinct Field of Study," edited by Yoshikazu Saleamuto and Ruth Klassen. Paper presented at the 9th General Conference of IPRA, Toronto, Canada, June 21-26. Published in the IPRA Proceedings of the 9th General Conference of IPRA.

Brock-Utne, Birgit. 1983a. "Research on Women and Peace." Paper prepared on request for the expert group meeting on the participation of women in promoting international peace and cooperation held in Vienna, December 5-9. An extract is available in UN Document no. AWB/EGM.83.1/CS/2.22 (November 1983).

Brock-Utne, Brigit. 1983b. "Likestilt til a drepe" (Equal to kill). NY Tids Kronikk (April 12).

Brock-Utne, Birgit. 1984. "The Relationship of Feminism to Peace and Peace Education." Bulletin of Peace Proposals, Vol. 15, No. 2, pp. 149-154.

Brock-Utne, Birgit. 1985. Educating for Peace: A Feminist Perspective. New York, Oxford, and Toronto: Pergamon Press (2nd printing, 1987; translated into Korean in 1986, into Norwegian 1987, and into Italian in 1988).

Brock-Utne, Birgit. 1986. "Kvinner og Fred po Forum, po den offisielle Konferansen og framover" (Women and peace at Forum, at the official conference and in the future). PRIO-INFORM 4/1986.

Galtung, Johan. 1969. "Violence, Peace and Peace Research." Journal of Peace Research. Vol.6. no.3; pp.167-191.

Green, Frankie. 1983. "Not Weaving but Frowning." In Breaching the Peace.

Ishida, Takeshi. 1969. "Beyond the Traditional Concepts of Peace in Different Cultures." Journal of Peace Research,Vol. 6, No. 2, pp. 133-145.

Jaggar, Alison and Paula Rothenberg. 1984. Feminist Frameworks. New York: McGraw Hill.

Kelkar, Govind. 1983. Women and Structural Violence in India. Paper presented at the UNESCO/IPRA consultation on women, militarism, and disarmament in Gyor, Hungary, August 25-28.

Lall, Betty Goetz. 1979. "SALT and the Coming Public Debate." Women Lawyer's Journal. Vol. 65, No.2.

Pietilo, Hilkka. April 1985. What Eoes the United
    Nations Mean to Women? An NGO View. Geneve:
    United Nations Non-Governmental Liason Service.
Reardon, Betty. 1985. Sexism and the War System.
    New York: Columbia University.
UN High Commissioner for Refugees. 1980. "The Situation
    for Women Refugees the World Over." Document
    No.A/CONF.94/24, presented to the World Conference
    of the United Nations Decade for Women.
Wiberg, Hakan. 1981. "Journal of Peace Research 1964-
    1980--What Have We Learned About Peace?" Journal of
    Peace Research, Vol. 18, No.2, pp.111-148.
Woolf, Virginia. 1938. Three Gunieas. London: Hogarth
    Press (reprinted by Penguin Books, New York, 1977).

13

Women, Science Education and Action for Peace

Robin Burns

WOMEN, SCIENCE EDUCATION AND ACTION FOR PEACE

In this paper I wish to examine the following propositions:
1. That science is a cultural phenomenon and should be examined as such;
2. That the failure to recognize scientific culture and to examine its claims has led to a failure to distinguish between other cultures co-existing within particular societies and to take over scientific worldviews and legitimations as the best method of generating knowledge and of steering a society;
3. That the examination of scientific culture is essential to understandits claims and limitations;
4. That the methods of recruitment of scientists into the dominant scientific culture indicate ideological presuppositions which are sexist, racist and militarist;
5. That the teaching of science without an understanding of its cultural base and without a critical examination of its relationship to society is a barrier to the attainment of peace.

These are widesweeping propositions. At a time when scientific results can be used to save or to destroy the world, and when the scientisation of education and society is leading to an uncritical attempt to recruit individuals to science, in the name of social progress, the myths of science urgently require examination.

SCIENCE AS A CULTURAL PHENOMENON

Two features of science as culture are especially relevant to the consideration of its role. The first is its pattern of recruitment, socialisation and enculturation, and the second is its worldview.

Entry into Scientific Culture

Welch (1978) provides a concise history of the rise of science in the universities of Europe in the 19th century and points to three publications, Darwin's Origin of Species (1859), and Marx's The Communist Manifesto (1848) and The Capital (1867), as vital steps in propagating a "more secular, less mythological view of the world" (p.124). The actual acceptance of science, and with it a more practical, even vocational, definition of education, has been a protracted and more complex process, with national variations, in turn determined by the particular definitions of knowledge, education and the role of both in society (see e.g. Burns, 1979; Cowen, 1971). But it now has a firm place in higher education, though Meyer (1984) suggests that in the Moslem world science rests uneasily with other epistemologies.

The path into science today is clearly through the formal educational system. More than any other area of curriculum, science is sequenced, so that it is difficult to enter after certain basic learnings have been undertaken. And while it is compulsory in most basic education, encouragement to continue is given to those considered the most apt pupils. Nations differ in the forms of post-compulsory education, and hence it is difficult to make more than broad generalizations, however it seems clear that factors which contribute to the success of pupils in science include "resource" variables (availability and qualifications of teachers, laboratories and equipment, timetabling considerations) and "motivational" ones (a complex including encouragement by teachers, parents and peers, perceived career opportunities, self-perception).

Two apparently conflicting principles of recruitment are at work: merit and the ascribed characteristics of sex and socio-economic status. In a society where access to high status jobs requires success in science subjects, equity principles play little role in the recruitment to, and distribution of resources for, scientific education.

What happens to those who are admitted? There is a prolonged period of "initiation," which bears some simililarities with pre-20th century notions of apprenticeship. While there may be certain extra-curricular activities involving initiative, for example talent quests, special camps and prizes, science curricula right up to the post-graduate level largely involve the mastery of techniques and a given body of knowledge. The student learns the rules, and is rewarded for assiduously applying them. Those who do well are invited to continue, but mostly require a "sponsor" to gain access to resources such as laboratory space and equipment, and the most common practice even for doctoral degrees is for the "supervisor" to include the student in a project on which he is currently working. In most cases access not only to resources but to outlets for results is controlled by the supervisor, for example, co-authorship of research papers. One must become part of a team, and one is dependent on continued sponsorship in order to disseminate one's work through conferences, journals and the like, all controlled by "proven", "eminent" elders. And while this pattern may differ little in the social sciences and humanities, the lower reliance on equipment makes it a little more possible for the individual to work alone, though the elders still control rewards. One gains admission, status and employment through compliance, as with any society or culture. The amount of "deviance" allowed depends on the discipline and its particular reward structure, which may in turn be partly dependent on its status vis-a-vis other disciplines (bio-technology, for example, seems to be enjoying current high status) and the capacity and willingness of the users of scientific results to pay for certain types of research and development.

The Scientific Worldview

Since the time of Bacon, a key element in the scientific worldview is its place in relationship to nature: science is to "conquer and subdue her, to shake her to her foundations" (quoted in Brock-Utne, 1985:113), thus science is for the conquering, subduing, penetrating of nature so that man can control not only his own destiny but that of the world at large, defined in material terms (I am deliberately using the male terms, since the opposition nature: culture, male: female is a pervasive one in most cultures and languages; the implications of this will be discussed later).

Both the human beings, the natural world and society become technically manipulable objects, knowable through certain observational methods characterized by "objectivity", and constructed into a system of "laws", according to which the truth or falsity of a statement or finding can be determined. The system is "closed" insofar as it determines the way in which knowledge which is legitimate is to be generated and therefore precludes challenges based on other premises. Specifically precluded are statements of values, in fact empirical science asserts as <u>credo</u> its value neutrality. That this value neutrality is mythical is seen when a scientific paradigm is considered as a social and cultural phenomenon, as well as an epistemological one. Science does have a worldview, which is translated into an ideology for socio-political practice through the application of empirical or pseudo-empirical techniques to the solution of social problems. It also has a power and interest structure, which because it contains in itself no adequate means for evaluation of its normative aspects, its myths and applications become self-perpetuating. This worldview has the political function of acting as a legitimating ideology for the application of scientific knowledge to the solution of problems outside its area of avowed application, especially to the solution of social and political problems. Its cultural function comes from the models of the person, society and knowledge inherent in it, which provide ideals for and critiques of practice in the continuous process of culture.

A normative feature of the scientific worldview in its unacknowledged value and interest (normative) structure, and its inability to be used for dialogue with other worldviews as a result of this denial and the absence of terms outside its own frame of reference for determining legitimacy. It lacks an "ethical groundplan" for evaluation of the contribution of science or scientists to wider society, and must therefore rest for its appeal on its own reward structure. This can even be maintained in the face of wider opposition, through recourse to the "proven" nature of the results which it produces and the superiority of its methods, although it seems currently more common for scientists to accommodate to the wider society, in the interests of their survival as scientists who require resources from others. It is at this point of interface between science and society that the unacknowledged interest structure of science becomes most apparent and the role of scientist qua scientist and qua citizen most blurred. It can at least be hypothesized that it is at this point, too, that the claims of science as a superior form of knowing, essential for proper social functioning, become most apparent. A method used to "protect" science and to continue its command of economic, political and social "capital" is to assert its superiority as a basis for social practice, which both de-legitimates the other bases and the worldviews on which they are premised, and discloses the cultural nature of science itself.

Implications of Science as a Dominant Worldview

If it is part of human cultural life to generate a worldview which is at least held as binding on its members and determines who shall, and who shall not, be admitted to membership, then it follows that the scientific worldview is but one of many. It also follows that those living within any society in which scientific activity takes place, but who are not themselves scientists, at least in part hold another worldview. This can even be seen within science, in its broader sense, where it is now recognized that, even if they do not currently hold as high a status or legitimacy, other ways of generating knowledge may be found. These ways include the hermeneutic and critical approaches or paradigms (see e.g. Burns, 1979, 1986; Easlea, 1973; Galtung, 1972; Lindholm, 1985; Naess, 1972; Radnitzky, 1972).

The previous section argued that the role of scientific culture in the wider society is a powerful one. That power is enhanced by reference to the merit principle, since it disguises the fact that non-compliance with its worldview is one basis for low merit and performance in science. And holders of other worldviews cannot argue, since they have no ground rules accepted by scientists for challenging it. Differential status is thus seen to be acquired and legitimated without reference to values, or by reference to scientific values which, because of their formal exclusion from the practice of science, are not open to question. Those whose worldviews are thus de-legitimated, are "legitimately" precluded from power.

Thus, through the transposition of the culture of science to a generalized, scientized culture, dominant over members and others within the structures within which it is maintained, a self-perpetuating basis for social inequality is established. And this inequality includes unequal access to the means to acquire a self concept to enable participation in politically effective alternative cultures.

Challenges to the Dominant Scientific Culture

The case has been made that it is difficult, in epistemological, political or personal terms, to challenge the dominance of the scientific culture, and that formal education is an important means for maintaining its position. Myths tend to be difficult to discredit, though like a knowledge paradigm, can eventually fail to provide a satisfactory guide to explain and symbolise human sociocultural life. It is argued that one step towards "de-mythologising" science is through its examination as a culture, which indicates the limits of its claims.

Sexism, Racism and Militarism in the Scientific Worldview

That science has been historically a male activity hardly needs repeating. It was developed by men, white men, and is linked to the control of the physical, social and human world. Symbolically, it can be seen to be anti-nature and anti that depiction of the female which is linked to nature and to characteristics of women as opposed to men. With the extension of "social needs" for a more educated population and for more people of talent to be selected for higher education and for scientific research and development, a rhetoric has developed which attempts to be more inclusive in the provision of opportunities for higher, and scientific education.

Sexism. Two sets of interests appear to coincide in the present attempts to increase participation in science, including the participation of women. One is the need for numbers to maintain the status of science and for "talent" to take it forward, and the other is the attempt by feminists to increase the participation of women in high status and non-traditional careers. As mentioned above, neither attempt has achieved a great deal so far, despite studies which show a small number of girls opting for non-traditional careers and figures showing the increase in female enrollments in science-related courses. A great deal of effort appears to be devoted to "explaining" why so little change has occurred, with explanations ranging from the biological ("it is women's destiny to bear and rear children and this is incompatible with devotion to a career") through the social (women just aren't acceptable at least in high-level jobs) to the psychological (women have different interests in selecting a career; women fear success and have lower motivation and expectations). A fourth, rarely-mentioned reason, is that the nature of science is not as attractive to women as to men.

In an extensive study of the characteristics of students entering tertiary science courses, Beswick and McDougall (1977) distinguished the following factors affecting female participation rates examines male and female students over a three year period, and finds that although the women dropped out less than the men, seemed confident and had as high an orientation to science as men, their career choices differed. Other studies note similar findings, and similarly fail to come to grips with issues in the nature of science and science education which might account for these differences, thus tending to perpetuate the myth either that science is less attractive to women and will remain so, or that they must change their attitudes because that is the way in which more of them will be admitted to scientific careers. And while feminists are concerned at the under-representation of women, the issue of change in science or even a critique of its knowledge and ideological base is more disputed.

A starting point for such a critique is in the analysis of cultural production itself and the fact that public culture is male culture, and women are admitted to it and have to attempt to find their identity within it according to male rules and criteria. Science is also male as is social science (see e.g. Acker and Esseveld, 1981; Westkott, 1979).

The inter-relationship between the nature of science and science education rather than the supposed deficiencies of women and girls plays an important part in the attitudes of the two sexes to scientific activity. "Girls don't want to do science partly because they are brought up to think that it is a male subject and partly because it is a male subject" (Curran, 1980: 37). It is not just through attempts to increase female participation based on equality of opportunity, nor changes in the curriculum, including the implicit as well as explicit socialization that goes on within schools and the wider community, that desirable change will be achieved (e.g. Yates, 1983). Rather, recognition of the sexual bias of science and its use to oppress women, overtly through its use in the allocation of status and power and covertly through technology, including bio-technology, and the denigration of women's knowledge, is essential for what Callaway (1981) calls "re-vision as looking again, a deliberate critical act to see through the stereotypes of our society as these are taken for granted in daily life and deeply embedded in academic tradition" and what Shelley (1984) invites as "unashamedly build[ing] a new structure on our values, arising from our experience; there could be a Mathematics which delights in diversity and which brings with it 'an awareness of the oneness of things'" (p. 12). The linking of mathematics and science may be an important step: girls tend to value mathematics more highly than science, and to be equally discouraged from participation in it (e.g. Gill, 1984 and 1985).

Racism. Not only has science been developed by men; those men were white. And just as the assertion of the superiority of the scientific worldview downgrades the knowledge more characteristically associated with women, it also affects other knowledge systems, sexist or otherwise. The traditional anthropological approach to worldviews considers a continuum from magic through religion to science, thus reproducing in the socio-cultural sphere a unilinear evolutionism which leads to such social practice as genocide, justified by the need to maintain the dominance of the "superior" race.

One way in which the racism of science can be specifically understood is through its use in imperial expansion and continued domination of developing countries by the industrialized ones. Mendelssohn (1976), while invoking the possession of science as a justification for the superiority of its possessors, nevertheless points to two important aspects of this possession: its ability to enhance predictability leading to technological and economic "advances" and the preclusion of following "blind" alleys (this is debatable), and its use in conquering the high seas, exploring the trade winds, determining the nautical position, and knowing the distribution of land and water over the globe which, "together with the possession of superior arms, were all necessary for the establishment of this domination [of whites]" (p. 23).

A key factor in this aspect of scientific domination as racism is the control of scientific resources. Cases are being uncovered where scientific results have been suppressed because they are not in the interests of dominant commercial enterprises, leaving scientists to fume and attempt to uncover this suppression (agriculture and medicine probably give most examples of this). However, in the selection of particular sorts of science for support and development, and in the failure of science to provide a value base for alternative processes, it is open to such manipulation. The United Nations is fond of using a rhetoric which emphasizes the social responsibility of science for the solution of world ills and the betterment of the human condition, but until it can produce a more equitable distribution of scientific resources, including alternative definitions of scientific processes and practices, there is likely to continue to be a widening gap between the originators of science and their "clients". Nor is the rhetoric of scientific co-operation for development likely to be implemented or, if it is in its present form, to change patterns of control. For this rhetoric is based on an aid "model" which is inherently inegalitarian, and asymmetrical, the western (or eastern) scientist helping the "southerner" to solve his problems with their methods.

It is not only in the use of science in the conquest of the tropical and southern world, or possession of it as a justification for this, but the actual effects of the application of western science and technology to the third world that important aspects of its connection with racism can be seen. These range from the application of high technology in agriculture, where traditional techniques were more ecologically sound or where the wealth requirements to use newly-developed grains lead to widescale land alienation, impoverishment of the poorest and increased burdens on them (see e.g. Rogers, 1980), to the exploitation of the resources and environment of third world countries where multinational corporations undertake scientific production free from the legal constraints and production safeguards of the countries in which they developed their techniques (the U.C. Bhopal disaster is a dramatic example). No longer merely the resource-provider for industrialization, the third world has become its scientific testing-ground as well, from the testing of drugs to the testing of nuclear bombs.

While it could be argued that it is not science itself but its use which is part of the perpetuation of structured inequality, which is at least implicitly racist, this overlooks two clusters of factors which implicate science per se. The first is the unrecognized interest structure of science, and the second is the acceptance of the fact of and results from "scientific imperialism". To be able to test one's hypotheses, free from ethical considerations or laws applicable in western societies, is an opportunity of great temptation. And that the lives of those which may be affected are of less worth, must surely be implied, else why would atomic tests in the Pacific or Australian desert not only fail to remove the inhabitants first, but regard any effects that they might suffer as important scientific data? Similarly, the testing of drugs on "captive" populations (e.g. contraceptives on third world women, the mentally retarded or prisoners) flows from the same logic. And the types of highly funded and prestigious research which is supported is based on a choice, not just of those who fund it or not, but of those who agree to accept the funds, carry out the research and wipe their hands of any active role at any level of the decision making. The direct recruitment of scientists (and social scientists must be included) to serve the interests of ruling elites is an explicit case of scientific imperialism, as is the promulgation through education, either through assistance with establishment of educational institutions abroad or the training of selected third world people in developed countries. Both rely on the "achievements" of science, pure and applied, for their justification of intervention, and have the effect of serving, "by interest or default, the interests of elites from the advanced industrialized countries and dependent Third World countries, and hence contribut[ing] to structural violence against the poor" (Toh, 1984: 18).

A further aspect which needs consideration is part of the myth which equates scientific achievement with supposed possession of certain mental aptitudes. "Modernization" will only occur, it is still assumed, when the superstitious ways and thought patterns are replaced with more rational ones. This will only occur through "modern" education, which has the dual function of propagating these ideas to the detriment of alternative ones, and controlling the resources so that only limited "catching up" is possible. The "readiness" of certain cultures (especially China, at present) to turn to modern science is used to rank societies in terms of progress and to provide extra encouragement for them to reach or exceed the "take-off" stage. Some of the confusions about the relationship between supposed inate characteristics and aptitude for science can be exploded by reference to research on women and science, which indicates some aspects of the role of culture in facilitating or inhibiting "performance". The International Association for Research in Education science and mathematics studies have been extended to developing countries, where an almost inverse relationship is found between the achievement of women and the Gross National Product of the country in question! (Kelly, 1978) It may be a more selected sample of girls in the schools in third world countries, but this does not explain away the fact that they do as well as boys, or better, while their sisters in developed countries do less well. Those who invoke culture to explain differences in achievement, without acknowledging the cultural base of the object to be explained, science, and then inter-relate individual and cultural "worth" as a rationale for differential treatment, are on shaky grounds indeed.

Militarism. Skjelsbaek (1983) identifies four dimensions of militarism: the behavioral (characterized by the excess use of violence), the mental or ideological (disregard for human life, ethnocentrism, dehumanization of others, emotional "underdevelopment"), the structural through the near-monopoly by nations of the legitimate use of violence either against other governments or against their own citizens and the international (through the system of alliances which are not only for military purposes but which are patterned along military lines, and through the internationalization of military expertise, armaments and training: pp. 5-14). Further analysis of militarism indicates both racist and sexist aspects, such that Reardon (1981) asserts that "the common values basic to these interrelated belief systems socialize, indeed 'educate', human beings to the acceptance and pursuit of warfare" (p. 1).

Brock-Utne (1985) and Reardon (1985) have summarized findings and argued a detailed case, especially for the links between sexism and militarism, and it does not require much extension of their logic to include racism in this value complex. While sexism and racism rest on a construction of social reality based on hierarchy, authority and biologically based inequality, which provides access for the dominant elite to superior force if other methods for maintaining the legitimacy of their position fail, militarism is more overtly based on the use of force. It can be argued that the interests of the holders of all three sets of beliefs coincide: the maintenance of a global system, by force if needs be, which is premised not only on existing power structures but on control of resources, including legitimacy, to convince others of the rightfulness of that order.

There are two major ways in which science is implicated in that power structure: through the means it provides for its maintenance in physical terms and through its reinforcement of the ideology of control. The employment of scientists in military-related research rather than in life-enhancing projects is one aspect of the contribution of science to militarism; that it is not merely financial convenience or necessity is indicated by the aim of science to create a "utopia" for itself where the conditions for its practice are a dominant consideration in social organization (Saunders, 1977) and by the extent to which it is scientists and not the military that keep the search for new means of destruction "progressing" (Brock-Utne, 1985). In terms of ideology, there is little difference between the values which support control of nature and control, by structurally or physically violent means, of human life. The power of the ideology requires that not only those whom it directly benefits, but others as well subdue their own interests, with values such as "loyalty" placed high on the list of desirable traits which will be rewarded by "protection", and there is a direct connection between behavior according to such values within the family and within the nation at war.

And one component of the legitimation of an order is adherence to an ideology based on "scientific principles", in the making of which women have a weak role. (p. 2). One could go round and round in circles of mutually-reinforcing connections between science, militarism, sexism and racism. It is important to uncover the connections and the means by which they are reinforced. One powerful myth which is dressed up in objective terms and which is used to support the "naturalness" of such an order of life comes from anthropology, in which the deduction that hunting in a particularly organized way can be used to distinguish human from sub-human societies, and that hunting is a male prerogative necessary for the survival of a whole group. As Slocum incisively points out, this "theory" is not only unbalanced, but "leads to the conclusion that the basic human adaptation was the desire of males to hunt and kill. This not only gives too much importance to aggression, which is after all only one factor of human life, but it derives culture from killing" (1975: 39).

Science Education and Education for Peace

The foregoing has indicated the masculine image of science, and some relationships between science and sexism, racism and militarism as both the practical and ideological underpinnings of dominant forms of social and cultural relationships. The high status of science and the role it plays in society is reflected in the attempts to recruit the best students to its service, and its important role in the curriculum. Since formal education plays a vital role in social reproduction, despite the role of other social agencies in giving content to values and influencing behavior, one place in which social transformation can be initiated is in the classroom. However, at present those classrooms not only form part of the structural and ideological status quo, but actively promulgate it, not only in all its sexist and racist forms but, as Reardon (1981) indicates, in militarist ones as well.

While it is unrealistic to single out science education as the only important area for change, it is argued that the present unquestioned teaching of science and the advocating of change simply through recruiting more women into science through educational programmes, is detrimental to producing people who can challenge the status quo and contribute to alternative cultural forms. And, given the unacknowledged value basis of science, its support of dominant values in the wider society, and the desperate need for an alternative value basis in order for humanity not only to survive but to move towards a more just and sustainable life, new definitions of legitimate knowledge and new educational contents and practices and urgently required.

Thus we have a double bind: science is taught as if it were value free, and this downgrades other forms of knowledge leading to such situations as whole courses on nuclear physics without any reference to the effects of nuclear bombs (Brock-Utne, 1985) and histories which emphasize only the positive outcomes of war with scant reference to destruction or the effects on civilians except insofar as they support the war effort, and treat science as an autonomous actor while scientists are subsequently glorified as contributing to the war effort (Burns, 1986). Nor is there an assured place in the curriculum for education for participation in the critique and development of values: a recent survey of science programmes in secondary schools indicated that not even the history of science is taught in any systematic way though reference is sometimes made to famous scientists (predominantly male, often with the sole exception of Marie Curie).*

Thus the capacity which is being uncovered through feminist research for women to develop a different "science", and a different educational, social, cultural and ethical practice, is not only under-rated, under-resourced and denigrated by reference to male canons and norms, but systematically deformed through formal education.

DISCUSSION

The structure of education and its relationship to the powerful scientific legitimating ideology perpetuates an ethical and political illiteracy through its fragmentation and through a failure to include the study of values, and of social aspects of science and technology, in any core curriculum, including teacher education curricula. The perpetuation of this illiteracy is not, it is suggested, because we do not know any better or have any resources to do so, but because the scientization of culture and politics has ignored an alternative source for such literacy.

Aspects of alternatives have been suggested in writings on the nature of science and the need for more holistic and integrated approaches (see e.g. Bohm, 1981; Brock-Utne, 1983; Lindholm, 1985; Nudler, 1979). Biggins

(1977) suggests that the recognition of other values, alternatives to control, will arise when scientists recognize that knowledge seeking is not only based on interests, but that other interests, for example those represented by ecology, can become the basis for scientific thought, and that this recognition implies a radical transformation of modern scientific knowledge. In attempting to integrate another aspect of science, "facts" and "experience," Nudler (1979) suggests that the additional notion of a "desirable future" and a recognition that the interactions between analytical levels becomes more complex when the "human reality" is studied, implies a need both for a more holistic perspective and a way of taking the observer into account. Not only the observer, but the observed also need to be taken into account (Mushkoji, 1979), and also co-operation for change, recognizing the political nature of research on human beings (Huizer, 1979). In such ways, it is suggested, not only can people "reclaim" science and hence gain tools, through dialogue, for its evaluation especially in order to selectively apply it to their own lives, but science, in its broadest sense of Wissenschaft, may then become a tool of liberation rather than of oppression.

Yet when it comes to science teaching, researchers are still claiming that half of those who begin its study, females, "will have to become more assertive" even if the system can be changed "to reduce the difficulties for females in science" because "both men and women need an understanding of science in our highly technological society, and it would be unfortunate if we could not effectively utilize the brain power of the large number of women who currently are avoiding careers in science" (Welch, 1985).

It is difficult to avoid the conclusion, when women's writings on science and when women's perspectives on knowledge are taken into account, that it is different science that is required, and that women's perspectives provide firm guidelines on which to base this. In the ways in which feminist research is being undertaken (e.g. Brock-Utne, 1985; Callaway, 1981) new relationships between "subject" and "object" are being explored which provide a basis for co-operation for change. And the ways in which women's approaches to ethical-moral issues differ from men's indicate further bases for apprehending the effects of different ways of seeking and applying knowledge. Some proposals for improving the "understanding" of science indicate that there is a need to let pupils understand the risks and benefits, evaluate these and make value judgments, based on greater "scientific" literacy (Science and Society Committee, 1983), but this in itself does not constitute "moral literacy". Manthorpe suggests that: "A truly alternative feminist science must be almost possible to imagine for it must be involved with an alteration in the relationship between men and women, and thus with an alternative society and consciousness" (1982: 76), rather than either a radical restructuring of science or a "feminization" of its contents. This transformation is necessary because science is constituted by social relations (loc. cit) which at present are characterized by domination.

Thus, liberation, on the basis of which a more peaceful society can be invented, can begin in the classroom as a microcosm of the wider world. It is easy to point to the difficulties of change in the classroom since it is embedded in the wider society and conceived as dependent on that society. However, the choice is whether to comply with that dependence or struggle to transform it. The foregoing has indicated the extent to which formal education, especially science education, is a way to ensure that compliance, and the nature of the alternative resources of knowledge and knowledge application, and their inter-relationships, both theoretical and ethical, which women and other oppressed groups can contribute. Boulding (1981) has shown how women researchers conceive their agendas in the fields of international relations and peace; similar studies are needed in other spheres, including pedagogy. Once it is recognized that the power of the scientific culture is constituted by unwarranted normative claims which have enabled it to de-legitimize other forms of knowledge seeking, then it is possible to re-write curricula and research agendas, and methods of conceiving and transmitting ideas. The need is desperate, for human survival is at stake.

Bibliography

Acker, J. and J. Esseveld (1981). 'Issues in feminist research'. Stockholm, _____mimeo, draft.

206

Aas, B. (1982). 'A materialistic view of men's and women's attitudes to war'. Women's Studies International Forum 5 (3/4):355-364.

Bernard, J. (1973) 'My four revolutions. An autobiographical history of the A.S.A.' American Journal of Sociology 78 (4): 773-791.

Bernstein, B. (1971). Class, Codes and Control. London, Routledge and Kegan Paul.

Beswick, D. and A. McDougall (1977). 'Characteristics of women entering science'. Paper presented to the ANZAAS Congress, Melbourne (mimeo).

Biggins, D.R. (1977). 'Scientific knowledge and values: the case of ecology'. Paper presented to the ANZAAS Congress, Melbourne (mimeo).

Bohm, D. (1981). 'Insight, knowledge, science and human values'. Teachers College Record 82(3): 380-402.

Boulding, E. (1981). 'Perspectives of women researchers on disarmament, national security and world order'. Women's Studies International Quarterly 4(1):27-41.

Brock-Utne, B. (1983). 'Are universities educating for war?' Paper presented to the IPRA Conference, Gyor, Hungary, August.

Brock-Utne, B. (1985). Educating for Peace. A Feminist Perspective. London and New York, Pergamon.

Burns, R. (1979). The formation and legitimation of development education with particular reference to Australia and Sweden. La Trobe University, Melbourne, unpublished PhD dissertation.

Burns, R. (1984a). 'International Student Mobility: Neo-imperialism, Brain-Drain or Development Co-operation?' In A. Hetland, ed. Universities and National Development. Stockholm, Almqvist and Wiksell International.

Burns, R. (1984b). 'Getting there, staying there, going on: women in universities'. In R. Burns and B. Sheehan, eds. Women and Education. Melbourne, ANZCIES.

Burns, R. (1985). 'Peace eduation: is it responding sufficiently to children's fears of the future?' Australian Journal of Early Childhood 10 (4): 16-23.

Burns, R. (1986). 'Conflict and mass destruction: a content analysis of Australian involvement in World War II in history textbooks in Victoria'. Paper presented for the Ipra Conference, Brighton, Sussex (mimeo).

Callaway, H. (1981). 'Women's Perspectives: Research as Re-Vision'. In P. Reason and J. Rowan, eds., Human Inquiry: A Sourcebook of New Paradigm Research. London, John Wiley and Sons.

Carlson, R. (1972). 'Understanding women: implications for personality theory and research'. Journal of Social Issues 28(2).

Cass, S., M. Dawson, D. Temple, S. Wills and A. Winkler, eds. (1983). Why So Few? Women Academics in Australian Universities. Sydney University Press.

Charlesworth, M. (n.d.). 'The anthropology of Science'. Deakin University (mimeo).

Cowen, R. (1971). 'The Utilitarian University'. In B. Holmes and D. Scanlon, eds. World Yearbook of Education 1971/2. London, Evans Bros.

Curran, L. (1980). 'Science education: did she drop out or was she pushed?' In Brighton Women and Science Group, eds. Alice through the Microscope. London, Virago.

Easlea, B. (1973). Liberation and the Aims of Science. London, Chatto and Windus.

Galtung, J. (1972). 'Empiricism, criticism, constructivism'. Synthese 24.

Gill, J. (1984). 'Hanging rock revisited: the not so mysterious disappearance of girls along certain educational paths'. In R. Burns and B. Sheehan, eds. Women and Education, Melbourne, ANZCIES.

Gill, J. (1985). 'The wood between the worlds: constructing an understanding of gender relations in schooling on the basis of a comparative study'. In J. Maddock and C. Hindson, eds. Quality and Equality in Education. Adelaide, ANZCIES.

Gilligan, C. (1981). 'In a different voice: women's conceptions of self and morality.' Harvard Educational Review 47(4): 481-517.

Gilligan, C. (1987). In a Different Voice. Cambridge, Harvard University Press.

Gray, A. (1984). 'Concepts of disadvantage and models of remediation'. In R. Burns and B. Sheehan, eds. Women and Education. Melbourne, ANZCIES.

Hill, H. (1984). 'Women, war and Third World development'. Paper presented to the Third National Conference of Labor Women, Adelaide, January.

Huizer, G. (1979). 'Applied social science and political action'. In G.Huizer and B. Mannheim, eds. The Politics of Anthropology. The Hague,

208

Mouton.

Kelly, A. (1978). Girls and Science. Stockholm, Almqvist and Wiksell International.

Lindholm, S. (1985). Kunskap. Fran fragment till helhetsyn. Stockholm, Liber Forlag.

Lovejoy, F. and E. Barboza (1984). 'Feminine mathematics anxiety: a culture specific phenomenon'. In R. Burns and B. Sheehan, eds. Women and Education. Melbourne, ANZCIES.

Manthorpe, C.A. (1982). 'Men's science, women's science or science?' Studies in Science Education 9:65-80.

Mendelssohn, K. (1976) Science and Western Domination. London, Thames and Hudson.

Meyer, B. (1984) 'Knowledge and Culture in the Middle East: some critical reflections'. In K. Watson, ed. Dependence and Interdependence in Education. London, Croom Helm.

Mushakoji, K. (1979). 'Scientific revolution and inter-paradigmatic dialogues'. Japan, United Nations University HSDRGPID-14/UNUP-65.

Naess, A. (1972). The Pluralist and Possibilist Aspect of the Scientific Enterprise. Oslo, Universitetsforlaget.

Nudler, O. (1979). 'Notes for an epistemology of holism'. Japan, United Nations University HSDRGPID-13/UNUP-65.

O'Donnell, C. (1984). The Basis of the Bargain. Gender, Schooling and Jobs. Sydney, George Allen and Unwin.

Pietila, H. (1983). 'To develop an alternative peace policy of woman'. Paper presented to the Women's Peace Movement, Aland, June.

Poole, M.E. (1983). 'Adolescent perceptions of teachers and school subjects'. South Pacific Journal of Teacher Education 11(2):23-29.

Radnitzky, G. (1972). Contemporary Schools of Metascience. Goteborg, Akademiforlaget.

Reardon, B. (1981). 'Militarism and sexism: influences on education for war'. This paper was prepared for a special peace education edition of the Bulletin of Peace Proposals and accepted by the editor, but not published because another feminist paper was also accepted and the general editors considered two 'on this topic would be too much'.

Reardon, B. (1985). Sexism and the War System. New York, Teachers College Press.

Rogers, B. (1980). The Domestication of Women. London, Tavistock. Saunders, J.R. (1977). 'Scientists for Utopia'. Paper presented to the ANZAAS Congress, Melbourne, August.

Science and Society Committee, National Council for the Social Studies (1983). 'Guidelines for teaching science-related social issues'. Social Education 47(4): 258-261.

Seddon, T. (1984). 'Science in the classroom'. Peace Studies October:24-26.

Sharpe, S. (1976). 'Just Like a Girl'. How Girls learn to be Women. Harmondworth, Penguin.

Shelley, N. (1984). 'Women, culture and mathematics'. Paper presented to the International Conference on Mathematics Education, Adelaide, August (mimeo).

Skjellbaek, K. (1983). 'Dimensions a modes of militarism'. In B. Huldt and A. Lejins, eds. Militarism and Militarization. Stockholm, Swedish Institute for International Affairs.

Slocum, S. (1975). 'Woman the Gatherer: Male Bias in Anthropology'. In R. Reiter, ed. Toward an Anthropology of Woman. New York and London, Monthly Review Press.

Spender, D. and E. Sarah, eds. (1982). Learning to Lose. Sexism and Education. London, The Women's Press.

Toh, S.H. (1984). 'The seamy side of expertise: social scientists and Third World violence'. Peace Studies October: 16-19.

Welch, A.J. (1978) 'From dalliance to connubial bliss. Science and higher education in the nineteenth century'. In D. Davis, ed. Education and The Economy. Sydney, ACIES.

Welch, W.W. (1985). 'Sugar and spice and all things nice?' Australian Educational Researcher 12(1): 5-23.

Westkott, M. (1979). 'Feminist criticism of the social sciences'. Harvard Educational Review 49(4):422-430.

Willis, P. (1977). Learning to Labour. How Working Class Kids get Working Class Jobs. London, Saxon House.

Yates, L. (1983). 'Counter-sexist strategies in Australian schools'. In S. Acker et al, eds. World Yearbook of Education 1983/4. London, Kogan Page.

Yates, L. (1987). 'Australian research on gender and

education 1975-1985'. In J.P. Keeves, ed. <u>Australian Education: Review of Recent Research</u>. Sydney, Allen and Unwin.

14

Neo-Conservatives and Controversies in Australian Peace Education: Some Critical Reflections and a Country Strategy

Toh Swee Hin

INTRODUCTION

In both Britain and the United States, recent years have witnessed considerable public controversies over peace studies or peace education. 1/ Likewise, as peace perspectives gained interest and implementation at all levels of Australian formal and non-formal education, there has been a burgeoning of criticisms and debate over such developments. A strident campaign, led by prominent members of the neo-conservative movement in Australia, has seen numerous attacks on programmes (e.g. courses in schools and universities), organizations (e.g. Catholic Commission for Justice & Peace, Australian National University's Peace Research Centre), and individual peace educators or researchers. That this conservative reaction against peace education is occurring should not surprise us. Such critics perceive peace education as a "tool" of the general peace movement to spread its "influence" among uncommitted Australian youths and ordinary citizens, thereby undermining the not-to-be-disputed "truths" of maintaining "peace through strength".

It is incumbent, however, on peace educators to respond directly to neo-conservative criticms by demystifying the assumptions and valued embodies as well as the distortions cast on what peace education is or ought to be. If peace education is to maintain and increase its urgent momentum, we need to be fully aware of the opposition's case and tactics, and plan a constructive, peaceful strategy to counter and defuse the criticisms. This paper takes an initial step, within the Australian context, towards such awareness. It should be seen, however, mainly as an exploratory study with some tentative suggestions for action, and further research, now underway, will be needed to yield a more systematic, viable counter-strategy.

The prevailing campaign against peace education has its roots in a determined effort by a vocal minority sharing common beliefs and values, and inter-linked by membership in or affiliation with a small group of neo-conservative organizations. There is to date no generalized public outcry over peace education -- indeed, recent public opinion polls would indicate that a majority of Australians consider peace-related issues to be legitimate components in the school curriculum. 2/ Despite this advantage, peace educators cannot afford to be complacent about the neo-conservative challenge. Although small in size, its considerable resources, well-focused organization and polemical intensity are significant factors in manipulating public opinion.

Critiques in Quadrant

As the "premier" conservative journal in Australia and major activity of the Australian Association for Cultural Freedom, 3/ Quadrant has led the way in "intellectual" censure of peace education or peace studies.

The constant stream of poorly research opposition to peace edution in its pages perhaps reflect a willingness to serve as a ready outlet for such criticisms. See e.g., Whitehall 1984, 4/ Burns 1983b 5/ Jacobs 1985 and Parkington (1986) and the rebuttals by Begley (1984) March 1986. In part confirmation of this point, the very latest issue of Quadrant (1986) includes in its editorial columns an unsubstantiated attack on peace and development education courses in my academic department, labelling them as "tendentious rot". If Quadrant's editors had bothered by enquire into how these topics are taught, they would have seen that while the teachers may hold views on peace issues which generally diverge from neo-conservative beliefs, students are exposed to a variety of theoretical, including neoconservative positions.

The South Australian Red Cross Kits

In late 1985, public controversy erupted over the distribution of an Australian Red Cross Society (South Australian Division) kit entitled "Understanding Conflict" (Redden, 1984). Designed for years 8-12 Humanities and Social Science courses, the kit presented eight case-studies in human conflict from the personal to international levels, such as the situation of teenagers caught in a bushfire, community conflict over a communications tower, the issue of live sheep exports, and Northern Ireland. Opposition to the kit came from some farmer groups who objected to the live sheep export case-study as "biased", a claim quickly echoed by neo-conservatives in a more general opposition to peace education policies being planned by the S.A. Department of Education. The controversy led the Red Cross itself to withdraw the kit from distribution in early January, 1986, as society officials became worried that its image of "political impartiality" could become tarnished. 6/

In demystifying the Red Cross kit controversy, it is crucial to note that the actual case-studies were written with "objectivity" as a primary pedagogical principle. Students are given "maximum exposure to the variety of interests and opinions held...(then) encouraged to develop their own analytical basis for making decisions and judgements that will positively affect the future." 7/ In the specific case-study on live sheep exports, the positions of farmers, exporters, meat workers and animal liberationists are all presented. Redden had also consulted with relevant organizations like the United Farmers and Stockowners, the Australian Meat Industry Employees Union, and the Animal Liberation Movement who approved the arguments cited for their respective cases. The charges of political bias and "indoctrination" are therefore difficult to sustain. Hence, when the controversy is viewed in the wider context of conservative reaction, one strongly suspects it provided an expedient spark for resisting and undermining official South Australian moves to highlight peace studies in the International Year of Peace.

Apart from the Red Cross' withdrawal of the kit, the controversy may possibly influence some school principals or teachers to proceed more cautiously with integrating peace education into their curriculum. Nevertheless, the S.A. Department of Education has defended the legitimacy of peace education and proceeded with the appointment of a Peace Education Officer. 8/

Teaching for Human Rights

In 1984, the Human Rights Commission published a resource manual for teachers to use in treating issues of human rights across years 5-12 (Pettman, 1984). Trialling of the manual "Teaching for Human Rights" has proceeded in some 150 government and non-government schools throughout Australia, except in the Queensland state system, where it was banned by the Department of Education (Symon, 1985). The manual essentially provides a series of learning activities through which students come to understand various dimensions and levels of human rights, and develop humane values and empathy consistent with that understanding. Specific issues areas include human rights and the law; freedom of conscience and opinion, or of assembly and public participation; economic, social and cultural wellbeing; racism, sexism, the family and education. Emphasis is placed on learners applying human rights principles to their own environment (e.g. negotiating classroom rights and responsibilities) before looking at global abuse of human rights.

In mid-February 1986, however, Federal opposition members of Parliament, during debate on the government's Bill to reconstruct the Human Rights Commission, strongly raised questions about the manual. One liberal Senator, Jim Short, branded it as "hardcore Communist" propaganda promoting anti-free enterprise, anti-family and anti-Western values. He pointed to passages which described Australian society as having a "highly stratified class structure, a value system that is secular, racist, sexist and materialist", and which criticizes advanced capitalist countries for "mass assassinations" through structural violence in the development and operation of the capitalist world-economy. 9/

A close reading of the manual's discussion and activities, however, reveal such charges to be highly distortive and emotionalized. As the manual's author Pettman said, the opposition Parliamentarians based their criticisms on very selective quotations out of context. 10/

The short-term effect of the controversy, which faded soon from media view as parliamentary debate moved beyond the Human Rights Commission, might be in Pettman's view to induce some caution among principals and teachers about trialling the programme in their schools. The controversy, however, is unlikely to have significant long-term effect, as trialling and revision of the manual proceeds apace admidt the current strongly favourable public opinion towards human rights learning. 11/

Controversies in the Catholic Church

Increasingly, the peace and development education role of some Catholic church agencies, notably the Catholic Commission for Justice & Peace (CCJP) and the Australian Catholic Relief (ACR), and priests or Catholics identified as followers of "liberation theology", has received strong criticism from conservative groups and individuals. One recent major controversy ensued with the publication of the CCJP's social justice discussion document "Work for a Just Peace" (CCJP, 1985). In the paper, the Commission raises issues and questions about the perils of the arms race.

Upon the document's publication in September, the newspapers reported "severe" criticisms by rank-and-rile Catholics and priests, some of whom apparently refused to distribute the document in their parishes. 12/

Criticisms were also made by a leading Opposition senator and right-wing trade unionists, 13/ a Quadrant article (Scarrabelotti, 1985), and even the U.S. embassy who protested to the Catholic bishops over "serious distortions and misrepresentations of U.S. foreign policy" in the paper. In response, the CCJP has defended its position by emphasizing that the peace document is a discussion paper, rather than imposed political prescriptions, and the CCJP statements have been misunderstood or misinterpreted.

A second major controversy related to the Catholic Church's involvement in peace and development education has been the attack on the Australian Catholic Relief's (ACR) aid programmes to the Third World and its emphasis on development education, which in the eyes of the critics, advance radical liberation theology.

In response to the various criticisms of its philosophy, aid and development-education activities, the ACR has produced literature to clarify what it deems as distortions and half-truths designed to stimulate deep-seated community fears (e.g. of communism).

For example, with regard to the charges of being "Marxist" or "quasi-Marxist", ACR and CCJP officers quote the well-known Brazilian bishop Helder Camara, who said: "when I feed the poor they call me a saint; when I ask why the poor have no food, they call me a communist".

Conferences, Peace Bus and Peace Theatre

A vital expression of the growth of interest in peace education has been the supportive and pioneering role played by teacher unions and professional organizations. For example, both major teachers unions -- the Independent Teachers Federation of Australia (ITFA) and the Australian Teachers Federation (ATF) -- have held national conferences to explore curriculum issues in educating for peace. Given the strident conservative opposition to peace studies thus far observed, it is not surprising that such kinds of conferences have also encountered reaction. Hence the ITFA National Conference on Peace Education, held in the most conservative Australian state, Queensland, drew the ire of conservative spokespersons.

The Tenth biennual conference of the Australian Geography Teachers Association (AGTA), entitled "Teaching Geography for a Better World," which included major papers on education for peace, political literacy, multiculturalism, human rights and Third World underdevelopment, was criticized in the conservative Bulletin magazine even before it was held! (Duncan, 1985).

These criticisms, appearing well before the actual conference, appear calculated more to create public fears than to inform rationally and fairly about the curriculum issues on key topics with contemporary geography courses.

Another innovative project in peace education, the "Peace Bus", has also not escaped criticism. Organized by the People for Nuclear Disarmament (PND) with Federal government funding, the project involves sending around a double-decker bus, with videos on peace issues, curriculum material and resource persons, to suburbs and country towns in a number of states. One Opposition Parliamentarian labelled the spending of $96,000 under the Community Employment Program as "absurd" given the economic restrictions on social welfare and services spending. 14/ Similar grants to other organizations for peace education purposes were also labelled as "training professional protesters".

Operation Peace Studies

In late 1985, Operation Peace Studies: War in the Classroom was published and claimed to examine "the threat peace studies pose to our educational system, to the rights of students, and to freedom of thought and speech." Its author, pseudo-named "Pat Jacobs", is a former government intelligence analyst. Jacobs' litany of charges against peace studies included its "blaming" of wars, conflicts and injustices on capitalism; its "hostility" to "free societies"; and its "promotion" of Soviet foreign policy and strategic objectives. Peace educators are said to be "subversives...imbued with fanatical self-righteousness bordering on political megalomania", and exploiting "psychological and political vulnerabilities and anxieties of school children".

TOWARDS A POSSIBLE COUNTER-STRATEGY

In demystifying the various controversies over peace education or peace studies, several substantive arguments have been raised to refute the neo-conservative charges, or to clarify stereotypes and distortions on the theory and practice of peace educators. I would like now to draw together the threads of this demystification exercise into a possible counter-strategy which peace educators might use to defuse such controversies and conservative attacks. But one caveat applies: the suggested strategy remains exploratory, requiring substantiation on the basis of more systematic empirical research on the everyday practices of peace educators in Australia.

Responding to Criticisms of Bias

The charges of "bias" and "indoctrination" have been the staple diet of the neo-conservative campaign against peace education. It is valid of course to counter this charge by analyzing how social knowledge is never value-free or neutral, and that the producers and reproducers of dominant knowledge expediently employ the guise of "neutrality" or "value-freeness" to legitimize their assumptions, values, ideas and policies (Freire, 1985; Burns & Aspeslagh (1984: 140) noted,

> however much our educational aim is to encourage a positive expression of opinion towards equality, justice and disarmament...this does not mean that we deny students the possibility of arriving at other opinions. The freedom to come to one's own decision must always be possible for students.

What does this mean in pedagogical practice, though? To begin with, there is a need for peace educators to more systematically and explicitly include neo-conservative or "peace through strength" literature and information in their curriculum resources. I say "more" because contrary to neo-conservative perception, many peace educators in practice do expose learners to arguments rejecting "pro-peace" ideas. Indeed, good analytical texts or readings used for peace studies usually do fairly describe "peace through strength" views prior to and/or during their critiques of such views, and alert readers to their literature. Hence, it would be helpful when such readings are listed in say a resource bibliography, users should be explicitly alerted to citations to citations or passages within which do accurately portray the opposition's case.

Nevertheless, to preempt effectively charges of "bias" and "indoctrination", curriculum guides and resources aimed at the potential peace educator should definitely identify-clearly sections where the "peace through strength" and other neo-conservative ideas are treated explicitly. For example, in my own course material, students receive a fair dose of the modernization paradigm in development-education, or to neo-conservative arguments and literature on disarmament, militarization, the "Soviet threat" thesis, ANZUS and the U.S. bases. Indeed, since the conservative critics constantly harp on the charge of "pro-Sovietism" among peace educators, all curriculum material should include as a rule literature sensitive to the deficiencies of the Soviet system, albeit of course geared towards rational and objective analysis rather than promoting the hysteria favoured by neo-conservatives. Also, noting that deficiencies do exist should not become an excuse for leaving unquestioned "Western" systems.

A further important tactic to defuse the "bias"
charge is to include among any invited speakers or
lecturers those of neo-conservative leanings. Their views
deserve to be heard, as part of a democratic learning
process whereby alternative positions are critically
assessed and independently accepted or rejected in part
or whole by learners themselves. And where peace
education texts or guides list resource organizations to
contact, it is important to also identify "peace through
strength" groups. Such steps will make it harder for
neo-conservatives to justify their claims of "bias."

A second major kind of response to "indoctrination"
charges is to reflect the neo-conservative yardstick --
that democratic learning requires exposure to the whole
spectrum of opinions (which is no less shared by peace
educators) -- back on prevailing mainstream "academic"
theory and practice. To what extent are traditional
subjects like geography, history, economics and english
being taught on what basis, so that learners at least
have an opportunity to query the wisdom of dominant
paradigms or theories? This question needs to be high on
the agenda of peace educators, for as critical
sociologists have increasingly shown, contemporary
educational structures and processes serve largely to
reproduce the dominant social, cultural and political
values, attitudes and skills of society, albeit not
without contradictions and certainly not in a monolithic,
mechanistic fashion (Apple, 1982; Whitty & Young, 1976;
Giroux, 1981).

More specific research also indicate that textbooks
often legitimize political bias in their selective
appraisal of problems (Haavelsrud, 1980; Hicks, 1981;
Fien, 1982; Toh, 1984:9-11). I have also encouraged
post-graduate research in which several students are
investigating how traditional subjects like Geography and
Economics are treating Third World issues. Some
preliminary findings suggest that many school teachers
have been socialized by their previous academic training
into the modernization paradigm; that resources relied on
also tend to underemphasize or ignore PEACE paradigm
views; and that the students hence usually believe in
major tenets of modernization thinking about
underdevelopment. 15/ Likewise, university programmes
in "development economics" or "agricultural economics" by
and large train their candidates to subscribe to
modernization orthodoxies on causes (e.g. lack of
advanced technology and capital) and solutions (e.g.

Green Revolution and TNC investments) to Third World poverty, which in turn has significant implications for the overseas training of Third World professionals. Similar kinds of curriculum evaluation research should also be directed at for instance, International Relations, Economics and Politics courses to assess what bias there might be with regard to peace and conflict issues.

By such demystifying research, it will be possible to demonstrate "hard" evidence to the neo-conservatives that their reference points for "unbiased" academic study may in fact be oriented pedagogically towards sustaining dominant values, assumptions, theories and concepts. Consequently, the abstract defense of "educational standards" loses its "neutral" gloss, and the neo-conservatives will be obliged as responsible scholars to justify why existing pedagogy in "traditional" academia is inherently superior.

Organizing for Peace Education

As Fien (1982) has stressed, peace educators have a responsibility to clarify to the general public, and allay any fears or correct misrepresentations about what we actually do in teaching, say, nuclear issues. There is a need for developing curriculum packages in a participatory mode, involving parents, teachers, community members, non-governmental organizations, and politicians. Through such public participation, the general citizenry directly knows all points of view are exposed to children and students, and is assured that the teaching of peace and conflict issues is no more or less "academic" than traditional topics or disciplines in the curriculum.

However, involving interest groups and the community is no guarantee that neo-conservatives will thereby be satisfied, as the South Australian Red Cross kit controversy illustrates. Although the case-study on live-sheep exports did not involve prior consultation with and prior approval of their own position by livestock owners, it was still attacked as biased. Perhaps this controversy suggests another important factor, namely the organizational "vulnerability" of any organization promoting peace education. In this case, the Red Cross' established public image and expectation of "neutrality" meant neo-conservatives could raise enough embarrasing controversy to the point where society officials, while not necessarily agreeing with the charge of "bias", were forced to withdraw the kit for fear of upsetting its contributing constituencies. The incident might have turned out differently if the kit was sponsored by, for example, a professional academic or teacher body, the Education Department or other government agency, as the charges of bias could then be demystified without any threat to organizational survival. The "Teaching for Human Rights" controversy provides a case in point. When the Human Rights Commission stood its ground and strongly defended the criticisms, apart from perhaps a short-term caution within the schooling community, no long-term negative effect is expected. A corollary tactic is for non-governmental organizations involved in peace education to cooperate closely with professional-based bodies (e.g. teachers' subject associations), which also fulfills the earlier discussed participatory principle of peace curriculum development. Official teacher in-service courses or workshops provide another legitimating, less organizationally vulnerable channel of introducing peace studies into the curriculum.

A related point in organizing for peace education concerns how spokespersons are reported by and perceived by the popular media. As earlier analyzed, much of the thrust of the anti-peace studies campaign has been based on the assumption that peace educators are demanding seperate peace studies subjects. While there are those within the peace movement and peace eduation community who make this case, it is essential not to give the (mis)impression, especially through public announcements, that this is a monolithic view shared by all peace educators. Indeed, much of the prevailing opinion on peace education expressed at conferences or workshops in the eighties has tended towards the integration of peace perspectives throughout the whole curriculum. The latter emphasis presents less of a strawperson target for the conservative critics, as they then have to present substantiated arguments for why peace issues could not be "academically" included in the existing and "traditional" subjects.

With respect to responding to the media, much of which tend to farour anti-peace studies arguments, 16/ one can only keep trying to correct stereotypes, distortions and any grossly biased commentary or reporting. The ACR, for example, noted that one major newspaper ran several stories on the aid to Communist countries issue without bothering to contact its office. But apart from speaking to the media, or writing corrective letters to editors, ACR found it more important and effective to directly approach the Catholic community in a grassroots oriented publicity campaign. While a leaflet was produced to demystify the conservative criticisms, emphasis was placed on a <u>positive</u> approach towards clarifying ACR's aid and development-education work. Timely visits by African development personnel and messages of solidarity from Third World grassroots organizations further reinforced the message that aid is not merely giving material help, but requires restructuring rich world-poor world relationships. Hence, while directly countering negative media treatment is an on-going task, the ACR's experience suggests that "going around" the media-assisted controversies and educating the general community on the positive achievements of a specific peace and development education programme would be a more effective strategy.

Last but not least, it is increasingly clear that the campaign against peace studies has emanated from a relatively small number of sources or critics. While not subscribing to or implying a "conspiracy theory", it is nevertheless useful to be aware of the "power-structure" behind such conservative vision of the "good society", and its reassertion of so-called "traditional values" in economic, political, cultural and social spheres. <u>17</u>/ In Australia, there appears to be a consolidation of the "new right" involving old conservative groupings (e.g. Australian Association for Cultural Freedom, which publishes <u>Quadrant</u>; Institute for Public Affairs; National Civic Council; anti-communist trade unions) and more recent associations (e.g. Australian Association for Defense; Centre for Independent Studies; Australian Council for Educational Standards) (Carey & Pows, 1985). Some leading members of the conservative Opposition parties have also been associated with "new right" philosophy, and the Liberal Party (1985) itself has issued policy statements on disarmament and deterrence within the "peace through strength" mould, and rejecting the peace studies. <u>18</u>/

Many of the "new right" think-tanks involve leading conservative Australian intellectuals (e.g. Chipman, Kramer), and obtain generous financial support from the business community. Among the latter, the Chairman of Western Mining Corporation, Hugh Morgan, has been one of the "new right's" most enthusiastic supporter and vocal spokesperson on diverse social issues. The international links of Australian neo-conservatives are also interesting, given that controversies and conservative opposition have also been prominent in Britain and the United States. Indeed, while the contexts are different, the same themes and arguments resurface again and again in this internationalized politics of anti-peace education. Hence the Australian Lecture Foundation, whose chairman is WMC's Hugh Morgan, and think-tanks like IPA and CIS, regularly invites leading overseas neo-conservative thinkers to speak in Australia. For example, Roger Scruton, editor of the Salisbury Review and vocal critic of British peace studies, delivered the 1984 Latham Memorial Lecture (organized by the Australian Association for Cultural Freedom). Scruton (1984) warned of radical threats to the state and criticised notions of multi-culturalism. Norman Podhoretz, the influential editor of the conservative U.S. Commentary magazine, is said to have met Hugh Morgan and leading Quadrant intellectuals on a 1981 visit, and now dispenses a regular dose of neo-conservative commentary in the Weekend Australian (Clark, 1986). Edwin J. Feulner (1985), president of the U.S. Heritage Foundation, delivered the 18th Latham Memorial Lecture on the important influence think-tanks can have on government policy, including his foundation's success in the U.S. attack on UNESCO and in pushing for Reagan's Strategic Defense Initiative. Milton Friedman (1981) was invited to lead a seminar organized by the Centre for Independent Studies, and most recently in March 1986, leading U.S. neo-conservative Jeane Kirkpatrick was a keynote speaker at conferences in Melbourne/Sydney held by the IPA. Owen Harries, neo-conservative academic and former ambassador to UNESCO, served as a Heritage Foundation fellow in Washington before recently becoming co-editor of Irving Kristol's new U.S. magazine, The National Interest. Harris (1984, 1985) warns regularly of the "Soviet threat" and the importance of ANZUS, and won friends in Washington's neo-conservative community with his vocal criticisms of UNESCO (Hewitt, 1985).

In drawing attention to the internal power-structure and linkages within the Australian neo-conservative community, and relationships with British and U.S. counterparts, there is no necessary suggestion that the campaign against peace education is a well-coordinated "conspiracy". However, it would be surprising if there is not at least some inspiration drawn by Australian critics from their overseas colleagues, or vice versa. One immediate practical implication for Australian peace educators hence would be to try and learn from parallel experiences overseas in terms of coping tactics and strategies. Another implication is for peace educators to present a more unified stand against the distortions and criticisms. This process is underway with the recent formation of an Australian Association for Peace, Justice & Development Education (AAPJDE) and the Australian Peace Studies & Research Association (APSARA). The former has made clear as one of its goal to act as a spokesbody for peace educators which will coordinate constructive clarification of what peace education really is to the Australian community at large.

The third implication of realizing that this network, formal or informal, of neo-conservative critics exists is not to engage them purely within the parameters of their critique. Rather, by close analysis of their overall social, political, economic and cultural ideology of the neo-conservative community, we may instead of responding piecemeal to specific charges defensively, take the initiative in positively questioning their credibility as self-proclaimed spokespersons and defenders of "democratic" tradition. For peace educators, one strategy towards this initiative would be to reconceptualize the debate on peace education.

Reconceptualizing the Debate

It is obvious that many of the neo-conservative critics in Australia have centred on issues of disarmament and national security. Particular attention is paid to the "Soviet threat" thesis and on political instability in the Third World which may result in movements or governments unreceptive to advanced industrialized capitalism. While it is certainly important to engage the neo-conservatives on these points, it is crucial to broaden the parameters of the debate to focus more attention on the "processes" and more "micro" dimensions of peace education. Hence is is not merely content (e.g. disarmament; deterrence; structural violence); it also inherently needs to be consistent in practice. Peace educators are ethically obliged to teach about and for peace peacefully, which means not indoctrinating. It would be a form of cultural violence if learners are not given opportunities to be aware of various perspectives and values, and encouraged to develop analytical skills which leads to critically informed choices and jugements.

Furthermore, peace education is also about conflict resolution, and for learners, this means not just reflecting on possible resolutions of larger conflicts (e.g. superpower tensions, wars, world hunger) , but even more fundamentally applying it to their everyday learning and living environments. Schools embody the well-known hidden curriculum, and often organizational and inter-personal relationships among individuals or groups express values (e.g. authoritarianism, aggression) wittingly or unwittingly in contradiction to official values considered desirable for youth and later adult life (e.g. democratic consensus-building; civility). Peace education has useful ideas, skills and techniques for helping teachers, students, parents and the wider community to create more harmonious environments. The experience of the West Australian peace education project is a useful case in point. When initially formed, it received the usual criticisms of promoting anti-deterrence views and the like. However, as the project developed by emphasizing the utility of conflict resolution to schools and communities, positive support grew for its work now perceived as relevant and non-threatening.

Indeed, one recent public opinion poll commissioned by a state Department of Education shows an overwhelming majority of the representative sample of respondents supporting the following initiatives:
- school children becoming more aware of the causes of conflicts and disputes between peoples, groups and countries
- school children being encouraged to learn skills to resolve conflicts non-violently
- more opportunities for schoolchildren to learn about the U.N. Declaration of Human Rights and the work of the U.N. international cooperation, social justice and peace
- schoolchildren dealing with issues causing strong fears, lack of hope and powerlessness about the future
- opportunities for schoolchildren to study various views on how to create a less violent, more peaceful and secure world
The results of this study would suggest that there is a pool of acceptance within the wider community for peace studies or peace education in its multi-dimensional

context, and disconfirms the "public fears" which the
neo-conservatives cite to support their position. It
also means though that peace educators should even more
continue to clarify to the public how peace education can
positively contribute to personal, community, national
and global peace, and enlist their active participation,
so as to preempt neo-conservative-led controversies from
sowing seeds of doubt and confusion.

Last but not least, as argued eariler, peace
educators will also need to reconceptualize the
neo-conservative's debate in terms of their presumed
status as defenders of "tradition", "morality" and the
like. While this task is beyond the scope of this paper,
it means in brief to demystify the neo-conservative
agenda on various social, political, economic and
cultural issues. Will their economic policies improve
conditions for the poor and unemployed even in so-called
"developed" societies like Australia? Will the
environment be conserved for posterity, or suffer
continual destruction in the quest for
profit-maximization? Will their politics of Third World
"stability" in the guise of protecting "natinal security"
and the interests of the "free world" help the poor
majorities obtain their basic needs with dignity and
self-reliance? Will their cultural policies pay due
respect to the richness and strengths of minority
cultures in multiethnic societies? Will their criticisms
of affirmative action principles and policies continue to
perpetuate structural inequities facing half of
Australia's population? Above all, will their
educational principles and practices create citizens
unafraid to question and act to improve the quality of
democratic life? Open, peaceful discussions of such
questions will likely begin to shake the "moral" high
ground assumed by many neo-conservatives. Hopefully, it
will awaken the majority's consciousness and conscience
that the ideal neo-conservative society will not be good
for most human beings in an increasingly fragile,
conflict-ridden and unequal world.

NOTES
    1.   See for example reports in The Times Higher
Educational Supplement 1/6/84, 21/8/84, 19/10/84,
26/10/84; Reagan (1984); Cox & Scwton (1984):
Social Studies Professional (1984): Social Education
(1983): Phi Delta Kappan (1983).

2. On this point, see my concluding section "Reconceptualizing the Debate".

3. For a self-account on the history of the Australian Association for Cultural Freedom, see Coleman (1984).

4. See two other Quadrant articles by Whitehall (1982, 1983) who again uses faulty "guilt by association" premises to prove pro-Soviet dominance of the Australian peace movement and the related nuclear-free and independent movement. Whitehall seems unwilling to consider alternative conceptions of the "Soviet threat" thesis which are bases, not as a priori pro-Soviet sentiments, but on national analysis of the relative roles of the superpowers in global militarization.

5. See Burns (1983) on a more general case against the present Australian Foreign Minister's view's on peace issues.

6. The Weekend Australian, Jan 4-5, 1986:1

7. The Advertiser, Jan 4, 1986:4

8. The Advertiser, Feb 2, 1986:3

9. Sydney Morning Herald Feb 19, 1986:3

10. Personal communication from Dr. Ralph Pettman, Senior Research Officer, Human Rights Commission, Commonwealth of Australia.

11. See my concluding section "Reconceptualizing the Debate".

12. Gill, A. "Catholics bitterly divideds over aid to Communist Countries" Sydney Morning Herald, Sep 9, 1985:12; Weekend Australian, Feb 1-2, 1986:17.

13. The Weekend Australian Feb 1-2, 1986:17; The Bulletin Feb 11, 1985:30.

14. The Weekend Australian June 8-9, 1985:1

15. See forthcoming M.Ed. thesis by P. Bergin (1986). "An Evaluation of Development Education: Selected N.S.W. High Schools", Centre for Social and Cultural Studies, University of New England, Armidale, N.S.W.

16. E.g., Sydney Morning Herald, Editorial, Mar 12, 1983; Editorial; Nov.24, 1984; Editorial; Nov. 15, 1985; The Australian, Editorial, Jan 6,1986; Editorial, Feb. 5, 1986; The Age, article by Michael Barnard, April 9, 1985; The Bulletin, article by Greg Sheridan, Nov. 8, 1983.

17. See Manne (1982) for a fairly recent collection on Australian neo-conservative ideology; Duncan & McAdam (1985) on a sympathetic account of the New Right; and the

228

leading conservative journals <u>Quadrant</u> and the IPA
(Institute of Apublic Affairs) Review.
    18. "Strict Guidelines Needed for Peace Studies",
media statement by Peter Shack, MP, Shadow Minister for
Education and Youth Affairs, Jan, 26, 1986.

BIBLIOGRAPHY

Adelson, J. & Finn, C.E. (1985). "Terrorizing Children",
    Commentary, April: 29-36.
Apple, M.W. (ed.) (1982) Cultural and Economic
    Reproduction in Education, London, Routledge and
    Regan Paul
Barnard, M. (1982). "The Soviet Danger" in R. Manne
    (ed.) The New Conservatism in Australia, Melbourne:
    Oxford University Press.
Begley, P. (1984). "John Whithall's 'Peace Studies in
    the Classroom", Quadrant, June:5-6.
Burns, A. (1983a) "Mr. Hayden on War and Peace",
    Quadrant, Sept:45-49.
Burns, A. (1983b) "Peace Research at ANU" Quadrant,
    Dec:49-53.
Burns, R. (ed.) (1981). "Peace Education", Special
    issue Bulletin of Peace Proposals, 2.
Burns, R. & Asqeslagh, R. (1984). "Objectivity, Values
    and Opinions in the Transmission of Knowledge for
    Peace", Bulletin of Peace Proposals, 15 (2):
    139-148.
Carey, M. & Paws, T. (1985). "The New Right Think
    tanks", National Times, Sept 13-19:14-15.
Catholic Commission for Justice and Peace (1985). Work
    for a Just Peace, Surry Hills: CCJP.
Chipman, L. (1982). "The Children of Cynicism", in R.
    Manne (ed.), The New Conservatism in Australia,
    Melbourne: Oxford University Press.
Clark, A. (1986). "How a Radical Thinker Became a
    Neo-Conservative Opinion Moulder", The Bulletin, Jan
    7:68-70.
Connell, W.F. (1983). "Curriculum for Peace Education",
    New Horizons in Education, 68:6013.
Cox, C. & Scruton, R. (1984). Peace Studies: A Critical
    Survey. London: Institute for European Defense &
    Strategic Studies, Occasional Paper No. 7.
Denborough, M. (ed.) (1983) Australia and Nuclear War.
    Fyshwick: Croom Helm, Australia.
Diwakar R.R. & Agrawal, M. (eds.) (1984). "Peace
    Education", Special issue, Gandi Mary:64-65.

Duncan, T. (1985). "Radical left bid to hijack geography course", The Bulletin, Dec 3:62-63.

Duncan, T. & McAdam, A. (1985). "New Right: Where it stands and What it means", The Bulletin, Dec 10, 1985:38-45.

Dunn, D.J. (1985). "The Peace Studies Debate" Political Quarterly, 56 (1):68-73.

Feith, H. (1982). "Repressive-Developmentalists Regimes in Asia", Alternatives, 7(4):491-506.

Fuelner, E.J. (1985). "Ideas, Think-tanks and Governments", Quadrant, Nov:22-26.

Fein, J. (1982). "Bias in Geography Textbooks", Paper presented to the Australian Geographical Research Association Conference, Sydney.

Fein, J. (1984). "Peace Education: Countering the Critics", Radical Education Dossier, 23:19-22.

Fein, J. & Gerber, R. (eds.) (1986). Teaching Geography for a Better World, Brisbane: Jacaranda.

Freire, P. (1985). The Politics of Education. New York: Bergin & Garvey.

Friedman, M. et.al (1981). Taxation, Inflation and the Role of Government, Sydney: Centre for Independent Studies, Occasional Papers 4.

Giroux, H.A. (1981) Ideology, Culture & the Process of Schooling, Landa & Falmer

Haavelsrud, M. (ed.) (1974). Education for Peace: Reflection and Action. New York: IPC Science and Technology.

Haavelsrud, M. (1980). "Indoctrination or Politicization through Textbook Content", International Journal of Political Education, 3(1):8-81.

Haavelsrud, M. (ed.) (1981). Approaching Disarmament Education Guilford: Westbury House.

Haavelsrud, M. & Galbunt, J. (eds.) (1983). "The Debate on Education for Peace", special issue, International Review of Education 29(3).

Harries, O. (1984). "The Case Against Best Case Arguments", The Bulletin, June 5, 1984:97-102.

Harries, O. (1985). "Crisis in the Pacific", Commentary, June

Hewitt, J. (1985). "From Sydney to Reagan's Right-Hand", Sydney Morning Herald, June 6, 1985:11.

Hicks, D.W. (1981). Bias in Geography Textbooks: Images of the Third World and Multi-Ethnic Britain,

Bedford Way, Working Paper No. 1, Centre for Multicultural Education, University of London Institute of Ecuation.

Hicks, D.W. (1986). Studying Peace: The Educational Rationale, Lancaster: Centre for Peace Studies, St. Martin's College, Occasional Paper No. 4.

Hicks, D.W. (1986a) "The Geography of War and Peace" in J. Fein & R. Gerber (eds.) Teaching Geography for a Better World. Brisbane: Jacaranda.

Jacobs, P. (1985). "The ANU's Peace research Centre", Quadrant, Nov:39-44.

Jacobs, P. (1985). Operation Peace Studies: War in the Classroom, Melbourne, Rosa Research & Publication.

Jastrow, R. (1984). "Reagan vs. the Scientists: why the President is Right About Missile Defense", Commentary, Jan: 23-32.

Jopson, D. (1986). "The Liberation Priests", National Times, Feb 28-Mar 3:10.

Kirkpatrick, J. (1981). "US Security and Latin America," Commentary, Jan: 29-40.

Kirkpatrick, J.J. (1984). "Threats", Quadrant, Sept:39-42.

Kristol, I. (1986). Foreign policy in an Age of Ideology", The National Interest, 1(1) (Reprinted in Quadrant, Jan/Feb:80-87).

Letham, V. (ed.) (1985). Education for Peace, Justice and Hope, Freemantle: Freemantle Education Centre.

Liberal Party of Australia, (1985). "Statement of Principles on Disarmament and Deterrence", Canberra: Liberal Party.

Luttwak, E.N. (1985), Delusions of Soviet Weakness", Commentary, Jan:32-38.

Mack, A. (1986). "The ANU Peace Research Centre: Disinformation and Pat Jacobs", Quadrant, April:41-52.

McAdam, A. (1982), Imperialism and the Third World: Western Marxist and Conservatives", in R. Manne (ed.), The New Conservatism in Australia, Melbourne: Oxford University Press.

McCoy, A.W. (1984), Priests on Trial, Ringwood: Melbourne.

Manne, R. (ed.) (1982) The New Conservatism in Australia. Melbourne: Oxford University Press.

Partington, G. (1985). "(Im)moral Education in Australia: The South Australian Experience", Quadrant, June:18-24.

Partington, G. (1986). "The Peace Educators", Quadrant,

Jan/Feb:58-66.

Peace Studies Curriculum Group (1984). Peace Education
in New South WAles North Ryde:PSCG

Pettman, R. (1984) Teaching for Human Rights.
Canberra: Australian Human Rights Commission &
Richmonds: Hodja Educationa; Resources Cooperative.
Phi Delta Kappan (1983) 64 (8) April & 64(9) June,
articles for an against disarmament education.

Pipes, R. (1984) "How to cope with the Soviet Threat",
Commentary Aug

Podheretz, N. (1983). "Appearance by Any Other Name",
Commentary, July: 25038.

Redden, J. (1984) Understanding Conflict. Adelaide:
Australian Red Cross Society (South Australian
Division).

Regan, D. (1984). "The Threat of Peace Studies",
University of Nottingham Gazette of Nottingham
Graduates 4(1):8.

Robinson, G. & Pollack, A. (1984). "War and Peace-pas
des enfants" National Times, June 8-14: 13-15.

Santamaria, B.A. (1982). "Why I Disagree with the
Catholic Commission for Justice and Peace", National
Outlook, Feb: 10-12.

Santamaria, B.A. (1982). "The Australian Strategic
Environment: an Overview" in R. Manne (ed.) The
New Conservatism in Australia, Melbourne: Oxford
University Press.

Santamaria, B.A. (1986). "CCJP not merely the
statements, but the Philosophy, News Weekly, Jan
8:7-9.

Scarrabelotti, G. (1985). "The Catholic Commission for
Justice and Peace", Quadrant, Dec:29-33.

Scruton, R. (1984). "The Ursupation of the State",
Quadrant, Nov:9-14.

Sharp, R. (1984). "Varieties of Peace Education" Paper
presented to the IFTA National Eduation Conference
Brisbane, May 11-13, 1984 (Also Chap 12 in Sharp
(1984)

Sharp, R. (1985). Apocalypse No. Sydney: Pluto Press.

Sheridan, G. "The Arguments about Teaching Peace" The
Bulletin Nov 8:58-64.

Simper, E. (1986). "Catholic at War over Peace",
Weekend Australian, Feb 1-2:17.

Social Education (1983) "Viewpoints on Nuclear Education"
Nov/Dec:187-492.

Social Studies Professional (1984). "Conference in
Teaching About Nuclear Weapons" 74(Nov): 1, 6-7.

232

Stannard, B. (1984) The Fr. Brian Gore Story. Sydney: Collins/Fontana

Steinle, J. (1986). Education for Peace Memorandum Principles of schools and Chairpersons of School Councils. Adelaide: South Australia Director-General of Education

Symon, A. (1985) "Battle over the Teaching of Human Rights" The National Times, Sep 27/Oct 3, 1985:43.

Tanter, R. (1982) "The Militarization of ASEAN: Global Context and local Dynamics", Alternatives 7(4):507-532.

Toh, S.H. (1981) "Social Peace and Third World Development", in C. Fox (ed.) Peace Education Conference, Sydney: United Nations Association of Australia (NSW) & Australian International Independent School.

Toh, S.H. (1984). "No Peace Without Development: Solidarity with the Third World in Australian Classrooms", Paper presented to the IFTA (Independent Teachers Federation of Australia & New Zealand Academy for Advancement of Science) Conference, Monash University, July

Toh, S.H. (1986) "Third World Studies", in Fein J. & R. Gerber, (eds.) Teaching Geography for a Better World, Brisbane: Jacaranda

U.S. Dept. of Defense (1985) Soviet Military Power, Warhgta: US Govt Printing Office

U.S. National Conference on Catholic Bishops (1984) The Challenge of Peace, Melbourne: Dove

Warden, I. (1986). "How can we best teach our children the virtues of peace", The Canberra Times, Feb. 25, 1986.

Whitehall, J.S. (1982) "Who's Who in the Australian Peace Movement" Quadrant Sept:13-23.

Whitehall, J. (1983) "Peace Movements in the Pacific" Quadrant Oct:42-47 Nov

Whitehall, J. (1984) "Peace Studies in the Classroom" Quadrant, Jan/Feb: 82-86

Whitehall, J. (1985) "Liberation Theology" Quadrant, Jan-Feb: 22-28

Whiteley, M. (1986) "Where Does ACR Stand?" Sydney: Australian Catholic Relief.

Whitty, G. & Young M. (eds.) (1976). Explorations in the Politics of Knowledge, Naffertan: Naffertan Books

15

A Survey of Peace Education in Canada

Wytze Brouwer

INTRODUCTION

Many definitions of peace education exist on which one might base a survey on peace education curricula in Canadian schools. In looking at any particular global conflict situation, one notes that elements of human rights, social justice, underdevelopment, militarism and even agricultural and ecological concerns enter into a possible resolution of such conflicts. One could therefore define peace education as that education in which all of the above topics are brought to bear on the analysis of global conflicts. Although the ultimate goals of peace education might indeed be to equip students to be able to resolve complex world problems, such a peace education program would be very complex and difficult to fit into a school system.

An alternative approach is to include each of the above mentioned components separately into a definition of peace education. In such a definition, development education is already peace education; human rights education is peace education; in fact, education for social justice, for ecological balance, and education in militarism, arms races and security are all elements of peace education. This definition is much broader than the former and is based on the hope that students will develop the attitudes and skills required to integrate the knowledge gained in the study of each separate component and apply them to interpersonal, community and global problems as the students mature.

Another advantage of a broad definition of peace education is that it builds on topics that are already integral parts of the education of Canadian students. The topics of world hunger and development, human rights and social justice, and ecological concerns are already included in all the provincial programs of education. Moreover, a broad definition of peace education places

disarmament education in somewhat a less central position
as only one component of peace education, not necessarily
the most important.

For the purpose of this survey, the knowledge
components were selected from Barbara Wien's (1984)
survey of US and Canadian University Peace and World
Order Studies. The topics chosen include Global
Understanding, Current Global Issues, Human Rights and
Social Justice, World Hunger and Development, Peacemaking
and Nonviolence, Multiculturalism, Ecological Balance,
International Law and International Organizations
(including the United Nations), and Religious
Perspectives on War and Peace.

Beside cognitive objectives, Canadian curriculum
documents also reflect the importance of developing the
skills, and values or attitudes that promote effective
citizenship. These values include the development of
self-confidence and self-worth, tolerance for differences
in culture or views, respect for evidence, appreciation
of the values that promote a more equitable distribution
of wealth and resources, and the willingness to
participate in the democratic process and in the
resolution of the world's problems.

One of the ways of making explicit the goals of
peace education is to describe the characteristics of
(ideally) successful graduates of a peace education
program. If we use our imagination to see such graduates
ready to enter the adult world, we would hope to see that
peace education prepares:

young people who have developed a positive
self-image, a feeling of self-confidence and competence,
based on the recognition that they can influence the
conditions under which they live;

young people who have developed a feeling of
community with others in their own country, or across the
globe, who often face life under very different and
difficult conditions;

young people who have developed an appreciation, or
esteem, for the customs, cultures and beliefs of other
societies;

young people who have gained a great deal of
knowledge and insight into the circumstances in which
others live;

young people who have developed the skills and
habits of sifting the truth from the propaganda which
surrounds them in every culture;

young people who have developed the respect for the wise use of resources and appreciate more than just the materialistic aspects of life;

young people who can tolerate and respect different points of view, who can see their world through the eyes of others and who have the skills to resolve any conflict in non-violent ways;

young people who have the desire and the skill to participate in shaping society, in their own community, their nation and in the world.

It is clear that such values, if they are to be achieved at all, cannot be taught in a few lessons, but must be part of a long-term process that involves parents, teachers, school board members and requires also the political will to achieve such goals. Moreover, such values cannot be taught in a verbal way, like a set of doctrines, if they are to result in real behaviors. Bartelds (1984) suggests that these attitudes develop best in an environment in which:

(1) responsibility and independence are stimulated;
(2) there is room for experimentation with behavior and learning styles;
(3) educators do not preach values, but model these values by their conduct;
(4) attention is paid to the emotional feelings and well-being of others;
(5) cooperation is emphasized rather than competition.

Based on the different provincial curriculum documents and on the considerations outlined above, the values or attitudes by which teachers' opinions were sampled included the values of cooperation, conflict resolution, empathy, mutual interdependence, participation in society, appreciation for cultural differences, development of responsibility and self-worth, and tolerance for the opinions of others.

In order to review the state of peace education in school systems across Canada it is also necessary to describe the organization of Canada's educational system. Since education is a provincial responsibility, the overall educational policies are set by ten provincial ministries of education and the two territorial (Yukon and the North West Territories) ministries. Consequently, a survey of the provincial policies and regulations must take into account as many as twelve provincial educational documents.

Within each province, the various school divisions, or school boards, have considerable local flexibility. The various provincial goals of education are general enough to allow school boards to develop more explicitly themes such as education for social justice, multicultural education, and even nuclear awareness education. In such cases, school boards may simply encourage their teachers to develop such themes, or the boards may set up task forces to develop curriculum in these areas.

Provincial educational documents generally prescribe the educational objectives that should be achieved during each year and in each course, but do not prescribe the specific ways the objectives must be achieved. Since the provincial educational objectives have knowledge, skill, and attitude components, teachers have considerable local responsibility for designing the educational strategies for achieving the objectives. For example, the educational objectives encouraging global understanding, tolerance for cultural differences, and participation in society from a local to global level, allow teachers to discuss topics related to militarism and the arms race.

Many provincial educational documents prescribe a "core curriculum" that can be achieved in about 80% of the classroom time available. Although many topics may be suggested for the remaining 20% of time, school jurisdictions and local school teachers often have the freedom to choose topics of special or local interest. It therefore appears that teachers in Canada do have the freedom to address issues related to war and peace in a balanced manner in their classrooms.

Teachers' federations also have an important influence within each province or territory. The Canadian Teachers' Federation is the umbrella organization of the different federations, but each province has at least one teachers' federation with some provinces having four or five.

The survey addresses each of the four constituencies mentioned with respect to the policy statements, curriculum documents and other questions related to peace education.

PROVINCIAL CURRICULA RELEVANT TO PEACE EDUCATION

Most of the topics associated with peace education, with the exception of Ecology and Religious Perspectives on War and Peace, fall in the domain of what is often called Social Studies. The topic of Ecology falls within science programs in the elementary school, or in general science, biology or chemistry in the secondary schools. The topic Religious Perspectives on War and Peace usually falls within religious studies programs which are offered primarily in Roman Catholic or independent Protestant schools.

Canadian Social Studies programs generally spiral out from the study of the family and the local community in Division I (K-3) to the study of global community by Division IV (grade 10-12).

While adhering to this vertical opening up from the local to the global scene, some of the provinces, Manitoba and Alberta in particular, also provide for a local to global opening up in a horizontal sense by including topics such as Neighborhoods around the World in grade 2 and Culturally Distinct Communities in grade 3, for example. All provinces offer at least one World Issues course in high school, with Alberta offering two compulsory World Issues courses in grades 11 and 12.

Another important characteristic of Canadian society, which is reflected in all provincial curricula, is Canada's multicultural heritage. This heritage, together with the continuing influx of immigrants and refugees, requires a special educational emphasis on the value of various cultural, linguistic, racial and religious origins. The requirement of Canadian students to live harmoniously in a multicultural Canada should, in principle, equip them well to be citizens of an increasingly interdependent world.

A feature of the high school programs in a number of provinces is in the flexibility of the programs. In Saskatchewan, Manitoba and Alberta, for example, topics specified in the curriculum guides cover only about 70-80% of the teaching time available. The remaining time may be devoted to important current issues such as the nuclear arms race and disarmament. In a variation of this model, the Nova Scotia Modern World Problems course for grade 12 lists up to 18 possible topics, six of which might constitute a full year course. One of the suggested topics is NATO, the Warsaw Pact and the Nuclear

Arms Race, so that teachers in Nova Scotia do have the opportunity to address the topic in the classroom. The Manitoba World Issues course looks at the issues of Lifestyle and Development, and Global Organization, explicitly from an East-West and a North-South Perspective and includes a unit on Future Studies.

Whereas most topical outlines of Social Studies courses emphasize the knowledge objectives, the various provincial programs also emphasize the development of inquiry and communication skills. Students are expected to develop the skills required to recognize problems, to gather information, to analyze and reach tentative conclusions and to communicate their findings and opinions in a clear and logical way. Various provincial programs also place a great deal of emphasis on the development of those skills that will enable a student to participate effectively in society from the local to the global level.

In principle, it appears that the knowledge, skill and value goals of Social Studies education in Canada are in close agreement with those of peace education. The topics of world hunger and development, human rights and social justice, and multiculturalism are included in all provincial programs. At least half of the social studies curriculum guides identify issues related to the nuclear arms race, or global conflicts explicitly as topics that may be selected as part of a world issues course. However, some provincial ministries in current reviews of Social Studies programs are weighing the possibilities of including these topics in the core of the programs.

On July 10, 1985, the Quebec Cabinet decided to approve the principle of official Quebec participation in the celebration of the International Year of Peace. A working group was set up to plan ways of involving the public and the schools in celebrating the International Year of Peace. Under the guidance of an advisory committee, which included representatives of parent groups and school boards, the group designed a poster representing a call for global understanding and disarmament, a folder outlining possible ways in which students can be actively engaged in the pursuit of peace, and a teaching unit entitled Eduquer a la paix: c'est contribuer a batir la paix, designed to be used on October 24, 1986, United Nations Day. The major themes of the teaching unit are "Peace at the Personal Level" and "Peace at the Societal, Global Level."

TEACHER SURVEY

The teacher survey included teachers who were identified by school board superintendents as being interested or involved in peace education at various grade levels. These teachers were asked to respond to a number of questions related to their experience in peace education, the components of peace education considered most important, the attitudes and values considered most important and the areas in which support materials are required.

Table 1 indicates the percentage of teachers who regularly include various components of peace education in their program. The peace education topics most widely taught by the elementary school teachers are Human Rights and Social Justice, Peacemaking and Nonviolence, and Multiculturalism. Of the topics listed in Table 1, only Peacemaking and Nonviolence is not explicitly mentioned in provincial curriculum guides. Secondary school teachers indicated a greater exposure to Current Global Issues, World Hunger and Development, Human Rights and Social Justice and Global Understanding.

Table 1: Components of Peace Education Most Frequently Taught in Canadian Classroom

Topic	Elementary (K-6) N=22	Secondary (7-13) N=69
Global Understanding	39	63
Current Global Issues	33	75
Human Rights and Social Justice	33	63
World Hunger and Development	56	65
Peacemaking and Nonviolence	56	57
Multiculturalism	50	43
Ecological Balance	33	30
International Law and Organizations	28	37
Religious Perspectives on War and Peace	22	32

The figures indicate the percentages of responses in which the topics were mentioned.

It should be noted also that the topics of Ecology and Religious Perspectives on War and Peace do not receive a high emphasis by the (primarily) social studies teachers surveyed, even though Ecology is taught in essentially all Canadian science programs. Religious Education courses are common in Roman Catholic schools but not in public schools in Canada.

Teachers were also asked to indicate the peace education topics they considered most important. The differences between the responses of the elementary and secondary school teachers are rather interesting. The topic Peacemaking and Nonviolence, which does not occur in the provincially mandated curriculum guides, is considered by far the most important component of peace education by the elementary school teachers, whereas Global Understanding, Human Rights and Social Justice, Current Global Issues and World Hunger and Development are ranked as important as Peacemaking and Nonviolence by the secondary school teachers. Perhaps surprising is the relatively low rating for Multiculturalism, and International Law and International Organizations (UN, UNESCO, World Court), especially at the secondary level.

Table 2: Peace Education Topics Considered Most
Important for Canadian Schools

Topic	Elementary N=22	Secondary N=69
Global Understanding	30	75
Current Global Issues	45	61
Human Rights and Social Justice	35	67
World Hunger and Development	45	61
Peacemaking and Nonviolence	75	73
Multiculturalism	45	34
Ecological Balance	35	28
International Law and Organizations	15	15
Religious Perspectives on War and Peace	20	21

Table 3 indicates the value components of peace education that teachers consider important enough to require greater emphasis in Canadian schools. All the values listed, except for the attitude (and skill) of nonviolent resolution of conflicts, are frequently mentioned as important in current Social Studies curriculum guidelines.

The elementary school teachers identified the values of nonviolent conflict resolution, cooperation, and the development of responsibility and self-worth as the three values that most required increased emphasis.

The secondary school teachers rated these three values along with tolerance, and participation in society as essentially equally important. The

Table 3: Value Components of Peace Education that
Should Receive Greater Emphasis in
Canadian Schools

Topic	Elementary N=22	Secondary N=69
Cooperation, Local and Global	77	72
Nonviolent Conflict Resolution	91	72
Empathy Towards Others	73	65
Mutual Interdependence	55	59
Participation in Society (local to global)	68	72
Appreciation for Cultural Differences	59	66
Developing Responsibility and Self Worth	82	71
Tolerance for Opinions	73	74

total range in percentage mention for each value was 36% for elementary school teachers, but only 15% for secondary school teachers. Aside from sample size, this may be a reflection of the emphasis on cognitive objectives in Canadian secondary schools.

The emphasis on the value of nonviolent conflict resolution is reflected in a number of recent curricula. The Vancouver Branch of the United Nations Association of Canada, for example, has published a number of teaching units on Conflict Resolution for elementary and intermediate grades. The North York School Board (1985), and the Commission scolaire St-Exupery have identified conflict resolution as a topic important enough to serve as a focus for some curriculum development for elementary schools. The topic has clear relevance for the personal lives and family situations of school children and has obvious implications for society as a whole.

The teachers participating in the survey were also asked to indicate which peace education topics required additional resources, and also the type of resources that would be most helpful to the teacher. The responses indicate that the vast majority of elementary school teachers wanted more resources to teach the topic Peacemaking and Nonviolence. Secondary school teachers also indicated this topic as most in need of additional resources, with the topics of Human Rights and Social Justice, and Global Understanding also receiving frequent mention.

Teachers were also asked the types of resources needed on the peace education topics. Topical films were mentioned most frequently as a valuable resource. These results appear to be consistent with the results of a National Film Board of Canada survey, in which the most-requested audio-visual resources for peace education were videotapes and/or films. The need for up-to-date, factual materials in the form of fact sheets was listed second in importance and the need for classroom-ready units and teachers' guides was next. A number of teachers also indicated a need for topical educational kits containing slides, overheads, fact sheets and teachers guides. It is not clear whether the teacher responses indicated a dearth of available resources or a lack of familiarity with the resources.

A common element in Tables 1-3 is the importance of Peacemaking and Nonviolent Conflict Resolution. In the teacher survey but also in a number of teachers' federations policy documents, the skills of constructive conflict resolution are not only prerequisite to peacemaking on the international stage but have especially important benefits for students' personal, family and community lives. In the Burnaby unit <u>Conflict</u>

and Change (Draft 1985) students analyze conflicts in
their own experience and practice a variety of conflict
resolution strategies in these situations. Throughout
the unit the scale of conflicts studied is slowly
expanded to the global stage. In some of the peace
education units produced in Canadian schools, the
assumption is made that the skills required for
constructively resolving interpersonal conflicts are
identical to the skills required to solve international
conflicts. There is clearly a need to familiarize
teachers with a greater variety of conflict resolution
strategies such as the ones discussed in the Christian
Movement for Peace (1984) peace education program, or in
Alternatives to Violence (1984), a peace education
program prepared by the Quakers, or in Perspectives: A
Teaching Guide to Concepts of Peace (1983). In these
three curriculum projects students are exposed to a wide
variety of conflict resolution strategies, and the
curriculum projects avoid the naive over-simplification
that the solutions of global conflicts are as simple as
the solutions of interpersonal conflicts might be.

CONCLUSIONS

The survey shows that many of the components of
peace education are reflected in Canadian Social Studies
programs and are beginning to become part of subject
areas such as Science, Religious Education, Literature
and Drama courses. Teaching peace education, including
nuclear arms education, is consistent with all the
provincial statements of the goals of education. Some
provinces are beginning to introduce specific nuclear
awareness and war-and-peace units into the curriculum.
School boards throughout Canada have grappled with
the problem of peace education and a fair number have
taken the opportunity to set up task forces to
investigate further the feasibility of developing curriculum in the area. The prime concern has been the
development of Nuclear Awareness Units, with Conflict
Resolution and Social Justice units generally added for
primary grades.
In general, there is greater support for peace
education from teachers' federations than from any other
constituency. Almost all teachers' federations encourage
peace education activities, and some federations support

the development of curriculum units and peace education associates.

Several hundred teachers interested in peace education were identified by superintendents of education. These teachers indicated considerable experiences in teaching about human rights, social justice, multiculturalism and global issues but regarded the topic of peacemaking and nonviolence as the most important component of peace education, with global understanding also ranked high for secondary school teachers.

The teachers also supported a greater emphasis on peace education values, especially the values of nonviolent conflict resolution, developing responsibility and self-worth, cooperation, tolerance for other opinions and the value of participating in society at all levels.

In addition to the organizations and teachers surveyed there are, of course, many other organizations involved with peace education. Volunteer organizations such as Educating for Peace, Educators for Social Responsibility, and other organizations such as Learner Centers are also active in providing expertise, curriculum resources and teaching strategies in peace education.

NOTES

Alberta Education. 1981 Social Studies Curriculum Guide. Edmonton: Curriculum Branch, 1981.

Bartelds, C. Gandhi Marg 64-65. July-August, 1984, pp. 308-312.

Department of Education (Newfoundland). The Master Guide for Social Studies, K-XII in Newfoundland & Labrador. St. Johns: Division of Instruction, 1980.

Manitoba Education. Social Studies Grade 7-12. Winnipeg: Minister of Education, 1985.

Ministere de l'Education de les Saskatchewan. Programe de sciences humaines des Ecoles Designees, Quatrieme Cycle. (Version Experimentale). Regina: Bureau de la minorite de langue officiale, 1981.

_____. Programe de sciences humaines des Ecoles Designees, Troisieme Cycle. (Version Experimentale). Regina: Bureau de la minorite de langue officiale, 1981.

Ministry of Education, British Columbia. Social Studies Curriculum Guide,

Grade 8-11. Victoria: Publication Services Branch, 1985.

North York Board of Education. White Paper on Nuclear Awareness. Toronto: North York Board of Education, 1985.

Ontario Ministry of Education. History and Social Studies Curriculum Guide. Toronto: Ontario Ministry of Education, 1985.

_____. Science Curriculum Guide. Toronto: Ontario Ministry of Education, 1986.

Wien, B. Peace and World Order Studies. New York: World Policy Institute, 1984.

16

Education: A Force for Change in the Northeast of England: What Are the Global Implications?

David Menham

This chapter is extracted from a study originally researched at Bradford University School of Peace Studies in March 1986.

INTRODUCTION

> "Our society is a multicultural, multiracial one, and the curriculum should reflect a sympathetic understanding of the different cultures and races that now make up our society. We also live in a complex, interdependent world, and many of our problems in Britain require international solutions. The curriculum should therefore reflect our need to know about and understand other countries."
>
> D.E.S. Consultative Document 1977
> "Education in Schools"

What has come to light during the course of my investigation into education policy in the North East of England is the following:

An expressed desire amongst local education authorities (LEAs) to

- study conflict resolution
- improve the quality of teaching and the ethos of the school
- provide a harmonious atmosphere in the classroom
- increase pupils' participation in decision making processes
- give a more global or international perspective in the classroom
- provide in-service training to achieve stated objectives

246

- improve and expand upon existing teaching resources
- implement policies through the process of consultation rather than conflict
- involve the community in its plans and decisions.

There is no reason to believe that these moderate objectives could not be achieved in every nation regardless of its avowed political affiliations. Some form of structural violence is present in all educational establishments due to the limits imposed by state education itself. To break free of this requires a concerted effort. Cross-cultural comparisons need to be made in order to bring more knowledge to the surface. Growing number of nations are now multi-ethnic - multi-ethnicity demands a multi-dimensional response. The more clearly that the aims of multi-ethnic education, world studies, development education, disarmament education, human rights education, environmental education, peace studies and global peace education are defined in terms of education for world citizenship, the more precisely the natural boundaries of human existence will be demonstrated to the world at large.

BACKGROUND INFORMATION

The North East of England is composed of a number of Metropolitan and non-Metropolitan Counties. They include Northumberland, Durham, Cleveland, North Yorkshire, West Yorkshire, Humberside and South Yorkshire. The region houses a total population of 7 1/2 million people which account for 14% of the population of the British Isles. The land covered stretches for 192 miles from North to South and some 85 miles or so from West to East. Within this area there are 19 local Education Authorities servicing 4,456 schools with a combined total of 1,163,183 pupils excluding Sheffield.

Except for Northumberland and North Yorkshire most of these counties are densely populated, ranking amongst the most densely populated counties in the whole country. In addition they have been between them 525,311 unemployed. Although the industrial base of the area is becoming more diverse the region has traditionally provided vital branch industries in key field such as coal mining, steel manufacture and shipbuilding. Textiles have also figured highly, especially in West Yorkshire, and in Bradford in particular. Only

Northumberland and North Yorkshire have kept their rural character intact and are consequently more dependent on agriculture than industry. However even they are interconnected. These two areas also have much less dense populations as a result. All areas throughout the region have depended upon their prosperity coming from these traditional industries, and since they have declined the social and economic climate of the area has also declined.

Due to this common industrial inheritance working class traditions and values have strongly permeated the region. The political composition of the Councils reveals a 60% Labour majority, with Conservatives in second place accounting for 25.5% of the total number of Council seats. The SDP/Liberal Alliance takes up 11.3% of the remainder and the final 3% or so is a mixture of Independent and other Councillers. This no doubt has some bearing on the composition of Education Committees and the formulation of their policies.

Within the confines of Government finance and control the local education authorities have been given relative freedom in developing their own policies and devising the shape of the curriculum. To some extent the schools and colleges that they service also have similar rights, although they are not so clearly defined.

DEVELOPMENTS IN EDUCATIONAL REFORM

The educational reforms of the 1950s and 1960s helped to bring about a Comprehensive system of education based on merit, but they did very little to promote the conditions necessary for equality of opportunity to flourish. The reforms of the 1970s tried to restore this balance but a number of important factors were left out. The position of ethnic minorities and the position of females had been grossly overlooked. So too had the environment in which education is delivered. The concept of structural violence was not an accepted fact and the effects of institutionalization were not taken very seriously. The interdependence between the educational system and the industrial system that it evolved within was not fully understood. The links between the domestic economy and the international economy were not seen as important until a very real crisis occurred.

The increase in crime and domestic violence towards the end of the 1970s and the beginning of the 1980s brought things to a head. Questions were raised as to the sources of violence and anti-social behavior. Was it the individual or group that were to blame? Was it society? Was it the Government? Or was it something more fundamental to all of us? Was there any way of halting this destabilizing process without the need to refer to increasingly Draconian methods?

The policies of the various LEAs began to reflect the answers more and more coherently. By examining the nature of conflict in a professional and scientific manner they began to catch up to the Peace Researchers who had first begun to examine these questions for themselves in the 1950s. In the words of Geoff Driver this became immediately obvious when it was realized that "many long established school aims and activities have ceased to be directly related to the external realities." Competition for many schoolchildren in areas of high unemployment seemed pointless. It also made them question what it was that they were in fact being educated for. The learning process was coming under heavy criticism. The conditions in other parts of the world brought this home to many pupils and students.

The concept of community is perhaps the key to understanding this. 1/ Education must be able to relate to the community but in order to do so the community must first be defined. Traditional communities everywhere no longer exist in isolation from one another. Britain has always been a multi-nation state. Since the Second World War it has gradually become a multi-ethnic state. Multi-ethnicity has brought with it the concept of multiculturalism.

PEACE EDUCATION, WORLD STUDIES AND
MULTICULTURAL EDUCATION:
THE SUPPORTIVE NETWORK

Multicultural Education

The emergence of multicultural education in Britain shows the desire for people to communicate on an entirely new basis. The validity of what were previously viewed as purely foreign cultures in our classrooms, today, shows a shift in consciousness and a move towards accommodation which at the same time represents a move away from assimilation. It has proved difficult to achieve integration by demanding that our ethnic minorities should accept the British way of life without question.

In fact as a means of complying with European legislation the British Government and Parliament have instead had to introduce new legislation designed to combat discrimination' against our ethnic minority communities. We have also had to introduce Equal Opportunities Legislation in order to protect the rights of women in addition to this. This has led to an upsurge of interest in human rights generally. No coherent human rights legislation yet exists in this country. The Universal Declaration of Human Rights has not been ratified and the European Covenant has not been fully incorporated into our legal system. Britain's role in Europe has not been clearly defined as it seems to be a fairly arbitrary one. 2/ Britons have a tendency to orientate themselves to developments that are taking place across the Atlantic instead. This of course has a historical basis.

Fortunately the ideal of multiethnicity also came from the U.S.A. Together Britain and America have produced a wealth of material on racial and multicultural issues. This has helped to open up the debate further. Local Education Authorities are now beginning to benefit from the debate and are rapidly gaining expertise in this field. Some LEAs have been able to set up special Multicultural Education Units. In the North East of England they are quickly becoming a regular feature in a number of Teachers Centres or otherwise they are housed in their own set of offices. The National Association of Multicultural Education supports this process and actively promotes it. There are also many community based initiatives which link in with this work. 3/

World Studies

World Studies is a rapidly evolving discipline which has been taken up by a number of LEAs throughout the country. One of the main centres for this is the World Studies Teachers Training Centre in York (WSTTC). Since 1982 the Centre has grown from a Development Education Centre into a nationally recognised educational establishment housed as it is within the vicinity of the School of Education at York University. Almost all of the LEAs in the North East have had contact with this centre and many teachers have received in-service or pre-service training there. 4/

World Studies, due to its broad ranging character, concerns itself not just with issues of race or culture but also with issues of human rights, the position of women in world society, international relations, development education, environmental education and peace education. The idea of Education for World Understanding has been around for a number of decades going back as early as the 1920s and 1930s but it has relatively remained a fringe concern until the growth of development agencies in the 1960s through to the 1980s. This resurgence has boosted the work of such organizations as the Council for Education in World Citizenship which was originally founded in 1939. (This organization also helped in the founding of UNESCO after the Second World War.)

The modern response is probably also tied up with the revival of the peace movement and the increase of international organizations world wide. Britain is the International Headquarters for hundreds of such organizations. One of the explanations for this is connected to the role that Britain played in the world prior to the dissolution of the British Empire. It is hardly surprising then that since many countries have gained their political independence from their former colonizers that they should seek contact on a more equitable basis. This has upset traditional based relationships and produced a number of uncertainties for countries such as Britain. The New Commonwealth agreements and the inclusion of many African states in the Treaty of Rome has done much to push these uncertainties to the forefront of peoples minds. The demand for cultural equality and racial harmony is not just a domestic affair, it is an international concern. Socialist countries in Eastern Europe also have their problems in this respect, so the issues are not just confined to countries with market based economies. 5/

The growth of debate since the publication of a series of reports on what are now termed as North-South issues has turned organizations such as Oxfam and Save the Children Fund into multi-million pound concerns at a time when Britain's official aid is at its lowest ever.

This demonstrates the increasing level of grass roots support that has spontaneously arisen just in the last 3-4 years. The World Studies Teachers Training Centre is financed by the EEC, the Rowntree Trust and Christian Aid. It is also linked into an expanding network of other organizations including the Council for Education in World Citizenship, World Studies Project (of Centre for Peace Studies), the One World Trust, the World Studies Teacher Education Network, the National Association of Development Education Centres, the UNESCO Associated Schools Project and the Standing Conference on Education for International Understanding. It also has links with the with the Peace Education Network. 6/

Peace Education

Peace Education is not as easy to define as Multi-cultural Education or World Studies. Many people in Britain associate the word Peace with the Peace Movement and with the activities of CND in particular. It is not entirely fair to do this as the peace movement was in existence long before CND and its associated organizations. (Some of the earliest Pact Societies were formed at the turn of the century in the USA.) The Peace Movement in Britain did not really begin to crystallize until just before the First World War. Peace Education, 'Has its roots in ecumenism, pacifism, reformist education and international work camps'. The concern for curricula development also goes back many years and is not just a contemporary phenomenon. 7/

Peace Research first became formalized in Britain in the 1950s in the shape of Conflict Studies. The first establishment in this country was the Lancaster Peace Research Centre which was founded in 1959. The first Vice-Chancellor of Lancaster University was involved with this movement and secured a Rowntree funded Fellow in Conflict Research for his University in 1965. Today Richardson Institute for Conflict and Peace Research is attached to the Lancaster Department of Politics.

In 1983 the Richardson Institute for Conflict and Peace Research published the results of a survey conducted on Peace Education in Great Britain. They consulted 125 LEAs on the kind of topics which the LEAs considered should be included in peace studies. Further, they covered seven other areas including their views on peace studies as a discipline. The results suggest that, "while there are differences of interpretation between Labour and Conservative councils, and between 'nuclear free' and 'non nuclear free' councils, there does appear to be some consensus on the central topics to be considered by peace studies."

I would argue that such statements tend to add to the confusion surrounding the nature of 'Peace Education' and 'Peace Studies'. Thus, in the introductory leaflet produced by the Centre for Peace Studies also at Lancaster (St. Martin's College) they make the following statement. "Education for peace is not a new subject. Rather it is a dynamic perspective which can enhance all areas of the Curriculum and indeed the whole ethos of the school. It has the backing of Her Majesty's Inspectorate, Local Education Authorities, teachers' unions and a wide range of other educational organizations." This particular centre acts in a very similar way to the WSTTC at York. Their view of Peace tends to coincide with the WSTTC's view on global education. So the word 'Peace' is used in a number of different ways. Peace Studies and Peace Education are perhaps as often misunderstood as the two words Racism and Racialism. Peace Education and World Studies are used interchangeably.

Most critics tend to react to the word peace as it relates to the peace movement and in particular the unilateralist movement. 8/ Peace Education and Disarmament Education are also confused with one another. Some LEAs such as Wakefield got around this problem by calling their document 'Education for Peace'. Barnsley LEA chose to avoid the confusion altogether by calling their document 'Education for a Less Violent World'. North Tyneside used the title 'Peace Studies' and then continued a discussion on Multicultural Education and Peace Education. Some LEAs decided not to devise a policy statement at all but went ahead with a programme on World Studies, in the absence of any conflict.

THE EMERGENCE OF THE GLOBAL DIMENSION
IN MULTICULTURAL EDUCATION

Despite the level of support which now exists for Multicultural Education, it still has its critics on both sides of the political fence. THese antics either see it as too weak in its application and therefore too compromising, or as a direct threat or challenge to traditions which for many British people are held sacred and inviolable. At its best it is a challenge to the creative ability of most teachers to re-orientate their basic world view to one which is more accommodating to a pluralistic sense of cultural identity. This dual legacy devolves from the remnants of the British Empire. It therefore affects our ideas and concepts in relation to "the rights and duties of citizenship."

New Commonwealth citizens in particular realize this dichotomy which exists between their traditional understanding of the world and their newly acquired understanding which has come to them through their participation as citizens of the United Kingdom. It has created an identity crisis for many of their offspring. It has confused their sense of community also. For the emerging new young generations whose family background is that of the Commonwealth it is a double dichotomy. Many choose to reject both their home culture and their host culture in favor of 'youth culture' or what is termed by a number of sociologists as 'pop culture'. In fact their essential dilemma is no different from that of many British people who also hold the family in high regard, and recognize the need for cultural continuity as a means of preserving and conserving cultural identity.

In World Studies

The World Studies approach recognizes that this 'cultural crisis' is a 'common crisis' and an essential part of the process of change. It has its roots in how we as individuals, families and groups see ourselves in relation to the rest of the world. It is therefore fundamentally a matter of perspective. Our sense of cultural perspective also contains political elements and is tied up with the concept of the Nation State and the sense of patriotism that the State invariably demands from us. In the past this has led nations into competition with one another in defense of the glory of their country.

The World Studies approach challenges this concept of patriotism and asks us to recognize it as a negative characteristic. The critics assert that this has a detrimental effect on the country's morale. They say it negates our sense of citizenship for something they see as too big and too difficult to grasp. Besides, the defense of the nation is seen as paramount to our collective security.

In Global Peace Security

The opening sections concentrated on a number of factors that have contributed towards the shaping of the British Education System. They also concentrated on the more recent responses to curriculum innovations which have led to the fundamental aims of education being reviewed and reconsidered in a new light.

The official response was identified as concerned with the controversial nature of these revised aims and objectives but not so much they have been rejected altogether. The peace movement has developed too broad a platform to be ignored and has become too strong and widespread to be held back. Much evidence points to its permanent character as it has transcended the stage where it can be dismissed as a passing fad or fashion of an extreme Left wing minority. The issues have found their way into Church gatherings and onto the agendas of many moderate and politically neutral organizations, many of which have come to recognize them as educational issues alone. The prominence of these issues is part of the natural dialectics of human experience since the aftermath of two world wars which have left the world in a condition of uneasy peace.

Multicultural Education is the forerunner to a global education. World Studies is the intermediate stage that has to be reached in order to provide the necessary framework of understanding for the concept of education for World Citizenship to take root. Education for peace can help provide the social skills for a global education to emerge but unless it is universal in nature and concept it will be as divisive as education for war. Disarmament Education, although very useful, is limited too. Multicultural Education is enlightening but it is too limited. Peace Education is an ongoing movement tied up with the process of change and is only limited by the absence of its ultimate goal. It is not however an illusory concept, only a slippery one. Political Literacy is a good foundation for it to rest upon but this foundation will only be as strong as its basic components. Global literacy goes some way to strengthening such a foundation. World Studies attempts to provide this so it therefore has more immediate applications in the field of education. It can provide the necessary model for advancing civilization along humanistic lines and in so doing it can redress the imbalances caused by previously incomplete and entirely secular educations. It does not reject the need for a technical education in addition to a social education. In fact technical education can be improved within its sphere of influence. 9/

In British society there is an obvious dichotomy between technical education and social education. One has been promoted at the sacrifice of the other. There has been a lack of harmony and integration. World Studies provides the necessary integration and also can help to promote the necessary harmony. The goals of industry and the goals of peace should not be in basic conflict with one another as they invariably are. An efficient economy can be devised without the present concentration on arms production and arms sales. A global outlook can help provide the global security that is now lacking. Common Security can only be arrived at through common solutions. In the past NATO and the Warsaw Pact have tried to provide this common security but only for a limited number of individuals, groups and families within an exclusive club of nations. These clubs are showing signs of distrust not of common concern for the virtues of humanity. They need to be revised, reviewed and reassessed within the context of a global setting, otherwise these two competing systems will drag the rest of the world into a conflict far more devastating than any that has been previously achieved. Although the immediate future appears quite dark and uncertain it has the potential to be lifted out into the light of day.

NOTES

1.   This idea is explored by Professor James O'Connell in his Lecture Notes of 21st January 1983. The lecture was entitled "Towards an understanding of the concepts in the study of peace". Section 2 A "Belonging, Making, Developing" deals with the concept of community. School of Peace Studies, Bradford.

2.   For a discussion of the Council of Europe's approach to multicultural education see "Education for the 21st Century", Council of Europe Forum Magazine 2/85.

3.   For a discussion of LEA responses to multicultural education see NAME Journal Vol. 7. No. 3. Summer 1979.

4.   This information came to light during the course of interviews with the various LEAs involved in this study.

5.   eg. Minority Rights Group Report no. 37 on "The Hungarians of Rumania", and Paul Kelletts Dissertation 1985 (U.G.) School of Peace Studies "The Multinational Nature of the Soviet Union and its Implications for Stability: The Cases of the Asian and Baltic Republics".

6.   Information taken from "A Statement of Intent" WSTTC Autumn 1982.

7.   For a detailed discussion see page 20-28 of "A Global Peace Study Guide" compiled by G.K. Wilson; Housmans Publishers London, 1982.

8.   This view is also held by Michael McCrum (former Head of Eton) as expressed in a statement made at the Annual Conference of the Council for Education in World Citizenship in 1983.

9.   "Global Pi - World Studies in the Science and Maths Classroom" WSTTC York 1985.

258

TABLE I: POPULATION STATISTICS

Local Authority	General Population	Number of Unemployed	Unemployment %
1.2 Northumberland	300,700	16,949	17.0
1.3 North Tyneside	193,400	15,162	20.7
1.4 Newcastle	278,400	26.356	20.7
1.5 South Tyneside	159,100	16.084	20.7
1.6 Gateshead	209,700	17,368	20.7
1.7 Sunderland	293,400	29,432	20.7
1.8 Durham	603,700	44,097	19.7
1.9 Cleveland	562,700	56,424	23.0
1.10 North Yorkshire	691,100	29,589	11.6
1.11 Leeds	712,200	44.321	14.5
1.12 Bradford	464,400	30,965	14.5
1.13 Calderdale	191,200	10,588	24.5
1.14 Kirklees	372,700	20,857	14.5
1.15 Wakefield	310,700	20,862	14.5
1.16 Humberside	851,600	60,106	17.8
1.17 Doncaster	288,200	25,185	19.1
1.18 Rotherham	252,500	20,547	19.1
1.19 Barnsley	224,800	18,479	19.1
1.20 Sheffield	540,500	42,802	19.1
TOTALS	7,501,000	546,173	

STATISTICAL SOURCES: 1. Municipal Year Book (1986)
Municipal Publications Ltd.
2. Britain 1986 (1986) HMSO

TABLE II: POLITICAL COMPOSITION OF COUNCIL

Local Education Authority Area	NP	IND	C	LAB	L	SD	ALL	RA	O	V	TOTAL SEATS
Northumberland	-	2	13	30	-	-	20	-	-	1	66
North Tyneside	-	-	20	33	2	-	4	-	1	-	60
Newcastle	-	-	22	45	10	1	-	-	-	-	78
South Tyneside	-	-	3	47	1	-	-	1	-	-	66
Gateshead	-	-	7	57	1	-	1	-	-	-	66
Sunderland	-	-	13	52	-	-	7	-	2	1	75
Durham	-	4	5	50	-	-	7	-	5	-	71
Cleveland	-	-	20	51	-	-	6	-	-	-	77
North Yorkshire	-	7	43	20	-	-	26	-	-	-	96
Leeds	1	34	53	10	1	-	-	-	-	-	99
Bradford	-	-	43	41	6	-	-	-	-	-	90
Calderdale	-	-	16	22	15	-	-	-	1	-	54
Kirklees	-	18	36	14	-	3	-	-	1	-	72
Wakefield	1	4	54	-	4	-	-	-	-	-	63
Humberside	-	-	35	36	-	4	-	-	-	-	75
Doncaster	-	-	11	51	1	-	-	-	-	-	63
Rotherham	1	3	61	-	-	1	-	-	-	-	66
Barnsley	1	3	60	-	-	1	1	-	-	-	66
Sheffield	1	35	22	-	-	10	-	-	1	-	69

KEY: NP=No party, IND=Independent, C=Conservative, LAB=Labour, L=Liberal, SD=Social Democrat, ALL=Alliance, RA=Ratepayers' Association, O=Others, V=Vacancy

TABLE III: EDUCATION STATISTICS

Local Authority	Total no. of schools	Total no. of pupils in fulltime education	£m/1985 Education expenditure rates	£m/1985 Education Government Grant
1.2 Northumberland	219	50,034	69,302	66.2
1.3 North Tyneside	102	31,551	49,517	42.8
1.4 Newcastle	133	41,070	70,076	56.1
1.5 South Tyneside	98	25,556	43,076	35.5
1.6 Gateshead	118	32,538	47,845	45.0
1.7 Sunderland	147	53,006	72,235	70.5
1.8 Durham	400	99,780	137,452	134.4
1.9 Cleveland	290	102,303	153,062	147.7
1.10 North Yorkshire	498	100,974	147,182	146.7
1.11 Leeds	373	112,205	166,876	160.8
1.12 Bradford	293	81,362	120,836	121.2
1.13 Calderdale	122	33,363	46,190	46.5
1.14 Kirklees	223	67,304	94,938	95.9
1.15 Wakefield	201	51,754	75,068	72.6
1.16 Humberside	513	146,969	212,043	205.9
1.17 Doncaster	174	50,747	72,565	71.1
1.18 Rotherham	147	45,683	62,694	63.6
1.19 Barnsley	145	36,987	53,043	52.6
1.20 Sheffield	260	-	-	120.0
TOTALS	4,456	1,163,186	1,694,848	1,794.8

TABLE IV: PEACE ORIENTATION

Local Education Authority Area	Peace Education Policy	Nuclear Free Zone
Northumberland	No policy, no developments	Yes
North Tyneside	Written policy, part implementation, good support	Yes
Newcastle	No written policy. Support M.E., W.S., P.E.	Yes
South Tyneside	Support all three areas, developing policies	Yes
Gateshead	Developing policy through Personal and Social Education	Yes
Sunderland	Recognize P.E. as part of Political Literacy	Yes
Durham	Support M.E. and W.S. as approach to Social Sciences	Yes
Cleveland	Policy on M.E., not on P.E., strong support for W.S.	Yes
North Yorkshire	No policy, no plans, informal network only	No
Leeds	Recognize P.E. as part of Political Education	Yes
Bradford	Concentrate on M.E. and Multifaith Education	Yes
Calderdale	Support M.E. and W.S., P.E. partly explored	No
Kirklees	Policy devised and implemented	Yes
Wakefield	Policy devised and implemented	Yes
Humberside	No formal policy but level of support exists	Yes
Doncaster	Policy exists but not fully implemented	Yes
Rotherham	No policy and no plans	Yes
Barnsley	Policy on Education for a Less Violent World	Yes
Sheffield	Policy developed, being implemented	Yes

KEY: M.E. = Multicultural Education, P.E. = Peace Education, W.S. = World Studies

17

Hunger for Weapons: Education on 'Armament and Development' for Twelve to Sixteen Year Olds

Clara Venema

INTRODUCTION

This chapter describes one possible way to teach about the theme "armament and development." First, it considers why the theme should be taught. The main part of the chapter discusses the process of developing educational material on this theme and describes the final product.

This chapter is a reflection of my own experience in this area. As a staff member of the Polemological Institute of the University of Groningen, I participated in the national Educational Project on Development Cooperation (EPOS) from 1982 to 1986. The aim of this project is to integrate development education in the regular secondary education for pupils of 12-16 years of age. One of the activities of this project was the development of educational material on armament and development, entitled "Hunger for Weapons." In this way peace education was combined with development education. The Polemological Institute has a longer experience in the field of peace education than in the area of development education. Since the foundation of the Peace Education Working Group in 1972, peace education and its integration into secondary schools have been developed systematically. Since 1976, the educational activities of the Polemological Institute have expanded to include development and environmental education through participation in a project aimed at the integration of world studies in secondary education (1976-1986).

262

SOME REASONS TO TEACH ABOUT
ARMAMENT AND DEVELOPMENT

The theme of "armament and development" is a very complicated one. It is a subject of considerable scientific and political discussion. It is difficult to grasp. Nevertheless, there are good reasons to introduce the topic, even to pupils of about 14 years of age.

The Importance of Development Education

The first reason is general in character. It concerns the importance attached to development education by the Dutch government and by Dutch teachers. In the laws on both primary and secondary education, the government states that education should contribute to the personal and social preparation of the pupils for participating in society later in life. Education on the North-South issue is part of social and political education. Last year, the Dutch Parliament included in a motion two reasons in favor of development education. Development education can contribute both to an awakening of consciousness of the North-South issue and to the strengthening of national support of development cooperation.

In the opinion of teachers, the North-South issue should be taught because it belongs to the biggest world problems of this time, and young people should be able to contribute to the solution of these problems. Another reason often mentioned by teachers is that students learn of the North-South issue from the media and thus ask questions about it in the classroom.

That the Dutch government attaches importance to development education may be seen from the following:

1. In 1970 the National Commission for Instruction on and Awareness of Development Cooperation (NCO) was set up. This institution has the task of stimulating the national awareness of Third World issues and international cooperation.

2. In 1982 the minister of development cooperation took the initiative in starting the Educational Project on Development Cooperation which was planned to last three years. It was subsequently extended until August 1986. EPOS is a national project, in which several institutes throughout the country cooperate. The

national Foundation for Curriculum Development (SLO) coordinates the project. Through curriculum development,
in-service training, and development of educational
materials (teaching packs), the project has been working
on the integration of development education into the
regular secondary education for pupils of 12-16 years of
age. The activities of EPOS will be continued and
expanded to the regular education for the age groups 4-12
and 16-18 in a so-called National Network for Development
Education, which is to start in August 1986.

The Present Topicality of "Armament and Development"

The second reason to teach about armament and
development is related to the topicality of the theme.
The arms industry has become the largest industry in the
world. In 1984, the military expenditures were around
$800 billion. The Third World countries are responsible
for some 23 percent of these expenditures. The trade in
arms is also very extensive; probably $30 billion a year
are spent on the import of weapons. About 65 percent of
the arms trade is directed to the Third World. The war
between Iraq and Iran has led to an increase in the
profits of the arms trade.

At the same time, one-fourth of the world population
is starving. The gap between the rich and the poor is
still widening in many countries. It is therefore not
surprising that in the past few years many reports have
been published on this alarming situation. Examples of
international reports are the report by the
Brandt-Commission (1980) and the report by the United
Nations on the relation between armament and development
(1981).

The Dutch government has also expressed its deep
concern about the growing armament increasing
underdevelopment throughout the world. According to its
statement of May 1984, military expenditures have a
negative effect on economic growth. The Dutch government
is in favor of setting up an international fund for
disarmament and development.

Through the media members of the general public,
including students, are confronted with this contradictory situation. Teachers should focus on this aspect
of the development issue, not only because of its

topicality but also because it touches on the essence of the North-South issue.

The theme of "armament and development" relativizes such stereotypes as: "The people of the Third World countries are poor and starving while the wealthy countries in the North have enough money to buy weapons." This theme clarifies the fact that the gap between the rich and the poor is a gap not only between the North and the South but also within several countries, both in the North and the South.

Military expenditures have negative economic, social, and political consequences in countries of both the North and the South. The theme also illustrates the close relationship between peace and development. Peace and security are threatened not only by the arms race but also by the unequal distribution of wealth and power between and within countries.

The Many-Sidedness of "Armament and Development"

The third reason for education on "armament and development" concerns the many-sidedness of the theme of "armament and development" which encompasses historical and geographical as well as economic and social factors. Dealing with questions such as the causes and effects of armament, one has to study the (im)balance of power between and within the concerned countries in the past and in the present; strategic and geographical positions, economic and political structures, and so on. Teaching about "armament and development" will therefore require historical, geographical, economic, and sociological approaches. As it is very difficult for only one teacher to combine all these approaches, education on this theme will tend to stimulate cooperation among teachers of different subjects. The approaches of the different teachers together will give students a more complete insight in the issue. Cooperation among teachers will also contribute to the desired integration of development education in the different subjects.

THE PROCESS OF DEVELOPING EDUCATIONAL MATERIAL
ON "ARMAMENT AND DEVELOPMENT"

We have developed the educational material on
"armament and development" in the framework of EPOS. The
project has been distinguished by
● cooperation with teachers in the development
the material;
● the restriction of the theme;
● the objectives of the lessons about the
theme; and
● the selection of a Third World country as an
example of the theme.

The Cooperation with Teachers

The education material we generated in the
Educational Project on Development Cooperation (EPOS) was
developed in cooperation with teachers of a pilot school.
The educational staff of the Polemological Institute has
worked in this way for approximately ten years. The
close cooperation with teachers ensures to a great extent
that the teaching packets are really suited for the
pupils for whom it is meant. The teachers' daily
experience with the pupils counterbalances the possibly
too "scientific" approach of the staff members of the
Polemological Institute. Furthermore, through this
cooperation with schools and teachers, try-outs of the
first drafts of the material in the classroom are made
possible. The resulting revisions are incorporated into
the final version of the material. Such cooperation has
enabled teachers to contribute directly to the
development of the material on "Hunger for Weapons."
EPOS could offer support facilities for the teacher
involved.
Quite frequently preporatory meetings were held in
which the progress of the work was discussed, the theme
"armament and development" was studied, and teaching
strategies were evaluated. These meetings were attended
by teachers and two staff members of the Institute. In
addition, we regularly called plenary meetings with all
the concerned teachers. During these meetings teachers
were informed and consulted about our plans. Thus more
teachers became involved in the development of the
material. Furthermore, one student-teacher did some

research activities during the development of the
material during his term of probation.

The Restriction of the Theme

In the small preparatory group consisting of the
geography teacher and two staff members of the
Polemological Institute, we studied and discussed the
theme of "armament and development." In our attempts to
outline the theme and to make explicit what we thought
students should know about it, we realized just how broad
the theme was. We decided to emphasize the following
factors: the increase of military expenditures in Third
World countries; the growth of the arms trade from North
to South; and the social, economic, and political
consequences of the increase of military expenditures and
armament for Third World countries.

Instead of using the concept of development in
relation to armament, we preferred to discuss the causes
and consequences of armament in Third World countries,
thus avoiding the difficulties of narrowly defining the
concept of "development"--that is, deciding whether
development should be limited to a measure of the gross
national product or the standard of living, or broadened
to include national power and prestige. The title of the
first draft of the material was "The Relation Between
Armament and Development" but the final version is called
"Hunger for Weapons", which better covers the content of
the teaching packet.

The Objectives of the Lessons about
"Armament and the Third World"

In the process of making explicit what aspects of
"armament and development" students should learn, we were
gradually describing the objectives of the lessons on
this theme. Taking into account the age of the pupils
(about 14 years), we determined the general objectives of
the lessons on armament and the Third World as follows:
  1. knowledge of and insight into the increase and
the dimensions of armament in Third World countries;
  2. insight into the causes of armament in Third
World countries;

3. insight into the political, social and economic consequences of armament in Third World countries, and

4. knowledge of and involvement in national and international attempts to spend less on armament and more on development.

The students must know and understand that, especially in the past twenty years, the military expenditures in and arms imports into the selected Third World country have increased enormously. Research on the arms trade to the Third World demonstrates that the total amount of military imports varies across regions and periods of time. For instance, the countries in the Middle East import many more weapons than the countries in South Asia, and the countries in the Far East imported more weapons during the mid-1960s than they did during the mid-1970s.

The pupils also need to learn about some of the general and specific causes of armament in the Third World. One general cause is the legitimate need for security. While learning about the differences among several regions and periods, the pupils will get a rough idea about the more specific causes of the armament in Third World countries. They should begin to understand that depending on the periods of time in question and the geographical situation of the countries involved, the following reasons could account for increased arming:

- the fighting of a war;
- racial, ethnic, or religious tensions;
- a regional vacuum of power and regional arms races;
- economic growth (e.g., by oil revenues);
- internal repression, often by a military regime.

The pupils should also understand why countries in the North supply Third World countries with weapons. The biggest arms suppliers of the Third World are the Soviet Union and the United States. These superpowers have political and strategic reasons to deliver arms to their "client-nations." Thus the East-West conflict has spread to the Third World. Both superpowers need support in the Third World as a guarantee for military bases and the supply of oil.

Most of the other big arms suppliers—countries such as France and Britain—have economic and industrial reasons to deliver arms to Third World countries. Their weapon industries can survive only if a vast part of their production is exported.

In addition, the pupils should get some insight into the consequences of armament for the Third World countries themselves. Depending on the circumstances in the country concerned, the nature of these consequences will be mainly political, social, or economic. Some possible consequences follow.

1. The national debt may increase. In this case many governments will decide to counterbalance the negative effects of their military expenses and increase their export production and decrease the production for the home market, at the expense of the poorest in society.

2. Political and/or economic dependence on the arms supplying country may increase. The receiving country is often obliged to admit a great number of technical specialists from the supplying country. Often the receiving country has to borrow money or make a "favorable financial arrangement" with the supplying country in order to pay for the arms. The superpowers, especially, will try to expand their political influence by establishing military bases or by intervening in conflicts or wars in return for the supply of arms to the country concerned.

3. The number of wars may increase. Since 1945 more than 150 wars have been fought: civil wars, border conflicts, and wars between neighbor and distant countries. Most of these have occurred in the Third World. Indeed, it is in the Third World, especially, that a reciprocal relationship exists between wars and armament. Wars lead to more armament, and armament leads to more (or more intense) war.

4. Military influence may increase. The military already exerts an important influence in many Third World countries: Two-thirds of the approximately 100 Third World countries are directly or indirectly ruled by military governments. In those countries the population has little political influence.

The development of an open and involved attitude of the pupils toward decreased armament in favor of development is a very important objective, but the realization of that objective is very difficult. Especially from a political point of view, the object of the lessons about armament in the Third World is a very sensitive theme. Teachers may be concerned that, as a result of these lessons, pupils may become convinced of the senselessness of financial aid to Third World countries as long as these countries buy arms.

On the other hand, simply moralizing about the sense of reducing armament and increasing development cooperation is not very useful either. Rather, teachers must inform their pupils about the national and international attempts being made to reduce armaments in the world. The pupils should be stimulated to form their own opinions about ways to reduce armament in the Third World. This goal will probably be reached much more easily in schools where the pedagogical climate is such that attention is paid to social and global issues, where pupils are accustomed to forming and expressing their own opinions and are stimulated to listen to and discuss with each other.

THE SELECTION OF A THIRD WORLD COUNTRY
AS AN EXAMPLE OF "ARMAMENT AND THE THIRD WORLD"

As the theme of "armament and the Third World" is very complicated, a scientific approach requires detailed studies of all its different aspects. From a pedagogical and didactic point of view, the theme should be treated in a very concrete way, as pupils of 14 years of age will lose interest if the information they receive is too general and abstract.

Therefore, we have selected just one Third World country that illustrates most of the aspects of our theme. The selection of this example proved difficult because the country or region had to meet the following criteria:

1. large expenditures for the purchase of weapons;
2. a high percentage of extremely poor people;
3. distinct national and international reasons for its armament;
4. visible consequences of the armament;
5. enough background information available for pupils about the armament in this country; and
6. close relations with the Netherlands.

After considering the Middle East, the Far East, Latin America, and North Africa, we selected India as an example. India is a good example for the following reasons:

1. The military build-up in India is influenced by international and regional power relations;

2. India considers strong military power to be proof of national status and prestige;

3. The Indian economy has a dualistic structure consisting of large technologically advanced industries with high production and small, distressed, traditional industries.

4. India has strong political and economic ties with the Soviet Union through the supply of arms and arms components, a situation it would like to change in the framework of its nonalightment policy;

5. There are strong ties between the Dutch government and Dutch industries, and India.

The example of India is not as illuminating, in the area of arms expenditures, however. Around three percent of the India's GNP is spent on arms--a percentage comparable to that of the industrialized countries of the North. Although 40-60 percent of the Indian population is starving, one must question whether that poverty can be related to the military expenses of India. Therefore, the example of India requires an approach toward theme of "armament and the Third World."

"HUNGER FOR WEAPONS"

Some General Requirements

During the preparation and try-outs of the teaching packet entitled "Hunger for Weapons," we agreed that the material had to meet certain requirements with respect to size, contents, and methods of teaching. First, we decided that, in order to keep the pupils' attention, the number of lessons about "armament and the Third World" should be no more than eighteen. Depending on the wishes of the school, it should be possible to spread the lessons over eight days, or to deal with them over a shorter period of only three days.

The content of the material should, of course, be consistent with the assumed foreknowledge of pupils of about 14 years of age. In order to determine the extent of this foreknowledge, an investigation was made at the pilot school, preceding the lesson series on "Hunger for Weapons." This test indicated that the 14 year-old pupils at this particular school had some general and superficial knowledge of international politics. But they did not have any specific knowledge of India. Based on this test, and on the experience of the teachers, the educational material contains concrete, detailed information about the economy, political situation, and military expenditures of India, set in an international context.

Another requirement was that the different approaches of the theme should be used so that teachers of different subjects could use parts of the material in their own lessons. The structure of the material is such that, the theme of "armament and the Third World" is pivotal; mutual coordination and cooperation are needed so that teachers of different subjects can contribute to the education on this theme. The material fits best in the curricula of history, geography, languages, mathematics, economics, and social studies. Furthermore, educators pay much attention to the methods of teaching. In order to attract the pupils' interest in the theme and to stimulate them to form their own opinions about it, they need to be given enough time to take in the information offered to them. A variety of methods is suggested in the material: individual and group tasks, role playing, the making of a radio program, and a structured discussion in the classroom.

THE STRUCTURE OF THE TEACHING PACKET

The teaching packet consists of a textbook for pupils, a series of twenty-four pictures and a guide for teachers.

The textbook contains the following chapters:

1. India as a "Developing country"

This chapter details development problems in India: the contrasts between rich and poor, and between the big and the small industries. A series of pictures is used to give an impression of the characteristics of India as a developing country.

2. India and Armament

This chapter examines the military build-up in India. The increase of its military expenditures is explained, and the armament of India is compared to the armament in some other Third World countries and in the Netherlands. In a related vein, the chapter suggests that the pupils make a radio program on a tape recorder. They decide for themselves what kind of program it is going to be: one that gives information in an objective way, one that tries to convince the listeners of either the rightness or the wrongness of the armament in the Third World, or one that calls on the listeners to join an upcoming demonstration against exports of arms to India.

3. The Consequences of the Armament

This chapter describes the political, social, and economic consequences of armament for Third World countries in general and for India in particular.
As a "warm-up" before studying this chapter, the chapter suggested that the pupils perform a role-playing exercise. In this exercise the Indian government has to decide whether a certain amount of money is going to be spent on defense armament or on development. The roles of the persons involved are given. The pro-defense party consists of the minister of defense, some high-ranking military officers, the director of an arms industry, and a scientist working on nuclear research. The pro-development party consists of the minister of development, two local representatives, and members of an association for medical care, urban development, and the fishermen's trade union. The roles of the prime minister and other ministers are also given. The government has to decide on two financial proposals—one by the minister of defense—the other by the minister of development.

4. The Prospects of Arms Reduction

This last chapter explores some possibilities by which to reduce armament in the Third World. The pupils discuss this issue on the basis of eight statements. In relation to these statements, some background information is provided. Examples of these statements follow:
- Armament reduction will endanger peace and security.
- Only if the wealthy nations in the North start reducing their armament can Third World countries be expected to do the same.

● The export of Dutch arms to Third World
countries can be justified in terms of the employment it
creates here.
● Each nation in the Third World has the right to
an army.

The teacher's guide to this educational material
consists of two parts. The first gives more detailed
information on the increase in causes and consequences of
armament in the Third World. The second part gives
suggestions as to the structure of the lessons and the
use of other teaching materials.

EVALUATION OF "HUNGER FOR WEAPONS"

The final version of the teaching packet "Hunger for
Weapons" was preceded by two draft versions. Both were
tried out at the pilotschool in three different groups.

The pupils reacted favorably to the lessons about
"Hunger for Weapons." They particularly appreciated the
making of the radio programme and the role play about the
Indian budget. Asked about his experiences during the
series of lessons, one pupil said: "I was really
startled by the high military expenditures of India. In
the role-playing exercise involving the Indian budget I
played a military man and had to stand up for an increase
of the military expenditures. But stepping out of that
role I was aware of the enormous poverty in India."

The lessons about the economic and political
situation in India have changed the images of India held
by most of these students. One pupil discovered that
India is "both a wealthy and a poor nation." Another was
amazed by the big industries and high military
expenditures of India. A number of pupils had
difficulty understanding all the different causes
underlying the increased armament in Third World
countries.

Asked about the causes of the arms trade to the
Third World, one pupil answered: "It's the profits that
count. Giving aid to the poor isn't profitable; selling
arms, however, is lucrative." Another pupil could not
believe that the government of India spends money on arms
when half the country's population is starving. But most
of the pupils obtained so much insight into the causes
and consequences of armament in the Third World countries
that they disapproved of the statement "Third World

countries with high military expenditures should not receive any aid."

These reactions demonstrate the importance of the varied method of teaching that was used. An issue this complicated can be taught effectively only if the pupils are given the opportunity to assimilate the information properly. Towards this end, concrete information, (illustrated by figures, tables, maps, cartoons) appeared to be helpful. The process of developing educational material in cooperation with teachers also proved worthwhile. Indeed, it contributed to a product very well suited for use in the classroom—in part, because the teachers themselves became involved in the issue.

PART TWO

Economic Aspects
of Peace

18

Peace and Development in a Counter-Elitist Perspective

Narindar Singh

INTRODUCTION

If Shakespeare were to write Macbeth once again, he might speak not just of security but of the national security state as the "chiefest enemy" of the human race. Indeed, if we focus upon the possibility of instant annihilation we are now confronted with, we can identify the cause as the military pursuits of the two national security superstates of today. Ironically, this state of ultimate insecurity is the direct and inevitable outcome of what these superstates have been doing for over forty years --each in the name of its own security. But this is not a situation with which we can afford to remain content. For it seems a miracle, according to Noam Chomsky, that the catastrophe has not occurred already. 1/ Its occurrence would be the ultimate crime that the "decision makers" wielding enormous amounts of power could commit. Therefore, if transformation for global peace is to mean anything at all, we must dispel this threat by attenuating the power of the ruling circles--and soon.

I am persuaded that it is the stark immediacy and the totality of this threat which has to be emphasized as the paramount problem of our age. This means that what we have to be concerned with is not what E.F. Schumacher once called "the cheerful brutality" of Keynes' oft-quoted remark that in the long run we are all dead. Rather, what we have to focus upon is the grim reality that it is in the very short run that we could all be dead. For in the long run in which Keynes expected us all to die, we would still be leaving our progeny behind. But in the situation we now face, the superpowers, or rather their managers, could make us all vanish in a holocaust so thorough that the progeny too would be abolished.

I am not saying that the nuclear holocaust is going to take place tomorrow. But it very well could and because it could, we cannot take even the continuity of our race for granted. It is in the threat of the abolition of human history itself that the fundamental novelty of our situation lies .

Indeed, this threat is so staggering that we cannot even expect to comprehend it much less cope with it unless we transcend our old modes of perception, irrespective of whether we have been conditioned by Liberalism or Marxism. Common to these conditioners, all their differences notwithstanding, is an identification of "progress" in human history with what is presumed to be an ongoing conquest of nature by human beings. However, given the distinct possibility of instant annihilation that we are now living with, the very idea of the Idea of Progress looks like a macabre joke. But what both ideological conditioners prevent us from seeing is the following: The kind of "weaponization" which has become the bane of our race today is both an effect and a cause of a continuing concentration of politico-economic power. It is interlocked in turn with the process of hyper-industrialization, based not on authentic science but on unbridled scientism, which the unwary see as a relentless conquest of nature. This is one reason why, basic to the success of general disarmament, there would have to be what Rudolf Bahro once called "industrial disarmament." And that is something which both Liberalism and Marxism would equate with a plea for setting the clock back. But both would be impervious to the grim meaning of the clock which regularly appears on the cover of The Bulletin of the Atomic Scientists. These considerations are more serious than those which seem to have persuaded Rajni Kothari, for example, to speak of an obsolescence of the prevailing ideological frameworks. 2/

It follows that what we need today more than ever before is liberation from both Liberalism and Marxism. This means that what we need is a radicalism so thorough and irrepressible that in order to perform its literal function of going to the roots of the crisis, it does not leave any of the prevailing modes of thought and of existence unexamined. For what we have to contend with here is the sheer tenacity of these apparently conflicting worldviews. Indeed, no matter what else the Bomb might have destroyed, it certainly did not manage to destroy the cultivated prejudices of the "decision makers" and their ideologues. Or, in Einstein's telling and generally misquoted phrase: "The unleashed power of the atom has changed everything save our modes of thinking, and thus we drift toward unparalleled catastrophe." The profound irony is that while individuals and groups could at worst have faced the prospect of "nasty, brutish and short lives" during what Hobbes imagined was a state of nature, our race as a whole faces this prospect during a very advanced stage of what anthropology would call culture.

THE NUCLEAR AUTUMN

Merely because we can no longer take for granted the continued existence of humanity we are obligated to re-examine the legitimacies of the prevailing modes of social organization and the prevailing modes of comprehending reality. Put in this light, the contemporary set of world polities can be seen to be entirely unsustainable. Indeed, if social sustainability is presumed to be the minimum necessary condition of national security, then most nation states of today, and the superstates in particular, have already lost their very reason to exist. This is a profound crisis of legitimacy which nation states almost without exception face and which can be traced to an unending accumulation of baroque and therefore militarily dubious and pointlessly expensive weapons systems. For such systems to spell disaster, there does not have to be a regular war. And closely associated with their fabrication and acquisition are a variety of tenacious and mounting social costs such as unemployment, inflation, homelessness and environmental degradation.

At stake is the legitimacy of the modern hyper-militarized state as such--not the legitimacy of this ism or that one. An ability to focus on the lack of validity of the state per se is the product of a worldview which I designate as "counter-elitist." But a consistently counter-elitist perspective precludes partiality of any kind towards one superstate as against the other. In being critical towards one and appreciative of the other, one may well be giving vent to one's naive prejudices. But one would also be ignoring a vital fact which Frank Blackaby has only recently drawn attention to: "Although each side accuses the other of making preparations for a first strike, neither side really believes this." 3/ Neither can believe this because each knows that either's first strike will leave neither undestroyed. Still each prefers to make the accusation because that is the only excuse it can have to persist with its own arms program. The compulsion to arm in each case is autonomous; the attempted justification in each case is heteronomous. This can be nothing but a recipe for an open-ended and relentless militarization; for a corresponding destruction of resources; for an inexorable compounding of insecurities, economic, military and political; and, as far as the superstates are concerned, for a complete elimination of legitimacy. What we need to take note of here is the fact that the establishments of the United States and the Soviet Union together have created the irrational world of today. There can be no question of accusing the one and excusing the other.

Those who fail to see the prevailing situation this way tend always to misperceive it. A case in point is Andrei Sakharov. I have an extremely profound respect for him on account of all that he has suffered and continues to suffer at the hands of his tormentors. But the sheer intensity of his suffering has so affected his perception that to him the United States fails to appear as an overly militarized state. He seems to believe that the U.S. is actually "striving to avoid a peacetime militarization of the economy, society, technology and science." 4/ In fact, he goes further and advises the West, if it seeks to avoid nuclear war or war as such, to make "certain limited economic sacrifices" and restore "strategic parity." This means that the managers of the Western bloc should continue to produce even more nuclear weapons and make a thermonuclear war even more likely.

As far as the security managers of the two powers and their ideologues are concerned, these are not the kinds of considerations which matter. For they may expect to remain installed in office if and only if they are able to manage a more or less uninterrupted escalation of military spending. To this end all they need is a generous "input" of artificially whipped up patriotic hysteria which in turn requires recurrent references to some sinister threat or other emanating from abroad.

This condition is not entirely new. For the power elite everywhere have always tended to consolidate their positions at home by creating crises abroad. Thus, Shakespeare himself made the dying Henry IV advise his son as follows: "Therefore, my Harry, be it thy course to busy giddy minds with foreign quarrels..." But in a situation in which mountains of destructive weapons are already available, creating external crises for reasons of domestic consolidation can be extremely dangerous and perverse. Given the immediacy of the threat of extinction which our race now faces, the ruling elite whould not promote even their short-term interests, much less their long-term objectives, by trying to remain installed through continuing to arm. But they must persist with arming "regardless of the cost and regardless of the peril," as President Kennedy once claimed. This is the reason why it is in power per se that we have to see the deadliest enemy of the human race as a whole; and that means that the power which the rulers wield is their own enemy as well.

The moment we become aware of the enormity of the hazards which accumulated and accumulating power congeals; the moment, therefore, we begin to focus on its irredeemable illegitimacy; and the moment, in turn, we begin to plead for its drastic attenuation, we convert ourselves to what I have chosen to designate as a counter-elitist worldview.

What needs to be emphasized here is the point that a self-consciously counter-elitist worldview alone permits us to articulate all the serious consequences of some of the more dangerous pursuits of the powers that be. One may refer here to Carl Sagan and his crusade against the nuclear madness. He is one of the original proponents of the Nuclear Winter Theory in which the nuclear war fighting doctrines meet their ultimate refutation. Even so, he manages to dismiss the Strategic Defense Initiative (SDI), also known as the Ballistic Missiles Defense (BMD), or the Star Wars program of the Reagan Administration not because it is diabolical but because it cannot possibly promise 100% success. Incidentally, this is strongly reminiscent of Robert Oppenheimer's rejection of Enrico Fermi's proposed plan to poison the "enemy's" food stock with radioactive isotopes not because the idea was revolting in itself but because for such a scheme to become at all worthwhile, the number of victims would have to be at least a half million. Which, in view of the uneven distribution of the isotopes was not likely to be case. 5/ Well, what Sagan says is this:

> Imagine some highly effective defensive shield over the U.S. The Soviet Union launches an attack of 10,000 strategic warheads, all of which reach the American shield, in effect go boing, and harmlessly slither off into the Gulf of Mexico. Or imagine a comparable shield over the U.S.S.R., so that if the U.S. attacks with 10,000 warheads, they all go boing, and slide off into the Sea of Okhotsk. What could be wrong with this? In my opinion, nothing.

We will see presently that the word used ought not to have been "nothing" but "everything." But in the meantime, let us reproduce the rest of Sagan's argument:

> If absolutely impermeable shields were miraculously emplaced, simultaneously and at reasonable cost, over the U.S. and the Soviet Union, the security of both nations would increase. But the moment the shields are a little permeable, the moment one is deployed before the other, the situation, I maintain, reverses; then the world becomes much more perilous, and the two superpowers—as well as all the other nations—would be far better off had the shield never been invented or deployed. 6/

The fallacy underlying this argument is its elitism which presumes the legitimacy of the modern state. Therefore, let me refer to the devastation which even paralyzed warheads must perforce cause, particularly when they run into thousands. If "judiciously" distributed, a mere ten pounds of plutonium (named after Pluto the Greek god of darkness) can expose all of humanity to cancer. And thousands of corporate and socialist warheads will contain hundreds of tons of it.

All this will be scattered all over the globe after the bombs have all gone "boing." One need not try here to figure out all the consequences of a full hundred per centum success of the strategic defense system. Even if it were possible it would hardly be necessary. What is immediately important are the consequences, in terms of human misery, of a frenzied and self-intoxicating obsession with arms of all kinds.

All these consequences can together be designated as "the Nuclear Autumn." This autumn, in my opinion, is more urgent than the Nuclear Winter which Sagan and his team have warned us about. For the winter which will be the very ultimate manifestation of human folly will still be one which no one, except perhaps some Mars-based scientists, will be able to observe or to write about.

In contrast, the Nuclear Autumn is already here and is suffered by the poor in the form of the opportunity costs of militarism. All over the world unemployment, inflation, lack of shelter, starvation, and ill health are some of the manifestations of the Nuclear Autumn. In other words, these are the insecurities to which only the poor are exposed and which cannot but intensify with increased military spending. In insisting that only if perfect BMD systems are deployed simultaneously by the United States and the Soviet Union "the security of both nations would increase," Carl Sagan fails to note the insecurities which are the lot of the world's poor and which I have described as The Nuclear Autumn. He is either unaware of them or does not consider them to be serious enough to merit even a passing reference. But had he taken due note of these insecurities and then asked what could be wrong with each of the two superpowers having a perfect BMD system, he could only have said, "In my opinion, everything."

What is involved here is the intense heat of the Cold War--a kind of heat, moreover, to which only the poor may be exposed and which cannot but produce an illusion of warmth for the rich. Indeed, by the very process of its preparation, the Third World War has become infinitely more ruinous than even the Second World War which to date has been the most destructive war ever fought in history. Therefore, no matter how "reasonable" the cost, even a theoretically perfect BMD system cannot but have a crippling effect on the socio-economic systems of the world. For, Carl Sagan's assertion notwithstanding, this cost will be added to the billions already going down the military drain. Little wonder that:

> The tattered ranks of America's homeless are swelling, and economic recovery that made this Christmas merrier than the last for most Americans has not brought them even a lump of coal. As sub-freezing temperatures settled in last week, scattered anecdotes gave way to chilly facts. Unemployment is at a two-year low of 8.4 per cent, but cities and voluntary groups across the country

are swamped with thousands more requests for shelter than ever. 7/

I wonder if anyone could still claim that at least a perfect BMD arrangement evolved by the superpowers would mean increased security for both. But one could ask: What kind of security and for whom?
  It is natural that the conditions in the Third World are no better. Rather, they are much worse:

> Typically, more than half the entire (urban) population lives in slums and squatter settlements and between one third and one half has no access to safe water supply or sanitary waste disposal facilities. Those with an education and salaried position or regular wage-paying job in the modern sector make up a relatively small minority. The great majority ekes out a living in a vast variety of ways in the informal sector--running small shops, doing domestic work, running errands, operating pedicabs, and picking up any odd job that will bring in a little cash. 8/

I submit that a poverty so tenacious cannot possibly be explained in isolation from the kind of military-industrialism with which the establishments of the world are more or less pathologically obsessed. Indeed, the mere fact that around 65 people die every minute of hunger and hunger-related diseases which the world cannot get rid of is explained largely by the fact that during that very minute the world also manages to spend $1.7 million on arms (which happens to have been the rate for 1986: The International Year of Peace). More specifically, the fact that most of these deaths take place in the Third World is expalined by the fact that the Third World is bearing a good part of the cost of the arms programs of the other two. Considering the escalating prices of most sophisticated weapons systems and considering also the fact that the Third World now accounts for around two-thirds of all imports of major weapons, 9/ this is the obvious conclusion to draw. But a simple computation shows that 65 people dying every minute means 93,600 people dying every day. And this means that the world or rather the Third World is experiencing one Hiroshima every day--and such is the fish-blooded callousness of our ruling elite that they continue to import baroque death machines and deposit the kickbacks earned in the process in Swiss bank accounts.

If, therefore, we do not redefine our notions of security and thus do not bridle the military-industrialism of our time, we will be moving closer to that dreaded Nuclear Winter against which eventuality Carl Sagan has issued so eloquent a warning.

TOWARDS A GLOBAL SPRING

The nuclear winter is precisely the "season" we must omit if we are to survive as a civilized species. We must move directly from the Nuclear Autumn of today into a Global Spring of the near future. Exactly how we do this is not for an individual to detail or describe. In fact, an attempt to describe the Utopia may serve as a distraction from the primary task which is to dispel the Dystopia. To this end, we would have to shatter a variety of illusions of progress and military security which the powers that be manage somehow to "sell." The prevention of the termination of our future is the immediate task of our generation. A precise structuring of the future is a task which lies only in the future. There can be little more futile an exercise than preparing blueprints of a future when we cannot even be sure that there indeed will be a future. Our primary task is to <u>so</u> change the <u>present</u> that a future becomes possible.

The desired direction involves an attenuation of power. For as long as the colossal pyramids of power remain in existence, we cannot feel secure in the present or be sanguine about the future. In the elitist perspective, the realization of a world without large masses of power may not be a feasible goal, and the best we may hope for is a working arrangement between different sets of powers. But because of an accelerating depletion of non-renewable resources and an increasing pollution of the environment such an arrangement cannot last for long, much less indefinitely. It cannot be <u>sustained</u> for an historically significant length of time. The elitist perspective is by its very nature self-defeating.

In what I call the counter-elitist perspective, a massive deconcentration of power is not only desirable but realizable. For the concentration of power, in the very process of causing resource-exhaustion, cannot but impose mounting costs on ordinary people. When these people begin to comprehend the hazards involved, power must begin to attenuate. It is a question of awareness so acute that the counter-elites begin to mobilize and to deny the resources to the power elite for an unending pursuit of armaments which can only have goals both dubious and diabolical.

It may not be possible directly to use nuclear weapons without causing the extinction of our race. But they can still be and are being used all the time, though only indirectly. For it is under the cover of the nuclear umbrella that the supposedly rival superpower establishments of our time continue to acquire conventional weapons which in turn are used for intervention and counter-insurgency abroad and for the imposition of a variety of costs on domestic populaces for reasons of state. The tacit assumption here is that the nuclear umbrella itself will never get burnt. However, with the proliferation of nuclear weapons continuing unabated, it can, even if accidentally. Such complacency can hardly be excused.

It is in this context that Paulo Freire's concept of "conscientization" begins to acquire an entirely new profundity and meaning. I am persuaded that in order to promote conscientization we must also redefine such casually yet commonly used terms as "developed," "developing," and "progress." One cannot assume that a species which has been carefully groomed for extinction by its own rulers is moving along the road to progress. No less untenable than the idea of "progress" is the current idea of "development," identified as it is with indiscriminate and even reckless industrialization. But since it cannot but cause an accelerating depletion of resources now known to be finite, and since it cannot but inflict a variety of penalties on ordinary people, it can hardly be sustained for long. This brings us back to Rudolf Bahro's idea of the "industrial disarmament of the West".

Right now, the world's need for industrial disarmament may not be as acute as its need for nuclear disarmament. But from the point of view of sustainability, which by definition is a very long-term objective, the "Whimper" is as grim a threat in the future as the "Bang" is in the present. This means that in order to be able to avoid self-destruction we would do well to be as wary of the "Whimper" as of the "Bang" and to plan to discard soon such lifestyles and modes of production as can be shown to be heedless of the basic constraints of ecology. One may refer here to the reckless clearance of the tropical rainforests now taking place at the rate of 157,000 square kilometers per year. If this process remains unchecked, these forests will all be gone by the year 2057A.D. 10/ This would mean in effect the destruction of the breathing organs of the Earth system. Which means that the ecological "Whimper" is in itself a very serious threat that we face.

Put in this context, much of what passes for economic activity is a contradiction in terms. The explanation is simple and lies in the fact that a frenzied consumption of the terrestrial capital which contemporary hyper-industrialism entails cannot possibly signify a nomos or law according to which our global oikos or house, or rather "habitat" in the present context, ought to be managed. It follows that we would do well to dispel the illusion of prosperity which is taken to define a contemporary hyper-industrial society--in particular, because built into its "output" structures are very heavy thermodynamic deficits. For example, modern "high-yield" chemical agriculture requires an input of about five calories of energy to give a food-energy output of just one calorie. And this kind of agriculture is not the worst offender, too. Sustainability therefore requires a worldwide focus on the basic needs of all and on ecologically nonviolent methods of meeting those needs.

It follows that in counter-elitist terms, a country like India ought never to try to hyper-industrialize itself. Instead, it ought to try to employ the millions who happen now to be reduced to redundancy to participate fully in shaping their own economic futures. Not until it does that may it arrogate to itself such a designation as "developing." But that is a designation for which the rest of the world also is not yet quite ready. Nor can it be unless it does away with concentrated power as an institution.

To conclude, in counter-elitist terms genuine peace and authentic development are perfectly compatible goals because they both require a drastic attentuation of state power. They are perfectly realizable goals as well because concentrating power cannot but be a self-defeating process in a finite environment. This means that while genuine peace requires something different from arrangements like "arms control," which the establishments seek in pursuit unending arms buildups, authentic development too requires a concern with something different from the insatiable demands of industrialization which cannot but devour energy and destory the environment.

NOTES

1. Noam Chomsky, "What Directions for the Disarmament Movement," Michigan Quarterly Review, Fall, 1982, p.601.

2. Rajni Kothari, "Masses, Classes and the State," Economic and Political Weekly, February 1, 1986, p.210.

3. The SIPRI Yearbook, 1986, p.8.

4. Andrei Sakharov, "The Danger of Thermonuclear War," Foreign Affairs, Summer 1983, p.1007.

5. Barton J. Bernstein, "The Oppenheimer Conspiracy," Discover, March 1985, p.24.

6. Carl Sagan, "Star Wars Won't Work," Discover, September 1985, p.68.

7. Newsweek, January 2, 1984, p.20.

8. Philip H. Coombs, The World Crisis in Education. New York: Oxford University Press, 1985, p.46.

9. The SIPRI Yearbook, 1986, p.325.

10. Nicholas Guppy, "Tropical Deforestation: A Global View," Foreign Affairs, Spring 1984, p.929.

19

The Limits of Import Substitution: Emerging Authoritarianism in Kenya

Peter Magnusson

INTRODUCTION

In an essay on "Armaments, Underdevelopment and Demilitarization in Africa," 1/ Robin Luckham notes that most of the institutions (the political parties, the elections, the parliaments, the independent trade unions and the free press) through which the colonial powers tried to establish pluralist democracy in Africa after independence, have either disappeared or fallen into disrepair. Conversely most of the instruments through which they established their hegemony (the bureaucracy, the legal and educational systems, the police and armed forces) have survived. The military may even have replaced the party as Africa's most important political institution. 2/

Until a few years ago Kenya in East Africa seemed to be a striking exception to this development. Kenya, one of the major African examples of a country adopting, in Immanuel Wallerstein's terminology, the strategy of "promotion by invitation," 3/ is known as one of the politically most stable and democratic countries on the continent. Consequently the role of force has been less significant in the political and economic development of Kenya than in most other African states. The attempted coup in August 1982, and the following drastic measures to restore law and order, may however indicate that the stable era has ended and that the ruling elite will begin to rely on a more authoritarian form of capitalist development. A stagnating economy, increasing social cleavages and rivalry of elites makes an increased role of force even more likely.

The purpose of this paper is to discuss the increasing authoritarianism and militarization in light

of the fragility of the Kenyan state. According to
Charles Tilly, a state is "an organization employing
specialized personnel which controls a consolidated
territory and is recognized as autonomous and integral by
agents of other states." 4/ Kenya, like most African
states, was created by aliens for their own purposes. It
derives legitimacy from recognition as part of the
interstate system rather than from being an "organization
which controls a consolidated territory."

We will trace the signs of authoritarian development
in Kenya to failures and contradictions in the
nation-building project of the Kenyan elite. In the
first section we will focus on the colonial era and the
formation of the Kenyan state. In the second we will
deal with the development strategy i.e. the attempts of
the ruling elite to create a material foundation for
state hegemony--the modernization imperative. In the
third section, we will focus on one of the major
obstacles to consolidation of state power in Africa--the
non-coincidence of state and nation.

THE COLONIAL STRUCTURE OF KENYA
BEFORE 1964

The colonial economic structure in Kenya rested on
plantations, ranches and so-called mixed farms which
produced coffee, tea, wheat, maize and meat for export,
and for the home market. The agricultural labor force
was overwhelmingly African. Europeans controlled larger
commercial and industrial enterprises, and Asians
functioned as middlemen, mainly within trading, in both
urban and rural areas. Some Asians controlled
small-scale manufacturing. European interests were
represented by both international capital, mainly
invested in plantations and ranches, and by settlers,
mainly occupied with mixed farming. During the first
half of the 20th Century the colonial administration
primarily supported the interests of the European
settlers, but when the system began to show strain the
administration gradually withdrew its support. The
presence of a large number of European settlers
concentrated in the highlands in the central parts of
Kenya had at least two important implications: First, a
peaceful transition to independence was, as in most
settler-colonies, impossible. Second, the struggle would

be dominated by the Kikuyus, who were most affected by the colonial mode of production.

The Kenya African Union (KAU), the first nationalist party in Kenya, was foundedin the mid-1940s. In 1947 Kenyatta became chairman, and the party became increasingly radical in its nationalist demands. In a sense he tried to Kenyanize Kikuyu nationalism. Kenyatta and other Kikuyu leaders, without broadening their political base, made themselves spokesmen of the entire African population.

By the early 1950s militant Africans were organizing secret associations, and political assassinations and other forms of armed resistance became increasing common. With the Mau Mau rebellion the struggle for independence assumed a violent character. Mau Mau was a movement among the Kikuyus, and oathswearing together with other traditional and ritual customs among the members made many the movement as a fanatical religious organization. But Mau Mau should be understood against the background of an increasingly conscious struggle against the colonial system. In 1952 Mau Mau was banned and the colonial administration proclaimed a state of emergency. Kenyatta and about 200 other African leaders were arrested and charged for cooperation with and organization of the rebellious groups. Political organizations, among them the KAU, were prohibited. Beside the struggle against the British the rebellion also had a dimension of tribal war against "loyalist" tribes and groups. This disintegration of the African community was supported by the colonial administration in its "divide and rule" policy.

In 1960 the state of emergency was lifted. In a strict military sense the British had won the war. In several years of bitter fighting 32 European civilians, 63 security troops and about 2,000 African loyalists were killed. About 12,000 Mau Mau were killed by soldiers and police or hanged. 5/ In a wider political perspective the Kikuyus appear as winners. It had become clear to the British and to the colonial administration during the state of emergency that a Kenya functioning according to the old system had passed an historical stage, and with the Mau Mau still raging, they began to initiate changes.

The Transition to Independence

Measures which aimed at a non-radical, gradual shift from the old colonial system to a new representative one were taken in a precautionary way as the precariousness of the old system became increasingly obvious. Some changes, ie. economic ones, came about as a result of changing conditions. There was, for example, an economic expansion following the Second World War which caused an agricultural change: Before the war almost the entire internal commercial sector rested on European settler agriculture, mainly "mixed farms". But by 1958 the "mixed farmers" owned no more than 15-20 percent of the foreign assets invested in Kenya. 6/

The colonial administration, backed by new international interests, seemed prepared to desert the settlers and ally itself with African leaders willing to accept continued private, including European, ownership and enterprise. These new tendencies formed the background of the so-called "multi-racial policy" initiated by the New Kenya Group (NKG) founded in 1959. The purpose of this policy was to increase Black participation in economic activities and establish a foundation for future common interests which in turn would prevent radical changes in the economic structure when the political power was handed over to the Black Africans.

One prominent feature of the NKG strategy was not to lift monopoly legislation which could result in a fast expansion of competing industry based on local Asian capital. Instead one was to maintain an adjusted monopoly system which would include some Black Africans supported by European capital.

A precondition for the overall strategy was to reduce discontent, and thereby neutralize the potential political force of the masses, particularly the Kikuyus. This could only be done by transferring land to Black African hands. However, proclaiming that European land was to be transferred to Blacks, one risked the settlers' saving what was possible to save, destroying the rest and leaving the country. The short-term economic consequences would endanger the entire economy. The essence of the plan to transfer land, then, in 1961, was that the British government together with the World Bank would offer the African farmers credit in order to make it possible for them to buy out the European settlers.

In accordance with decisions made at the Lancaster House conference elections were held in 1961, some seats in the legislative assembly were to be reserved for Europeans and Asians. Elections were approaching and a fragile African unity began gradually to crack up. Former KAU supporters, primarily Kikuyu and Luo, came together in a new party, the Kenya African National Union (KANU), while representatives of the minority tribes, fearing Kikuyu and to some extent also Luo dominance, soon founded a second party, the Kenya African Democratic Union (KADU). With Kenyatta still in prison, KANU was divided into two factions, one radical under the leadership of Oginga Odinga (a Luo), and one more moderate led by another Luo, Tom Mboya. KANU won the elections but refused to form a government as long as Kenyatta was held in detention. The colonial administration agreed to release him and, when free, Kenyatta accepted the leadership of KANU. He succeeded, temporarily, in uniting the two factions within KANU and formed a coalition government together with KATU representatives.

With strong Kikuyu demands on a land transfer without any compensation, it may seem strange that the KANU leaders accepted the NKG model for the transfer of land. This can partly be explained by a fear that the transition to independence would be delayed if they didn't accept, and a fear within KANU that KADU would accept the plan and thereby succeed in forming a government without KANU. Another important reasons was that after the Lancaster House conference, Kenya experienced a high and rapidly growing flight of capital. Leaders must have been anxious to restore the international confidence in Kenya. New elections were held in 1963 and KANU won. On December 12, 1963 Kenya became independent. In 1964 KANU and KADU merged and Kenya was proclaimed a republic with Jomo Kenyatta as the first president.

THE DEVELOPMENT STRATEGY: ATTEMPTS TO CREATE A MATERIAL FOUNDATION FOR STATE HEGEMONY

The development policy that emerged through cooperation among the British government, the colonial administration and the Black African leaders and which aimed at maintaining large parts of the colonial economic structures, continued, and during the first years of independence the foundation of the Kenyan development strategy was built in this spirit.

The Consolidation of the Strategy

The transition to independence in 1963 did not include any major structural transformation. The mode of development was confirmed in Sessional Paper No. 10 of 1965, "African Socialism and its Application to Planning in Kenya." 7/ It stated that the only permanent solution to the economic problems is growth, by maintaining inflow of foreign capital. Private ownership of capital was to be maintained and private property should not be expropriated without full compensation. This made nationalization of foreign property, with a few exceptions, unnecessary. The use of the word "socialism" in the title of what Kenyatta called "the practical bible for the development of Kenya" was probably motivated by the fact that the leaders wanted to forestall some of the opposition from the radical fraction within KANU.

In 1964 the leaders of KADU agreed to dissolve the party in exchange for seats in the KANU government. It soon became clear that the political differences and cleavages between the former KADU leaders and most KANU leaders were insignificant compared to the cleavage between these and the radical wing of KANU demanding nationalization and land transfer without compensation. By merging with KADU the moderate faction of KANU strengthened its position, and shortly afterwards the radicals who were purged out of influential positions in the party founded a new party, the Kenya People's Union (KPU). The government answered with harassment of the new party. In the 1968 elections most KPU candidates were prevented from participating due to "technical errors" concerning their nominations. Nevertheless, the KPU maintained a rather widespread support, particularly in the Western parts of the country inhabited by the Luos. It was of course not viable to exclude radicals from the government. If the new regime was to survive, it would have to ease political pressure from the masses demanding land, and from other groups calling for increased economic and political participation and also create an internal support-base.

Settlement Schemes

The New Kenya Group plans for transfer of land were embodied in so-called settlement schemes. The first one was initiated as early as in 1961 and in the following years the program was extended. During the 1960s 500,000 people obtained almost 1.5 million acres of land, mainly in the former "white highlands." 8/ In spite of, and actually partly as a result of, the settlement schemes, agriculture in Kenya maintained its colonial structures. However, during the transition to, and first years of, independence these schemes likely played an important role to ease political dissent. One of the most prominent features of the strategy for land transfers was that private ownership of land was to be maintained. The African farmers were to buy out former European settlers.

Great Britain was, together with the World Bank, the main supplier of credits to finance the schemes, and credits were given on favorable terms in the early, politically most strategic stages of the program. Credits were given only to freeholders, to increase the security of repayments. After the situation was more stable, the granting of credits was tightened and the financial terms hardened. As a result an increasing share of the land, in the form of large farms, was obtained by wealthy Black Africans. These "large farmers" came to play a role similar to the former settlers. They obtained a large portion of political influence which they used to make the government maintain some of the monopolies and favorable price fixing. The big export oriented plantations were more or less excluded from all new elements in the agricultural policy and continued to operate as before.

The Rise of an African Petty Bourgeoisie

Due to the transfer of land, foreign ownership within the agricultural sector decreased. But in the large-scale commercial and agricultural sectors foreign investment remained high. The only important exception to total foreign ownership and control was joint ventures between foreign companies and the Kenyan government. Monopoly legislation together with political hostility made most Asians refrain from long-term investments. Many tried to smuggle out their assets out of the country

and as a consequence the hostility between Asians and
Black Africans increased. Conditions favorable to the
foreign sector were furthered by political institutions
where the interests of foreign firms and parts of the
Kenyan elite mingled. The joint interests of the foreign
sector and the ruling elite were furthered by African
share-holdings and management posts in foreign companies.

During the first years of independence there was a
potential contradiction between the government's
encouragement of foreign investment and its political
dependency of a growing group of African traders,
small-scale manufacturers, transporters, etc. The
political support of this emerging, "petty-bourgeoisie,"
demanding government support in order to obtain larger
shares of the profitable non-agricultural sectors of the
economy, was crucial. The solution was to, in some
branches, integrate local African and foreign capital.
The result of the political activity of African
businessmen and the policy adopted by the government was
that a small group of African capital owners and
entrepreneurs emerged in sectors which to a large extent
were connected to foreign capital and protected by
monopolies and tariffs. In this way a triangular
alliance between leading bureaucrats, foreign capital and
an initially economically weak local petty bourgeoisie
was created. 9/

Africanization

Another way of preventing political discontent and
further strengthening joint interests between the elite
and foreign capital was through the so-called
"Africanization" policy. During the 1960s and early
1970s most parts of the civil service were "Africanized"
and the number of Black Africans in the managements in
foreign firms had increased.

The ruling elite thus succeeded, by settlement
schemes together with protection of an emerging local
petty bourgeoisie and "Africanization" of the civil
service and foreign firms, to reduce political unrest,
consolidate its position and pursue its strategy of
promotion by invitation. And the economy did expand.
International investment remained high and the gross
domestic product rose with an average close to 6 percent
during the first 15 years of Independence.

However, most options utilized to maintain political stability were preconditions for the entire strategy and are not available today. Some of these options, i.e. the creation of a Black African petty bourgeoisie, seems to have generated contradictions which today appear as threats to development and to stability. Today there is a degree of antagonism within the Kenyan elite among groups demanding a continued protected import-substitution and others, closely linked to international capital, want a more export oriented policy. The limited possibilities for continued import-substitution supports the forces looking upon exports of manufactured goods as the best source of expansion, and there have been recent moves in this direction. This shift in policy has caused unrest among the Kenyan manufacturers who rely on the internal market and quantitative import restrictions. Those involved in larger firms view the shift towards export manufacturing as feasible but want the government to take "more constructive action to boost industry, investment and exports." 10/

Kenyan exports face major problems. In the beginning of the 1970s about half of Kenya's export of products went to Tanzania and Uganda, markets protected by the external tariff of the East African Community. The collapse of the East African Community, the subsequent closing of the border between Kenya and Tanzania and the unstable political situation in Uganda have led to major losses for Kenya, the more so since the events in Tanzania and Uganda have cut off the markets of Rwanda, Burundi and Zambia. It is unlikely that Kenya can easily regain her position as a regional exporter of manufactured goods even though the border of Tanzania now is re-opened and even if the situation is normalized in Uganda. The transition to Black majority rule in Zimbabwe has meant the emergence of a new strong competitor in these markets. The establishment of a new South-East African Community--the SADDC--with Zimbabwe and Tanzania, but not Kenya, among the members, makes the picture even gloomier for Kenya. The protectionist import substitution policy made a relatively fast development of wages possible, which together with the stagnant economies, and subsequently protectionist policies in the industrialized countries, increases the difficulties of obtaining shares in these markets.

Major problems are indicated irrespective of the path of development Kenya follows: increasing internal antagonism and conflict, due to an increasing shortage of arable land and declining standards of living and harsher wage policies, especially if Kenya is to compete for markets in the industrialized world. Africanization is more or less completed and the unemployment figures keep rising. The agricultural sector, forming the backbone of the country's economy, is stagnant and Kenya is no longer self-sufficient in food production. The social inequalities generated by uneven capitalist development are together with the stagnant economy creating severe and deepening tensions in the society. The rapid population growth, perhaps the highest in the world, leads to major problems concerning employment and land. Some 80 percent of the population live in the rural areas. Since under 20 percent of the total acreage is considered arable, the population growth will result in major problems concerning the access to land. The uneven distribution of land will lead to political unrest. The trade unions have no formal right to make any statements concerning political questions and the Central Organization of Trade Unions (COTU) is subject to government control. A recent demand to increase the minimum salary by several hundred percent may, however, be an indication that COTU will try to play a more active role in the future.

STATE VS. NATION: ETHNIC DISSENT
AS THREAT AGAINST THE STATE

A recurrent reason for opposition and conflict in Kenya is ethnic dissent. The Somali population has, since the transition to independence, demanded autonomy in order to unite with neighboring Somalia. The central government has refused to meet these demands and the political situation has several times forced the government to proclaim a state of emergency in the region.

The Non-coincidence of State and Nation

Robin Luckham stresses the artificiality of the state framework established under colonial rule as one of the main sources of conflict in Africa. According to

Luckham the non-coincidence of state and nation surfaces at basically three levels. First, in struggles for control of the state among different class factions. Second in the problems of keeping a number of precapitalist social formations or "nations" with different cultural and social organization within the framework of the same state. Third, the non-coincidence of state and nation have affected interstate relations. 11/

In Kenya all three levels are relevant. Although ethnic identification tends to be comparatively low among the ruling classes of most African countries, ethnic politics and political mobility based on ethnic belonging continues to be an important feature of the political life. In Kenya this is illustrated by the cleavage between the two dominant ethnic groups, the Kikuyus and the Luos. There are over ten major ethnic groups in the country. The problem of keeping social formations with different cultural, social and economic organization within the framework of the same state manifests itself in the demands for political autonomy raised by the Somali population who are living next to a Somali state. Somalia has territorial claims on Ethiopia and Kenya, and although the land dispute between Somalia and Kenya never has been as explosive as the conflict between Somalia and Ethiopia, it has been a recurring reason for violent government action and strengthening of the armed forces.

Ethnicity and Class

Although the non-coincidence of state and nation is a major reason for intra-as well as inter-state conflict in Africa, ethnic differences and contradictions between nation and state are in most cases not manifest until they are politically activated. Differences in culture and social organization tend to result in ethnic conflict when they become intertwined with class conflict. First, there are the relations between capitalist and precapitalist modes of production initiated during the colonial period--the adoption of precapitalist modes of production for commodity production for the world market and the manipulation of "traditional" political forms to consolidate political control. Second, class factions have manipulated ethnic ties when they have struggled for power or, when in control of the state, sought legitimacy

beyond class divisions. This has been possible because
class relations are not solid enough to consolidate one
particular class's state hegemony nor fixed enough to
impede tribal, regional or ethnic manipulation. Third,
ethnic conflict has been affected and sharpened by the
development strategies of the ruling class. Dependent
capitalism has tended to generate uneven development and
has thus sharpened interethnic competition. Fourth,
uneven development has caused for instance, rebellion
against starvation and neglect but it has also created
the fear of redistribution of wealth and resources among
privileged ethnic groups.

Ethnicity and the Modernization Imperative

African states today derive their legitimacy largely
from the international state system in general and from
the African state system in particular. Accordingly the
Organization of African Unity's most cardinal principles
concern the integrity of the present boundaries and
noninterference by one state in the internal affairs of
another. However, we find no "nation" that is
co-extensive with the state boundaries. On the contrary
we find relatively "overdeveloped" 12/ states struggling
to extend and consolidate their position by "capturing,"
economically, politically and culturally, traditional
social formations in promoting development characterized
by an economic modernization and a political and cultural
homogenization corresponding to the Western model. The
Western type of development pattern is reflected in the
terminology used to describe and explain political change
and conflicts in Africa: describing traditional social
formations as "precapitalistic" rather than
"noncapitalistic" or when explaining ethnic conflicts as
a result of the state- and/or nation building process.
According to Karl Deutsch the twin processes of
"cultural assimilation" and "social mobilization" give
birth to nations and nationalities. Cultural
assimilation is the process by which smaller, subordinate
communities or nationalities are absorbed into the
information and communications network of larger dominant
"nations." Cultural assimilation has usually, in the
Western experience, been accompanied by "social
mobilization," that is, the process by which men and
women are uprooted from their traditional agrarian

settings as a result of social, economic and technical development, and thereby mobilized for more intensive communication. 13   As the modernization process has proceeded, however, even the nation states in Europe have experienced an excess of mobilization to assimilation, "leading to growing cultural differences and eventually reactive ethnic nationalism among the fully mobilized population who stress their cultural identity." 14/   A similar political development can be found in many parts of Africa.

> As urbanization proceeds apace, as commerce and industry make inroads into the traditional agrarian economy, as educated publics are formed, so various ethnic groups begin to aspire to national status and even statehood.   In so far as modernization is at all responsible, it appears to be an agent of "state-destroying" through cultural differentiation rather than "nation-building" through any cultural assimilation." 15/

Given the fragility of the African state system, these tendencies may continue to be major obstacles to state hegemony in large parts of Africa.   In light of this they are likely to nourish the prevalence of authoritarian and repressive forms of state government.

STATE, SECURITY AND MILITARIZATION--
SOME CONCLUDING REMARKS

Some of the contradictions the ruling elite of Kenya have to cope with in order to secure Kenya's position and strengthen the power of the state are generated by the development strategy and by the non-coincidence of state and nation, which impact upon the way in which the ruling elite of the state will intervene in the economic and political development process.   With respect to the strategy, we have argued that the dependent capitalist development, based on export of agricultural primary goods and industrialization by import substitution sustained by foreign investment, today has reached its limits.   The stagnating economy and increased political tensions tend to make the ruling elite more dependent on authoritarian forms of government--the more so since the options used to reduce political unrest at an earlier stage of the strategy are not available today.   It is against this background one must understand the detention of several oppositionals in 1981-1982 and the proclamation of Kenya as a de jure one party state.

Authoritarianism and force are likely to be more conspicuous in the future whatever economic strategy the state pursues. Attempts to transform the economy in order to establish the conditions necessary for, in O'Donnels' terminology, a deepening of the industrialization process will lead to political unrest. Force and repression may be the only way in which the state can guarantee political stability. The cracks in the above-mentioned alliance between different factions of the economic and political elite tend to result in rivalry over state power between the segments opting for an export oriented strategy and those in favor of a continued protected import substitution policy. Even if the latter alternative really isn't a feasible strategy any longer, one must not forget that the "protected petty bourgeoisie" emerged as an important political base for large parts of the ruling elite and they will do what they can to defend their position.

One prominent feature of the future political development of Kenya will be struggles between different factions of the elite trying to obtain state hegemony in order to safeguard increasingly divergent interests and policies. In this respect we thus consider what has been labelled "nervous authoritarianism" 16/ to be a consequence of the built-in contradictions of the Kenyan development model. The deadlock of the strategy, the stagnant economy, increasing political tensions, reduced political rights and the need for political stability thus add up to a picture indicating an increased role of force and repression.

Turning to the questions of state versus nation as threats against the ruling elite and obstacles to state hegemony, we note that ethnic dissent tends to be activated as a consequence of the stagnating economic development. We also find it relevant to comprehend the relations between force/authoritarianism on the one hand and modernization and state/nationbuilding as such on the other. Even though the divergent economic interests transcend ethnic ties, ethnicity may be one conspicuous factor in the struggle for state hegemony. The rivalling factions within the elite are likely to mobilize whatever loyalties, including ethnic, they can in order to strengthen their position. In this way ethnicity becomes intertwined in the contradictions generated by the development strategy and thus, as blocked accumulation sharpens inter-elite rivalry, ethnic dissent may emerge as a major threat to political stability and as a source to state repression. These tendencies are discernible in the relations between the two dominant ethnic groups, the Kikuyus and the Luos.

Considering the other aspect of ethnic dissent it seems clear that the importance of ethnicity has not always receded with modernization and industrialization. Often these processes instead seem to accentuate ethnic diversity, particularly in Third World societies. Anthony Smith even argues that we are fully justified in isolating a broad historical trend in the modern era, and designating it as an "ethnic revival," but that such a "revival" of ethnicity is also a transformation, and that it possesses a unique character, shared by no previous ethnic revival. 17/ It is tempting to connect this ethnic revival with "the modernization imperative" of the state. The modernization imperative can be defined as an external and internal pressure on the state of a less developed society to increase the productive capacity in order to survive and to consolidate the political system to avoid being swallowed by other states or of breaking up because of internal conflicts. 18/ Irrespective of the nature of the particular development strategy pursued by the state, the needs to increase the productive capacity, tends to generate contradictions which activate ethnic dissent and as a consequence--violent state action against ethnic minorities. In Kenya these tendencies are most prominent in the northern parts of the country. By using large acreage of the most fertile land for plantations and other forms of cash crop production, poor and landless peasants have been forced to settle on seemingly free acreage with a lower potential for agriculture--"seemingly free" in the sense that this land is often used as pasture grounds for the herds of nomadic people. 19/ The increased scarcity of land tends to create rivalry and clashes between ethnic groups. The government has used violence to crush the hostilities and during 1984 there were several reports of executions, even massacres, carried out by government forces. 20/ In this way ethnic dissent also becomes directed against the state--which tends to perceive it as an internal security threat and meet it with increased repression. In the Northeastern Province where the Somali people can identify themselves with a neighboring Somali state the situation is particularly explosive.

The major task of the armed forces is to be responsible for the external security. But, "... in cases of strong resistance to the state-building project the military becomes heavily involved also in the maintenance of internal security. This is the norm in the Third World. 21/ The contradictions and conflicting interests provide a fertile internal soil for the seeds of militarization. When irrigated by military aid, generated from external ambitions of protecting economic and political interests and globalization of the cold war, these seeds grow and flourish. Signs of a more active political role of the military, signs which are already facts in many other African countries, are accordingly discernible in the contemporary political development of Kenya.

A harsher economic climate and increasing economic, political dissent and the expansion of the armed forces have paved the way for military involvement in the politics of Kenya. In August 1982 parts of the Kenyan Air Force were involved in an attempted coup d'etat. Some, referring to the broadcasts made by the mutineers in the initial stages of the attempt and the assumed connections between the revolting officers and radical university lectures and students, have seen parallels in Jerry Rawlings' takeover in Ghana and Samuel Doe's in Liberia. Others say that the initiative was taken within one of the rivalling factions of the elite. A third interpretation is that the ethnic cleavage between the Luos and the Kikuyus played a major role. Whatever forces one may recognize behind the coup attempt, the military will most probably play a more active role in the future economic and political development. As the former stability is put under increased strain, force and repression are bound to be decisive instruments for the ruling elite in its attempts to secure its position. At the same time the professional character of the armed forces will most likely decline as they are pulled into the internal political struggle. Their own economic and political priorities, depending on factors such as recruitment, training, possibilities of promotion, salary and duties, will affect their loyalties towards the ruling elite as economic and political (and ethnic) cleavages are deepening. A sign of the growing political significance of the military establishment is President

Moi's concern for the well-being of the soldiers and their families--something which is reflected in increased salaries, special shops with respect to goods as well as prizes, building of advanced educational institutions for officers' children, etc. Whether this is enough to keep the troops in their barracks remains to be seen.

NOTES

1. Robin Luckham, "Armaments, Underdevelopment and Demilitarization in Africa," Alternatives, VI, New York: Institute For World Order, 1980.
2. Ibid., 217.
3. Immanuel Wallerstein, The Capitalist World-Economy, Cambridge: Cambridge University Press, 1979, 81.
4. Charles Tilly, "The Formation of National States in Western Europe," Princeton, NJ: Princeton University Press, 1975, 70.
5. O. Bethwell (ed.), Politics and Nationalism in Colonial Kenya, Nairobi: East African Publishing House, 1972, 121.
6. Colin Leys, Underdevelopment in Kenya: The Political Economy of Neocolonization, London: Heinemann, 1975, 42.
7 Republic of Kenya, Sessional Paper No. 10 of 1965, "African Socialism and its Application to Planning in Kenya," Naitobi: Government Printers, 1965, pp.6.
8. Colin Leys, 1975, 76.
9. This triangular alliance is one of the most typical features of the promotion by invitation strategy, see for instance Luckham 1980 and Wallerstein 1979.
10. M. Godfrey, "Kenya: African Capitalism or Simple Dependency, in Bienfield and Godfey (eds.), The Struggle for Development:, 1982.
11. Robin Luckham, 1980, 235-236.
12. Anthony Smith, State and Nation in the Third World, Brighton: Wheatsheaf Books, 1983, 125.
13. Karl Deutsch, "Social Mobilization and Political Development," American Political Science Review, 35, 1961, 493-415.
14. Anthony Smith, 1983, 11.
15. Anthony Smith, 1983, 11-12.
16. Africa Now, September 1982.
17. A.D. Smith, The Ethnic Revival," Cambridge: Cambridge University Press, 1981.
18. Bjorn Hettne, 1984, 22. (needs full citation)

19.   Interview with Gudrun Dahl in Fjarde Varlden, No. 2, 1984.

20.   During 1984 there were several reports of government action against the Degodias of the Northeastern Province and the Pokots in the northwestern parts of the country. See for instance Africa Now, June 1984 and Weekly Review, April 13, 1984.

21.   Bjorn Hettne, 1984, 23.

20

Arms Manufacture: The 'Pulling' Industry in Industrialization Aimed at Import Substitution: The Case of Turkey

Judit Balazs

The invasion of Cyprus by Turkey in 1974 brought Greece and Turkey to the brink of war. At this point the United States ordered an arms embargo against Ankara. The embargo acted as an incentive for Turkey to build up an industry specializing in weapons and strategic devices. Priority in the Turkish industrial development went to a strategic concept under which the country would devote the production capacity of its processing industry, or at least a good part of it, to ships, submarines, anti-tank missiles, hand guns and ammunition. In essence, the concept of building up domestic manufacture of strategic devices and of achieving an independent defense system coincided with the economic management guideline for import substitution approved in 1963.

The Turkish government aimed at "independence" in national defense. Although it invested an impressive sum of money in building up a military industry, that this was clearly not a task that could be handled in a short medium term. So it did not seem likely that Turkey would be capable, within a projectable time period, of pushing itself up among the leading countries that have advanced technologies and are manufacturing weapons on their own.

The viable course for developing countries in building up military industries of their own assumes that a multiphase of development is followed:

1. Strategic devices are imported and the recipient country handles repairs and servicing,
2. Manufacture of the strategic devices takes place in the recipient country on the basis of a license, while the seller country gives the technological guidance and assistance,
3. The domestic assembly industry is built up,
4. Subassemblies are put together from imported parts, which may be returned to the seller country,

5. The parts for the strategic devices are made by the domestic industry from imported raw materials,

6. Domestic production provides the raw materials,

7. The arms program becomes completely independent and with production taking place domestically. This procedure includes the designing, output of the raw materials as well as the entire production process.

Looking back on the history of arms manufacture in the developing countries up to the 1980s, we find that not a single country was able to reach phase seven.

Despite the fact that the technological development level of Turkish industry put restrictions on even building up a military industry based on licenses and by no means one embodying the most advanced military technology, in the opinion of the Turkish Ministry of Defense and the military administrations the six programs of manufacture given in detail below are feasible, given the country's current technical and industrial conditions:

1. Assembly of military fighter-bombers (most likely F 16-79 or F 18 L models);

2. Manufacture of short- and intermediary-range AIM-7E2 guided air fighter missiles and, following that, of AIM F missiles, which are more advanced;

3. Manufacture of laser controlled anti-tank missiles and cannons, as well as 105mm ammunition for M-48 tanks, achieved in cooperation with European countries;

4. Modernization of 188-M48 tactical armoured vehicles according to the M60-A1 standard, with ammunition set onto a ballistic course by computer;

5. Construction of guided-missile carrier frigates of the Oliver Hazard Perry class;

6. Establishment of a domestic base for production of rubber for military purposes, including tyres for strategic and tactical devices.

Despite optimistic forecasts, Turkey will not likely be able to build up an independent strategic industry within the foreseeable future. However, in the current phase it is still worthwhile to examine the economic consequences of efforts to build up a military industry.

NATIONAL ECONOMIC CONSEQUENCES OF BUILDING UP AN ARMS AND STRATEGIC-DEVICE INDUSTRY

Bourgeois theory defines import substitution as an economic strategy issuing from industrial development and growth impulses. That theory qualifies arms manufacture as the most dynamically developing sector and the pulling force of technical development. Moreover, given its influence, which rapidly flows into other sectors of the national economy, it stresses the stimulating effects of the arms industry when looking at the whole of the national economy. The argument analyzing these effects includes: (1) the long-term national economic efficiency of the production processes, which take a comparatively long time to build up, (2) the monopolized certain market "realization," and (3) the "imported technology" entering the country through license purchases, which can be made to give a yield not only in production directly for military purposes but also in numerous other sectors of the national economy. It is worth thinking about the part of this argument that emphasizes increased demands on education and training and the objective growth in research and development potential. The absolute requirements for "adaptation" and the operation of advanced, imported technology to domestic conditions underlines the technological development role of the military industry.

This argument, although it appears to be based on economic motivation and to refer to the national advantages utilizable through the operation of the economic interest mechanism, cannot, in fact, justify the need for armament. I feel that within the current framework there is no need to discuss that at any greater length. Nevertheless, it appears worthwhile to trace all the flows that have taken place in the development of the national economy, induced by the realization of the military development strategy.

It is generally known that, as far as ratios are concerned, armament in the developing countries takes a far heavier toll on their national economies than in the industrially advanced countries, because in the developing countries there is no operation of transitional stimulants of the kind induced by military production in profit-orientated economies. On the other hand, it does distort supply and demand relations, since military expenditure creates significant purchasing and directed solvency demand without contributing to the establishment of production capacities that will be at the service of future consumption. At the same time, it deforms the investment pattern and the rational allocation of available development funds. And all this is concomitant with a growth in technological dependence.

THE TURKISH ARMS INDUSTRY

As a point of departure, I should comment that a good number of subsectors of Turkish industry are directly dependent on military orders. There are also a good number of industrial subsectors that make a significant profit in either a direct or indirect form, from participation in production for military purposes. This gives an unusual "institutional" framework to the "Armed Forces Mutual Aid Fund" (Ordu Yardimlasma Kurumu or OYAK).

OYAK was founded in 1960 and, over the course of several decades, grew into a venture that has infiltrated just about every sector of economic life, through a conglomeration of state, private, bank, industrial, foreign, and military capital. Today it has gained dominance over a good number of areas. The operational mechanism of the OYAK venture is derived from the fact that active officers are compelled to pay 10 percent of their salaries to the OYAK fund, and these funds are used to buy shares in companies.

OYAK came about under the patronage of the army, through what was basically a capital association of military and civilian personalities. Its objective was to capitalize a part of the expenditure devoted to maintaining the army to use in the military industry, to gain military control over an increasingly great share of the economy, and to build "military capital" into civilian production so as to gradually reshape it to serve the war machine.

A clear illustration of OYAK's success is that in barely ten years it purchased the majority of shares of the Turkish car industry, the agricultural machinery assembly industry, the complete sales network for the latter, the OYAK insurance company, the TUKAS food processing company, cement factories with millions in capital, giving it a controlling interest in them; and 20 percent of the shares of the PETKIM petrochemical company. It also developed a 42 percent interest in the Renault car factory, an eight percent hold in the state-owned TURK PETROL and 7 precent of Goodyear's shares.

Obtainable data on OYAK activity reflects conditions in the 1970s. It is probable, though, that OYAK's sphere of activity has also expanded significantly over the past fifteen years and that it has entered more and more sectors of the economy, gradually gaining control of an entire series of companies. This assumed growth is made particularly probable by events in 1980 such as the military take-over. Although the growth in military expenditure is not followed linearly by capitalization, it is impossible to draw any clear conclusions even on the growth in the volume of production for military purposes. At any rate, the outstandingly high growth rate of military expenditure does make the above assumptions probable: With a growth rate of 23.5 percent in 1980-1981 and one of 9.3 percent in 1981-1982, Turkey far surpassed the growth rate in military expenditure for the NATO countries. At the same time, with half a million mobilizable men, Turkey maintains the largest army within NATO.

Thus, there can be no mistaking the fact that the political elite in power has a clear interest in increasing military expenditure, while its direct or indirect production for military purposes on the given level of industrial and technological development is clearly connected to imported technologies. This elite interest has a decisive influence on the course, trends, and dynamics of industrialization. Once this is known, the question to be answered is whether building up a sector of the manufacturing arms and tactical devices industry can operate as a "pulling force" on industry as a whole.

In the 1960s and particularly after the arms embargo took effect, Turkey's rising expenditure for arms purchases was a very heavy load on the balance of payments. In the time between 1975 and 1978, direct arms imports rose from 9.8 percent of total imports to 15.1 percent. Over the same period, imports of capital good and inputs connected to foreign capital goods and inputs connected to foreign capital and directly serving production for military purposes grew from 23.7 percent to 49.3 percent. However, despite massive investments of capital and the creation of domestic arms production, the building up of a "self-defense" ability may take decades at Turkey's level of technical development.

The production programs discussed earlier really involve local assembly under the management of specialists from abroad and the local mounting of imported subassemblies. Yet realization of even this program assumes the existence of a definite technico-industrial basis.

THE INDUSTRIAL BASIS FOR MANUFACTURING
ARMS AND STRATEGIC DEVICES

The implementation of arms manufacturing programs depends fundamentally on the technical development levels of the following industrial subsectors:
    chemical industry (manufacture of explosives)
    iron and steel industries
    light metal industry
    metal-working
    manufacture of gauges
    manufacture of industrial motors
    machine production
    production of electrical machinery
    ship-building
    metal industry
    rubber industry
Taken together these industrial subsectors make up the industrial and technological basis that provide the "potential defense ability."

Table 20.1 provides a good illustration of the ratio of industrial subsectors that make up the "potential defense ability" as compared to total industrial capacity. The ratio is noticeably high, whether the role is examined on the basis of employment figures, production capacities, or value added. The comparatively high ratio and the extensive scale of production indicate a relatively high level of technical development. However, a detailed analysis gives a fundamentally different picture.

Using the data of the Yearbook of Industrial Statistics (ISIC categorization), 33 of the products in the 64 six-digit subgroupings of machine manufacture are not produced in Turkey. This means that fundamental products of machine manufacture such as steam turbines, gas turbines, hydraulic turbines, forging, compressing,

Table 20.1

Ratio of Industries Making Up "Potential Defense Ability"
Within Total Processing Industry

ISIC nomenclature	Numbers employed (1000 capital)	1980 Output a/	Value added a/
Iron and steel	55.6	37.29	16.42
Nonferrous metals	19.8	9.74	3.71
Metal products	30.7	12.67	4.96
Machinery	40.5	17.17	6.59
Electric-powered machinery	28.1	16.02	6.26
Ship building and repairs	7.4	1.69	1.09
Vehicles	32.6	24.06	8.38
Total PDA b/	214.7	118.64	47.41
Total PDA b/ in % of processing industry	28.4%	28.7%	30.8%

a/   in billions of Turkish pounds

b/   "potential defense ability"

Source: Yearbook of Industrial Statistics, Vol. 1 (1982, Edition).

(TL=Turkish Lira=Turkish Pounds)

extrusion and injection moulding machines, metal working machinery, rolling mill facilities, and electromechanical instruments are not made at all in Turkey. The lack of these machines not only testifies to the limits in the output capacity of the sector. In addition, considering that their manufacture would be essential from the point of view of military output, the result is that production is strongly dependent on imports.

To take another example; in ten subcategories (ISIC 384) of motor vehicles, Turkey manufactures only four products (passenger cars, buses, tractors, and loaders) and here too the work involves only the mounting of imported subassemblies.

Thus we see a circle of problems surrounding the myth of a Turkish economy creating "a self-sufficient military industry basis resting on own abilities." A single pair of import-export statistics well illustrates the problem. In the late 1970s nearly 50 percent of Turkey's total import was input for industrial subsectors in the "potential defense base," while the very same subsectors contributed only 3.3 percent to producing the Turkish export base.

Knowing all this, we can draw the conclusion that up to the 1980s, endeavors both to substitute for imports and to build up a self-sufficient military industry were not "crowned with success." In addition, they did not induce the industrial development resting on a foundation of advanced technology that had been so favourably forescast for the Turkish economy.

In 1980 the economic management concept proclaiming the establishment of stabilization raised the prospect of a complete revaluation of the policy that has been followed until that time. The new government inaugurated on November 6, 1983, reiterated this policy, and the import substitution policy gave way to world economic confrontation. World market isolation and the industrial-technological gap indicated a total defeat for that economic management.

The reevaluation of economic policy and the concept set down on paper at the same time did not in themselves yield results, since doing away with restrictions that regulate imports does not make Turkish commodities competitive. On the contrary, the economic policy must be accompanied by an external industrial-technical basis with a potential for development that makes it possible for it to close the gap with the world market.

Considering that technical progress in Turkey is clearly linked to foreign capital, creating competitiveness on the world market is possible only if there is foreign capital.

So it is no surprise that following the change in economic management, government policy was aimed clearly at attracting that capital. Although between 1954 and 1980 the total capital accumulation invested in Turkey came to US$ 228 million, in only two years that figure grew to US$ 400 million. If a comparison is made of Tables 20.2, 20.3 and 20.4, we can draw a number of conclusions.

It is obvious even at first glance that during the course of a single year (1984) capital investments in the processing industry increased to almost US$200 million, or by the same amount as increased between 1954 to 1983 (see Table 20.4). New investments came to US$130 million of that. But it is even more worthwhile to examine how the ratio of total capital investments for 1984 for the strategic subsectors grew to double (82 percent) of what its ratio within accumulated investments had been (42 percent) (see Table 20.2). Aircraft manufacture tops the list: It came to nearly 80 percent of total new investment. We can count an entire series of newly founded companies. Thirteen of the twenty-seven companies operating in the chemical industry were founded in 1984, and there were eleven new investments in the area of electronic machine production.

It is clear from a comparison of the tables that foreign capital investments received an unprecedented impetus, and that the strategic subsectors enjoyed particular priority. Swiss investments were highest in capital, but the United States had the strongest position. This is clearly indicated by the United States' position of strength in the most sophisticated subsectors--electronics and aircraft production--where its ventures are highest relative to all foreign investors, with a 78 percent share. The FRG's production, which is also primarily for military purposes, consists mainly of ship building and submarine manufacture and is in second place.

The conclusion we can draw is that, although Turkey has fundamentally reevaluated its development concept, development linked to the foreign capital of the strategic subsectors continues to be the top priority. In

Table 20.2
Equity Capital in Joint Ventures in the "Potential" Defense Sub-Sectors
(December 31, 1984)

	No. of firms	Total company capital	Ratio of foreign capital%
Production of electric and electronic machinery	18	14, 442	43.5
Machine manufacture	11	10, 316	24.3
Chemical industry	27	11, 590	76.7
Motor vehicle production	9	31, 768	34.9
Metal working	11	7, 753	26.5
Iron and steel production	6	9, 550	33.2
Rubber manufacture	4	3, 836	55.0
Vehicle component manufacture	9	14, 220	37.8
Miscellaneous	7	3, 441	48.96
Non-PHS a/ total		78, 320	
Processing industry total	167	185, 236	38.7
Processing industry/PDS a/ = 42%			

a/ Potential defense subsectors.

Source: Near East Briefing, (January-March 1985);
          calculations by author

Table 20.3
Breakdown of Foreign Capital Operating in Turkey
According to Country of Origin
(December 31, 1984)

Country	No. of firms	Foreign	Capital	
		Million TL	Ratio within total foreign capital	Ratio in total joint venture capital
Switzerland	51	20, 163	17.10	43.02
United States	36	17, 983	15.25	78.6
Federal Republic of Germany	47	14, 404	12.21	45.5
Libya	2	11,000	9.32	50.000
France	6	3,657	3.10	42.90
Others				
Foreign capital total	267	117,902	100.00	46.2

Source: Near East Briefing, (January-March 1985); calculations by author.

Table 20.4

Investments of Foreign Capital Permitted in "Potential
Defense Ability" Subsectors in 1984

	No. of firms	Sum of investment	Million US$ Type of investment		
			New	Expansion	Increasing Capital
Manufacture of electric and electronic machinery	11	11.90	0.13	9.0	2.77
Iron and steel manufacture	7	1.4	0.1	1.11	0.19
Motor vehicle manufacture	7	7.17	0.15	-	7.02
Chemical industry	13	3.96	0.78	0.37	0.41
Machine manufacture	5	1.33	0.35		0.98
Aircraft manufacture	2	123.29	123.29	...	...
Vehicle component manufacture	3	1.41	...	1.41	...
Metal-working	4	1.79	1.19	1.60	...
Rubber production	3	0.77	...	0.77	...
	58	33.05			
Processing industry total	99	186.04	130.14	24.45	28.5

Processing industry/PDA = 8.2%

Source: **Near East Briefing**, (January-March 1985); calculations by author.

other words, objectives set down a long time ago appear to be imbedded in a new economic policy concept.

This is illustrated by the growth in expenditure in the military industry, and by trends in imports directly or indirectly serving production for military purposes (see Table 20.5 and 20.6). The expansion of industrial subsectors for direct or indirect military purposes is continuing but is clearly connected to the activity of foreign capital: in the early 1980s approximately 20 percent of the capital goods imported were for investments in the subsectors making up the "potential defense ability."

The existence of a military government, stable administration, and political consolidation in Turkey provide security for foreign venture capital and a guarantee of high profits. The re-regulation of capital activity has resulted in significantly wider and more plastic institutional framework and sphere of operation. Thus, it is no surprise that Turkey has appeared on the market for arms and strategic devices as a seller.

This fact, however, has not been an incentive to create a domestically based R&D inasmuch as the expansion of the subsectors continues to be based on licenses. In reality, the arms-manufacture orientation of Turkey's industrial development policy is truly profitable to the owners of the foreign capital and to their domestic partners, whereas their real interests are not at all connected with or conducive to building up a domestically based R&D potential. This is all the more true given that, at the current level of development, implementation of production programs based on licenses clearly appears to be more economically viable; hence maintenance of a dependency on licenses really strengthens the positions of foreign capital in Turkey while further operating toward what are obviously profit interests. As a result, the international scale of the redistribution of the surplus value produced in Turkey is accelerating.

NOTES

1. Here I would primarily refer to: Kennedy, G. The Military in the Third World, Duckworth, 1975, pp. 291-293.

2. World Development, Vol. 11, No. 9, p. 813-823.

322

3. Economist Intelligence Unit, The Economic Effects of disarmament (1963), p. 1.

4. Delvet Istatistik Yilliginin Enstitusu/1980, Ankara.

Table 20.5

Trends in Military Expenditure in Turkey

	Military expenditure (in million US$)		Military Expenditure in % of national income
	In TL, at current prices	At 1980 prices	
1974	15,831	1,793	3.9
1975	30,200	2,870	5.8
1976	40,691	3,295	6.2
1977	49,790	3,173	5.8
1978	66,239	2,906	5.2
1979	93,268	2,578	4.3
1980	185,656	2,442	4.3
1981	313,067	3,015	4.9
1982	447,790	3,296	5.2
1983	556,738	3,214	5.0
1984	803,044	3,051	5.0

Source: SIPRI Yearbook (1984-1986).

(TL=Turkish Lira)

Table 20.6
Direct Imports of Machinery for Production of Infrastructure
(in million US$)

	1979	1980	1981	1982
Nonelectric machinery	941,960	865,333	1,254,998	1,407,346
Of this:				
Power machines	182,473	261,255	267,695	355,493
Agricultural machinery	12,710	31,564	38,138	101,283
Metal-working machinery	129,995	66,639	74,488	93,603
Textile machinery	72,458	65,174	145,182	121,553
Electric machinery	265,828	308,337	372,306	411,798
Of this:				
Power installations				
Switches	116,871	174,544	173,266	175,333
Control facilities	16,275	7,057	10,530	11,334
Telecommunications installations	38,439	34,694	53,535	80,206
Means of transport	207,638	195,830	323,508	494,913
Of this:				
Aircraft	2,462	1,320	1,619	77,644
Ships	16,849	30,212	80,945	126,865
Processing industry production	57,882	56,799	84,603	119,110
Of this:				
Instruments	20,238	24,500	42,965	56,704
Of this: measurement and control instruments	13,798	17,733	29,611	35,490

21

The Right to Work and
the Situation of Workers

Ines Vargas

In this chapter we discuss frames for analyzing the situation of workers. We examine different approaches to "work," the relation between main international standards on the "right to work" and the realities of labor life. The focus is Latin America and we also address employment-related concepts.

We begin by addressing different approaches to work as a human activity, because such a perspective is important for identifying the situation of the workers concerned. It is also important to contrast the corresponding discussion with the realities of labor in the Third World, in this case Latin America. Secondly, even though "work" encompasses a far wider range of activities, we will mainly frame the situation of workers in employment. And we will discuss the related definitions and problems they raise.

Closely linked to the problems of working life are policies implemented to promote development. In Latin America, employment has generally not been considered a major target of economic policy, and this trend has dramatically deepened with the adjustment processes now under way. The depth of the current recession has been such that Enrique Iglesias, Executive Secretary of CEPAL (ECLA, the UN Economic Commission for Latin America) has pointed out on several occasions that the economic phenomenon cannot be divorced from political considerations, since in some cases it has strained the limits of social and economic tolerance in certain countries of Latin America. (Iglesias, 1984).

The Latin American regional crisis, aggravated by the renegotiation of the external debt, is today the main cause for the worsened situation of labor in the area. The recommended formula and guidelines imposed by international financing organizations upon Latin American countries have had a tremendous social cost. These

circumstances and the international economic situation
have played an important role in the present state of
affairs but national policies adopted for such adjustment
have not contributed to a minimization of social costs.
PREALC (the Regional Employment Program for Latin America
and the Caribbean) has concluded in a recent study that
those policies have led to an even greater worsening of
the situation for the poorest groups of the population.
(PREALC, 1984).

Since the human factor is still the major production
factor in Latin America, increases in the already high
rates of unemployment and underemployment have dramatic
implications. The situation of workers is an important
element in the dynamics of the societies concerned:
among other things, it figures prominently in the
explosive events and social movements of that region. In
this context, the importance of trade unions is obvious.
Only by organizing themselves can the workers be in a
position to express their demands and improve their
social conditions. At the same time, the process of
political, economic and social development influences the
way in which labor relations, worker organizations and
procedures as well as trade union movements operate.

THE RIGHT TO WORK

The Meaning of "Work"

Attitudes and approaches to work through history
have been based on differing views. The meaning of
"work" itself and the norms and values concerning its
role and relation to society have determined, for
example, the place of the slave in slavery, the serf in
feudalism and the wage laborer in capitalism. However,
we need not resort to history to observe the different
conditions of working life. For obvious reasons, there
is little value in attempting to compare the
possibilities and positions of workers in developing
countries with those of workers in industrialized countries. An additional and often dramatic difference is
that in the Third World the situation is one of living on
an income on the one hand, or barely existing on the
other. For the Third World worker, losing a job means
facing a life of misery and destitution: this is due
first to the lack or inadequacy of social security
arrangements, and second to the tight labor market,

leaving behind a massive reserve army of labor. With this critical demand for employment, the wages are kept low, barely at existence level.

From Aristotle through the Roman period to our time, views concerning the nature of work have tended to follow two distinct approaches: (1) a realistic one envisaging work in terms of the corresponding social reality, and (2) a more idealistic approach, involving the dignity of work as a human value. In the twentieth century the first trend has had as its main exponents Taylorism, Fordism and related schools of thought. The second has served as the impetus in establishing "the right to work" among fundamental rights and freedoms.

Current discussions about "work" and the future of "work" have changed drastically in comparison to the focus in former times. Arguments today concentrate on the social consequences of scientific and technological development and the impact of those on the level of employment. Contemporary discussions deal with the structure, content and organization of work and division of labor. They present different sets of values about work, including various views and opinions on "work humanization," "self-realization in work," "industrial democracy," "post-industrial societies," and also "leisure societies." Since the 1960s, much sociological, psychological and labor research has been undertaken on these questions in many industrialized countries. At the same time, however, issues of this kind are rarely touched upon in developing countries. Here priorities are quite different, and are bound up with links between poverty, unemployment and underemployment. Working is simply a question of survival.

Traditionally, the term "work" has been generally related to "job" or "employment," even if it is recognized that there are activities which, although not directly providing material means for surviving, are also work: housework and activities carried out by unpaid family workers. In developing countries, however, a great percentage of the labor force is not engaged in wage employment. Development Report, 1979, estimates that the majority of workers in the Third World are self-employed or unpaid family workers, while only a smaller percentage is engaged in wage employment. While there is considerable variation among countries, analysis reveals clearly that wage employment accounts for a much larger proportion of the labor force in industrialized countries than in developing ones. (Squire, 1981, 57)

Moreover, interpreting the "right to work" as the right to have a job is less than adequate. Working life is a highly complex reality which cannot be properly understood by only taking into account the employment/unemployment situation. This distortion is further aggravated by the complexity of work relations, ranging from wage labor in a free-choice employment situation under just and favorable conditions, to overexploitation and subjugation.

An analysis of the Yearbook of Labour Statistics for 1977 to 1983 indicates not only that wage employment is far more significant in the labor force in the OECD countries than in Latin America, but also that the corresponding proportions act in very different ways because of the dissimilar activity rates among them. Costa Rica ranks first with 75.26 percent wage earners, but this is of an economically active population of only 34.70 percent. Or take Mexico, registering 62.31 percent of wage earners for an economically active population of only 28.80 percent. The insignificance of wage employment, on the one hand, and the high rates of poverty prevailing in this region, with large numbers of laborers remaining in very low productive activities, have led the ILO and analysts to emphasize the underemployment problem—not only in Latin America, but also in all developing countries.

What, then, is the meaning of the discussion about the "right to work" for the larger majorities of the Latin American population? Certainly, much of that population is too young or too old for labor activity, or is impaired from working. However, the data speak for themselves in relation to the quantitative aspect of "the right to work."

Apart from its relative quantitative status and reward, work has also certain recognized aspects that are not purely economic: including the right to meaningful work and a safe working environment. Blauner suggests that the "meaning" of labor activity is related to the workers' relationship to the product, process and organization of work. (Blauner, 1964) Also the meaning of work has been analyzed in the contradiction between labor activity and its control, division, monitoring and standardization favoring productivity. For Braverman, a loss of meaning is inherent in every phase of the

de-skilling process that characterizes the actual designs
of work processes, making them efficient and productive.
(Braverman, 1974)

These questions may be important, but they are of a
different character than the meaning of work in the Third
World, for instance for a laborer in Latin America who
may not even have a place in the productive system. Our
traditional measures of analysis simplify the nature of
"work" and employment. Low levels of GDP and information
do not express the essence or the realities of the
situationfor the great majority of the worker in the
world: for example, those in the developing countries.

GDP levels and the way laboractivity is recorded
provide onlylimited information about the economic basis
of the poor majority in the developing nations. The
inequality on which most of the Third World societies are
founded manifests itself in the fact that half the
national income is earned by a tiny percentage of an
elite population.

International Standards on the Right to Work

The "right to work" has received recognition in
international law and in the constitutions, basic
charters,legislation and other official documents of many
nations. Perhaps the best illustration is found in the
Universal Declaration of Human Rights adopted and
proclaimed by the General Assembly of the United Nations
in 1948, which specifies in its Article 23:

> 1. Everyone has the right tow ork, to free choice
> of employment, to just and favourable conditions or
> work and to protection against unemployment. 2.
> Everyone, without any discrimination, has the right
> to equal pay for equal work. 3. Everyone who works
> has the right to just and favorable renumeration,
> ensuring for himself and his family an existence
> worthy of human dignity, and supplemented, if
> necessary, by other means of social protection. 4.
> Everyone has the right to form and to join trade
> unions, for the protection of his interests.

This is further amplified in the International Covenant
on Economic, Social and Cultural Rights adopted in 1966.
Its Article 6 provides:

1. The States Parties to the present Covenant recognize the right of everyone to the opportunity to gain his living by work which he freely chooses or accepts, and will take appropriate steps to safeguard this right. 2. The steps to be taken by a State Party to the present Covenant to achieve the full realization of this right shall include technical and vocational guidance and training programs, policies and techniques to achieve steady economic, social and cultural development and full and productive employment under conditions safeguarding fundamental political and economic freedoms to the individual.

Through the framing of the ILO Conventions and Recommendations (the International Labor Code), International Labor standards formally illustrate various facts of the right to work and the range of policies, programs, legal aspects and administrative arrangements involved in the realization of this right. Main ILO instruments concerning the right to work (even if they do not expressly mention it) are the Employment Policy Convention, 1964 (No. 122) and Recommendation, 1964 (No. 122). These provide the basis for the ILO's World Employment Program comprised mainly of large-scale research, especially upon the links between employment promotion, income distribution and the international division of labor.

These questions may be important, but they are of a different character than the meaning of work in the Third World, for instance for a laborer in Latin America who may not even have a place in the productive system. Our traditional measures of analysis simplify the nature of "work" and employment. Low levels of GDP and information do not express the essence or the realities of the situation for the great majority of the workers in the world: i.e. those in the developing countries.

GDP levels and the way labor activity is recorded provide only limited information about the economic basis of the poor majority in the developing nations. The inequality on which most of the Third World societies are founded manifests itself in the fact that half the national income is earned by a tiny percentage of an elite population.

International Standards on the Right to Work

The "right to work" has received recognition in international law and in the constitutions, basic charters, legislation and other official documents of many nations. Perhaps the best illustration is found in the Universal Declaration of Human Rights adopted and proclaimed by the General Assembly of the United Nations in 1948, which specifies in its Article 23:

1. Everyone has the right to work, to free choice of employment, to just and favourable conditions or work and to protection against unemployment. 2. Everyone, without any discrimination, has the right to equal pay for equal work. 3. Everyone who works has the right to just and favourable renumeration, ensuring for himself and his family an existence worthy of human dignity, and supplemented, if necessary, by other means of social protection. 4. Everyone has the right to form and to join trade unions, for the protection of his interests.

This is further amplified in the International Covenant on Economic, Social and Cultural Rights adopted in 1966. Its Article 6 provides:

1. The States Parties to the present Covenant recognize the right of everyone to the opportunity to gain his living by work which he freely chooses or accepts, and will take appropriate steps to safeguard this right. 2. The steps to be taken by a State Party to the present Covenant to achieve the full realization of this right shall include technical and vocational guidance and training programs, policies and techniques to achieve steady economic, social and cultural development and full and productive employment under conditions safeguarding fundamental political and economic freedoms to the individual.

Through the framing of the ILO Conventions and Recommendations (the International Labour Code), International Labour standards formally illustrate various facts of the right to work and the range of policies, programs, legal aspects and administrative arrangements involved in the realization of this right.

Main ILO instruments concerning the right to work (even
if they do not expressly mention it) are the Employment
Policy Convention, 1964 (No. 122) and Recommendation,
1964 (No. 122). These provide the basis for the ILO's
World Employment Program comprised mainly of large-scale
research, especially upon the links between employment
promotion, income distribution and the international
division of labour.

International principles and provisions concerning
the workers' right to organize consist partly of
provisions concerned with freedom of association, but
also of principles and patterns referring to freedom of
association in the trade union sphere (Freedom of
Association and Protection of the Right to Organize).
The Universal Declaration of Human Rights, besides
recognizing the right of all individuals to "freedom of
peaceful assembly and association" (Art. 20), specifies
that "everyone has the right to form and to join trade
unions for the protection of his interests" (Art. 23).
These principles have been developed further in the
International Covenants on Civil and Political Rights and
Economic, Social and Cultural Rights, both of 1966. The
ILO's basic instruments in these matters are Convention
No. 87, 1948, concerning Freedom of Association and
Protection of the Right to Organize; and Convention No.
98, 1949, concerning the Application of the Principles of
the Right to Organize and to Bargain Collectively.

The Realities of Working Life

Ideally, the right to work (or the right to a "job")
may be included in international law and in most
constitutions of the world's nations. In reality,
opportunities for earning a living are becoming more and
more difficult for an increasing number of people both in
the industrialized world and the Third World. This is
true not only in terms of getting and maintaining a job
but also in satisfying the basic needs of workers and
their families. By this, we refer primarily to income.
Though questions about having meaningful employment which
can enable people to realize their talents and ambitions
are important in other contexts, these have little
significance from a Latin American perspective.

This dual nature of work is perhaps most dramatically illustrated by Studs Terkel in Working. He writes:

> This book, being about work, is by its very nature, about violence - to the spirit as well as to the body. It is about ulcers as well as accidents, about shouting matches as well as fistfights, about nervous breakdowns as well as kicking the dog around. It is, above all (or beneath all), about daily humiliations. To survive the day is triumph enough for the walking wounded among the great many of us ... It is about a search, too, for daily meaning as well as daily bread, for recognition as well as cash, for astonishment rather than torpor; in short, for a sort of life rather than a Monday through Friday sort of dying. (Terkel, 1974, xi)

In Latin America the social consequences of the labor situation are extremely critical. In Chile, for example, where more than 30% of the labor force suffers some form of underutilization, the future looks bleak. Studies of malnutrition among children, drug addiction and prostitution of young people, together with reports and testimonies about miserable occupation disguising unemployment for men and women of all ages, are increasing. This deterioration has been experienced over the past ten years by the majority of workers. A generalized worsening of nutritional standards, time dedicated to recreation, quality of housing, health attention and sanitary services have produced a deterioration which finds dramatic expression in an increase of morbidity for the privileged workers who still have jobs. Moreover, the increase in productivity and the instability of the work situation have meant a higher trend for workers to get sick. (Echeverria, 1984)

Scientific management methods, mainly along Taylorist lines, have been spreading everywhere. This has occurred not only in the industrial sector, but also in business and service activities, where mass production and "people processing" have gradually become the norm. In consequence, a system of job fragmentation has evolved, with the assembly line the prime example. In the developing countries, these developments have become widespread: first in industrialization processes and then in other areas. Although criticism of Taylorism has a long history and there have been some efforts at implementing non-Tayloristic forms of work organization in the industrialized countries, the system still dominates in the organization of the processes of labor and production. Thus we still find the fundamental contradiction between declared principles concerning "the right to work" and the realities of working life.

While recent decades have witnessed some attention to work itself as a human activity (even though the discussion is relatively meaningless in the Third World), many aspects of work have been left unexamined. These mainly involve imbalances between "work" in the industrialized countries and in the developing ones. It is beyond the scope of this investigation to explore further different theoretical propositions about this distinction, or to take a stand in the ongoing discussion. It is, however, important to underscore the disparities between the nature and meaning of work for regions at different levels of development. This inadequacy is representative of much that has been found lacking in the analysis of different studies on the consequences of trade on employment in both industrialized countries and developing ones. Such research has often tended to treat the problem as a static one, rather than take into account the implications of differential policies and realities of development and underdevelopment.

Medium- and Long-term Prospects

ILO estimates show that the world population in 1987 will amount to some 5 billion people, 75% in developing countries (ILO, 1980). In Africa, Asia and Latin America today, no less than 40 to 45% of the total labor force -- almost 330 million adult men and women -- are either out of work or underemployed (ILO, 1982b). It is in these regions where the active population is growing faster -- at an estimated rate of 2.5% annually between now and the end of the century, against a world average of only 1.8%. ILO estimates that for the labor force increase from 1980 to December 1987 (250 million persons) 30 million jobs would have to be created each year in the developing countries just to absorb potential laborers in work. As of 1985 this has not happened, with the employment situation deteriorating further every day. The current sharp increase in unemployment and underemployment and the uncertainty about the long-term global economic situation make it difficult to foresee how this concrete aim might be achieved. Moreover, in 1980 ILO estimated that, taking 1979 as a statistical basis, 332 million jobs would have to be created in the world between 1980 and 1987 in order to solve the unemployment situation and provide jobs for the newcomers of the labor force. This is an unlikely accomplishment. From these data on the economic and social situation of these countries, it clear that there is very little chance for the 800 million people living in absolute poverty to improve their situation in the foreseeable future.

The long-term prospects are even gloomier. Here we will refer only to one aspect among many: the annual number of persons reaching working age is expected to be about 100 million by the end of the present century, most of them in the Third World. This forecasts a massive employment problem, further aggravated by labor-saving technological progress. This increase in the labor force further worsens the situation of the working poor. Nor is it financially feasible, in these circumstances, to rely on social assistance programs or public work projects to create employment opportunities.

For Latin America, the growth of work force 1980-1987 will be some 25-31 million individuals. This corresponds to a general population growth in Latin America in the same period of some 100 million (ILO, 1980). In a situation with increasing insufficiency of productive employment with adequate income, this sharp increase in the labor force will but exacerbate further the imbalance between labor supply and demand in the region. This imbalance is the main cause of increasing "informal" activities that absorb the excess of labor force supply. In the informal sector, people usually work as self-employed in activities linked with improductive services -- representing forms of hidden employment -- or in traditional, very small enterprises with very low productivity. The further outlook seems difficult indeed. Even the mechanism of informal activities may prove insufficient for absorbing the excess of labor. The probable future social price of this situation for the people of the continent will obviously involve riots and social violence.

International Action

In the face of this situation, the International Office of ILO has tried to discover and test new approaches. It has been concerned with systematic studies of new forms of work organization, and in 1976 it launched the International Programme for the Improvement of Working Conditions and Environment (PIACT). Under this program the organization of work was to be a key area of research and action. With the World Employment Programme (launched officially in 1969) the office began to provide national policy-makers and planners with practical guidelines to enable them to accelerate growth rates in productive employment. ILO activities consisted of comprehensive and exploratory employment missions, research efforts and regional/country employment teams. A central contribution to the conceptual field is the "basic needs" approach adopted in 1976. At the same time, ILO has continued its efforts to set international standards, promote their application, denounce their violation and combat discrimination.

In Latin America the provision of direct support has become a principal means of action for the Regional Employment Programme for Latin America and the Caribbean (PREALC). Under this program, many governments have been advised by the ILO on national and sectoral employment policies. Other ILO centers acting in the region are the Inter-American Vocational Training Research and Documentation Center (CINTERFOR) and the Inter-American Center for Labour Administration (CIAT). These efforts, as well as analysis of employment in different countries and activities, have helped to improve the situation of labor in Latin America. But those and similar programs face a tremendous uphill struggle. The situation in this and other regions of the Third World is proceeding from bad to worse.

ILO is aware of these problems. In its Report VI on Employment Policy prepared for the 69th Session of the International Labour Conference in 1983, it noted that since the adoption of the Employment Policy Convention (No. 122) and Recommendation (122) in 1964, new issues have arisen. Those include the necessity of restructuring national economies in the light of the international division of labor; the energy crisis and inflation; development, choice and transfer of technology; gaps between employment and income levels within countries; integration of the urban informal sector, South-South cooperation, and international migration (ILO, 1982b, 3-4).

However, the contradiction between stated principles concerning "the right to work" and the situation facing workers -- especially in developing countries -- makes it difficult to ponder on the possibilities of normative rules. What is at stake is the ability of the economies to further appropriate employment policies to broaden the labor markets and give opportunities to those seeking work.

EMPLOYMENT, UNEMPLOYMENT AND UNDEREMPLOYMENT

Employment is but one form of human labor, though the current magnitude of the employment problem lies at the heart of the worker's situation and should not be considered only in its quantitative dimension. But even in this limited aspect, the size and extent of the employment problem is not adequately covered by current dominant frameworks for employment and unemployment, framed as these are on the conventional "labor force" approach with its market criteria.

The Labor Force Approach

The labor force approach is based on the notion of economic activity. "Economically active" are those persons above a specified age (often 10 or 15 years old), who have worked for pay or profit during a particular reference period (frequently one week) or who have been looking for work. (ILO, 1984, 3). The labor force approach, with its point of departure in the "gainfully occupied population," was formally introduced to the ILO at the Sixth International Conference of Labour Statisticians in 1947. The definitions have been reviewed at later conferences, as have methods of implementing the corresponding resolutions. At the Thirteenth International Conference of Statisticians in 1982, a new reorientation, clarification and extension of the labor force approach was adopted. This approach raises many problems, even if its use has been formally recommended by the ILO and the United Nations for all population censuses carried out in or around 1970.

The main criticism of this approach is that it is based on "economic activity." This limits and distorts the analysis of the low income countries. The other side is that "economic activity" is a concept related to a given economic and social organization, so that in any given country such "economic activity" is recorded in the national income statistics. This means that certain important activities are not included in the labor force approach -- for example, housework, taking care of the family, producing and preparing food for the family.

Generally speaking, this approach does not cover Third World conditions, where heterogeneity of labor realities do not fit within this framework, i.e. the urban informal sector. This is especially true for female work. In addition to the activities already mentioned, rural women in developing countries carry out such socially vital work as fetching water and gathering wood for household use, gardening, storing crops, processing food and working directly in crop production on family farms supplying the market. Very often the woman has to walk long distances in order to accomplish these tasks. (See Werneke and Broadfield, ILO, 1979)

The Economically Active Population and the Concepts of Employment, Unemployment and Underemployment

According to ILO guidelines, the "economically active population" comprises all persons who furnish the supply of labor for the production of economic goods and services during a specified time reference period. This can be quantified by measuring the "usually active population," in relation with a long reference period such as a year; or by measuring the "currently active population" or the labor force at a given point in time, typically a period not longer than one week (Resolution I of the Thirteenth International Conference of Labour Statisticians, 1982, paragraphs 5 to 8).

In the Third World, a large percentage of the population lives in rural areas where the primary way of producing is still by traditional agricultural methods. Thus the family remains the basic production unit. In these rural areas, it is very difficult to separate work accomplished on the basis of labor force activity from other forms of work. Most individuals will present a mixed situation, especially because of the seasonality of work activities. Concerning Latin America specifically, there are large areas in many countries with the problem of the minifundia, where the scarcity of land and other capital-inputs determines a very low pattern of labor use. This is due to the unequal land distribution, where the latifundia coexists with minifundia. Latifundia involves the concentration of lands in few hands, with large amounts of lands owned by one person or family. Generally, the best lands belong to the latifundia. Minifundia exists on the remaining lands, with considerable fragmentation and subdivision of rural property. Usually the minifundia is found together with family production. In large number the minifundia predominant work objective is self-subsistence. The latifundia-minifundia system has led to inefficiency and slow growth; these have led to underutilization of most of the land and underemployment of labor. Obviously this situation, widespread in Latin America, is very difficult to measure through the labor force approach.

Even though control of the rural economies has been steadily slipping away from the traditional Latin American landholders' oligarchies into the hands of commercial farming, trade and industrial enterprises, rural labor has not benefitted from such a transformation. The agrarian structure changes with modern agricultural enterprises, but the situation of land tenure and advancing technology does not provide peasants with opportunities for bettering their situation. Former tenants are transformed into wage earners and evicted from their lands: if they are dismissed, they may find it very difficult to get a job or a plot of land elsewhere. While some landowners are selling parts of their farms, these are going to their better-off tenants or to professionals; others are going into contract farming with local business or small holders. All these new systems are simply creating more unemployed and homeless in the rural area. This problem of land distribution lies at the root of the underutilization of labor and poverty in Latin American rural areas.

Process of Urbanization. Evaluating Unemployment Measures in the Urban Sector in Latin America

Very likely all of the reasons mentioned previously and income differentials constitute the major factors in determining the persistence and, in some cases, the acceleration of rural-urban migration in Latin America. This rate is the highest in the Third World. Besides the problems, threats and pressures of all kinds that this trend causes in the cities, it also has a serious impact on the general labor situation. Indeed, there is a rural employment crisis, and prospects for improving this situation are grim. The picture of employment in agriculture gives no ground for optimism. However, through migration the rural excess of labor is transformed in urban unemployment and urban underutilization of labor because the expansion of the modern urban employment is not able to accommodate the increase of the urban labor force, neither in this natural growth nor in its migration component. PREALC states that "no matter how fast 'modern' outputs grow, even if achieved without introducing labor-saving innovations, the absolute size of the modern sector is too small to perform such a task." (PREALC, 1978, 21)

This is also linked with the way that the urbanization process has taken place in Latin America. In these countries, as in the Third World in general, the situation has differed from that in Europe in earlier stages of economic development. Paul Bairoch specifically points to the sharp contrast of these different experiences, emphasizing that in Europe the urbanization rate remained below the share of the active population engaged in manufacturing until 1890. By contrast, in the Third World and in Latin America the process of urbanization takes place in advance of, instead of as a consequence of, economic growth and industrialization. Bairoch also analyzes the limited possibilities of employment opportunities in the manufacturing sector in these countries, and comes to the conclusion that industry has been able to absorb only a very small proportion of the surplus active rural population (Bairoch, 1973).

Rural-urban migration and the substantial increase of the urban population and urban work force in the developing countries have resulted in a large distortion that has given rise to an enormous increase of various urban "informal" activities. It is in the urban informal sector that the surplus of labor has created their own means of survival. Defining the urban informal sector is

not easy, yet there exist a number of labels to describe
the activities included in it. Such activities are
generally defined negatively, as those which are not
effectively subject to "formal" rules of contracts,
licences, taxation, labor inspection, etc. They involve
a vast range of activities: casual construction labor,
domestic service or any kind of service provided by a
small-scale self-employed unit which may also employ one
or two others or include family workers.

No doubt, many of these persons included in the
urban informal sector do not clearly fit within the
categories defined by the labor force approach, even if
their tasks may be related to productive activities. The
problem is that this sector represents a large percentage
of the urban working force, and particularly those likely
to have labor problems: young and old laborers, women,
migrants and illiterates. The concept of unemployment is
very hard to apply to those working for themselves.
Sometimes the activity of these self-employed persons is
so little that the borderline to unemployment is very
vague, as they may be able to manage only occasional
work. At times they will be included among the
underemployed, and at other times they will be listed
among the underemployed, or they may not be included in
any category of the labor force at all.

Measuring Unemployment

In the final analysis, unemployment is measured by
the number of people looking for jobs. Thus, the standard definition of unemployment includes a highly
controversial point in the criteria: work-seeking
activity. How should this be determined, for example, in
the case of the self-employed? It also becomes very
difficult to get an accurate picture of this factor with
family workers. Thus the unemployment concept is far
better suited to the industrialized countries than to the
Third World, and even in the former it may yield a very
narrow image of the true situation. Concerning this
aspect, the Report prepared for the Thirteenth
International Conference of Labour Statisticians clearly
stated: seeking a job is essentially a process of search
for job information and therefore relates mainly to paid
employment and is meaningful where channels for exchange
of such information exists and are used. This is

generally the case in the industrialized countries, where most of the workers are employees; information about labor exchanges is common; and people refer to such information when searching for a job. The Report also states that the situation in the Third World is absolutely different, with the bulk of workers being self-employed or engaged in household enterprises, and the labor exchanges and similar institutional arrangements not fully developed, often limited to certain urban sectors only. (ILO, 1982c, 43)

As regards Latin America, PREALC studied the increase in open unemployment that appeared to accompany the decrease in the activity rates in recent years, concluding that this situation suggests the presence of discouraged workers. This interpretation is supported by the decline in activity rates caused mainly by a reduction in labor participation by young laborers and women. PREALC is aware that this produces a distortion in unemployment rates, because if the labor market is reactivated, participation rates will again increase (PREALC, 1984, 17-18). Therefore, the fact that discouraged workers are not included in the economically active population means a distortion of the already high rates of existing unemployment.

These illustrations are only some aspects of the difficulties involved in measuring unemployment. It is much harder to evaluate the unemployment situation in developing countries than in developed ones. In fact, unemployment is rarely estimated on a consistent basis in developing countries because of conceptual and statistical problems. In addition to those aspects, it is necessary to consider the lack of resources to carry out research properly and the political use of the data. Another problem is the way borderline cases are classified. Such cases represent a large proportion of the labor force. Thus, even if unemployment statistics are available in developing countries they will not give a very realistic picture of the employment situation, at least not the dimension of underutilization of labor.

A very important issue in evaluating the situation of labor in the developing countries concerns the problem that unemployment is the most acute problem facing workers; however, in quantitative terms, underemployment is the most important form of underutilization of labor. And it is not possible to form a reliable estimate about its extent and composition. The gravity of this situation is illustrated by the fact that the considerable reserves of labor force necessarily have major consequences for the general situation of labor in the affected country.

From the data available, PREALC estimates that the degree of overall underutilization of the labor force in Latin America by 1970 was around 27.4%. Of this figure, only 5.8% was open unemployment: one-fifth of underutilization was attributed to open unemployment, meaning that four-fifths of the problem remained hidden, when approached through the most traditional estimate. (PREALC, 1978). Further, the total underutilization rate was 29% for rural areas and 25% in towns. In a more recent study, PREALC (1984) points out that for 1983 the rate of open unemployment rose to levels over 10%, and that underemployment had also risen. According to PREALC, unemployment now represents one third of total underutilization.

Gauges of underemployment are receiving increasing attention not only in developing countries, but also in developed ones. At present, however, virtually no industrialized country is producing official statistics on this topic, although a number of alternative measurements may be derived from regular published data of certain countries, e.g. the United States. (ILO, 1982c, 19)

SUMMARY AND CONCLUSIONS

All the considerations presented above lead to the general conclusion that the labor force approach yields only a narrow frame for analyzing the magnitude of the problem presented by labor. Employment-related concepts seem better suited for assessing the employment situation in the developed countries. In practice, these concepts are also applied to the developing countries, where societies are fundamentally different from the developed ones to which the notions of "employment" and "unemployment" originally referred.

Official unemployment figures are merely the tip of the iceberg. Although unemployment is a major issue in most countries today, statistics say nothing about the realities of underemployment or hidden unemployment, nor of the discouraged workers whose number is increasing daily. This basic situation exists for the developed and developing countries.

In the developing countries, the problem is most pronounced. Open unemployment is not the major form of underutilization of labor. Underemployment is certainly more important in quantitative terms, but empirical study in this field is hindered by the difficulty of measuring the phenomenon. Some countries have included in their employment surveys questions intended to detect forms of underemployment or estimate the discouraged workers, but they have serious limitations. The growth in population and the increase in work force projected for the Third World, the rural-urban migrations and the growth of urban informal sectors present truly alarming future prospects for these countries. In addition, the repercussion of slow or negative growth in developed and developing countries serves to aggravate issues that will continue to pose serious challenges during the coming years.

BIBLIOGRAPHY

Oscar Altimir, "Poverty in Latin America: A review of concepts and data," in Cepal Review, Santiago, Chile, April 1981.

Paul Bairoch, Urban Unemployment in Developing Countries. Geneva: ILO, 1973.

Daniel Betaux, "Stories as Clues to Sociological Understanding: The Bakers of Paris," in Paul Thomson, ed., Our Common History: The Transformation of Europe, London: Pluto Press Limited, 1982, 93-108.

Robert Blauner, Alienation and Freedom. Chicago: University of Chicago Press, 1964.

Harry Braverman, Labor and Monopoly of Capital. New York: Monthly Review Press, 1974.

CEPAL (ECLA), El Desarrollo Latino Americano en Los 80 (Latin American development in the 80s), E/CEPAL/G 1150, 1981; and "Los problemas centrales del desarrollo," (Central Problems of Development). In Notas sobre Economia y Desarrollo de America Latina, prepared by Servicios de Informacion (Information Services), No. 335, February 1981.

Magdalena Echeverria, Enfermedades de los Trabajadores y Crisis Economica, Estudio de Casos, Chile 1970-1980, Programa de Economia del Trabajo; Academia de Humanismo Cristiano, Programa de Investigaciones

Sociales sobre la Poblacion en America Latina (PISPAL), Editorial Interamericana Ltda., Santiago, Chile, 1984.

Jules Geller, "Forms of Capitalist Control over the Labor Process," Monthly Review, Vol. 31, No. 7, December 1979, 39-46.

Michael Hopkins, "A Global Forecast of Absolute Poverty and Employment," International Labour Review, Vol. 122, No. 4, July-August 1983, 565-577.

_____, "Employment trends in developing countries, 1960-80 and beyond," International Labour Review, Vol. 122, No. 4, July-August 1983.

Enrique V. Iglesias, "Begin to grow. The only option of Latin America," Notas Sobre la Economia y el Desarrollo de America Latina, prepared by ECLA Information Service, Santiago, Chile, No. 393/394, 1984.

ILO, "ILO Medium-Term Plan 1982-1987," Report on programme implementation, 1978-79, ILO, 66th Session, Geneva, 1980.

ILO, The Urban Informal Sector in Developing Countries. Employment, Poverty and Environment, edited by S.V. Sethuraman, International Labour Office, Geneva, 1981.

ILO, "Report of the Director General, International Labour Conference, 68th Session 1982, Geneva, 1982.

International Labour Conference, 69th Session 1983, Report VI (1), Employment Policy, ILO, Geneva, 1982.

ILO, Labour Force, Employment, Unemployment and Underemployment, Thirteenth International Conference of Labour Statisticians, Report II, ICLS/13/II, Geneva, 1982.

ILO, World Labour Report, Vol. I, "Employment, incomes, social protection, new information technology." Geneva: International Labour Office, 1984.

Jean Mouly, "Employment: A concept in need of renovation," in David H. Freedman (ed.), Employment Outlook and Insights, Geneva: ILO, 1979, 111-117.

OECD, Economic Outlook, No. 35, Paris, July 1984.

PREALC, Employment in Latin America, New York: Praeger, 1978 (in cooperation with the Regional Employment Program for Latin America and the Caribbean (PREALC) of the International Labour Office (ILO).

PREALC, "Despues de la Crisis: Lecciones Y Prespectivas

(After the Crisis: Lessons and Perspectives," PREALC Working Paper, mimeo, Santiago, Chile: PREALC/250, October 1984.

Lyn Squire, Employment Policy in Developing Countries: A Survey of Issues and Evidence, New York: Oxford University Press, 1981, a World Bank Research Publication.

Guy Standing, Labour Force Participation and Development, 2nd ed., Geneva: ILO, 1981.

_____, "The Notion of Voluntary Unemployment," International Labour Review, Vol. 120, No. 5, September-October, 1981, 563-579.

_____, "The Notion of Structural Unemployment," International Labour Review, Vol. 122, No. 2, March-April 1983, 137-153.

_____, "The Notion of Technological Unemployment," International Labour Review, Vol. 123, No. 2, March-April 1984, 127-147.

Studs Terkel, Working: People Talk About What They Do All Day and How They Feel About What They Do. New York: Random House Pantheon Books, 1974.

Diane Werneke and Robin Broadfield, "A needs-oriented approach to manpower," in David H. Freedman, (ed.), Employment Outlook and Insights, Geneva: ILO, 1979, 137-148.

22

The Arms Trade: Facts and Implications

Michael Brzoska and Thomas Ohlson

RECENT TRENDS

The spectacular growth of trade in major conventional weapons came to a halt in the early 1980s. This is particularly noteworthy since the arms trade during the 1970s was labeled the "fastest-growing business" in the world. The spectacular increase in arms transfers that was recorded for the second half of the 1970s resulted from orders placed earlier in the 1970s. It was then that increases in oil prices, the use of arms exports to recycle oil money, changed superpower policies and some major international crises stimulated an unprecedented proliferation of arms.

By the early 1980s the framework for worldwide arms transfers had changed. There was no increase in the wealth of the countries in the Third World and no sign of an emerging "new international economic order." Instead, external debts reached record levels. A global economic crisis, leaving deep scars in many industrialized countries, is still soaring in most Third World regions. Financial institutions and banks in the Western industrialized countries have a tighter grip than ever on many Third World states.

SIPRI statistics for the imports of conventional weapons reveal large differences from region to region. 1/ Arms imports by the most important region, the Middle East, remain on a high level throughout. A stable, slightly upward trend is visible also in South Asia. In Africa, on the other hand, a sharp increase in the late 1970s has been followed by substantial decreases in the 1980s. The economic crisis has hit Africa particularly hard. Specific relevant facts are that Libya, for example, imported far more weapons in the late 1970s than could be assimilated by its small armed forces, and therefore imports have decreased substantially in the

1980s; and the mandatory UN embargo on arms sales to South Africa of 1977 has so far proven unsuccessful in political terms, but it has substantially reduced South African arms imports. Many weapons are now produced domestically and imports have shifted to components and dual-use technology. Far Eastern arms imports have been dominated by the Korean situation and more importantly by the relationship between Vietnam and its neighbors. Latin American arms imports were kept at a stable level into the 1980s due to conflicts in Central America, unresolved border disagreements in South America and the Falkland/Malvinas War. In the mid-1980s economic problems became apparent in the regional arms import pattern.

The economic crisis had a different effect on the supply side. A number of supplier countries had used their arms export policies as instruments to ward off effects of increased earnings from oil and other raw materials in certain Third World countries. This proved a successful strategy in the cases of the USA, the USSR and France. Other countries tried to follow this path and in the late 1970s the UK, FR Germany and Italy were able to expand their arms exports. Arms production capacity was markedly increased. When demand was reduced, the competition among producers increased considerably, prompting a number of effects described in the following section. It is the expanding gap between demand and supply which explains many of the changes in the arms market between the 1970s and the 1980s.

There are differences from country to country on the recipient side. In the USA the arms transfer policy came under heavy criticism in the mid-1970s and it was a major issue in the 1976 presidential campaign. President Carter introduced a number of restrictions which led to a reduction in USA arms exports. But the restrictive policy was gradually eroded by the Camp David agreement of 1978, and by 1980 few of the restraints were effective. The incoming Reagan administration reversed the Carter policy, but the level of arms transfers has not reached the heights of the mid-1970s. Additionally, the Reagan administration's emphasis on restrictions of technology transfers has had some effect on arms transfers. In the Soviet Union arms transfers in the late 1970s were an important money maker. Still, the USSR entered into arms transfer talks with the USA in 1978. It is questionable whether the USSR, around this time, also introduced a more restrictive arms export policy. The data show a decrease in Soviet arms exports in the early 1980s; this may, however, be explained by Soviet difficulties in adapting to the structural changes in the arms market. Soviet arms exports are concentrated in a few countries with which the USSR is politically aligned.

In the Western European countries, arms exports are an important source of economic revenue. The French arms industry, to take a pertinent example, is highly export dependent -- this produces the general consequence that economic considerations increasingly influence arms export policies. As a group, these countries have considerably expanded their market share at the expense of the superpowers (See table 1). The change of government in France in 1982 did not, despite election rhetoric from leading socialist politicians, change France's arms export policy. The Mitterand government has instead sought to improve French marketing and competitiveness. This tendency is also found in the UK where the arms industry gained comparatively little from the global boom in the early 1970s. In FR Germany the restrictions introduced in the early 1970s were gradually eased. In Italy the expansion of the arms industry was unhampered by government control. The same is true for Spain which became an important arms exporter in the early 1980s.

Arms imports use up scarce currency in a way that does not contribute to the future repayment of debts. They contribute to indebtedness and economic crisis in the Third World. They have fueled political crises and increased the probability of war. In the early 1980s, the net outcome was a reduction of demand; a reduction which, to some extent, is explained by saturation due to the huge import volumes of the 1970s. The described trends have resulted in structural changes in the arms market, some of which are described in the next section. An example of some consequences of the changed patterns in the arms market is the supply of weapons to the belligerents in the Iraq-Iran War.

Table 1: The Leading Major-weapon Exporting Countries:
The Values and Respective Shares for 1981-1985

Figures are Stockholm International Peace Research Institute trend indicator values, as expressed in US $ m, at constant (1975) prices; shares in percentages. Figures may not add up to totals due to rounding.

Country	1981	1982	1983	1984	1985	1981-5	Percent exported to Third World, 1981-1985
USA	5,325 39.2	5,726 40.4	5,425 40.6	4,995 36.1	4,187 36.5	25,659 38.7	44.3
USSR	3,905 28.8	4,095 28.9	3,233 24.2	3,613 26.1	3,460 30.2	18,306 27.6	74.1
France	1,454 10.7	1,274 9.0	1,410 10.6	1,553 11.2	1,319 11.5	7,010 10.6	80.5
UK	536 4.0	638 4.5	494 3.7	825 6.0	654 5.7	3,146 4.7	66.3
FR Germany	487 3.6	325 2.3	639 4.8	790 5.7	420 3.7	2,662 4.0	61.6
Italy	545 4.0	695 4.9	396 3.0	460 3.3	405 3.5	2,501 3.8	93.9
Third World	409 3.0	454 3.2	764 5.7	510 3.7	297 2.6	2,434 3.7	95.5
China	161 1.2	252 1.8	255 1.9	555 4.0	293 2.6	1,516 2.3	95.3
Others	737 5.4	701 5.0	729 5.5	523 3.8	423 3.7	3,111 4.7	67.3
Total	13,559	14,160	13,345	13,824	11,458	66,345	64.1

DRIVING FORCES AND STRUCTURAL ADAPTIONS

Any attempts to restrain the international trade in conventional weapons requires an insight into the factors that propel the trade in arms.

Supply Factors

The incentives to export weapons are multiple. They can be grouped into two basic categories: political factors and economic factors. They are at work on different levels: the international, the national and the sub-national (industrial) levels.

At the global or international level, the political factors are determined by the world-wide East-West conflict. One instrument in this hegemonic struggle is arms transfers. The factors on the international level are primarily applicable to the major powers, the USA and the USSR. But other suppliers, such as France or Sweden, can use global rationales by pointing out that their weapons come free of political, military or economic strings. In the hegemonic conflict arms transfers are intimately intertwined with attempts to exert political leverage. Arms sales are seen as a means to establish or maintain influence in a region or a country, or to prevent other countries from becoming influential. Buying a modern weapon system normally involves a long-term commitment from both parties, and with the direct acquisition follows supply of spare parts, technical assistance, maintenance, training and education throughout the life of the weapon. Economically, the aim is to ensure the stability of civilian markets and the inflow of necessary raw materials.

From a national point of view, there are factors such as the influence on the military elites of the recipients; burden sharing; and access to transit rights, facilities and spares. Furthermore, the longer production runs resulting from arms exports are claimed to be beneficial for a number of reasons: they lower national arms procurement expenditures through lower unit prices and help recoup some of the research and development costs; they ensure a stable employment level; and they provide an industrial capacity to increase production for national defense, should such need arise. In times of pressure to economize on domestic procurement expenditures, such arguments become very powerful. Finally, there is the suggestion that arms exports, at least in the short run, help to improve the balance of payments, and that arms transfers open doors for civilian exports; conversely, restrictions on arms exports, it is argued, will cause other hidden losses to the economy.

On the sub-national or industrial level, the pressures to export arms are of a purely economic nature. First of all, in the West there are often specific, structural differences between the arms industry and the ideal free market enterprise. For example, prices of weapons do not normally fall with reduced demand; instead they tend to rise. Added demand from abroad holds the price rises down and the firm remains competitive. Another difference is that supply does not always adjust to demand because of the need for excess capacity in case of war. Second, arms exports are a highly profitable business for the arms industries. Third, in many arms industries arms exports account for a substantial part of total turnover, and with relatively large barriers to entry and exit this comprises yet another strong and built-in pressure to export. A substantial number of companies entered the arms business in the 1970s when demand was great and they found it difficult to move back to civilian production in times of general slack in civilian markets. Nevertheless, economic constraints in the recipient countries have so far caused a slow-down of the international arms trade in the 1980s. The slow-down has led arms manufacturers to intensify their marketing effort, illustrated, for instance, by the increasing number of arms fairs and exhibitions.

There is also a tendency for arms industries to dissociate themselves from their respective governments. From an arms control perspective there is an important point to be made here: The various determinants listed above are not always pulling in the same direction. There is an inherent tendency towards a collision of interests between the political and economic determinants. This has most often occurred in countries with restrictive arms policies, such as Sweden and FR Germany, taking the form of a clash between the government and the industry; but a clash also occurred in the USA when President Carter's policy was aimed at restraining US arms exports.

Demand Factors

The pressure to import arms can be identified on levels similar to those for the pressure to export. On a regional or subregional level, there is the almost automatic pressure arising from circular arms procurement patterns. The key phrase is "enhancement of national security." It is an ill-defined proposition, used to legitimize both the preparation to counter-attack and the acquisition of large weapon arsenals for internal repression.

On the national level it is argued that the import of modern weapons and weapon technology enhances prestige, industrialization and development. On the sub-national level, the vestel interests of the military elite is the most important, often exerting a major influence on arms procurement decisions. Inter-service rivalry is a related factor which often leads to excessive arms imports.

The obvious restraining factor on the demand side is cost. When measured against the national security needs of a country plagued by economic problems, the cost of modern and sophisticated weapons systems may be deemed too high, particularly if the weapons do not seem appropriate for the relevant conflict scenarios.

Enhanced Position of Buyers

The international market for arms is becoming a buyer's market. This is primarily the result of the simultaneous occurrence of two factors: fierce competition among a growing number of suppliers, and budgetary constraints among the recipients. A number of features of the arms market exemplify this.

First, there is the great number of offset deals involving technology transfers. While previous arms transfers were usually concluded on cash or credit terms, it is now difficult for a seller to avoid offset arrangements with the arms recipient. This is true in the case of sales not only to industrialized countries, but also to countries in the Third World. The offsets often equal, and sometimes even exceed, the value of the arms transfers.

Industrial offsets may include: (a) joint production of a weapon; (b) production under license of the weapon; (c) subcontracting in the purchasing country for components and spare parts for the weapon; (d) transfer of research and development capabilities; (e) the right to market the weapon on behalf of the supplier; (f) maintenance contracts for regional users of the weapon; and (g) imports of other industrial goods from the weapon recipient by the supplier country.

Second, there is the related issue of financing. The financial conditions in many cases determine success in the race for contracts. An obvious case is that of the "Al Thakeb" air defense deal between France and Saudi Arabia. In 1982 the French government had borrowed about $4 billion from the Saudi government. The Al Thakeb deal settles this French debt: Saudi Arabia will not have to make payment. The funds for the development and production of the missiles and launch systems will come from the French government. 2/ Both industrial offsets and financing agreements generate resource flows in addition to the arms flows; they are both expressions of the trend of suppliers to increasingly subsidize their own arms exports. It is noteworthy that the arms industries themselves, particularly those in western Europe, seldom have to bear the burden of the subsidies.

Third, there are frequent reports about the intensity of competition for contracts. The new Nigerian military government, which claimed irregularities in arms purchases as one of the reasons for taking power in 1984, found that bribes had been handed out on a regular basis in connection with arms imports.

Fourth, there is the case of "export" weapons. In western Europe many weapons are tailor-made to the specifications of Third World recipients--this has largely been considered a commercial success. In the Soviet Union and the United States the term "export" weapons has a different meaning and refers to weapons with down-graded capabilities. (The US FX fighter is one example.) The USSR also tries to export less capable versions of their front-line aircraft. Customers in the Third World are skeptical: They demand, and often receive, top-of-the-line aircraft, such as the US F-16. Soviet clients also prefer more advanced systems if they can afford them: The Soviet Union sold an aircraft type (the MiG-29) to India that it had not even supplied to its own forces. In this case, India could capitalize on Soviet fears that India would continue to diversify its arms imports and move away from the Soviet Union.

Fifth, there is an increasing demand among cost-conscious recipients for modernization of existing stocks of weaponry. The suppliers have responded to this: There is an increasing flow of enhanced components, upgrading and modernization kits and so on in order to prolong the life of the aircraft, armored vehicles and other weapons in the inventories of the armed forces.

Finally, the increasing leverage of recipients is illustrated by the fact that certain countries, e.g. Jordan, Kuwait and Nigeria, have all bought weapons from both the USA and the USSR in recent years. The sellers' grip on recipients is no longer the trademark of the arms trade. If one superpower declines to supply certain equipment, some customers simply turn to the other superpower.

THE IRAQ-IRAN WAR AND THE ARMS TRADE

The Iraq-Iran war, now in its sixth year, has developed into a military and diplomatic stalemate: a war of attrition in which neither adversary appears to have the military strength to defeat the other or the will to negotiate a peaceful settlement of the conflict. Recent developments, however, have increased the likelihood of a technological and/or geographical escalation of the conflict--thus making the war a global concern. Arms resupplies continue to reach the adversaries in sufficient quantities for the war to continue.

The Iraqi invasion was obviously based on a misperception of Iran's military capability and will to defend itself. The Iraqi leadership envisaged a quick victory against an enemy weakened by internal turmoil, purges of the officer corps, and arms resupply and maintenance problems. Instead, the protracted and bloody war, with more than 500,000 soldiers and civilians killed, has put severe strains on the economies of both countries. Iraq seems to be in the worse situation: it has used up its financial reserves, civilian development programs have been abandoned, and the country has been forced to reduce its oil exports drastically. The Gulf War has become an economic war in which both sides try to disrupt the main source of revenue of the other--the flow of oil.

The United States and the Soviet Union have both declared their neutrality in the war, they both envisage unpredictable advantages--or losses--from the war, and they have both, directly or indirectly, supplied both belligerents with weapons during the course of the war (see table 2). Although diplomatic relations with Iraq were resumed in 1984, the United States had, by the beginning of 1986, no diplomatic relations with Iran and little leverage with either. The Soviet Union has diplomatic relations with both Iraq and Iran, a friendship treaty with Iraq and Syria, and strong military ties with Libya. Libya and Syria are among the main weapon suppliers to Iran. The USSR is thus in a complex situation, with Iraq, Iran and their allies making their claims a test of Soviet credibility.

There are several points to be made regarding U.S. and Soviet positions in the Iraq-Iran war. On the one hand, the fact that the war continues reflects their limited abilities to stop the war through diplomacy. On the other hand, they do not perceive the war, in its present and still limited form, as a serious threat to their interests in the area. After the war, Iraq and Iran will have to rebuild their civilian and military structures. The continued limited war thus creates the conditions for Iraq and Iran's future reliance on the major powers. The nature of this reliance, however, remains obscure. The USA and the USSR do not, therefore, wish to limit their future options by committing themselves too deeply at the present stage.

Arms Resupply During the War 3/

Arms resupply during war is generally more complex, covert and difficult to verify than in peace-time; the table undoubtedly under-estimates the complexity of the situation. These are some of the main points to be made:

First, and most noteworthy, no less than 15 countries had by early 1986 rendered support to both belligerent states. Second, the number of arms suppliers delivering major weapons increased dramatically after the outbreak of the war: in the case of Iraq, from 3 to 18; and for Iran, from 5 to 17. Third, the supply patterns have changed. Fourth, unlikely groupings of countries emerge as suppliers, or supporters, of the same party. Iran, for example, has received weapons from such

Table 2: Arms Resupply and Other Support to Iraq and Iran, 1980–1985

Country*	Iraq			Iran		
	Major weapons before war	Major weapons during war	Other support during war	Major weapons before war	Major weapons during war	Other support during war
Supporting both parties						
Austria		x	x			x
Brazil	x	x	x		x	x
Chile			x			x
China		x			x	
Ethiopia		x			x	
France	x	x	x	x	x	x
German DR		x	x		x	
Italy		x	x	x	x	
Korea, North		x	x		x	x
Spain		x	x			x
Sweden		x				x
Switzerland		x	x		x	
UK		x			x	x
USA		x	x	x	x	x
USSR	x	x	x	x	x	x
Supporting Iraq						
Belgium			x			
Czechoslovakia		x	x			
Egypt		x	x			
FR Germany		x	x			(x)
Hungary		x				
Jordan		x	x			
Kuwait			x			
Morocco			x			
Pakistan			x			
Philippines			x			
Poland		x	x			
Portugal			x			
Saudi Arabia			x			
Sudan			x			
United Arab Emirates			x			
Yugoslavia		x				
Supporting Iran						
Algeria					x	x
Argentina						x
Greece			(x)			x
Israel					x	x
Libya					x	x
Korea, South					x	x
Mexico						x
Syria					x	x
Taiwan					(x)	x
Turkey			(x)			x
Viet Nam						x
Yemen, South						x

* In many cases without official sanction or knowledge; in some cases illegal.

politically disparate countries as Israel, Libya, North and South Korea, South Africa, Syria and Taiwan. Finally, both countries rely to a significant extent on private arms dealers and circuitous delivery routes via third countries for their supply of small arms, spare parts and munitions.

Iraq has tried for several years to extend the sources of its weapons and move away from dependence on the Soviet Union. The main Western benefactor of this policy is France, although the USSR is still the largest single arms supplier. France has sold Iraq approximately $7 billion worth of arms since the start of the war--a great deal of credit to extend--but the deal included an exchange for oil. Egypt, Italy and Spain are also among the main suppliers of arms to Iraq. Egypt has retransferred weapons from a multitude of original suppliers.

Iran's main suppliers of major weapons are Libya, Syria and North Korea. Support has also been given by Israel and Taiwan, often referred to as pariahs in the international system. There are unconfirmed reports of substantial Chinese arms supplies. With foreign assistance, Iran is also in the process of enhancing its significant, indigenous capacity to produce weapons and munitions. Otherwise, Iran is heavily dependent on the private, international market for supplies. The most absurd example is probably the case of the private arms dealer who purchased captured Iranian equipment--M-47 tanks, howitzers and mortars--from Iraq, and then resold it to Iran. 4/

Effect on Regional Arms Procurement

Since late 1980, all of the six Gulf Cooperation Council (GCC) members (Saudia Arabia, Iran, Iraq, Kuwait, The United Arab Emirates and Dubai) have purchased major warships or missile-armed fast attack craft, sophisticated jet fighters, helicopters, main battle tanks or other modern armored vehicles, and a wide range of anti-air, anti-ship and anti-tank missiles.

The main threats currently seen by the GCC states are Iraqi and Iranian attacks on tankers passing through the Gulf. This is of not only regional but also global concern. From the outset of the war, the U.S. and the USSR have striven to keep the conflict from spreading beyond Iraq and Iran. The U.S. has pledged to protect free shipping through the Gulf. U.S. policy in the region is focused on protecting Western access to Gulf oil by supporting friendly regimes and building up U.S. military installations in the Gulf.

Lessons

The main conclusions to be drawn from the facts concerning the arms trade in the Iraq-Iran war are the following:

1. The weapons flows are in many ways different from those before the war. There is a dramatic increase in the number of suppliers, the patterns of supply are different from those before the war, and there are supplier groupings and interests which are not easily explained along standard political lines.

2. The procurement methods of wartime supply are different. Secret trade routes and arms merchants play a more significant role than in peace-time. The private, international arms market is booming. Many governments also profit markedly from the war.

3. The United States and the Soviet Union are maintaining a low profile—support is primarily given indirectly to both parties, often through their allies.

4. Except possibly for France, very few of the states involved in the arms resupply show signs of wanting to see an end to the war.

5. A massive rearmament process is likely to emerge in Iraq and Iran once the war ends, particularly in the field of high-technology weaponry. This will affect arms procurement policies throughout the region.

6. The prospects for arms trade restraint in the area seem bleak. The flow of arms illustrates the fierce competition between supplier states and the general commercialization and privatization of the arms market.

ARMS PRODUCTION IN THE THIRD WORLD

The volume of Third World arms production has risen dramatically since 1965. In 1984 the volume was almost 600 times the 1950 volume. Before the mid-1960s, production was limited to a few countries, such as Argentina and Egypt. Since then, many more countries have started producing conventional weapons. By 1985, 26 countries had produced major weapons (aircraft, armored vehicles, missiles, ships). If other equipment is also included, such as small arms and munitions, 54 countries are (or have been) involved in some form of arms production activity. In the early 1980s there were signs of stagnation in some countries: the overall growth rates of the volume of Third World arms production were not so high as during the 1970s. 5/

Third World production of major weapons is concentrated in only a few countries. Ranking orders have changed over time and there are still newcomers, like the ASEAN countries. During the five-year period 1980-84 Israel, India, and Brazil accounted for some 58 percent of the volume of Third World major weapon production. Another 38 percent were accounted for by Taiwan, Argentina, South Africa, South and North Korea and Egypt; the remaining four percent is shared among a handful of smaller producers.

The primary motive for Third World arms production is the quest for political and military self-sufficiency. There is ample evidence of the difficulties in trying to reach this goal. Arms production requires the inflow of technology from the major industrialized countries.

The costs associated with Third World arms production are high. The more up-to-date the technology, the higher the costs. Length of production runs and the share of domestically made pre-products also affect costs. Cost advantages appear only when robust and "simple" weapons—often much in demand by other Third World countries—are produced. Both costs and economic spillover to civilian industry depend heavily on the (as a rule insufficient) strength of the industrial base. But the use of scarce resources for arms production is always at the expense of more productive, civilian production.

Third World arms production is currently in a structural dilemma. The armed forces demand high-technology weapons which, as a rule, cannot be produced. Domestic demand for what can be efficiently produced is reaching the point of saturation. Exports are the obvious way to reach a market, and Third World arms exports are increasing. Major markets are found in crisis areas and in countries at war. But competition is fierce and the global market for weapons is shrinking.

The spread of arms production technology affects attempts to reduce the level of armaments in the Third

World. The risks and intensity of conflicts are increasing. On the other hand, arms production in the Third World to some extent eliminates the discrimination between the haves and the have-nots inherent in earlier arms control proposals. Third World arms reductions might be more feasible now if the political will to achieve it can gather momentum, both in Third World and in industrialized countries. Disarmament does not generate development, but given the scantiness of resources, it is in many cases one important prerequisite for development.

ARMS TRANSFERS LIMITATIONS

International efforts to limit the global arms trade have come to a virtual halt. None of the various suggestions and initiatives of the past decade has led to any action. The need for control of the trade in conventional weapons has become even more urgent now than in the past. Some of the basic rationales for arms transfer limitations are now more relevant.

1. The transfer of arms is often a political act, and with the present tension between the USA and the USSR there is a danger that a conflict between their respective arms clients could escalate into a major power confrontation.

2. The arms market is today a buyer's market due to the global over-capacity of arms production and the proliferation of arms production capabilities.

3. The imports of arms and military technology in general are an economic burden for all countries, but especially for those with limited foreign exchange earnings. The current extreme indebtedness of many countries in the Third World is aggravated by arms imports.

However, prospects for increased Third World military security through a reduction of conventional armaments do not appear encouraging. It can even be argued that the risk of conflict is increased through enhanced capabilities to sustain war efforts. Similarly, it can be argued that most tensions within and among Third World countries are largely the result of local or regional economic, social and political problems. Such problems might be exacerbated through arms imports and arms production via diversion of scarce resources or distortion of the domestic industrial structure.

Furthermore, the current structure of the arms market may in itself complicate attempts at arms reductions. Offsets and barter agreements have commercialized and privatized the arms market. The civilian sectors are now more enmeshed in arms sales than before through civilian offsets, transfers of civil and dual-use technology and so on. Commercialization and privatization are detrimental to arms control, since control is by definition the responsibility of the governments.

Prospects for the Future

New attempts at control of arms transfers will have to be based on experience gained from the failures. Control has to lie in the interests of the participating parties. There are various options for action, such as: supplier versus recipient control; unilateral, bilateral, regional/global multilateral measures; quantitative or qualitative restrictions, and so on. Among the proposals, most attention should be given to those that: (a) combine diverging interests; (b) help to change or re-evaluate interests; or (c) provide countervailing interests.

For those suppliers that use arms exports as a foreign policy instrument, the danger of horizontal escalation is such a countervailing interest. It has led to tacit self-restraint in the past in nuclear technology, and also in conventional armaments. In North and South Korea, for example, the Soviet Union refrained from supplying mobile air defense systems and the USA did not supply any advanced aircraft until 1981, when the Reagan Administration decided to sell F-16 aircraft to South Korea. Currently, the perception of such a common interest does not seem to be very strong despite the recent conflicts, and the experiences learned from them, in the Middle East.

The economic determinants of arms exports, now so prominent for a large and growing number of suppliers, are at least partly outweighed by the so-called opportunity costs of arms; resources can only be used once, either for arms or civilian use. Furthermore, the long-term development potential, and thus the prospects for world trade in general, grow if civilian goods rather than arms are traded. As the economic benefits now accrue differently than they would if more civilian goods were exchanged, a compensation scheme would have to be devised. If this were achieved, a multilateral limitation involving suppliers with economic motives could be in the interests of all of them.

In the light of the detrimental effects of arms exports, this would seem to be an attractive development for all parties involved, especially the recipient countries. However, a very serious objection to such arms transfer limitations is raised by a number of recipient states. They are afraid that their security interests are not fully appreciated. This claim is based on the assumption that security can be bought through arms--a crucial and highly controversial assumption. The Brandt Commission, for instance, stated: "More arms do not make mankind safer, just poorer." 6/ It seems vital for Third World countries--and, indeed, for all countries --to re-examine the issues of militarization and security needs in the light of the costs and consequences. One important aspect here is that Third World conflicts-- real or perceived--are regionally based, even if they are often enmeshed in and fueled by the competition between the major powers. Therefore, there is much room for initiatives toward arms limitations from the recipient's side. This should be paralleled by continued similar efforts on the part of the supplying countries.

One important confidence-building measure for any such discussion is open reporting on trade in and production of conventional arms. Secrecy promotes suspicion. More openness would also stimulate public debate of arms transfers, both in supplier and recipient states. Public debate, in turn, stimulates reconsideration and re-evaluation of the interests and determinants of the arms trade and the ways to control it.

Finally, any action to reduce the over capacity in arms production will reduce the economic pressures to export arms--pressures which are an important determinant of the current level of the arms trade, independent of the security needs of the recipients or suppliers. There is increasing activity by trade unionists working in the arms industry to move away from arms production for exports. The arguments in favor of planning conversion from arms production to civilian production, put forward by the UN expert committee on disarmament and

364

development, 7/ are further strengthened when seen in connection with arms exports.

NOTES
1. SIPRI figures are estimates of the deliveries of major conventional weapons (aircraft, artillery and armor, missiles, ships). The sources and methods are described in SIPRI Yearbooks.
2. Armed Forces Journal, No. 11, 1984, 72.
3. Major conventional weapons are as defined in note 1. "Other support" includes deliveries of small arms, ammunition and spare parts, provision of financial aid, transit rights, military advisors or troops and training. Excluded are deliveries of civilian ships and aircraft, so-called dual technology and industrial assistance. In a number of cases information is unconfirmed or questionable.
4. Der Spiegel, November 21, 1983, 16.
5. Figures are from: J. Brzoska, T. Ohlson (eds.), Arms Production in the Third World, London: Taylor & Francis, 1986.
6. Independent Commission of International Development Issues, North-South. A Program for Survival, Cambridge: MIT Press, 1980, 117.
7. United Nations, Study on the Relationship Between Disarmament and Development, A/36/356, October 5, 1981, 172-176.

23

Third World Debt Bondage

Jomo Sundaram

THE GROWING DEBT PROBLEM

The most remarkable features of Third World debt are its rapid growth and immense size. As seen in Table 1, long-term debt of Third World countries grew especially rapidly in the mid and late seventies. The average annual growth rate rose from 18.3 percent during 1970-73 to 21.3 percent during 1973-80, before tapering off to 13.5 percent in 1981, 11.9 percent in 1982, 13.5 percent in 1983 and 10.8 percent in 1984. Throughout this period, private debt grew much faster than official debt, at least until 1983. In 1984, the official debt increase exceeded private debt increase, an observation to which we will later return. As Table 1 demonstrates, the biggest borrowers appear to have been the middle-income countries, including the oil exporters, while the low-income countries, especially in Asia, have generally been borrowing less.

Not surprisingly then, as Tables 2 and 4 show, the external debt of all (indebted) developing countries jumped from US $68 billion in 1970 to US $141 billion in 1984, US $334 billion in 1977 and US $747 billion 1982, before tapering off to US $865 billion in 1985. By 1985, the Americas accounted for 41 percent of total debt to developing countries, followed by Asia with 26 percent, and Africa with 15 percent.

As Table 3 shows, the nature of capital flows to developing countries has changed significantly. Direct foreign investment as a proportion of new capital flows to developing countries has fallen from 20 percent during 1960-65 to 13 percent during 1980-83. The nature of foreign debt has also changed significantly. The average maturity period for new public debt commitments has declined from 18 years during 1960-65 to 14 years during 1980-83. Recent uncertainties in the capital market have meant that loans with floating interest rates as a

TABLE 1

GROWTH OF LONG-TERM DEBT OF DEVELOPING COUNTRIES, 1970-84
(Average annual percentage change)

Country group	1970-73	1973-80	1981	1982	1983*	1984*
Debt outstanding						
and disbursed	18.3	21.3	13.5	11.9	13.5	10.8
Official	15.3	17.6	9.7	10.4	9.8	13.2
Private	21.1	24.0	15.7	12.8	15.6	9.5
Low-income countries						
Debt outstanding						
and disbursed	12.9	16.0	5.5	8.0	6.3	10.8
Official	12.5	14.1	7.7	10.1	8.2	10.5
Private	16.0	24.9	2.3	1.0	2.2	12.3
Asia						
Debt outstanding						
and disbursed	11.1	13.2	2.9	8.6	7.8	14.1
Official	11.6	11.2	6.2	10.1	7.4	10.6
Private	4.3	33.2	12.4	0.1	10.5	36.0
Africa						
Debt outstanding						
and disbursed	19.7	22.6	10.2	6.9	3.7	4.7
Official	17.3	24.2	10.9	10.6	10.1	10.2
Private	24.4	19.7	8.5	2.0	13.5	14.6
Middle-income oil importers						
Debt outstanding						
and disbursed	19.7	21.0	14.9	12.9	11.5	10.3
Official	17.8	18.5	12.1	11.0	13.4	15.0
Private	20.8	22.2	16.1	13.7	10.7	8.3
Major exporters of manufacturers						
Debt outstanding						
and disbursed	22.6	20.8	14.7	13.0	12.1	10.2
Official	21.0	18.9	10.5	9.1	12.6	18.8
Private	23.2	21.4	15.9	14.1	12.0	7.9
Other middle-income oil importers						
Debt outstanding						
and disbursed	13.4	21.5	15.4	12.8	9.9	10.5
Official	14.6	18.0	13.9	13.0	14.3	11.0
Private	11.9	25.8	16.8	12.5	5.8	10.0
Middle-income oil exporters						
Debt outstanding						
and disbursed	19.6	24.9	14.6	11.8	19.9	11.5
Official	15.5	20.6	7.9	9.4	4.9	12.8
Private	22.6	27.1	17.5	12.7	25.8	11.1

* The increase in debt outstanding and disbursed and the shift from private to official sources is in part due to the impact of rescheduling.
Source: World Bank, World Development Report 1985, p. 153, Table A.10

TABLE 2

INDEBTED DEVELOPING COUNTRIES: OUTSTANDING EXTERNAL DEBT
1977-86
(US$ billion)

			As at the end of			
	1977	1982	1983	1984	1985*	1986+
Total Debt	333.5	749.1	796.9	829.5	865.1	895.7
By Region						
Africa	61.0	117.5	125.4	130.4	133.9	135.3
Asia	83.6	182.6	201.5	212.3	229.0	247.5
Europe	38.9	74.7	76.9	80.6	84.5	86.7
Non-oil Middle East	25.4	48.7	52.9	54.9	58.8	60.2
Western Hemisphere	124.6	325.5	340.2	351.3	358.9	366.0

* - Estimate
+ - Forecast

Source: IMF World Economic Outlook, August 1985, in Economic Report 1985/86,
p. 37, Table 3.3

TABLE 3

COMPOSITION AND TERMS OF CAPITAL FLOWS TO DEVELOPING COUNTRIES
IN SELECTED PERIODS

Component and term	1960-65	1975-80	1980-83
Direct foreign investment as a percentage of net capital flows	19.8	15.5	12.9
Floating interest rate loans as a percentage of public debt	-	26.5	37.9
Average years maturity on new public debt commitments	18.0	15.0	14.0

Source: World Bank, World Development Report 1985, p. 4, Table 1.1

TABLE 4

DEBT INDICATORS FOR DEVELOPING COUNTRIES IN SELECTED YEARS, 1970-84

(ratios in per cent; amount in billions of dollars)

	1970	1974	1976	1978	1980	1981	1982	1983	1984
Debt disbursed and outstanding		135.4	194.9	301.2	411.6	470.1	525.6	597.6	655
Disbursement		36.4	49.8	80.6	97.5	114.2	105.6	86.4	85
(from private creditors)		25.6	—	61.2	69.2	85.6	75.6	55.2	55
Debt service			19.7	25.9	47.5	71.1	83.0	91.1	85.4
Principal repymts			13.1	16.9	31.9	40.4	44.3	45.3	40.7
Interest			6.6	9.0	15.6	30.7	38.7	45.8	44.6
Net transfers*			16.7	23.9	33.2	26.4	31.2	14.5	1.0
Ratio of debt to GNP	14.1	15.4	18.1	21.0	20.9	22.4	26.3	31.3	33.8
Ratio of debt to exports	108.9	80.0	100.2	113.1	89.8	96.8	115.0	130.8	135.4
Debt service ratio	14.7	11.8	13.6	18.4	16.0	17.6	20.5	19.0	19.7
Ratio of interest to GNP	0.5	0.8	0.8	1.1	1.6	1.9	2.3	2.3	2.8
Total debt outstanding disbursed	68.0	141.0	204.0	313.0	430.0	488.0	546.0	620.0	686.0
Private debt as percentage of total	50.9	56.5	59.0	61.5	62.9	64.1	64.6	65.8	65.0

Note: Interest and debt service for 1970-83 are actual (not contractual) service paid during the period. Interest and debt service for 1984 are projections of contractual obligations due based on commitments received through the end of 1983 and take into account reschedulings through the end of 1984.

Source: World Bank, World Development Report 1985, Table 2.6

proportion of the public debt increased dramatically, from 27 percent during 1975–80 to 38 percent during 1980–83.

Table 4 clearly shows how the growth of debt has outpaced other growth indicators for developing countries. As a proportion of the gross national product (GNP), foreign debt has risen from 14 percent in 1970 to 21 percent in 1980 and 34 percent in 1984. As a proportion of exports of goods and services, foreign debt fell from 109 percent in 1970 to 80 percent in 1974, rising to 113 percent in 1978, dropping to 90 percent in 1980, before rising steadily to 135 percent in 1984. The declines around 1974 and 1980 are largely attributable to unsustained primary commodity (especially oil) price booms at those times. The debt service ratio has been subjected to similar influences, but has nonetheless risen from 14.7 percent in 1970 to 19.7 percent in 1984. However, the ratio of interest service to GNP has risen steadily from 0.5 percent in 1970 to 1.6 percent in 1980 and 2.8 percent in 1984. During the seventies, the proportion of private debt also rose rapidly from 50.9 percent in 1970 to 56.5 percent in 1974 and 62.9 percent in 1980, before tapering off to 65.0 percent in 1984.

SERVICING THE DEBT

Sooner or later, the chickens would have to come home to roost as a consequence of this rapid growth of LDC debt. The fear of a breakdown of the whole system has affected international bankers and the major OECD governments. But greed for the handsome profits to be made from lending to the South has proved too tempting. In 1982 alone, 22 governments had to reschedule debts as they could not make their payments in time.

As we can see from Table 5, by March 1984, seven Third World countries had been forced to reschedule over US $200 billion in debt, with Mexico and Brazil – who have announced that they do not have the foreign exchange to service the loans – accounting for US $125 billion. As we shall see later, if one or several of these countries were to default, some of the largest U.S. banks could go bankrupt. However, this is unlikely as the U.S. Federal Reserve would probably intervene to keep the banks afloat. Nonetheless, fear has crept into the hearts of bankers, making them far more cautious in their

TABLE 5

COMMERCIAL BANK RESCHEDULING

Country	Total bank debt ($ billions) at March 1984
1. Mexico	63.9
2. Brazil	61.1
3. Argentina	24.5
4. Venezuela	22.3
5. Chile	11.7
6. Philippines	9.0
7. Nigeria	8.7
	201.2

Source: International Currency Review, (Journal of the World Financial Community) Vol. 16, No. 2, Sept. 1984.

TABLE 6

US BANK CLAIMS BY SECTOR
December 1984 $ billion (% change 1982-84)

	Public sector	Banks	Other private
Brazil	11.9 (+63)	8.1 (−7)	2.9 (−14)
Mexico	13.5 (+39)	4.4 (+11)	8.6 (−19)
Latin America	37.7 (+48)	19.2 (−11)	17.3 (−22)
Asia	8.6 (+6)	10.4 (−20)	8.2 (+0)
Africa	1.7 (−28)	1.7 (+43)	0.9 (−3)
Non-OPEC	48.0 (+33)	31.3 (−12)	26.4 (−16)
OPEC	10.3 (+14)	6.1 (−14)	7.7 (−15)
Developing countries	58.3 (+30)	39.4 (−12)	34.1 (−16)

Source: Henry S. Terrell & Rodney H. Mills, "US Bank Lending: How Big A

lending policies. Yet, lend they must, for otherwise borrowers may not be able to keep up their contractual payments.

Default has been avoided thus far by prompt intervention led by the U.S. government, various multilateral agencies under its control (IMF, World Bank, Bank for International Settlements) and other central bankers, thus shifting part of the private creditors' risks to the public.

As Table 6 shows, these measures have actually rescued the private lenders involved, rather than potentially defaulting countries, which have, in fact, fallen deeper in debt as a result. This in turn renders the international financial system even more vulnerable. Table 6 shows that during 1982-84, public sector lending to the Third World rose by 30 percent, while private sector lending dropped by 14 percent. Public sector lending to Brazil rose by 63 percent, to Mexico by 39 percent, and to Chile by 144 percent, while private lending to Brazil and Chile dropped. Table 7 shows what has been happening to Third World debt. Already, by 1972, 56 percent of new debt actually went to debt servicing. New borrowing continued to grow until 1981, when 73 percent of new debt went to debt servicing. As new borrowing declined after that, this proportion rose rapidly to 86 percent in 1983 and 108 percent in 1984. As long as new borrowing was increasing rapidly in the seventies, net proceeds (i.e. debt servicing minus new borrowing) continued to increase, i.e. until 1978. From 1979, net proceeds actually began to decline each year, though new borrowing was still growing until 1981, and from 1984, only two years after new borrowing began to decline, net proceeds were negative, i.e. debt service payments exceeded new borrowing in 1984 and probably continue to do so since then as well.

Three factors have contributed to this decline in net proceeds since 1979, thus precipitating the recent crisis. Realizing their over-exposure to Third World debt, banks began to reduce overall lending, lending a greater proportion on a short-term basis (thus raising annual amortization payments) and raising interest rates. Beyond its size and rate of growth, another aspect of concern about Third World debt is the fact that until recently, an ever-increasing proprtion has been from private banks, rather than governments and multilateral agencies.

TABLE 7

DEBT SERVICE ON EXTERNAL DEBT OF THIRD WORLD COUNTRIES
(US$ billion)

Year	New Borrowing (1)	Debt Service (1)-(2) (2)	Net Proceeds (3)	Debt service as a per cent of new building (2) x 100 (1)
1972	21.3	12.0	9.3	56.3
1974	36.7	19.8	16.9	54.0
1976	49.9	26.1	23.8	52.3
1977	61.5	33.1	28.4	53.8
1978	80.7	47.9	32.8	59.4
1979	94.2	62.3	31.9	66.1
1980	97.5	71.1	26.4	72.9
1981	114.2	83.0	31.2	72.7
1982	105.6	91.1	14.5	86.3
1983*	86.4	85.4	1	98.8
1984+	85	92	-7	108.2

Source: World Bank, World Debt Tables, 1984/85
Notes: * - Preliminary figures
        + - World Bank Estimates

For example, while debt to developing countries more than doubled during 1974-79, lending from private sources more than tripled. As we can see from Table 4 above, private debt as a percentage of total debt rose from 51 percent in 1970 to 66 percent in 1983, before declining slightly to 65 percent in 1984. This trend is also reflected in Table 1, which shows private lending growth much faster than official lending until 1982; in 1984, for the first time since at least the seventies, official lending exceeded private lending.

Private lending generally involves much higher interest rates, and hence greater debt service burdens. Hence, according to the World Debt Tables, during 1974-79, the private proportion of disbursed debt rose from 54 percent to 63 percent, while the private proportion of interest payments rose from 72 percent to 79 percent, and the private proportion of debt servicing rose from 77 percent to 83 percent!

BANKS ON A LIMB

The high proportion of Third World debt in the loan portfolios of the large banks has also alarmed financial circles. The exposure of these banks to Third World debt can be appreciated by comparing such loans as a proportion of the banks' capital. According to Table 8 then, if Mexico defaults or declares a unilateral moratorium, 60 percent of the capital of the nine biggest U.S. banks would be needed to keep the bank afloat. If both Mexico and Brazil default, the nine banks would go bust as more than 100 percent of their capital would be required to keep afloat. South American countries alone account for 210 percent of the banks' capital, compared to 341 percent for the entire Third World.

As we can see from Table 9, at the end of 1982, debt exposure to five countries (Argentina, Brazil, Mexico, Venezuela and Chile) as a percentage of capital in major U.S. banks was extremely high, reaching 263 percent in the case of Manufacturers Hanover. Over-exposure to individual countries, especially Brazil and Mexico, was also very high. The six largest U.S. banks had US $40 billion on loan to these five countries, i.e. these loans exceeded their total capital of US $23 billion by 72 percent!

TABLE 8

THIRD WORLD DEBT EXPOSURE OF THE NINE LARGEST
U.S. BANKS, 1982

	Loans extended (US$ billions)	Loans as a percentage of banks' capital
OPEC members	<u>16.2</u>	<u>71.2</u>
Venezuela	7.1	31.4
Indonesia	1.9	8.4
Saudi Arabia	1.7	7.5
Non-OPEC South American countries	<u>40.7</u>	<u>178.6</u>
Mexico	13.6	59.8
Brazil	12.3	54.2
Argentina	5.6	24.6
Non-OPEC Asian countries	<u>17.3</u>	<u>75.9</u>
South Korea	5.1	22.3
Philippines	3.7	16.1
Taiwan	2.7	11.6
Non-OPEC African countries	3.6	15.7
Total of all developing countries	77.7	341.4%

Source: Hearing Before the Committee on Banking, Finance, and Urban Affairs, House of Representatives, International Financial Markets and Related Matters Serial No, 97-99, p. 54, cited in Magdoff & Sweezy (1984)

Note: The above data are as of June 1982. The nine largest banks and their capital in US$ billions - Bank of America (4.1); Citibank (5.1); Chase Manhattan (3.2); Manufacturers Hanover (2.0); Morgan Guaranty (2.3); Continental Illinois (1.8); Chemical Bank (1.6); Bankers Trust (1.4); 1st National Bank of Chicago (1.2). Their total capital is $22.8 billion. Capital consists of the sum of a bank's preferred stock, common stock, surplus, undivided profits, and reserves for contingencies and other capital reserves.

TABLE 9

EXPOSURE TO ARGENTINA, BRAZIL, CHILE, MEXICO & VENEZUELA
AS PERCENTAGE OF CAPITAL, MAJOR BANKS, END-1982

	Brazil (%)	Mexico (%)	Total* (%)	Capital (million)	Exposure (dollars)
Citibank	73.5	54.6	174.5	5,989	10,451
Bank of America	47.9	52.1	158.2	4,799	7,592
Chase Manhattan	56.9	40.0	154.0	4,221	6,500
Morgan Guaranty	54.3	34.8	140.7	3,107	4,372
Manufacturers Hanover	77.7	66.7	262.8	2,592	6,812
Chemical	52.0	60.0	169.7	2,499	4,241
Continental Illinois	22.9	32.4	107.5	2,143	2,304
Bankers Trust	46.2	46.2	141.2	1,895	2,676
First National Chicago	40.6	50.1	134.2	1,725	2,315
Security Pacific	29.1	31.2	82.5	1,684	1,389
Wells Fargo	40.7	51.0	126.6	1,201	1,520
Crocker National	57.3	51.2	196.0	1,151	2,256
First Interstate	43.9	63.0	136.0	1,080	1,469
Marine Midland	47.8	28.3	n.a.	1.074	-
Mellon	35.3	41.1	n.a.	1,024	-
Irving Trust	38.7	34.1	n.a.	996	-
First National Boston	23.1	28.1	n.a.	800	-
Interfirst Dallas	10.2	30.1	49.2	787	387

[n.a. - Not available] [* Total - including Argentina, Venezuela, and Chile]

Source: William Cline (1983) International Debt and the Stability of the
          World Economy, Institute for International Economics, p. 34, Table
          6.

As the saying goes: "If you borrow one million and cannot pay, you are in trouble, but if you borrow one billion and cannot pay, the bank is in trouble." As we can see from Table 10, U.S. bank claims on developing countries at the end of 1984 amounted to US $130 billion, with the 9 money centre banks alone accounting for US $84 billion, or 64 percent of the total. Latin America accounted for US $74 billion, or 57 percent of the Third World total, with Brazil and Mexico together accounting for US $50 billion, or 38 percent.

As we can see in Table 11, in 1980, eight of the major private U.S. banks had combined foreign assets, mainly loans, amounting to US $249 billion. Of this, 58 percent of the banks' revenues came from all foreign (not just Third World) sources.

Evidence suggests that defaults on foreign loans to governments or loans guaranteed by foreign governments have hardly occurred in the post-war period. Data on Citibank debt losses during 1974-80 show that the loss ration on domestic loans (0.70 percent) was more than double the loss ration on foreign loans (0.29 percent). During the seventies, Citibank's outstanding loans more than quadrupled, while the foreign percentage of Citibank's loan portfolio rose rapidly from 40% in 1971 to 53 percent in 1975 and an average of 62 percent during 1976-80 (Franklin, 1982: 21).

WHO IS BORROWING?

Debt data clearly show that many of the poorest countries borrow most from official sources. Predictably, it is the relatively better off countries which have been considered to be more creditworthy to the private creditors. As Table 12 clearly shows, the top 25 debtor developing countries have all borrowed in excess of US $5 billion each by December 1983. As Table 13 highlights, Mexico alone accounted for 18 percent of bank claims on developing countries. The five largest borrowers accounted for 48 percent, or almost half of the total, with the next five accounting for 14 percent, and the following ten for 19 percent, leaving another 19 percent for the 59 remaining countries.

Such evidence belies the popular belief that Third World debt peonage is largely due to current account deficits for oil-importing countries as a result of OPEC

TABLE 10

US BANK CLAIMS (END 1984)
(US$ billion)

9 money centre banks	All US banks	
15.8	23.9	Brazil
14.7	26.5	Mexico
45.5	74.2	Latin America
17.7	27.2	Asia
3.3	4.4	Africa
66.4	105.8	Non-OPEC developing countries
17.4	24.1	OPEC
83.8	129.9	Developing countries

Source: Calculated from Henry Tenell & Rodney H. Mills, "US Bank Lending: How Big A Stimulator? The Banker, Sept. 1985, p. 67.

TABLE 11

1980 FOREIGN REVENUES AND ASSETS
OF EIGHT MAJOR U.S. BANKS

	Revenues in billions of $		Foreign revenues as % of total	Foreign assets in billion of $
	Total	Foreign		
Citicorp	14.2	9.1	64.1	68.0
Bank of America	12.1	6.3	52.5	44.3
Chase Manhattan	8.0	5.1	63.5	40.1
J.P. Morgan	5.2	3.2	62.0	27.3
Mfrs. Hanover	5.2	2.8	54.5	28.2
Chemical N.Y.	4.3	2.1	49.4	17.5
Bankers Trust N.Y.	3.7	2.0	55.3	16.4
First National Boston	2.3	1.3	57.2	7.2
Totals	55.0	31.9	58.0	249.0

Source: Forbes (July 6, 1981), pp. 92-93, cited in Franklin (1982: 20)

TABLE 12

DEVELOPING COUNTRIES RANKED BY DEBT TO BANKS, DECEMBER 1983 <1>
(in billion of U.S. dollars)

1.	Mexico	84.96	2.	Brazil <2>	73.71
3.	Argentina	24.07	4.	Korea	23.43
5.	Venezuela	21.21	6.	Philippines	14.65
7.	Yugoslavia	14.51	8.	Indonesia	13.25
9.	Egypt	11.96	10.	Chile	11.91
11.	South Africa	10.61	12.	Malaysia	9.99
13.	Algeria <3>	9.58	14.	Portugal	9.40
15.	United Arab Emirates	9.01	16.	Romania <4>	9.00
17.	Kuwait	8.94	18.	Turkey <5>	8.81
19.	Hungary	8.62	20.	Saudi Arabia	7.95
21.	Nigeria <5>	7.75	22.	Colombia <6>	6.32
23.	Israel <5>	5.67	24.	Thailand	5.64
25.	Greece	5.58	26.	Peru	4.22
27.	China, Peoples Rep. of	4.13	28.	Morocco <6>	4.02
29.	Iran, Islamic Rep. of <7>	3.77	30.	Ecuador <8>	3.63
31.	Ivory Coast	2.30	32.	India	2.01
33.	Syrian Arab Republic <5>	1.80	34.	Uruguay <5>	1.76
35.	Costa Rica <7>	1.56	36.	Pakistan	1.52
37.	Bolivia <5>	1.35	38.	Tunisia	1.34
39.	Sri Lanka	1.28	40.	Jamaica	1.27
41.	Sudan	1.24	42.	Iraq	1.23
43.	Nicaragua <4>	1.12	44.	Cameroon <5>	1.06
45.	Zambia	1.04	46.	Dominican Republic	1.00
47.	Libya <9>	0.97	48.	Zimbabwe <10>	0.92
49.	Trinidad and Tobago	0.87	50.	Oman	0.86
51.	Burma <5>	0.84	52.	Congo <5>	0.84
53.	Jordan	0.80	54.	Zaire <4>	0.77
55.	Guatemala	0.65	56.	Papua New Guinea	0.64
57.	Senegal	0.62	58.	Kenya	0.60
59.	Cyprus	0.59	60.	Gabon <5>	0.58
61.	Honduras <5>	0.48	62.	Qatar <5>	0.45
63.	Paraguay	0.44	64.	Bangladesh	0.40
65.	Tanzania <5>	0.30	66.	Niger	0.28
67.	Mauritania	0.25	68.	Yemen Arab Republic	0.24
69.	Ghana	0.22	70.	Sierra Leone	0.22
71.	Mali	0.21	72.	Benin	0.17
73.	Guyana <10>	0.17	74.	Madagascar <11>	0.17
75.	Malawi	0.17	76.	Haiti <10>	0.14
77.	Somalia <5>	0.13	78.	Mauritius	0.11
79.	Viet Nam <12>	0.11			

Source: International Monetary Fund, IMF, International Capital Markets, Developments and Prospects, 1984, Statistical Tables, p. 89, Table 30.

<1> Figures are the sum of cross-border interbank accounts by residence of borrowing bank and international bank credit to nonbanks by residence of borrower. As of the end of December 1983 unless otherwise noted.
<2> Latest published data for cross-border interbank accounts (CBIA) are Fund staff estimates.
<3> Latest published data for CBIA are as of end of September 1982.
<4> Latest published data for CBIA are as of end of June 1983.
<5> Latest published data for CBIA are as of end of September 1983.
<6> Latest published data for CBIA are as of end of December 1982.
<7> Latest published data for CBIA are as of end of December 1981.
<8> Latest published data for CBIA are as of end of December 1980.
<9> Latest published data for CBIA are as of end of June 1982.
<10> Latest published data for CBIA are as of end of December 1978.
<11> Latest published data for CBIA are as of end of December 1979.
<12> No CBIA data are available.

prices. Mexico, the largest borrower, and Venezuela both export oil, while Argentina imports very little.

In fact, the so-called newly industrializing countries (NICs) - such as Brazil, Mexico, South Korea and Taiwan - have been among the biggest borrowers. Some bankers reason that even if some NICs actually default on loans, the banks would still have access to and control over the tangible productive capacity already built up in the NICs.

CURRENT ACCOUNT DEFICITS

The financial dependence of the South on the North can in turn be-traced to the chronic balance of payments deficit experienced by most of the Third World. Much of this deficit is due to foreign exchange payments for shipping, insurance, dividends, royalties and interest. Such obligations cannot be postponed. Hence, imports to meet people's needs and to facilitate production are necessary. With policies maintaining economies open and dependent, further foreign investment and foreign borrowing appear to offer short-term solutions, which actually bring about ever greater deficits.

As mentioned earlier, OECD governments, especially the U.S., and the various multilateral agencies have moved in to take over some of the risks from the private creditors, and coerce potential defaultors to undertake austerity measures, such as currency devaluation, trade liberalization, cuts in public expenditure, mass consumption and imports, to restore private creditor confidence. In the process, of course, more profits are to be made, e.g. fees for renegotiating old loans and raising interest rates on new or renegotiated loans. These multilateral agencies play a key role in coordinating the programmes, overseeing domestic policies and disciplining debtors - which ultimately ensure the preservation of debtors' interests and the existing economic system.

As can be seen from Table 14, the current account deficit of developing countries rose by leaps and bounds in the late seventies, from US $57 billion in 1978 to US $113 billion in 1981, before dropping off equally sharply to US $38 billion in 1984. Net external borrowing followed this trend, rising from US $63 billion in 1978

TABLE 13

BANK CLAIMS ON DEVELOPING COUNTRIES, DECEMBER 1983

Country or Group	Percentage Composition of Amounts Outstanding
Mexico	17.9
Brazil	15.5
Argentina	5.1
S. Korea	4.9
Venezuela	4.5
Subtotal, 5 largest borrowers	47.9
Next 5 borrowers	14.0
Next 10 borrowers	19.4
All others	18.7
79 developing countries	100.0
Amount (US$ billions)	474.39

Source: calculated from Table 12

TABLE 14

DEVELOPING COUNTRIES: CURRENT ACCOUNT DEFICIT AND NET EXTERNAL BORROWING

(in billions of U.S. dollars)

	1978	1979	1980	1981	1982	1983	1984
Current account deficit	57	62	77	113	103	59	38
Net external borrowing	63	70	98	120	98	66	47

Source: IMF, Annual Report 1985, p. 22, Table 8

to US $120 billion in 1981, before falling to US $47 billion in 1984.

But the various austerity and other measures imposed have helped. Devaluations, for example, raise import costs and thus hinder the growth of productive capacity, while contributing to inflation and weakening domestic effective demand. Trade liberalization wipes out local industries, while public spending cuts tend to undermine welfare.

The question now is how much more the Third World countries can and will take of such medicine without retaliating, e.g. by debt repudiation. Even if Third World balance of payments deficits can be cut, this will not solve the crisis. New borrowings would still be needed to finance even the reduced deficits. As the debts accumulate, the debtors' payment burdens will mount, requiring yet more borrowing. It all seems somewhat hopeless.

Ultimately, however, we can only find a solution by challenging some of the very premises on which the financial system has been built. For example, neither bank capital nor profits are sacred. Such questions will have to be faced.

24

Debt and Dependency:
The Case of Latin America

Jacobo Schatan

The 1980s have witnessed the explosion of the Third
World external debt crisis, which has its epicenter in
the Latin-American region. 1/   Whereas in the past it
was simply a matter of concern for specialists in trade
and financial matters, this phenomenon has now acquired a
universal dimension, occupying front page coverage in the
most well-known newspapers with unusual frequency.   This
concern is shared today by political leaders, business-
people, financiers, members of national and international
organizations, economists and other social scientists,
and other working people.   The average Latin American
person is becoming conscious of the fact that she or he
is bearing the weight of an external debt of more than $1
thousand each, an amount that for many represents the
income of several years.

The external debt is only one of the more visible
manifestations of the profound crisis that has been
affecting the Latin American region for a good number of
years.   In its present stage the crisis represents the
end   of   a   long   phase   in   Latin   American   economic
development.   It is a crisis that requires a fundamental
redefinition of the region's external economic relations,
internal   development   patterns,   prevailing   social
relations and values.

Prevailing   patterns   of   production,   industrialization, consumption, and so on--in sum, of development--led
many Latin American countries to considerably increase
their imports of all kinds of goods since the mid1970s,
when the Western economic powers were suffering a severe
recession and the world was floating in the petrodollar
sea that resulted from the Yom Kippur War of October
1973.   Such imports were only partially financed with
export earnings; the rest came from foreign loans from
both the public and private sectors of these countries.

The idea was to make a big leap forward in order to emerge from the situation of "underdevelopment" and, with the usual unfulfilled hope, to be able to repay such loans with the product of exports that would result from new investments. It was the era of the Latin American "miracles": the Brasilian miracle, the Chilean miracle and several others. But such miracles were short-lived. External indebtedness, which was one of the pillars sustaining those economic "prodigies," grew beyond all expectations. Easy money, which stimulated waste, corruption, and capital flight, together with its increased cost in international financial markets, combined to push the Latin American foreign debt to the enormous level of nearly $400 billion recorded today.

It is urgent that systematic and thorough studies of these processes and phenomena be carried out, and that a wide debate, at national and international levels, be opened on these issues; however, new approaches need to be taken so that propositions that are also new can be formulated. These should represent a general option that is viable both technically and politically. In the following pages we shall explore a few of the fundamental aspects of such a problem.

THE DEBT AND ITS ORIGINS

It is interesting to note that the present Latin American debt situation is not an entirely new phenomenon. About one hundred years ago something similar happened when the main financial markets in Europe began feverishly lending to South American countries, which thus became the major market for European capital. The external debt of South American nations persistently grew, fed by new loans that mainly served to repay older ones. This process was interrupted by World War I; interest in the South American market, however, was not renewed when the war ended. It was not until the 1970s that private international banking "rediscovered" Latin America. When the first oil shock took place at the end of 1973, as a consequence of the Yom Kippur War in the Middle East, and oil prices skyrocketed, a financial process began that can be summarized as follows: (1) The most important oil-exporting countries, unable to utilize domestically the huge financial surpluses generated by oil price increases, made huge deposits in various OECD financial institutions. (2) At the same time, a good number of middle- and high-income oil-importing nations-- particularly those with a higher degree of industrializa- tion--decided to accelerate their rates of economic growth, notwithstanding the increase in oil prices and that policy sharply contrasted with the "stagflation" situation prevailing in the OECD countries. (3) The OECD banks, with great liquidity and a weak domestic demand for funds started a wild competition to export capital to the more dynamic of the less-developed nations, which, at that point, applied to the international private banking system to obtain the money required to implement their expansive economic policies. (4) In order to diminish the risks of those operations, the international private banks decide to change the terms and conditions of the loans, shifting from the fixed rates of interest that had prevailed until then to variable rates. (5) By 1980 the situation had changed dramatically. Alongside a world economic recession, inflation had become increasingly acute in the United States and other industrial nations, and rates of interest had escalated. The economic recession in central nations provoked a sharp drop in prices of raw materials exported by Third World countries, precisely at a time when financial charges due to interest payments had become heavier and the inflow of fresh capital to the Third World had begun to slacken. (6) In 1982 the crisis in Mexico acquired full force, followed by similar crises in other Latin American countries as well as in other regions of the world.

Numbers show with dramatic clarity the development of the indebtedness process. According to reliable data from the World Bank and the OECD, the external debt of developing nations grew from $90 billion in 1970 to nearly $1 trillion in 1986. The average rate of interest, five percent in the early 1970s, increased to 11 percent in 1982. Since then it has declined, but it still remains at quite a high level (8.25 percent, U.S. prime rate).

Latin America has been hit hard by these events. Its overall debt increased from $40 billion in 1970 to its present level of nearly $400 billion. Its debt services increased even more rapidly: whereas total remittance of interest and profits was less than $3 billion in 1970, during recent years it has reached over $35 billion. As a result, Latin American nations have had to compress their imports drastically and, for the first time, this region has become an important net capital exporter. The net capital outflow during the 1982-1986 period has been estimated at over $130 billion.

THE PHILOSOPHY OF INDEBTEDNESS

For "neoliberal" or "developmentalist" economists, foreign indebtedness is seen as something positive that is inherent in economic growth. Thus, the majority of development models applied by Third World countries of mixed or market economies have relied on a permanent net transfer of financial resources from Western industrial nations (and Japan). They maintain that the position favoring indebtedness is of a "technical" nature, whereas the opposite position is a "political" one. They are of the opinion, therefore, that the "economic" response to the determination of the optimum level of indebtedness corresponds to the "technicians" and not to the "politicians."

These and other similar arguments look like simple fallacies to us. First, it is not possible to separate the "economic" from the "political"--a fact that only the staunchest technocrats would deny. Second, a substantial portion of the capital that enters Latin America by way of "development loans" leaves through the back door and finishes in private accounts in the United States, Switzerland, or the Bahamas. Third, because not all the investments made with foreign loans are socially useful and profitable, they do not all contribute to the self-sustained development of debtor nations. In addition, there are strong reasons--linked not to a given economic or political position or ideology but, rather, to the need of preserving the wealth of resources with which humankind is endowed--that point toward a policy of "nonindebtedness."

THE MATERIAL BALANCE

In order to better understand the meaning of the present Latin American foreign indebtedness situation and the subjection that its annual service implies, we designed a "package" demonstrating the 18 main basic commodities exported by this region (in 1982) and calculated the amount of the debt, services, and global repayment outflow in terms of that "package." For this purpose we used the price of each commodity in several reference periods to obtain the average price of one metric ton of the "package" (which we baptized as MAPRAL, the Spanish acronym for "Latin American Raw Materials", with the following results: $136 in 1976-1977, $217 in 1980, $191 in 1983, $171 in 1985 and approximately $130 by March 1986.

Considering that Latin American countries have been paying during the last few years a sum of $40-45 billion to service the debt (interest plus amortization), the physical outflow in MAPRALES was around 220 million tons in 1983 whereas it increased to nearly 350 million tons in 1986. With an interest rate of 10 percent per year, the total debt (without further indebtedness) would be repaid in some 24 years and the overall physical outflow, at 1986 prices, would reach the exorbitant level of 8 billion tons. This is an intolerable burden for a stock of finite resources.

Therefore, unless debt services are drastically reduced and export resources are adequately revalued, Latin American and Third World nations in general will be condemned to the virtual plunder of their strategic resources. Politically, this would be equivalent to a territorial conquest of the South by the North, without a military war and in the name of the sacrosanct concepts of "development" and "interdependence." Economically and ecologically, the repercussion for the South would be equally disastrous: deterioration and exhaustion of resources, both renewable and nonrenewable, such as minerals, topsoil, and water. What nature takes eons to build will be razed by the neoconquerors in a matter of years. But the responsibility does not rest exclusively upon the latter; to a great extent it also lies on the shoulders of debtor nations. We shall examine separately these two major sources of responsibility.

THE RESPONSIBILITY OF CREDITORS

The fundamental causes that have pushed up the rates of interest and other financial charges in world markets are well known: applied initially at the beginning of 1980 to contain the sharp inflationary process in the United States and to stop the decline in the value of the dollar vis-a-vis other currencies, the measures taken have become a self-sustained mechanism as a result of the Reagan administration's policies. The increase in defense expenditures, coupled with the reduction of taxes, resulted in monumental fiscal deficits as well as trade deficits, both of which are today in the range of $180-200 billion.

At the same time, prices of raw materials exported by Latin American countries and other Third World nations have steadily declined since 1980, to the point of collapse. The strangling effects of the above-mentioned opposing trends in the cost of money and in the prices of raw materials forced a steady increase in the physical resource outflow from South to North, as discussed. When one compares the differences between outflows calculated at an interest rate of six percent and those estimated at an interest rate of 10 percent, the results are astonishing. They are more so if we add the price factor. With a 10 percent rate and 1986 prices of raw materials, the total outflow is five billion tons higher than that considered at a rate of six percent and 1980 prices of raw materials. This difference can be be considered a true "gift" from Latin America to the North, particularly the United States. One could very well think, in this regard, that the metals Latin America has been "donating" to the Reagan administration are used by that Administration to manufacture the armaments that are being employed against some of the Latin American nations themselves.

THE RESPONSIBILITY OF DEBTORS

Capital Flight

This is a wide category in that it includes both the capital that left the countries (in order to evade taxes, to hide income obtained through doubtful means, to buy real estate abroad, etc.) and the capital that ought to have entered the southern countries but never did, (instead it remained abroad, as a result of fraudulent operations, illicit "commissions," or other similar wanton tricks).

According to a number of reliable sources, estimates of capital flight range from a minimum of $150 billion to a maximum of more than $200 billion for the Latin

American region as a whole. It is generally argued that
many of the operations leading to such massive flight
were not illegal; it is also maintained that an
overvalued currency makes it "convenient" to purchase
almost anything abroad. But, although it may be
convenient for an individual or a corporation to have
both a financial surplus large enough to have it invested
abroad and the domestic operation that generated such
surplus, it is not convenient for the nation. A good
portion of the money lent to these countries originated
in productive and mercantile operations carried out on
Mexican, Brazilian, or Chilean soil. That is, Latin
American savings were siphoned away only to return in the
form of loans, for which these countries had to pay
interest.

Waste, a Result of Social Irrationality

A large portion of the Latin American external debt
derives from imports of nonessential goods, be they
capital, intermediate, or final goods. The production-
consumption mode of Latin American countries, by
following a wasteful pattern in imitation of United
States or European lifestyles, is forcing Latin American
societies to depend increasingly upon imported goods and
technologies, thus leading to a situation of growing
foreign indebtedness.

The economy of industrialized capitalist nations
and, to a lesser extent, that of socialist countries is
characterized by its high level of waste of energy and
other basic resources. The blessings of the highly
praised "market competition," which has transformed the
northwestern economies into something like a cornucopia,
are more apparent than real because a large part of what
comes out of such "abundance horns" is nothing but waste!

Let us examine some of the sources from which such
waste originates—source that have also affected Third
World societies under the stimuli of the "inexorable laws
of market exransion" and their vanguard forces, the
publicity agents. We first identify the category of
excessive consumption. All of the food that is consumed
over and above the biological requirements of the human
body (taking into account activity and other external
factors) can be considered as waste. Further, in
addition to all the useless expenditure of material

resources involved in the production, transportation, storage, processing, distribution, and cooking of food that the human body does not need, we must consider the resources spent in the elaboration of medicines and in the building and maintenance of hospitals, pharmacies, and medical schools, that are devoted to curing hypertension, arteriosclerosis, diabetes, and other illnesses caused by excessive food consumption. Those resources could have been utilized to satisfy the needs of people suffering from illnesses resulting from underconsumption. Therefore, we should also charge to the account of irrational excessive food consumption the social cost of medical attention related to malnutrition and undernutrition, as well as the loss of the productive capacity of millions of undernourished adults. We must further add all the food that is thrown into the trash can, whether left over or rotten.

Second, we should consider the production of goods and services of a nonessential nature, such as armaments, luxury items, toxic products, financial-speculative services, and so on. Examples of socially unnecessary production abound. The quantities of steel, rubber, oil, labor and other resources employed to transport a single person by automobile are many times greater than those utilized to transport the same person by bus, tram, or train. The quantity of materials of all types that go into a luxurious house of, say, 1,000 square meters, which will probably lodge no more than five or six individuals, is many times higher than that employed in building a modest house of 80-100 square meters, which will provide shelter for the same number of people. A given function can be performed in many ways, but the one generally chosen in these societies is not the simplest, the most direct, or the one requiring a lesser amount of resources of any origin and of imported components. The "modernization" of central and peripheral economies has brought with it a remarkable increase in this type of waste. Moreover, as such waste contributes to the growth of GNP, it is hailed as an evident measure of "progress."

Production and consumption of socially nonessential goods pose severe demands on the external sector, as their local manufacture requires not only imported components and parts but also capital goods. In addition, the more extravagant manifestations of conspicuous consumption are satisfied with imports of luxury finished goods. To assess the order of magnitude of such "superflous" imports, we examined the foreign trade statistics of Brazil, Chile, and Mexico during the 1978-1981 period--a time of rapidly growing indebtedness in all three countries. Using a number of assumptions and criteria of "superfluity," and applying varying percentages of "discount" (i.e., the portion of a given import category that we deemed to be superfluous), we arrived at some staggering conclusions. In the case of Mexico, the import waste was close to $14 billion for the whole 1978-1981 period--a sum that represents roughly one-sixth of Mexico's total external debt by end-1981. For Brazil, the corresponding figure was $10 billion, or one-ninth of its foreign debt by end-1981. In the case of Chile, which constitutes the most pathetic example, the import waste reached a figure of $5 billion, or one-fourth its total outstanding debt. Comparing these figures with those for India (whose GNP is in between those of Brazil and Mexico) we assessed an import waste of around $4 billion, or one-fifth its total debt. In per capita terms the contrast is even sharper: $6 in India, $79 in Brazil, $200 in Mexico, and more than $500 in Chile!

THE LIMITS TO CONSUMPTION

From both a Third World and a planetary viewpoint, an indefinite continuation of "American Sytle" consumption patterns is unbearable. Emerging in response to this awareness, various schools of thought have postulated "zero growth" in industrialized nations. But this concept has not yet received sufficient support either nationally or internationally. Conversely, proponents of other schools of thought state that resources are practically unlimited and that their utilization depends more on technological factors and on their market prices. Even demands made by Third World countries revolve around their wish to have a larger share of the world's "economic pie," on the understanding that the "pie" will have to continue growing indefinitely. Poorer nations trust that the richer ones will continue to expand at ever-increasing rates, so that they may buy more goods from them and thus remain in a position whereby these poor nations can maintain their own political and development schemes--schemes that often are similarly inequitable and destructive.

But such a state of affairs cannot continue for much longer. The tempo of the "production-destruction" process has accelerated to the point where it is seriously threatening the future of humankind. The gap between rich and the poor widens, and the repression against the latter becomes stronger. Unless profound political, social, and economic changes are undertaken, the earth will become a battleground in which the dominant group will exert the utmost brutality not only against the subordinate one, to extract from it the maximum possible surplus, but also against the planet earth itself.

IN THE SEARCH FOR A NEW PATH

In order to conceptualize the possible solutions to the intertwining problems of external indebtedness and maldevelopment of Latin America, we shall deal separately with the two central issues: repayment of the present debt, and the elimination of the basic causes underlying it.

Debt Repayment

Latin American governments have long (but earnestly, only since 1983), studied how to overcome their debt burden. The most important mechanism utilized so far has been the renegotiation process, whereby services of the principal due in 1983, 1984, and 1985 have been transferred to some future period. Interest has had to be paid punctually, however. Renegotiations have been carried out on a country-by-country basis. The idea of establishing a "debtor's cartel" or "debtors club" has been rejected by both debtors and creditors. With the exception of Cuba's Fidel Castro, who has proposed that Third World debt be totally cancelled because it is "unpayable and uncollectable" (to such end, the industrialized world should devote a mere 12 percent of its military expenditures), and the president of Peru, Alan Garcia, who decided that no more than 10 percent of Peru's export earnings will be devoted to repaying or servicing the Peruvian foreign debt, no authorized voices have been heard in favor of a drastic change in the terms and conditions for tackling the debt problem, including a possible cessation of payments.

The main reasons for not considering a radical solution derive from the fear of an abrupt cutting of commercial and financial relations with the capitalist world, which might retaliate with measures such as an embargo of property and deposits abroad, sequestration of air and sea vessels, embargo of any merchandise coming from the debtor country that touches foreign ports, and other like measures.

Obviously, if all the concessions being contemplated and sought by Third World countries were to be granted, the economies of the Third World undoubtedly would be relieved from the pressure of the debt. However, there are certain deficiencies in the approaches that are being taken at present, the most important of which, in our view, is the rather lukewarm attitude toward tying prices of raw materials to rates of interest.

We shall illustrate with the case of oil. Mexico has seen its foreign interest bill mount to an annual figure of approximately $9 billion. Using March 1986 oil prices of US$13 per barrel, we find that this sum would represent 700 million barrels of oil. However, if the average interest paid by Mexico remained at the level of six percent that prevailed during the mid-1970s, instead of the recent and current 10 percent (average), the volume of oil necessary to pay the annual interest would decline to some 240 million barrels. In other words, Mexico is giving away nearly 500 million barrels of oil a year in exchange for nothing--no new service or product as a payment for those 500 million barrels of oil.

The destruction and despoiling of Latin American and other Third World resources are totally unacceptable. It is for this reason that current proposals for tackling the debt problem are utterly insufficient as well as deficient. We believe that a more appropriate formula should contemplate at least the following steps: (1) the diminution of the size of the debt, through (a) the elimination of all artificial increments suffered by international interest rates during the last ten years, above a basic rate of six percent per year, and (b) compensation for the decreased prices of raw materials since 1980, a decline that has greatly favored the economies of industrial nations; (2) the repatriation of all the capital that "flew away" from Latin America during the last ten years, under different schemes and modalities; (3) for the remainder of the debt, application of the following conditions: (a) transformation of the monetary value of such debt into a given amount of raw materials (or their equivalent in manufactured products), (b) utilization of reasonable commodity unit prices (e.g., those prevailing in 1980), (c) a six percent annual rate of interest, as a maximum; (d) a 25-year repayment period; and (e) stabilization of such basic unit prices during the whole repayment period. Finally, no new debts would be contracted during the repayment period. We examine these proposals in more detail.

Deflation of the principal. It can roughly be estimated that Latin American countries have disbursed more than $100 billion during the last ten years on account of excessive interest rates. If we apply a differential rate of four percent (10 percent minus six percent) to the outstanding debt throughout the whole 1976-1985 period, we reach a figure of around $105-110 billion. This is a sum that Latin America really does not owe and should not be recognized as legitimate, since it originated exclusively in the monetary and financial problems of industrial nations, mainly the United States. Had the interest rates remained at their 1975-1976 levels, the Latin American countries would not have faced the huge disbursements required in the following years, and therefore their need to borrow would have been much smaller.

If, at the same time, prices of raw materials had stayed at their 1980 levels, export earnings would have been some $25 to $30 million higher than what they actually were. Had this been the case, Latin America's borrowing needs would have declined by the same amount.

Summing up, we reach a total of some $130-140 billion, which corresponds to about one-third the total current Latin American debt. In any serious negotiation with creditors, this amount should be deducted from the principal, which would thus be reduced to around $260 billion.

Capital Flight. As indicated above, it is estimated that not less than $150-200 billion left the region as capital flight in the course of the last ten years alone. These are savings generated within the region, which "flew away" as a consequence mainly of the very unequal wealth and income distribution patterns prevailing in Latin American countries. It is not the industrial worker, or the peasant, or the white-collar worker who buys dollars to open accounts or acquire real estate abroad; it is the relatively small group of people who benefit from the economic and political systems that send their money away. It is clear that such a process is also directly responsible for the increase in Latin America's indebtedness. Had those savings remained within the region, the need to borrow would have decreased by the same proportion. Since such monies are deposited or invested mostly in creditor countries, strongly helping their economies, it is neither logical nor just that Latin American should pay interest on that money.

Instead, it would be fair to pursue the establishment of an agreement to repatriate that capital between debtor and creditor institutions and governments. By means of capital extradition procedures, owners of those capital assets abroad would have the opportunity to return them to their places of origin and convert them into national currencies for local investment in activities of general interest--subject, of course, to the laws, regulations, and fiscal charges prevailing in the respective countries of Latin America. There is no reason whatsoever that "an appropriate climate of confidence" should be established to promote the return of the fugitive capital that certain groups in the United States and Latin America request as a prior condition. The return of this capital would simply mean reinforcement of existing advantages in terms of earning rates, lower taxes, salaries, and so on. It would also mean a broadening of the income gap between different social groups. There would be no guarantee that the increased capital would not "fly away" once more, as soon as some clouds gather in the economic sky of the Latin American countries.

If a repatriation process gets under way, debtor countries could apply the foreign currency thus recovered to the repayment of the principal. If we assume, conservatively, that the amount to be repatriated under such a scheme is on the order of $125 billion, another third of the standing debt would be slashed from the present bill.

Deleting the amounts estimated in the sections on deflation of the principal and capital flight, we arrive at a net figure of some $135 billion. This figure might be considered the "legitimate" portion of the debt, notwithstanding the fact that even this reduced fraction contains some elements of illegitimacy (such as all those superfluous imports made by Latin American nations, which undoubtedly favored the economies of creditor countries). If the "legitimate" debt is paid in 25 years, with an annual interest rate of not more than six percent, the total service would amount to $13.5 million in the first year. These are figures that seem to be manageable by Latin America, even under conditions of economic stress (as at present). Annual services should be converted into a basket of selected raw materials at prices that are fixed beforehand (e.g., 1980 prices). Otherwise, through further price manipulation and depreciation, creditor countries could well extract the same or similar volumes of basic resources, even after the debt has been deflated to one-third its original (current) size.

With such a solution, Latin American countries would not require further borrowing to repay the debt, nor would they have to force the export of all kinds of goods in order to service such debt. Simply by devoting an average of 10 to 12 percent of their present export earnings they could see the burden of their foreign debt disappear.

BEYOND DEPENDENCY: ELIMINATION OF STRUCTURAL CAUSES OF INDEBTEDNESS

The adoption of such a scheme would represent a gigantic step toward the reduction of economic dependency. Decisions on what and how much to export and import would no longer be dictated by the obligation of meeting high foreign financial commitments; rather, they would be dictated mainly by national real development interests. However, if there is no movement beyond this point, the entire problem would not be totally solved. For this to happen, the deep causes underlying the process of indebtedness must be totally eradicated, so that the present situation of financial, commercial, technological, and cultural dependency can be radically transformed. If basic patterns of social behavior—which currently entail high waste and high import coefficients—are not modified, the outflow of resources will not diminish substantially; indeed, they will most likely increase to a considerable extent.

As long as relations between the South and the industrial North remain intact, and the "development philosophy" does not change, southern nations will continue to be easy prey for cultural penetration from the North. It is critical, therefore, to start a "delinking" process that allows Southern nations to achieve a high degree of national and regional autonomy and self-sufficiency, and, more important still, to achieve a more advanced stage in the path toward a "rationally ordered society." 2/ We have already seen the result of our societies' irrational behavior, one manifestation of which is the imported goods that are consumed, in excess, by a minority of people trying to imitate the lifestyles of richer people in richer countries. It is neither possible nor desirable--indeed it is absurd--to "democratize" excessive consumption; first, because what is consumed over and above that which is necessary for a "reasonable" or "decent" standard of living is pure waste; second, because in any case there would not be enough for everybody, particularly if by "everybody" we mean not only the present population of the world but future generations as well.

What should be "democratized" is equitable and rational behavior pattern, which would imply not only renouncing the exploitation of other human beings but also the thoughtless exploitation of nature. Such behavior, in turn, would necessarily imply a drastic recomposition of demand and supply of goods and services. The present emphasis on the production and consumption of superfluous, noxious, or luxurious goods would have to give way to an increase in the production and consumption of those essential goods and services that large segments of southern populations are lacking today. Because of their useless nature, many activities that are characteristic of capitalist "developed" societies would have to be suppressed, but many others would have to be created, in areas of science, culture, recreation, sports and so on. Human toil would be rewarded according to the effort made, not at the whimsical demand of rich minorities. Both responsibilities and benefits would be "democratized." If the total quantity of work needed to produce the overall mass of goods and services required by the community turns out to be lower than the total availability of human power (given a certain technological level), then free time should be equitably shared. Contrary to what happens today, in a "rationally ordered society" there would be no reason why some people should overwork while others have to face "forced" unemployment.

An initial step in the road toward solving the foreign debt problem--and the political and economic dependency associated with it--could be the compression of imports made from industrialized nations to a minimum compatible with the true requirements posed by "rational" behavior patterns. Most essential goods and services are of a simple nature, and can easily be produced domestically with the resources and technologies that are available. Food, clothing, housing, transportation, education, health services, recreation, and culture do not need to depend on inputs from the industrialized world. Latin American countries are in a position to develop suitable capital-goods industries that can construct the machines that will process the Latin American raw materials and produce the finished essential goods that are required. If the superfluous portion in consumption is eliminated, the need to import will be significantly reduced. If, in addition, an aggressive import-substitution policy is pursued, as it was a few decades ago, Latin America could become economically self-sufficient and politically sovereign. In such a situation, the need to count upon large quantities of hard currency would disappear, as dollars, marks, yen, and so on, would be required for a relatively few selected operations; thus, the countries involved would be exempt from the "obligation" to borrow for their development and, consequently, from the compulsion to transfer their physical resources by way of exports. By not borrowing and not having to pay interest and other charges, these countries would dispense with the juggling of the U.S. (or European, or Japanese) financial and fiscal administration; even more important, they would be able to retain for their own benefit the fruits of Latin American work.

It might be said that the slackening of the commodity flow from South to North would strengthen and accelerate the process of substitution for resources that are more readily available within the North itself. But in fact such a substitution process has been taking place for a long time, and has accelerated considerably during the last few years. Perhaps the "de-linking" process could be initiated by the northern countries. Such a decision would be taken on the basis of what for them is easiest and cheapest, either to secure (in whatever way) the resources located in the South, or to liberate themselves through technology.

The dissociation of the South implies, therefore, the disconnection from a lifestyle that favors waste, injustice, fictitiousness, and ostentation. It also implies breaking with a false notion of "progress" (as such "progress" results in greater deterioration in the quality of life of vast numbers of human beings) as well as dissociating from cultural patterns that favor quantity over quality. The issue is not, therefore, simply an economic or commercial matter, nor merely a confrontation between two blocs, the one very powerful and the other very weak. In essence, it is a new way of understanding human relations.

We have covered a great distance, having started with the consideration of a phenomenon that might be seen as occasional and temporary—the external debt—and having concluded by questioning the current forms of social organization. We believe that until the veils that conceal the true roots of the debasement and misery of our societies are lifted; until the rusty analytical tools that are currently used to approach the economic, social, and political problems are abandoned; until many of the premises and fetishes that serve as a frame of reference for carrying out such analysis are thrown overboard; it will be truly difficult, if not impossible, to effect a change in values that will lead to that "rationally ordered society" we think is the only option left to stop the progressive "Frankensteinization" of today's societies.

NOTES

1. A much more thorough and extended discussion of the issues discussed in this chapter is found in Jacobo Schatan, World Debt: Who Is To Pay? (New York, Zed, 1987), from which this chapter was drawn.

2. A concept drawn from Paul Baran's The Political Economy of Growth (Modern Reader Publications, New York, 1968).

25

Transforming the
International Order

Jose A. Silva Michelena

The transformation of the international order results from simultaneous and multiple forces at work. In the beginning of the 1970s, political economists placed a great deal of emphasis on what had come to be known as the New International Economic Order. The world economic crisis was perceived by Third World social scientists and politicians as an opportunity for Third World countries to reinsert themselves into the world economy on more favorable terms than had previously been the case. This opportunity was considered to be favorable because of the almost-universal withering away of colonialism, the new sense of national self-reliance, and the significant development (relative to the recent past) of the productive forces in Third World countries.

Within this framework the so called North–South dialogue was launched. A few years later, however, it became clear that the northern countries, except when points beneficial to their own economies arose, were not active participants in the dialogue. A case in point was industrial redeployment. Today, the North–South dialogue is dead and South–South cooperation is too modest to be considered significant.

Politically, there were also hopes that the climate of detente would provide enough room for Third World governments and semiperipheral states to experiment with new forms of government. From collective self-reliance to various "new roads" to socialism, new forms of political organization emerged on the world political scene. Today it is clear that both the political and the economic room for maneuvering of the Third World and semiperipheral countries of the South have been significantly reduced.

Following a brief overview of the main Third World schools of thought on the nature of the present and historical international order and on the possibilities of its transformation, the primary forces currently transforming the international order are analyzed. The chapter concludes with a consideration of future alternatives for Latin America.

THEORETICAL BACKGROUND

Until the 1950s, in Latin America as well as in other Third World continents, the transformation of the world was viewed basically from two theoretical perspectives, both of European origin. Academic social science was clearly dominated by what had come to be known as the theory of modernization; and critical social science was mostly inspired by the Leninist theory of imperialism.

The theory of modernization was widely accepted among Third World academic circles because it represented a new synthesis of a long tradition of thought in sociology, anthropology, and economics (In particular, I refer to the works of Marshall, Durkheim, Tonnies, Weber and Redfield.) Moreover, this new synthesis of social thought appeared at a time when African and Asian countries were being decolonized; new nations were being built; and movements of liberations were emerging everywhere.

The theory of modernization contrasted with the rather simplistic view prevailing in the immediate postwar period in academic and policy circles in the United States. It was believed then that those revolutionary movements were mainly the product of the Machiavellian influence of the Soviet Union, which was relentlessly seeking to expand communism; hence the main policy objective was to "contain" such expansion by militarily opposing these movements.

The theory of modernization implies a profound revision of the historical evolution of the world. It not only reinforces the idea that development would spread from Europe and the United States to backward or traditional countries, but most significantly it also postulates that social and political movements that were seeking to transform the established order were the result of conditions of backwardness, misery, and disruption of values. These conditions prevailed for the majority of the population of traditional countries, in contrast to the affluent modernity or urban minorities and power cliques.

International aid programs were inspired by the theory. These programs greatly influenced government planning in the Third World. The theory held that the transition of a traditional society to a modern one, (such as that of the United States or Europe) would be motivated by foreign investment and the technological transference accompanying it. The emergence of modern middle sectors would soon bring political changes, which in turn would facilitate the modernization of both the agrarian structure and industry. Further, theorists believed that international commerce would benefit from further specialization in raw materials, which would reinforce the comparative advantages enjoyed by these countries.

This conception of world order and international change prevailed in Latin America until the early 1960s. In other Third World continents it remained dominant for a few years more. Nevertheless, as of the late 1940s, a group of economists working for the UN Economic Commission for Latin America (ECLA), under the leadership of Raul Prebish, were already questioning basic premises of the economic theory of modernization. In particular, they questioned the International Commerce Theory:

> Raul Prebish, a pioneer in the analysis of Latin American underdevelopment, expressed that long term weakness in the price of raw materials invalidated the positive results which, supposedly, were derived from the comparative advantages. After analytically dividing the world in a developed Center and an underdeveloped Periphery, Prebish demonstrated not only that there has not been any technological progress from the center to the periphery, but that, on the contrary, productivity growth in underdeveloped countries was being rechanelled toward the center, through the mechanism of "deterioration of the terms of trade." (Munoz, 1985, p. 22)

A new "developmentalist" strategy was suggested by the ECLA; involving inward-oriented growth through import-substitution industrialization, diversification of exports with manufactured products, agrarian reform, modernization of the state to make it more consonant with its new interventionist role, and institutional reforms at the international level in order to favor peripheral countries.

Many Latin American governments, urged by programs such as the Alliance for Progress, incorporated the ECLA's strategy in their development plans. However, in face of the continued failure of such plans and the persistence of underdevelopment a new interpretation of the center-periphery relation emerged in the mid 1960s. This new vision of international relations and development came to be known as the theory of dependency. This interpretation broke away from the notion that development spread from the center to the periphery. It also left aside the Keynesian-Parsionan paradigm that formed the basis for both modernization and developmentalist theory. Instead it proposed a historic-structural interpretation of the capitalist world order. This theory was inspired by the Marxist-Leninist theory of imperialism but went beyond the Eurocentric bias of the latter. Underdevelopment of the periphery was seen, in part, as a consequence of the development of the center, within the context of the expansion of capitalism throughout the world. This theory emphasized that as peripheral economies were incorporated into the capitalist system, their economic structures became heterogeneous and organically linked to the international economy in such a way that there was a deterioration of the terms of trade, unequal exchange, and super-exploitation of the labor force. Third World dependent economies thus contributed to the development of the center and became underdeveloped themselves.

In recent times the increasing transnationalization of the productive apparatus and the internal market as well as the role of national and international class alliances were emphasized. The nation-state did not disappear from the analysis, but it was complemented with class analysis. Moreover, analysis of the transformation of the world included considerations of both changes in the capitalist and socialist camps.

Dependency theory greatly influenced analysis in other Third World continents, as well as in some academic circles in the United States and Europe. But this wide influence in the intellectual sphere greatly contrasted with the meager impact it had at government levels. This outcome was undoubtedly a sign of the ideological dependency and self-imposed restrictions of the dominant local elites. Dependency theory has been criticized from different points of view, but no clear theoretical alternative has yet emerged.

Meanwhile, disenchantment with "real socialisms" was almost parallel to the bitter questioning of consumer society. The prolonged economic crisis of the world economy since the late 1960s resulted in the withering away of the last of the "true believers" in development. If it is true that the crisis gave rise to new hopes for a "new international order," it is also true that the continued failure of the North-South dialogue soon revealed that more "joint" approaches like those proposed by the Brandt Commission, the RIO Project, or the Club of Rome to the question of developing a more just international order were needed.

Instead, old economic theories were revived in the center. The adoption of neoliberal policies by the United Kingdom and the United States was followed everywhere in the capitalist world. In Latin America, a new wave of dictatorships quickly adopted such ideas. Whereas, at the beginning these countries, as well as some democracies that also followed these neoliberal ideas, experienced some economic growth, they soon failed, leaving those countries in a deep and prolonged recession and literally mortgaged to the international banking community.

In face of this complex and confused panorama, Third World social science (or that elsewhere) has not produced a new theoretical approach to face the crisis. Important theoretical advances have been made, however. Indeed, Third World scientists have made important contributions, but these have to be yet integrated into a coherent theoretical body. Understandably, governments have tried to revive neoliberal or developmentalist policies, but their efforts have met with little success. In other words, in addition to the profound crisis the world economy is undergoing, there is a profound crisis in the social theory of the transformation of the world. In the following pages we shall attempt to understand the main forces behind this transformation.

THE WORLD ECONOMIC CRISIS

Since the end of the 1960s, the world economy has been undergoing a crisis that is likely to last for a few more years. The causes of this crisis are profoundly rooted in the present world economic mode of accumulation and there is reason to think that the conditions for its transformation are not yet ripe. Since the crisis started, periods of recovery, (as in 1983-1985) have been brief. As Martner (1985, pp.1-11) pointed out recently, forecasts made by international organizations for the period 1985-2000 are not optimistic with respect to a sustained recovery of the industrialized economies that would contribute to the economies of Third World countries. Martner cites the conclusions of the "World Development Report" of the World Bank, studies made by the International Social and Economic Affairs Department of the United Nations, as well as studies made by UNCTAD. All three conclude that at best there will be slow growth, unless serious progress is made in transforming dominant tendencies in the world economy mode of accumulation.

As Frank (1974, p. 2) pointed out some years ago, the crisis can be overcome in a more or less permanent way only if a new model of accumulation is reached. It is true that the model based on cheap energy has been substantially changed, but the other components of the model, such as consumerism and militarization, remain very much based on past theories of development. The truth is that a new model can only come into being only if technological breakthroughs are realized--that is, breakthroughs that would open new opportunities for accumulation on a world scale.

Some authors (Perez, 1983; Herrera, 1984) have argued that microelectronics, though only in its beginning phase, may be one such technological breakthrough. Bio- technology and exploration of the sea bed are also frequently mentioned as providing new sources of accumulation for the world economy. However, nobody can predict when all these new sources will be capable of initiating a wave of prosperity.

With respect to the new international division of labor, transnationalization of the world economy remains the most general tendency. In other words, transnational corporations (TNCs) seem to be playing an ever more important role in both developed and underdeveloped economies.

In the developed economies TNCs are playing the most important role in the transformation of the social division of labor. The most significant consequences of this transformation seem to vary across their various centers. For the United States, the main negative consequence seems to be slow growth in productivity as compared to Europe and Japan. For Europe, the main problem seems to be growing unemployment, and for Japan it is the dependence of its economy on expanding foreign markets (see Thurow, 1985). Further, these problems may result in a growing tendency for the major world economies to isolate themselves as a mean of solving the above-mentioned problems (Thurow, 1985).

Transnationalization, however, conspires against such a scenario. As their name indicates, transnational corporations operate on a world scale, while states can effectively act only on a national level. Thus States have to control multinational monopolies, financial flows, and fiscal and monetary policies.

The impact of transnationalization on Third World economies is quite clear: external and internal macroeconomic disequilibria, growing external debt, disintegration of internal productive activities and further integration of national economies into the international circuit of accumulation, elementary insecurity, urban and rural famines, and the irrational use of natural resources. As mentioned before, a new and more favorable interaction with the world economic order is becoming less and less likely.

Evidently, the situation varies according to the degree of transnationalization of the national economies. But there is a problem that seems to be equally burdening all underdeveloped economies: the external debt. During the last fifteen years Third World debt to the international banking community has increased very rapidly reaching the frightening sum of nearly $800 billion in 1986. Latin American debt accounts for about half of that figure, but some countries in Africa and Asia also have the dubious honor of being in the list of the most highly indebted countries of the Third World.

The question of why the Third World nations became so highly indebted was addressed in a previous analysis by Silva Michelena (1985). In short, Silva Michelena argued that Third World indebteness is due to a combination of factors, among which the most important are the prolonged and pronounced recession, a variety of errors committed by both the international financial institutions and Third World governments, and, above all, the tendency of increasing transnationalization of Third

406

World economies, which has generated accumulation
mechanisms that have inevitably resulted in balance of
payment and fiscal deficits. To cope with these
problems, Third World governments have resorted to
external borrowing from an international community that
has been overeager to lend at low interest rates.

With the possible exception of four Asian export-led
economies, all underdeveloped economies, regardless of
their particular model of accumulation, seem to be at the
brink of debt. Governments have not defined strategies
for getting out of this situation, because they
apparently have no choice but to apply the politically
risky IMF austerity policies. This situation worsened
considerably from 1981 to 1984 because of the rising
interest rates, which unexpectedly caused Third World
countries to face the dilemma of paying the debt or
starving their populations. The fact is that the
economies of these Third World countries, which exacted
great sacrifices by their populations, were being
swallowed by increasing interest rates. Since 1984
interest rates have come down a bit, but most of these
countries have had to devote a third or more of their
income derived from exports to service the debt.

This problem is also potentially dangerous for the
financial security of "developed" countries and for the
peace and security of the whole world. But the negative
effects on Third World populations are real and present.
As an example, we can mention the draconian policies
under which the people of Mexico and the Philippines are
suffering; and due to the debt problem, families in
Nigeria, Zaire, and Venezuela, which until now were
barely subsisting, can cope no more. Thus, it is not
surprising that delinquency and personal insecurity in
the capital cities of most underdeveloped countries are
reaching alarming proportions. Discontent is everywhere
and open protests are multiplying throughout the world,
as evidenced by massive street demonstrations in
Argentina, Egypt, Sierra Leon, Liberia, Indonesia, and
Colombia. General strikes and states of emergency have
occurred in Bolivia and Peru; coups d'etat have taken
place in Morocco, Tunisia, the Dominican Republic, and
Haiti; in Brazil hungry masses have looted supermarkets
and silos; in Chile, in the midst of the fight against
dictatorship, hunger marches have alternated with
political protests. There are examples of many such
protests of popular masses against the set of policies

being imposed by the IMF, which have left hundreds dead, thousands wounded and imprisoned, and Third World states more and more repressive. In short, this multiplication of conflicts is jeopardizing world peace, particularly in light of the new and more tense world political situation.

THE WORLD POLITICAL SITUATION

At the end of President Carter's administration, the policy of detente began to deteriorate until it became once again a situation of cold war (Halliday, 1983). Today, this new situation dominates the world political scene and determines changes in the global strategic scheme. Events have occurred since 1985 that would seem to indicate a gradual easing of this tense situation—events such as the resumption of the Geneva talks and the summit conference of November 1985 in Geneva. However, such initiatives have not had any practical effects beyond fostering the illusion that nuclear holocaust is a bit further off than before.

The main consequences for the rest of the world of this new period of confrontation between the two superpowers are greater control of dissidence within each bloc, an attempt to strengthen alliances and military pacts, and, for the Third World, a reduction of the political room for maneuvering of each individual country. In sum, political and social experiments are not likely to be tolerated.

These conditions are true both in the capitalist camp, where leaders are attempting to diminish the new wave of revolutions that began in the 1970s, and in the socialist camp, where they are coping with the anxieties caused by Soviet intervention in Afghanistan and the prolonged confrontation between Vietnam and Kampuchea. In other words, an attempt is being made by the hegemonic powers to keep order in their respective zones of influence. As a consequence, underdeveloped countries have suffered an important loss in the degree of freedom that they had reached to autonomously define policies oriented toward the transformation of their societies and toward the achievement of a more favorable reinsertion into the world economic order.

One of the factors leading to the new cold war was the realization by U.S. leaders of the progressive weakening of the U.S. military, political and ideological influence vis a vis the USSR, and economic deterioration vis a vis Europe and Japan. This so-called crisis of hegemony prompted Reagan's administration to overreact, in the sense of defining a policy that would recover for the United States its former position of absolute hegemony in the world scene. The Reagan response implied the abandonment of the policy of defense of human rights and, acting through the Trilateral Commission, which characterized the Carter administration, the Reagan administration has concentrated on an overall policy based on force, militarism, political and economic pressures and direct intervention in the internal affairs of countries within the U.S. sphere of influence. This is demonstrated by the nuclear redeployment imposed on European countries in spite of the massive opposition of the population and, above all, by the United States' insistence on carrying forward the Strategic Defense Initiative, which apparently is changing the whole strategic scheme of the postwar era.

The scant attention paid by the superpowers to the results of the summit meeting of Argentina, Greece, India, Mexico, Sweden, and Tanzania, held in New Delhi in January 1985 for the purpose of fostering peace and disarmament, is indicative of the inability of the peripheral countries to change this tendency.

It is important to mention that within the new strategic scheme being put into effect by the Reagan administration there is a plan to cope with revolutionary movements in the Third World. One of the military elements of this strategy is the Rapid Deployment Force, which is designed to place in any part of the world, rapidly and without warning, a combat force strong enough to put down any insurgency. However, as demonstrated in Nicaragua, intervention may be preceded by political and economic intervention.

Nevertheless, it is important to mention that at the beginning of 1986, when this chapter was being written, there were some signs that the United States may have been introducing important changes into its policy toward the Third World, in the sense of relying less on dictatorships to keep Third World countries in order and to help new democratic movements to reach power. The overthrow of Baby Doc in Haiti and the case of Marcos in the Philippines may be examples of these changes. To be sure, the new democratic movements must demonstrate their allegiance to Washington before receiving any kind of backing, but there does seem the new possibility of transformation under these conditions.

LONG-TERM TRENDS

We have already mentioned that one long term trend in the transformation of the international order is toward the increasing isolationism of the United States, Europe, Japan, and the socialist bloc. This fragmentation of the world market will come about because no country is really capable or willing to pay the price of managing the world system, and because the particular problem that each power is now facing apparently can find no real solution within the present world economy. For the Third World, there would probably be a severing of ties with the South and, perhaps, with other powers zones of influence. However, if competition among the powers sharpens, then more room for Third World maneuvering may result.

A longer-term vision of the trends transforming the international order may give a totally different perspective. Wallerstein (1985) argues that, as in many other periods throughout history, the expansive phase of the world economy has given way to a new and prolonged recessive phase. As in other such historical phases, the reorganization of the world affects not only economic relations among countries, but also the system of interstate relations and the overall cultural-ideological configuration.

One possible transformation may be the establishment of a new axis integrated by the United States, Japan and China. This new axis would seek to establish selective cooperation with the semiperipheral states of the South; Thus, of course, implying not only a certain redistribution of surplus but also a significative increase in capital accumulation. Moreover, the cost of such distribution would be more than compensated by the decrease of political explosions in the South.

The formation of such an axis would certainly imply the formation of another axis that integrates the USSR, Western Europe, and Eastern Europe. As both the United States and the USSR would have to face growing internal dissidence and disorder, they would probably pay less attention to Europe. Hence the tendency towards the reunification of Europe would be accentuated.

Wallerstein discusses a series of considerations on the basis of these two main hypotheses. Perhaps it worth mentioning here that such reorganization of the world order would provide new opportunities for the process of capital accumulation, but with it "a considerable proportion of the world population would continue to be scandalously exploited and who knows if worse than ever" (Wallerstein, 1985, p. 23).

However, such a scheme may be necessary for a truly radical ideological and cultural change resulting in the dethronement of established social ideologies. And this intellectual revolution may be what is needed to re-evaluate the strategic options of world antisystemic movements, so as to remove them from the historical cul-de-sac in which they have found themselves since 1945.

FUTURE ALTERNATIVES FOR LATIN AMERICA

Political and economic trends in the international setting certainly have a great deal of influence on the alternatives open to any particular country, but the viability and feasibility of any project are affected by the extent to which significant social and political movements assume the responsibility for concrete projects of their own. I shall attempt to summarize the different proposals being put forward in Latin America by the social and political forces now present. Some of these proposals were initiated in the past but continue to be backed by significant social forces awaiting the opportunity for a comeback. Others are just intellectual constructs, but they may be also considered messages with a destiny.

The Neoliberal Proposal

The neoliberal proposal is usually backed by internal forces linked to transnational corporations, conservative politicians, and the authoritarian military. Although it was recently defeated in Argentina, Uruguay, and Brazil, it still appears to be a latent alternative. Even in countries with a more or less democratic tradition, such as Costa Rica, Mexico, and Venezuela, there are strong sectors favoring this alternative, which is also backed by the Reagan administration. The worsening of the new cold war and the consolidation of the new U.S. hegemony sustain an attitude tending to favor this alternative in the short run.

The neoliberal proposal is formulated within the context of a reordering of the world capitalist system under the hegemony of the United States. The supporters of this proposal usually argue that the factors blocking further capitalist development include: (1) excessive democracy and the consequent deterioration of government's legitimacy, (2) state gigantism and its effect on the fiscal deficit and inflation, (3) too much growth in the power of labor unions and their participation in the formulation of public policies, and (4) excessive nationalism. With respect to the international perspective, this proposal argues in favor of greater integration with the U.S. economy in a global system of mutual complementarity.

The Proposal for Liberal Democracy

For the countries that have recently become democratic, such as Argentina, Uruguay, and Brazil, the main objective would be the consolidation of a restricted democratic regime. For countries such as Costa Rica, Mexico, Colombia, and Venezuela, which have a certain democratic tradition, the main objective would be to achieve a better redistribution of wealth. This proposal is backed by the elites: entrepreneurial, labor union leaders, the technobureaucracy, the main political social democratic parties, the church, and the armed forces. A social pact among these elites would guarantee both democratic stability and an appropriate management of interests conflict. Negotiation and consensus are the general principles orienting politics. The policy implies a restricted participation of popular sectors, which have been reduced to participating in national, state, or municipal elections.

Given the present circumstances of the debt problem, the main policy concern of sectors favoring this alternative today is to pay the debt through tacit or open agreements with the IMF. They favor bilateral negotiations, although they are willing to participate in international meetings such as the Quito Conference

(January 1984) or the Cartagena Consensus. There is a growing resistance among the advocates of this alternative to blindly follow IMF recommended policies. However, resistance is more rhetorical than practical. In short, these advocates lack an alternative economic program.

Projects of Social Transformation

The advocates of these proposal share the idea that a self-reliant Latin America for the year 2000 depends a great deal on the type of transformations that may take place now. These transformations require new social actors that are expressive of popular interests. These new actors should have a profound democratic vocation and be capable of generating a new hegemony within each state. This proposal would benefit from international trends such as those envisaged by Wallerstein.

Within this general characterization, it is possible to identify two main versions in Latin America: the deepening of Liberal Democracy and the Popular Regional Transformation.

Deepening of Liberal Democracy

This alternative radically questions the idea that economic growth is the main objective of development. It advances a new conception of development according to which the main purpose of productive growth is the betterment of the quality of life, a reordering of the logical order of needs, and the assignment of resources geared to satisfy the new order of priorities.

Politically it implies a coalition in power clearly able to meet the needs of the popular sectors. Hence measures to avoid a reconcentration of power must be taken. Elite corporatism must be replaced by the organized participation of the popular masses, in decisions concerning the economy. Decentralization is essential to guarantee effective participation as is a change in the social relations of production. A third form of ownership has been suggested: comanagement and cooperatives.

Finally, basic structural transformation should facilitate the economic autonomy of Latin America in the

world economy by substituting markets and reorienting
exports and imports.

Popular Regional Transformation

This alternative is basically structured along the
same lines as the previous one, but it is adapted to the
particular conditions of the Caribbean and Central
American states. Here, more emphasis is given to real
regional integration, so as to cope with the fact that
most Central American and Caribbean countries are
mini-states. This integration should recognize the
existence of such varied situations as those in Puerto
Rico, Panama or Cuba (Gorostiaga, 1985).

Socialism

The existence of Cuba makes socialism a real
alternative for Latin America. Advocates of this
alternative constitute significant social and political
forces in various countries but they are most important
in Peru, Nicaragua and El Salvador. In the rest of Latin
America there is a new ideological and political hegemony
of the overwhelming bloc constituted by Social and
Christian Democracy which for the time being seems to
have the appeal of the masses.

The disenchantment with socialism is due to a
complex set of phenomena, including the failure of
guerrilla movements in the early 1960s, the realization
that "real socialism" has not been able to find a way of
effectively guaranteeing civil and political liberties,
and the pragmatic assessment of the costs involved for a
socialist experiment in a climate of cold war and
interventionism of the United States.

Finally, there is a certain widespread optimism due
to the fact that in the last ten years Latin America has
changed from having predominantly dictatorial regimes to
having predominantly democratic ones. This fact may not
have a great deal of influence in the global strategic
scheme, but it certainly provides a stimulus for
democratic movements all over the Third World. There may
be no direct linkage between Latin American democratization process and, for instance, the overthrow of
Marcos in the Philippines. But these events certainly

assist the rise of democratic movements elsewhere. If democratization of the Third World becomes a steady tendency, there may be new hope for greater South-South coordination and interchange. Perhaps this is the first step toward a truly new international order.

BIBLIOGRAPHY

Frank, Andre Gunder. 1974. "World Crisis and Latin American International Options." Paper presented to the symposium on Latin America in the International System Royal Institute of International Affairs. London, May 1.

Gorostiaga, Xabier. 1985. "Condicionantes para una Alternativa Regional a la Crisis Centroamericana." In Heraldo Munoz ed., Crisis y Desarrollo Alternativo en Latinoamerica. Santiago de Chile: Editorial Aconagua.

Halliday, Fred. 1983. The Making of the Second Cold War. London: Verso Edition and NLB.

Herrera, Amilcar. 1984. "The New Technological Wave and the Developing Countries.: Brazil: UNICAMP, mimeo.

Martner, Gonzalo. 1985. "La Insercion de America Latina en la Economia Mundial--Una Vision del Future." Caracas: PROFAL-UNITAR, June, pp. 1-11.

Munoz, Heraldo. 1985. "Vias al Desarrollo despues de la Crisis y el Neoliberalismo," In Heraldo Munoz, ed., Crisis y Desarrollo Alternativo en Latinoamerica. Santiago de Chile: Editorial Aconcagua.

Perez, Carlota. 1983. "Structural Change and the Assimilation of New Technologies in the Economic and Social System: A Contribution to Current Debate on Kondratiev Cycles." Paper presented at the International Seminar on Innovation, Design and Long Cycles in Economic Development at the Department of Design Research, Royal College of Art, London, April 13-15.

Silva Michelena, Jose A. 1985. "Los Intereses Estrategicos Globales y la Problematica de la Seguridad en la Ordern Internacional: America Latina y Europa." In EURAL; La Vulnerabilidad Externa de America Latina y Europa, Buenos Aires: GEL.

Thurow, Lester. 1985. "The World at a Turning Point." Paper presented at the Seminar Crisis and State Regulation: Policy dilemmas for Latin America and Europe. Buenos Aires: EURAL, October 14-16.

Wallerstein, Immanuel. 1985. "European Unity and Its Implications for the Interstate System." Paper presented at the seminar The Role of Europe in the Peace and Security of Other Regions. Austria: Schlaining Castle, May 2-4.

PART THREE

Security and Conflict

26

Uncertainties About WTO and NATO Military Doctrines

Laszlo Valki

The political and military nature of military doctrines has been a subject of debate for a long time. It has also made its way onto the agenda of the Warsaw Treaty Organization (WTO). The Appeal of the WTO, published on June 12, 1986 stated that:

> From the point of view of the actual intentions of military-political groupings or of individual states, the issue of military doctrines is no less important. Mutual suspicion and distrust, which accumulated over the years, have to be eliminated, and each other's anxieties should be thoroughly analyzed. For the security of Europe and the entire world, the military concepts and doctrines of the military alliances have to be of defensive character.

The "thorough analysis of each other's anxieties" should logically mean that the Western experts tell their Eastern colleagues what worries them in the military doctrine of WTO and the latter report on their threat perceptions of the NATO doctrine. This paper proposes a third way. It addresses both doctrines and (1) the criticisms expressed by the Western experts themselves concerning their own doctrine, (2) the presumptions which have emerged in the West concerning the content of the WTO doctrine. It is a particular feature of the present situation that (1) the actual content of NATO's Flexible Response doctrine, which was originally of a defensive character, has become unclear as a result of criticisms and proposals such as Follow-on Forces-Attack (FOFA); (2) with regard to the content of the WTO doctrine -- which according to its stated intentions is also defensive -- Western opinions are divided.

In the opinion of the critics, the official military doctrine of NATO is not suitable for exercising credible deterrence against the potential enemy. According to the doctrine, in the event of an external attack NATO would not immediately use its whole available conventional and nuclear arsenal, but would react gradually. If it could not hold up the advance of the enemy by conventional means, it would, at a certain point, use its nuclear arsenal. In this way the response would be "flexible." But since the conventional forces of the WTO countries are allegedly superior to NATO forces, the Western alliance would be unable to contain an attack with conventional forces, so nuclear weapons would sooner or later be used. However, after launching the first short-range missile, the Soviet Union would obviously launch its own missiles, which would probably be answered by NATO's medium-range nuclear missiles. The operators of similar Soviet weapons would not remain idle, consequently an armed conflict between the conventional forces would escalate with a high grade of automation into a general nuclear war. In such a conflict, people in the densely populated part of Western Europe would perish. Thus the announced threat, that at a given point NATO would use its nuclear weapons, does not have a deterring effect because, practically, NATO would be threatening suicide. 1/ The attacker would reckon with cold rationalism that its attack launched with conven-tional forces would be successful, because of its conventional superiority, and there would be no realistic fear of a nuclear counter-strike. Kissinger says:

> It is absurd to base the strategy of the West on the credibility of mutual suicide... The West Europeans should not keep asking us to multiply strategic assurance that we could not possibly mean or if we do mean, we should not want to execute because if we execute, we risk the destruction of the civilization. 2/

According to its critics, Flexible Response is con-troversial for the additional reason that it presumes that a nuclear war can be limited to Europe. This presumption follows from the stipulation that in the case of an unsuccessful defense with conventional arms, NATO would not immediately launch all available nuclear weapons, but only the short- or medium-range nuclear missiles. This stipulation was probably formulated assuming that the enemy would end its aggression after a few "minor" nuclear exchanges. The elaborators of this doctrine imagine that the conflict would not extend to other continents and that the United States would not receive devastating nuclear strikes. It is interesting, other critics continue, that this presumption is essentially compatible with President Reagan's well-known declaration of October 1981, that a limited nuclear war in Europe is not inconceivable. Although, after a general outcry, this declaration was refuted by official sources, analysis of the doctrine's internal logic reveals that it was not a slip of the tongue.

The critics have explained that escalation is more likely than "self-restraint." Although one cannot predict the scenario of a European armed conflict, one would not be launched with limited aims. If, despite the doomsday risk involved in the use of nuclear weapons, one party carried out an offensive operation, it would probably not be satisfied with limited results. Operations are carried out to win. Neither of the parties can be sure that the other party will adhere to the rules necessary to fight a limited war. The critics note that war experience acquired in the past forty years cannot be used analogously because neither of the two global powers has ever met in a direct military conflict, and no such conflict has occurred with a third nuclear power. Wars in the Third World have been limited because the two global powers have avoided direct conflict, and because most states fighting limited wars have not possessed limitless destructive capabilities. The continuation of the war has had physical limits. According to Barnaby and Borg,

> The doctrine of flexible response is based on the assumption that both NATO and the WTO will be able and willing, in the case of war, to escalate from conventional via tactical nuclear to all out nuclear warfare in a slow and orderly fashion, so that hostilities can be broken off before the worst happens. This implies a state of mind, which is more to be found at a card table than at the battlefield. 3/

Another contradiction of Flexible Response is connected with escalation dominance. This means that in a military conflict only one party would be able to cause unacceptable damage to the other party by escalation, without the latter answering with comparable counter measures. Practically, this capability is identical to military superiority. But no escalation dominance exists with regard to the two global powers. The concept of the gradual application of more and more destructive weapons seems to be a rational action only if it promises some result. If the aggressor has the same capability of escalation as the defender, then escalation does not produce credible deterrence on either side.

Do we have to take seriously the various critical statements? According to Marek Thee: "As never before in the history, contemporary military doctrines and strategies are by their nature intuitive and highly speculative, because of the unremitting revolution in military technology and the impossibility of real-life-testing of the nuclear arsenal." If this is a speculative doctrine then its criticisms cannot be free of speculative features either, and we do not know whether Flexible Response is credible and whether the above critical statements are correct or not.

The most important question is whether the WTO considers this military doctrine credible, not what the elaborators of the doctrine think about their own concept. No single official NATO document says anything about which doctrine would be applied if NATO launched an attack against a WTO country. And no WTO experts have published anything concerning the reverse. Both alliances have declared a defensive doctrine and describe the other as the potential aggressor. The WTO, as far as I know, has produced no document or analysis which would doubt the credibility of Flexible Response.

In other words, whether one has deserved it or not, whether one has offensive intentions or not, one is deterred. I have not met any East European expert who would presume that a European military conflict could be kept within limited and conventional frameworks, and that NATO would not eventually use its nuclear weapons. This is ignored by NATO analysts because they are willing to evaluate the credibility of their doctrine only within their own system of logic. This is what western peace research literature calls "self-deterrence," and whose inconsistency has frequently been pointed out, without any result. The expressed doubts concerning Flexible Response give East European observers the impression that

some politicians and military experts of NATO would
themselves undermine the credibility of their own military doctrine, if their aim were to make the WTO
leadership believe that if attacked with conventional
weapons, NATO would defend itself solely by conventional
means -- that it is not serious about the nuclear option.

Whatever we think about it, we have to accept
Flexible Response as a fact. The problem is that this
fact has unfavorable consequences. Two alternatives have
been offered. Unfortunately, NATO has picked the concepts of Follow-On-Forces-Attack (FOFA) and AirLand
Battle, which has resulted in the lowering of the nuclear
threshold, and in the increase of offensive war-fighting
capabilities.

The alternative, "alternative security," "defensive"
or "nonprovocative defense," would have raised the
nuclear threshold and increased defensive capabilities.
Regrettably the latter is supported only by opposition
politicians, peace researchers and a few companies,
interested in the production of defensive weapons.

The declared acceptance of the FOFA and AirLand
Battle doctrines raised anxiety not only in the East but
in the West. The FOFA was formally adopted by the
Defense Planning Committee of NATO in November 1984 and
considered the official battle doctrine. Although according to several declarations the AirLand Battle of 1982
is a doctrine of only the US Army, evidence indicates
that, practically, it would be applied in the European
theatre. 5/

The essence of these doctrines is that in the case
of an assumed attack by the WTO it is not advantageous to
try to contain the offense on the frontiers because in
such a case the West would have to fight the war entirely
on its own territory. Therefore, with various conventional armed forces (primarily with the use of
non-nuclear short-range missiles, precision-guided
artillery weapons and unmanned aircraft) powerful strikes
should be made at the beginning of the conflict on the
first echelons and then on the second, the third, and so
on. The aim would be to cut the supply lines of the
attacking echelons. They would have to destroy airports,
stores, railway lines, bridges, radar stations and
communications equipment, etc., at a depth of 50 to 400
km. within enemy territory, then quickly penetrate enemy
territory. The AirLand Battle, according to the official
American source:

... operations carried out on the basis of the AirLand Battle are quick, powerful and successfully utilize the shortcoming of the enemy... In a constantly changing situation, the attacking (NATO) forces keep the initiative in hand and destroy the unity of the enemy's defense. Applying the various supporting and reserve forces in a flexible manner, they continue the attack until they acquire victory... Independently of whether they initially attack or defend themselves, the American units have to capture the initiative at any point of the globe and have to use this in an aggressive manner... Penetration deeply into the enemy's territory is not an unimportant or secondary operational task but part of a co-ordinating operational plan which cannot be neglected. 6/

Up to now the quoted source has spoken exclusively about operations with conventional armed forces. The following lines contain more:

The use of nuclear and chemical weapons dramatically increases the possibility to suddenly change the field situation which the attacker will be able to successfully utilize... By extending the battlefield and integrating conventional, nuclear, chemical and electronic means... the US Army can quickly begin offensive action to conclude the battle on its terms.

General Starry, the former commander of Training and Doctrine Command (TRADOC), and originator of the AirLand Battle told a congressional committee in 1984 that in a Central European battle "the delays that are attendant upon asking for and receiving nuclear weapons release always creates a situation in which if you wait until they get into your territory to ask for the use of nuclear weapons, it is always too late..." 7/

D.T. Plesch is right when writing that the use of nuclear weapons in AirLand Battle is therefore substantially different from the orthodox view of Flexible Response ... AirLand Battle appears to envisage a deliberate lowering of the nuclear threshold at a time when public concern has centered on the need to raise it. 8/ This doctrine not only lowers the nuclear threshold but practically terminates it, for in any type of European armed conflict it envisages the almost immediate use of weapons of mass destruction. This is a dangerous concept as it considers nuclear weapons identical to conventional ones, except that they are somewhat more destructive. Essentially this is described by Dieter Senghaas as "die konventionalisierung der nuklearen Strategie." 9/

Those who have elaborated on this doctrine believe that the Third World War could be conducted in a similar way to the Second. Bjorn Moller is correct when he points out:

> The FOFA was presented as an evolutionary development of the NATO doctrine. What was new about it was, two things both of which entailed revolutionary consequences—but of which only one was admitted in public: First of all, it raised the tempting prospect of "conventionalizing" the deep strike missions, hitherto the domain of the nuclear forces... Secondly, it raised the perspective of a gradual adoption by NATO of the new American doctrines of the extended and the integrated battlefield, centrally connected with the AirLand Battle doctrine of the U.S. Army, but having its counterparts in the U.S. Navy and Air Force. 10/

This concept becomes dangerous when we think about the possible consequences. In the case of a WTO attack it seems a really sensible alternative that NATO should destroy the WTO air bases with an attack against the second echelons, before the attacking aircraft have returned to them. However, in a crisis situation, there is a major temptation to attack the air bases before the aircraft have taken off. Thus, the development of deep interdiction capabilities inspires a pre-emptive strike. And because this idea is not overlooked by the WTO, in a crisis the risk increases for both parties.

Let us now examine Western literature with regard to the military doctrine of WTO. It is characteristic that Western literature refers not to the military doctrine of the Alliance but to that of the Soviet Union, presuming that the two are identical, thus I adhere to this terminology. In the following I will examine the most important points of moderate views, and not extreme assessments, according to which, for example, the Soviet

Union is able and ready to attack and occupy an overwhelming part of the West German territories within two weeks.

According to Western experts, there was no essential change in Soviet strategies during the first years following the Second World War; they remained the same as they were during the Great Patriotic War. Thus, the appearance of nuclear weapons did not induce the then Soviet military leaders to re-evaluate doctrine. Although Stalin regarded the development of nuclear weapons of major significance, he considered it more a means, which represented a new and larger destructive power, than something which could decide the outcome of a war. The fact that after the Second World War there was less disarmament in Soviet conventional forces than in the West, was not due to the appearance of the nuclear bomb.

Western sources seemed to know that the Soviet Union was not prepared for a surprise NATO attack. The nuclear bombs were kept in store. No Soviet airplane was engaged in "nuclear patrol," in contrast to the American Air Force, whose squadrons were continuously circling along the frontiers of the Soviet Union with nuclear bombs on board. At that time the American nuclear bombers could easily have reached Soviet airports and other targets before the Soviet planes loaded with nuclear weapons could take off. Western evaluations do not have the explanation for this rather reserved Soviet strategy. According to some, the Soviet Union simply did not fear a surprise American attack. According to others, it did not want to provoke the Americans.

After Stalin, the essence of the doctrine did not change, but more emphasis was placed on nuclear weapons. Western sources reported on military maneuvers, which paid more attention than earlier to the consequences of the use of nuclear weapons. At the same time, in a 1954 speech, Malenkov warned that a new world war is unimaginable, as nuclear destruction would mean the annihilation of human civilization.

The decisive change in the Soviet military doctrine was brought about by the launching of the first Sputnik, which put an end to the invulnerability of the territory of the United States. The post-1957 period was characterized by the advancement of nuclear weapons. According to the Soviet doctrine of that time, any armed conflict between the two military alliances would bring about a total nuclear war. The Soviet intercontinental missiles would immediately be used in the first "decisive" phase of the conflict. Clashes would also soon develop in the European theatre, but the Soviet conventional forces would only be used when the fight had been decided in the nuclear field.

The Soviet military doctrine of that period was characterized by an <u>overestimation of the role of nuclear missiles</u>. Khruschev said the following at the session of the Supreme Council in 1960:

> Our state has a powerful rocket technology. Given the present development of military technology, military aviation and the navy have lost their importance. This type of armament is not being reduced but replaced. Military aviation is now being almost entirely replaced by missiles. We have now sharply reduced and probably will further reduce and even halt the production of bombers and other obsolete equipment. In the navy, the submarine fleet is assuming greater importance and surface ships can no longer play the role they played in past.

Khruschev's insistence on the primacy of the rocket forces confirmed for Western analysts that the Soviet doctrine at the beginning of the 1960s was, in many respects, similar to the American <u>Massive Retaliation Doctrine</u>, according to which, any attack against the WTO would be answered with the use of all the ICBMs of the Soviet Union. It is an interesting feature of that period that the Soviet rocket forces were still under-developed. The target precision of the ICBMs was low, and their number was small. According to McNamara, the Soviet Union possessed about 200 strategic warheads during the 1962 Cuban Missile Crises, while the United States had 6,300. <u>11/</u> At the same time, Khruschev spoke about essentially higher nuclear forces in his public speeches and announcements. He probably deployed short and medium range nuclear rockets to Cuba in order to counterbalance the enormous superiority of the American ICBM forces.

The reduction of the long distance bombers was stopped during the Khruschev period and further research and development programs were initiated. The first experiments were launched to set up antiballistic missile systems. As the Soviet air defense became suitable for increasing achievements, the opinion emerged that something similar could be developed against the American missiles. A long time had passed before each realized the senselessness of building ABM systems.

The situation did not change essentially during Khruschev's last years in office. The emphasis remained on the nuclear weapons of "massive retaliation." Nevertheless, taking into consideration the number of these weapons, the Soviet doctrine of that period cannot be compared to that of the United States, and it should rather be called "minimal deterrence."

Military Strategy by Sokolovsky 12/ was, for another two decades, considered by Western experts the only authentic work about Soviet military doctrine. Published in 1962, the year of the Cuban crisis, it was the first work since the 1930s which dealt with the basic issues of strategy. According to Western reviewers, it carried the signs of compromise which emerged in practice between those who were in favor of missiles and those who were in favor of the development of conventional forces. The book found the development of all branches of the services equally necessary, not deciding about disputed strategic questions. Some chapters anticipated a prolonged war, while others expected short nuclear exchanges. In places, it alleged that a limited European war would necessarily broaden into a nuclear world war. In other places limited war was considered possible. Later, numerous Western authors used Sokolovsky's book to justify their own "worst case scenario."

Sokolovsky (or the team of authors who in fact compiled the book) undoubtedly placed great emphasis on the study "of how a future war may break out," which included a "detailed study" of, among other things, "methods of delivering the first blow." According to the authors, "the main task of Soviet military strategy is working out means for reliably repelling a surprise nuclear attack by the aggressor." The initial phase was described as "fierce and destructive"; it would "pre-determine the development and outcome of the entire war." "Unless these weapons are destroyed or neutralized, it is impossible to protect the country's vital centers from destruction, and one cannot count on successfully achieving the aim of the war even if the [enemy] troop formation deployed in the military theatres are destroyed." Some Western analysts drew the conclusion that if necessary, Soviet forces would be able to make a preventive attack against the strategic rocket forces of the United States. Others alleged that only the principle of "launch-on-warning" was introduced into the Soviet rocket forces, and only upon being informed of the launching of American missiles would the Soviet military command order the launching of its ICBMs. There was a great difference between the two interpretations, for the first saw the Soviet intentions essentially offensive, while the other presumed a reactive, defensive intention. The supporters of the two interpretations never reached an agreement.

After Khruschev, a considerable change occurred in the evaluation of the role of rocket weapons. Western sources quoted Tyoushkevitch, a Soviet expert in this connection:

After the 1964 Plenum of the Central Committee of the CPSU, certain incorrect views within the military-scientific circles connected with the over-evaluation of the potential of the atomic weapons, its influence on the character of war, and on the future development of the Armed Forces were overcome. 13/

This meant that the leading military circles regarded a limited war as possible. According to another Soviet author, Kiryan:

Bearing in mind that a war may begin without the employment of nuclear weapons, the armies of the world's largest nations, primarily those possessing nuclear weapons, are endeavoring to maintain ground forces which could successfully carry out combat assignments with the employment not only of nuclear weapons, but also conventional weapons. 14/

In 1968, Sokolovsky and Tcherednyichenko wrote the following in a military magazine:

The possibility is not excluded of wars occurring with the use of conventional weapons, as well as the limited use of nuclear means in one or several theatres of military operations. 15/

According to Western analysts, these statements indicate that Soviet strategic thinking had become similar to American thinking. The same factors which had induced the American military and political leadership to give up the doctrine of Massive Retaliation had induced Soviet leadership to make a similar amendment. Thus, the acceptance of the doctrine of Flexible Response by the United States was followed in the Soviet Union by something similar. According to the new doctrine, the Soviet army would not answer with the use of its ICBMs or use its battlefield nuclear weapons immediately, but would beat off the aggressor with its conventional forces and continue the counter-attack as long as necessary. A Soviet document from 1966 indicated that during such combative actions the military leadership would know that it was "under the constant threat of the use of nuclear weapons by the enemy."

Only in Brezhnev's speech at the 1967 conference of the European Communist and Workers' Parties were the changes mentioned. At that time, the Soviet general secretary announced that the Soviet Union did not consider a general nuclear war the unavoidable consequence of a European conflict. The introduction of the new Soviet doctrine was confirmed by public sources late in the 1970s. Ogarkov wrote in 1979:

> Soviet military strategy regards it as possible that a world war may begin and may be conducted for a certain time with only the use of conventional weapons. However, the expansion of military operations may result in it developing into a general nuclear war. 16/

Some official Soviet sources -- particularly since the mid-1970s -- have written about the fearful and destructive force of nuclear weapons and about the pointlessness of a war fought with such weapons. As a recurring formula, certain hints are made about the final victory of Socialism, even in the case of a total nuclear war, but the conclusion is unambiguous: such a war must not be fought or launched. Western authors also quote Col. Gen. Gareyev from his work published in 1985:

> "The modernization and accumulation of rocket-nuclear weapons achieved such extremes that

massive use of these weapons could result in
catastrophic consequences <u>for both sides</u>. <u>17</u>/

Ogarkov formulates in a similar manner:

> The quantitative accumulation of nuclear weapons ...
> has led to radical qualitative changes in the
> condition and potential use of these weapons, ...
> ending the possibility of carrying out so-called
> disarming strike, and ... ensuring that an immediate
> shattering response even with limited number of
> nuclear weapons ... will deprive the aggressor after
> this of the opportunity to conduct not only war, but
> any serious operations. <u>18</u>/

Certain Western sources seemed to know that
reservations were expressed in Soviet military circles
not only concerning the application of ICBMs, but also
concerning the use of shorter range nuclear weapons. In
fact, according to Soviet strategic planners, in a war
launched with conventional weapons, no battlefield
nuclear weapons must be used. Such weapons would not
serve either defensive or offensive aims. After the
first explosions the situation would become chaotic; the
commands controlling the military operations would be
unable to measure the losses and take measures to replace
them. After nuclear explosions most of the means of
communication would be gone, and there would be a break
between the control and C^3 posts and the units, or among
the units themselves.

According to Western experts, the Soviet Union would
consider the deployment of Pershing and cruise missiles
an especially dangerous step because their use would
immediately broaden a European nuclear war into an
unlimited general war. The present Soviet leadership
regards a limited nuclear war as unimaginable. This is
indicated not only by numerous official statements, but
also by the unpublished recognition that the Soviet Union
would be unable to differentiate between a limited and a
total nuclear attack. The Soviet military leadership
would be brought to consider the limited use of certain
NATO nuclear weapons an indication of total nuclear
attack; it would be compelled to launch a <u>pre-emptive</u>
strike against every nuclear launching station of NATO.

The general <u>stage of alertness</u> of the Soviet army,
according to Western evaluations, has not changed

appreciably since the 1950s. There are still no nuclear
bombs on board the strategic aircraft, at least not
continuously. A considerable portion of the submarines
are also in port and only the ballistic missile forces
are able to strike the enemy immediately upon warning.
Civil defense would need several weeks to reach the
necessary stage of alertness. The ground conventional
forces are far behind the level necessary to engage in
any type of operation. To reach a normal level at least
5-10 days would be necessary. Moreover, there are
reserve forces whose mobilization would take 60-90 days.
If the Soviet Union were compelled to transport
significant forces from a far distance to the European
theatre, it would be weeks until the desired quantity
reached its destination. The stage of alertness of the
C^3 network is very low.

Western sources say that the present Soviet military
doctrine considers a surprise American or NATO attack
improbable. According to Soviet sources, the danger of
such an attack could exist only as a consequence of some
prolonged crisis, e.g. a war in the Middle East which
gravely affected Soviet interests. In such a case, the
Soviet military command would probably have sufficient
time to reach the necessary stage of alertness. It is
reassuring that the Soviet Union has not prepared itself
for a surprise attack either. According to even the most
pessimistic NATO critics, Western reconnaissance would
sense Soviet mobilization at least one week prior to any
planned military operation, thus allowing sufficient time
for preparation.

Official skepticism notwithstanding, some Western
analysts consider the Soviet renouncement of the first
use of nuclear weapons credible. According to those
analysts, the Soviet Union has no interest in the first
use of nuclear weapons because Soviet conventional forces
supplemented by East European allies are superior to NATO
forces; in an eventual NATO attack, such a broad
protective zone (the territory of East European states)
exists along the Soviet borders that its conventional
forces stationed at distant territories would have time
to mobilize against an initial enemy advancement and
counter-attack; and if the WTO launched an attack against
NATO, the war could be kept outside of the Soviet Union
only by conventional means. The use of nuclear weapons
would obstruct the advance.

According to Western evaluations, the Soviet doctrine agrees with <u>Flexible Response</u> in that in a European armed conflict, it would regard conventional defense as sufficient. The Soviet version differs from the American doctrine in that it does not assume the development of a situation in which the Soviet Union would be pressed to engage in the first use of nuclear weapons.

Western sources draw attention to the fact that the Russian terminology differentiates between the character of the military doctrines of the United States and the Soviet Union. It describes the previous as "ustrashenyi" and the latter as "sdierzhivanyi." In English terminology, this could roughly be described as "deterrence by punishment" and "deterrence by denial." It means that the emphasis in the American doctrine is on deterrence with ultimate threatened nuclear retaliation in an enemy attack. The Soviet doctrine offers several alternatives for the military-political leadership. Although ultimately the Soviet Union also threatens with a nuclear counter-strike, the opportunity has been provided for the Soviet armed forces to respond to every challenge on an appropriate level, and with the use of appropriate weapons or branches of the services. This would be accomplished by keeping the quantity, armament and military abilities of conventional forces on a high level. Thus, the Americans threaten with <u>subsequent punishment.</u> The Soviet Union threatens with its ability to <u>prevent</u> an attack.

According to Western sources, the Soviet Union modernized its air force at the end of the 1970s, making it possible to strike successfully with conventional bombs and air-to-surface rockets against deep NATO targets. It created the so-called operational maneuver groups, which are able to penetrate the first defense lines of NATO and paralyze the enemy. Its weapons, ammunition and fuel stores were brought forward from the hinterland (most to East European countries) and filled with 60-90-day reserves. It improved the C^3 network, ensuring better communication with headquarters, with the individual army units, or with the East European allied forces.

With the improvements, the Soviet Union has apparently confronted the NATO strategic planners with a serious dilemma. In the event of a prolonged and gradually increasing crisis, NATO would have to take

434

preventive measures (e.g. remove and redeploy the mobile nuclear launchers and the aircrafts from the bases, and place bombs and rockets on board aircraft, etc.) in order to reduce the losses caused by an eventual unexpected Soviet attack. At the same time, the strategic planners are aware of the fact that these measures may be interpreted by the Soviet leadership as NATO preparation for a pre-emptive strike. The circle is completed because a pre-emptive strike can be prevented only with a pre-emptive strike. In this situation, crisis stability is considerably decreased and would probably continue to decrease.

The conclusion could be drawn from the above, that originally both military doctrines were of a defensive character but certain concepts of a deep interdiction and conventional weapon systems suitable for its accomplishment, have appeared on both sides. The primary danger is that the accelerated development of conventional military technology might, during a period of serious tension, inspire both parties to engage in a preventive strike. It can not be presumed that any party would initiate a surprise attack in a calm international situation. However, during a prolonged and escalating crisis, the danger of such an attack can emerge. Neither can allow itself to await the initiative of the other party, because the precision-guided and highly destructive weapons of the latter would make a counter-strike nearly impossible.

NOTES

1.   Such a statement was made first by Robert McNamara as early as 1963.
2.   Henry A. Kissinger, "NATO: The Next Thirty Years," Survival, Vol. 3, 1979, 266.
3.   Frank Barnaby and Marlies ter Borg, "Which way NATO? Problems facing the Alliance," paper presented at conference on "Emerging Technologies and Military Doctrine," Amsterdam, July 1985.
4.   Marek Thee, "Military Technology, Military Strategy and the Arms Race: Their Interaction," PRIO-Report, Oslo, 2/1985.
5.   D.T. Plesch, "AirLand Battle and NATO's Military Posture," ADIU Report, Vol. 7, No. 2, March-April 1985, 8 ff.

6.   Field Manual 100-5 and 7-1, 7-2 quoted by Horst Afheldt, Defensive Verteidigung, Reinbeck bei Hamburg, Rowohlt, 1983. The text is retranslated from German.

7.   Quoted by Plesch, op. cit.

8.   Ibid.

9.   Dieter Senghaas, "Noch einmal: Nachdenkens uber Nachrustung, Leviathan, 12 Jg. 1984, Heft 1, p. 5.

10. Bjorn Moller, "The Strategy of NATO and the Prospects of Non-Offensive Defence," working paper of the Centre of Peace and Conflict Research at the University of Copenhagen, No. 6, 1985.

11. Michel   Charlton,   "'Star   Wars'   or Peace-in-the-Skies: A Short History of Dreams and Nightmares," Encounter, No. 1, 1986, 14.

12. V.D. Sokolovsky, ed., Voyennaya Strategiya, Voyenizdat, Mosdva, 1962.

13. S.A. Tyushkevich, Sovietskiye Vooruzhonnie Sili: Istoriya stroitelstva, Voyenizdat, Mosdva, 1978, 476.

14. M.   Kiryan,   "Factors   Influencing   the Organizational Structure," Selected Readings from Soviet Military Thought 1959-1973. Systems Planning Corporation, Arlington, 1980, 39.

15. V.D. Sokolovsky, Tcherednyichenko, "Military Strategy and Its Problems," Selected Readings from Soviet Military Thought 1959-1973. Systems Planning Corporation, Arlington, 1980, 383.

16. N.V. Ogarkov, "Military Strategy," Sovetskaya Voennaya Entsiklopediya, Voyenizdat, Moskva, Vol. 7, 1979, 558.

17. M. Gareyev, The Views of M.V. Frunze and Contemporary Military Theory, Voyenizdat, Moskva, 1985, 240.

18. N.V. Ogarkov, "The Defence of Socialism: The Lessons of History and the Modern Period," Krasnaya Zvezda, May 9, 1984, 3, and History Teaches Vigilance, Voyenizdat, Moskva, 1985, 89.

27

No-First-Use of Nuclear Weapons and Non-Offensive Defense

Bjorn Moller

INTRODUCTION

In this article I shall sketch the interconnection between no-first-use of nuclear weapons (NFU) and the restructuring of defense in the direction of a non-offensive defense (NOD). Although I am in favor of both ideas, I will deal with their mutual inter-connection, rather than deliver any comprehensive argument for either. My point is that NFU and NOD are connected in several ways:

1. Both NOD and NFU serve the same strategic purpose: Stability. Both aim at avoiding any unintentional armed confrontation between the blocks.

2. NFU implies conventionalization of defense structures. But apparently the only alternative to NOD is presented by the various deep-strike strategies -- e.g. AirLand Battle (ALB) and FOFA --which will make matters worse.

3. NOD will make NFU possible by increasing defensive potentials.

4. NOD will necessitate NFU both because of its essential objectives of damage limitation and stability -- and because of its tactical and operational principles.

5. NOD, in a "zonal" version, will present a logical follow-up to NFU, and on the nuclear weapons-free zones (NWFZ) connected herewith.

THE CONCEPT OF NFU
(NO-FIRST-USE OF NUCLEAR WEAPONS)

NFU can assume several different forms. NFU may be:
- A declaratory policy with no implications for strategy or posture -- i.e. a mere renunciation of the "right" of nuclear first-use;

- A strategic reform, implemented either by the abolition of all nuclear arms not compatible with NFU, thus eliminating first-use-incentives (the "hardware" approach). Or by revising doctrines, command structures, field manuals, etc. (the "software" approach).

As a declaratory policy NFU has already been adopted by China and the Soviet Union and (in an extremely emasculated form) by NATO nuclear powers, in the form of a conditional pledge not to use nuclear weapons against non-nuclear states.

But a declaratory NFU is of little avail as a stabilizing or confidence-building measure unless it is implemented. And as a minimum the logical implication of NFU is the removal of all nuclear weapons which could only be used if they were used first, i.e. in contravention of the pledge. This applies first of all to nuclear weapons in vulnerable positions (e.g. near the inner-German border): Atomic Demolition Munitions (ADMs) and nuclear artillery shells as well as short-range ballistic missiles (SRBMs): Lance, Pershing 1, SS-21, SS-12 mod. Aircraft with insufficient shelter fall into the same category as, for instance, NATO's quick reaction alert (QRA) aircraft. Such nuclear weapons are inevitably under the "use-them-or-lose-them" spell and will entail great incentives for preemption and first use.

The nuclear arms which are most incompatible to an NFU policy are those which, in addition to the above characteristics, also place the opponent in an analogous situation, i.e. nuclear weapons with hard-target-kill capability and providing very short warning. They thus place time-urgent targets at risk and create incentives on the part of the opponent for preemption and first use. This applies especially to modern stationary ICBMs and IRBMs with a low Circular Error Probable (CEP) as e.g. the Pershing 2.

Nuclear weapons which may be compatible with a NFU-policy are those which are deployed in invulverable positions and which may thus be withheld for strictly retaliatory purposes: submarine-launched ballistic and cruise missiles (SLBMs and SLCMs) (the latter, however, entail a range of other negative effects), intercontinental bombers in association with an efficient system for early warning (DEW/BMEWS) and with the option of airborne alert, and finally, mobile intercontinental missiles (ICBMs) (which, however, also pose other risks).

It applies to neither tactical aircraft nor missiles, however, because of the extremely short warning they provide.

The most NFU-compatible nuclear weapons would be those which possess all these characteristics and which lack any capability of threatening the time-urgent targets of the opponent, due to their lack of hard-target-kill (HTK) capability by virtue of their high CEP.

Even after the removal of all nuclear weapons which are incompatible with NFU (and thus removing the first-use incentives) the first-use option remains. It can hardly be totally eliminated except by complete nuclear disarmament. But it can be almost achieved by the above precautions as well as by a deliberate vulnerability to retaliation. In addition, institutional barriers might be raised against first-use, be it in the form of a congressional veto on presidential nuclear clearance or (but perhaps far-fetched) by the handing over of all American, British and French nuclear weapons to a Multilateral Force (MLF) which could only initiate nuclear use with the approval of all members. A dual-key arrangement for a Joint Task Force (as proposed by former second-in-command of the US Army in Europe, A.S. Collins, 1/) would be a step in the same direction.

CONCEPTS OF NOD (NON-OFFENSIVE DEFENSE)

A non-offensive defense might best be defined in a negative sense: As a defense with no capability for offensive (or counter-offensive) operations against enemy territory. This can be secured in various ways:

1. By totally renouncing all components, which (in combination with others) would form an offensive capability: Strategic mobility, deep interdiction-capability, etc.

2. By deliberately (and credibly) omitting at least one necessary component, thus deliberately "emasculating" one's offensive capability: In the case of islands this component might e.g. be a major navy or deep strike systems. Terrestrial powers might instead renounce bridge-building equipment, air support over foreign territory, long range C3I systems and logistics etc. 2/

3. By a reduction in quantitative terms of offensive components, eliminating the option of even limited offensives under optimal circumstances.

4. By a dispersed deployment of "traditional" forces in the rear, combined with strictly defensive forward defense measures as e.g. fire barriers (by means of passive munitions) or an infantry-network -- as proposed by e.g. Eckhardt Afheldt, 3/ the Starnberg research team, Alvin Saperstein, 4/ Manfred Bertele 5/ and Sverre Lodgaard. 6/ Such zonal arrangements would give the opponent ample warning time and thus adequate mobilization margin. If the force ratio is not too uneven this would also eliminate any genuine offensive capability.

Verification problems make the second way sub-optimal, because the option of simply adding the missing component (or hiding it "up one's sleeve") could never be eliminated. Neither the second nor the third way can be considered optimal because of the problem of context: They would have to be implemented for the entire alliance, taking into account not only existing formal alliances, but including also potential "worst-case-alliances" as the Soviets might perceive them. The fourth way is of course a very sub-optimal and temporary expedient because deployments could always be altered upon relatively short notice. On the other hand, it may well be the most realistic option, at least for the short term.

Unless otherwise indicated, I shall, however, refer below to the "ideal model": The total absence of all "offensive components." Until now the best proposal is probably the model developed by Horst Afheldt for Central Europe: 7/ A territorial defense consisting of three overlapping networks, aiming at the attrition of a ground force invasion:

1. A stationary network of "techno-commands:" Infantry in dispersed positions covering the entire territory and armed with precision guided munitions (PGMs) for anti-tank and air defense purposes.

2. A dispersed network (also covering the entire territory) of missile-commands for concentrated fire against massive breakthroughs.

3. A redundant and decentralized C3I-network -- e.g. for target acquisition for the missile commands.

THE REASON WHY BOTH NOD AND FNU ENHANCE STABILITY

The most likely danger of armed conflict between the blocks is an unintentional war initiated with preemptive strike or (less likely) a preventive operation with the aim of preventing assumed enemy plans for aggression. Theoretically one might thus eliminate the risk in two ways: By political confidence-building and by non-offensive military strategy and posture. I shall deal with the military aspects.

The prime objective of defense must be stability: first of all, crises must be avoided. Second, crises must not escalate into war. And third, war -- if it should break out -- must not be allowed to escalate into all-encompassing nuclear destruction. We are thus dealing with multiple thresholds which should not be transgressed. NATO's strategy of Flexible Response, however, is the exact opposite of this, planning to employ various forms of military escalation as "tools" for crisis management: Deployment of U.S. reinforcements in Europe, manning of forward defense positions, placing missile batteries in launch position, delegating "pack-ages" of nuclear munitions to field commanders 8/ (...) nuclear clearance ... Every single step may be perceived by the opponent as threatening. He will therefore counter-escalate, etc., until one of the parties finally initiates armed conflict with a preemptive strike aimed at the time-urgent targets of the opponent in order to prevent him from preempting against one's own time-urgent targets.

When the threshold of war is crossed, the incentives to cross the nuclear threshold are enormous. Even if nuclear clearance is given according to the Athens guidelines (after due consultation with allies, etc.) 9/ -- and one cannot assume it -- commanders in the field will still be facing the familiar use-them-or-lose-them dilemma. This applies especially in the case of forward deployed nuclear storage sites and means of delivery, which would be vulnerable to even conventional attacks. But in any case the fear of enemy nuclear preemption would haunt those in command. Their incentives for nuclear preemption would thus be ample.

According to Bernard Rogers, the crossing of the threshold would occur after a few days of conventional fighting. This prediction might even prove too optimistic, at least as far as the Central Front is concerned, considering e.g. the Soviet option of using Operational Maneuver Groups (OMGs), 10/ parachute units, 11/ or speznaz-units 12/ as well as deep-interdiction systems to threaten nuclear targets. After crossing the nuclear threshold control of escalation would be extremely unlikely, 13/ and the threshold of global holocaust (500-2000 EMT) would probably be transgressed after a few days or earlier.

This unstable situation would be somewhat mitigated by an implemented NFU: A number of time-urgent targets would be removed (ADMs, artillery systems, SRBMs, IRBMs, QRA-aircraft with associated command, control and communications (C3I) installations, etc.), and the incentives of the opponent to preempt against these targets would thus be eliminated. If nuclear preemption could thus be avoided, stabilization might be expected to "spread downwards," reducing likewise the incentives for conventional preemptions: There would be no nuclear targets against which to preempt by conventional deep interdiction means. Current dual capable systems would become strictly conventional -- and thus less tempting to preempt against, etc.

A NOD reform would remove most of the remaining incentives for preemption: There would be no threatening forces to neutralize. There would be no lucrative targets for massive attacks (neither conventional nor nuclear). There would be only dispersed light forces. And there would be no front-line to break through by a massive, "blitzkrieg" offensive because the defense is territorial in its coverage.

The defense could of course be defeated, but only by military means which would imply risks of escalation, as e.g. chemical weapons (targetted for area coverage) or nuclear weapons. This would entail irrationally big risks, however, because neither the retaliatory nor the first-use option would have been eliminated. And any other version of attack would be time-and resource-demanding, and therefore irrational, at least according to Soviet strategy. 14/

Both NFU and NOD thus enhance stability by eliminating incentives for preemption. They eliminate the most likely form of war: the inadvertent war. However, there remains the (very unlikely) possibility of premeditated war with the aim of conquering foreign territory. In the section below I shall attempt to argue the case that neither NOD or NFU make this more attractive, rather the contrary.

THE REASONS WHY NFU NECESSITATES NOD

Most proponents (and all critics) admit that NFU would necessitate changes in conventional strategy and posture. But whether this change would imply higher armament levels (in quantitative terms) and/or transarmament (in qualitative terms) and if so, in which direction, is disputed. The quantitative proposal is seldom heard because of the huge financial and demographic problems the attainment of a conventional "balance" on the Central Front would imply. 15/

The transarmament proponents form two different wings: Those who advocate greater reliance on (conventional) offensive capability, and those who propose a self-sufficient, strictly defensive defense posture. The new offensive strategies, however, rarely aim at a genuine NFU but rather at a No-Early-First-Use (NEFU) strategy and posture, and they can be divided into three categories, depending on the priority they attach to the various means. None of the three concepts would solve the problems created by NFU for conventional defense. They would rather reduce stability, and they would probably not attain their objective.

1. Increasing deep interdiction-capability, including Offensive Counter Air (OCA): FOFA 16/ ESECS 17/ and others. 18/

2. Increasing the offensive capability of NATO ground forces: S. Huntington. 19/

3. Increasing both deep interdiction and offensive ground force capabilities: Air Land Battle 20/ and others.

Raising the nuclear threshold by a NEFU posture: 21/

- The increased capability for deep interdiction would, albeit by conventional means, place the time-urgent targets of the WTO at risk, including their prime airfields (M.O.B.s) 22/ and nuclear installations. This implies an increased incentive for preemption, and thus a reduction of stability.

- The same applies to a certain extent to the offensive ground forces capability which would likewise pose a threat to vital installations, including nuclear ones. In addition, it might create the possibility of intervention in internal WTO-conflicts, a prospect which would worry the USSR. 23/

- The offensive ground-forces capability would demand a forward deployment of weapon systems and personnel. This would increase the number of time-urgent targets (e.g. POMCUS-depots) for the deep interdiction systems (and OMGs), of the WTO and thus put an increased premium on WTO-preemption.

- The logical WTO response to the threat against its second echelon forces would be to assign a higher priority to its first (strategic) echelon, especially the Group of Soviet Forces in Germany (GSFG) with perhaps an increased emphasis on OMGs.

- The deep interdiction capability relies to a great extent on dual capable systems: current DCAs as e.g. Tornado 24/ and, in the longer run on E.T.-weapons as e.g. CAM-40, MRASM, Boss, T-16, T-22, etc. 25/ This will increase WTO uncertainty concerning the character of the interdiction, with the potential risk of an early crossing of the nuclear threshold by the Pact.

- A logical WTO response would be deployment of its own conventional or dual capable deep-interdiction systems (SS-21, SS12-mod, SS-23), 26/ thus revealing deep strike as a "fallacy of the last step." - As long as the official goal is only NEFU (and not NFU), the WTO might still suspect "integrated use" of nuclear weapons (as in the ALB-doctrine, 27/) and the threats mentioned above would therefore most likely meet with a nuclear response. The same result would probably follow from the use of "quasi-nuclear" weapons with a collateral damage in the same range as for sub-kiloton (or enhanced radiation, "neutron") nukes. 28/

While the first potential consequence of NFU seems excluded (financially and politically), and the second will only make matters worse, we are left with the third option: combining NFU with NOD, in either a comprehensive or a partial version.

The partial solution, adding "NOD components" to current forces, perhaps in combination with a limited increase in force levels, has e.g. been proposed by W. Kaufmann 29/ and by the Union of Concerned Scientists 30/ who both advocate permanent tank barriers along the West German border. The UCS wishes to supplement this with infantry anti-tank groups in the border areas.

More radical solutions, in the form of a comprehensive NOD in combination with a NFU, have been

proposed by Horst Afheldt 31/ and Jochen Loser. 32/
That such defense models would make nuclear weapons
obsolete for any other purpose than for deterring nuclear
attack is the point I intend to make in the following
paragraph.

NOD should make a "genuine" NFU possible by its
increased defense potential. Under a NFU/NOD regime,
defense has fewer threats to meet, and would be able to
meet these threats even better than the current posture.
Whereas we can now ignore the risk of inadvertent war, we
are left with the possibility of a premeditated WTO
aggression against NATO.

In this case, however, the only likely form of
aggression would be a massive attack against an area
representing an intrinsic value sufficient to make an
aggression appear worthwhile. To achieve his objective
the aggressor must, first of all, establish control of
the society attacked. 33/ Territorial control alone will
not do, because mere territorial gain would seem absurd
on the part of the USSR: Square miles is not in
excessive demand in the Soviet Union! Secondly, this
control, according to Soviet military doctrine, has to be
achieved quickly, partly because a protracted war would
bring the superior force potentials of NATO into action:
The vast economic resources, etc. 34/ Finally, the
aggression must not escalate to the nuclear level. The
conflict has to remain limited.

It is this kind of aggression that NOD should be
able to deter, and it implies three strategic
imperatives:

- An attack should be made time-consuming, thus
making a blitzkrieg strategy futile;

- An attack should require forces out of proportion
to the values which the aggressor might lay hands on by
establishing control;

- The aggressor should be unable to secure his
conquest in the long run.

A non-offensive defense should thus aim at an
efficient attrition of enemy forces, making a quick
breakthrough impossible. The risk of early defeat should
be avoided by the territorial and decentralized character
of defense. It should avoid the great confrontation
battle which is a conditio-sine-qua-non for victory in a
blitzkrieg. 35/ On the contrary the defense should
fight according to a strategy of "non-battles" 36/ in a
"guerrilla-like" manner.

The defenders might, of course, be defeated one by one by infantry, but this would critically hamper the momentum of the attack: The invader would not only have to move forward, but also outward, because the entire territory would have to be conquered, and the defenders might simply go into cover only to re-emerge later. To achieve the defeat of such a defense, very large forces would be required, perhaps an unattainable number even for the USSR, and at the very least, altogether out of proportion with the expected gains.

Alternative forms of attack such as area-covering attacks by chemical or nuclear means would inevitably escalate the conflict and thus blunt the intentions of the invader. On the one hand, the aggressor would risk nuclear retaliation (only first-use is excluded, not retaliation), and on the other hand he would negate his very purpose of the attack by turning the conquered territory into a heap of radio-active rubble.

Combining non-offensive military defense with civilian-based defense measures would make a longterm control of society unlikely. A fall-back strategy for civilian defense as proposed by e.g. J. Galtung and the Nolte brothers 37/ and by the British Alternative Defense Commission 38/ might thus be advisable.

We are now left with the question of whether a NOD/NFU posture might in fact increase the defense potential. Because it has never been put to the test of actual combat -- a deficiency it shares with current postures -- we must confine ourselves to evaluating the evidence by theoretical means alone. Several things indicate that the NOD/NFU posture might live up to the demands made on it:

- It can take advantage of the natural and man-made defensive positions provided by terrain 39/ -- and especially so if the forces consist of locals, possibly of militia-character.

- It can take advantage of specializing on pure defense, e.g. by giving priority to tactical mobility over strategic and to firepower and precision over mobility and armor.

- It can meet the imperatives of modern sensor technologies by remaining hidden by virtue of renouncing mobility and concentration. 40/

- It can increase the relative weapons effect by emphasizing weapons, rather than platforms and thus achieve a better "teeth-to-tail" ratio.

- It can re-allocate resources from nuclear to conventional forces, both financially and (to a certain extent) materially.

-It might perform the role of a common denominator for multinational forces along the Central Front, thus avoiding current incompatibilities between the various front sectors. 41/

-It can avoid self-deterrence, inevitably connected with the nuclear option and thus make timely mobilization possible.

These factors seem to indicate that an NFU/NOD strategy would be able to meet all "reasonable" defense needs as well as the present defense, and without its apocalyptic perspectives!

THE REASONS WHY NOD NECESSITATES NFU

If you adopt an NFU, NOD is recommended. But if you adopt a NOD posture, you will inevitably have to adopt an NFU strategy: The prime characteristic of NOD is its strict defensiveness, i.e. the deliberate avoidance of posing threats to the opponent. This characteristic is impossible to sustain while retaining the first-use option and posture.

But NOD might (and probably should) be combined with a nuclear retaliatory capability. This capability, however, does not necessarily have to be materially linked to conventional defense, since its only mission would now be to deter nuclear threats or attacks. NOD could therefore be complemented with a minimum deterrence strategy and posture, implying neither vertical nor horizontal "extended deterrence." 42/

In addition to this political/strategic imperative a tactical/operation imperative applies: A NOD has only a limited capability of point defense. This necessitates a reduction of the number of potential targets. And such targets would inevitably be nuclear storage sites and means of delivery as well as associated command centers. That these targets have to be avoided makes an NFU-posture necessary.

WHY NOD MIGHT BE A LOGICAL FOLLOW-UP ON NFU

There thus seems to be a logical interconnection between NFU and NOD: They both aim at the same goal (stability), and they function reciprocally: NFU without NOD might worsen the problems it was supposed to solve, and NOD without NFU is impossible. But this logical interconnection might prevent the implementation of both concepts, if one (by being unrealistic) blocks the way for the other and vice versa. This fortunately does not have to be the case, as the logical interconnection may be implemented by a step-by-step approach: There are several proposals for this strategy, both from peace researchers and from the political arena. Sverre Lodgaard from SIPRI has thus proposed a follow-up on the so-called "Palme-corridor" in Central Europe: 43/ He proposes to supplement the 150 km. stretch on both sides of the border free of tactical nuclear weapons 44/ with a parallel zone free from potentially offensive conventional weapon systems: Heavy and medium artillery (over 200 t./caliber over 100 mm). (The rule automatically would exclude dual-capable howitzers, etc.) Bridge building material, air defense systems of a certain range, etc. should also be withdrawn. Instead the zone should be defended by light infantry, VTOL-aircraft requiring no regular runways, drones (RPVs) etc. This should provide longer warning as the zone would simply act as an early warning system. 45/

On the political arena in the SPD Andreas von Bulow has proposed a model very similar to a zonal model. 46/ And the British Labor Party has likewise committed itself to a strictly conventional strategy, with NFU as a first step and "defensive deterrence" as the second. 47/ Such ideas, however, seem to demand a certain reciprocity and might be obtainable with a step-by-step approach: A draft treaty for a chemical weapons-free zone has already been negotiated by the SED of the GDR and the West German SPD 48/ and it will be followed by negotiations on a NWFZ for Central Europe.

The logical third step would be an OWFZ (offensive weapons free zone) with a depth of e.g. 200 km.s. As a minimum this zone would require a restructuring and perhaps withdrawal of the GSFG. This process might provide an impetus for a restructuring of defense doctrines in the smaller WTO countries as a non-offensive trend. There are many indications that these countries yearn for this development, 49/ which Romania has already realized in the form of a Yugoslav-inspired doctrine at territorial defense. 50/ That this kind of trend would encounter obstinate Soviet resistance may be taken for granted.

One might, on the other hand, imagine a "GRIT-process" along the lines of Charles Osgood's 51/ description, consisting of limited, reciprocating, unilateral steps gradually leading to a NFU/NOD posture along the Central Front. The steps need not be (and maybe cannot be) symmetrical. Unilateralism might alternate with bi- or multilateral negotiations (MBRF, CSCE, etc.). The schedule might for instance look something like this:

1. NATO reciprocation of the Soviet NFU declaration.

2. Soviet withdrawal of SS-21 and SS-12.mod from the GDR and the CSSR.

3. Treaty on establishing a NWFZ in Central Europe.

4. Withdrawal of ADMs and nuclear artillery munitions.

5. Treaty on a CWFZ in Central Europe.

6. Non-aggression treaty between NATO and the WTO.

7. NOD measures along single NATO front sectors (British Army of the Rhine (BAOR) and RAF or the Bundeswehr), e.g. redeployment of tank divisions, infantry anti-tank barriers, etc.

8. NOD measures in the GSFG (as e.g. splitting up divisions, removal of bridge building equipment, dual capable artillery, etc.)

9. Withdrawal of SRBMs and chemical weapons.

10. (......)

11. (......)

12. Withdrawal of GLCM, Pershing 2, SS-20, etc.

13. Complete NOD-implementation in the Bundeswehr and/or the BAOR.

14. (......)

15. Withdrawal of GSFG and Soviet troops in CSSR.

16. Withdrawal of the US Army and USAF from the FRG (except Berlin).

The ideas are not new; they are gradually acquiring a political constituency, and one might be optimistic if e.g. the Labor Party and the SPD regain power. One cannot predict Soviet response, but a favorable reception for such a development is not out of the question.

NOTES

1. A.S. Collins, "Current NATO Strategy: A Recipe for Disaster," in G. Prins (ed.), The Nuclear Crisis Reader. Vintage Books, New York, 1984, 40.

2. E. Muller, "Dilemma Sicherheitspolitik -- Tradierte Muster Westdeutscher Sicherheitspolitik und Alternativoptionen: Ein Problem und Leistungsvergleich," in E. Muller (ed.), Dilemma Sicherheit -- Beitrage zur Diskussion uber Militarische Alternativkonzepte. Baden-Baden: Nomos Verlag, 1984.

3. Eckhardt Afheldt, "Verteidigung ohne Selbstzerstorung. Vorschlag fur den Einsatz einer leichten Infanterie," in C. F. von Weizsacker (ed), Praxis der defensiven Verteidigung; and (in abbreviated version) in Horst Afheldt, "Defensive Verteidigung," Spanhola, Hamburg, 1983.

4. A.M. Saperstein, "Non-Provocative Defense and Disengagement Zones" paper for conference on "European Security Requirements and the MBFR Talks," University of Toronto, May 1985; and A.M. Saperstein, "Depletion Zones and Enhanced Non-Provocative Defence in Europe," paper for Stockholm International Peace Research Institute workshop on "Measures to Reduce the Fear of Surprise Attack in Europe," Stockholm, 1-3/12 1983.

5. Manfred Bertele, "Struktur und Dislozierung von Landstreitkraften in Europa. Mogliche Funktionen Vereinbarter Beschrankungen bei der Schaffung Militarischen Gleichgewichts," in U. Nehrlich (ed.), Die Einhegung Sowjettischer Macht. Kontrolliertes Militarisches Gleichgewicht als Bedingung Europaischer Sicherheit. Nomos Verlag, Baden-Baden, Wamas, 1982.

6. Sverre Lodgaard, "Policies of Common Security in Europe," in Stockholm International Peace Research Institute, Policies for Common Security, Tayland Francis, London, 1985.

7. Horst Afheldt, Verteidigung und Frieden: Politik mit Militarischen Mitteln. Munchen/Wien; Defensive Verteidigung, 1976.

8. Department of the Army: Field Manual FM101-31-1/Marine Corps. Fleet Marine Force Manual FMFM 11-4: Staff Officers Field Manual: Nuclear Weapons Employment Doctrine and Procedures, 1977, p. 4 og 9ff.

9. Cf. L. Freedmann, "The No-First-Use Debate and the Theory of Thresholds," in F. Blackaby, S. Lodgaard and J. Goldblatt (eds.), No First Use, SIPRI, 1984, 75; and J.J. Holst, Moving Toward No First Use in Practice,

450

in JD Steinbummer and LV Sigal (eds.), Alliance Security: NATO and the No-First-Use Question, Washington, D.C., The Brookings Institute, 1982, 173f.

10. C.N. Donnelly, "The Soviet Operational Manouvre Group: A New Challenge for NATO," International Defense Review, No. 9, 1982, 1177ff; C.N. Donnelly, "Soviet Operational Concepts in the 1980's," in European Security Study Group, Strengthening Conventional Deterrence, London, 1983, 125ff; J.G. Hines, "The Soviet Conventional Offensive in Europe," Military Review, April 1984, 9ff.

11. D.T. Isby, "Soviet Airmobile and Air Assault Brigades," Janes Defence Weekly, 14/9, 1985, 561ff.

12. V. Suvorov, "Speznaz: The Soviet Union's Special Forces," International Defence Review, No. 9, 1983; G. Hoden, "Defining the Spetznaz Threat," ADIU Reports No. 7, 4, 6ff; Cf. the story of speznaz agents at Greenham Common, Janes Defence Weekly, 25, January 1986.

13. R.S. MacNamara, G. Kennan, McGeorge Bundy and G. Smith, "Nuclear Weapons and the Atlantic Alliance," Foreign Affairs, Summer 1982; A.S. Collins, op. cit, 40/. J.M. Lee, "The Role of Nuclear Weapons," paper for Niels Bohr Centennial, Copenhagen, 1985, 18ff.

14. N. Leites, "The Soviet Style of War," in D. Leebaert (ed.), Soviet Military Thinking, Allan & Unwin, London, 1981, 192ff; and P.H. Vigor, Soviet Blitzkrieg Theory, St. Martins Press, New York, 1983.

15. G. Krell, T. Risse-Kappen and H.-J. Schmidt: "The No-First-Use-Question in Germany," in J.D. Steinbruner & L.V. Sigal (eds.), Alliance Security: NATO and the No-First-Use Question, Washington: Brookings, 1983, 160ff, cf. Bundesministerium der Verteidigung (Federal Ministry of Defense): Weissbuch, 1985, 386ff.

16. B. Rogers, "Sword and Shield: ACE Attack on Warsaw Pact Follow-On Forces," NATO's 16 Nations, vol. 28, no. 1, February 1983; B. Rogers, "Follow-On Forces Attack," NATO Review, no. 1, 1985; R. Colsaat, "NATO Strategy: Under Different Influences," ADIU Report no. 6, 1984; J.S. Wit, "Deep Strike: NATO's New Defense Concept and Its Implications for Arms Control," Arms Control Today, vol. 13, no. 10; R. de Wijk, "NATO Plans for the 1990s," ADIU Report no. 5, 1985; D.T. Plesch, "Airland Battle and NATO's Military Posture," ADIU Report No. 7, 1984; Institut fur Friedensforschung und Sicherheitspolitik an der Universitat Hamburg, "Angriff in die Tiefe," (Information Paper) Ein Diskussionsbeitrag zum Rogersplan, Hamburg 1985.

17. ESECS (European Security Study Group), Strengthening Conventional Deterrence in Europe: Proposals for the 1980s, Macmillan, London, 1983; ESECS, "A Program for the 1980's. Report of the special panel," London, 1985, reviewed in J. Steinhoff, "Dream or Reality: Hardware for FOFA," NATO's Sixteen Nations, April-May 1985, 24ff.

18. Die Grunen, Angriff als Verteidigung, Dic Gunnenim Burdsstag, Bonn, 1984; P. Berg and G. Gerolff, "Deep Strike: New Technologies for Conventional Interdiction," SIPRI Yearbook, 1984; J.E. Tegnelia, "Emerging Technology for Conventional Deterrence," International Defense Review, no. 5, 1985; North Atlantic Assembly Military Committee, Subcommittee on Conventional Deterrence in Europe: Interim Report, 1984.

19. S. Huntington, "Conventional Deterrence and Conventional Retaliation," International Security, vol. 8, no. 3, cf. the critique of this concept: K.A. Dunn and W.O. Staudenmeier, "The Retaliatory Offensive and Operational Realities in NATO," Survival, no. 3, 1985.

20. Headquarters Department of the Army, "Field Manual 100-5: Operations," 20/8, 1982.

21. I have dealt somewhat more elaborately with this question in B. Moller, "The Strategy Crisis of NATO and the Concept of Non-Offensive Defence," working paper no. 6, Centre of Peace and Conflict Research, Copenhagen, 1985.

22. ESECS, op. cit. 1983 (#17), 21f and 152f; cf. D.R. Cotter, "Potential Future Roles for Conventional and Nuclear Roles in Defence of Western Europe, ibid., p.220ff; Rogers, "Sword and Shield," p.26; Subcom. on Conventional ..., op. cit. 21ff.

23. Cf. S. Tiedtke, "Abschreckung und ihre Alternativen. Die Sowjettische Sicht einer Westlichen Debatte," Texte und Materialien der Forschungsstatte der evangelischen Studiengemeinschaften, Reihe A no. 20, Heidelberg, 1986.

24. G. Dorgerloh, "Der Tornado wird fur FOFA armiert," Europaische Wehrkunde nr. 5, 1985, 271ff; or the B-52 (M. Feazel, "NATO Deploys Boeing B-52s in Deep-Strike Attack Exercise," Aviation Week & Space Technology, Sept. 9, 1985.

25. M.C. Gordon, "Technology and NATO Defence: Weighing the Options," in J.R. Golden, A.A. Clark and B.F. Arlinghouse, Conventional Deterrence - Alternatives for European Defense, Banks, Lexington,Ky. 1984, 150ff,

452

esp. 158f; K.K. Stratman, "Prospective Tasks and Capabilities Required for NATO's Conventional Forces," Supp. Paper for ESECS op. cit.(#17), 186ff; D.R. Cotter loc. cit.(#17), 209ff.

26. Janes Defence Weekly, 2/11, 1985, 975f.

27. Field Manual 100-5, p. 2.3 and 7.3.

28. J.P. Robinson: "Quasinuclear Weapons," in W. Gutteridge and T. Taylor, The Dangers of New Weapon Systems, Macmillan, London, 1983, 151ff, c.f. Cotter loc. cit., 228ff, who is all too happy to mention their "nuclear equivalence" as an argument for conventionalization.

29. W.K. Kaufmann, "Non-Nuclear Deterrence," in J. Steinbruner and L.V. Sigal (eds.), op. cit. 68f.

30. Union of Concerned Scientists, No First Use Report, Council of Concerned Scientists, Washington, 1983, 28f.; cf. J.M. Lee, op. cit.

31. H. Afheldt, "Defensive Verteidigung,"; H. Afheldt, "The Necessity, Preconditions and Consequences of a No-First-Use Policy," in F. Blackaby, S. Lodgaard and J. Goldblatte (eds.), op. cit., 57ff.

32. J. Loser, "Weder rot noch tot - Uberleben ohne Atomkrieg" - Eine Sicherheitspolitische Alternative, Munchen, 1982, 176 et passim.

33. P.H. Vigor, Soviet Blitzkrieg Theory, St. Martin's Press, New York, 1983, 27ff.

34. Ibid., 1-7 et passim. Cf. C. Donnelly, "Soviet Military Doctrine," Military Review, August 1982, 42ff; C. Donnelly, "Soviet Operational Concepts in the 1980's," 114ff.

35. Vigor, op. cit, 79.

36. Cf. G. Brossollet, Essai sur la Non-Bataille, Editions Belin, Paris, 1975.

37. J. Galtung. There Are Alternatives, London: Spokesman, 1985; H.H. Nolte and W. Nolte, Ziviler Widerstand und Autonome Abwehr, Baden-Baden: Nomos Verlagsgesellschaft, 1984.

38. Alternative Defence Commission, Defence Without the Bomb, Taylor & Francis, London, 1983, p.244.

39. Cf. F. Uhle-Wettler, Gefechtsfeld Mitteleuropa -- Gefahr der Ubertechnisierung von Streitkraften, Guthersloh, 1981, 27ff; Union of Concerned Scientists, op. cit., 27.

40. H. Afheldt, "Defensive Verteidigung," 53f.

41. Cf. J.A. Blackwell, "Conventional Doctrine: Integrating Alliance Forces," in Golden, Clark and Arlinghouse, op. cit., 141ff.

42. Cf. "historical" varieties: (1964): L. Szilard, "'Minimal Deterrent' vs. Saturation Parity" in H. Kissinger (ed.), Problems of National Strategy, Praeger, New York, 1965, 376ff; and L. Freedman, op. cit., 245ff og two modern versions: J.M. Lee, op. cit., 26f. Cf. H.A. Feiveson, R. Ullman, F. von Hippel, "Reducing U.S. and Soviet Nuclear Arsenals," Bulletin of the Atomic Scientists, August 1985, 144ff.

43. Report of the Independent Commission on Disarmament and Security Issues, "Common Security: A Programme for Disarmament," London, 1982.

44. A range which S. Lodgaard, however, proposes to reduce to 100 kms.: "Disengagement and Nuclear-Weapons Free Zones: Raising the Nuclear Threshold," in S. Lodgaard and M. Thee (eds.), Nuclear Disengagement in Europe, Stockholm: Stockholm International Peace Research Institute, 1983, 157ff.

45. S. Lodgaard and P. Berg, Disengagement in Central Europe, in Shadgaard and M. Thee (eds.), Nuclear Disengagement in Europe, Taylor & Francis, London, 1983, ibid, p.248ff.

46. A. von Bulow, "Strategie Vertrauensschaffender Sicherheitsstrukturen in Europa: Wege zur Sicherheitspartnerschaft," Blatter fur Deutsche und Internationale Politik, no. 5, 1985, 1267ff.

47. Labour Party, "Defence and Security for Britain," Statement to the Annual Conference 1984 by the National Executive Committee, Manchester, 1984, 20 et passim.

48. Fur eine Chemiewaffenfrie Zone in Europa, Gemeinsame Politische Initiative der Sozialistischen Einheitspartei Deutschlands und der Sozialdemokratischen Partei Deutschlands, Verland List im Bild, Dresden, 1985.

49. Chr. Jones, Soviet Influence in Eastern Europe: Political Autonomy and the Warsaw Pact, Praeger, New York, 1981; Chr. Jones, "Soviet Military Doctrine and Warsaw Pact Exercises," in D. Leebaert (ed.), op. cit., 225ff; Chr. Jones, "National Armies and National Sovereignty," in D. Holloway and J.M.O. Sharp (eds.), The Warsaw Pact: Alliance in Transition, London, 1984, 87ff.

50. Studies and Research Centre for Military History and Theory, "National Defence: The Romanian View," Military Publishing House, Bucharest, 1976. Cf.

R. Lukic, "La Dissuassion Populaire Yougoslave: Cahiers d'Etudes Strategiques," CIRPES, Paris, 1985.

51. C.E. Osgood, "An Alternative to War or Surrender," Univ. of Illinois Press, Urbana, IL, 1962. Cf. D. Granberg, "GRIT in the Final Quarter: Reversing the Arms Race through Unilateral Initiatives," <u>Bulletin of Peace Proposals</u>, no. 3, 1978, 210ff.

28

Common Security and the Concept of Non-Offensive Defense

Anders Boserup

Under "classical" strategic conditions, before the advent of nuclear weapons, force could be treated as a general instrument of national policy. The use of force and the threat of the use of force could serve a variety of different purposes, including offensive ones. But the situation in Europe is no longer classical. Any war in Europe, even strictly non-nuclear war, would take place in the shadow of the nuclear arsenals of the two super-powers and of the risk of escalation to ultimate disaster. In the event of war, avoidance of nuclear escalation would be the overriding concern of all belligerents. I refer to such a situation as "sub-nuclear."

Because Europe is a central area of confrontation between the two main nuclear powers, the European states are "trapped" in this sub-nuclear situation. It is a context which they must always take into account in their defense policies and in their military planning. While they cannot withdraw from this sub-nuclear situation, suitable military policies can make it less deadly.

In a sub-nuclear situation the political aims that may be pursued by military means are severely limited. The use of force to achieve goals is excluded and the only use that can be made of the military instrument is as a deterrent to avert war and, if this fails, to try to terminate it without disaster. While this is generally recognized, its implications in terms of defense policy have not been fully drawn. This paper is an attempt to analyze these implications at the most general level, contrasting them with the conditions which prevailed in the past.

The fact that in Europe today military force can be used only to prevent war is generally conceived in terms of the notion of "deterrence." This is an extremely vague concept which can be used to justify any military

455

program whatever, and yet it provides a perspective on the question of war-prevention which is much too narrow. To speak of "dissuasion" rather than "deterrence" is already an improvement, because the term "dissuasion" does not assume that the prevention of war can be based only on terror and threats. In a more realistic discussion of war-prevention two causes of war must be distinguished: (1) deliberate, premeditated attack by one side based on a calculation (however mistaken it may be), of the likely costs and benefits and (2) crisis-escalation where both are drawn against their will into a spiral of hostile acts through their very efforts to avoid it.

It is generally agreed that the prospect of a deliberate attack is remote, while the risk of unintended escalation in a crisis is quite real. Nevertheless, present efforts seem designed to minimize the former risk, even at the price of enhancing the latter.

In fact, crisis-escalation cannot be "deterred" or "dissuaded", least of all by further argument and more credible threats, because what needs to be contained here is not the aggressive inclinations of the opponent but panic and overreaction on both sides. The propensity for crisis-escalation depends on the instabilities built into the opposing military forces and on the commitments, threats, and fears generated in a crisis and it has to be dealt with in those terms. The build-up of forces in peace-time and their mobilization in times of tension is more likely to precipitate a crisis than to avert it.

Even in the case of premeditated attack, dissuasion cannot be reduced to "raising the price of aggression." There are other means of dissuasion because a deliberate attack has a political purpose, not just a military aim. It presupposes a specific political purpose as well as adequate military capability. It must be possible for the aggressor to draw up an attack plan which seems likely to succeed in achieving that purpose. Prudence demands that we assume the worst of motives, but this does not mean that we can just assume them and focus all attention on capabilities. By such action dissuasion would be impossible (except through threats of retaliation) because even with the best defence, a successful attack is always technically feasible if the area is small enough. But for the attacker, a small area has value only as a stepping stone in relation to wider aims, and this introduces a calculation of cost and benefit whose terms the defense can influence. Here the political purpose reasserts itself. In a sub-nuclear situation dissuasion is completely political. So is "deterrence," for under nuclear parity and mutual assured destruction, the decisive factor in deterrence is not capability but credibility.

MUTUAL DEFENSIVE SUPERIORITY

Military <u>security</u> presupposes that our defense capability is superior to the offense capability of potential opponents. The condition for overall military <u>stability</u> among several states is that each state or alliance is strong enough to defend itself but too weak to attack others with any prospect of success. For two opponents "A" and "B" the condition for military stability therefore takes the form of mutual defensive superiority:

$$D(A) > O(B) \quad \text{and} \quad D(B) > O(A).$$

Here D and O refer to the strength of the forces when fighting in a defensive and in an offensive mode respectively. These expressions are shorthand forms, not true inequalities, for the terms are not numbers that can be defined in the abstract. "The defensive capability of country A," for example, is meaningless, except in the context of a precisely specified attack.

Virtually all discussion of military stability in Europe ignores the simple and obvious condition of stability expressed in the above inequalities and is

based instead on the notion of a "balance of forces" which one could express in the following form:

$$F(A) \approx F(B)$$

This form is nothing more than a condition of <u>symmetry</u>. It is totally unrelated to the question of <u>military</u> stability. The latter does not arise from an <u>equality</u> of force, but from the <u>unequal</u> force of offense and defense.

The "fallacy of symmetry," the belief that the pursuit of "balance" is also will ensure military stability is widespread. New weapons programs are said to be needed to "restore the balance," without which, it is implied, stability would be endangered. The need to maintain "balance" is also the dogma underlying all disarmament and arms control negotiations. In fact, the pursuit of "balance" can have catastrophic consequences, especially when military technology undergoes the rapid change of today. Forces which are particularly suited for attack but not for defense (for example weapons which are both threatening and vulnerable) invite pre-emptive attack and encourage early use. To pursue symmetry in such weapons is to promote instability. The symmetry condition is also meaningless because it is impossible to compare "forces" in the abstract without specifying their mode of fighting. The military "balance," therefore, cannot express a real ratio of force. It is necessarily a mere numerical "gun count."

In contrast, the set of inequalities which describe the condition of mutual defensive superiority compares forces in terms of a specified mode of fighting and expresses the relation of forces as if they were tested against each other, first with country "B" in the offensive (and, by implication, with country "A" in the defensive) and then the other way around. It is true that in an actual war both will often fight partly in one mode, partly in the other. It may even be impossible to distinguish the two modes, as in a pure war of maneuver. But this does not invalidate the condition of stability which refers only to what would happen if the two adopt the defensive and the offensive, respectively.

Since the ability to fight in a certain mode depends on the weapons available, on their types, quantities and combinations, it is meaningful to speak of the overall defensive and offensive capabilities of a country or alliance vis-a-vis a specified opponent. But it is of course meaningless to speak of certain weapons as "defensive," others as "offensive." The contribution of a piece of hardware to offensive and defensive capability depends on what other weapons and forces are available on both sides. Even the Great Wall of China can be regarded as a contribution to offensive capability if, by strengthening defense on one front, it releases forces for offensive action on other fronts. "Defensive," therefore, is not an attribute of weapons, it is a mode of fighting. A "defensive" or "non-offensive" defense is not a defense which relies on "defensive weapons" but a defense designed to fight in the defensive mode and to take full advantage of the possibilities offered by that mode of fighting.

There are several different types of stability requirement and, correspondingly, several different conditions of stability, but all of them have the general

form of mutual defensive superiority, as expressed in the above inequalities. One can distinguish:
- stability in relation to premeditated attack, which presupposes such overall defensive superiority on both sides that neither can devise an attractive attack strategy.
- stability in relation to pre-emption in crisis, which will prevail if all force components on both sides are most effective when used in the defensive mode. If so, there is an incentive for both to "wait and see" and no advantage in surprise attack or pre-emption.
- stability in relation to escalation in war, which prevails if both sides have a defensive superiority at all higher levels of warfare and in each geographical sector. If so, military prudence would preclude the escalation of hostilities and the opening of new fronts. War, if it does erupt, will tend to remain confined.
- stability in relation to competitive arming, which presupposes that force procurement on both sides remains within the bounds of mutual defensive superiority. In this case there is no justification for "balancing" arms acquisitions by the other side.

These aspects of military stability are also the components of security. Their aggregate effect is what I call "military stability" or "military security," using these two terms almost interchangeably; the former to refer to the state of the system as a whole; the latter to refer to the situation of each state individually.

INSTABILITY IN CRISIS

The general perception in the West is that the Warsaw Treaty Organization has an overwhelming superiority in conventional forces and could push through to the Rhine in a matter of days. Other studies of "the Soviet Threat" suggest that when all the factors are taken into account there is an approximate equality of strength. Others again promise that if military expenditures were raised by a few percent, the present western inferiority could be remedied, western reliance on nuclear deterrence could be diminished, and the "nuclear threshold" could be raised. In my opinion all of these positions miss the real issue. There is indeed a conventional disequilibrium in Europe which could have disastrous consequences in the event of war. But it is

460

not a disequilibrium between East and West. It is a disequilibrium which is built into the force structures on both sides and which makes the present military situation explosive.

The disequalibrium results from the fact that the heavily armored, mobile military formations that constitute the bulk of the fighting forces on both sides in Europe are designed for a symmetric kind of warfare in which the distinction between defense and offense at the tactical and operational levels is blurred. These formations are suited for a war of maneuver, for disrupting the defenses, and for swift penetration into enemy territory. They are unsuited for the tasks which conventional forces ought to fulfill in a sub-nuclear situation: to impose a mutual stalemate on the battlefield to facilitate a political settlement. Stability, stalemate and de-escalation, which always depend on defensive superiority, cannot be achieved with forces as they are now deployed.

This is particularly true of air forces. Air superiority is held to be decisive in relation to ground combat, and one can predict that once war begins to seem unavoidable, there would be a race to destroy the radar, airfields and ground-to-air missiles of the opponent. There is an enormous advantage in striking first, and in a matter of hours one side could be left with a temporary advantage in the form of air superiority which would have to be exploited at once, leaving the other side with a fatal vulnerability which it might feel compelled to cover up with threats of nuclear escalation.

In a war of maneuver, numerical superiority is no guarantee against defeat. More than numbers it is skill, information, surprise and sheer luck which matter, as was clearly demonstrated in the opening phases of World War II. No commander therefore, would want to fight a war of maneuver with forces that are merely equal to those of the opponent. This again underscores the deception involved in the call for "balance." Even if it could be measured unambiguously, equality would not provide security and would not be seen as sufficient by either side. When responsible commanders speak of "the forces needed for balance," they mean forces which are significantly stronger than those of the opponent.

Reluctance on the part of the West to give up the option of first use of nuclear weapons is always justified by reference to its presumed conventional inferiority. It is evident, however, that building more conventional forces of the type we have now would not diminish the risk of nuclear escalation. The problem with our present conventional forces is not that there are too few of them but that if they were brought into action they would give rise to precisely that kind of swift-moving, high-risk, decisive war which would be an invitation to nuclear escalation.

. The immense dangers involved in any military operation in Europe are evident. If an attack plan is to look attractive it must therefore promise quick, decisive results; it must seem quite unlikely to escalate, yet it must hold out the prospect of very significant gains. The only thing that could tempt the opponent to premeditated attack is the prospect of a swift operation establishing a fait accompli almost overnight. Slow-grinding salami tactics that accomplish nothing significant, massive nuclear strikes which are likely to be reciprocated and the prospect of a long war of attrition cannot tempt an aggressor.

Not only, therefore, are our present forces of a kind that could both precipitate an unintended war through the mechanism of crisis-escalation; and enhance the risk of deliberate aggression. It is precisely in a swift-moving war of maneuver that an attacker might imagine that a surprise attack could succeed, that a few quick successes would lead to military or political collapse and that the chaotic, escalation-prone character of a war fought with such forces might paralyze both the nuclear and the non-nuclear forces of his opponent. In our excessive concern with the remote likelihood of a deliberate attack we have thoughtlessly continued to develop force structures which (1) enhance the real danger of stumbling into unintended war, (2) and which are so destablizing that they might create the opportunities for quick victories they were meant to foreclose.

FORCE IN A SUB-NUCLEAR SETTING

In a classical pre-nuclear situation the military security of each state depended only on its ability to match in defensive strength the offensive potential of its opponent. Each of the opponents sought defensive superiority for itself. Mutual superiority and, with it, overall military stability, did not arise by design. If it did arise it was only as the combined effect of the independent actions of the two sides.

But in a sub-nuclear situation it is in the interest of each to try to ensure that both of the above inequalities are satisfied. To pose an offensive threat that the other side cannot "fend off" is to invite it to base its "security" not on defense in the proper sense of that word but on "nuclear deterrence" with all the contradictions and instabilities that this implies. In a sub-nuclear situation the opponent, by definition, always has the option of "plugging the holes" or of trying to plug the holes in his conventional defenses by threatening nuclear escalation. To threaten the opponent is to invite counter-threats and to slide from a situation of joint security into a nuclear "balance of terror," where the inherent threat that one is willing to face mutual annihilation rather than accept defeat, has to be shored up with sabre-rattling, trip-wire deployments and the rhetoric of uncompromising enmity. In a sub-nuclear situation security cannot be one-sided: there is either common security through mutual defensive superiority or there is common insecurity in the form of absolute confrontation, temporarily held back by the threat of mutual annihilation.

In a sub-nuclear situation the political purposes of the military instrument can only be to prevent war and, if war comes, to bring about a stalemate and try to terminate it without disaster. Therefore the aim to be pursued in military operations cannot be victory as it is under classical conditions. It can only be to stall the act of war and impose a pause, so that politics can take over. The need, therefore, is not for forces which can strike and win but for forces which can absorb a blow, hold back, win time and avoid any battle that might prove decisive. In a sub-nuclear situation decision in battle, be it in one's favor or in favor of the enemy, is the surest way to nuclear disaster.

In a sub-nuclear situation each side is always in a position to refuse defeat by escalating so there cannot be a real decision on the battlefield. Whatever else it can do, military force cannot impose a decision. In a classical situation, force decides the outcome of war, directly or indirectly, because war is a real trial of strength, involving, if need be, all of one's forces and all of the forces of the opponent. In a sub-nuclear situation it would be madness to engage in a real trial of strength involving all of the weapons of the opponent. Force, therefore, cannot decide the issue; only <u>politics</u> can decide. Those who think in classical terms have the greatest difficulty in grasping the importance of this point.

One implication is that whereas "strength" is a fairly adequate measure of the effectiveness of the military instrument under classical conditions, this simply cannot be the case under sub-nuclear conditions. Military strength matters, but it matters only in so far as it helps ensure mutual defensive superiority. In a sub-nuclear situation the criterion of strength is subordinate to the criterion of stability, and it is against this criterion that the effectiveness of the military instrument should be measured. A rational military policy in a sub-nuclear situation is one that maximizes crisis-stability in a systematic way while maintaining sufficient defensive strength to discourage all adventurism. It is a policy which emphasizes defensive capability while reducing offensive capability to a minimum.

It is often asserted that for deterrence to be effective it must be possible to threaten enemy territory with retaliation in the form of destruction or conquest. This seems to be based on the frivolous notion that states decide on the issue of war and peace on the basis of a cost/benefit calculation, much like a businessman contemplating an investment. In any case it reflects an inadequate understanding of the conditions of warfare in a sub-nuclear context. In that context no one is immune and no attack is without danger. The anticipated gains from a successful attack have to be important enough to compensate for the risks. But the risks are in direct proportion to the importance of the stakes and in contrast to the classical situation large gains are impossible without a large risk. Here, not force but politics decides. All submission, including the surrender of territory, is a free decision which can be reversed at any time by resorting to nuclear escalation, to counter-threats, or simply by taking up arms again under cover of the nuclear umbrella which, if it works one way also works the other way. In a sub-nuclear situation, the spoils of war can only be acquired by mutual consent. Since the forces of the opponent cannot be crushed because of the risk of escalation, force is no

longer a means of compulsion. Therefore the position of
troops on the ground if and when a settlement is worked
out cannot be decisive. In a sub-nuclear situation
military force has lost its privileged position as the
ultimate arbiter because force held back by
self-deterrence cannot decide.

THE CONCEPT OF ATTRITION NET

The idea of basing conventional defense in Europe on
attrition through essentially stationary forces deployed
in depth derives from two different considerations. One
is the sub-nuclear character of the strategic situation
in Europe. As we have seen this implies that security
must be sought in mutual defensive superiority. To this
end, the forces on each side must be designed to maximize
defensive capability while minimizing the capability to
threaten the opponent, and they must be designed to avoid
decision and seek indecision and stalemate instead.

The other consideration is the pressure of current
developments in military technology, particularly the
development of target-seeking munitions resulting from
improvements in sensor-, data- and missile technology.
It means that weapons can be highly accurate and
essentially independent of the range. The two combine to
create the conditions for more efficient forms of
defense, while at the same time threatening present forms
with obsolescence.

In an engagement in which the opponents use ordinary
unaimed or poorly aimed fire the numerical strength of
the opposing forces is the decisive factor. The smaller
force will have less firepower, but it will have more
targets to cover. Its inferiority is therefore literally
"raised to the power of two," as expressed in
Lanchester's square law. This means that there is a
massive premium on numerical superiority in each separate
engagement. To subdivide one's forces into smaller
detachments is to invite defeat because the enemy, if he
keeps all his forces together, can then crush these
detachments one by one with few losses to himself. This
is the basic reason why the concentration of force at the
point of battle has always been one of the most firmly
established principles of strategy.

As precise ammunition becomes the norm this
situation will change radically. If virtually every shot

hits and every hit kills, then the problem is not to hit the target but to find it. In this situation losses no longer depend on numbers but on who is <u>seen</u> first, by eye or by sensor. Then, numerical superiority in an engagement serves no purpose; it is a handicap because it provides the enemy with many easy targets. Instead of superiority in numbers, superior concealment becomes the paramount factor in war and this puts a premium on dispersion rather than concentration. Two kinds of dispersion matter in this context: dispersion into very small units because these are more easily concealed; and dispersion over the entire theater of operations because it diminishes the need for troop movements and minimizes exposure. At the most abstract level this is the rationale for deploying forces in the form of an <u>attrition net</u>. Ideally such a net consists of tiny defense units dispersed evenly over the entire theater of war so that there is no way of bypassing the net and no need to move forces about.

The development of "smart" weapons with very high kill-probabilities will obviously favor the defense much more than the offense because the defense can remain hidden whereas an attacker cannot. Sooner or later he must come into the open and expose himself to the sensors and to the fire of the defense. And this asymmetry between offense and defense is not affected by the fact that certain counter-measures can be developed. They can delay the impact of the new weapons but they cannot change the overall trend. The most visible evidence of this trend toward greater cost-effectiveness for defense is the rapidly escalating cost and increasing vulnerability of tanks, warships and aircraft which are indispensable for attack but for which a well concealed, widely dispersed defender will have no use.

Precise suggestions for the organization and equipment of the fighting units of an attrition net were first made by Brossollet in a partly different context. His design was later adopted by Afheldt as the core of his network of "techno-commands" and developed into a comprehensive concept of non-offensive defense. In this approach the defense forces are organized into a network of small, evenly dispersed units of maybe a dozen men; each unit is assigned to an area a few kilometers in radius. Their task is not to "defend" the area against enemy incursion—which, of course, they cannot do—but to see that enemy forces passing through will suffer significant losses—much higher than those of the defense. To this end, the defense units would be equipped with armor-piercing infantry weapons, land mines, anti-aircraft missiles and whatever is needed to prepare and booby trap the area.

The stationary character of the defense net precludes the use of these forces for offensive purposes and at the same time allows the defense to exploit fully the advantages of fighting in the defensive, adapting to local conditions and making use of natural or man-made obstacles. Moreover, a stationary force cannot engage in large-scale maneuvers and therefore cannot be driven to accept a major, possibly decisive battle.

To be effective, a stationary attrition defense must combine area coverage with adequate firepower and staying power. For firepower the units have to rely heavily on various types of smart weapons; for staying power on concealment and camouflage. Because they are so small, know the terrain and need not move around in the presence of enemy forces, the units can hide easily. With remote controlled response they need not give away their position when firing. Their vulnerability is further diminished by the fact that the need for centralized command and control and for supplies and support from outside the area is not great. If the defense setup is composed entirely of small autonomous units of this kind and renounces the use of aircraft, airfields, warships, and tanks most of the weapons of the attacker would be useless.

There are three ways for the attacker to deal with an attrition net:
- One approach is to ignore the defense, push right through and accept the casualties this implies. The problem is that if the defense net is equally dense everywhere there is not much to push through to: no poorly defended sanctuary in the rear to invest and no major army detachments to crush. Little is achieved by clearing a corridor to nowhere while leaving the bulk of the defense forces intact. And if only the units within a narrow corridor are destroyed, the reinforcements and supplies coming through would still be exposed to the fire from neighboring units.
- The second approach is to engage in a major "combing" operation to find and destroy the defense units one by one. This would cause long delays and impose great losses on the attacker.

- The third approach is to destroy the units with area weapons without engaging them directly. With nuclear weapons this is possible, but only by escalating the war to genocidal proportions which, in a sub-nuclear context cannot be an attractive option for the attacker. Each soldier is vulnerable to nuclear fire, but the defense network as a whole is essentially invulnerable.

The attacker is forced to choose between three unattractive options: pushing through to an objective of no real military value, settling for a long and costly war of attrition, and escalating to large-scale nuclear war. A quick, decisive blow, the only truly attractive option, is precluded by the dispersion of the net.

To pose a significant threat to enemy forces in concentrated formation a network defense must be able to concentrate substantial fire-power in any given spot. This general problem was solved by Afheldt by superimposing two nets: a finely meshed net consisting of a large number of "techno-commands" as described above, and a coarse net consisting of fewer units equipped with medium-range missiles with target-seeking munitions designed for attacks against concentrated formations. These missile forces can be regarded as a substantially improved functional equivalent of the tank formation. Their fire can be concentrated at any point almost instantaneously because it is only the warhead, not the platform, which is brought to the battle area. Unlike tanks, the missiles can remain dispersed and hidden in the distance, even while fighting, and they do not give themselves away until they fire, at which time there would be nothing but an empty launching tube to fire back at.

The effectiveness of these missile forces hinges on their combination with the infantry units. Because the finely-meshed infantry net keeps the entire theater of operations under constant surveillance its units can supply accurate target coordinates, thereby obviating one of the main shortcomings of long-range missiles when used in combination with present-day forces. The infantry network also obviates the other difficulty associated with the use of long-range target-seeking ammunition: the difficulty of distinguishing friend from foe. In its ideal form the defense would renounce all use of armored vehicles, aircraft and ships. Missiles and sub-munitions can therefore home on anything whose radiation signature is approximately right without any risk of hitting one's own forces. Above all, the infantry net constitutes a protective shield for the missile units. If the latter are properly concealed, the attacker is faced with the dilemma noted above. He can silence the missile units by fine-combing vast areas, but this is a time-consuming operation exposing him to the fire of all the infantry units. Instead, he can push forward regardless, clearing only a narrow corridor, but if so the corridor remains under fire from the missile units.

The infantry units need several types of weapons to meet the different challenges they may face, such as armored vehicles, dismounted infantry, low-flying aircraft and, near the shores, enemy vessels. Similarly, missile units are needed to cope with concentrated enemy formations of each of these types. The optimum design and the relative density of these nets must depend on geographical conditions, on the character of the enemy forces and on the type of attack that is anticipated. The general aim is to impose roughly the same degree of attrition, irrespective of the type of forces used by the enemy, of the degree of concentration, and of the invasion routes chosen. It is also evident that the weapons must be sufficiently varied to confront an intruder with a complex threat which cannot be circumvented by any simple device.

Over the past decade a considerable number of different models of non-offensive defense have been proposed, most of them explicitly relating to the "Central Front" in Europe. While they differ in many important aspects the common core of all of these models is a system of net-like, area-covering, essentially stationary attrition forces as described here. On closer examination it is easy to see that the way in which these models ensure greater stability always hinges on their net-like components. It is these which promote crisis-stability in peace, stalemate in war and which preclude a quick decision or a significant breakthrough. The stationary, essentially reactive attrition net is clearly the logical core of a non-offensive defense system, even though in terms of manpower and hardware it is not necessarily the most prominent component in all of the existing models.

A pure attrition net is a theoretical model, whereas practical alternatives for the foreseeable future must be a "bricolage" based on presently available forces and equipment with modest but decisive changes in structure, deployment, training and armament. A model which is meant to be implemented in practice is a compromise between the ideal and the possible.

Some authors believe that a transition to a more defense-oriented force structure would only give enough guarantees against calculated aggression if accompanied by equivalent steps by the other side; others envisage a unilateral process of transarmament, but combine a net defense with other types of force structure, mostly in the form of successive zones, to achieve high defense capability as well as high crisis stability. In front of the net there might be placed a "fire-belt" where earthworks, dense minefields and intense artillery fire would cause significant delay, disruption and attrition of the attacking forces before they meet the net. In its rear there might be operational reserves consisting of traditional mobile armored units, strong enough to cope with the weakened enemy forces that might have fought their way through the net, but too weak to constitute a threat of aggression.

A stationary defense system can take full advantage of the military geography of the region in which it is deployed. A non-offensive defense system would therefore be differently designed on different sectors of the front, even though the underlying principles would be the same. Many different models have been proposed. Most differ not in principle, but in the way these principles have been adapted to different conditions and different regions.

29

From Deep Strike
to Alternative Defense:
The Role of Technology

Gunilla Herolf

Future NATO doctrines and strategies are now a
subject of much debate in Europe. The US Army AirLand
Battle Doctrine of 1982 has been seen as a sign of a
change of direction towards a more offensive type of
strategy for NATO. While SACEUR Bernard Rogers has
repeatedly assured us that AirLand Battle is not
applicable to Europe, other US officials have disagreed
and cite the existing diversity of national doctrines.
The Follow-on Forces Attack (FOFA) concept developed by
NATO appears similar to the AirLand Battle Doctrine
although in FOFA no troop attacks into the rear areas of
the enemy are envisaged. As with AirLand Battle, the
FOFA plan argues for such attacks with long-range
weapons. Many technological development resources are
now devoted to weapons systems for deep strike missions
against both fixed and moving targets. A vital component
of these systems is guided submunitions which can be
ejected in large numbers from missiles or aircraft
dispensers. Missiles would be preprogrammed against
fixed targets or led to moving targets by information
from the aircraft-based Joint Stars radar. Complex
information systems are being created to handle the
collection, evaluation and dissemination of this
information.

Much criticism has been voiced against these
systems. The efficiency of the weapons is questioned.
The guided submunitions, the airborne radar and the
information system are considered vulnerable to
countermeasures. Also questioned is whether the Warsaw
Pact countries, if attacking the West, would deploy their
forces in a manner that would provide a sufficient number
of targets in the rear areas. The Soviet emphasis on
mobility and forward penetration would make deep strikes
less viable through attacks on (Command, Control,
Communications and Intelligence System) C^3I installations

necessary for deepstrike weapons. This emphasis would also create interspersion of WTO and NATO forces, making targeting more difficult.

The deepstrike weapons create, for both sides, an advantage in launching preemptive attacks, thereby decreasing crisis stability. To the extent that the missiles can be mistaken for nuclear missiles, they lower the nuclear threshold since they might trigger a nuclear response. Further, they give impetus to increased armaments. The offensive character of the weapons, as well as the offensive character of a doctrine such as AirLand Battle, further serves to create an atmosphere of antagonism.

ALTERNATIVE DEFENSE CONCEPTS

Alternative types of defense are based on a concept of security which is not attained at the expense of other nations. When such a system is created, whether unilaterally or bilaterally, one of its most important characteristics is transparency—that the system is not only defensive but also clearly recognizable as such. This is demonstrated by the choice of weapons, command and control systems, infrastructure and doctrines. Another demand is that it be at least as efficient as the system it is replacing. A deficiency in one area can, up to a certain point, be offset by strength in another.

Some alternate defense components, particularly the weapons, are important both for transparency and for efficiency. For example, a large number of alternative defense concepts have been outlined for Central Europe. Many include a narrow fire or barrier zone close to the border, followed by a zone in which mobile groups can attack advancing forces from positions in the terrain with the aim of delaying, disrupting or destroying them. In the rear, tanks and longer range weapons would be deployed. Deterrent weapons are sometimes proposed for basing at sea only.

An alternative defense system is further characterized by its decentralization, although the degree of autonomy within the system can vary. Decentralization would increase the flexibility as well as lower vulnerability. Mobile groups would be equipped with precision-guided munitions (PGMs). The development of PGMs has been considered a precondition for this type of decentralized defense as their increasing capabilities as compared with the development of protective measures against them, indicates an advantage. Although added protection of tanks has made it difficult for missiles to penetrate the front of a modern tank, missiles have been developed which attack tanks from above where they are less well protected. Other missiles can attack the sides of tanks; plastic mines, which are hard to detect, can destroy tanks from underneath. Protective measures such as smoke emmission, would be difficult to implement while moving, especially under time pressure.

Future technologies, such as sensor technology (for detection and homing) and miniaturization (for including advanced technology in small weapons), are thought to favor the defensive side more than the offensive, and are expected to become increasingly cost-effective.

TRANSITION TO ALTERNATIVE DEFENSE SYSTEMS

Deepstrike plans are already moving toward implementation. Alternative security would not, however, necessarily lead to abandonment of all development of these technologies. The Joint Stars radar, with targeting capability far into enemy territory, and the long-range missiles are offensive parts of deep strike, however, which would have to be abandoned. A characteristic, typical of deepstrike systems, such as overloading them with the latest technology, should be avoided because the systems become expensive and are capable of functioning only under ideal circumstances. Complex systems, where each part affects the whole system, are generally unsuitable.

It is important that an alternative defense system be as unpredictable as possible and that it be capable of a flexibility which creates a need for information in real time. Under current plans, information would be supplied mainly by the Joint Stars radar, flying parallel to the border between East and West Germany and looking some 150-200 km. into Eastern territory, but information can also be obtained through remotely piloted vehicles (RPVs). These RPVs would circle over an area and relay information via a data link over a transmission distance of some 50 km. The RPVs in a defensive system would cover the territory to be defended and give mobile groups the needed time to react. A weakness of a real-time system based on RPVs would be the vulnerability of the data link to jamming. The latest ones are said to be invulnerable but electronic warfare and its countermeasures are in continuous development. It would be possible to use RPV-mounted cameras as a back-up system, but information from these cameras is not immediately available. While surveillance can be seen as offensive, a surveillance system is also a necessity for any type of defense and therefore would not necessarily indicate malicious intent.

The ability to attack moving-point targets beyond line of sight is an asset for defending forces. To attain this capability the Joint Stars radar and missiles are being developed for long range attacks along with RPVs which provide real-time information for artillery. The artillery would use the same submunitions as the long-range missiles. The shorter range (up to 30 km.) of the artillery makes its integration into another defense system possible. Compared to the lighter infantry weapons, the artillery has more firepower. It also has a longer range capability and is therefore better able to take advantage of the terrain, so that it is less vulnerable to direct fire. While submunitions for deepstrike weapons are said to be diverted easily, diversion would be more difficult to carry out in such a setting. The attacking forces crossing a border would meet a number of short range missiles and artillery-launched guided submunitions. A variety of guidance types, such as infra-red, millimeter-wave radar guidance, wire guidance and various types of laser guidance, exist for short-range anti-tank missiles. The necessary variety of protective measures would slow the attacker down considerably.

Deep strike is a long way from alternative defense and change would have to be gradual. But the examples given show that a major break in technological development is not a necessary first step. Some concepts and technologies which have been developed for deep strike strategy could even be transferred to another type of defense system. The doctrines of today assign an important role to technology, where fast decisions are necessary and human error dangerous. Yet the search for technological solutions continues. In the alternative defensive concept, the role of technology would be reduced and a more robust type of defense would be emphasized.

The road to alternative defense implementation can take different directions. If implemented unilaterally, an alternative defense system would have to be effective against the traditional type of defense. An alternative defense system can also be implemented as a part of disarmament and confidence and security building efforts and gradual approaches to alternative defense could be brought into the political process. The progress made in the field of alternative defense would pave the way for disarmament efforts and turn the two approaches into mutually supportive ones.

Prospects for the implementation of an alternative defense system might appear to be weak. But there is an awareness of the dangers of destabilizing weapon systems in Europe as was clearly shown by the negative reaction of Defense Minister Worner of the FRG and Prime Minister Thatcher of the United Kingdom to United States proposals to deploy conventional silo-based missiles in Europe. Although it has been adopted by NATO, FOFA has met with little enthusiasm in Europe and weapon development is proceeding slowly. The contribution for FOFA implementation expected of European NATO members has added to the negative reactions. European proposals for commonly developed weapon systems have concentrated mainly on short-range weapons of the type referred to earlier. Although it does not share such views, the USA is conscious of the necessity of new roles in NATO. A stronger European position within NATO might eventually contribute toward turning the present doctrinal and technological trend in another direction.

30

Getting Theory and Practice Together: The Conflict Resolution Working Group

Paul Wehr and Ann FitzSimmons

THE PROBLEM

Two recurrent difficulties plague conflict resolution researchers. The first is our, as yet, modest ability to analyze conflict from an interdisciplinary perspective. We are inhibited in that by our own training and by the organizational structure of the university. Our discipline-bound languages and conceptual frameworks, and our jealous guarding of home turfs compound the problem. Game theoretical analysis is the most transdisciplinary of the conflict research areas because mathematics can function as a common language. It is a notable exception. Yet, we know from experience that the most revealing analysis of conflict is done through a mix of theoretical perspectives.

A second obstacle to good conflict analysis is the meager opportunity to test our work. If we do the research for policymakers, our recommendations are often too threatening to established policy and structures, too arcane in presentation style, or too little thought through in terms of policy implications to be useful. Whatever the reason, conflict resolution research only rarely 1/ finds its way into policy in a direct and visible way.

While the impact of conflict resolution on policy has grown only slightly in the last quarter century, the need for it has been steadily increasing. Classroom use is one expanding application. A recent survey of 294 U.S. colleges and universities identified 838 courses on conflict resolution. 2/

A second group of conflict research consumers is the growing number of dispute resolution professionals in fields ranging from industrial arbitration to divorce mediation. These practitioners are generally heavy on

475

experience and light on analysis beyond the specific case. The theoretical underpinning of their profession is underdeveloped.

Finally, policymakers and public officials are beginning to seek counsel from conflict resolution researchers. The increased frequency, intensity and cost of disputes is stimulating growth in alternative dispute resolution. In the area of environmental conflict, for example, the search for alternative dispute resolution methods is producing a profession, a literature, and a demand for the new product. 3/ Yet the melding of theoretical analysis with practical resolution of disputes has not kept pace.

The Approach

Our faculty group at The University of Colorado at Boulder decided to tackle these three problems: disciplinary insularity within the university, lack of opportunity to test theory, and distance between academician and policymaker. We would identify an interesting local conflict, hear the views of the conflict parties, collect additional data, pool our diverse disciplinary insights, and produce an analysis. We hoped that profitable working relationships among conflict research faculty would provide a base for a permanent conflict resolution research program.

The Model

With support from the university's vice-chancellor, we identified faculty in law, sociology, the business school, psychology, geography and political science who were known to be interested in conflict management. We grouped them into four analysis clusters to produce multiple theoretical perspectives for sharing in roundtable sessions. Each cluster had a research assistant for data gathering.

We identified a conflict to study and secured the participation of the major parties. We heard the dispute in three panel sessions: (1) the opponents of the policy in dispute, (2) the proponents of the policy and (3) a panel of press, survey consultants and other impartial observers. These three panels presented the conflict to the our Conflict Resolution Working Group (CRWG) over a two-week period. The CRWG then divided into subgroups to prepare analyses. These were shared in two seminars and used in the preparation of two reports -- one for the panels and a second for CRWG members. A final meeting of panel members and the CRWG modified the reports and produced a critique of the process.

THE CONFLICT

The case chosen for study was a complex of episodes -- disputes within a conflict within a controversy. The conflict centered around a temporary downzoning order (TDZ), which would increase the minimal size of building lots, imposed by the Board of County Commissioners (BOCC). The disputes were between the BOCC and indivi- dual property owners who would be disadvantaged by the proposed downzoning if they wanted to subdivide. Most of these disputes were resolved either in the courts or through case-by-case negotiation during the study period. Disputes, such as these, are generally resolvable. Conflicts, such as these over downzoning, are generally not resolvable but can be managed or limited. Controversy (prolonged opposition of interests and opinion) is impossible to resolve and difficult to manage because it does not present itself in episodic form.

The disputes were part of a broader conflict surrounding a secretly prepared proposal to downzone certain rural areas of Boulder County. The conflict did not lend itself as easily to resolution as did the disputes, though it was sufficiently time-bound to be identified as a case or episode. Both the disputes and the conflict were episodes in a still larger continuing controversy over the Boulder County Comprehensive Plan (BCCP) and how best to implement it. The CRWG analysis focused on both the downzoning conflict (over what was being done) and the TDZ conflict (over how it was being done).

The BCCP was adopted in 1978 to guide county land use decisions. Since then, the county's zoning resolution had been updated to make land uses conform as closely as possible to the plan without rezoning. It was impossible to fully implement the BCCP, however, because of incongruities between the county's zoning and Compre- hensive Plan maps. The commissioners and the Planning

Commission (PC), therefore, instructed the Land Use Department (LUD) staff, in January of 1985, to draw up a rezoning proposal.

> The purpose of this proposal is to ensure that those lands which are located outside of projected urban development areas (also referred to as Community Service Areas) as designated within the Boulder County Comprehensive Plan are properly zoned so as to prevent their premature urbanization, while at the same time preserving the established residential character of many of these areas. (Docket #AR 85-4)

That proposal to rezone part of Boulder County provided the basis for the conflict and the disputes. It surfaced on July 5 when area newspaper publishers were briefed on the proposal and copies were delivered to interested parties. The media carried stories the following day. The LUD staff would be asking the commissioners, on July 23, to enact the proposed rezoning on an emergency basis for a period not to exceed six months. The temporary resolution (TDZ) became the initial point of conflict as the Board voted 2-1, Commissioners Heath and Stewart for and Commissioner Smith against, to implement rezoning on a temporary basis. This was justified, claimed the planners, as an emergency action to prevent a "flood" of building permit requests from landowners whose property would be downzoned. Approval of a building permit or type of development would give them a vested right to use their land in ways contrary to the Comprehensive Plan. This could have resulted in substantial amounts of new residential and commercial/industrial development. The effect of the BOCC action was that, as of July 23, persons whose land was proposed to be downzoned would have use of their land under the proposed zoning (i.e. rezoned/downzoned) categories. They would not be able to exercise their rights to use the zoning which existed prior to July 23. With development "on hold" for unincorporated zoned land, citizens would be able to react fully to the rezoning proposal in a series of nine neighborhood meetings and various public hearings.

Mapping the Conflict

One approach to presenting a conflict formation for analysis is conflict mapping 5/ whereby different key elements of the conflict are identified in relation to one another (see map). Conflict mapping is most thoroughly done through interviews with the major conflict parties and neutral observers, who then check the diagram for accuracy. In the case of the downzoning dispute the time and resources for such in-the-field mapping were unavailable, and it was done using information from the presentation sessions and other data.

A conflict occurs within certain contexts, has a structure, and usually displays a certain potential for management. The mapping process afforded us a comprehensive view of the dispute.

Contexts

The contexts of the conflict included the historical, economic, and decisional settings out of and within which it developed. The downzoning proposal and TDZ resolution were developed to complete the implementation of the Boulder County Comprehensive Plan (BCCP). The Plan had been a source of controversy between the controlled growth orientation of Boulder City and the regulation-wary rural areas of Boulder County. There was a longstanding antagonism between rural landowners who cherish the right to use and sell their property as they wish and planners who interpret those rights more narrowly. Growth pressures in the County, greatly stimulated by Metro Denver development, have increased land values, landowner resistance to regulation, and concerns of planners for controlling growth.

Changing land use is an important contextual factor. As Boulder County agriculture becomes increasingly tenuous, landowners desire to sell their land

The Conflict Map

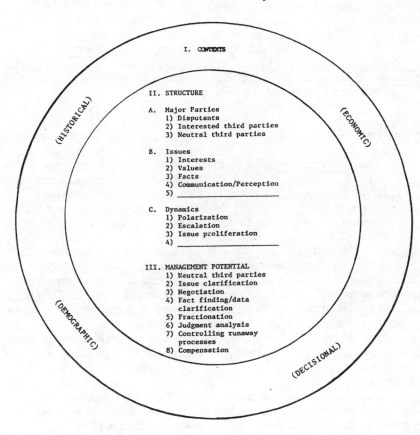

I. CONTEXTS

II. STRUCTURE

A. Major Parties
   1) Disputants
   2) Interested third parties
   3) Neutral third parties

B. Issues
   1) Interests
   2) Values
   3) Facts
   4) Communication/Perception
   5) _____

C. Dynamics
   1) Polarization
   2) Escalation
   3) Issue proliferation
   4) _____

III. MANAGEMENT POTENTIAL
   1) Neutral third parties
   2) Issue clarification
   3) Negotiation
   4) Fact finding/data
      clarification
   5) Fractionation
   6) Judgment analysis
   7) Controlling runaway
      processes
   8) Compensation

(HISTORICAL)

(ECONOMIC)

(DEMOGRAPHIC)

(DECISIONAL)

for development. Inevitably, speculators become involved and agricultural land becomes concentrated in fewer hands, anticipating the development boom. Rising housing costs in Boulder have caused a shift of population growth to other parts of the county.

The <u>decisional</u> context of the conflict centers around a board of three county commissioners elected at large. Boulder County has a long tradition of open and consultative government with a high level of citizen policy-attentiveness. The Commissioners work within a planning process managed by their staff, the Land Use Department, and two advisory planning commissions. In January 1985, a change in BOCC membership permitted initiation of a rezoning procedure for bringing unincorporated areas into line with the plan.

Structure

The structure of the conflict includes its key elements and how they interrelate.

<u>Parties</u>. Major actors in the conflict and the disputes shifted somewhat over a five-month period. Included were preexisting units such as county agencies and the courts and certain interest groups like PLAN Boulder County, the Boulder Board of Realtors, the Chambers of Commerce, and the Sierra Club. There were also organizations created by the conflict itself: committees to recall Commissioners Heath and Stewart, and a new group supporting the Comprehensive Plan (Citizens for Boulder County's Future). The creation of new groups and coalitions is an important function of the conflict process. <u>6</u>/

While Commissioners Heath and Stewart were strongly, and Smith generally, in favor of BCCP implementation, the latter disassociated himself from TDZ and for a time was a leading opponent. Smith, unlike his counterparts, saw the Comprehensive Plan more as a guide for growth policy, saw no emergency requiring drastic action, and felt that rezoning was a better approach than downzoning. The TDZ issue, then, alienated the two commissioner-proponents from their colleague and from a substantial number of their constituents.

Opposition to downzoning was concentrated in two efforts. A small group of landowners, the Committee Against Downzoning (CAD), took the issue to court and subsequently had TDZ nullified. A recall committee was formed as the opposition became increasingly directed against Heath and Stewart. The recall group included landowners of diverse political orienta- tion, as well as ultraconservatives and property rights advocates. Their explicit goal was to force recall of the two downzoning commissioners.

Landowners in the areas to be downzoned were not of one mind. Leading the opposition to it was a major landowner who would lose substantially through lost development potential. Smallholders, however, were divided in their positions. Some were against downzoning for economic, philosophical or practical reasons. Some, however, were for it as protection for their rural lifestyles.

Active in support of downzoning were the old-line environmental groups and the new Citizens for Boulder County's Future (CBCF) created in support of both the beleaguered commissioners and controlled growth in the county. The press was important. It was the major provider of information about the dispute. Without its usual inside access to policymakers, however, it was not always an accurate provider in the conflict. As is often the case in community conflict, the press both fanned and damped down the controversy.

One can view this conflict as drama. 7/ The parties were actors playing characters and assuming roles in various public encounters such as hearings, neighborhood meetings and press interviews. The actors played to both their constituents and their opponents. As the conflict progressed, it took on the character of a medieval morality play, and the personification of good and evil was determined by whose script was being used. These well-defined, well-rehearsed roles were perfected by Commissioner Heath, among others, as the defender of good planning and majority environmental values, and by developer Dollaghan, as the defender of property rights and consultative government. The scripts in this conflict assumed lives of their own, with set lines and emotional slogans: "Can't confiscate a right or justify a wrong," and "Public stewardship of the land above all." Getting disputant actors to modify their scripts was a major conflict management tactic.

2. <u>Issues</u>. Issues are the manifestation of the different <u>interests</u>, <u>values</u>, <u>facts</u>, and <u>perceptions</u> motivating the conflict parties. They are the verbal

expression by the disputants and observers of the root causes of the conflict. Salient issues in this conflict included: (1) the legal property rights of landowners abrogated by downzoning (i.e. justice in policymaking); (2) the appropriateness of TDZ and the denial of due process and public involvement because of secrecy and suddenness (i.e. honesty in policymaking); and (3) the presence or absence of the need for TDZ (i.e. justification in policymaking).

Interests: Through analysis of the social, political and economic structures of Boulder County one could immediately see latent conflict becoming manifest as the interests of slow-growth and environmental conservation commissioners collided with economic and influence interests of major landowners. Familiarity with interest group formation 8/ helps us understand the conflict. If there is not a genuine common interest to protect, false interest groups and coalitions such as the recall committees grouping large and small landowners will not survive. In this conflict those having substantial speculative capital in large holdings had relatively little in common with the small farmers and owners of small businesses whose individual disputes could be negotiated to settlement with the planning authorities.

There are really three groups of interests involved here: individual interests, collective interests of the community as a whole (such as a quality environment), and institutional interests of governmental and corporate agencies which can be seen as quite separate from the collective ones. The county planning agencies, for example, had a professional interest in implementing the Comprehensive Plan. They felt obligation and justification to do so. Members of the press felt obliged to get the facts and cover the downzoning conflict as best they could, but they felt thwarted by official secrecy. The interests of institutions are as vigorously pursued as private ones.

Values: Interests interconnect with philosophical and social values. It is difficult to know where interests leave off and values begin. One normally justifies pursuit of one's personal interests in terms of general societal values (e.g. constitutional rights, environmental protection, sound planning, honesty in government, participatory democracy, fair compensation). The interests of certain policymakers, landowners and environmental activists thus are presented as values, which reflect the interests of those individuals as well as certain classes and categories in society. Values are more difficult to negotiate than interests, and the shift toward emphasis on the former over the latter probably rendered the disputes less tractible than they would otherwise have been.

Values especially prominent in this conflict included: property rights, sound planning, open space, fairness and equity of treatment, protection of the underdog, environmental and esthetic quality of life in Boulder County, and participatory government.

Facts: The data on which the downzoning proposal and TDZ were based and those on which opponents based their challenge were often in conflict. Figures on recent growth trends and building levels in the disputed areas varied greatly from proponent to opponent, with both producing "facts" to support their position. A case in point was the scope of the emergency that TDZ was intended to preclude. The number of building permits issued during the last ten years in the areas temporarily downzoned varied from the 67 cited by downzoning opponents to 3000 claimed by the proponents. The data presented by county officials changed three times as the proposal was discussed, renegotiated and revised. The size of the area affected was not clear to all parties and it was certainly not clear to the public. The downzoning proposal affected 10% of the unincorporated land in the county. The impression the public appeared to have was of a much larger area. Inflated too, was the number of landowners affected negatively by TDZ. Not only was this number considerably smaller initially than the public at large appeared to believe, but it diminished as individual variances were granted and agreements were reached with county officials. In sum, data calculation and presentation tended to confuse rather than clarify, producing uncertainty and escalating the conflict.

Finally, the degree of consultation by officials with their constituents was at issue. The Commissioners could claim many years of consultation with citizens throughout the Comprehensive Plan development process. In their view downzoning was in line with what the large majority in the county wanted. The opponents, approaching it more narrowly, pointed to the secrecy, surprise and total absence of constituency consultation in the preparation of the downzoning proposal. Hampered by the lack of its usual access and foreknowledge, the press could not perform its normal role of clarification. It had been brought into the process too abruptly and too late. Since data were being used as ammunition to buttress opposing positions, there was no source of objective information.

Communication and Perception: In crisis, human behavior loses much of its predictability and tends to short-circuit and shortcut the communication channels normally available to it. 9/ Communication between the disputants in the early stages was either nonexistent (the downzoning proposal was pre- pared in secrecy) or occurred under conditions not conducive to accurate communication. Where proponents and opponents met in public forums, much posturing and little mutual understanding occurred. The commissioners were not present at the neighborhood meetings. Often opponents delivered their speeches at hearings and did not stay for subsequent discussion. Effective communication did begin to take place as commissioners and planning officials began case-by-case negotiations with individual land-owners, which led ulti- mately to the resolution of most disputes. Social judgment theorists claim that direct communication between disputants often inhibits conflict resolution. This view would have found some support here from how disputants communicated in public.

The press, public meetings and official communiques -- modes by which community information normally travels -- were inadequate in this time of crisis. People created their own news 10/ in the form of new "facts," rumor, and misinformation.

Dynamics. Conflict is a process that originates somewhere, goes somewhere, accelerates, decelerates, escalates, deescalates, and often terminates. One perspective represented in the CRWG suggests that one need not see this or any public policy conflict as discrete in itself but as a dimension of a larger process: the managing of community growth and power allocation. This larger process is normally handled within prescribed channels and procedures but occasionally spills into unpredictable struggle, as was the case with downzoning and TDZ. Still, for those of us who look at conflict through lenses other than those of policy analysis, the characteristic conflict dynamics were there: the precipitating event, the personalization and bipolarization of the conflict, the proliferation of issues, the escalatory spiral, and the termination. 11/

Conflict Management Potential

A third and final dimension of the conflict map concerns the possibilities for managing the conflict. These are contained either within the conflict itself or within the surrounding contexts. This element is of particular interest to those parties with a special concern for avoiding or decelerating the dispute. Assuming certain general principles of conflict management, the CRWG identified a number of such potentials for mitigating the conflict.

MULTIPLE ANALYTICAL PERSPECTIVES

The conflict map was useful for descriptive analysis, but it failed to furnish the deeper theoretical analysis the CRWG was seeking. We moved toward that analysis in the roundtable sessions. The CRWG "clinicians" listened, questioned, observed, gathered data, and formulated their "diagnoses" through their respective disciplinary lenses.

Political Conflict

The policy science diagnosticians found much of the conflict to be a normal and functional part of the planning process, to help keep community growth in stable equilibrium. Certain social theorists[12] would agree that such conflict could produce new relations or indicate values/norms disynchronization. The disputes were simply a reflection of the use of power by those who had it: disputants rationally pursuing their interests. Whether a conflict like this develops depends very much on what other issues are competing for public attention at the time.

The problem, then, was not the conflict itself or the errors in judgment or the public costs of the conflict, which were minimal. These are characteristic of policy formation and implementation. Problematic was how disputes within the conflict were generated and

-- the stereotyping, the disinformation, the open
hostility and namecalling -- which led the dispute away
from settlement.

Perception of fairness and misperception of support
were influential in several respects. Leaders of the
recall movement mistook negative public reaction to how
the downzoning was being done, for agreement with their
"property rights" and "individual vs government"
arguments. Many who criticized Heath and Stewart on
grounds of violating principles of fairness and open
government later rejected the effort to recall them as
equally unfair.

The social conflict group acknowledged that the
downzoning conflict was part of a continuing controversy
over how fast growth should occur in the county, and that
it should be analyzed as a dynamic process in its own
right, with particular attention given the runaway
processes of escalation and personalization. With a
better understanding of how those processes can be
anticipated and controlled, the inevitable conflict that
growth issues produce can be less costly and more
productive of sound policy.

Human Judgment

Disputant motivation was a major theme of analysis
running through the views of three of the analysis
groups. The fourth, or human judgment team, however,
felt that such an emphasis might lead to an incorrect
diagnosis of the problem. Such policy conflicts, they
argued, often have roots not in the motivation of disputants but in a flawed policymaking process and in
cognitive misperceptions. Disputants' motivations may be
irrelevant for understanding and resolving a dispute. If
the Boulder County Comprehensive Plan were based on areas
of value agreement among all major policy actors
(officials, business leaders, environmentalists,
landowners), such conflict could be mitigated, perhaps
even avoided entirely. One tested approach 13/ is to
capture the judgment policies of these actors and to
design proposals based on the convergence of these
policies. Proposal development (e.g. downzoning of
unincorporated areas) could be accomplished with minimal
conflict by building judgment analysis into the policy
process.

Prescription

The diagnoses emerging from the roundtable sessions led to certain prescriptions. The policy scientists suggested certain minor modifications that might improve the policy process (e.g. objective data supporting proposals; compensation for loss caused by growth, policies to reduce litigation and increase citizen satisfaction).

The law and business diagnosticians, who largely agreed that the conflict management system was working reasonably well in this instance, suggested some strategic and tactical considerations which might make a difference in such conflict (e.g. neutral procedures for policy proposal discussion, objective fact-finding, alternative dispute resolution on call).

The social conflict analysts suggested a more thorough understanding of the conflict process and some guidelines for controlling it:

a. Avoid surprising people. At times secrecy in government is warranted, but in Boulder County, where citizen participation and consultation are important norms in public business, the costs would normally outweigh the benefits.

b. Fractionate the conflict. Breaking the conflict down into manageable disputes is one approach to reducing it. 14/ Negotiating with disputants singly rather than collectively is often effective. This is exemplified in the commissioners' case-by-case negotiation with smallholders.

c. Maximize direct communication under the right conditions. For example, more neighborhood meetings with all parties present, facilitated by professional neutral third parties, might have resolved the disputes earlier.

d. Maximize accurate information. The absence of solid data aggravated this conflict. Empirical truth was in short supply, stimulating disputants to invent their own.

e. Maximize options and alternatives. The ability to respond to contingencies with an array of strategies can reduce conflict.

f. Utilize neutral third parties. This is possible in all negotiable disputes. Neutral third parties are those, who by virtue of their training, experience and/or status in the community, command the credence and trust of the disputants. Whether academic conflict specialists can play this role depends very much on how their relationship to the disputants is structured.

g. Control the runaway processes of conflict. Regulating those processes reduces conflict costs to an acceptable level. Personalization, polarization, information distortion, and escalation can all be anticipated and modified.

The human judgment specialists prescribed a cognition-based policy process substituted for or added to the current motivation-based model. They would, for example, capture the judgment policies of the disputants and design policy alternatives that accommodated their respective value hierarchies.

THE OUTCOMES

The settlement of the TDZ disputes and the management of the downzoning conflict were acceptable to most. One could compare the July/ August hearings, jammed with confused and angry people, to the final hearings in December with low attendance and few citizen comments. In December the downzoning plan was passed unanimously. The TDZ order -- the major source of citizen hostility and resentment -- had been overturned by the courts in October. Negotiation with individual disputants eliminated some major debatable measures from the original proposal. The fairness principle operated rather well throughout the conflict in favor of both county officials and individual landowners. Not all, however, thought the outcome fair. The losers, mostly large landowners, mounted a drive to expand the BOCC to give downzoning opponents more influence.

Was the body politic healthier after the conflict than before? Were some immunities to growth regulation disputes in the future built up in the process? Has open and fair government in Boulder County gained or lost in the conflict? Such questions will be answered in the future. Boulder County and its BCCP consensus on growth equilibrium will collide with growth-minded communities in the county as they increasingly use the annexation rights they have under state law.

THE FUTURE OF THE CRWG

In evaluating the conflict roundtable experience, we learned that multidisciplinary communication and collaboration are possible, even enjoyable. We had sustained participation from most members. We were able to get sufficient data from the presentation sessions and graduate assistant research to analyze the conflict. Disputants had a fair and quiet forum in which to make a clear presentation of their view of the conflict and this was valuable for them and for us. On the other hand, the productivity of the four subgroups varied considerably. Providing them with more time, stronger research assistance, clear delineation of the database each needed, and a common set of research questions would have helped produce a more balanced and integrated analysis.

If the CRWG approach is to evolve further it must be economical in providing high return to participating disputants and faculty for relatively low time investment. It must be selective in establishing a process and criteria by which only the most appropriate conflicts are analyzed. Our analyses must be intelligible to both academic and lay readers as we work to advance both theory and practice.

We might, perhaps, meet these criteria with a "clinical" model. An intake panel would decide whether or not a conflict was appropriate for CRWG intervention and if it were so judged, the intake panel would form a consultation panel drawn from the CRWG pool. A typological checklist might help the intake panel to identify the appropriate disciplines and persons for a particular dispute. The consultation panel would hear the case presented jointly and respond with a diagnostic "package." This might include a conflict map, negotiation counseling, communication facilitation techniques and other resources. An analysis matrix sheet might provide data on each case study for periodic CRWG roundtable assessment of theoretical and methodological knowledge gained.

The experience gained with the CRWG is the basis for a formal proposal now being developed at the University of Colorado for a permanent Conflict Resolution Consortium (CRC). The CRC will incorporate the conflict roundtable as an important continuing element and would enhance it with small research grants, a research publication program, a computerized information exchange, a practitioner-researcher forum, and a conflict resolution information bank of published literature. We

492

assume that close researcher-practitioner-disputant collaboration will be the sine qua non of our future understanding and regulation of contentious relations.

NOTES

1. A. Etzioni, "The Kennedy Experiment," Western Political Quarterly. 20, 1967, 361-380; C. Osgood, An Alternative to War or Surrender. Urbana, IL: University of Illinois Press, 1962.

2. P. Wehr, et al, "Dispute Resolution in Higher Education," Dispute Resolution Forum. Washington, DC: National Institute for Dispute Resolution, April, 1986.

3. L. MacDonnell, "Natural Resources Dispute Resolution: An Overview," The Natural Resources Journal. Special Issue, Evnironmental Dispute Resolution, 1987. G. Bingham, Resolving Environmental Disputes: A Decade of Experience. Washington, DC: The Conservation Foundation, 1986.

4. K. Hammond and L. Adelman, "Science, Values, and Human Judgment," Science, 194, 1976, 389-396; P. Wehr and J. Rohrbaugh, "Citizen Values and Forest Policymaking," Western Sociological Review, 9, 1, 1978, 39-48.

5. See chapter 1, P. Wehr, Conflict Regulation, Boulder, CO: Westview Press, 1979.

6. L. Coser, The Functions of Social Conflict, New York: The Free Press, 1956.

7. E. Goffman, The Presentation of Self in Everyday Life, Garden City, NY: Doubleday, 1959.

8. R. Dahrendorf, Class and Class Conflict in Industrial Society, Palo Alto, CA: Stanford University Press, 1959.

9. J. Coleman, Community Conflict, New York: The Free Press, 1957.

10. T. Shibutani, Improvised News: A Sociological Study of Rumor, New York: Bobbs-Merrill, 1966.

11. J. Coleman, Community Conflict, New York: The Free Press, 1957.

12. L. Coser, The Functions of Social Conflict, New York: The Free Press, 1956; R. Merton, Social Theory and Social Structure, New York: The Free Press, 1957.

13. K. Hammond and J. Grassia, "The Cognitive Side of Conflict: From Theory to Resolution of Policy Disputes," in S. Oskamp (ed.), Applied Social

<u>Psychological Annual</u>, 6, Beverly Hills, CA: Sage, 1985, 233-254.

14. R. Fisher and W. Ury, <u>Getting to Yes: Negotiating Agreement Without Giving In</u>, Boston: Houghton Mifflin, 1981.

31

Unintended Nuclear War: An Emerging Academic Concern

Paul Smoker

INTRODUCTION

During the past few years there has been an increasing amount of literature which suggests that the risk of unintended nuclear war, particularly during a crisis, is likely to deviate significantly from zero. There are a number of major reasons, including the decrease in decision time associated with modern nuclear weapons technology and the increasing role of computers in the command and control systems, that appear to be increasing the risk of unintended war at times of crisis or under conditions of urgency of decision. 1/ And there are a number of apparently less important factors, including drug abuse, stress, psychological disorders and human error that further complicate the picture. Past incidents could be relevant to our understanding of the risks involved.

MAJOR PROBLEMS-ACCIDENTS

There are many examples of nuclear accidents involving weapons. According to Beres 2/ the Defense Monitor estimates that "an average of one US nuclear accident has occurred every year between 1945 and 1948, with some estimating [that] as many as thirty major nuclear accidents involving weapons and 250 minor nuclear accidents have occurred during that time" (1978). On March 11, 1958, a B-47 bomber accidentally dropped a nuclear weapon in the megaton range over Mars Bluff, South Carolina. The conventional explosive "trigger" of the nuclear bomb exploded leaving a crater 75 feet wide and 35 feet deep. It is possible to argue that the various interlocking safety devices render such situations harmless, but historical examples show that this

494

assumption is open to question. On January 23, 1961 a B-52 bomber had to jettison a 24 megaton bomb over Goldsboro, North Carolina. On this occasion five of the six interlocking safety devices were set off by the fall. A single switch prevented the bomb from exploding; the explosion would have been 1,800 times more powerful than the Hiroshima bomb. Had the sixth switch failed, an unintended nuclear war would probably not have resulted, despite the widespread devastation and damage. Replacement of mechanical switches by electronic devices has its own problems. According to the New Internationalist, a plane carrying a thermo nuclear device had its electronic key activated and the weapon armed by a tune from a Spanish radio station.

It seems reasonable to argue that an unlikely event of this nature becomes more probable if more planes carrying nuclear weapons are airborne. In an intense crisis situation more planes carrying nuclear weapons are likely to be airborne, and the probability of unintended nuclear war would almost certainly deviate significantly from zero if an accidental nuclear explosion occurred on the territories of either of the superpowers during a crisis. The US Department of Defense acknowledges that at least seven weapons have been dropped accidentally, and in four cases the conventional explosives involved exploded. Britten reports that the remaining three were lost and that "The high explosive of at least five nuclear weapons has been detonated accidentally in other circumstances, and at least two other nuclear weapons have been lost. Eight others have been destroyed, and six more damaged, all with radioactive contamination." 3/

Alistair Edwards, the Research Coordinator for Accidental Nuclear War of the British Scientists Against Nuclear Arms, has with the aid of Sandy Harcourt, also of SANA, compiled a database on "accidents which have caused, or might have caused, firing of, or damage to, a nuclear weapon." As of October 1985 this database included 98 such accidents including 53 cases of the delivery system being destroyed, 14 cases of radioactive release, 13 cases of delivery system damage, 12 cases of non-nuclear explosion, 12 cases of weapon release, nine cases of fire, six weapons damaged, five transport accidents, five false attack warnings, three weapons destroyed and two cases in which weapons were lost. 4/ The number of actual incidents, as Edwards points out, is probably much higher since only 14 of these events are ascribed to the Soviet Union.

Accidents involving airborne planes carrying nuclear weapons have occurred in a variety of contexts. On January 17, 1966, an American B-52 bomber collided with a KC-135 refueling tanker causing the deaths of five crewmen and the dropping of four hydrogen bombs which were recovered after an intensive ground and sea search. During a sustained crisis situation the probability of such incidents increases and an accidental nuclear explosion from such a source cannot be ruled out. Take off and landing too have their problems. On January 21, 1968 a B-52 attempting an emergency landing at Thule Air Force Base, Greenland, crashed. The high explosive components of all four nuclear weapons aboard detonated, producing plutonium contamination over an area 300-400 feet wide and 2,200 feet long.

Information on such accidents is not always available. Britten comments that in cases where radioactive spillage is involved the governments concerned often manage to keep the accident secret. Thus one of the most serious accidents known occurred in Britain on July 27, 1956 at Lakenheath Royal Air Force Base and was not acknowledged by the United States Department of Defense until 23 years later in 1981. While landing, a United States bomber had crashed into a storage igloo containing three Mark-6 nuclear bombs. The resulting fire damaged the bombs but failed to explode the conventional explosive trigger each contained. A retired, then active, United States Air Force general who was in the United Kingdom at the time subsequently wrote that had the conventional triggers exploded "It is possible that a part of Eastern England would have become a desert." Another Air Force officer who was present at the time commented that "It was a combination of tremendous heroism, good fortune and the will of God." Stewart Britten describes the events surrounding the incident in some detail, including various other nuclear incidents such as the well-publicized events of November 2, 1981. In this accident a US Poseidon missile was being winched from the US submarine support ship USS Holland when the winch ran free and the missile fell 17 feet, until the automatic brakes on the winch brought it to rest just above the submarine's hull. Britten discusses the likely consequences had the missile hit the hull and had the submarine contained a warhead (information that is not available) given that the warhead contains a highly unstable plastic explosive which detonates 50 percent of the time when subject to a metal weight dropped from 15 inches. Britten also observes that shortly before the Poseidon incident a crew member of the USS Holland had been sentenced for trading in LSD, cocaine and amphetamines. The possible interaction among various factors in a given situation should be of major concern to scholars interested in the subject of unintended nuclear war.

Missiles have been involved in a number of accidents. In September, 1980 a small explosion caused by a technician dropping a wrench socket and breaking a fuel tank caused a huge explosion in the silo of a Titan II Inter Continental Ballistic Missile. Britten reports that "The explosion blew off the silo's 740 ton door and catapulted the re-entry vehicle with its 9 megaton warhead six hundred feet into the air." An increasing number of accidents at Titan sites have resulted because of aging missiles and human error. New missiles are not immune to similar problems. On January 10, 1985 a Pershing 2 missile caught fire near Heilbronn, Germany. White hot rocket parts were hurled to within 250 yards of a store of nuclear warheads. Soviet accidents are of course less well publicized, although incidents such as the Soviet runaway missile that crashed on frozen Lake Inari in Finland at the end of 1984 are well reported. Britten also reports on nine accidents involving "submarines, some armed with nuclear weapons," that have collided with hostile vessels in Soviet waters.

Accidents involving bombers and missiles are numerous. But those involving the command and control systems are potentially much more dangerous. The explosion of a single nuclear weapon by accident would be a catastrophy and could cause the deaths of many tens of thousands of people, but mistakes in the command and control system are more likely to start an unintended nuclear war. There are many well documented examples. On October 5, 1960, the central war room of North Atlantic American Defense System (NORAD) received a top priority warning from the Thule, Greenland, Ballistic Missile Early Warning System station indicating that a massive missile attack had been launched against North America. A radar malfunction was responsible.

MAJOR PROBLEMS-SOFTWARE AND COMMUNICATION

On November 9, 1979 a "war game" scenario was accidentally fed into the US early warning system. The simulated missile attack was read by operators as being a "live launch." During the six minutes it took to discover that the attack was not real, fighters from bases in the United States and Canada had taken off and missile and submarine installations worldwide has been placed on alert. On the day following the incident, Tass, the official Soviet news agency, criticized the error and warned that another error "could have irreparable consequences for the whole world." This incident illustrates the way in which training procedures could, under some conditions, reinforce the belief of human operators that messages on their monitors correspond to reality. Because none of the operators have experienced an actual missile attack, their image of such an event is to a considerable degree influenced by the various training procedures involved in simulation exercises. An error of this kind, particularly under conditions of heightened stress and fatigue, is likely to increase the probability of unintended nuclear war during a crisis.

On June 3, 1980 a 45-cent computer chip failed early in the morning, causing the "detection" of a Soviet missile attack by the NORAD system. About 100 B-52s were prepared for take off, as was the President's airborn command post. Thousands of miles away the United States commander in the Pacific took off in his looking glass aircraft. In this incident the computers had indicated that an attack was coming from two Soviet submarines, then that more submarines had joined in, and finally, after the B-52 pilots had scrambled, that a full scale Soviet ICBM launch had begun. This serious incident illustrates another possible source of unintended nuclear war, namely failure or malfunction of an electronic component conveying incorrect messages to human operators.

Organizations such as Electronics for Peace in the United Kingdom have been particularly concerned with this problem. At the Manchester Conference on Unintended Nuclear War organized by the Richardson Institute for Conflict and Peace Research, Tim Williams presented a paper that reviewed some of the problems involved in the reliability of military electronics.[5] In considering the question of failure in electronic systems Williams examines component failure and allegations of short cuts by major defense contractors in the necessary "burn in" process that screens out components that would fail in the first few hours. Williams considers several aspects of the problem of reliability of military electronics and concludes that the reliability of electronic systems is inversely proportional to their complexity. Unfortunately the trend in C3I systems is towards greater complexity, and towards more reliance on electronic components. Williams argues that incidents of failure in C3I systems appear to be increasing. Examples like the 45-cent computer chip illustrate the global ramifications of failures in the worldwide electronic control systems. Recently Pentagon officials revealed that millions of micro chips used in modern weapons systems might be faulty, including those used in Britain's chevaline warhead.

The Center for Defense Information, using the United States Freedom of Information Act, obtained official figures for false alarms in the NORAD system during the years 1978-83. The increase in computerization is accompanied by an increase in false alarms. During this period, according to the Center, there has been a ten-fold increase in the number of false alarms from about 25 in the first half of 1978 to approximately 250 in the first half of 1983. It is likely that this trend will continue.

Lt. Col. Charles A. Wood, Acting Director of Public Affairs for the North American Aerospace Defense Command, has provided David Morrison of the Center for Defense Information with a list of emergency action conferences during the period 1977 to 1984. 6/ These include routine missile display conferences, which are called "with any indication of a possible missile launch." These routine missile display conferences involve the four command posts, at NORAD, Strategic Air Command, National Military Command Center and the alternate NMCC. Lt. Col. Wood describes how "Information on the launch is relayed to the Commander in Chief of NORAD, who assesses the presence or absence of a threat to North America. If he determines there is no threat to North America, the Missile Display Conference is terminated." If the NORAD Commander in Chief decides there is a threat possibility, a Missile Threat Conference is convened. Lt. Col. Wood says that "This brings into the evaluation process more

senior personnel within the Department of Defense. If
the threat continues, even more senior personnel are
added up to and including the President."

NORAD does not consider the overwhelming majority of
these incidents false alarms, a concept they define as
"any event which would cause an increase in the alert
status of United States strategic forces when there was
no valid event," although the July 1980 incident was
classified a false alarm under this definition. It can
be argued that NORAD is wrong in defining only a handful
of incidents as false alarms even under their own
definition. It can reasonably be argued that many more
of the hundreds of incidents "would cause an increase in
the alert status of United States strategic forces when
there was no valid event" if they occurred during a
period of international crisis. The important question
is not whether past mistakes have caused such an increase
in alert status, but whether such mistakes would under
certain conditions lead to an increase in the alert
status. A refusal to address this question represents a
refusal to recognize the extent to which the overall
context, within which errors occur, influences the
possible outcomes from such errors. The frequency of
occurrence of the missile display conferences and of
conferences called to evaluate possible threats is
reported by NORAD as follows:

Routine Missile Display Conferences		Threat Evaluation Conferences
1977	1567	43
1978	1009	70
1979	1544	78
1980	3815	149
1981	2851	186
1982	3716	218
1983	3294	255
1984	2988	153

The frequency with which potentially serious events are
now known to be occurring within this one system
highlights the need for further exploration of worst case
studies.

Two of the most important problems for command and
control centers are computer equipment and programming
techniques. Daniel Ford observes that "The radar of

Thule, Greenland, was designed in the late 1950s. Until
a modernization program is completed, it will remain an-
tiquated by today's technological standards. Two
companion radar installations, using essentially the same
equipment, are sited at Fylingdales Moore, Yorkshire and
Clear, Alaska." 7/ Ford also comments on the fragility
of the electrical supply feeding NORAD, and the inappro-
priate decision made in 1970 to install, despite NORAD's
protext, the Honeywell 6000 series. This batch processor
that handles information in a step-by-step sequence is
not suited to the computational problems involved in
"real time environments," where the demand is to obtain
immediate access to key data and to keep up with rapidly
moving events.

David Bodanis points out that even if modern
computers have been installed, the software often
presents insurmountable obstacles. 8/ In the June 1980
incident, when failure of a computer chip caused
"detection" of a Soviet missile attack, for example, he
points out that NORAD officials "were terrified of the
software responsible. They had no monitors to let them
know what messages were being sent out, as patching in
such monitors could interfere with the flow of data.
They had no comprehensive checking software to pick out
equipment faults such as the one at the heart of the
alert, because no one had been able to design software
that would do the checking and yet not interfere with the
original software. ... they were scared to hook their
computer up with the surveillance people because they
could not guarantee that the program doing the hooking up
would not make things worse."

Bodanis, who advocates structured programming
techniques for such complex computer systems, also points
out that the radar at Fylingdales can detect only a few
dozen individual Soviet warheads because the software was
designed in the early 1960s. It would be impossible from
this source to distinguish between a limited attack and a
full scale Soviet assault, a technical situation that
raises serious doubts about any doctrine of limited
nuclear war. Ford makes similar arguments when he points
out that even if warning systems work, and this is by no
means to be taken for granted, the information from such
systems goes into 1960s computers built to handle
situations involving perhaps 50 warheads. Ford argues
that in a modern strike, involving thousands of missiles
and decoys, they would be unable to handle the data, and

be incapable of telling the size of an attack or predict the likely targets.

These problems are likely to become more severe as technological imperatives dictate future weapons systems. While President Reagan has been forthright in advocating high tech space based systems under the rubric of the so-called Strategic Defense Initiative (SDI), many computer specialists predict insurmountable problems in achieving the goals of the "Star Wars" program. Defense Secretary Caspar Weinberger in an interview with Omni magazine argues that "The goal would be to try it against thousands of missiles, including missiles that carry ten independent warheads, and missiles whose warheads can change direction. It is, I am told, essentially a problem of enormous and extraordinarily rapid computer capability. We must develop that to the point where we can identify, track and destroy several thousand targets in a very, very short space of time." Weinberger concedes in the same interview that this "very, very short space of time" would be less than three minutes to activate the first layer of the proposed system. Such a schedule requires completely autonomous computer control with no time for human beings to identify false alarms.

Patricia Mische writes: "It has been estimated that the software would require nearly ten million lines of code. This would, by far, be the largest program ever written." 9/ These severe software problems must be seen in the context of the unavailability of sufficiently powerful computers. Thus the Union of Concerned Scientists in discussing the problems of "Star Wars" argues that "hundreds of space weapons, each capable of delivering hundreds of energy beams or non-nuclear kill devices, would have to be aimed at some 1,000 targets in the course of only five to eight minutes. (After this short period, the enemy missiles would begin releasing their multiple warheads and the number of targets would increase by a factor of up to ten.) Computers capable of accomplishing this sort of massive, instantaneous data processing do not exist." 10/

David Parnas was a member of the Panel on Computing in Support of Battle Management convened by the Strategic Defense Initiative Organization (SDIO). His resignation from the panel was accompanied by eight technical papers he had produced to explain why "systems of the sort being considered by the SDIO cannot be built." 11/ The second of these papers, "Why the SDI Software will be Untrustworthy," concludes that "All of the cost estimates indicate that this will be the most massive software project ever attempted. The system has numerous technical characteristics that will make it more difficult than previous systems, independent of size. Because of the extreme demands on the system and our inability to test it, we will never be able to have any confidence, that we have succeeded. Nuclear weapons will remain a potent threat."

It can be argued that the problem of unintended nuclear war is becoming increasingly serious in proportion to the progressive computerization of the command, control and communications systems. This trend is almost certainly bound to continue, as is the pressure for launch on warning systems. Alan Borning of the Department of Computer Science, University of Washington, is particularly concerned with the problems of computer system reliability and nuclear war. 12/ He details the various applications of computers, noting that "nuclear forces in particular depend heavily on computer systems for such tasks as guiding missiles, analyzing sensor data and warning of possible attack, and controlling communications systems." Borning sees "a number of disturbing facts and trends" and in common with most if not all who have considered the problem, he expresses doubts as to the reliability of such systems during times of crisis. Broning elaborates on the highly interactive and coupled nature of the Soviet and Western systems and points out that "To be at all confident of the reliability of complex systems there must be a period of testing under conditions of actual use. As far as is publicly known, the command and control systems of the US and the USSR have never been 'tested' under conditions of simultaneous high alert." The trend towards launch on warning systems is also criticized by Borning, who doubts the practicality of such policy because of considerations associated with computer systems. The risks of unintended nuclear war are increased further by launch on warning systems. Borning's excellent annotated bibliography on computer reliability and nuclear war 13/ is of great value in this regard.

In normal times the inevitable errors and the problems involved in command and control are not necessarily dangerous. But in times of heightened tension not only does it seem likely that the probability

of various types of accidents and malfunctions is likely
to increase as the number of flights, take-offs,
landings, levels of alert and information flow all
increase, but the consequences of accidents is likely to
increase significantly the probability of unintended
nuclear war.

OTHER FACTORS

The various human problems associated with
maintenance of nuclear weapons systems should not be
overlooked. In August 1969 an Air Force major was
suspended for allowing three men, described as having
"dangerous psychiatric problems" to guard nuclear weapons
at a base near San Francisco. One of the guards was
accused of going berserk with a loaded carbine while at
the base. The major testified that although he had
received unfavorable psychiatric reports on the three
guards, he had not removed them because he was short of
staff. These incidents are not uncommon.

Maurice Bradley of the Psychology Department at
Strathclyde University is particularly interested in
psychological processes increasing the risks of
unintended nuclear war. 14/ His documentation includes
340 references on risks and the relevant psychology of
accidental nuclear war; 85 recent relevant news items;
and 32 surveys of attitudes to nuclear war. Bradley
argues that "The psychology of risk shows how we perceive
the many dangers in life quite precisely on one level,
but that, on another level we seem to operate denial
processes that allow us to behave as if some known risks
did not exist, especially when we believe we can do
nothing to avoid them." Bradley relates this literature
to nuclear systems by asserting that "If we traditionally
accepted the risk of accidents, in the sincere belief
that mistakes can be forgiven, it now seems obvious that
we have reached a stage of denying that there are any
risks involved with nuclear weapons, in order to avoid
facing the consequences that will arise if such systems
seriously malfunction."

Bradley presents survey evidence that suggests that
nuclear decision makers accept that nuclear war would be
catastrophic but deny there is any serious possibility
that it will occur "presumably believing in deterrence,
the sophistication of leadership, and that only a

rational decision could launch such weapons." A similar argument is developed by Kringlen 15/ in his essay on the myth of rationality in situations of crisis. Bradley also reports on many cases of nuclear accidents involving boredom, misread signals, practical jokes and serious departures from safety procedures.

In some of the reported incidents the use of drugs has been a significant factor, for example, the USS Nolland incident involved LSD. Hard drugs have been a factor in a number of cases including the case in 1969 when a Cuban defector flew a MIG jet through radar defenses and landed in Florida. The potential for increasing errors from such sources cannot be ignored in any serious consideration of unintended nuclear war. In the early 1970s an Army code specialist said he was sometimes under the influence of marijuana while he worked with secret materials while stationed at a United States nuclear missile base in Germany. He said soldiers sometimes were "high" when they attached nuclear warheads to the missiles and when making missiles operational. Such a claim may be false, but the number of similar stories raises important questions concerning drug abuse.

During the years 1975-1977 about 5,000 persons per year were removed from access to United States nuclear weapons programs because of alcohol abuse, drug abuse or mental illness. Stress, boredom and isolation are inherent in contemporary nuclear weapons systems. General George Blanchard, Senior Field Commander in Europe, "now estimates that eight percent of all GIs stationed in Europe are using hard drugs. Mike D'Arcy, a drug counselor for the Berlin Brigade, is quoted in the Bulletin of Atomic Scientists as saying "I would estimate the true statistic to be roughly 65 percent recreational abuse of heroin, hard drugs: 85 percent soft drugs, considered to be hashish, mad dog, soft drugs that are not addictive. Hard core heroin abuse I would estimate between 7-10 percent." The screening process for those involved with nuclear weapons is much more strenuous than for regular forces, and the level of abuse is almost certainly much lower, but the problem still represents a part of the overall picture in considering possibilities for accidental nuclear war.

Mental and drug problems are not limited to the lower echelons of decision making. There are a number of documented historical examples that suggest such problems can extend to the very highest level. For example United

States Secretary of Defense Forrestal (1948–49) was responsible for the United States nuclear weapons program. For a full year before he resigned he was mentally ill with severe depression and paranoia. He committed suicide 55 days after he resigned. His successor Louis Johnson began showing mental instability after one year and was asked to resign in 1950.

President Nixon during the final stages of the impeachment process boasted to a group of congressmen: "I could go into the next room, make a telephone call, and in twenty-five minutes seventy million people will be dead." Secretary of Defense Schlesinger took the unusual precaution of requesting the various nuclear command and control centers to report to him "any unusual message from the President." British Prime Minister Eden was "practically living on Benzedrine" during the Suez Crisis, although his performance was not necessarily impaired by his medical condition. Kennedy too had a similar problem.

Mental instability or drug abuse at the very highest levels may not be a common problem, but some of the particular personality requirements associated with achieving such high political office may be a relevant concern for students of unintended nuclear war. Highly charismatic and emotive leaders, such as President Reagan, may hold particular personal beliefs and have a number of personality traits that, under certain conditions, become very relevant to nuclear war. Studies of the personalities and beliefs of such decision makers could make an important contribution to the prevention of unintended nuclear war.

INCREASED DANGER AT TIMES OF CRISIS

During the Suez crisis of 1956 and against the background of Soviet communiques concerning the consequences of worldwide nuclear war, a series of events were recorded by western intelligence sources on the eve of November 5th. Unidentified jet aircraft were flying over Turkey (the Turkish Air Force went on alert); 100 Soviet MIGs were reported over Syria, a British Canberra bomber was shot down over Syria, and the Soviet fleet was moving through the Dardanelles out of the Black Sea (an event associated with the start of Soviet hostilities). The US General Andrew Goodpaster feared that these events could "trigger off all the NATO operations plan" (at that time all out nuclear strikes on the Soviet Union.)

In fact the jets over Turkey were a flock of geese, the 100 Soviet MIGs were a smaller routine escort returning the President of Syria from a state visit to Moscow, the Canberra crashed through mechanical failure, and the Soviet fleet were engaged in a long scheduled exercise. Bracken, an authority on the command and control of nuclear weapons, argues that the "detection and misinterpretation of these events, against the context of world events from Hungary to Suez, was the first major example of how the size and complexity of worldwide electronic warning systems could, at certain times, create a crisis momentum of its own." 16/

Professor Michael Wallace (University of British Columbia) and Brian Crissey (Applied Computer Science Department, Illinois State University) have used the data on false alarms to estimate how soon a "use them or lose them" situation would develop during any future international crisis. 17/ Using just the data from the NORAD system, and assuming Soviet computers are as good as those in the West and that it takes four minutes to resolve a false alarm, they used a computer simulation to calculate probabilities. If we assume no increase in false alarms during a crisis then it is 95 percent probable that a use them or lose them situation will occur during the first week of any future world crisis, given the expected flight times of forward based Yankee and Pershing missiles.

In normal times when the Soviet Yankee submarines are not close into the American coast and Pershing II is not on high alert, the longer false alarms do not constitute a dilemma. But during a crisis, with heightened levels of tension and massive information overload, the "use them or lose them" pressures will almost certainly dominate. At such times the Permissive Action Links (PALs) which release the command of nuclear weapons to brigade level commanders are activated, and the probability of unintended nuclear war through human error is further increased.

Previous studies of crisis clearly show a substantial increase in information to be processed and consequently greater opportunity for false alarms to be generated and for spurious events to be misinterpreted. In addition, Soviet computer technology lags behind the West, and there is evidence that some of the Soviet software has been spiked through selling such programs to the Soviets on the blackmarket. An article in Computer Weekly points out that the Soviet Union depends on the United States for 60 percent of its advanced software (computer programs) and that many of the programs which are being filtered through illegal trading sources to the Soviets from the United States have deliberate faults built into them.

Crises have not in recent years been a dominant feature of the international system, but during the past five or six years there has been a resurgence of interest among academics in theoretical and empirical studies of crises. In part this is due to the deterioration in relationships that accompanied the Soviet invasion of Afghanistan, and the election of President Reagan in the United States and Prime Minister Thatcher in the United Kingdom. These events contributed significantly to a new cold war and a major upturn in the nuclear arms race. It is not an unreasonable hypothesis to suggest that the probability of a significant crisis involving the United States of America and the Soviet Union is greater now than in the mid-seventies.

An unfortunate aspect of some previous crises has been the speed at which they have developed. In addition this paper has argued that the changed political, psychological and military conditions associated with a crisis tend to increase the probability of events which could cause an increase in the alert status of nuclear forces when, in the words of NORAD, "there was no valid event." Additionally Bracken and others argue that the size and complexity of the worldwide C3I systems can under such conditions create their own crisis momentum.

CONCLUSION

This paper has considered some of the problems associated with the possibility of unintended nuclear war. Various authors have made a number of suggestions for lowering the statistical probability of such a war, including joint crisis control centers and an international satellite monitoring agency. A discussion of the various suggestions is beyond the scope of this paper.

The problem of unintended nuclear war is complex since it involves various known and unknown interactions between human, mechanical and electronic components under a broad range of psychological, social and political conditions. As yet the problem is not adequately delineated in detail, although aspects of its general nature are now clear. Most authors agree that the probability is not constant and varies according to the particular conditions prevalent at any one time. The problem is unlikely to become less complex in the future.

The establishment of an international multidisciplinary academic committee is an important first step in moving towards an understanding of the nature of the problem. Groups such as the International Peace Research Association can play an important part in such developments.

NOTES

1. Sven Hellman, Chief Engineer, Adviser National Security Affairs, Ministry of Defense, Stockholm, discusses this in "Risks of Nuclear War by Mistake—An Overview" in the Swedish publication.

2. Louis Rene Beres, Apocalypse, Chicago University Press, 1980.

3. Stewart Britten, The Invisible Event: An Assessment of the Risk of Accidental or Unauthorized Detonation of Nuclear Weapons and of War by Miscalculation, Menard Press, 1983.

*4. Alistair Edwards, "Accidents have Happened,"

*5. Tim Williams, "The Reliability of Military Electronics,"

*6. Letter dated February 13, 1985 from Lt. Col. Charles Wood, Acting Director of Public Affairs, NORAD, to David Morrison, Center for Defense Information.

7. Daniel Ford, The Button, Simon and Schuster, 1985.

8. David Bodanis, "The Catastrophe Program," The Guardian, June 27, 1985.

*9. Patricia Mische, Star Wars and the State of Our Souls, Winston Press, 1985.

10. UCS briefing paper number 5.

*11. David Parnas, "Software Aspects of Strategic Defense Systems,"

*12. Alan Borning, "Computer System Reliability and Nuclear War,"

*13. Alan Borning, "An Annotated Bibliography on Computer Reliability and Nuclear War,"

510

*14. Maurice Bradley, "Psychological Processes increasing the Risks of Accidental Nuclear War,"

15. Kringlen, The Myth of Rationality in Crisis Situations, in Swedish publication.

16. Paul Bracken, The Command and Control of Nuclear Weapons, Yale University Press, 1983.

*17. Michael Wallace, "Accidental Nuclear War: A Risk Assessment."

*Papers presented at the Manchester conference and available from the Richardson Institute.

32

The Settlement of Border Conflicts: A Theoretical Model with Empirical Illustrations

Kjell-Ake Nordquist

INTRODUCTION

This paper is an attempt to formulate a model for analyzing border conflicts and to present some results from preliminary research based on R.L. Butterworth's compilation of data on interstate security conflicts 1947-74: Managing Interstate Conflict: Data With Synopses.

Although the pattern of Third World armed conflicts after World War II is dominated by colonial and internal wars, "border conflicts" are also frequent -- whether they are disputes that take place in border areas or disputes about the location of the border, or both. Since "nation-building" presumes control of a territorial area, border disputes may be one of the most crucial issues in establishing statehood. At the same time, a border is a matter of common concern between states. No state can have "sovereignty" over a border.

New weapon technology may reduce the military role of borders. At same time, "natural" borders such as mountains, rivers, forests or deserts, and artificial borders, such as the Maginot Line or walls, are all militarily more easily mastered with modern weapon technology. Most studies of borders and international conflict try to associate violent interstate conflicts with geographical proximity or with the number of bordering states. These studies relate the border to certain traits in the international system (distance, fragmentation). The focus of this paper is different in that only conflicts over the location of the border are analyzed.

Defining "border conflict:" A "border conflict" is defined here as a militarized conflict over the definition, delimitation or demarcation of an interstate border. Conflict behavior may take place in a border

511

area, but if the conflict is not over the location of the border it will not be considered a border conflict.

A conflict is militarized if some kind of military operations or demonstrations have been included in the parties' conflict behavior. The analysis covers interstate borders only. The primary party in a conflict will be a government, although various political groups may be involved at different levels. Finally, the conflict is terminated if the parties explicitly state that the conflict is settled. A cease-fire is not considered a settlement.

Empirical Data: The set of independent variables used is drawn from a comprehensive compilation of post-World War II conflicts: Robert L. Butterworth, Managing Interstate Conflict 1945-74. It contains 301 synopsi of "interstate security conflicts." Each synopsis covers one conflict "case." Butterworth has analyzed each of these cases using 47 variables, of which about half concern conflict management efforts. Butterworth's synopsi actually describe only 197 different conflicts, however, because he treats some long-term conflicts as different cases. Taking this into account, in this paper, Butterworth's distinction between border conflicts and others is used as a basis for the discrimination of border conflicts. The application of the definitions previously mentioned in Butterworth's conflict data results in 24 militarized interstate border conflicts between 1947 and 1974 (see Table 1).

Table 1.   Interstate Militarized Border Conflicts 1947-74

Parties	Conflict Area	Agreement Year
Ecuador - Peru	River Amazon Basin	--
Italy - Jugoslavia	Trieste	1954
Burma - China	Border area	1960
Oman/Abu Dhabi - S. Arabia	East Arab Boundaries	1975
Ethiopia - Somalia	Haud Reserve and Ogaden	--
Cambodia - Thailand	Temple of Preah Vihar	--
China - India	Aksai Chin; North East Front.	--
India - Pakistan	Rann of Kutch	1969
Honduras - Nicaragua	Dep. of Gracias a Dios	1960
Argentina - Chile	Beagle Channel Islands	--
Egypt - Sudan	Wadi Halfa	1959
China - Nepal	Border area	1961
Mali - Mauretania	Hodh desert province	1963
China - Soviet Union	Alma Ata region; N East Amur	--
Cambodia - Thailand	Border area	--
Kenya - Somalia	Kenya Northern Frontier	--
Guyana - Venezuela	Essequibo region	--
Algeria - Morocco	Tindouf; Western Sahara	1970
Dahomey (Benin) - Niger	Lete Island (River Niger)	1965
Ghana - U. Volta (Burkina)	Border area	1966
Argentina - Uruguay	Rio de la Plata	1973
Iran - Iraq	Shatt al Arab; Border area	1975
Equatorial Guinea - Gabon	Corisco Bay Islands	1972
Iraq - Kuwait	Warba and Bubiyan Islands	--

Source: R.L. Butterworth, Managing Interstate Conflict 1947-1974, Pittsburgh, 1976.

The regional distribution of the conflicts is the following: 7 in Africa, 7 in Asia, 6 in Central/South America, 3 in the Middle East, 1 in Europe.

Eleven of these conflicts have a symmetric power relation at the initiation of conflict. This symmetry is determined from a power ranking model by Cox and Jacobson and applied by Butterworth. Butterworth made a classification of five categories of states, from "super" to "smallest," and those border conflicts in which both states fell into the same category are defined as "symmetric." These 11 symmetric conflicts are listed below in Table 2.

Table 2. Symmetric Interstate Border Conflicts 1945-1974

Settled	Year	Not Settled (comment)
Algeria - Morocco	1970	Iran - Iraq (war since 1979/80)
Honduras - Nicaragua	1960	Iraq - Kuwait (stalemate)
Dahomey (Benin) - Niger	1965	China - India (negotiations)
Mali - Mauretania	1963	Ecuador - Peru (periodical fighting)
Equat. Guinea - Gabon	1972	
Ghana - U. Vol. (Burkina)	1966	

THE ANALYTICAL FRAMEWORK

A basic assumption for the framework is that one has to investigate developments during three different phases/processes of conflicts, as presented below:

The conflict generating process:
- incompatibility formation
- military planning/preparation
The conflict process:
- conflict behavior
- settlement behavior
The settlement implementation process:
- agreement vs. extra/intra-party factors
- formal/nonformal party interaction

The shift between processes is defined so that a conflict passes from I to II when it fits the criteria for a militarized border conflict and from II to III when an agreement comes into force.

Two main types of variables will be used: structural and contextual. Structural variables are long term variables and are not changed by the actual conflict. Contextual variables are a result of other (economic, political, personal, etc.) circumstances of the actual conflict.

THE CONFLICT GENERATING PROCESS

Main Aspects

This first phase of a conflict is a process ending in a militarized or nonmilitarized border conflict. It has an "open beginning." It consists of a mixture of latent and manifest variables of contextual and structural type. Our task is to trace the emergence of a border conflict. Two areas seem important:

(1) political incompatibility formation (through rhetoric, diplomatic moves, propaganda, etc.) and
(2) military activity: Is there some planning/preparation with special relevance for border actions?

516

Analytical Framework

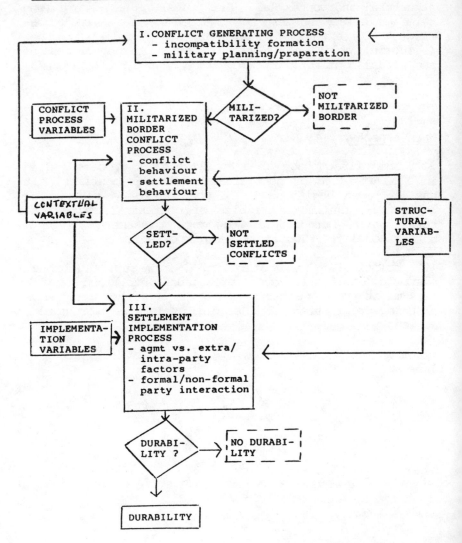

The reason for discriminating between structural and contextual variables may be better understood as seen in Table 3 below, which refers to the formation of value incompatibility and the military policy and preparation for carrying out a border conflict.

The factors in the table are proposals of variables that can be used for the analysis of this process.

```
Table 3.  TYPE OF VARIABLES

                        CONTEXTUAL          STRUCTURAL

INCOMPATIBILITY   Border area assessment  Traditional historic
FORMATION         Leadership relations    animosity
                  External penetration    Cross-border ethnic/rel.
                  (mining, oil fields)    similarities/differences

MILITARY          Build-up in border      Long-term build-up
PREPARATION       areas                   ---> increasing unbalance
                  Deployment of new       Power relations between
                  weapon systems          adjacent states
```

Structural and contextual variables represent to some degree two different traditions of research. Where the contextual variables generally are analyzed through qualitative methods, the structural variables often are analyzed quantitatively.

Contextual Variables

The incompatibility formation part of this process is dependent on the nature of the border issue itself. What type of border area assessment is emerging? Prescott (1978) argues for a three-fold division:
1) territorial boundary disputes; which "result from some quality of the neighboring border-land which makes it attractive...";
2) positional boundary disputes; "concern(s) the actual location of the border, and usually involve(s) a controversy over the interpretation of terms used in defining the boundary";

3) functional boundary disputes; "concern(s) the use of some transboundary resources ..."

Prescott's categories can be related to the general view of a conflict as a "value incompatibility." Values can be of very different character, and there are four basic types of value characteristics. These can help us to clarify the conditions for a settlement of a conflict.

Table 4. FOUR TYPES OF CHARACTERISTICS

	INDIVISIBLE	DIVISIBLE
Material	An unexploited river A piece of art	Territory Capital
Nonmaterial	Sovereignty	Influence

If we relate these four categories to Prescott's different types of border conflict and exemplify with the eleven symmetric border conflicts, the following table emerges:

Table 5. Four Types of Border Conflict Incompatibilities

	Indivisible	Divisible
Material	Positional dispute - border location (Dahomey-Niger, Mali-Mauretania Iran-Iraq Ghana-Upper Volta)	Functional dispute - resource development (Honduras-Nicaragua, Algeria-Morocco, Iraq-Kuwait, Egypt-Sudan, Eq. Guinea-Gabon)
Nonmaterial	Territorial dispute - high value in the territory as such (Ecuador-Peru)	(Political dispute) - influence in the region (China-India)

The bottom, right cell, dispute over political influence, covers an aspect of border conflict which is not included in Prescott's categories, but it applies to his stress upon the function of borders.

Generally one could assume that conflicts over divisible values are easier to settle than those over the indivisible. Whether conflicts over nonmaterial values are easier to settle than conflicts over material values is more difficult to hypothesize--nonmaterial things are often bound to principles, and the attitude toward them is dependent on a variety of factors. Analyzing the very nature of the value contended could be a useful start for the analysis of the succeeding processes since it directs attention towards the unregulated positions of the parties.

A second type of contextual variable mentioned in Table 3, is the role of leadership. Personal relations between national leaders may aggravate a latent conflict or smooth out contention. Examples of these two effects are the Ghana-Upper Volta conflict (Nkrumah vs. Yameogo) and Dahomey-Niger (Maga and Diori). This situation should not be confused with regime change and the personal changes followed by that, of which the Iran-Iraq conflict is an example. Although Khomeiny has a hostile personal attitude towards Iraq, he also represents an ideology that supports hostile attitudes towards the Iraqi Suni government.

A third type of contextual variable is foreign economic penetration. In the cases of Equatorial Guinea-Gabon, Honduras-Nicaragua and Algeria-Morocco, the use of natural resources became an important conflict aggravating factor.

A second main group of contextual variables are--<u>military preparation</u>, more specifically, buildup in border areas and deployment of new weapons systems. These are not found in Butterworth's border data. Additional case studies of each pair of states would be required in order to obtain information.

Structural Variables

All hypotheses in the literature referred to in this study use what we call structural variables when analyzing the causes and origins of border conflicts. As was noted in the introduction, very few studies analyze the special form of international conflict called "border conflict."

Mandel (1980) tests two hypotheses on the outbreak of border disputes, the first illuminating the incompatibility aspect, the other the military aspect:
- border disputes occur with greater frequency and severity between states with low technology than between states with high technology.
- border disputes occur with greater frequency between states of roughly equal power than between states of highly unequal power.

Mandel finds these hypotheses strongly confirmed, using data from Butterworth.

One type of structural variable often considered a cause of conflict is the ethnic and/or religious factor. Butterworth includes the ethnic factor among his independent variables, and a comparison of the 24 border conflicts and all other interstate security conflicts listed by Butterworth gives the following result:

Table 6. Ethnic Factors in:	Non-Border Conflicts	Border Conflicts
No relevant ethnic factor	90 (52.0%)	13 (54.2%)
Slight ethnic factor	21 (12.1%)	5 (20.8%)
Strong and salient	62 (35.8%)	6 (25.0%)
In Sum:	173 (99.9%)	24 (100.0%

Although the number of border conflicts is limited, it seems that the ethnic factor is not particularly associated with border conflicts.

THE CONFLICT PROCESS

This process contains two main aspects:
1) "conflict behavior"
2) "settlement behavior."
These forms of behavior can be related to either contextual or structural variables. Each variable can be described both in conflict-behavioral and settlement-behavioral terms.

"Conflict behavior" is defined as behavior aimed at depriving the counter-party of something valuable. In actual conflicts it means all forms of conflict extending efforts, violent as well as nonviolent. "Settlement behavior" means behavior that facilitates settlement. It can in principle be everything from military surrender to negotiation of "a fair deal" from a (militarily) superior position. An important factor for the choice of conflict mechanism, i.e. for the choice of means to carry out a conflict, is the ability of the mechanism chosen to take care of and use, to the benefit of the party, his resources devoted to the conflict. It seems self-evident and is for that reason omitted from the conflict theory literature.

Nevertheless, in the conflict process this factor becomes crucial to the shift between the two types of conflict process behavior: When are settlement means a better mechanism? When can they use resources best? Theoretically one can split this process into two parts:

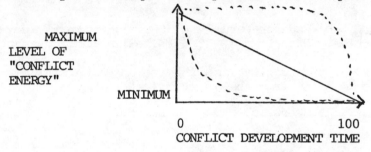

MAXIMUM
LEVEL OF
"CONFLICT
ENERGY"

MINIMUM

0   100

CONFLICT DEVELOPMENT TIME

The continuous line indicates the theoretical 50/50 share between conflict-extending and settlement-directed behavior, respectively, during a full conflict process. The upper dotted line indicates a conflict with the opposite pattern: The settlement directed behavior dominates. An example of a border conflict illustrating the upper line is the on-going war between Iran and Iraq, while the Honduras-Nicaragua conflict is a good illustration of the lower line. Per definition the structural variables of the first process will also influence this process. But there might be such structural variables that were not relevant for the first process but are now. One such variable is for instance "membership in an international governmental organization." Do IGOs' actions, as third parties, have a positive influence on the settlement of border conflicts?

The 11 symmetric border conflicts are distributed in the following way between settled and not settled conflicts and international organizations as third parties:

Table 7. International Organization as Third Party

	Yes		No
Settled	Honduras–Nicaragua	(OAS,x)	Mali–Mauretania
	Algeria–Morocco	(OAU,x)	
	Eq. Guinea–Gabon	(OAU,x)	
	Egypt–Sudan	(UN ,–)	
	Ghana–Upper Volta	(OAU,–)	
	Dahomey–Niger	(CE,–)	
Not Settled	Ecuador–Peru	(OAS,x)	China–India
	Iran–Iraq	(UN,LAS)	Iraq–Kuweit

("x" after organization abbreviation marks involvement of a commission from the organization)

IGOs seem to have a positive effect upon the outcome of border conflicts. Of special interest are the Ecuador-Peru and Iran-Iraq cases. Do they differ from the others in any significant way that can explain their position? Ecuador-Peru is the only conflict that concerns an "indivisible" and "territorial" dispute; in Prescott's sense, the territory as such is so valuable for the parties (or at last one of them) that the efforts of an IO were not satisfactory for the parties. The Iran-Iraq case concerns one of the most torn border areas throughout history: a vital strip of land needed for Iraq's access to the Gulf. With a pronounced hostile attitude from the Iranian side this strategic weakness makes the whole war much broader than the border location. In both of these cases, state core values are threatened through the conflict: for Ecuador and Peru their status as "Amazonian states," and for Iraq a matter of territorial integrity and position in the Arab world.

Making a comparison among all of Butterworth's interstate
nonborder conflicts and the 24 border conflicts shows the
following pattern for "number of fatalities:"

Table 8.   Number of Fatalities in Conflicts

	Nonborder Conflicts		Border Conflicts	
FATALITIES None	33	(19.1%)	9	(37.5%)
1 - 100	49	(28.3%)	7	(29.2%)
101 - 1000	41	(23.7%)	6	(25.0%)
1001 - 2000	13	(7.5%)	2	(8.3%)
greater than - 2000	37	(21.4%)	0	(0.0%)

Border conflicts seem to be less violent than nonborder
conflicts. In fact, over 90% of all border conflicts
have 1000 or less fatalities and over one-third have none
at all.

But is "fatalities" interesting with respect to the
settlement probabilities? Data from the 24 border
conflicts may provide some answers.

Table 9. Number of Settled/Not Settled Conflicts

		Settled	Not Settled
FATALITIES	None	8	1
	1 - 100	3	4
	101 - 1000	3	3
	1001 - 2000	0	2
	greater than - 2000	0	0

The figures in this table point to the fatalities as a
threshold for settlement. It seems that this factor is
of interest for further analysis in the search for
settlement conditions.

The nonmilitary part of the conflict process may
include the leadership-discussion from above. Here, we
shall continue the thread from the discussion of value

incompatibility and ask how the issue is formulated. Is it clearly stated or merely a number of diffuse accusations? Is the issue the only, or clearly dominating issue in the border conflict, or are there other competing interests articulated?

Table 10. Conflict Issue Specification and Connection to Other Issues

THE BORDER ISSUE IS:

		Specific	Diffuse
ISSUE CONNEC- TION TO OTHER ISSUES	Weak	Stability, instrumental situation, good chances for settlement	Instability, low priority, risk for connection to other issues; turns either to square 1 or 4
	Strong	Instability, competitive situation, if border issue gains upper hand it moves to square 1, otherwise to square 4	Stability, the border issues is dominated by the connection; pro- tracted conflict

---

From this we hypothesize that specific and independent border issues are more often settled than diffuse and strongly connected issues? A start is to investigate the moves of the 11 symmetric conflicts.

handled. Two examples were the absence of objective data, which fueled the conflict and the lack of any means for compensating losers in the conflict.

Law and Business

Our colleagues in the law and business schools found the conventional conflict management processes in this dispute working normally. Nor could they diagnose illness or dysfunction. The business community responded to the downzoning proposal and the TDZ order like an immune system mobilizing against infection. Working as an interest group through its chamber of commerce, business and industry representatives did what they normally do: identify superordinate goals and form coalitions to further these goals. Here is the mobilization of true interest groups (in contrast to the recall committees.) Business, while it rejected the downzoning approach and TDZ in particular, reaffirmed its support for the Comprehensive Plan.

The lawyer-analysts felt that the conventional systems handled the problem reasonably well, and suggested actions which might have increased the effectiveness of government. The commonly used judicial fact-finding process might have reduced "heat" and in-creased "light" in the conflict. An alternative measure to TDZ (e.g. a permit moratorium) that was less likely to prejudge the proposal review outcome, anger opponents, and disappoint supporters might have been used. The conventional win/lose legal and administrative procedures might have been facilitated by the introduction of alternative dispute resolution methods such as mediation and arbitration by neutral "masters."

Social Conflict

The social conflict diagnosticians performed a battery of tests on the "patient," using a range of concepts and methods. One of them looked for disputant motivation in the larger social, political and economic structures of Boulder County. He saw basic economic and political interests in conflict and the actors making strategic decisions in pursuit of those interests. Another saw "pathologies" in communication and perception

Table 11.

Conflict Dynamics Before Settlement
(Settled conflicts are underlined, position changing
conflicts in boxes.)

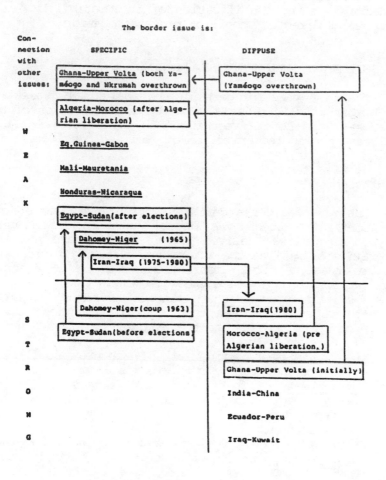

Table 11 shows that all settled conflicts are specific and have weak connections to other issues, and that the moves of the conflicts are (all but one (Iran-Iraq)) moving towards settlement. This move means a clarification of the issue of contention. Some of the reasons for the moves are indicated in the table. The Iran-Iraq move may depend on the change of Iranian government which made the border issue broader when the Alter agreement from 1975 was signed.

This table indicates that de-linking of connected border issues and clarification of incompatibility is a "settlement directed" conflict process behavior.

THE SETTLEMENT IMPLEMENTATION PROCESS

The last phase/process in the analytical framework for border conflicts deals with the implementation of an agreement, and before reaching this point, the conflict will have passed the criterion of "settled conflict."

Main Aspects

One may consider a durable settlement a function of the conflict process. A durable settlement inherits certain qualities derived from the parties' value priorities as well as the interstate system. In order to explore these a first distinction would be to discuss what factors can influence the agreement.

The intra-treaty factors concern two major issues:
- the relation between the value distribution agreed upon in the treaty and the parties' internal ranking of the disputed value/s.
- the management/regulation of future conflicts, either related to the regulated issue or other.

Extra-treaty factors are more numerous and of intra-party and extra-party nature, respectively:
*intra-party:
- social/economic/political changes that make the conflict issue become a) absorbed, b) split into autonomous issues, c) de-priorited, getting lower relative importance, or d) re-prioritied, getting higher relative importance.

*extra-party:

- change in relations with other parties on non-border issues,

- change in relations with a party and non-party,

- change in the international environment, economically, ideologically, etc.

Our discussion of the last aspect of the settlement implementation starts from the assumption above, that the general pattern of peaceful relations between the signing parties influence the durability of a border agreement. State relations can be either formal or nonformal, the last type means private forms of transborder contacts, for tourism, work, trade, family contacts, etc.

The relative share of these types of contacts between states may indicate some important aspect for settlement durability. Table 12 illustrates the case.

Table 12.		Level of Formal Contacts	
		High	Low
LEVEL OF NON-FORMAL CONTACTS	HIGH	Nordic countries	Israel-Jordan
	LOW	USA-USSR	North Korea-South Korea

The high/high and low/low are in a sense very stable "systems." There is reason to believe that an agreement should be harmonious with the general interaction pattern between the parties. Although the conflict as such could be beneficial for the parties in terms of reshaping attitudes and increased internal strength, one should not expect an agreement over a specific issue to resolve other issues, to which the commitment from the parties and their negotiators has been relatively low. Testing this hypothesis for possible ways of analyzing conditions

528

for durable settlements of border conflicts would be interesting.

SUMMARY

This paper is a discussion of a proposal for a theoretical model for the analysis of border conflicts. A review of the literature over border conflict studies shows a severe lack of theorizing about causes of border conflicts and conditions for settlement. Most studies are case studies or regional studies.

BIBLIOGRAPHY

Border and Territorial Disputes, Day, A.J. (Ed.), A. Keesing's Reference Publication, Longman London, 1982.
Butterworth, R.L., Managing Interstate Conflict 1945-74: Data with Synopses, University of Pittsburg, Pa. 1976.
The International Regulation of Frontier Disputes, Luard, E. (Ed.), Thames and Hudson, London, 1970.
Midlarsky, M., On War. Political Violence in the International System, The Free Press, New York, 1975.
Prescott, J.R.V., Boundaries and Frontiers, Croom Helm, London, 1978.Randle, R.F., The Origins of Peace, A Study of Peacemaking and the Structure of Peace Settlements. The Free Press, New York, 1973.
Richardson, L.F., Statistics of Deadly Quarrels, Quadrangle Books, Chicago, 1960.
Starr, H. and Most, B.A., "The Substance and Study of Borders in International Relations Research," International Studies Quarterly, Vol. 20, No. 4, 1976.
Studying Boundary Conflicts, Tagil, S. (Ed.), Esselte Studium, Lund, 1977.Wallace, M. and Wilson, J.M., "Non-Linear Arms Race Models," Journal of Peace Research, Vol. XV, No. 2, 1978. Universitetsforlaget, Oslo.

33

The Dynamics of Reform and Repression in the South African Conflict and the Emerging Role of the South African Defense Forces

Elling Njal Tjonneland

> The process of ensuring and maintaining the sovereignty of a state's authority in a conflict situation has, through the evolution of warfare, shifted from a purely military to an integrated national action ... The resolution of a conflict in the times in which we now live demands interdependent and coordinated action in all fields ... We are today involved in a war ... The striving for specific aims must be coordinated with all the means available to the state. --(White Paper on Defense and Armaments Supply, 1977)

From the perspective of the early 1970s the ruling National Party in South Africa had seemingly gone from strength to strength in the postwar period: high growth rates in the economy; further elaboration and development of the apartheid policy and a Black population apparently under control; remarkable improvement in the relative social and economic position of the Afrikaners vis a vis the English-speaking Whites; the Afrikaner ethnic identity and unity continuously strengthened and consolidated; and -- in a process probably unique in a comparative perspective -- the National Party had managed to increase its support among the White population in almost every election since 1948. By the early 1970s the Party had already created an image of itself as an almost monolithic bloc.

By the late 1970s South Africa was surrounded by militant Black ruled states which were committed to the liberation struggle and eradication of apartheid. South Africa had to prepare for war at the border and maintain an increasingly costly military occupation of Namibia. The economy was in crisis, poverty was deepening and a massive unemployment was accelerating, creating an explosive social situation. The reemergence of Black nationalism and a new tide of Black resistance underscored the inability of the regime to achieve legitimacy and obtain support for the apartheid policy from the majority of the population.

Faced with the combined and interlinked effects of regional developments, the economic crisis and an increasingly explosive social and political situation, the apartheid regime became unable to formulate a coherent policy response which could unite die volk and lay the foundation for economic recovery and political stability. In the end Prime Minister Vorster was forced to resign and was replaced by Defense Minister P.W. Botha. In this paper I will argue that P.W. Botha's coming to power was much more than a change of the head of government. Botha's arrival marked the beginning of a wide-ranging reorganization and restructuring of White politics and the apartheid state and has led to the emergence of an increasingly authoritarian military-bureaucratic regime.

FROM VORSTER TO BOTHA

The change from Vorster to Botha was generally welcomed by South Africa's allies in the West. Chester Crocker, the influential assistant secretary of state for African affairs in the Reagan administration, and an architect of the policy of change through "constructive engagement" and dialogue with the regime, saw the shift as a "drawn-out coup d'etat" which brought a new group of modernizing afrikaners to power. 1/

It is partially correct to say that P.W. Botha's rise to power was characterized by attempts to map out a new strategy. But to present the policy changes introduced by the new regime as a break with apartheid and as reforms which pointed towards a future nonracial South Africa is untrue. Neither the statements, nor the policies of Botha give substance to such interpretations. The strategy introduced by the new government and associated with the names of Wiehahn and Riekert, the Koornhof Bills, the new constitution and the proposals for the Constellation of States in Southern Africa are summarized as follows.

The new administration had intended to facilitate the emergence of new allies among the Blacks. Its leaders had begun to realize that the Homeland leaders and the bureaucracies set up there were too weak and isolated to be able to act as "buffers" between the Whites and the Black majority. This realization led to a change of policy in two directions. First, the regime tried to incorporate the two Black minority groups, the Asians and the coloreds, into the political system; with the right to vote and to elect their own representatives to the new tricameral parliament. Second, Botha tried to obtain support from the urban Africans -- the 2-4 million with residential rights in the townships around the "White" cities in South Africa. Incorporation was to be achieved partly by improving their material living conditions through upgraded housing conditions, educational reforms and services, and by gradual incorporation into government and administrative structures in the townships (at a later stage, perhaps, even at the national level). Of particular importance in these policy changes was the attempt to stimulate the emergence, expansion and consolidation of a Black middle class and the coopting of the rapidly expanding Black trade union movement through changes in the industrial relations system.

The policy changes toward the urban Blacks was a de facto recognition of their right to remain in "White" South Africa, and as such it was a break with the past and a "violation" of the basic principles and aims of apartheid. The second "package of policies" introduced by Botha, however, represented a continuation of apartheid principles directed towards the vast majority of Blacks who lived in the "homelands" and serviced "White interest" as migrant workers. The pressures created by the impoverishment and breakdown in the "home-lands," the massive unemployment and the increasingly efficient methods used by Blacks to circumvent the system led the new regime to introduce new and more advanced forms of control to ensure that the "outsiders" remained "outside" in the "homelands" and only passed through the "influx" control and moved "inside" in accordance with economic needs and legal procedures. In brief, these policy changes were introduced to rationalize and modernize apartheid and to make apartheid machinery run more smoothly.

A less explicitly articulated aspect of the new strategy were the (vague) ideas inspired by monetarist ideology and liberalist conceptions of the role of the state that underlay much of the Botha regime's thinking on the need for changes. By reducing public expenditures, stimulating the private market and freeing the market forces from state regulation, influential ideologists within the regime expected to be able to lay the foundation for an economic recovery, create job opportunities and solve the pressing social problems. Changes along these lines, they believed, would not only ensure continued expansion of the "free enterprise system," but would also lead Blacks to struggle and bargain through the market mechanism rather than to attempt to control the political system. By leaving as much as possible to the market forces, and by relying on the private sector to solve the pressing social and economic problems, the regime expected to be able to create a "legitimacy," if not for the government, at least for the ideology of free enterprise and capitalism, that would be acceptable to the Blacks. Beyond these policy changes two additional and closely interrelated dimensions of change, represented by the shift from Vorster to Botha, must be analyzed: The restructuring of the apartheid state and the new developments within Afrikaner nationalism and White politics.

Centralization of State Power and the Military

The apartheid state had already developed into a highly interventionist state requiring the coordination of a vast army of state bureaucrats. In the Vorster-era this gave rise to a highly bureaucratic, complex and increasingly inefficient administration which in the end, at the height of the "information scandal," forced Vorster to resign. 2/

The need for a major overhaul and a thorough rethinking of the role of the state itself became urgent. P.W. Botha initiated a technocratic and managerial revolution and streamlined the political and administrative structures. A major reorganization and rationalization of the decision-making process was undertaken. Its main characteristics were increased power and influence of the executive; a growing centralization of power in an expanded Prime Minister's office (and later, with the new constitution, the institutionalization of a strong presidency); and a corresponding decline of the role of the White parliament and the National Party.

Closely linked to this restructure of the policymaking process, a restructure which increasingly insulated broad state policymaking from the party-legislative arena, Botha also attempted to develop a corporatist system of national economic management and planning. This development paved the way for a closer alliance and working relationship among the new regime, business organizations and major corporations.

This centralization and concentration of state power was coupled with an increase in the political influence of the military with a strong presence of military officers in the formulation, coordination and implementation of public policy. (The heads of the military played the key role in advising P.W. Botha; close personal relations had been forged between SADF officers and P.W. Botha during his period as minister of defense.)

The South African Defense Forces (SADF) had, historically, been a loose and weak organization, but gradually, from the early 1960s, it became a highly rationalized devise for the preservation of White supremacy and the apartheid state. This change is illustrated by the rapid expansion of military forces, improved operational capabilities, increases in the military budgets and in the growth of an armaments industry. In addition to quantitative expansion and growth, the militarization also implied a qualitative shift in the role of the military in apartheid politics, a shift which has given SADF increased power in almost every sphere of South African life. SADF had traditionally been anchored in the liberal British model, based on separation of political and military functions and the predominance of civil over military authority. The dynamics of militarization -- a product both of international isolation (in particular the arms embargo) and domestic and regional pressures created by Black nationalism -- began to change the SADF during the 1970s. The change led to the incursion of military personnel into political decision-making and civil law enforcement. 3/

SADF officers began to advocate what they termed the "total national strategy." They pointed to the need for coordinated actions among all government departments and institutions to counter what they perceived as a multidimensional "communist onslaught" against the Republic of South Africa, in the ideological, cultural, political and diplomatic fields.

The 1977 White Paper on defence and armaments supply was the first major public indication of the growing influence of this still vague notion of a "total strategy." With the elevation of Defense Minister P.W.

Botha to prime minister in 1978 the foundation was laid for military involvement in top decision-making bodies. The State Security Council (SSC) emerged as the single most important decision body in the new centralized system developed under Botha. The military -- more precisely, the whole security establishment, centered on the SADF -- now has a substantial and increasing, if not yet preponderant, influence in the SSC and it exerts a major influence on the political process as adviser, coordinator, supervisor and, to some extent, executor of public policy.

Cleavages within Afrikaner Nationalism and Restructuring of White Politics

The latent tensions and contradictions within the ruling National Party became manifest toward the late 1970s and in the end led to a full split within the Afrikaner circle, the formation of the breakaway Konservatiewe Party, the flourishing of other rightwing groups and the resurfacing of an anti-capitalist fascist corporatism. The Party found it more and more difficult to appeal to ethnic identity and volkseenheid across dividing socio-economic interests and conflicting conceptions of key themes and dimensions within Afrikaner nationalist ideology.

A deep and irrevocable split developed along class and ideological lines while the traditional distinction between the political cultures of Afrikaners and English-speaking Whites became blurred, leading to reduced ties of loyalty and identification between political parties and the electorate. 4/ The net result of these new patterns of cleavages and alliances was to reduce the importance of ethnic identity as a source for party affiliation among Whites. It led to the emergence of new groups of more technocratic leaders in the National party, leaders more receptive to the authoritarian positions favored by the military, and more prepared to attempt to solve the crisis by following the strategy of reform outlined above.

THE POLITICS OF FAILED REFORMS

The escalating opposition in the townships to the government since 1984 leading to direct involvement of military troops, the symptoms of the deepening economic crisis, and spreading international hostility, are indications of the failure of the Botha regime's strategy of reform and attempts to regain control. Three main reasons can be identified.

First, conflicts within the White community tended to slow down, and even block the decision-making process and the implementation of the reform strategy. The conflicts within the party-legislative arena and fear of losing voters to the right were of particular importance here. However, the enormous state bureaucracy with the task of running the apartheid machinery and maintaining control, also played an increasingly more manifest political role. Obstruction, and even direct sabotage, have prevented reform and change. The role of racism and the deeply ingrained herrenvolk mentality of the White society was also a powerful force against change. It seemed to prevent the emergence of pragmatic flexible attitudes crucial to foster the development of Black groups willing to collaborate with the regime.

Second, even when reforms and changes have been implemented as planned, the intended effects have generally not materialized. They have often been contradictory and sometimes have even stimulated new resistance and increased support for radical Black nationalism. There are groups which have benefited materially from the reforms, but this has not generally led to increased support for the regime's policies. (Indeed many of those who have benefited have become prominent leaders of the resistance). With the intensity of the conflict in South Africa, the strength of the opposition and the widespread support for the nationalist cause, any Black who wishes to collaborate with the regime immediately becomes isolated and is unable to act as a "buffer," and can be in no position to increase the legitimacy of the regime.

The fate of the economic reforms, which were intended to reduce public expenditures and give new stimulus to the market forces in an attempt to restore growth and solve the pressing social problems, is particularly instructive. It has proved extremely difficult to curb government expenditures. The regime has cut down subsidies on items such as food and transport, but has increased its spending in areas like defense and maintenance of internal security, salaries to White civil servants and subsidies of farmers. The rising interest rate has reduced demands and has led to massive layoffs of Black workers, while the policy of allowing the exchange rate to float has boosted inflation via higher import costs as a result of the falling value of the rand. The policy of monetarism has led, in South Africa as it has elsewhere where this antidote has been tried, to a rise in unemployment combined with downward pressure on wages and a rising cost of living. The social and economic problems underlying the unrest have thus increased and the political pressure upon the regime has intensified.

Third, and most important, the Blacks have not been available for manipulation. They have not been passive recipients of the changes, but active subjects in the process, rejecting and resisting the regime's strategy for reform and control. Often they have managed to put the regime on the defensive and have even made it more difficult to stabilize the situation than it was before the process was initiated. The reforms of the industrial relations system are illustrative. The intention was to gain control of the rapidly expanding independent trade union movement through cooptation rather than through the costly and increasingly inefficient methods of crude repression. By recognizing the unions and tying them to the established and heavily bureaucratized concilation machinery for settlement of wages and disputes, the regime expected to be able to restrict the activities of the unions to economistic "bread-and-butter" issues and force them to follow the "rules of the game" (a strategy which has been successfully pursued vis a vis White workers since 1926). The Black unions, however, accepted the benefits contained in the new strategy, but refused to accept the restrictions. Today the independent trade union movement has emerged as one of the most powerful supporters for the elimination of Apartheid and for other radical changes.

The regime's strategy for cooptation of the urban Africans through reform of local government structures is equally telling. Botha intended to shift the responsibility of administering "urban African affairs" from White officials to "city councils" elected by and among the urban Africans themselves. In 1983, 38 such councils were established. The intention was to have 104 councils functioning by the end of 1984. By April 1985, all but three had collapsed because of Black boycotts and pressure upon council members to withdraw. In the end the government had to intervene with police and military troops and, from July 1985, with the proclamation of a

State of Emergency. President P.W. Botha now finds himself in the same position as his predecessor, Vorster. With a stabilization strategy in ruins, a regime and a White community deeply split, demoralized and frustrated, and with former allies calling for his resignation; Botha finds himself unable to formulate a coherent policy response beyond the use of massive repression.

TOWARDS A NEW STRATEGIC OFFENSIVE

One can reasonably conclude that a return to apartheid fundamentalism is unlikely. It is true that the right wing of Afrikaner nationalism has a substantial following and that its support is likely to expand as Black resistance continues and the regime remains incapable of moving into the offensive. The right wing, however, is in no position to become a government alternative. Neither are there any reasons to expect a reunion of the right wing and the National Party. The preconditions for a successful mobilization of die volk on an ethnically exclusive program no longer exist. The majority of the Afrikaners have realized that some changes and adaptations are necessary in order to survive. (This should not be interpreted as saying that the Afrikaner right wing will not continue to exert a strong influence on the National Party. Frighteningly enough, "Ku-Klux-Klan"-type terror organizations which physically assault and kill Blacks and White traitors, kaffirboeties, may develop.)

The economic and political pressure upon the regime is likely to continue and accelerate. A return to the situation of the 1960s -- when the apartheid state following the Sharpeville massacre managed to crush the Black resistance and silence the organized opposition -- is not probable; the liberation forces today are strong, prepared and organized, support is widespread, and the state's ability to create fear among the Blacks by use of repressive powers and physical strength alone is limited. The regime will probably remain incapable of formulating a coherent policy response beyond the massive use of violence, and thereby also increase general frustration and demoralization. The fear of losing control in the streets, the quarters and the townships which is beginning to characterize the White community may increase and create shockwaves throughout the White community. But there is no reason to expect the National

Party to lose its position as the dominant political party in the White parliament.

Elements within the White society have been attempting to map out a new strategic offensive aimed at defusing political conflict and restructuring the economy. This is a strategy which goes well beyond the reforms analyzed above and takes as its starting point the inevitability of the political incorporation of the Blacks. This inevitability has led to the emergence of a new strategy -- still vague and contradictory -- where the emphasis seems to be on the need to remove all racial discrimination still in the statute books; to abandon the political and territorial premises of apartheid, though not necessarily of race and ethnicity; to (possibly) reintegrate the "homelands;" to create new local and regional structures and eventually to establish some of federal South Africa. 5/

There are two main components in the offensive. The first is the formulation of a new regional strategy designed to regulate population movements and settlement within newly defined regional units and centered on the metropolitan areas and embracing neighboring homelands or parts of homelands deemed to fall within the labor supply catchment areas. The new residential areas will be on the suburban periphery of the metropolitan areas to increase employment and income through the fostering of informal sector activities and industrial decentralization.

This strategy is, basically, a continuation of the traditional policy of decentralization of industries. It has been pursued with limited success since the early 1960s in an attempt to reap the benefits of cheap labor without the burden of having Black Africans living on the "White man's land." Some important changes are, however, contained in the new proposals: the emphasis on economic needs and market forces; the reintegration of "homelands" with "White" areas and establishment of new regional units in economic planning and management; and the albeit slow, recognition of the inevitability of raising the level of Black African urbanization. Through these changes the government expects to be able to solve some of the pressing social problems. To lay the foundation for an "orderly urbanization" and to legitimize capitalism.

The second component in the emerging strategy is the reform of local and regional government structures with corresponding constitutional changes. The need for a political incorporation of the Black Africans is recognized, but the importance of avoiding majority rule is also emphasized. The ideologists and planners fear that African rule within a unitary state might lead to administrative chaos, devastating ethnic conflicts and even socialism. There has been an intensive search for alternative political models lying somewhere between apartheid and majority rule. The ideas of federalism and the notions of constitutional protection of group interests and minority rights have emerged as the most popular themes in this debate.[6]

The federal model is attractive to its protagonists because it may secure economic freedom and private enterprise, as well as protect the White minority. The model, combined with relatively autonomous local and regional political entities, can fragment a national majority regionally and serve to "localize" conflicts. Federalism easily lends itself to a system of institutional checks and balances both regionally and within the central state (from veto rights to independent bodies) which limit any one group's access to political power. Federalism is envisaged as a prescription for a minimal or limited government which would be incapable of implementing radical social change. The hope is that a federal constitution may place the central state above political conflicts, making it difficult to mobilize nationwide forces around any demands of a national scope. A federal state would, they expect, by default, leave intact the foundations of the economy and expose only marginal or localized elements of the economic system to modification.

In an assessment of this emerging strategy and its chances of success one can raise the same questions that were posed on Botha's failed strategy. But one is generally left with the same answers. If implemented the way it is intended the strategy is unlikely to achieve its aims. The new regional strategy can hardly create employment and income and solve the pressing problems of poverty. Above all the strategy would be unable to satisfy popular demands and aspirations. A key element and precondition for the further development of this strategy -- Black participation in local government -- is not forthcoming.

The most likely scenario in the short to medium term is continued militarization and concentration of crucial functions in executive organs isolated from the party-legislative arena and insulated from electoral pressures and public scrutiny. The military has been able to accumulate political influence and social power and lay claims to increased fiscal resources. The future is likely to see a continuation or acceleration of this "creeping coup," a growing but gradual and low-key penetration of the military into key public decision-making bodies and into the social institutions and collective psychologies of the White community.

The ideology of "total strategy" is, at the present level of development, primitive, transparently self-rationalizing, and largely devoid of any practical positive content. The guiding spirit stems from rationalized and essentially authoritarian conceptions of the uses of power. Judging from experience, the level of state violence and repression is likely to accelerate dramatically. One may expect, under martial law and a total news blackout, house-to-house searches backed by uninhibited use of firepower; torture (on a larger scale than is now practiced) and execution of suspects; deportation and concentration camps; and intensified military destablization of the neighboring states.

Militarization also gives rise to new dimensions to the division, frustration and fear within the White society, as witnessed in the debates on conscription, the economic costs and increased tensions between SADF and the business community. (The private sector has been receptive to the burgeoning defense industry and the ties to SADF, through the military-industrial complex are very close, but the burden of war and lack of skilled manpower following the extensions of military service for White males, is beginning to be felt).

CONCLUSION

The dilemma of the South African regime is classic. The Apartheid leaders have realized the need for political changes, but at the same time they want to avoid and prevent a radical social transformation. The result has been a combination of repression and authoritarian "reforms" from above. When these reforms are rejected by the Blacks, the regime resorts to the use of massive violence and repression in an attempt to regain control. The dynamics of this development has led to a growing militarization and the emergence of an increasingly military-bureaucratic state.

Structural movement in the apartheid society and in its international environment (partly also the close personal relations forged between P.W. Botha and the heads of SADF) has resulted in a strong and increasing military influence over public policy formulation, coordination and implementation. This increased role of SADF is likely to exacerbate the racial cleavages and tensions, and the costs will be paid in civil liberties, human rights, elimination of political institutions and tightly controlled participation. The analysis of apartheid politics under Botha has, however, also pointed out that the state's ability to retain the initiative, to set the pace, and to "form" the terrain of political struggle, has weakened considerably. Despite the militarization and expansion of the repressive powers of the state, it is the African National Congress and the Blacks themselves who are on the offensive. The future development of South Africa is increasingly dependent upon the strength, the strategy and the tactics of the liberation forces.

NOTES

1. See Crocker's article "South Africa: Strategy for Change," Foreign Affairs, 59, 1980–81, 2:323–51.

2. Cfr. Dan O'Meara, "'Muldergate' and the Politics of Afrikaner Nationalism," supplement to Work in Progress, 22, 1983; and Hermann Giliomee, The Parting of the Ways, South African Politics 1976–1982, Cape Town: David Philip, 1982.

3. The major study of the dynamics of militarization and the political role of the SADF is an important book by Philip H. Frankel, Pretoria's Praetorians: Civil-Military Relations in South Africa, Cambridge: Cambridge University Press, 1984. (This is actually the first book-length inquiry into the SADF and my major source of information on the issues raised in the sub-title.) Cfr. also K.W. Grundy: The Militarization of South African Politics, London: I.B. Tauris, 1986; and G. Cawthra, Brutal Force -- The Apartheid War Machine, London: International Defence and Aid for Southern Africa, 1986.

4. Cf. C. Charney, "Class Conflict and the National Party Split," Journal of Southern African Studies, 10, 1984, 2:269–82.

542

5. This section is indebted to an excellent analysis provided in W. Cobbet et al, "Regionalism, Federalism and the reconstruction of the South African state," South African Labour Bulletin, 10, 1985, 7:87-116.

6. A major theoretical contribution emerging from this tradition is Arend Lijphart's Power-Sharing in South Africa, Berkeley: Institute of International Studies, University of California, 1985 (Policy Papers in International Affairs No. 24). Cfr. the critical examination of this strategy in R. Southall, "Consociationalism in South Africa: The Buthelezi Commission and Beyond," Journal of Modern African Studies, 21, 1983, 1:77-112.

34

National Security in the Third World: Need for a New Framework

K. P. Misra

In the post World War II years the traditional concepts of security have undergone significant transformation for a variety of reasons. Profound innovations in science and technology, including the advent of nuclear weapons, and the acquisition of independence by nearly 100 new states (the so-called Third World) have contributed to the new situation. This paper highlights the fact that the old concept of security has been rendered inadequate by the distinctiveness of both the domestic and the international situation of the countries in the Third World. We will examine some of the contradictions of the old security concept focusing upon Third World national security and stressing the importance of research to delineate the conditions that will increase security for the peoples of the Third World.

The problems of security at various levels--individual, sub-national, national, regional and international--though somewhat different, are inextricably interwoven; they are different points along a continuum. Their integral nature is evidenced by the fact that if security, at one point, is endangered, the other points cannot remain wholly unaffected. Yet we find that security studies generally limit their scope to national security. The reason for this is evident. Notwithstanding the influence of some schools of thought which have emphasized the pivotal position of the individual in any durable security arrangement, and in spite of the growth of internationalism, the nation-state continues to be the most decisive, socio-political organization in the world today. Our allegiance to it clearly surpasses our other loyalties and national security has a primacy over the security of all other units and organizations. But is this proper? We

recognize the primacy, though not the exclusiveness, of
security at the national level, and although "security of
the Third World" hardly exists, as such, one would not
suggest that the Third World countries cannot
meaningfully co-ordinate their several efforts in dealing
with problems of national security.

While identifying the components of security, some
key problems confront us. One of these is the
bewildering complexity of contemporary technology. This
development has serious implications which extend beyond
security matters and which have contributed to political
complexity. Leaders do not have the capacity to absorb
the implications of these technological intricacies and
they are often dependant upon technologists to draw
conclusions. It is no wonder, therefore, that the
average citizen finds it almost beyond one's competence
to understand security problems. This is particularly
dangerous for the democratic political systems, as today
few problems are more important for citizens than those
relating to the security of their nation. Briefly,
today's technological and political complexity and the
inability of citizens and their decision-makers to
comprehend it, mark the modern security situation.

AN UNSATISFACTORY APPROACH

Until a few decades ago, the concept of security was
confined to narrow limits; it was routine to think of a
nation's security problems in terms of military hardware.
This kind of thinking promoted wars and armed conflicts
and placed the security of large parts of the world in
jeopardy. Two world wars were fought within the span of
a single generation and numerous local conflicts have
erupted from time to time. It also became manifest that
during war the industrial resources and economic strength
of a nation were decisive factors in its ability to
defend itself. Since the Second World War, violence and
conflict have continued to plague the world. The Third
World has endured conflict situations more frequently
than have other countries. Some regions of the Third
World have witnessed especially bitter conflicts, and the
issues which generated these conflicts are still alive
and may lead to conflict again.

What factors have been responsible for these
conflicts in the Third World? The basic factor has been
that the new nations are engaged in a desperate endeavor

to build viable political systems out of what are often unpromising and divided elements. Their efforts at socio-economic reconstruction are generating tensions. Most of these countries are weak and poorly defended. Taking advantage of these sources of insecurity, powers external to the region have moved in and through supply of arms and the sinews of war and, through extension of support to unpopular and undemocratic regimes, added fuel to the fire. The irony of the situation is that these outside powers have taken such actions ostensibly to strengthen their own security. They appear oblivious to the basic point that they cannot find their equilibrium in themselves alone. Theoretically, there is now a fairly wide agreement about the components of security. The tragedy is that the powerful countries are unable to practice them. They ignore the lessons of history and still conceive of security, substantially, in terms of military hardware.

AN ENLIGHTENED APPROACH

Because the old approach has been unsatisfactory in many respects, many enlightened people have pleaded for a wider approach to the concept of security. This approach may or may not be appropriate for the developed countries of the world, but it would certainly benefit the Third World. If all relevant factors and forces are kept in view, in general terms, one may define the security of a nation as a condition of being protected or of not being exposed to danger. It implies freedom from danger and from a fear of danger. Last, a nation's security rests in the stability that it enjoys. Thus viewed, the framework of any valid concept of security must be multi-dimensional and rest on socio-economic, politico-cultural, ethnic, and ideological considerations as well as military.

In the post-World War II period when many areas of Asia and Africa became independent, their leaders, most notable among them Jawaharlal Nehru, enunciated a set of principles which later came to be know as non-alignment. Non-alighment envisaged a foreign policy orientation which was different from the traditional model. Though negative in appearance, its basic motivation was to positively create a situation conducive to the maximum socio-economic development of states. The assumption was that non-alignment would serve the real needs and requirements of security.

Robert McNamara points out:

> In a modernizing society security is not military hardware, though it may include it; security is not military force though it may involve it; security is not traditional military activity though it may encompass it. Security is development and without development there can be no security. A developing nation that does not, in fact, develop simply cannot remain secure for the intractable reason that its own citizenry cannot shed its human nature. 1/

It is ironic that in practice McNamara's own country ignores this approach. The United States identifies security largely with the military in all major conflict areas in the Third World. By relying on military hardware it has committed a grievous mistake. Consequently, in security terms the countries of these regions have had to pay a heavy price, and the United States has failed to strengthen its own security. An inescapable conclusion is that whatever hinders the development of a country hinders security also. There is an organic connection between socio-economic development and security.

But this is not to say that development is the only basis of security. Security of a country depends not only upon what it does to itself as well but also on the impact of external factors. There are many instances where the security of one country becomes the insecurity of another. This happens when national security objectives are pursued either without reference to the security of others or by impairing the security of others. Thus development is alone will not necessarily provide security, particularly external security. The security of a country is invariably relative; it has never been absolute.

In the Third World a variety of complex factors have threatened national security, and lack of development was one of the most important of these. Numerous situations of internal violence have arisen in Burma, Ceylon, India, Indonesia, Pakistan, and many other countries in the Third World, largely because of socio-economic hardship and lack of opportunities. Although there were other causes, many revolts, agitations, and insurgencies were caused by religious differences, ethnic variations, ideological cleavages, territorial loyalties and, significantly, foreign interventions, whether implicit or explicit.

It is in the context of development that oil and other resources become important security dimensions. After the Arab-Israeli conflict of October 1973 the price of oil was raised fourfold and some countries were not able to afford oil at this price. Similarly aid and trade have serious direct implications for security. The policies and behavior of the countries that provide aid have direct and serious implications for development and, therefore, for security. According to one school of thought, if the United States had not supplied huge quantities of arms to Pakistan and Israel, thus feeding the belligerency of the ruling classes in those two countries, South and West Asia would not have had to make huge sacrifices of scarce economic resources in fighting futile wars. The resources wasted during the war could have been used to achieve a better level of development which in its turn would have certainly strengthened the security of the nations concerned.

The socio-economic or development approach to security is not reflected in many proposals, writings, and movements. The Soviet concept of collective security in Asia, initially proposed by Leonid Brezhnev, General Secretary of the Central Committee of the Communist Party of the Soviet Union in 1969, is vague and open to different interpretations. But it is undeniable that there is a measure of socio-economic content in the proposal. An official Soviet publication on the subject clearly states that "extensive development of economic and other kinds of cooperation will make it possible ... to provide the necessary material basis for Asian Security." 2/ Also, "the peoples need security so as to satisfy their essential requirements and in this respect Asia is no exception." 3/ The ASEAN proposal to ensure their security and a proposal by the littoral countries of the Indian Ocean to create a zone of peace in this area also have explicitly emphasized the development dimension of security.

This approach was given powerful support by the United Nations, where the question of international security was discussed at length during the 25th session of the General Assembly in 1970. Most of the discussions took place in the First Committee which considered four drafts of declarations or resolutions, as well as various amendments. The relation between economic development and international security was described as vital by many member states. 4/ Ultimately a resolution (Resolution No. 2734 (XXV)) was, as recommended by the First Committee, A/8096, adopted by the Assembly in December. One hundred twenty nations supported the resolution; only one nation opposed it; and there was one abstention. Paragraph 21 of the resolution states that the UN General Assembly emphatically reiterates the need to undertake, within the framework of the Second United Nations Development Decade, urgent and concerted international action based on a global strategy and aimed at reducing and eliminating, as soon as possible, the economic gap between developed and developing countries, strength the security of all nations and establish lasting international peace.

Some theorists portray closing the gap as unrealizable and plead for only a minimum level of development. Such debate does not invalidate the main point which is made here. The concept of security was given an almost unanimous development mandate by the members of the United Nations. Thus, in a sense, the UN resolution provides international legitimacy to the development approach.

CIVILIAN DEFENSE APPROACH

The civilian defense approach is mentioned in this discussion not necessarily because we have faith in it but because it represents a line of thinking and action which is important enough to be considered in any discussion on security. Yet the approach has been popular with peace researchers, Gandhians, pacifists and other similar groups, and even some scholars, notably Thomas Schelling.

Civilian defense is different from civil defense. The former is based on the idea of nonviolent national defense while the latter refers to the efforts put in by the civilian population during wartime—efforts which may or may not be of a civil nature. Civilian defense has been defined as "a policy for the preservation of a society's freedom against possible internal threats (as coup d'etat) or external threats (as invasion) by advance preparations to resist such usurpation by action of the civilian population." 5/ The object of "preservation of a society's freedom" is accomplished through nonviolence, through attempts to change the heart of the invader and to create conditions--such as general non-cooperation and civil disobedience which Gandhi tried in India during its freedom struggle--which would make it impossible for the invader to succeed in his designs. This approach offers an alternative to military defense and nuclear deterrence by a nonviolent defense policy.

The advocates of civilian defense maintain that spontaneous nonviolent resistance movements under conditions of occupation have proved efficacious. The illustrations given from history are Hungary, 1849-67; Denmark and Sweden, 1940-45; and the East German uprising, 1953. Two recent cases are: Czechoslovakia, 1968, and Bangladesh, 1971. Without going into the circumstances of each case, we may note that a common feature of all of them is that a militarily weaker political entity, pitted against an overwhelmingly large military power, had organized its resistance and security on a basis that was essentially civilian and achieved some success. The claim is that if the tools of civilian defense are more cohesively organized and perfected along nonviolent lines, they can prove effective.

The various elements of the civilian defense approach have not yet been woven into a logical, well-knit, theoretical system. Different thinkers, practitioners and scholars have expressed their views, but a widely accepted theoretical framework is yet to emerge. One aspect which is relevant to our discussion may, however, be highlighted. This is the relationship between security and social justice. The advocated security through nonviolent methods does not answer the question of whether a social order organized along unjust lines is entitled to resist aggression and counter threats to its security. The approach is essentially political and practical in character. It asks if a society, whether just or unjust, can protect its security effectively by nonviolent means. The ability of a social order which contains structural violence, to ensure its security through nonviolent means is questionable. Security through nonviolent means can be achieved only if society is based on justice. According to Gandhi, a just social order is one in which all those conditions exist which enable each individual to secure maximum development in various situations. When development is hindered, violence begins--whether it is direct or indirect or structural. Yet the civilian defense approach has some crucial elements in common with the development approach to security.

There are many reasons why an unjust social order cannot achieve security through nonviolent means. First, a social order which is not just at all levels cannot organize nonviolent security efforts: It does not have the necessary will and the moral integrity to do so and it is incapable of reaching a level of social discipline and cohesiveness which makes nonviolent efforts effective. Only a social order free from all forms of exploitation can organize effective nonviolent security efforts.

THE AMBIGUOUS SYMBOL

There is general agreement that the foreign policy of a country is based on its national interests and that security interests take precedence over all other national interests. In fact demands of security unite the people of a country as nothing else can. All differences are set aside when the people of a country perceive that their security is affected.

The security interests of a nation do not exist in a vacuum. The components of security may be somewhat different under different sets of circumstances, but there is still a common ground. When it comes to identifying and making concrete the elements of security, there is a consensus that a nation's security policy should attach the utmost importance to the interests and security of the nation as a whole. The elements within a nation, such as individuals and groups and regions of various types, have to adjust and reconcile their security interests to those of the nation as a whole. Similarly, the situation today requires that interests of mankind or international bodies and organizations also be put in a subordinate category. There is practically no difference of opinion that some concrete security interests are paramount. They are: survival of the nation as a reasonable independent political system, political unity, territorial integrity, accepted social values, basic institutions and honor and prestige. These should not be eroded or undermined. Hence much effort is called for in protecting the sovereign status of a nation. That this is a fundamental preoccupation of security is not open to doubt. Keeping these general elements in mind, the concept has been defined as the ability of a nation to protect its internal values from external threats. The field of study, therefore, encompasses attempts to analyze the manner in which nations plan, make and evaluate the decisions and policies designed to increase this ability.

The above concept of security so defined and described is neither particularly enlightening nor helpful because when these general principles are applied to concrete cases, differences of opinion may arise. Ultimately, precise identification of the elements of security is made by the ruling elite of a country. But the diagnoses of those in charge of making decisions are not necessarily correct. At any rate there are always people who hold a different view. Two interconnected points follow from this situation. First, the perception of the ruling elite is decisive. Second, it is not possible to generalize or theorize on the concept of security to cover all situations because of the wealth of and variety of points of view that have to be taken into consideration. 6/

SECURITY FOR WHOM AND AGAINST WHOM?

The major difficulty arises when the security of the country and that of the ruling elite are considered identical. This situation may arise for many reasons. It may be that the two are really identical, that if the ruling elite is endangered, the political unity, territorial integrity and general strength or basic values of the country would be jeopardized. It is, however, instructive to remember that the opposite may be true. If a country has an undemocratic or a puppet regime, sustained in power by suspect sources, as was the case in the states of Indochina until recently, the security of the country is better served in real terms if the regime is removed. Thus, whether security is threatened or not in any given case depends upon the merit of that particular case. Additionally, when a threat is perceived it may be perceived honestly. But there may be a gap between the reality and the perceptions of the ruling elite, and the danger may be more apparent than real. Here threat is determined not on the basis of its actual existence but on the basis of the perception of the people in power. In most situations there is an interrelation between an actual threat and an imagined threat, and the ideal situation is one in which there is no gap at all. Finally, a regime may be so self-centered as to deliberately and dishonestly identify its security with that of the country.

The security of individuals or groups, whether ruling elite or another type, must not be confused with that of the state. The security interests of a country, though connected to those of the groups within it, are distinct because they relate to all the groups, to the totality of the country, to all its social values and organizations, and to its international personality. If this position is accepted as it should be, the answer to the second part of the question--security against whom--becomes relatively simple. The security of a nation has to be maintained against whatever undermines its various components. These components may be military, economic, political or ethnic. They may be domestic or external. Security consists of thwarting all such undermining forces.

NATIONAL AND INTERNATIONAL SECURITY

The security of a nation is closely connected to international security. If the security of the constituents of humankind is ensured and this security is not in conflict or contradictory but in harmony with the other, the security of humankind is almost automatically insured. This is the reason why enlightened statesmen have always attempted to remove the wider and larger sources of insecurity. They are concerned, for instance, about the gap between the rich and the poor nations--which is growing because of the economic policies of the former--and over the implications of this gap, for national as well as international security. It is widely realized that in the world as it exists today there are over 100 countries which are passing through a difficult modernizing and developing process. Their growth rates are not at all satisfactory. We should give these "seething caldrons of change" the attention they deserve before it is too late for us to do so. The security of the human race is threatened, not so much by a potential nuclear holocaust, as by the hopeless socio-economic situations which generate tension and endanger security. It is this fact which gives strength to the development approach to security.

SMALL AND BIG NATION'S SECURITY

Do small and big nations have similar security problems? Looking closely at history as well as at the contemporary situation, it appears that in certain basic respects the two sets of nations have to deal with different problems. Internally, the resources of the two types are different, though there may be some exceptions to this rule. Externally, they face different types of challenges and have different opportunities.

One-fourth of the countries in Asia-China, India, Indonesia, Japan and Pakistan are either medium or great powers. The rest are "small" nations. Recent events have shown that a small country can guard itself against the overwhelming military might of a "great" or "super power" if it relies more on political weapons than on the military. It is almost impossible for a small power to match its strength in military terms against that of a great power, but politically it can face the challenge successfully. Many illustrations can be cited to substantiate this view: In Asia the awesome military might of a super power--the United States--lost its fight with tiny states in Indochina. The Soviet inability to control Yugoslavia and Romania, France's loss of Algeria and Indochina, and the British debacle in Ireland and Cyprus are additional examples.

In the period since the Second World War, big nations with their greater military strength have treated small nations in a manner calculated to erode their security. They have, according to a recent study, 7/ perpetrated high-handed acts of the following types:

(1) outright incorporation of a state into another state;

(2) turning a small nation into a colony or satellite;

(3) imposition of an unpopular regime;

(4) subversion;

(5) undue influence over a small nation's internal policy; and

(6) undue influence over a small nation's external policy.

Military power has been the main instrument of domination. Traditional military strategy does not provide resistance to domination. If a small nation succeeded in the past in maintaining its security against overwhelming military power, it did so almost exclusively through political means. The hallmarks of the new strategy are courage, confidence, self-determination, and sacrifice for causes.

Big nations are in a different position. The attitude of the existing international system, which is dominated by certain powers, becomes important. The dominant actors in the system follow two types of policies. We have already noted their attitude towards small nations. With regard to big nations, they follow a different strategy. This strategy is to contrive a situation in which big nations, which have the potentiality of disturbing the status quo, are checkmated and are unable to act. The dominant nations endeavor to keep their club as exclusive as they can so that their primacy in the international system, which confers on them a variety of advantages, is not disturbed. The last half-century has witnessed many examples where the major actors of the international system have adopted such policies to achieve these ends.

The manner in which Russia was treated after 1917 and China after 1949 vividly illustrates this point. The way India is being treated at present by a super power is in line with the above policy. In a sense, while dealing with the big countries of a continent like Asia, the major actors on the international scene have greater opportunities to undermine their security through direct or indirect means, economic, technological, political, ethnic, and military measures. It is not surprising if the big countries of Asia have had to face bigger security problems on account of the omissions and commissions of some of the non-Asian actors of the international system.

While military hardware has general relevance, in the Third World context, development is a more important component of security. Whatever obstructs this process poses a threat to the security of the countries of this region. The development of strategic nuclear capability as a deterrent is certainly important for the super power, but within the context of Third World nations, it is of relatively less significance.

In conclusion, we have attempted to spell out a number of dimensions, and contradictions, in the concept security with special concern for national security in the Third World. We have illuminated the particular significance of development, combine defense, security against center elites, security against big powers and internal security to Third World countries. It is important that peace researchers attempt to delineate more clearly those conditions that provide security for Third World peoples and insight on how this security might be attained.

NOTES

1. Robert S. McNamara, The Essence of Security, Harper & Row, New York, 1968, 149.

2. Vladimir Pavlovsky, Collective Security for Asia, Moscow, 1973, 52.

3. Ibid., 48.

4. They included Algeria, Australia, Bulgaria, The Cameroon, Chile, Ecuador, Ethiopia, France, Indonesia, Iraq, Israel, Italy, the Ivory Coast, Japan, Kenya, Kuwait, Laos, Lebanon, Lesotho, Liberia, Mali, the Netherlands, Nigeria, Peru, the Philippines, Romania, Sierra Leone, Trinidad and Tobago, Tunisia, Turkey, Uganda, the United Arab Republic, The United Republic of Tanzania, the United States, Venezuela, Yugoslavia, and Zambia.

5. Gene Sharp, A Dictionary of Nonviolent Action and Civilian Defense, Cambridge, Mass., 1969, 63.

6. This is vividly illustrated by the events which occurred in Czechoslovakia in August 1968. The countries of the Warsaw Pact, under the leadership of the Soviet Union, thought that they were ensuring Czechoslovak security against the West, while an important section of the leaders thought of protecting the security of the country against the East. Thus in the same set of circumstances security was differently perceived by different people. The gaping chasm between image and reality creates such situations.

7. V.V. Sveics, Small Nation Survival, New York, 1969, 25-26.

35

Peace and Security:
Concepts and Strategies

Georg Sorensen

INTRODUCTION

Broad and dynamic concepts are needed in order to reflect the contradictions of peace and security in the real world. One of the most obvious contradictions is between individual and national security. To take but one example: the singularly most polluted industrial area in the world is Cubatao in Southeast Brazil, north of Sao Paulo. The physical and mental damage inflicted by pollution upon adults, children, newborn babies and embryos is alarming. Because of the economic importance of the area in terms of industrial output it was, in the last years of military regime, declared an area of national security. Small wonder that the population of Cubatao was readily able to point to a contradiction between national and individual security.

In order to address these contradictions, priorities must be made, in the form of concrete security strategies. Strategies cannot be formulated outside specific historical contexts. Against this background, the last part of the paper addresses the issue of a security strategy for Denmark, admittedly not very detailed, but outlining some principal priorities. But first, the concepts of peace and security are explored.

THE CONCEPT OF PEACE

In a recent article, Johan Galtung reiterates his position that peace has to do with absence of violence. This brings us to the question: what is violence? Galtung provides the following response: 1/

The best approach is probably to root violence in
the concept of basic human needs, in spite of the
shortcomings of that concept...

Based on this logic, Galtung poses four classes of needs
(survival, welfare, freedom and identity), whose
fulfillment creates peace. As indicated in Table 1, the
negation of each of these needs (holocaust, silent
holocaust, KZ/Gulag and spiritual death) is a form of
violence. In Galtung's scheme, the destruction involved
in holocaust and the repression involved in KZ/Gulag can
largely be attributed to specific actors (direct
violence), whereas the misery of "silent holocaust" and
the alienation involved in "spiritual death" can be
attributed more to social structures (structural
violence).

Table 1.   Four Classes of Needs
           Four Classes of Violence

	Direct violence: Actor-generated	Structural violence: structure-generated
More somatic Material	SURVIVAL violence HOLOCAUST	WELFARE misery SILENT HOLOCAUST
More spiritual Non-material	FREEDOM repression KZ, GULAG	IDENTITY alienation SPIRITUAL DEATH

In many ways, this is an attractive definition of
peace. It is broad enough to include the most important
dimensions of peace/violence, and precise enough to point
to pertinent foci of peace research. Note that defining
peace in terms of absence of violence, or fulfillment of
needs, brings the content of the concept of peace very
close to the content of the concept of development. This
latter concept is also defined in terms of needs by Galtung, the same four types mentioned above: survival,
welfare, freedom and identity. The overlapping of
definitions is not accidental. In his discussion of the
definition of peace, Galtung notes that "... what has

been said in this section could just as well be taken as a point of departure for development studies as for peace studies. The two are very similar, and should be regarded as two sides of the same coin." 2/

But there are also problems with the definition above. Here "peace" becomes an almost utopian value, because it is impossible to pinpoint societies that are free from both direct and indirect violence; moreover, it is difficult to devise strategies of development that would lead to such societies. 3/ In addition, broad concepts are often burdened with serious internal contradictions, and the above concept of peace is not an exception. Examine a society with a very high level of indirect (but also direct) violence against the majority of the population--e.g. Stroessner's Paraguay, Somoza's Nicaragua or Batista's Cuba. In these societies, it becomes almost logical for the people to resort to direct violence against the ruling elite in order to get rid of the indirect violence ... of the unequal social structure. One kind of violence is employed to get rid of another; one kind of peace is sacrificed to obtain another.

There are situations, in other words, where we cannot have the best of both worlds: absence of both direct and indirect violence. This being the case, we need to set priorities in order to get some sense of what aspect of peace is the most important in the concrete case. Setting priorities is what strategies are all about. What we need is strategies of peace 4/ for relevant parts of the world system.

Surprisingly, Galtung opposes this setting of priorities:

> One very basic point in this connection: I belong to those who very strongly oppose any attempt to impose priorities on these four classes of needs. In a trivial sense--with the biological organism close to death from direct or structural violence--it is empirically true that human beings fight for survival and welfare (food, clothes, shelter, and so on) more than anything else. But I refuse to accept those very extreme conditions as the basis for a general theory of priorities. ... The task of peace research is less modest, devising policies for all four goals, avoiding all four classes of violence. 5/

In a very abstract sense, Galtung is right: it would be wrong to focus entirely on any single aspect of needs/violence. But it is not true that the setting of priorities only has relevance for what Galtung calls "very extreme conditions." On the contrary, often the setting of priorities becomes necessary, as demonstrated in the examples above.

Several of Galtung's critics, including Kenneth Boulding, 6/ think that focus should be exclusively on negative peace, i.e. direct violence, the avoidance of war. But this position does not do away with the problems mentioned above. It obscures the existence of other forms of violence and moreover, it presupposes that the avoidance of direct violence, the prevention of war, always has first priority. This is the position contested in the examples given above.

We need a broad and comprehensive concept of peace, but as soon as it is formulated we are haunted by the contradictions built into it. There is even (at least) one additional difficulty with Galtung's definition which has not yet been addressed. It has to do with the fact that this notion of peace connects exclusively to the level of the individual. Galtung is aware of this. He emphasizes that his approach is "very anthropocentric." But although he hints that the implications of his position must be "explored in the social space of societal constructions and the global space of world systems, as well as the ecological dimensions attached to nature as such," 7/ it is difficult to see which consequences this "individualized" concept of peace has for state structures, the policies of one state versus another, the relations among groups of states in the world system. A notion of peace tied to the level of the individual may produce the dangerously ambiguous symbol once outlined by Wolfers which "while appearing to offer guidance and a basis for broad consensus ... may be permitting everyone to label whatever policy he favours with an attractive and possibly deceptive name." 8/

I think the problems mentioned above explain why Galtung's attractive notion of peace has remained on the sideline of the debate over peace strategies. Indeed, he makes no significant use of it himself when discussing European roads to peace and security. 9/ And perhaps this is what should be done: leave the broad concept of peace at the side as an attractive, utopian vision of the ultimate goal; and then proceed to combine this vision with more concrete strategies for security. The notion of security as a tool has certain advantages over the notion of peace.

THE CONCEPT OF SECURITY

When peace is defined as absence of violence, the logical corollary is to define security as absence of threats. But in that case, the logical answer to the question of defining threats would be: "threats" has to do with the risk of being exposed to various forms of violence. What is violence? Violence has do with basic human needs ... And we would short-circuit the discussion by regressing to the conceptual problems addressed above.

Instead, let us take the penetrating contribution by Barry Buzan as a starting point. 10/ He notes that there is no agreement on a general definition of security, and he does not try to formulate any brief definition. Buzan's intention is to "develop a holistic concept of security which can serve as a framework for those wishing to apply the concept to particular cases." 11/ The basic contention is that the problem of security must be analyzed at three distinct levels: the individual, the state, and the systemic level, including the interplays among these levels. Only then will we have a full understanding of the security problem.

Security is a relative concept, says Buzan. And it is much more difficult to apply the concept to people than to things. At the level of the individual, there are a number of factors to take into consideration (e.g. life, health, status, wealth, freedom). Out of the vast number of possible threats to the individual, Buzan focuses on what he calls social threats: physical threats, economic threats, threats to rights, and threats to position. 12/ In the present context, we are mostly interested in discovering how the state can be a source of threat to the security of the individual. There are four ways in which this can be the case, according to Buzan.

The first has to do with domestic law making and enforcement. The state can exercise a broad range of powers against its citizens in the name of the common good, from the "neutralization" of individuals considered a threat to the state for one reason or another, to the manipulation of the economy resulting in unemployment, increasing prices, etc.

Second, such threats can arise as part of an explicit state policy directed against certain individuals or groups. In highest danger are those seen by the state as dangerous "dissidents" of some kind, cf. Stalin's purges against opponents, Pinochet's hunting down of leftists, etc. Indeed, in most states, various categories of the populations tend to be singled out for some kind of "special treatment."

Third, there is a group of threats arising from political disorder, which in turn has to do with struggle for control over the state's institutions.

Only a minority of states have developed stable mechanisms for the transfer of political power. In the rest, violent conflicts over the reins of office pose an intermittent, and frequently serious threat to large sections of the population. The archetypes for this situation are countries like Argentina and Bolivia where military factions play an endless game of push-and-shove around the high offices of the state, while at the same time fighting an interminable, and often savage internal war against a variety of mostly left-wing revolutionary groups." 13/

Threats to individuals stemming from political terrorism also belong to this category; in addition to constituting a direct threat, terrorism can also have the side effect of making the security measures of the state more obtrusive.

The final group of threats has to do with the foreign policy of the state. It is an important raison d'etre of the state to provide its citizens with some protection against foreign attack or interference. In doing so, however, the state must impose risks and costs on its people. This can range from measures against individuals in the name of national security, to nuclear deterrence, where "The apparent end of a long tradition of national defense is a situation in which states seek to preserve themselves by offering each other their citizens as hostages." 14/

But the state does more than pose threats to individuals. The state is the single most important provider of security for its citizens. The state provides security against a wide range of threats: physical threats, economic threats, threats to rights, and threats to position or status. It is difficult to see how these needs of security can be met without state structure (a central problem to political philosophy since the Hobbesian image of individuals in the risky and chaotic state of nature versus the society where much freedom is sacrificed with the erection of a state structure capable of providing some measure of security). And it is even more difficult to envisage the decay of state structures in the present world system. The state is with us, and so is the unavoidable contradiction between individual and state security.

Let us turn to the security issue at the level of the state. The first problem is to identify the object of security. The state is not mainly a visible apparatus; the basic existence of the state is on the social plane, as an "idea held in common by a group of people." 15/ For the purpose of discussing the security issue, Buzan identifies three component parts of the state: 1) the idea of the state; 2) the physical base of the state; 3) the institutional expression of the state. 16/ Against this background, it is emphasized that states vary substantially,

> not only in respect of their status as powers, but also in respect of their weakness or strength as members of the category of states. When the idea and institutions of a state are both weak, then that state is in a very real sense less of a state than one in which the idea and institutions are strong.

> Strength as a state neither depends on, nor correlates with, power. Weak powers, like Austria, the Netherlands, Norway and Singapore, are all strong states, while quite substantial powers like Argentina, Brazil, Nigeria, Spain, Iran and Pakistan, are all rather weak states. 17/

In the case of strong states, the security issue is relatively straightforward. It has to do with protection of the components of the state from outside threats (military, economic, political) and interference. In the case of weak states, the concept of national security is much more ambiguous:

> it is probably more appropriate to view security in weak states in terms of contending groups, organisations and individuals, as the prime objects of security. The concept of national security

requires national objects as its points of reference, and in a state like Amin's Uganda these hardly exist aside from the national territory. 18/

The third and last level to take into account when addressing the security problem is the systemic level. Buzan takes the well-known realist assumptions of the international system as his starting point: the characteristics of the international system are very important for the security issue; as the system consists of nation-states above which there is no central author-ity, international anarchy becomes the main characteristic of the international system. But there are many shades of anarchy, from immature to mature. Mature anarchy, still a utopian vision, would mean a rather high level of security for the participating states. 19/

In discussing the systemic level, Buzan is again at pains to emphasize the interplay between system and state level:

> State and system are clearly so closely interconnected that security policies based only on the former must be both irrational and inefficient. 20/

> To consider states as the prime focus of the national security problem is mainly useful because it concentrates attention on the principal source of policy. But the problem which that policy seeks to address can only be defined in terms of the state-system nexus as a whole. Not only does sovereignty at level 2 (the state level, GS) define the general condition of anarchy at level 3 (the system level, GS), but also the character of the units generally provides a major input into the character of the system. 21/

The great merit of Buzan's contribution is that he sets a stage for the analysis of security which succeeds in combining radical and more conventional views of the issue. According to conventional views, security has to do with states having a sufficient level of armed force to be able to withstand threats from other states. Stable mutual deterrence based on armed force is as close as we can get to peaceful conditions in the international system. 22/ According to radical views, weapons are part of the problem rather than part of the solution. A decrease in the level of armament, in particular the level of nuclear armament, is seen as basic precondition for a more peaceful world. In addition, security and threats are treated as much broader notions than in the conventional view, involving social, economic and other issues, and giving special attention to the level of the individual. 23/

Both the conventional and the radical view of security is given attention in Buzan's discussion. Moreover, there is a clear emphasis on the contradictions involved in the security issue, especially when considering the interplay among the individual, the state, and the system level. It is made clear that enhanced security on one dimension (e.g. state security against external military threats) can mean less security on other dimensions (e.g. social and economic security of individuals). Buzan convincingly demonstrates that the list of such contradictions of security is very long.

The existence of contradictions means that we cannot have the best of all possible worlds: maximum security on all levels and dimensions. This problem is similar to the one mentioned above in relation to the concept of peace, where it was emphasized that the task of getting rid of both direct and indirect violence had to be put in an order of priority. Indeed, it may sometimes be necessary to resort to direct violence in order to get rid of structural violence. This means that priorities are necessary 24/ to the formulation of specific security strategies. This involves at least two sets of problems. One has to do with deciding the relative importance of various types of threats, with military and non-military threats as the two main categories. The other has to do with formulating security strategies regarding each group of threats.

The latter problem will be addressed below. Here, we concentrate on the issue of relative importance of threats. Two types of threats have been of prime importance in recent years, when looking at Europe in general and Denmark in particular. One is the threat of war stemming from increased tension between East and West in the so-called Second Cold War. 25/ The other is the threat to welfare stemming from the general economic crisis.

The importance of these categories is confirmed by the polls attempting to measure the subjective perception of threats by individuals. In the Danish case, the "danger of war" has competed with "unemployment" and "pollution" as the thing feared most. Since the beginning of these polls in Denmark in late 1983, unemployment has topped the list for most of the time, but the threat of war has not been disregarded. The issue was on top of the list in late 1983 and a good part of 1984. 26/

When translated into priorities of security policy, this means a reduction of the threat of war in Europe, and a move towards a more peaceful and stable situation, in a way which does not jeopardize welfare. 27/

What are the obstacles in the national context of Denmark?

THE NATIONAL CONTEXT: DENMARK'S OPTIONS

The constraints on Danish security strategies

Denmark's options on the security issue are determined partly by the international context, partly by the clashes of interests and viewpoints taking place between political forces on the national scene. This also means, of course, that the Danish security options are no objective entity; there is no such thing as objective truth when making security strategies. Everything depends on the assumptions made regarding the behavior of opponents and alliance-partners under specific circumstances.

The international context is not limited to the above factors. It also consists of a firmer element, having to do with the country's economic and political relations of dependency. Neither of these latter aspects will be considered in depth here. As far as the economic side is concerned, Denmark, like most small states, is heavily dependent on external trade, both because of the high volume of raw materials as well as sophisticated technologies which it imports, and because of the high export ratio of the country's own output. Danish foreign trade amounts to more than 35 percent of GNP, the greater part of which is exchange with other countries of Western Europe, notably West Germany, England and Sweden. 28/ Politically, Denmark has also tied its destiny to the Western allies, through membership in the EC and in NATO. Both memberships are supported by a majority of the population. 29/ In the foreseeable future, this is the

international framework in which Danish security
strategies are going to be formulated.

When looking at the national framework, we have
already noted (in section 3) that security strategies
must be formulated in a way which does not jeopardize
welfare. In other words, changes in security strategies
which have a negative impact on welfare goals
(employment, tax burden, etc.) are not likely to gain
approval, and this holds for "traditional" right-wing
demands for increased military expenditure as well as for
costly alternative propositions, for example in terms of
decentralized, high-technology defense systems.

We know that changes in the security strategy will
require the building of a new dominant coalition with
sufficient political muscle to instigate such changes.
Given the constraints on Danish security strategies
already mentioned, the interesting question is the
following: Is it possible to detect some kind of "middle
road" between conventional and alternative security
strategies which holds the promise of a changed security
policy with sufficient political support, and if yes,
what are the contours of this "middle road"? Let us take
a brief look, first at the problem of nuclear weapons,
then at conventional forces, with this question in mind.

The "middle road" I: nuclear weapons

While there are no nuclear weapons on Danish soil in
peace time, the role of nuclear weapons in NATO's overall
posture for the defense of Western Europe is of vital
importance to Denmark. But there is a lack of clarity
regarding assumptions underlying the deployment and use
of nuclear weapons which is reflected in the Danish
context. The center-right government supports the
current NATO doctrine of Flexible Response involving the
possible use of nuclear weapons against a conventional
attack from the East. The argument is that Western
European security is assured, through a possible
step-by-step escalation to nuclear confrontation in the
case of conventional aggression in Europe by the East.
However, is the first-use of nuclear weapons by the U.S.
likely at all in a situation where the American military
superiority is no longer present? In no way, according
to Dieter Senghaas. He argues that the threat of
first-use is not credible in a situation where American
overall superiority is absent:

> Should it come to a military conflict in Europe, ...
> any American president would, from an easily
> understandable self-interest, hesitate to use
> nuclear weapons. And furthermore, the Western
> European governments would request the US not to use
> nuclear weapons. 30/

The situation for this position seems to be that either
the threat of first-use lacks credibility, and the
deployment of INF-missiles is rendered useless, or there
is a possibility for a limited war in Europe involving
nuclear weapons (hinted at by Reagan in 1981), 31/ in
which case the problem is to make a convincing case that
such a scenario is of benefit to Danish (and European)
security.

The Danish Social Democrats 32/ have gone one step
further than the government. They support the notion of
"No First Use," but on the other hand they continue to
support the basic NATO strategy of Flexible Response.
The contradiction is obvious: if the policy of "no First
Use" wins over, the present strategy of Flexible Response
will have to be profoundly revised, either in the
direction of additional conventional armaments on the
Western side, or in the direction of alternative
stabilizing measures, such as the removal of offensive
conventional weapons from both sides.

The left wing in Denmark and the large majority of
the peace movement favor the abolition of nuclear weapons
outright, for both the West and the East. But how viable
is such a position in a situation where nuclear
capability has already proliferated to a number of other
countries outside the two alliances (China, India, and
maybe Brazil, Pakistan, South Africa and Israel)? Would
the major nuclear powers move to a level of nuclear arms
below that of such powers? And is it not possible that
the absence of nuclear weapons will mean less restraint
on the major powers, thereby increasing the probability
of conventional war? 33/ Moreover, nuclear weapons
cannot be disinvented. It is to be expected that nuclear
arms would rapidly be produced in the event of war
between countries capable of manufacturing them.

There is already a political majority in Denmark
favoring "No First Use" of nuclear weapons. The next
logical step would be in the direction of the concept of
"minimum deterrence," involving a substantial reduction
in nuclear arsenals on both sides, leaving only a few
systems to be used to retaliate a nuclear attack. 34/

For the peace movement, supporting such a measure would mean the abolition of the simplistic notion that the security problem is taken care of through complete disarmament. 35/ It would also help to put the discussion on nuclear free zones in a proper context, emphasizing that such zones are means towards a specific end: the reduction of nuclear arsenals.

For the Social Democrats, taking up "Minimum Deterrence" would mean facing in a more serious way the contradiction involved in favoring both "No First Use" and the basic principles of the current NATO strategy.

The "Middle Road" II: Conventional Forces

It is clear that Denmark has a severely limited military defense capability. This insight has led in two directions. One is the "What's the use?" attitude, according to which complete disarmament is the logical corollary, with the additional argument that such a measure would constitute an important step towards peace.

The other goes in the opposite direction: In critical situations Denmark needs help from the outside, from NATO. The latter position has prevailed in Denmark in the postwar era and is supported today by both the present government and by the Social Democrats.

The standard criticism of this position has been directed against Denmark's NATO membership: An alliance with the U.S. puts Denmark in a less secure, more tension-prone situation. 36/ An even more fundamental criticism is, however, possible. This has to do with the assertion that Denmark faces a severe defense dilemma in the conventional field. A large-scale conventional battle on Danish soil, involving substantial assistance from NATO forces, cannot avoid destroying what it is supposed to defend. 37/

On the other hand, there is little political and mass support for complete disarmament. And it could certainly also be debated whether complete disarmament is at all attractive. Denmark is in a delicate geo-strategic situation, and in the case of superpower conflict, both parties would wish to control the Danish straits. A completely defenseless Denmark would not be secure in such a situation. This raises the question of whether it is possible to escape Denmark's defense dilemma without rendering the country defenseless. Transarmament is probably the central concept here, working towards models of credible, non-provocative defense—and there are a number of possible models. 38/ Isolated Danish moves in the field of transarmament are not interesting as such, but only insofar as they contribute towards a more stable, less war-prone situation in Europe. 39/ Changes in the direction of transarmament/disarmament will not come in spectacular single moves. It is a step-by-step process which involves rethinking in other NATO countries as well. Significant advances along this road will also have to involve similar moves on the side of the WTO countries.

It has been suggested that an initial step in the right direction could consist of the establishment of a zone from which offensive conventional forces on both sides were withdrawn, for example a tank-free zone. "Such an initiative would correspond to more than a step towards mutual confidence-building in the face of the possibilities for rapid deployment of both land- and air-forces. But it could be the first step towards the erection of a non-offensive defense-potential, with the long range aim of developing a military potential which is structurally incapable of attack." 40/

CONCLUSION

The first argument in this paper was that broad concepts of peace and security are necessary. Without broad concepts, a substantial number of relevant issues threaten to escape the debate on peace and security. In addition, there are serious contradictions involved in obtaining peace and security, and these contradictions have to be faced in a conscious manner. This can only be done on the basis of comprehensive concepts, allowing such contradictions to be formulated in the first place.

On the other hand, as long as there can be agreement on the need for broad and dynamic concepts, there is little need to argue in favor of final definitions that are acceptable to everyone. Galtung is probably right in arguing that "peace" is like "development" in this regard: as long as we have a dynamically changing world, there can be no final definition of either. 41/

It is productive, in other words, to move swiftly from the level of concepts to the level of strategies. And here the argument was that the concept of security is the better starting point.

Unfortunately a broad and dynamic concept of security has often been used by people critical of the conventional agenda as an escape route to avoid the confrontation with conventional security issues. Put briefly, the argument—in a simplified version—has been the following: "let us have complete disarmament starting with nuclear weapons, and the threat of war is no longer a problem." 42/

The argument is both wrong and dangerous in that it threatens to leave the whole issue of military strategy and hardware to conventional wisdom. Consequently, it was the third argument of this paper that even those critical of the conventional agenda with its narrow concept of security will have to face the issue of external military threats in a world consisting of separate nation-states.

The fourth argument was related to the third. It stressed that changes in the given security strategies of countries will require the building of a new dominant coalition with sufficient political muscle to press through such changes. In other words, abstract debates over security may be stimulating, but without political clout they won't get anywhere in the real world.

Against this background, the paper briefly discussed some basic priorities for a Danish security strategy, without making a comprehensive contribution. The primary aim was to point out a possible meeting ground for both "conventional" and "critical" contributors to the debate over security strategies. The premise was that future changes in Danish security strategy would have to be formulated within the framework of such a meeting ground to make any implementation possible. The "meeting ground" gives a general idea of where we are going. The precise outcome, however, will depend on which political coalitions dominate the formulation of a Danish security strategy. Hopefully, security issues will not be left to any narrow groups in the future; a "democratization" is needed if the content of security policy is to be changed.

NOTES

1. Johan Galtung, "Twenty-Five Years of Peace Research: Ten Challenges and Some Responses," Journal of Peace Research, vol. 22, no. 2, 1985, 146.

2. Ibid., 147.

3.   Which does not stop Galtung from trying, of course. See also Hans-Henrik Holm, Vaekkelsespraedikant eller superstar - om udviklingen i Johan Galtungs videnskabsbegreb, Aarhus: Institute   of   Political Science, 1975, 25.

4.   In the same way that strategies for development are needed, cf. Georg Sorensen, "Some contradictions in a rich concept of development," working papers, no. 17, Development Research Group, Aalborg University, 1985.

5.   Galtung, 1985, op. cit., 147.

6.   Ibid., 157, fn. 5.

7.   Ibid., 147.

8.   Arnold Wolfers, quoted from Barry Buzan, People, States and Fear, Sussex: Wheatsheaf Books, 1983, 5.

9.   Johan Galtung, There are Alternatives! Four Roads to Peace and Security, Nottingham: Spokesman, 1984.

10. Buzan, 1983, op. cit.

11. Ibid., 11.

12. Ibid., 18.

13. Ibid., 26.

14. Ibid., 29.

15. Ibid., 38.

16. Ibid., 40.

17. Ibid., 66.

18. Ibid., 67.

19. Ibid., 96.

20. Ibid., 122.

21. Ibid., 246.

22. Cf.   for   example   Kjell   Goldmann,   Det internationalla systemet, Stockholm: Alons, 1978, part I.

23. Hakan Wiberg and Jan Oberg, "Concepts of Security and their Implications," Scandinavian Journal of Development Alternatives, III, March 1984, 15-36. Hans-Henrik Holm, "En ny sikkerhedspolitik?" Mimeograph, Institute for Political Science, Aarhus, 1985.

24. A commonplace observation perhaps, but not all that trivial against the rich notion of security discussed in the text.

25. Cf. Fred Halliday, The Making of the Second Cold War, London: Verso, 1983.

26. Jørn Thulstrup, Weekendavisen, January 10-16, 1986.

27. This raises the complicated question, whether it is at all possible to achieve both peace and welfare

given the basic structure of modern society. Cf. Bjorn Hettne, "Peace and Development: Contradictions and Compatibilities," Journal of Peace Research, 20, 4, 1983, 329-43; and Georg Sørensen, "Peace and Development: Looking for the Right Track," Journal of Peace Research, 22, 1, 1985, 69-78.

28. See for example N. Pultz, "Om international økonomisk integration og økonomiske unioner, in N. Petersen & C. Thune (red.), Dansk Udenrigspolitisk Arbog 1986, Kobenhavn: Samfundsviden-Skabeligt Forlag.

29. This does not mean that there is a popular majority behind NATO's concrete military strategy, cf. below.

30. Dieter Senghaas, "Die Zukunft der Sicherheit Europas," in Ulrich Albrecht et al. (eds.), Stationierung – und was Dann? Berlin, 1983, 164.

31. Cf. Galtung, 1984, op. cit., 9.

32. Cf. Hans-Henrik Holm and Nikolaj Petersen, "Dansk INF-politik," in Hans-Henrik Holm and Nikolaj Petersen (eds.), Slaget om Missilerne, Copenhagen: Det Sikkerheds- og Nedrustningspolitiske Udvalg, 1983, 211-249.

33. Cf. same argument in Egbert Jahn, "Tiden kan ikke skrues tilbage til før 6. August 1945," Information 27-28, October 1984.

34. Cf. Senghaas in Albrecht et al., op. cit, 162.

35. See for example, Inger Søndergaard, "Magten taler gennem din lukkede mund," GRUS nr. 11, 1983, 68-90.

36. See for example Galtung, 1984, op. cit.

37. Gert Petersen, "Nedrustning – sadan!" Information, February 26, 1986.

38. Galtung 1984, op. cit. See also Bjørn Møller, "Kort oversigt over ikke-offensive forsvars-modeller," Centre of Peace and Conflict Research, Copenhagen, 1985.

39. Bjørn Møller, "Vabenkontrol og defensivt forsvar," 10th Nordic Conference on Peace Research, Marstrand, Sweden, August 18-20, 1986.

40. Senghaas in Albrecht 1983, op. cit., 166. The argument is developed further in Dieter Senghaas, Die Zukunft Europas – Probleme der Friedensgestaltung, Frankfurt am Main: Suhrkamp, 1986, 103-116.

41. Galtung in Journal of Peace Research, 1985, op. cit.

42. This is not a quotation, but it is the gist of the argument offered in Inger Søndergaard, "Magten taler gennem din lukkede mund," GRUS, No. 11, 1983, 68-90

36

Understanding the European Security Configuration Through Concepts of Security

Egbert Jahn, Pierre Lemaitre, and Ole Waever

INTRODUCTION

This paper attempts to clarify certain methodological questions in 'conflict analysis' on the East-West conflict in Europe. 1/ Surprisingly, peace researchers usually present this conflict--often successfully-- as a pseudo-conflict, e.g. a bi-product of the arms race, a domination technique for ruling elites; a psychological macro structure. This article analyzes the East-West conflict in its traditional sense, as a conflict between East and West Europe. It focuses on the use of the concepts of security as lenses through which some elements of the structure of the conflict can be discerned. This approach to what is usually called 'conflict resolution' opens up potentially useful approaches for achieving what is better termed 'conflict continuation'. The main inspiration at the meta-methodological level is the 'socio-genetic' approach of Norbert-Elias. 2/

EUROPEAN PEACE ORDER OR EUROPEAN SECURITY?

European security, instead of European peace order, is preferred as the focus of research because the concept of (positive) peace is much more comprehensive and far-reaching than is the concept of security. The concept of security is more 'realpolitical', i.e. accepts more elements of present reality. Deciding which elements of this reality are to be changed, constitutes the problematic nature of security.

Security is open to a plurality of interpretations as regards social systems, whereas the concept of peace often is linked to the existence and promotion of a specific system. Thus, security as a fundamental

573

category is more 'open', more variable than 'peace'.
Barry Buzan has demonstrated how the concepts of 'power'
and 'peace' take one-dimensional, total, and absolute
stands on the questions of international anarchy and the
arms race, whereas 'security' is more open to different
versions. 4/

THE EAST-WEST CONFLICT IN EUROPE AS A
MULTI-DIMENSIONAL CONFIGURATION

The East-West conflict has to do with two kinds of
motivations, each with corresponding fears. 5/ One
motivation is physical security and the classical fear of
being annihilated by another. The other is security of
social orders (of structures and values) and the fear of
being situated in a power relationship where military
superiority can be used to enforce changes. There is
widespread feeling that the second is as important as the
first.
1) 'Threats' and 'defenses' are not necessarily
military. The social fears pose an open question
regarding methods and vary according to the specific
weaknesses of the state in question. 6/
2) Different social groups may have different security
interests and fears. Especially in relation to some of
the non-military threats (political, ideological, and
economic) certain elite groups have the most to fear.
They also have by far the most to fear in an all-out
defeat 7/ but in most societies the degree might be less
relevant than widespread consensus about the
undesirability of this event. Therefore, these
considerations about diverging security interests in
societies might be more important when combined with a
greater understanding of the non-military dimensions of
security and insecurity.
Decisions about influence upon other societies and
defense against the introduction of unwanted influence
will necessarily produce controversy about limits of the
concept of security. At the same time controversies
arise over differing costs and societal implications of
handling various security interests. For instance, the
choice of an alliance partner may generate controversy:
Even if different groups within a society perceive a
threat and a common basis for a security policy,
interests may still diverge because of the likely

domestic implications of aligning with a powerful state which has a specific social system. 8/

    There is an additional argument for taking into account variation in security policies among different groups--or among segments with different political orientations. Perceptions and interpretations of security conditions are shaped by images and perceptions of crucial historical experiences which are likely to vary among social groups or political orientations.

    The East-West Conflict is more complex than it is often presented. Security problems involved are likely to be different from state to state. Therefore, a study of European security should not start by defining 'security'. The different definitions of security is a crucial part of the European security situation. Additionally, security cannot be analyzed with respect to the state only. A researcher will have to look at different political programs; different understandings of security. Sometimes, different groups act independently across borders, and more often they are a part of the process which creates the product, 9/ national policy. European security must be seen as a configuration of different levels of understandings and praxises which aim in different directions. Understanding this socio-historical development requires that we investigate the composition and workings of the configuration.

    Concepts cannot be understood in isolation. On the other hand, the situation can be understood using different concepts. A study of concepts of security can be a way of picturing the European security figuration.

    In general, peace research tends to underestimate the importance of officially declared policies. 'Critical' thinking tends to prefer secret explanations, secret intentions, hidden structures, etc. But declared policies are a significant factor in the political processes, since they have some relation to actual views. 10/ Political actors advance views to make people understand the situation in a way supportive of their program and they need to signal their positions for the sake of bargaining. 11/ In political programs and in the ideologies of the East and the West it is said that the East-West conflict exists, basically, because of different views of history, of society, of the reasons for war and peace, and of international politics. Recent analyses have concluded that ideologies have consequences for the main direction of policies. 12/ Therefore, (notwithstanding areas of common interest) there are good reasons for taking seriously this stated conflict.

CONCEPTS OF SECURITY AND THE
CONCEPT OF SECURITY

Elaboration of different concepts of security is useful in avoiding misunderstandings when people use the same words but for different content or use different words for the same content. Another reason to examine the different concepts of security is that they are expressions of political and societal differences, an examination of which may expose fundamental traits of the East-West conflict. Barry Buzan describes security as "the pursuit of freedom from threat." 13/ When the state is strong and coherent enough to concern itself mainly with external threats, "national security can be viewed primarily in terms of protecting the components of the state from outside threat and interference." 14/ These components are the idea, the physical base and the institutions of the state. For any state the concrete meaning of security will depend on its existing strengths and weaknesses, its structure and its self-definition. 15/

An essential part of a research project must be to understand and to respect the relevant processes, forces, and actors. Understanding the problems of security means analyzing the East-West conflict and the concepts of security held by the actors are part of this analysis. On the other hand, mapping the existing views and policies is necessary but not sufficient. More precise concepts can be constructed by understanding the mechanisms and processes.

Concepts are involved at two levels: At the first level the main object is the attainment of an accurate understanding of the relevant political programs and actions and includes a description of the precise concepts used in the actor's thinking. At the second level, concepts are developed according to their effectiveness in grasping the dynamics of the situation. 16/

The first level consists of a characterization and criticism of political programs or policies in order to find their roots, their illusions, their pretentions and thereby to decide the margins and the possible alternatives in the given context. This task requires interaction with the second level-- understanding the situation. Understanding can be developed by criticizing the views of the actors and by engaging the scientific literature. In this way the criticism of real programs serves first, to clarify the character of the specific policy and its possible alternatives; second, to develop a substantial alternative view of the relevant problems. Taken on its own the second element leads to the development of possible models of security and more abstract analytical insights. Without the first element, however, we lack detailed understanding of the actual problems and dynamics of the situation to be changed. If isolated, the first element lacks a firm analytical founding and a coherent view of the situation even if it can construct valuable insight into the situation of various countries. Clarifications are needed on the level of existing programs and on the level of figuration and dynamics.

This structure might be seen in the parallel (in this methodological sense) between the present framework and Henry A. Kissinger's, 'A World Restored." 17/ Kissinger's study on European security (1812-1822) offers some methodological tools for our study of contemporary European security problems. Essential in both projects is to understand what was thought by whom, and why. Further, why they had to have certain perceptions and priorities, given certain specific conditions of political culture, geography, etc. Also important is to show the open questions of history, especially the possibility of developing different over-all forms of interactions. For this purpose, Kissinger introduced the concepts 'legitimate order', 'the legitimizing principle', and 'revolutionary situation' into theoretical concepts, while using concepts of security, of equilibrium and views regarding interference and non-interference to characterize the understanding of individual states and other forces.

With a similar conceptual duality we can attempt a partially defined security. We do not intend to close the concept by giving it a fixed meaning, however, as concepts of security are something to be identified in the existing world of European security. We need demarcations to tell us what is relevant to a study of European security. An interest in existing political programs does not mean a compulsion to involve whatever is used in relation to the word 'security'. Adherence to different, real, existing concepts of security puts an

upper limit on the concept of security. We are held to
the lower limit by the contexts we deal with here—hence,
the need for demarcations to clarify the 'constant
element' of security. The 'floating element' of the
concept is left to empirical analysis of existing
understandings of security, influenced by factors of
geography, political system, historical experiences, etc.

EUROPEAN SECURITY PROBLEMS

In recent years there is increased use of "security"
as a political term and also a widening of the security
concept. 18/ Today both very narrow and very wide
interpretations of security coexist and compete in
political language.

For analytical and practical purposes of peace
policy, it is useful to focus attention on those specific
problems that have provoked a political and scientific
debate on European security in a specific historical
situation, as opposed to other ongoing debates and
thoughts about security. This recent political debate
centers around two closely connected problems: (1) the
prevention of war and, (2) the prevention of aggression
in Europe. They are discernible from discussions on
political and military stability from debates about the
prevention of ecological castrophies, economic crises and
various crimes and accidents which threaten lives. The
debate on European security centers around the problem of
the political order within and between the European
states, which seems threatened both by military and by
non-military means.

The discussion of one problem, West European
security, assumes an actual or potential Soviet and East
European threat against the social and political order of
Western Europe and that this threat is different from the
Soviet threat against the United States. The term
'European security' implies some community of security
interests among different West European nations and
certain relevant differences of security interests
between Western Europe and the United States. European
security in this sense means security against aggression.
It implies a concept of extended—allied or
coordinated—national (West) European security. The
corresponding problem in Eastern Europe is discussed as
'security of the Socialist Community' and assumes an
actual or potential Western capitalist or imperialist

threat. The mutual threats are not so much directed against the very existence of European states or their borders (with the exception of the two German states) as against the 'idea' of states (Buzan) or their socio-economic and political order.

Another discussion of 'European security' deals with security against developments leading to war and includes arms control, arms reductions, confidence building measures, detente, diplomatic negotiations, economic cooperation and human contacts across the East-West border in Europe. In this sense European security means All-European security, and new terms have emerged while old terms are given new contexts. Such terms include 'common security', 'mutual security', 'equal security', 'security partnership', 'coordinated security' and 'complex security'. Used in this way 'European security' is a special regional case of international security referring to East-West relations in Europe, military as well as non-military.

Both discussions are two sides of the same coin, namely, the East-West conflict in Europe and so research on European security must therefore involve itself in the theoretical debate on the inter-relationship between individual and domestic, national and international security. 19/

Security against war and security against aggression are different. And we can choose to focus upon the threats from one or more specific actors or upon a process (the interaction). Security against aggression rests on the assumption that there is a threat—known or unknown, actual or potential—from another state. All measures for national security, alliance security and collective security rest on the assumption of such a threat.

Security against war rests on the assumption that all states of a system are involved in threatening international processes. The threat does not come from particular known or unknown states, but is rooted in the societies of all states and in inter-state interaction. Such kinds of threats include the arms race, mutual suspicion and distrust, national prejudices, insufficient information, the internal contradictions of the deterrence systems, crises in the world economy, ecological catastrophes and insufficient instruments for crisis management. These kinds of threats can often be dealt with only by international measures. They are not directed against particular states.

European security cannot be understood as a static order of military and non-military affairs in Europe. The reduction of military capabilities for aggression and war and the reduction of the political will for aggression and war must be seen as mutually dependent components in an historical process. Changes in the military order can bring about a political will to reduce the political intentions and social incentives for aggression and war. The change of the political will and the promotion of social conditions for such a change are also important preconditions for the change of the military order.

European security is thus much more than a specific military order. It is a political East-West order that permits a non-military continuation of the East-West conflict under the condition of military mutual security. European security must be seen as a non-military continuation of the East-West conflict. Otherwise one is restricted to assuming, in a 'real-political' sense, that the present socio-political and inter-state status quo should be 'eternally' stabilized. Moreover, this assumption excludes a more utopian concept of European security which would permit the possibility of a future political constellation in which both capitalist and communist systems would vanish and be replaced by a common European socio-political order.

European security in the described political and non-military sense is a wider concept than the concept of military order, and a narrower concept than that of a social (including economic and ecological) order. European security in this sense aims at establishing a historical process of dynamic stabilization or stable dynamization of the East-West order by overcoming peace oriented and mere real-political power oriented thinking. It is a historical compromise. 20/

In the current European situation the diverging security concerns make themselves felt clearly in several debates. The West emphasizes security against the danger of military action, or (in reality) the danger of military imbalance being utilized politically. The East seems to have a broader concept of security, whereas solutions, are focused on a narrow field. A major threat presented by the East as a security problem, and the priority when looking for common solutions, is the danger of war. But, in the East this danger is placed in the military sphere, not in the political context, in which this security problem is placed in the West. A broader sphere of human, ideological and political contacts defined by the West as "normal" relations to be dealt with in their own right are, by the East, labeled security problems. Thereby these processes are legitimately addressed following the logic of threats, of security problems. 21/

These different definitions and concepts of security constitute an obstacle to increased contacts between East and West. They pose a danger of setbacks for any new detente. They have necessary consequences and they are political and conflict-relevant in a situation like the European, where the conflict is not merely an external state-to-state affair, but involves also existing and future social forces. Domestic and international conflict are linked to one another. Any detente (and the ensuing increased contacts) will necessitate regulation that will be controversial in the light of the East-West conflict. Therefore, the problem of diverging concepts of security has to be addressed and a greater awareness of these controversies is a precondition for future detente.

IMAGES OF EUROPE

One of the reasons for the new interest of many European countries in European security is the loss of attraction of the American and Soviet universalist programs for "one world" and for "proletarian internationalism". Outside the two countries these programs are regarded more or less as ideological labels of the "imperialism" or "hegemonism" of the two world powers. Since 1945 they have tried to impose their view of international peace by military means, not by peaceful and democratic changes. During the Second World War and after, the two powers gained a certain ideologically and intellectually dominant position, not only because of their victory over German national socialism, Italian fasism, and Japanese militarism, but also because of the bankruptcy of the traditional 'realpolitik' and pragmatism within the Concert of Europe of all European Great Powers.

During the seventies and early eighties 'Europe' became a political term, as well as an historical or geographical one. The bad conscience regarding European colonialism has been more or less soothed by the release of most of the remains of the colonial empires and by the

creation of a system of economic cooperation with the
Third World countries--a system which is still disputed
because of its one-sided economic dependency and social
injustice, but which nonetheless today meets with no
strong, fundamental opposition in the Third World. And it
cannot be attacked in principle on ideological grounds by
the United States, Japan, China or the Soviet Union in
the same way as the anachronistic colonial system was
criticized in the period 1917 to 1975 (when the
Portuguese colonial empire finally broke down).

An encouragement of a new European self-esteem stems
from overcoming the rightist dictatorships in Greece,
Spain and Portugal and the inclusion of these countries
into the political process of European integration. Even
the brief Eurocommunist wave emerged with the idea that
communism and socialism could no longer get new impulses
and inspiration from the Soviet Union, but from Western
Europe by combining, in a new way, socialism and
democracy with internationalism, thus taking up the
initiative of the emancipatory movements in the Third
World.

The United States and the Soviet Union, for decades
the much admired centers of progressive impulses for a
worldwide development and international integration, are
now increasingly looked upon as conservative bulwarks of
outdated hegemonial superpowers anxiously trying to keep
their political positions in the world by military
build-up and military threats and interventions. In
contrast to this dichotomous view, Europe regains the
image of an actor in a polycentric world which also
includes dynamic, economic and political forces in Japan,
China and certain Third World countries. Increasingly,
European security is considered different from American
and Soviet security and, most important, a concern of the
Europeans themselves. Ruling elites and parts of
national populations still want American and Soviet
protection but today there is a strong drive for more
European self-determination in security policy.

Soviet aggression is not expected to be directed
against North America, but against Western Europe. The
new debate on European security in almost all political
parties in Europe has much to do with the fear of the
oscillating character of the United States' foreign
policy between isolationism and universal commitment. It
also has much to do with the European fear that the
United States might decouple its own fate from the fate
of Europe and might victimize Europe in one way or

another (by limited nuclear war or by capitulation in case of a limited Soviet political-military pressure or attack upon Western Europe). The general direction of the answers which the Europeans are developing in the face of the new security problems is two-fold. One answer is to increase the American political and military commitment in Europe, often combined with an increase in the European share in the NATO defense endeavors. The other answer is to reduce the probability of Soviet aggression by radical detente policy and disarmament, beginning with unilaterial Western disarmament measures, 'structural non-attack capabilities', and 'non-offensive defense'. The common denominator of most deliberations is increased European responsibility for its own security.

In this security debate the small East Central European and South East European states (members and non-members of the Warsaw Treaty Organization) are often forgotten. Peace research should not ignore their problems. Although related, developments in Eastern Europe outside the Soviet Union differ in many respects from Western European developments. 'Real socialism' in these countries was more or less imported as a consequence of the liberation of Eastern Europe from Nazi rule by the Soviet Army. The exceptions are Yugoslavia and Albania. Since 1948-49, however, a new relationship between the ruling communist elites and the vast majority of the population in each of the East European countries has slowly developed. There is a strong trend of independent national thinking which includes delicate security problems once the prerogative of the Soviets under the term of 'socialist internationalism' and 'socialist foreign policy'. This independent national thinking is not restricted to the masses of the population but is expressed also by or within the East European communist parties and governments under the label of 'socialist patriotism'.

The Europeanization process in Europe necessarily includes a common political identity. European only in the sense that it is directed against American and Soviet influence or hegemony and contains a vague solidarity with similar national aspirations of other Europeans, that new European feeling seems to be much stronger in the smaller Eastern European countries than in Western, Central and Northern Europe. 'European security' represents many different concepts of Europe and of security, especially if 'security' is synonymous for a lasting peace order or even a future political union of Europe. The central topic of all political thinking about 'European security' is how Europeans can handle a Europe divided into two opposing military alliances and social systems and how to end that conflict. Europeans no longer find traditional answers satisfactory. Behind the on-going debates on military strategies and weapon systems and even on the peace promoting or security endangering functions of economic and cultural East-West cooperation, there are different non-military identities rooted in European history.

Non-military aspects of European security would involve research primarily on the <u>political identities in Europe which influence the definitions of enemies and friends, opponents and allies</u> and on the perception of security or insecurity, determining whether weapons are perceived as a protection or a threat. Much of the so-called military or peace debate of the last years is a disguised debate on the problem of political identity and includes the relationship between political identities and the military and economic realities which have their own immanent tendencies. Research must also discuss the military, economic, cultural, ideological and other impacts of different political concepts of European security. However, the term 'European' security, is first a political concept which should be discussed as a political problem in its own right and which deserves the attention of peace research, at least in Europe.

Europe will not be a single political actor for a long time. Thus, research on European security has, primarily, to deal with mutual threats of Europeans themselves against each other. Second, Soviet and American military and security policies are connected to European Security--with the actual or potential threats of the Soviet Union against Western Europe or of the United States against Eastern Europe. Taking Europe as a whole, i.e. Eastern and Western Europe, we have to face the problems of various concepts of East-West Europe in the political debate. The different uses of the term 'Europe' might be summed up in four main categories:

1) <u>Western Europe as Europe</u> with European security as a special problem of extended national or alliance security within the framework of Western security as a whole, or security of the NATO member-states.

2) The Europe <u>from the Atlantic to the Urals</u>. Traditionally West Europeans have understood Soviet appeals to common European interests and traditions as an

instrument to divide NATO and to bind Western Europe into an anti-American solidarity with Europe. 22/ Three quarters of the Soviet Union belongs to Asia in traditional 'geographic' terms. Thus, by calling the Soviet Union a European state, one makes a political statement.

3) Europe from Poland to Portugal. A political statement is likewise implied if the Soviet Union, explicitly or implicitly, is excluded in speaking of Europe as different from the world powers or in speaking of Eastern Europe as distinct from the Soviet Union. (Excluding or including the GDR among the East European states.) In a more traditional terminology these countries constitute East Central and South East Europe; Eastern Europe is then Russia, the Ukraine, and White Russia, whereas the Baltic republics are seen as a part of Central Europe. Eastern Europe can thus connote two completely different regions of Europe (1) as a region East of the river Bug (2) the region West of the same river. Finally, Eastern Europe can denote the two regions together.

4) The 'European security area' is seen as a problem area embracing all states with vested interests in Europe. It includes all 35 member states of the Conference on Security and Cooperative in Europe (plus Albania). The United States, Canada, and the Soviet Union are included only insofar as their security interests in Europe are concerned. For matters of security analyses in international, political and military relations, the United States and Canada are member states of the 'European security area' with no territory in Europe. The Soviet Union is a member because of political and military interests, power and influence based on the Asian territories of the Soviet Union.

Each of the 'Europes' has a reality of its own. The 'Europe from Poland to Portugal', excluding both world powers as 'superpowers', is a real, political force.

The 'Europe from the Atlantic to the Urals' has an historical, geographic and cultural 'reality', and includes the Soviet Union mainly as a Russian, Europe-centered state with a large Asian appendix. This Europe notes that whereas the Soviet Union is separated from its European allies by a river, the United States is separated from its allies by an ocean. Hence, proposals for troop and armaments reductions in Europe often include European parts of the Soviet territory. 23/ The political processes of the 1980s has proven this Europe to be a real competing force.

SUPRA CONCEPTS FOR UNDERSTANDING AND INFLUENCING THE CONFIGURATION

This section will consider the compatibility and incompatability of Eastern and Western security concepts and discuss the structure of a promising perspective on the present situation. From the understanding of the European security configuration follows the importance of common 'rules' or principles. 26/ Incompatible political goals will always exist. Whether they evolve into dangerous conflicts will depend on the extent of agreement on 'rules'. Incompatible concepts of security were and are sources of insecurity.

The different states and regimes have different security problems, and security concepts. Security concepts are interpretations and perceptions of security are not easily mollified. Certain crucial security-interests are to be respected, but others are security-menacing circles. 27/ The 'old detente' was legitimized as a way of winning the conflict of the two systems. As both legitimized detente as something they would win, the incompatible long range goals of the two systems made detente impossible. 28/

Detente as status quo of the two social and state systems, is now proposed by some specialists in Eastern Europe and by some social democrats in Western Europe. But this status quo has to be internal as well as international because internal changes are likely to have security effects. Political, societal, and cultural changes will come (in East and West). At that time we either have a system that reacts with war, or we have developed a system capable of handling and containing such processes. This is the reason for the interest in societal changes and in the possibility of living with different European security systems.

Detente as a regime of non-intervention is in one way the opposite approach. All changes are legitimate if they are domestically founded. This is a process definition in contrast to the preceding output-definition. The two are based on opposing logics, but in practice they are often used pragmatically for the same purpose. The difference is important. These intricacies show the difficulties in setting up a

'formula' for European detente. Absolute
non-intervention is: a) impossible today because of
interdependence; 29/ but 'degrees' of (legitimate)
intervention is an important research-area. b)
Impossible for reasons of security policy--purely
domestically based change can have consequences
detrimental to (the stability of) common security. This
shows the classical problem of international arrangements
regarding agreement on definitions of the status quo 30/
or the legitimate forms of change. 31/

The concept Common Security takes as its starting
point and core idea the necessity of security together .
32/ It excludes the possibility of unilateral security
against the other. However, neither the term nor most of
the writings contain an explicit duality of security with
and against the other. Even when it is important to
upgrade the 'security with², it will for a long time have
to be done in coexistence with 'security against'. The
problems are (logically) hard to handle from the basis of
'common security'. This creates problems, i.a. in
relation to the view of deterrence. There can also be a
status quo tendency. The command to enhance your own
security by also enhancing that of 'the other' easily
translates into making the existing regimes secure. It
is difficult to fit social change into the formula of
'common security' (cf. the problems between the SPD and
Solidarnosc).

Theoreticians on European security need to develop
supra-concepts which can incorporate the logic of the
situation, the processes at work and the crucial points
of actual and future processes, in order to produce
realistic options for peace and security policies. In
this article these are mainly represented by discussions
of terms such as conflict-culture, security-regime, and
common security.

Security Regimes is a popular concept in the
academic world. The essence is self-constraint and
mutuality. The aim is to turn evil circles or interaction into good ones. 33/ The essential formula is
less absolute than common security, but there is a clear
affinity regarding core-ideas. At the present stage the
main problem is the vagueness and contradictions in the
general theory of regimes as well as in the specific
theory of security regimes as well as the contradictions
between these two. The affinity to common security,
together with the roots of the term in classical
diplomatic history, (ie, the European Concert, classical

international relations 'realism', etc.), might indicate a repetition of the status quo problem mentioned in relation to 'common security'. This question requires careful scrutiny of the concept and of the theory.

A third more dynamic concept is <u>conflict culture</u> which begins with an understanding of the relationship as marked by conflict. It then attempts to introduce a higher awareness of (and responsibility towards) the products one contributes to understand the configuration domestically and internationally.

An implicit premise for most political activity is the thought-figure that politics is a two-step project of 1) getting power, 2) using it; that is, forming the world according to one's plans. In reality, this is almost never the case. <u>34/</u> If the reality of constant interplay and inevitable unpredictability is taken into account it might--especially in a fundamentally dangerous situation like the European--produce a development from the present de-facto compromise towards a more conscious compromise: It is necessary to develop a conflict culture, rules of the game, where the conflict is acknowledged, but where the acceptable forms of future competition is agreed upon. Specifically, this will mean a higher concord on the concept of security in relation to the concepts of intervention/non-intervention.

In order to further 'normal interaction' it is necessary to restrict the concept of security by redefining certain activities from threats to challenges. That is, to narrow (and strengthen) the non-intervention norm, which is mainly a task for the East. Strengthening the norm is the other side of the process, of the compromise, as the West will have to accept the necessity of stability on some socio-political dimensions, which probably means broadening of the non-intervention norm in contrast to present use. <u>35/</u> Thereby parts of the East-West security problem could be transformed into East-West politics. <u>36/</u>

NOTES

1. For a more general treatment of 'non-military aspects of European Security', the reader is referred to our research report "Europeansecurity - Problems of Research on Non-military Aspects", <u>Copenhagen Papers No. 1</u>, 1987.

2. Norbert Elias, <u>The Civilizing Process</u>, Vol. I-II, New York/Oxford 1978/1982 (1st edition in German,

1939) - especially Vol. I, pp. 219-263 (the introduction to the 1968 German edition). See also The Court Society, Oxford 1983 (first edition, 1969); pp. 1-34, 140-145, and 208-213.

3. Cf. Barry Buzan, Peoples, States and Fear. The National Security Problem in International Relations, Brighton, 1983.

4. Barry Buzan: "Peace, Power, and Security: Contending Concepts in the Study of International Relations" in Journal of Peace Research, Vol. 21:2, 1984, pp. 109-125.

5. Norbert Elias, Humana Conditio. Beobachtungen zur Entwicklung der Menschheit am 40. Jahrestag eines Kriegsendes (8.Mai 1985), Frankfurt 1985, mainly pp. 117ff.

6. Cf. Henry A. Kissinger, A World Restored. The Politics of Conservatism in an Revolutionary Era, Bost 1957. Barry Buzan, Peoples States and Fear. The National Security Problem in International Relations. Brighton, 1983.

7. Cf. Elias 1985, op cit, pp. 120-122, Egbert Jahn, "Social Reform Policy and Detente Policy in Eastern and Western Europe," in Egbert Jahn and Yoshikazu Sakamoto (Eds.), Elements of World Instability: Proceedingsof the IPRA Eighth General Conference, Campus Verlag, Frankfurt/New York 1981, pp. 323ff.

8. This is: theoretically one is inevitably case between the pure state-to-state logic of traditiona 'international politics' and non-security, social processes, national politics and ideologies, etc. Cf. Gordon Craig and Alexander George, Force and Statecraft, New York/Oxford 1983; Martin Wight, Power Politics, London 1982; Ernst-Otto Czempiel "Neue Kleider, aber kein Kaiser?" Politische Vierteljahresschrift, Heft 2, 1981; Machiavelli, The Prince.

9. Cf. Jahn, Lemaitre and Waever, "European Security..." op.cit., Chapter 10.

10. Cf. Ernesto Laclau & Chantal Mouffe, Hegemony and Socialist Strategy. Towards a Radical Democratic Politics, London, 1985; Josue V. Harari (ed.), Textual Strategies: Perspectives in Post-Structuralist Criticism New York, 1979.

11. Ole Karup Pedersen: Udenrigsminister P. Munchs opfattelse af Danmarksstilling i international politik - 'Minister of foreign affairs, p Munch's conception of Denmark's position in international politics,' Copenhagen, 1970.

12. Cf. e.g. Egbert Jahn, "Der Einfluss der Ideologie auf die sowjetische Aussen- und Rustungspolitik," in Osteuropa, May, June, July 1986.

13. Buzan 1983, p. 11.

14. Ibid., p. 67.

15. Ibid., chapters 2 and 3; Henry A. Kissinger, A World Restored. The Politics of Conservatism in a Revolutionary Era, Boston 1957, London 1977 edition, pp. 29f, 82f, 207ff, 305f and 324ff; Arnold Wolfers, Discord and Collaboration, Baltimore 1962, pp. 151ff.

16. The term 'configuration' is adopted from the work of Norbert Elias. For the precise meaning of the term see Elias 1982, pp.166ff, Elias 1983, pp. 18-21, 208ff, Elias 1978, Vol. I, p. 261 and Norbert Elias, Was ist Sociologies?, 5th ed., Munich 1986, pp. 139-45.

17. Kissinger 1977.

18. Cf. Gert Krell, "Die Entwicklung des Sicherheitsbegriffs" in Beitrage zur Konfliktforschung 3/1980, pp. 33-57. A shorter version of this article in English can be found in Egbert Jahn and Yoshikazu Sakamoto (eds.) Elements of World Instablity: Armaments, Communication, Food,International Division of Labour, N.Y. 1981, pp. 238-55.

19. In addition to the previously mentioned book by Buzan, cf. also Jahn/Lemaitre/Waever op.cit., pp. 47ff.

20. Buzan 1984; and John H. Herz, "Idealist Internationalism and the Security Dilemma," in World Politics, Vol. 2:2, 1950, pp. 157-180, especially pp. 178ff.

21. In reality also the West often seem to be worried about contacts and try--against the prevailing ideology--to limit the contacts. Cf. the 1962-criticism by Richard von Weizsacker, reprinted in: Richard von Weizsacher, Die Deutsche geht weiter, pp. 171-181. Munchen 1985.

22. Cf. Eberhard Schultz, Moskau und die europaische Integration, Munich-Vienna 1975; Gerhard Weittig, Europaische Sicherheit. Das europaische Staatenssystem in der sowjetischen Aussenpolitik 1966-1972, Dusseldorf 1972; Gerhard Wettig, "'Gemeinsame Sicherheit' aus Moskaus Sicht. Alte Doktrin mit neuem Etikett" in Europaische Wehrkunde, 9/1986, pp. 502-504.

23. Cf. the recent arms reduction proposals of the WTO and NATO regarding conventional weapons in Europe: Budapest-declaration of June 11, 1986 and Brussels-declaration of December 12, 1986.

24. Cf. Barry Buzan, The Future of Western European Security. Paper prepared for the conference on European Security-Various National Viewpoints on Non-Military Aspects, Copenhagen 25-27th of September 1987. Forthcoming.

25. A survey of the thinking on security in different European countries can be found in the papers written for the conference 25-27th September 1987 organized by the Centre for Peace and Conflict Research in Copenhagen on European Security. Forthcoming.

26. This is speculation parallel to and partly inspired by socalled 'regime'-thinking -- compare also with Kissinger's thinking about a 'Legitimate Order.' Cf. A World Restored, London 1977 (first edition 1957).

27. Cf. the discussion of the "defense dilemma" and the "power-security dilemma" by Barry Buzan, 1983, pp. 156ff.

28. Cf. Egbert Jahn: "The Tactical and Peace-Political concept of Detente", Bulletin of Peace Proposals 1/1981, p. 33-43. This text is closely related to "Social Reform Policy and detente Policy in Eastern and Western Europe" in Jahn & Sakomoto (eds.) Elements of World Instability: Proceedings of the International Peace Research Association. Eighth General Conference, Frankfurt/New York 1981; pp. 323-335. And to "Elemente eines friedenswissenschaftlischen Entspannungsbegriffes" in Schotter (ed.) Europa zwischen Konfrontation und Kooperation: Entspannungspolitik fur die achtzieger Jahre, Frankfurt/N.Y. 1982. See also "Friedliche Koexistenz und Entspannung in sowjetischer Sicht" in Deutsche Gesellschaft fur Friedens- und Konfliktforschung (Hg.) DGFK-Jahrbuch 1982/83, Baden-Baden 1983, p. 67-90.

29. Ernst-Otto Czempiel: "Das Phanomen der Intervention aus politikwissenschaftlicher Sicht," p.5-20 in Ernst-Otto.

INTERNATIONAL PEACE RESEARCH ASSOCIATION

STUDIES IN PEACE RESEARCH

(Selected Papers of the General Conferences)

Proceedings of the IPRA Inaugural Conference
    Groningen, Netherlands, 1965.

Studies in Conflict
    Proceedings of IPRA Second Conference, Vol. I
    Tallberg, Sweden, 1967.

Poverty, Development and Peace
    Proceedings of IPRA Second Conference, Vol. II
    Tallberg, Sweden, 1967.

Philosophy of Peace Research
    Proceedings of IPRA Third Conference, Vol. I
    Karlovy Vary, Czechoslovakia, 1969.

The International System
    Proceedings of IPRA Third Conference, Vol. II
    Karlovy Vary, Czechoslovakia, 1969.

Case Studies, Simulations and Theories of Confict,
    IPRA Third Conference, Vol. III
    Karlovy Vary, Czechoslovakia, 1969.

Proceedings of the IPRA Fourth Conference
    Bled, Yugoslavia, 1971.

Proceedings of the IPRA Fifth Conference
    Varanasi, India, 1974.

Peace Development and New International Economic Order
    Proceedings of the IPRA Seventh Conference
    Oaxtepec, Mexico, 1977.

Elements of World Instability: Armaments, Communication,
Food, International Division of Labor
    Proceedings of the IPRA Eighth Conference
    Egbert Jahn and Yoshikazu Sakamoto (eds.)
    Frankfurt am Main, FRG, Campus Verlag, 1981.

Key Issues of Peace Research
    Proceedings of the IPRA Ninth Conference
    Yoshikazu Sakamoto and Ruth Klaassen (eds.)
    Orillia, Canada, 1981.

Conflict and Crisis of International Order: New Tasks of
Peace Research
    Proceedings of the IPRA Tenth Conference
    Chadwick Alger and Judit Balazs (eds.)
    Budapest: Centre for Peace Research Coordination of
    the Hungarian Academy of Sciences, 1985.